Special Needs Offenders in the Community

Robert D. Hanser
Institute of Law Enforcement
University of Louisiana at Monroe

PEARSON
Prentice Hall

Upper Saddle River, New Jersey 07458

Library of Congress Cataloging-in-Publication Data

Hanser, Robert D.
Special needs offenders in the community/Robert D. Hanser.
p. cm.
Includes bibliographical references and index.
ISBN 0-13-118872-0 (pbk.)
1. Special needs offenders—Rehabilitation—United States. I. Title.
HV9304. H23 2006
364.8—dc22 2005055576

Executive Editor: Frank Mortimer, Jr.
Assistant Editor: Mayda Bosco
Marketing Manager: Adam Kloza
Production Management: GGS Book Services
Production Editor: Trish Finley
Director of Manufacturing and Production: Bruce Johnson
Managing Editor: Mary Carnis
Production Liaison: Brian Hyland
Manufacturing Manager: Ilene Sanford
Manufacturing Buyer: Cathleen Petersen
Design Coordinator: Mary Siener
Cover Designer: Lisa Klausing
Cover Image: Corbis Digital Stock
Printer/Binder: R. R. Donnelley & Sons

Pearson Education LTD
Pearson Education Singapore, Pte. Ltd
Pearson Education, Canada, Ltd
Pearson Education–Japan
Pearson Education Australia PTY, Limited
Pearson Education North Asia Ltd
Pearson Educación de Mexico, S.A. de C.V.
Pearson Education Malaysia, Pte. Ltd

PEARSON
Prentice Hall

10 9 8 7 6 5
ISBN 0-13-118872-0

To my wife Penny;
to our children Tiffany Johnson, Amy Jackson, and Adam Jackson;
to my mother Loretta Wheeler;
and to my brother Guy Hanser

CONTENTS

CHAPTER 5

MENTALLY DISORDERED OFFENDERS 111

CHAPTER 6
MENTALLY RETARDED AND LEARNING-DISABLED OFFENDERS 151

CHAPTER 7
EARLY CHILDHOOD OFFENDERS 173

CHAPTER 8

THE CHILD AND ADOLESCENT OFFENDER 205

CHAPTER 9

GANG MEMBERS AS SPECIAL NEEDS OFFENDERS 229

CHAPTER 10

CHAPTER 11

CHAPTER 12

CHAPTER 13

CHAPTER 15

RESTORATIVE JUSTICE AND SPECIAL NEEDS OFFENDERS 381

CHAPTER 16

PREDICTIONS AND SUGGESTIONS FOR THE FUTURE PROCESSING OF SPECIAL NEEDS OFFENDERS 405

PREFACE

The origins of this book come from a series of lecture notes and articles that were initially collected as the basis to a course that I was assigned to teach as a matter of last-minute happenstance. While a doctoral student, I was assigned to teach a course on special needs offenders and was told that there was no actual textbook available on this subject. Instead, prior professors had relied on a collection of handouts and photocopied sources that had been passed down from person to person. On examining the working tools of this teaching assignment, I found this collection to be inadequate in addressing (what I thought to be) the specialized groups of offenders in the criminal justice and, more specifically, the correctional system.

My initial search found that there were certain groups of offenders that repetitively came up in the literature. Although these offenders were of concern in the official written literature, it seemed as if the scholarly world often went through fads and trends where one type of offender or the other was given a disproportionate amount of attention. While it is good to shed light on an issue that has been left in the dark, this can generate a process of sensationalism and can also portray that group of offenders as having more impact on the overall criminal justice system than is objectively true. This should not be allowed to occur among the academic world. In fact, it is the academic world that should safeguard against this.

Thus, it was my intent to find those groups of offenders that genuinely seemed to affect the criminal justice system, the criminal justice practitioner, and society in general. These offenders tend to have unique characteristics that make them different from most other offenders (such as with elderly offenders), while other characteristics may require special services but may be common to many offenders (such as addiction issues). It was a difficult process to discern exactly what should, and what should not, be considered a special needs offender or a special needs issue.

As I generated my list of what I thought were special needs offenders, I found myself modifying my perception all the way until the end of writing this book. Some offender group selections were obvious (female offenders, geriatric offenders, and mentally ill offenders), while others were less prominent as special needs offenders (the learning disabled and/or the early childhood offender). However, I began to realize that all these offenders were not only unusual or exotic in nature but also had specific characteristics that were unique and that hampered their ability to refrain from offending unless some form of specialized intervention were given. Indeed, when devoid of any such intervention, these "side pocket" offenders would be likely to simply disappear into a virtual lockdown cesspool. This is largely because the public (and indeed many correctional officials) simply do not understand many of these offender populations. And, in reaction, it is easier to develop a "one-size-fits-all" approach to the offending crowd than it is to troubleshoot a program to optimize its ability to prevent future recidivism.

Further, the media tend to do an effective job of drawing attention to many of these types of offenders because they are controversial. The public loves its controversy, and while the media may have some responsibility, it is the public that has severe misperceptions about many of these types of offenders. And this is where the crux of my decision emerged when deciding on the intent of this book. In so deciding, I resolved to demonstrate that programs can be "tweaked" in a fashion that makes them more effective at providing both the security of the public and the treatment of the special needs offender. I also resolved to demonstrate that it is in the public's own best long-term interest to support the modification of these programs to better serve the special needs offender.

As time went on, however, I found myself relying more and more on my practitioner experience. I have been a prior correctional officer at a maximum-security facility, and this helped hone my understanding of the offending population and of the challenges facing the day-to-day practitioner. Further, I have also worked as a contract therapist with probationers and parolees who have presented with a number of adjustment and mental health issues. From my experience as a security-minded institutional staff member and a treatment-oriented professional, a bit of insight began to emerge. It seemed that in both cases, the ultimate success and outcome seemed to depend frequently on how the subject case was initially assessed at the very beginning. Indeed, I began to realize that the first stage in offender supervision and/or treatment was the basis for everything else that follows. Quite simply, I became convinced that input at the beginning was the strongest influence on output at the end.

As I taught institutional corrections and community corrections courses (as well as a wide array of course work that integrated psychology and/or counseling with criminal justice), I realized that my message continually came back to assessment at intake and how important this was when determining effectiveness in the future. Further, it became a contention of mine that supervision personnel and treatment personnel can and should work together for both causes. I had a tendency to transmit this to students who often saw the security and treatment fields as being contradictory to one another. This is a sad misperception on the part of many general citizens, and it is this misperception that prevents us from tweaking many of our current programs so that they are more able to optimally supervise the offender and reduce likely recidivism.

It was with this bit of insight that I determined that the intent of this book would be to present a series of offenders who require supervision and treatment programs that are tweaked so as to be relevant to those offenders. While there may be a variety of methods to listing the types of offenders who could meet the criteria for this book, they were eventually categorized to include the following groups:

- Offenders with learning disabilities and mental handicaps
- Offenders with communicable diseases
- Substance-abusing offenders
- Mentally disordered offenders
- Early childhood offenders
- Adolescent offenders
- Gang-related offenders
- Sex offenders
- Family violence offenders
- Female offenders
- Geriatric offenders

These types of offenders were selected as special needs offenders because all have various unique subjective and objective needs that are relevant to improving their prognosis. This means that these offenders genuinely require alterations in correctional processing to best lower their future likelihood of recidivism. By the same token, these offenders were selected because they do hold potential to be receptive to these alterations in treatment and supervision. This means that, if given the alterations noted, these offenders will be less of a threat to mainstream society. This improvement in public safety is the ultimate goal and litmus test of success in any community supervision program. Thus, the process utilized to maintain public safety is the component that must be tweaked on various levels and in a variety of capacities.

This book's main contention is that these programs can, for the most part, be most effectively implemented within the community setting. Indeed, there is a bit of irony to this contention because the community's long-term safety is actually most improved when the community itself is involved and when the majority (certainly not all) of these offenders are provided specialized security and treatment regimens.

INTENDED AUDIENCE AND INTENDED USE

This book is written for the undergraduate criminal justice student. Other disciplines, such as psychology, social work, or counseling, may benefit from this book as well if the content reflects some form of offender-based course. However, the terminology, concerns, and focus are germane to the field of criminal justice and are most specific to the subspecialties of institutional and community corrections. Further, this book is most ideal for any course that deals with special needs offenders. As noted earlier, this was the primary motivation for initially starting this book. Although some universities and colleges may offer courses on special needs offenders, many do not. And because of this, this book was also written to be a useful supplement to any community corrections– or correctional treatment–based course that a program may offer. This book uniquely handles both of these areas of concern for each offender group that is presented. *Indeed, this is the very point of the book—that special needs offenders should be provided treatment interventions that are administered within the community*. Given this emphasis, this book is perfectly suited as a primary or secondary text for each of the courses mentioned.

In addition, it should be noted that each chapter is written so that it can be used as a stand-alone chapter to provide a framework for a specific lecture on a certain type of offender. This is yet another strength of this book, as it serves as a compilation of research and practice pertaining to a variety of offender types and therefore allows instructors to pick and choose as from a smorgasbord. Thus, this is likely to be a handy reference work for anyone interested in multiple offender typologies. In fact, a number of the chapters address typologies (sex offenders, domestic abusers, and arsonists) of certain offenders whenever such information seemed relevant. This adds to the distinctiveness of the book and its utility as both a teaching and a reference tool.

ORGANIZATION OF THE BOOK

This book is organized to present each specialized group of offenders against the backdrop of some generalized concerns that are common denominators to each group. This book makes a specific and deliberate attempt to avoid theorizing on each type of offender and instead attempts to work from the perspective of the practitioner. *This book is also not a social justice text advocating for the rights of the special needs offender*. Rather, it simply contends that if society wants to improve safety from crime committed by the special needs offender, then society (through individual communities) will have to implement certain measures to effect that improvement. Nothing comes for free, and nothing is free of consequence. Cause and effect cannot be avoided; instead, it is simply more prudent to determine which effect we would like to see emerge out of what are sometimes a series of undesired choices. Nonetheless, we must react in some fashion, and this book provides one such remedy to optimizing public safety.

Chapter 1 addresses the introductory aspects of dealing with special needs offenders. It provides the background information on defining special needs and why the definition can be so important. However, the semantics of definition is not the main thrust of this chapter. Rather, the chapter provides an overview of community supervision programs and treatment intervention programs and demonstrates how both of these can and should be linked together to exponentially improve the odds of each orientation's success. This is an important chapter because it clearly lays out the focus of the book and the manner in which agencies can and should work together to improve their responses to the special needs offender.

Chapter 2 goes further and builds on Chapter 1. Specifically, this chapter addresses the methods for effective program supervision and evaluation of the special needs offender. This process of offender supervision is presented as having four general stages. These stages are important because they give specific feedback on step-by-step assessment, supervision, and evaluation of the special needs offender. This chapter also provides specific assessment and classification instruments that should be chosen by agencies seeking to improve their ability to improve supervision and treatment objectives with special needs offenders.

Chapters 3 through 14 are separate chapters for each of the special needs offenders included within this book. Each of these chapters provides some form of introductory information on that type of offender, typically presented as a general discussion or presentation of background considerations. Each of these chapters then discusses the given special needs offender from "behind bars," providing a view of incarceration conditions and concerns for each of these offenders. This is important in and of itself, and it is important when understanding the special needs offender on aftercare and/or parole. Each chapter then addresses the given special needs offender when in the community, typically on some form of community supervision. Finally, most of these chapters may contain a treatment-oriented section that provides the student with some insight on how intervention programs may address each of these offender groups. The underlying theme in each of these chapters has to do with the overall treatment prognosis that the specific special needs offender is likely to have. Thus, regardless of whether a specific section on treatment is included, the flavor of each of these chapters is reintegrative. Each of these broad sections will likewise include numerous subsections to add clarity to the interrelation between topics included in each chapter.

Chapter 15 presents restorative justice as the primary orientation that can join both the supervision and the treatment perspectives together within the community. This is the chosen method of operation throughout this book since the book is, after all, one on special needs offenders in the community. This chapter demonstrates the successes of restorative justice programs throughout the nation and the world and also discusses the limitations of this approach. All in all, given the economic concerns and the desire to ensure that the concerns of the victim and the community are not overlooked, it is thought that this approach is the most pragmatic way to address special needs offenders in the community.

Chapter 16 provides several concluding remarks on the future of special needs offenders and also on what will be the likely outcome for society and the criminal justice system. Current legal and courthouse trends provide some indication of how the next decade may progress. The developing characteristics of the future special needs offender are discussed, as are additional factors associated with our increasingly multicultural society. Community supervision agencies will face predictable and difficult challenges in the future, and it will require an "all-hands" effort among criminal justice professionals and the community to maintain public safety.

THE BOOK'S ORIENTATION AND THEME

As one might guess, this book has a strong community-based orientation. The notion of "community justice" in corrections has been advocated by others in the past, but this book specifically links this form of justice to the supervision and treatment of special needs offenders. This is one of the primary distinctions between this book and the scant few other works that have attempted to address the special needs offender. This text utilizes community justice as a basic theme when determining how communities can and should be involved in the treatment process with special needs offenders. The reasons for this become increasingly clear with the majority of these offenders once the full spectrum of considerations are given full weight. There is likewise an emphasis on the use of restorative justice throughout most of the chapters of this book, culminating with a more thorough discussion in Chapter 15. It is my hope that it becomes clear that this is the best umbrella under which the full range of services (community policing, community-based corrections, and community–citizen integration) can be covered to provide a coherent package that meets the needs of the public as well as those associated with the special needs offender.

ACKNOWLEDGMENTS

The idea of writing this book originated from my assignment as a doctoral student to a course that dealt with special needs offenders. While teaching this course, my primary mentor, Dr. W. Wesley Johnson (Sam Houston State University), had suggested that I consider writing a book on the topic after listening to my aggravation over the fact that no appropriate book existed for this type of course. Dr. Johnson took the time to notify a local Prentice Hall representative of my potential interest in writing such a book. As it turned out, it was not to be until after I had left Sam Houston State University that I had decided to pursue this opportunity. However, if it had not been for Dr. Johnson's initial "seed planting," my decision to write this book would have never come to fruition.

I would also like to acknowledge Dr. Judy DeTrude (Sam Houston State University). I have often referred to Dr. DeTrude as my "academic mommy" because she has been so instrumental in shaping me as a therapist. It is her professionalism, sheer competence, and ethical bearing that I have always admired and that I have likewise done my best to emulate as a therapist. The training and guidance that I received from Dr. DeTrude was invaluable. She has left a lasting impression on my own personal view of therapy and my view of people.

Most important, I would like to thank my "momma," Loretta Wheeler. My mother has always believed in me and has always supported me like no other human could. It is my mother who encouraged me to pursue my education, and it is also my mother who most encouraged me throughout my efforts to write this book. She has helped me through hard times, both as a child and as an adult, and I am not one bit embarrassed to admit that I was, without a doubt, a momma's boy.

Likewise, I would like to thank my brother Guy Hanser. My brother has always expressed pride in my efforts and has been a source of continued support throughout the entire journey. He has been loyal even during times where it would have been understandable to act otherwise. One could not ask for a better brother, and I am truly a lucky person to have such a committed and solid fan in my corner.

And, of course, I would like to acknowledge my wife Penny and my three children, Tiffany, Amy, and Adam. Each deserves a special note of gratitude for having tolerated my long nights at the computer when it might have been more fulfilling for the family if I had spent more leisure time as a husband and a father. I am very grateful for their patience, understanding, and humor as I embarked on this endeavor.

Lastly, thanks go to the following reviewers: Ronald Iacovetta, Wichita State University; Leon Cantin, Mount Marty College; Donna Nicholson, Manchester Community College; David LaRose, Denver Career College; Vivian Lord, University of North Carolina at Charlotte; Eric Lang, Mount Olive College; and Anne Lanning, Rockingham Community College. It is through their efforts and feedback that the manuscript was continually improved, up to the development of the final product.

ABOUT THE AUTHOR

Robert D. Hanser, Ph.D., is an assistant professor of criminal justice at the University of Louisiana at Monroe (ULM). In his role as faculty member at ULM, he teaches graduate and undergraduate courses in criminal justice, chairs multiple theses, and maintains an active research agenda. In addition, he is also the director of the Institute of Law Enforcement at ULM and coordinates in-service training for law enforcement officers and jailers within the northern Louisiana region. He also conducts preservice and in-service training for police officers at the North Delta Regional Training Academy and enjoys the interface that he has with the academic and the practitioner worlds of criminal justice.

In addition to his full-time position, Hanser is also a part-time member of the core faculty of the Graduate School of Criminal Justice at Kaplan University. As a part-time faculty member with Kaplan University, he helped develop that university's graduate program in criminal justice. He was involved in both curriculum writing and program design and assisted the design team in presenting the degree program to the appropriate accreditation board. He has taught as an undergraduate and a graduate faculty member for Kaplan University for over two years and enjoys his affiliation with his friends in Chicago and Boca Raton.

Hanser received his Ph.D. in criminal justice from Sam Houston State University and received a master of arts in counseling from the same university. He is also a licensed professional counselor (Texas) and a certified anger resolution therapist. He has worked in a community-level domestic violence facility and has practiced therapy with children, adolescents, and mothers who are victims of family violence as well as perpetrators of family violence. He has also taught at a private school for troubled adolescents, many of whom were on juvenile probation while attending the facility. He has likewise provided general counseling services to numerous married couples and families throughout the community. He still continues to work in treatment programs for drug-abusing offenders on community supervision and provides anger management training for prison inmates of various custody levels.

Hanser has likewise worked for the Texas Department of Criminal Justice—Institutional Division (TDCJ-ID) as a correctional officer in the Administrative Segregation Department of the Eastham Unit. During his time of employment with TDCJ-ID, he worked closely with gang members of the Mexican Mafia, the Texas Syndicate, the Aryan Brotherhood, and the Barrio Aztecas. Through this experience in institutional corrections, he acquired extensive knowledge of inmate prison gangs and has had direct experience with a variety of highly assaultive inmate populations.

Throughout his teaching career, Hanser has taught courses on the courts, corrections, comparative criminal justice systems, world conflict, diversity relations, correctional treatment, and human behavior as well as numerous introductory courses in both criminal justice and psychology. When in his "specialist" mode of teaching/researching criminal justice, his particular areas of interest have typically leaned toward the realm of globalized comparisons of criminal justice systems, multinational and multicultural treatment programs for victims and offenders, court system operations and their social effects, multinational applications of psychology to various criminal justice issues, and the use of psychological profiles with terrorist, organized crime, cult-related, and extremist group members. He first developed his interest in multinational issues while serving in the U.S. Navy as a cryptologic technician aboard the USS *Ticonderoga* (CG-47). During his period of service, he served honorably during the initial periods of Operation Desert Shield and Operation Desert Storm.

Hanser has published several book chapters and peer-reviewed articles in areas related to mental health issues in criminal justice and various aspects of cross-cultural and multinational studies. Topics of previous research and publication include prison suicide, prison and "free world" sexual assault, cross-cultural and cross-national trends in domestic violence, cross-national perceptions of crime and justice in the United States, psychological applications to organized crime, and treatment programs in the United States and abroad. His areas of interest have included and continue to include any and all therapeutic interventions for victims and offenders. He does tend to have broad and competing interests that reflect his eclectic and multidisciplinary approach to the behavioral sciences and his inability to decide what he most wishes to do in his pursuit of self-actualization—a state that he is constantly striving to achieve.

CHAPTER

THE NOTION OF SPECIAL NEEDS OFFENDERS

1

Chapter Objectives

1. Understand and discuss what is meant by "need" when referring to special needs offenders.
2. Identify and define the types of community supervision program delivery. Also identify the different supervision styles associated with differing community supervision personnel.
3. Identify and define the common types of correctional therapy that are used. Also identify the different types of therapeutic personnel and their professional orientations.
4. Demonstrate how collaborative schemes between criminal justice personnel and treatment personnel can assist both groups in better achieving their own agendas.
5. Identify how the various components of effective offender supervision and treatment interventions can improve the offender's likely prognosis from initial assessment to ultimate reintegration.
6. Understand the importance of assessment when tailoring supervision programs to fit special offenders with special needs.
7. Understand why community-based programs are better suited than institutional programs for tailoring supervision programs to fit special offenders with special needs.

Statistics show that 97% of the 1.3 million inmates now in prison eventually will be released and will return to communities. Many will leave prison with no supervision or services. A strong transition process through which inmates are prepared for release, leave prison, return to communities, and adjust to free living is needed to protect the public effectively (National Institute of Corrections, *Transitions from prison*, retrieved from http://www.nicic.org/WebPage_222.htm)

INTRODUCTION

Dangerous and repeat offenders have become a serious concern for society. This concern over the dangerous recidivist has also been used as a tool of leverage among politicians and criminal justice agencies alike. This has often led to the development of fairly haphazard programs designed to accommodate concerns for public safety. The problem with this is that often these programs have limited effectiveness, and the public comes away with no further trust in the justice system than was possessed to begin with. This is unfortunate, and it leaves a bad perception within the public conscience.

This perception is similar to the often-touted seminal research of Martinson in which it was purportedly surmised that "nothing works." But this perception is very dangerous both for the public and for the criminal justice professional because it ignores the reality that some things work with some offenders under certain conditions. However, getting all three of these variables to line up appropriately so that the equation ends in treatment success is a complicated process that does not have simple, linear, and straightforward answers. However, it is precisely this type of answer that the public seeks, and it is the public official who is frequently willing to give such a simple answer for the sake of popularity.

The result is that shortsighted and reactionary policies are crafted that ultimately cause a number of unintended problems. Further, because the prior programs appear to be nothing less than miserable failures, the public is likely to scoff at the notion of treatment for offenders. Indeed, the very notion that offenders may have specialized needs is a source of ridicule among critics of treatment orientations. By implication, it may then be believed that persons making such observations are simply fooled into having a "bleeding heart" for the convict, who is undoubtedly presented in the extreme as a rapist or an ax murderer.

But this is where three common lies are perpetuated. First is the lie that all offenders are dangerous and that all of them need to be incarcerated for their transgressions. Second is the lie that advocacy for treatment means that a person is soft on crime and weak on responsibility (most programs stress offender accountability). And third is the lie that all offenders are the same.

The reality is that the minority of offenders are dangerous. Likewise, the reality is that only a small minority of offenders become habitual offenders. And the reality is that if they are effectively treated, a substantial portion do not reoffend. Further, these results fluctuate with the area of the nation, which demonstrates that it may be as much how some action is done as it is that a specific action was done at all. Finally, offenders present with a conundrum of issues, some more complicated than others, meaning that there are a select group of offenders who are unique when compared to other offenders. It is often these offenders who are at an increased risk of recidivating. These are also the offenders who need treatment the most. These are the special needs offenders—the focus of this book.

Indeed, the premise of this entire book is as follows: *Some offenders are in "need" more than others, and if we can learn how to match up programs to meet these "needs," then crime will be significantly reduced* because those offenders who are most symptomatic will be "fixed," and they will then commit less or no crime. However, a word of caution must be provided to the would-be student of this book. There are five subthemes that are woven into this premise. Each of these subthemes is equally important and must be integrated together if the main premise of the book is to be clearly understood by the student.

First, if offenders are to receive treatment, they should be treated within the community whenever feasible. If offenders are provided the correct treatment intervention and can be fixed, they can be best fixed in the community because the community has better therapeutic services and support programs than most prison systems. In addition, these offenders will not have continual forced exposure to other offenders as they do within the prison environment. If the treatment program ensures that offenders do not return to their criminogenic family or peer group, if the treatment program is intensive for hard-core offenders (but not as intensive for low-key offenders), and if public safety is not compromised in the process, then crime can and will be considerably reduced through a process of reintegration.

Second, not all offenders can be fixed. There is a small segment of the offender population that seems destined to recidivate. Among this group, some are so dangerous as to completely invalidate taking any public safety risk for the sake of offender treatment. If these offenders wish to change, it will have to be of their own volition and not because of external reward of potential liberty since they have demonstrated that they cannot be trusted and that they simply have no sense of remorse. If they later wish to change such characteristics, this is to be commended, but it should simply be because of their own inherent motivation to change without any modification of their sentence. If they are to serve life behind bars, then that is what they serve, plain and simple.

Third, assessment is the key to distinguishing the difference between those who can be fixed and those who cannot. Optimal assessment programs and a strong commitment in personnel and funding are the primary means by which community supervision can ensure public safety. This is also the best bet for community supervision agencies to improve their image in the long term. While improved supervision techniques are good and getting better every day, they are still somewhat reactionary. An ounce of prevention is worth a pound of intervention on any given day, and assessment is the best method of preventing future incidents. Thus, only the best and most empirically sound assessment tools should be used. This will save agencies money in the long term (but will likely be costly in the short term) and will easily pay for itself within a 5- to 10-year period, depending on the size of the agency's caseload.

Fourth, even forced treatment has been shown to work if given adequate time and if the correct program is matched with the correct offender. This is an important point because many people opposed to treatment will make the claim that "you can bring a horse to water, but you cannot make it drink" as their rationale that offenders must desire change for it to take place. However, current research is clearly showing that even forced treatment can and does effect positive change on offenders, particularly in the popularized and effective drug courts. While the rate of change is slower than with those who wish to participate in treatment, it nonetheless has been shown empirically to be effective. Again, the main factor is whether it is the correct treatment for the correct offender. And, as is always the case, the person providing the therapeutic intervention is critical as well. Given these considerations, it would appear that we can force a horse to drink after all.

Fifth, the community must be involved in the supervision process. The community is our most plentiful resource in community supervision programs, and if community demands for safety are sincere, then the community must be empowered to help ensure its safety and should also be publicly held accountable. Probation agencies must collaborate with other community-based agencies and must overcome any political snafus that entangle the process. If this is unavoidable, then this should become a public platform within the community so that no interest group can escape accountability. Plain and simple is the fact that probation cannot read minds, including the minds of offenders, and therefore if supervision is to be more proactive, the offender must be under the watchful eye of an actual person as frequently as possible. This means that community members must be willing to assist in the process of keeping an "eye" on the offender. The use of Community Watch programs, Volunteers in Policing, and Citizen Corps programs can be integrated to visit offenders at random points in the community and throughout the week to help ensure that offenders know they are being observed and to show the public that they do have a direct effect on their own sense of safety.

It is with the main premise of this book and these five subthemes in mind that each of the unique types of special needs offenders is examined. The subsequent chapters will strive to provide an overview of each offender type and discuss how these offenders should or should not be therapeutically treated. One thing that should become apparent is that "one-size-fits-all" approaches are destined to failure. If we cannot improve more than half of this population, we would then be best off saving millions of dollars by flipping a coin when making decisions to release on community supervision. This book highlights the fact that we are indeed able to do much better than the mere flip of a coin, but improvement will require a clear and methodical approach that is tailored for each type of offender (e.g., pedophile, juvenile arsonist, or female drug addict), and this approach must be grounded in effective assessment.

However, if we are to provide better and more specialized treatment interventions to these unique offenders, we must be able to determine who are special needs offenders. This is important because the definition of the population can make all the difference in future outcomes. Besides, without definition it is impossible to measure whether our contentions are true. Thus, we proceed from this point by exploring the very notion of special needs offenders and determining how this notion has gained importance during the past decade or so of correctional history.

THE NOTION OF SPECIAL NEEDS OFFENDERS

Any reintegration program relies on the notion that we must be able to reliably and validly classify and determine the needs of offenders. This ability to classify offenders ensures that we are able to match our responses in a manner that optimizes the outcome of our program. Further, from a legal and historical context, the concept of "needs" has been pivotal in designing responses to different types of offenders (e.g., juvenile offenders, mentally challenged offenders, and so on). However, it should be noted that the idea of a "need" is something that is absolutely necessary, not something that is a mere desire or preference. Thus, if individuals do not have this need met, then they will experience some form of serious social, psychological, physical, or emotional impairment within their daily functioning.

Indeed, among mental health practitioners, disorders are diagnosed only when there is some form of impairment of day-to-day functioning for the individual. A disorder is not thought to occur without any such impairment since there is no deficiency in one's functioning. This is important because this means that if something is truly needed and if we are robbed of our ability to obtain this need, then health effects will follow. Within the field of mental health, these health effects manifest in the form of aberrant behaviors. The criminal justice system becomes involved when these aberrant behaviors fall within the realm of criminally aberrant behaviors.

For purposes of this book, the term **special needs offender** is borrowed from Ashford, Sales, and Reid (2000) and refers to the following: (1) offenders have some notable physical, mental, and/or emotional challenge; (2) these challenges prevent either a subjective or an objective need from being fulfilled for that individual; (3) the lack of this subjective or objective need impairs their day-to-day ability to function within the confines of the criminal law; and (4) these offenders tend to be statistically unique from the remainder of the offender population, and they also tend to be prone to recidivism.

Further, Ashford, Sales, and Reid (2001) distinguish between subjective and objective needs. **Subjective needs** are those felt by the offender and are those needs that the offender perceives to be important (Ashford et al., 2001). These needs can be expressed or unexpressed by the offender for a variety of reasons (e.g., insecurity, manipulation, not themselves certain, lack of trust for treatment providers, and so on). Regardless, subjective needs are included in many treatment structures so that offenders can take an active part in their treatment. **Objective needs**, on the other hand, are determined by society and the correctional agency and have to do with socially selected and acceptable levels of health and social functioning to ensure that legal conduct is maintained (Ashford et al., 2001).

The trick for correctional practitioners is to find an effective balance between these two needs so that the offender is optimally motivated to comply with the program regimen (even though forced treatment can work, sincere effort from the offender client maximizes the effect of the program) while at the same time meeting the offender's minimal level of objective needs. All this must be factored in with the idea that the risk of recidivism should be reduced. Indeed, the community will be concerned most with whether the offender recidivates rather than with whether the offender feels better about the needs that are met. This concern about reducing the offender's recidivism has been dubbed a societal need. **Societal needs** are more concerned with those needs that most directly influence the likelihood of the offender's recidivism, and as a result the agency must address these needs first. These have been referred to as criminogenic needs, and these needs are considered the primary concern when addressing short- and long-term public safety (Ashford et al., 2001). All other offender needs are noncriminogenic and thus of secondary concern. Thus, the priority is set in addressing special needs among offenders. First and foremost, societal needs must be squarely addressed, and this is restricted to those needs that are most likely to affect recidivism. Second, objective needs must be met, and this is largely to comply with minimum standards established by legal precedent. Finally, subjective needs are met simply to motivate offenders to slowly "buy into" the societal and objective needs and expectations. With this priority in mind, we now turn our attention to the topic of program and personnel delivery of security and treatment services.

RECIDIVISM AND COMMUNITY SUPERVISION

Before discussing the various types of intermediate community supervision sanctions, it should be noted that, generally, hard-core offenders tend to fare better on intensive supervision (Champion, 2002). It is generally thought that these offenders have less impulse control and are less conditioned to work with autonomy and that more stringent community supervision prevents these offenders from committing crimes that might otherwise go undetected or, if detected, would become more serious. Thus, the use of more intense forms of security and supervision is strongly recommended with special needs offenders who have committed violent crimes or if they are repeat offenders.

With less serious and nonviolent offenders, the situation is much different. It is becoming increasingly clear that these offenders can benefit from both treatment and community supervision. Further, their rates of recidivism go down dramatically if they are maintained along the less restrictive forms of supervision. It is not necessarily that they are getting away with crimes that are not being detected; rather, the application of technical violations is relaxed a bit. This small bit of leniency can make all the difference in the offender's complete reform. Thus, when dealing with property and drug-abusing (as opposed to drug-trafficking) offenders, probation departments should utilize lighter forms of intermediate sanctions.

Some other points should also be quickly mentioned before we proceed to the types of intermediate sanctions. First, in general, parolees tend to have a higher recidivism rate than do probationers (Champion, 2002). However, just as important, the new offenses that parolees commit are not usually any more dangerous than those committed by probationers. This is important because this means that parolees should be given more intensive supervision but that heightened concern for the physical welfare of the community is usually unfounded as long as the parolee was not incarcerated for a violent offense. In the case of special needs offenders being incarcerated for violent crimes, it is recommended that they not be released into the community, or, if this is inevitable, they should be placed on the most restrictive form of community supervision available.

Finally, Champion (2002) notes some common characteristics among recidivists. A few of these are listed here as they may be relevant to the special needs offender:

1. Recidivists tend to be male and under 30.
2. Recidivists tend to be unmarried, widowed, or divorced.
3. Recidivists tend to commit crimes that are similar to their earlier offenses.
4. Recidivists tend to have alcohol- or drug-dependency problems that are associated with their new offense.
5. Finally, and perhaps most important, recidivists tend to be under no correctional supervision when committing new offenses.

Thus, when addressing special needs offenders throughout the remainder of this book, it should become clear that a 40-year-old female offender has a low risk of recidivism. Recidivists with dual diagnoses (mental health and drug addiction) are at heightened risk of recidivism. Sex offenders are apparently more likely to reoffend through sexual assault than some other form of crime. Finally, all offenders should have adequate supervision since the lack of supervision is what correlates with the tendency to commit new crimes.

To be effective, intermediate community supervision programs should be used in a manner that is most suited for the particular offender based on the two basic premises: (1) likelihood to reoffend and (2) type of offender that they are. The type of security that they receive should then be determined accordingly.

TYPES OF COMMUNITY SUPERVISION PROGRAM DELIVERY

There are numerous "types" of community supervision programs throughout the nation. For purposes of this chapter, we will focus on the variety of sanctions known as intermediate sanctions. **Intermediate community supervision** sanctions are those sentences that have differing levels of supervision, making the offender's sentence more structured than standard probation, but these sanctions are also considered less severe than a full prison sentence. Thus, all the sanctions that are between a standard probation sentence and a standard prison sentence are considered intermediate sanctions. It is important to note that any of the recommended intermediate sanctions used in this chapter will not utilize split or shock incarceration methods since these are simply varieties of incarceration and are not the focus of this book. The contention of this book is that such offenders can and should, for the most part, be treated in the community. If they cannot be so treated, then true incapacitation should take place. The following paragraphs discuss the suggested major types of intermediate community supervision sanctions that should be considered with special needs offenders.

Probation with community service and restitution requires the offender to provide a certain number of designated hours of free labor to a given cause determined by the court. Restitution, on the other hand, is a stated amount of money that the offender must pay to the victim or to a state victim fund. It is the recommendation of this book that community service and restitution be used in *every single case* where special needs offenders are involved, including juvenile offenders. This means that this sanction should be combined with those that are listed hereafter.

Intensive supervised probation (ISP) is usually viewed as the most effective alternative to imprisonment. Officer caseloads typically do not exceed 40 offenders. The model for ISP was first established in Atlanta, Georgia, and it is this model that is in mind for purposes of this chapter and this book. Specifically, this type of supervision consists of the following:

1. Five face-to-face visits between the probation officer and the offender per week
2. A minimum of 132 hours of community service
3. A set curfew
4. Mandatory employment (note that this should be required in all cases)
5. A weekly search for any new arrests
6. Automated tracking of arrests using a state crime information system
7. Frequent yet random testing for drugs and/or alcohol

This form of supervision is conducted by a team that consists of a probation officer if the caseload is 25 or less or two surveillance officers if there are 40 cases or more. In Georgia, this program is used to divert low-risk offenders from prison, typically nonviolent property offenders and drug abusers.

Day reporting centers are treatment facilities that offenders are forced to report to on a daily (or near daily) basis. These are similar to residential treatment facilities except that offenders on intensive supervision are not required to stay overnight. In some states, these day reporting centers are designed so that offenders attend 8- to 10-hour intervention and treatment classes. The optimal programs (and in the case of this book the choicest programs) are those that have a sundry array of classes, such as relapse prevention, educational development, individual counseling, group counseling, structured bibliotherapy where clients complete their assignments as homework and return them each day for discussion in a bibliotherapy class, and so on. The point is that the offender is immersed into a treatment regimen that accomplishes three key tasks:

1. The offender is supervised on a face-to-face basis.
2. The offender is kept busy and thus cannot be out on the street offending.
3. The offender is forced to comply with treatment, and, as we know from our earlier readings, a certain amount of this will eventually be processed even if the offender is resistant.

Home confinement with electronic monitoring (EM) is used instead of incarceration for persons on community supervision. This type of supervision is the most restrictive form of community supervision without actual incarceration and has also been used with offenders who have violated the terms of lesser forms of community supervision (Champion, 2002). Most programs utilize this type of supervision for a period that ranges from two to six months. It is a strong contention of this book that this type of supervision be utilized for much lengthier periods when used with adult pedophiles, multiple rapists, or domestic batterers who present a long-term risk of violence. In addition, offenders presenting with mental illness that disposes them to violent behavior should be kept on this type of supervision, and this should be lessened only after reclassification procedures (such as a retest of the MMPI-2 and the LSI-R, both discussed in Chapter 2) indicate that the offender clearly qualifies.

Home confinement combined with EM is an effective option to prison because the offender is watched closely yet the cost of supervision is only a fraction of what a prison sentence would cost. A variety of methods may be used to maintain the EM. One is the use of programmed contact systems that have randomly programmed times during the day and/or night during which an automated system calls the offender's house (Champion, 2002). The offender is required to repeat certain words and phrases whereby a voice analysis determines if it is truly the offender who has answered the phone. If the phone is not answered or if it is found to not be the offender, then community supervision personnel are alerted (Champion, 2002). Other versions use visual verifications where a picture is taken and automatically sent via installed equipment.

Home confinement and **global positioning satellite systems (GPS)** use a series of satellites to monitor and locate offenders. The Florida Department of Corrections first initiated this program to track probationers in real time at any point during the day or night (Champion, 2002). This system is far superior to any other program of supervision because it ensures that probation officers have near-instantaneous notification of an offender's violation of their community supervision. With this system, supervision officers can track an offender within a computer system and can even tell which street the offender is at within any part of the country. Further, these programs can utilize areas of inclusion or exclusion within the acceptable limits of offender travel so that if an offender enters a certain area that is restricted, the supervision officer is instantly notified (Champion, 2002).

Residential treatment homes are designed to house the offender, but the offender is not ordered by the court to stay at the facility (Champion, 2002). Indeed, these facilities may also have "day students" who use the facility as a day reporting center. The only difference is that offender-clients stay at the facility full time (e.g., sleep overnight). The offender may still be allowed to go to work and/or leave for weekend family visits and so on, but treatment staff determine when and where this is appropriate for the client. These facilities may have some clients who are court mandated along with other clients who participate voluntarily. The point is that this is a treatment facility, and offenders have many more liberties to leave throughout the day, have visitors, and engage in personal activities than they would in a halfway house, a jail, or a prison (Champion, 2002). These facilities are often run by nonprofit private agencies and operate on a grassroots local community level. Most of these facilities offer some sort of substance abuse counseling, and many of these programs are based primarily on substance abuse recovery issues.

Official halfway houses are residential settings for offenders who are court ordered to stay at the facility as a supplement to their conditions of community supervision (Champion, 2002). In addition, offenders who are exiting prison will often be required to stay at one of these facilities. It is important to note that the restrictions on free movement are likely to be more than those of the residential treatment home. These facilities may be used for probation and parole violators as well, particularly while jail and/or prison systems are full. Most of these offenders will also have some form of community service. Substance abuse counseling is most often a service that offenders will be required to obtain.

The previously mentioned sanctions were presented from the lightest to the most intensive. It should be noted that, in most cases, the use of a higher sanction still assumes that the offender will meet the requirements of all the lower sanctions. Therefore, except in cases where it is unproductive, each sanction will also include the terms and conditions of the one before it. Thus, it is highly likely that offenders in a residential treatment home will also be on intensive supervision, and they might even have some form of EM. However, offenders at a halfway house would obviously not have EM since they are required to remain at the halfway house around the clock and thus have continual supervision.

It should be again pointed out that this section does not present the use of "split sentence" programs, such as shock probation, boot camps, or intermittent jail/prison sanctions. This is not an oversight but is quite deliberate. It is the contention of this book that such sanctions are more or less designed simply to incarcerate and that these types of sentences exist simply because insufficient prison space is available to fully incarcerate this offender. Thus, the orientation is more for the goal of incapacitation, deterrence, and/or fulfilling punitive functions because of public expectations. Programs that incarcerate offenders over the weekend typically do so to keep the offender out of trouble during "peak times" where they may be prone to commit violations (especially drug addicts or alcoholics who drink and drive). This is an incapacitation perspective. Or judges may give some form of added jail time with the probation to further demonstrate their stance on crime (a punitive response). Other sentences, such as boot camps and probation, are used to deter future crimes.

It is the contention of this book that if offenders cannot be effectively supervised in the community, then they simply should not be in the community at all. To make it simple, they should be in jail or prison. Because clarity in the purpose of the sentence, the sanction, and the treatment is thought to have primary importance, it is this book's contention that the two perspectives should not be combined so as to avoid competing goals within the correctional sentence. The use of competing goals will undermine the treatment process, and, as we will see later in the chapter, this will simply keep us from effectively "pairing" our community supervision plan with our reintegration and treatment plan.

TYPES OF COMMUNITY SUPERVISION PERSONNEL AND PROFESSIONAL ORIENTATIONS

Daniel Glaser (1964) conducted research on parole officers and the orientation by which they approach their job. The research that Glaser conducted will be utilized in this book to provide a general framework for all community supervision officers, both probation and parole. Glaser contended that community supervision officers tend to operate at differing points along two spectrums: offender assistance and offender control. These two spectrums seem to contradict each other, as each tends to put officers at cross-purposes when trying to balance their job as reformer and public safety officer. This means that four basic categories emerge that describe the officer's general tendency when supervising offenders. Table 1.1 illustrates the offender assistance and offender control spectrums as well as the four resultant categories of officer supervision styles.

Paternal officers use a great degree of both control and assistance techniques (Clear & Cole, 2003). They protect both the offender and the community by providing the offender with assistance as well as praising and blaming. This type of officer can seem sporadic at times. These officers are ambivalent to the concerns of the offender or the community; this is just a job that they do. Indeed, these officers may be perceived as being noncommittal by taking the community's side in one case and then the offender's in another. The officers do not tend to have a high degree of formal training or secondary education, but they tend to be very experienced and thus are able to weather the difficulties associated with burnout within the field of probation.

Punitive officers see themselves as needing to use threats and punishment in order to get compliance from the offender. These officers may also view the offender as a "lower class" of individual and are likely to see punitive methods of control as the only type of mechanism that the offender population will or can understand. They will likely have a morally judgmental view of their caseload. These officers will place the highest emphasis on control and protection of the public against offenders and will also be suspicious of offenders on their caseload. This suspiciousness is not necessarily wrong or unethical, however, as this is part and parcel of the supervision of offenders. However, these officers may never be content with the offender's behavior until they find some reason to award some form of punitive sanction.

Table 1.1. Role Orientations of Community Supervision Officers

		Control Spectrum	
		High	**Low**
Assistance	High	Paternal officer	Welfare worker
Spectrum	Low	Punitive officer	Passive agent

Source: Adapted from Glaser (1964).

In other words, the view is that those on the caseload are doing wrong but are not getting caught. The officer knows this to be true and makes it his or her duty to ensure that the offender gets away with as little as possible. Naturally, human relations between this officer and his or her caseload is usually fairly impaired and sterile.

Welfare workers will view the offender more as a client than as a supervisee on their caseloads. These individuals believe that, ultimately, the best way they can enhance the security and safety of the community is by reforming the client so that further crime will not occur. These officers will attempt to achieve objectivity that is similar to a therapist and will thus avoid judging the client (Clear & Cole, 2003). These officers will be most inclined to consider the needs of their offender-clients and their potential capacity for change. They view their jobs more as a therapeutic service than as a punitive service, though this does not mean that they will not supervise the behavior of their caseload. Rather, the purpose for their supervision is more likened to the follow-up screening that a therapist might provide to a client to ensure that the client is continuing on the directed trajectory that is consistent with his or her prior treatment goals.

Passive agents tend to view their job as just that: a job. They will tend to do as little as possible, and they do not have passion for their jobs. Unlike the punitive officer and the welfare officer, they simply do not care about the outcome of their work as long as they avoid any difficulties. These individuals are often in the job simply because of the benefits that it may provide as well as the freedom from continual supervision that this type of job affords.

Clear and Cole (2003) note that it is debatable whether officers would best be served using one consistent type of approach or whether they should attempt to use each orientation whenever appropriate. Thus, the community supervision process can be greatly impacted by the approach taken by the community supervision officer. Further, agencies can transmit a certain tendency toward any of these orientations through policies, procedures, informal organizational culture, or even daily memos. The tone set by the agency is likely to have an effect on the officer's morale and subsequently their approach to the supervision process.

Indeed, it is the notion of role identity confusion that is a primary source of burnout among community supervision officers. **Role identity confusion** occurs when officers are unclear about the expectations placed on them as they attempt to juggle the "policing"-oriented and the "reform"-oriented nature of their work (Clear & Cole, 2003). If the agency is unclear or sends contradictory messages (such as noting that attention should be given to each offender's needs to prevent recidivism yet weighing officers down with excessive caseloads), then the stress level for officers increases. Thus, it may be that in some agencies officers should strive to utilize each approach so that they can fulfill the multiple overt and covert expectations of the agency.

On the other hand, some agencies may be exceedingly clear about their expectations of community supervision officers. In this case, if the agency has a strict law-and-order flavor, officers may be best served by utilizing the approach of a punitive officer to ensure that they are a good fit with agency expectations. In another agency, the emphasis might be on a combined restorative/community justice model coupled with community policing efforts that are designed to reintegrate the offender. In an agency such as this, the officer may find that a welfare worker approach is the best fit for that agency and that community. Thus, it is the culture of the community service organization that will have a strong impact on the officer's orientation, and if the officer's personal or professional views are in conflict with the organizational structure, the likelihood of effective probation supervision is impaired. This can and likely does translate to lowered outcomes and is one of the many possible sources of recidivism among offenders since it shapes the manner in which officers address the offender and their special needs.

The personal interaction between the community supervision officer and the individual offender cannot be underestimated. This is particularly true when one considers that in many cases it is the supervision officer and the offender who develop a supervision or treatment plan for that offender. The supervision officer has significant latitude in designing this supervision plan and also enjoys a wide degree of discretion in how the terms and conditions of this agreement are enforced. Thus, the officer has an amount of leverage that can place the offender at his or her mercy in many respects. The manner in which the officer approaches this is likely to affect the motivation of the offender. If agencies wish to improve probation outcomes, they should ensure that the right type of officer is working with the correct type of caseload as determined by organizational outcomes for each offender group.

MODELS OF DELIVERY: HOW TO ASSIGN AND PLACE OFFENDERS

The **model of caseload delivery** has to do with the process whereby offenders are initially assigned their community supervision officer. This is often determined by the agency size and the number of offenders under the agency's jurisdiction. Some models of caseload delivery may use some form of random offender assignment or may base the assignment on the geographical location of offenders to make the task of face-to-face supervision easier for the community supervision officer (Champion, 2002). However, other issues, such as organizational culture and agency intent, can affect the manner by which offenders are assigned to a given caseload. Generally, it is the contention of this book that the specialized needs caseload model be used when dealing with special needs offenders (Carlson & Parks, 1979; Champion, 2002). Naturally, if and when it is possible, it would also be beneficial if the agency were to structure the caseload as geographically realistic as possible so that the supervision officer can reasonably make visits.

The **specialized needs caseload model** pertains to community supervision assignments to offenders who share common specialized needs such as substance abuse, sex offending, a given set of disabilities, and so on. This model is a derivative of the specialized caseload model presented in other works (Champion, 2002). With this model, the officer assigned to these offenders will have special skills or training related to these needs. Further, supervision officers will typically have a close rapport with the therapists and the treatment program that is utilized. Indeed, the supervision officer and the therapist should have a close working relationship even if this is conducted largely by phone. Informal ties between the two should be fostered by both agencies, and supervisors on both ends could accommodate work schedules so that both are able to occasionally have lunch or other meetings with one another. The main idea is that both work together as a team. This notion of a collaborative relationship will become more apparent in subsequent chapters.

Related to this collaborative method of operation is the notion that caseloads of special needs offenders should be focused on offender accountability, cognitive restructuring (cognitive-behavioral techniques discussed later in this chapter), and on **restorative justice principles** of case management (Champion, 2002; Ferns, 1994). This form of case management is based on the notion that offenders need to learn about the impact that they had on their victim(s) and that in the process they should develop a sense of accountability and remorsefulness (Champion, 2002). The intent of the process of supervision and case management is to provide a restorative purpose and function to offender case management. This gives a purpose and direction to the process of supervision offenders in the community that has typically been lacking in times past. The community supervision officer watches the offender's level of cognitive distortion and deficiencies associated with his or her set of special needs, his or her level of antisocial behaviors, and the offender's ability to provide restoration to communities and victims. It is important to note that one strongpoint of this type of supervision is that the victim is given consideration in the process and that, if done correctly and if the offender legitimately complies, the offender will gain some form of understanding and some bit of empathy. Empathy is naturally a characteristic that will lead to remorse, and remorse, guilt, and conscience are the hallmarks of long-term offender treatment. This type of program therefore stresses increased offender accountability, individualization of punishments from the range of sanctions listed earlier, and community safety (Champion, 2002). These elements are combined with the treatment goal of increased offender awareness through cognitive-behavioral intervention (Champion, 2002; Ferns, 1994). Thus, selection of the treatment agency and the therapist used should be a deliberate and methodical process based on the type of offender being processed, the therapist's skill or training with special needs offenders, and the treatment design used (cognitive-behavioral being preferred).

As will be seen, the use of restorative justice programming is a strongly recommended approach with special needs offenders who are in the community. This type of programming easily works within the scope of a community supervision framework and can also help augment the various intermediate sanctions that may be imposed. These two orientations will later be shown to work together in a complementary fashion. Indeed, so much is this the case that Chapter 15 is devoted entirely to restorative justice programming and special needs offenders. Further, both intermediate sanctions and restorative justice techniques can be effective tools to likewise augment therapeutic interventions. The intermediate sanctions serve as the short-term motivation to attend and to stay on track with the offender's treatment, while the restorative justice principles attempt to build empathy and remorse while reducing much of the community stigma so that the offender will be less likely to recidivate and the community will have direct input into the supervision of the offender, thereby improving community safety and satisfaction. In short, this combined model of specialized supervision, treatment, and community involvement can lead to a "win-win-win" approach for all parties concerned.

TYPES OF THERAPEUTIC PERSONNEL AND PROFESSIONAL ORIENTATIONS

Therapeutic personnel come in many forms, particularly when dealing with specialized populations. Further, state laws often have different distinctions between types of therapeutic providers and the level of credential and/or license that they may hold. For instance, while a person may be certified, this is not the same as licensure. **Certification** implies a certain level of oversight in that a minimum standard of competency exists, but it is **licensure** that provides the legal right to see clients and receive third-party billing. Third-party billing is when insurance companies, employment assistance programs, or state programs are billed to reimburse the therapist. Obviously, this is important for the therapeutic practitioner working in private practice or in a non-profit but private facility. In addition, not all mental health specialists can give assessment tests. Many of the tests discussed in the next chapter (e.g., the MMPI-2) require a fully licensed psychologist with a Ph.D., whereas the other tests may have little or no minimal criteria other than training to administer and score the test.

The reason that all this is worth mentioning is that the student should realize that when community supervision agencies contract with various providers, they must be cognizant of the abilities and limitations that these service providers have. Obviously, the more trained and educated the clinician, the more costly he or she is likely to be. Thus, agencies must be aware of who they network with to avoid paying a full-blown psychologist for something that a counselor with a certification can do, perhaps just as well and for much less the cost. Obviously, when deciding on adding better assessment scales to their programs, agencies must factor in the cost to pay a highly qualified mental health professional, such as a psychologist who is trained in psychometrics.

The following paragraphs discuss the types of therapeutic treatment professionals with whom most agencies are likely to work either full time or on a contract basis.

Counselors typically have training in a particular area, such as substance abuse. They tend to deal with specific populations that have specific problems. However, many counselors have a master's degree and full licensure; these counselors are referred to as licensed professional counselors.

Social workers might have a bachelor's degree, but most practicing social workers have a master's degree in social work. Their knowledge of social support systems, organizations, and groups (community aid organizations or support groups) along with their background in psychological interventions distinguish their fields of competence.

Psychologists have doctorates in psychology and typically have extensive education and/or experience in research, theories of human behavior, and therapeutic techniques. In addition to therapy and counseling, they specialize in the administration of psychological tests and assessments.

Psychiatrists are medical doctors and typically are involved with the criminal justice system only during times when inmates must be subdued with medicine or when dealing with seriously disturbed persons. Their ability to prescribe medication for anxiety, depression, anger, and other disorders truly distinguishes them from the other three categories of mental health provider.

TYPES OF THERAPEUTIC ORIENTATIONS AND PROGRAM DELIVERY

Throughout the remainder of the book, we will discuss different types of treatment programs for different types of offenders. The intent of this section of the chapter is to provide the student some basic theoretical orientations to treatment as a foundation for subsequent discussions on intervention programs with specific types of offenders. The primary thrust of this book deals with the nature of supervision of special needs offenders while they receive the treatment that they need to reintegrate and cease criminal offending. However, it is not the intent of this book to serve as a therapeutic handbook or guide in applying treatment principles to these specialized populations. Thus, the following paragraphs discuss various orientations that are likely to be used in criminal justice networks. This is by no means an exhaustive list of therapeutic orientations; rather, these are selected because of their applicability to contemporary correctional programs.

Cognitive therapy is based on the belief that faulty thinking patterns and belief systems cause psychological problems and that changing one's thoughts improves one's mental and emotional health and results in changes in behavior. It challenges all-or-nothing thinking and overgeneralizations (Corey, 2005). One branch of cognitive therapy is called rational emotive therapy and is based on the belief that our emotions result from our beliefs, interpretations, and reactions to life events. This type of cognitive therapy is based more on thinking and doing and is more active. It is appropriate with adult sex offenders (Chapter 10) and domestic batterers (Chapter 11).

Behavioral therapy holds that long-term change is accomplished through action and that disorders are learned ways of behaving that are maladaptive. If the client practices the new behavior long enough, then feelings will begin to change as well. These types of interventions target behavior on a mechanistic level with a more direct training approach using observable reinforcements, punishments, and stimuli

(Van Voorhis, Braswell, & Lester, 2000). It may incorporate elements of social learning and models in learning new behavior. It will utilize techniques such as role playing, performance feedback, and imitation. This type of therapy is used extensively with almost all types of offender-clients and is one of the favorites in criminal justice agency because it can be easily observed and measured.

Reality therapy uses forms of involvement between counselor and client to teach the client to be self-responsible. The therapist rejects irresponsible and unrealistic behavior and insists that the client assume responsibility free of denial or excuse making (Corey, 2005). Finally, the therapist teaches and instructs the offender-client how to fulfill his or her needs within the limits set by reality.

Solution-focused therapy begins from the observation that most psychological problems are present only intermittently. This type of therapy assists the client to notice when symptoms are diminished or absent and use this knowledge as a foundation for recovery (Corey, 2005). If a patient insists that the symptoms are constant and unrelieved, the therapist works with him or her to find exceptions and make this exception more frequent, predictable, and controllable.

Adlerian therapy is based on the belief that human behavior has a purpose and is goal oriented and that we strive for social connectedness and suffer our emotional difficulties because of feelings of inferiority (Corey, 2005). Therapy is a process or reeducation leading to greater social participation and few feelings of inferiority (Corey, 2005). This type of therapy frequently uses and borrows numerous techniques from cognitive therapy as well. It is important to note that this type of therapy tends to mesh well with restorative justice principles discussed previously in this chapter and discussed later in Chapter 14.

Less common types of therapy include **family systems therapy**, which looks at the entire family as a system with its own customs, roles, beliefs, and dynamics that affect and impact the offender more routinely than any other group. Each family member plays a part in the system, and family systems therapy helps individuals discover how their family operates, their role in that system, and how this affects their relationships inside and outside that family system. This type of intervention has been found to be particularly effective with alcoholics and other substance abusers and should be a mandatory form of therapy for families of early childhood offenders and juvenile offenders. This type of therapy should augment individual counseling and is very effective in getting the family involved in the offender's treatment. It is likewise effective with female offenders, particularly those with children, and is especially useful with the types of offenders featured in Chapters 7 to 9.

Gestalt therapy is a form of therapy used in group settings in most cases. It helps the offender-client become more self-aware and to learn responsibility for thoughts and actions (Corey, 2005). Techniques include confrontation, role playing, and empty-chair dialogue, where the client attempts to resolve issues with others who are not present but are sources of stress or trauma in his or her life.

Feminist therapy focuses on empowering women and helping them discover how to break free from some of the traditional molds that have kept them from succeeding. This type of therapy tends to be focused on strengthening women in areas such as communication, assertiveness, self-esteem, and relationships (Corey, 2005). This is useful with female offenders (Chapter 13) since so many of these offenders were themselves victims at an early age (childhood sexual abuse) or during adulthood (domestically abusive relationships).

Faith-based therapy is often a blend of cognitive and behavioral techniques grounded in scriptural instructions on the appropriate form of cognition or behavior. These types of programs are becoming increasingly more popular and have been particularly effective with substance-abusing clients. An example of one such program is provided in Chapter 3.

Note that in addition to each of these, most every therapist will utilize the basic techniques associated with client-centered therapy, though the full use and undiluted version of this type of therapy is not usually used with the offending population. The main point for this book is that **client-centered techniques** emphasize that the therapist must be genuine, accepting, and empathetic to the offender-client. The therapist attempts to create a safe environment where the offender-client feels free to talk about his or her issues and is free to gain insight from them.

Finally, **existential therapy** reflects more a kind of philosophizing. It is not a specific therapy but is designed more to help the client gain perspective on his or her life. This type of therapy focuses on free will, the responsibility for choices, and the search for meaning and purpose through suffering, love, and hardship. This type of therapy is presented simply to note that this is probably an excellent model to use with geriatric offenders (discussed in Chapter 13). These issues will likely be important to these individuals who are reaching an age where these issues become increasingly relevant.

As can be seen, there are numerous types of therapy that can be used, and all have a certain appeal or usefulness for certain types of offender-clients. Thus, with special needs offenders, knowing which therapy type is the right match for each of the types of offenders presented will prove to be very important in maximizing treatment success. Further, some therapists may have a certain therapeutic orientation, or, similar to probation officers, they may have specialized training with one type of offender population but not with another. Thus, a "one-therapist-fits-all" approach is not likely to work with special needs offenders. If a community supervision department has a caseload of adult sex offenders, the same therapist(s) who are identified as being skilled at working with that population should be employed. Likewise, the same would be true of domestic batterers, the elderly, and so on.

CAN PROGRAMS BE TAILORED TO FIT SPECIAL OFFENDERS WITH SPECIAL NEEDS?

At this point, several things should be clear to the student. First, the type of probation officer can affect the overall supervision outcome. Second, the type of probation supervision program can affect the outcome of the offender as well. Third, the type of therapeutic personnel chosen can greatly affect the treatment outcome of the offender. Finally, the type of therapeutic curriculum and/or program can have an equal effect on the final outcome of the offender's likelihood of recovery. Each of these previous four factors is somewhat able to be controlled by the agency. However, one factor that cannot be controlled by the agency is the type of offender and his or her motivation when initially being placed on the caseload. One final factor to consider when determining whether programs can be tailored to fit special needs offenders is the use of effective assessment.

Assessment is the foundation on which the first four previously mentioned factors are based. Without effective assessment, there is no way of knowing which type of probation officer will work best with the given offender in question. Without accurate assessment, it is unclear which type of community supervision strategy should be used with the offender. And, as one would suspect, ineffective assessment would prevent us from knowing which type of therapist and which type of therapeutic orientation we should use with a given offender. Thus, assessment is the foundation for supervision planning and for treatment planning. If the assessment is incorrect, the supervision scheme will be faulty and the treatment program less likely to work.

Therefore, community supervision programs and treatment programs can be only as good as their initial assessment ability. This is a critical point and illustrates why Chapter 2 is entirely devoted to the assessment and classification of special needs offenders. Indeed, Chapter 2 provides a specific rationale for each stage in the supervision/treatment process since all of these are designed to maximize the ability of practitioners to address both public safety and reintegration goals with special needs offenders. This process also serves to limit the amount of guesswork when placing special needs offenders on community supervision. Although supervision personnel cannot read minds, the ability to optimize the likelihood of offender outcome is well within our grasp and requires only a structured, step-by-step process of implementation. Although our interventions may never be perfect, they can be optimized to have a sound "goodness of fit" so as to pass any social cost and social benefit analysis on a macro level.

With this in mind, then, it becomes clear that with effective assessment, the effects of both community supervision and treatment interventions can be optimized. Likewise, the implementation of certain community supervision orientations can help augment the effects of treatment and vice versa. Thus, the offender given probation will be recommended on the basis of the **presentence investigation report (PSI)**, a comprehensive overview and summary of an offender's background, including prior offenses, educational level, mental health concerns, and other factors, that is designed to assist judges in determining the most appropriate sentence for that offender. The PSI is completed by a community supervision officer, and it is the recommendation of this book that the community supervision officer be familiar with the basic characteristics of the special needs offender population they investigate. For example, understanding the dynamics and nuances associated with the mentally challenged offender will likely improve the overall quality and focus of the PSI when a probation officer must present an investigation on an offender with such challenges.

Special Insert 1.1. PSI Information Provided from Offender Self-Report Questionnaire

U.S. PROBATION OFFICE UNITED STATES DISTRICT COURT DISTRICT OF NEW JERSEY

(NJ Form 1 [4/95])

This questionnaire, containing a total of six pages, is to be completed by you and presented to the Probation Officer assigned to conduct a presentence report for the Court. Your answers should be complete and truthful and printed legibly. All questions are to be answered, and it is to be signed and dated by you on the last page.

LAST NAME: FIRST NAME:
MIDDLE NAME:
Other NAMES/ALIASES/NICKNAMES used:
____

DATE OF BIRTH: PLACE OF BIRTH: SOCIAL SECURITY NO.:
SEX: RACE:
HOME PHONE # (WITH AREA CODE):
PRESENT ADDRESS:
Other phones? *(provide number if applicable):* Pager #: ______________
Cellular #: ______________
Your Legal Address, if different:
____

If born outside United States, are you a U.S. Citizen? _____ If yes, date and place of naturalization: ______________
If no, what is Immigration Status: ______________ Entry Port and Date: ______________
Alien #: ______________ Do you hold a valid passport? __________ Issued by what Country? ______________

PRESENT CRIMINAL CASE

Date of Arrest on this Case: ______________
Offense of Conviction: ______________
Bail or Jail? _____ If in custody, Name/Location of Jail: ______________
If on Bail, type/amount of Bond: ______________ Name of Pretrial Officer: ______________
Defense Attorney: name ______________
______________ address ______________
phone ______________

Name(s) of any Codefendant(s): ____________________

Name of Government Agent: ____________________

Your version of the offense, explain how you see it: ____________________

CRIMINAL HISTORY ***(include juvenile and adult arrests)***

DATE OF:
ARREST/CHARGE:
CHARGE(S):
CONVICTION:
COURT NAME:
LOCATION:
DATE OF SENTENCE OR DISPOSITION:
SENTENCE IMPOSED COUNSEL? YES or NO

Have you ever been on probation, pretrial, or parole? ________ If yes, explain: ____________________

Are you on probation, pretrial, or parole presently? ________ If yes, name of Officer: ____________________

Was your probation, pretrial, or parole ever revoked? ________ If yes, explain: ____________________

Do you have other criminal charges pending? ________ If yes, explain: ____________________

(***use reverse side if necessary***)

FAMILY: PARENTS & SIBLINGS ***(list biological parents; if raised by other than natural parents, add surrogates' names below space for natural parents; after parents, list all siblings, living or deceased).***

FULL NAME RELATIONSHIP AGE
PRESENT ADDRESS AND PHONE OCCUPATION
FATHER
MOTHER

MARITAL STATUS

(please check one that applies): single _____ married _____ divorced _____ separated _____ widowed _____ domestic partner _____

(continued)

Spouse's full Name: ____________________ DOB: ____________ Maiden Name (if applicable):____________________

____

Spouse's Education level: _____ Occupation (and where): ____________________
Date and Place of Marriage: _____ Spouse previously married? _____
Does spouse have prior criminal record?

____

CHILDREN

CHILD'S FULL NAME AGE MOTHER'S NAME
CHILD'S ADDRESS *(IF DIFFERENT THAN YOURS)*
Are you under Court Order to pay child support? _____
If yes, amount ordered $ _____ per month by (*name/location of court*):

____

Are you in compliance with the child support order? _____ If no, explain:

____

What is the amount in arrears? ___________

PREVIOUS MARRIAGES

FULL NAME OF SPOUSE DATE/PLACE OF MARRIAGE
DATE/PLACE OF DIVORCE ALIMONY? AMOUNT?
IN COMPLIANCE?

PRESENT RESIDENCE (*please check type*): apartment _____ private home _____
condominium _____ townhouse _____
Amount of monthly rent/mortgage: $ _____; number of rooms: _____ length of time residing there: ___________
I live with:

____

I also have vacation home/apt. at (*exact location*):

____

(please provide dates and locations of previous residences over past 15 years):
from _____ to _____ at

____

from _____ to _____ at

____

from _____ to _____ at

____

PHYSICAL HEALTH

Height: _____ Weight: _____ Eye Color: _____ Hair Color: _____

Scars/Tattoos (*describe*):

___

My present physical health is (*check one*): excellent _____ good _____ fair _____ poor _____

Describe any physical limitations or disabilities:

___

I am under the medical care of Doctor ______________ at (*full address*) ______ for treatment of __________.

I take the following prescribed medications:

___

List past hospitalizations for treatment of illness or surgery:

DATE(S) NAME/LOCATION OF HOSPITAL REASON(S) FOR ADMISSION RESULT(S)

MENTAL/EMOTIONAL HEALTH

My present mental/emotional health is (*check one*): excellent _____ good _____ fair _____ poor _____

I am presently under treatment for ______________ with ______________ (reason) (doctor or program)

at (*location*): ______________

I take following prescribed medications: ______________

(list ALL past treatment for mental or emotional problems, including gambling):

DATE(S) NAME/LOCATION OF DOCTOR/HOSPITAL/PROGRAM INPATIENT?

REASON(s) FOR TREATMENT RESULT

DRUG HISTORY (***indicate past or current use of any of the following***): alcohol _____ marijuana _____ cocaine _____ crack _____

(meth)amphetamines _____ heroin/opiates _____ barbiturates _____

hallucinogens_____ inhalants _____ other _____

When was alcohol or any controlled substance(s) last used? _____

Are you presently in any form of treatment for any of above? _____

If yes, type of treatment and location:

___

If intravenous user, have you ever been tested for HIV?

___

(list ALL past treatment(s) for drug and/or alcohol abuse problems):

DATE(S) NAME/LOCATION OF DOCTOR/HOSPITAL/PROGRAM:

IN- OR OUTPATIENT?

REASON(S) RESULT(S)

MILITARY SERVICE I was not in military service: _____

Branch: ____________ Service No.:__________ Date Entered: ___________

Date Discharged: ____________ Type Discharge: ____________

(*continued*)

Highest Rank: __________ Rank at Separation: __________
Decorations/Awards: __________ VA Claim No.: __________
____

Foreign Service? _____ Courts-Martial ? _____ Military Occupation Specialty: _____

EDUCATION/VOCATIONAL SKILLS

(***list schools attended, with most recent first; include vocational programs***)
NAME/LOCATION OF SCHOOL, DATES ATTENDED, DEGREE, DIPLOMA, CERTIFICATE RECEIVED

Do you have specialized training or skills? _____ If yes, identify:
____

Do you have professional license(s)? _____ If yes, identify:
____

Is retention of license affected by your conviction?
____

Do you have permit or license for firearms? _____ What type of weapon(s)? _____
Issued by: __________
Do you have a Driver's License? _____ Issued by what State? _____ License Number: __________

EMPLOYMENT

Presently I am (***check one***): working FT _____ working PT _____ unemployed _____ retired _____ in custody _____ disabled _____
My present employment (*name, location*):
____
Job function/title ________________________________
monthly gross income: $____________________
Is your employer aware of your arrest and conviction in this case? _____
If not working, I am supported as follows *(indicate amount received per month)*: Social Security $__________; Pension $__________;
Disability $__________; Unemployment Benefits $__________; SSI $__________;
Welfare $_____; Food Stamps $__________;
Supported by another $__________ (*identify person/relationship providing support:*__________)
(please list all past employment over past 15 years)

DATES NAME/ADDRESS OF EMPLOYER, JOB, MONTHLY WAGE, REASONS FOR LEAVING

from _____ to _____
from _____ to _____
from _____ to _____
from _____ to _____
from _____ to _____
from _____ to _____

FINANCIAL CONDITION

(You will also be provided a detailed financial statement for completion and submission to the probation officer; at the present time, please provide the information requested below.)

My monthly NET income is $ _______ My monthly necessary household expenses total: $_________

My spouse's monthly NET income: $__________

Provide the approximate present value of each of the following which pertain to you:

AUTO(S): $________________ list year, make, and models:

____

EQUITY IN HOME: $________ STOCKS/BONDS: $________ IRA/KEOGH PLANS: $__________

BALANCE IN SAVINGS ACCOUNT(S): $________ NAME/LOCATION OF BANK(S): __________

BALANCE IN CHECKING ACCOUNT(S): $________ NAME/LOCATION OF BANK(S): __________

Do you have or ever had any civil proceedings brought against you including mortgage foreclosures? __________

If yes, explain:

____

Have you ever filed for or declared Bankruptcy?_____ If so, year and location:

____

Have you filed yearly income tax returns with I.R.S. for past five years ? _____

If no, explain: _______________________________________

____

In my spare time, I enjoy the following activities:

____

List any religious, fraternal, or civic organizations or clubs you are or have been a member of:

____

____

____

____

THIS FORM WAS COMPLETED BY:

____

(YOUR SIGNATURE) (DATE)

____

Note: This form is an adapted version of the NJ Form 1 and is a U.S. government publication available from the **U.S. Probation Office of the United States District Court** system (District of New Jersey). The full form can be found at http//www.fpdnj.org/PDF/FORM1/formone.pdf.

Thus, it is the recommendation of this book that probation departments remain consistent with the tenets of the specialized needs caseload model and ensure that those officers normally responsible for supervising a specialized type of offender (e.g., the mentally challenged) are assigned the duty of conducting the PSI for that offender. Clear and Cole (2003) note that there is some debate as to whether some officers should be assigned to full-time PSI writing while others are full-time supervision personnel. It has been noted that this is somewhat inefficient because often the supervising officer must then learn the content of the PSI that the initial investigating officer already knows. This should be avoided at all costs when dealing with the special needs offenders presented in this book.

It is the intent of this chapter to demonstrate that the effective matching of resources with the specific offender population is critical to increasing treatment outcomes. With this in mind, the supervision officer must be as familiar as possible with his or her offender caseload. Therefore, officers supervising special needs offenders should be both trained specifically to supervise these offenders and trained in case investigation and PSI writing focused on that particular type of offender. Finally, contrary to popular belief, less is more with these reports for special needs offenders, and therefore it is recommended that a shortened, tightly focused PSI be written for these caseloads. This means that the officer is required to know the case extensively and also to be completely informed of penal code requirements with the specific type of offending in question. The emphasis should be on the specific offender typology and the officer's expertise in connecting the type of supervision given with the right type of therapist (the officer will already know this person formally and informally, as noted earlier in this chapter) and the type of therapeutic program.

Thus, assessment begins with the PSI and then progresses to and includes those types of assessment and classification schemes noted in Chapter 2. From the information determined during the PSI and through subsequent assessment tools, the specific matching between supervision and treatment is determined. It is in this manner that recidivism with most special needs offenders can be prevented on the longest-term duration.

CONCLUSION

While not all offenders can be treated, not all must be incarcerated. Even among those who are incarcerated, a return to the community is often inevitable. With this in mind, it is important that programs of community supervision are as effective as possible to minimize the risk of recidivism. The special needs offender is just that: an offender with specialized needs and considerations. It is in society's best interest to address these needs to prevent the likelihood of further criminality.

It is not the contention of this chapter or this book that the offender be treated lightly. Indeed, quite the contrary is the case. These offenders should be held accountable to the victim and the community for the crimes they commit. However, these offenders typically have certain challenges and impediments that may preclude their ability to effectively make amends for their crime or crimes. A failure to acknowledge this reality is nothing less than an exercise in fantasy. Thus, it is contended that a restorative justice modality that includes the concerns of the victim and community is the best venue for both supervising and treating these offenders.

Further, the efforts of both supervision personnel and treatment personnel should not be in conflict with one another. Rather, they should strive to enhance the functions of one another. Therefore, a collaborative relationship must be maintained between community supervision personnel and treatment personnel. This collaborative relationship must go beyond lip service and be a routine form of communication. Further, these professionals do not work in a social vacuum but rather operate against the backdrop of numerous community personnel and resources. Thus, in keeping with a restorative justice and/or community justice model, the supervision and treatment personnel must create a working partnership with agencies and persons within the community. It is in this manner that the offender will be best supervised throughout the continuum of his or her sentence.

Finally, the use of effective assessment techniques is the fundamental groundwork on which this process is built. If this stage is flawed, then the entire process will be flawed as well. Probation officers responsible for the offender with the identified special need must take an active part in this assessment, and subsequent assessment scales and schemes must be linked to the probations officer's PSI. It is in this manner that supervision personnel and treatment personnel work hand in hand from the assessment stage to the final reintegration stage in supervision and treatment planning. While no program can be absolutely perfect, such techniques that are presented in this chapter will be likely to improve the overall response to special needs offenders while ensuring that public safety is not compromised. This is the ultimate goal when addressing special needs offenders in the community.

KEY TERMS

Special needs offender
Subjective needs
Objective needs
Societal needs
Intermediate community supervision sanctions
Probation with community service and restitution
Intensive supervised probation
Day reporting centers
Home confinement with electronic monitoring
Global positioning satellite systems
Residential treatment home
Official halfway house
Paternal officer
Punitive officer
Welfare worker
Passive agent
Role identity confusion
Model of caseload delivery
Specialized needs caseload model
Restorative justice principles
Certification
Licensure
Counselors
Social workers

Psychologists
Psychiatrists
Cognitive therapy
Behavioral therapy
Cognitive-behavioral therapy
Reality therapy
Solution-focused therapy
Adlerian therapy
Family systems therapy
Gestalt therapy
Feminist therapy
Faith-based therapy
Client-centered techniques
Existential therapy
Presentence investigation report

REFERENCES

Ashford, J. B., Sales, B. D., & Reid, W. H. (2002). *Treating adult and juvenile offenders with special needs*. Washington, DC: American Psychological Association.

Carlson, E. W., & Parks, E. (1979). *Critical issues in adult probation: Issues in probation management*. Washington, DC: U.S. Department of Justice.

Champion, D. (2002). *Probation, parole, and community corrections* (4th ed.). Upper Saddle River, NJ: Prentice Hall.

Clear, T. R., & Cole, G. F. (2003). *American corrections* (6th ed.). Belmont, CA: Wadsworth.

Corey, G. (2005). *Theory and practice of counselling and psychotherapy* (7th ed.). Florence, KY: Brooks/Cole.

Ferns, R. (1994). Restorative case management: The evolution of correctional case management. *APPA Perspectives, 18*, 36–41.

Glaser, D. (1964). *The effectiveness of a prison and parole system*. New York: Macmillan.

Van Voorhis, P., Braswell, M., & Lester, D. (2000). *Correctional counseling and rehabilitation* (4th ed.). Cincinnati: Anderson.

LEARNING CHECK

1. Which type of therapy contends that long-term change is accomplished through action and that disorders are learned ways of behaving that are maladaptive? If the client practices the new behavior long enough, then feelings will begin to change as well.
   a. Reality therapy
   b. Solution-focused therapy
   c. Behavioral therapy
   d. Adlerian therapy
   e. None of the above

2. What are some common characteristics among recidivists?
   a. Recidivists tend to be under no correctional supervision when committing new offenses.
   b. Recidivists tend to be unmarried, widowed, or divorced.
   c. Recidivists tend to have alcohol- or drug-dependency problems that are associated with their new offense.
   d. All of the above
   e. None of the above

3. ______________________ is the foundation for supervision planning and for treatment planning.
   a. Prediction
   b. Intake
   c. Assessment
   d. Recidivism reduction
   e. None of the above

4. ______________________ are residential settings for offenders who are court ordered to stay at the facility as a supplement to their conditions of community supervision.
   a. Official halfway houses
   b. Day reporting centers
   c. Home confinement with electronic monitoring programs
   d. Jails
   e. All of the above

5. ______________________ occurs when officers are unclear about the expectations placed on them as they attempt to juggle between the "policing"-oriented and the "reform"-oriented nature of their work.
   a. Job stress
   b. Role identity confusion
   c. Recidivism
   d. None of the above

6. Which model of caseload delivery is recommended when initially assigning offenders to various community supervision officers?
   a. Special needs offender classification system
   b. Special needs recidivism prediction model
   c. Special unit assignment process
   d. Specialized needs caseload model
   e. None of the above

7. This form of sanction is usually viewed as the most effective alternative to imprisonment.
   a. Split-sentence jail and community supervision
   b. Intensive supervised probation
   c. Residential treatment home
   d. Probation with community service
   e. None of the above

8. Why is assessment considered so important in achieving optimal supervision and treatment case planning?
   a. Without effective assessment, there is no way possible of knowing which type of probation officer will work best with the given offender in question.
   b. Ineffective assessment would prevent us from knowing which type of therapist and which type of therapeutic orientation we should use with a given offender.

c. Without accurate assessment, it is unclear which type of community supervision strategy should be used with the offender.
d. All of the above
e. Both a and b but not c

9. The presentence investigation report is completed by the______________.
a. Judge
b. Therapist
c. Community supervision officer
d. Each of the above assists in writing this report.
e. None of the above

10. Which type of therapy assists the client in noticing when symptoms are diminished or absent to use this knowledge as a foundation for recovery?
a. Reality therapy
b. Solution-focused therapy
c. Behavioral therapy
d. Adlerian therapy
e. None of the above

ESSAY DISCUSSION QUESTIONS

1. Identify and define the types of community supervision program delivery. Next, identify the different supervision styles associated with differing community supervision personnel. Why are the types of program delivery and the types of supervision styles important when dealing with special needs offenders?
2. Identify and define the common types of correctional therapy that are used. Also identify the different types of therapeutic personnel and their professional orientations. Why might the types of correctional therapy and types of therapeutic personnel that are used be important when providing treatment to special needs offenders?
3. How are the various programs of offender supervision able to work together with treatment intervention programs to improve likely offender outcomes? Provide some reasons why community-based programs are best suited for such collaborative efforts.

CHAPTER

2 RISK ASSESSMENT, DIAGNOSIS, RECIDIVISM PREDICTION, AND CLASSIFICATION OF OFFENDERS

Chapter Objectives

1. Understand the importance of assessment in developing effective treatment programs for special needs offenders.
2. Know about the different types of assessment (subjective and objective) and assessment instruments that are presented in this chapter.
3. Know and fully understand the assessment, diagnostic, recidivism prediction, and classification stages of the supervision and treatment planning process for special needs offenders.
4. Understand the fundamental aspects of offender risk prediction.

INTRODUCTION

The purpose of this chapter is to introduce the student to the various considerations involved with monitoring and supervising special needs offenders in the community. Because of concerns with public safety, it is imperative that correctional agencies be as adept as possible at accurately assessing the future prognosis of any offender under their supervision. For purposes of this book, the term **prognosis** refers to the likelihood of an offender to successfully reform and to simultaneously refrain from further criminal activity. Thus, there is both a treatment-related component (reform) related to an offender's prognosis and a public safety (likelihood of further criminal activity) component contained within an offender's prognosis. Both must be considered simultaneously if the correctional agency is to fulfill its mission in a satisfactory manner.

It should be pointed out that there are four general stages of offender supervision and treatment planning for both institutional and community-based corrections: (1) the assessment stage, (2) the diagnostic stage, (3) the recidivism prediction stage, and (4) the classification stage. The **assessment stage** refers to both subjective methods of clinical interviews and observations and objective methods of test taking, including mathematical models of offender profiling. The **diagnostic stage** refers to the process of diagnosing offenders based on physical health or mental illness or the diagnosis of offenders based on the types of challenges they may face. The **recidivism prediction stage** takes assessment and diagnostic information into consideration to determine the basic level of risk that an offender holds for further offending, and this stage is usually the framework from which classification stage decisions are developed. These predictions may be based on both subjective and objective information. The **classification stage** includes housing, job, and educational assignments within institutions as well as treatment, vocational, and supervision schemes for offenders on community supervision.

It should be pointed out that these stages are not official stages that work in this exact format in all correctional agencies. However, this basic process (perhaps with other similar terms), modified to one extent or another, is commonly found in most all correctional agencies, though one stage may be given more emphasis than another. It is the contention of this book that all four stages are important, but the assessment stage is the most critical of all, as this stage is the basis of all subsequent stages. Therefore, the more effective the initial assessment of the agency, the less recidivism should occur. Agencies are able to save society substantial grief and financial expense if they are able to accurately assess offenders at intake.

Intake is the initial process that an offender enters into in the correctional system. This process is heavily tied to information obtained from the **presentence investigation report** that the probation department will provide to the presiding judge of an offender's case. The presentence investigation report is the file that includes a wide range of background information on the offender (as noted in Chapter 1). This file will typically include demographic, vocational, educational, and personal information on the offender as well as records on prior offending patterns and the probation department's recommendation as to the appropriate type of sentencing and supervision for the offender in question. In many respects, the presentence investigation report is the initial point of assessment, and it will often be utilized during assessment in the institutional setting or when the offender is officially placed under the jurisdiction of the probation department.

This points toward another source of importance related to assessment. If the offender is accurately assessed, then only those offenders who are a risk to public safety will be incarcerated. Indeed, those offenders who are a low risk for recidivism or even those who are a high risk but are most likely to commit nuisance or nonviolent crimes should not be placed in prison. This is because such forms of custody are expensive and are designed mainly to prevent the offender from hurting others in society. Despite the common notion that the loss of liberty (their punishment) is the basis for the prison, it is the contention of this book that such a punishment can in fact be fulfilled as well through house arrest or some other form of secure supervision that does not require the expense incurred by prison. Whether offenders are kept within the strict confines of a bedroom or the strict confines of a prison cell is not the main consequence of concern since both sufficiently restrict liberty in an identical manner. The only difference is that if offenders decide to violate their sentence and leave the confines of their bedroom, there is no one immediately there to prevent them, whereas in prison such an option is unlikely because of the physical facilities and the immediate reaction of prison staff who are available to respond with haste. Thus, it is the basis of the offenders' likelihood to comply with the mandate of their sentence, not the actual restriction of their liberty, that should be the criteria of their receiving the added expense of a prison cell. Otherwise, financial resources are wasted and squandered unnecessarily on offenders who could have been just as severely punished for their wrongdoings at a fraction of the cost.

Further, it should be noted that assessment is also critical because those offenders who have a high risk of committing violent crimes should not be placed on community supervision. This still occurs, however, because of jail and prison overcrowding, which then places institutions in the precarious position of choosing the "least dangerous" of the violent offenders when releasing to the public. This is a risky position that no administrator relishes and is also the most common source of criticism leveled at community release programs. Ideally, it is the stance of this book that these offenders should simply not be in the community at all. But given the reality of corrections in our society, it is the contention of this book that such offenders should be given forms of community supervision that ensure that these offenders are under the constant watchful eye of a human supervisory authority so that some form of immediate intervention can be provided just as if they were still within the prison facility itself. Regardless of the correctional system's situation, it is strongly recommended that *all security-level determinations be based solely on objective assessment instruments and that subjective criteria be avoided when issues of public safety are at stake.* This is prudent for agency and personnel liability purposes and provides the most mathematically precise, consistent, and effective means of protecting public safety. On the other hand, *when making determinations regarding treatment progress, the use of subjective criteria from the specific primary treatment provider should be utilized more than any other form of assessment.* Such subjective criteria should consist of feedback from both the clinical and the security staff who have had substantial "face time" with the offender. It is important that the student understand the distinctions between the two types of assessment and the appropriate times for their use.

Given this book's position on assessment for security and assessment for treatment, it would be fair to say that the offender supervision process revolves around two key forms of response to the offending population: the goals of (1) incapacitation and (2) treatment. **Incapacitation** is the process of simply removing offenders from society so that they cannot cause further harm to the public. There is no goal beyond this with incapacitation, nor is there any implied retribution or desire to deter other offenders from committing crime. Such goals are too lofty to be pursued with most offenders, and this is especially true with most special needs offenders because of their unique challenges. On the other hand, **treatment** is the process whereby offenders are provided some form of intervention that will help them function within society without resorting to criminal behavior. The student should make one key observation with each of these approaches: both have the same goal of simply reducing the likelihood of future offending from that specific individual offender. In other words, each of these approaches has the same purpose (to prevent the offender from committing future criminal behavior), but both pursue this purpose in a different manner.

It is important that the student understand that with special needs offenders, the two goals of incapacitation and treatment are simultaneously important. Special needs offenders are a highly heterogeneous group with diverse treatment needs and security considerations. These offenders include a host of challenges, and the types of offenders discussed in this book demonstrate that there are numerous physical health, mental health, and sociological factors that serve to exacerbate the ability of the criminal justice system to reduce future criminal behavior from these offenders. Indeed, since the reduction of recidivism is the goal of corrections with special needs offenders, incapacitation schemes will prove to be a short-term solution in any case that is less than a life sentence or death sanction. Since the majority of special needs offenders will ultimately be released into the community at some point, the issue of treatment is simply inevitable. Further, as we will see in Chapter 13, life sentences will eventually lead to increased geriatric offenders, who are roughly three times as expensive to house and incarcerate than typical young offenders. Specialized programs are then likewise necessary to accommodate the disabilities and diminished health that these offenders will increasingly possess.

Thus, it comes full circle that the need for some form of treatment is inevitable. If the vast majority of offenders will ultimately be released into the community and if those who are kept in prison will ultimately develop special medical and mental health requirements when serving a life sentence, then the issue of whether treatment should be provided becomes a completely moot point. Indeed, given the reality of corrections at this point, the need for treatment would apparently override even the notion of incapacitation, as over 60 percent of all offenders in correctional care

are on some form of community supervision, whether that be probation or parole (Clear & Cole, 2003).

Further, special needs offenders are represented within this population and consist of those offenders who are most likely to reoffend. Therefore, these offenders are at a heightened risk of further offending unless some form of intervention is provided to stop their trajectory toward further offending. Since it is the goal of treatment to prevent further offending and since incapacitation is, at best, only a temporary option, treatment becomes the primary orientation when dealing with special needs offenders. In fact, if we do not have some form of sound treatment approach for special needs offenders, we must then say to ourselves that we are openly inviting further offending. Failing to provide treatment programs for special needs offenders is then an act of negligence on a social level and is essentially saying that while we know these offenders have a high rate of recidivism, we do not wish to provide interventions that will lower this recidivism. Treatment for special needs offenders is therefore a necessary evil if nothing else. Treatment for special needs offenders is necessary if we wish to prevent further harm to new victims in our society. Treatment for special needs offenders is necessary if we truly wish to fight crime to the best of our ability.

SPECIAL NEEDS OFFENDERS AND THE ASSESSMENT STAGE: OBJECTIVE ASSESSMENT

As noted earlier in this chapter, when making determinations about security levels (especially when community supervision is involved), it is strongly recommended that determinations be based solely on objective assessment instruments. However, there are a variety of specific assessment instruments that are employed by agencies throughout the nation. These types of objective assessments can range from behavioral checklists that staff complete after a brief period of observation to paper-and-pencil tests completed by the offender to assessment formats that characterize the offender's social, demographic, and criminal history (Van Voorhis, Braswell, & Lester, 2000). Regardless of the type of objective assessment (and some are better than others), the objective assessment should *always be based on the response of supervision staff and should never incorporate self-report data from the offender*. Further, input from the victim (e.g., in programs that utilize a restorative justice element) should not be considered when making decisions to release to the community. Rather, the determination should be clearly restricted to objective mathematical "risk-factor" criteria devoid of all other considerations (e.g., prison or jail overcrowding, desires of the victim, apparent sincerity of the offender, and so on).

Perhaps one of the best-known types of risk assessment systems is the **Wisconsin Risk Assessment System**. This form of structured assessment has become the prototype for many probation and parole systems. Staff members use this instrument to score probationers on the predictors contained on the list, and from this point they classify them into either high-, medium-, or low-risk categories

(Van Voorhis et al., 2000). All the items on this list are statistical predictors of likely failure while on probation. All these predictors are based on previous probation histories among probationers and are based on the premise that the best predictor of future aggregate probationer behavior is the prior aggregate level behavior of probationers. As a result of tracking probationers over time, this instrument has been able to find those factors that are associated with failure and success while on probation. Some of the factors that are examined include the following:

1. Number of address changes in the past 12 months
2. Percentage of time employed in the past 12 months
3. Alcohol consumption problems
4. Other drug consumption problems
5. Offender attitude
6. Age at first conviction
7. Number of prior periods of probation/parole supervision
8. Number of prior probation/parole revocations
9. Number of prior felony convictions
10. Type of convictions or prior adjudications

It should be noted that not all risk factors are the same. Indeed, some risk factors are fairly permanent, or at least they occur because of no fault or cause of the offender. Other risk factors, on the other hand, are due solely to the offender. Further, some risk factors are more suited for security, custody, and control of the offender, whereas others are designed more for treatment. Factors such as age at first conviction, gender, sex, and even disabilities or mental impairments are not directly caused by the offender and are also unlikely to change. These permanent factors are often referred to as **static risk factors**. Thus, static risk factors are characteristics that are inherent to the offender and are usually permanent (Van Voorhis et al., 2000). These characteristics are often the best basis for security determinations. Opposite static risk factors are **dynamic risk factors**, or those characteristics that can change and are more or less influenced or controlled by the offender, such as empathy, motivation, drug use, and family relations (Van Voorhis et al., 2000). These characteristics are often useful to treatment providers but are not really a sound basis for security determinations because they have the possibility of changing when certain stimuli are presented in the offender's life. Special Insert 2.1 provides an example of a risk assessment form that incorporates both static and dynamic scales for juvenile sex offenders that are assessed. The student should note the specific subscales and the separate scoring sections for static and dynamic scores when examining this insert.

As noted earlier, the assessment of special needs offenders is very difficult because they are more heterogeneous than the remainder of the offender population.

Special Insert 2.1. Sample Risk Assessment Form for Juvenile Sex Offenders

Juvenile Sex Offender Assessment Protocol-II
Scoring Form

Scoring Code: 0 = Stable; 1 = Moderate; 2 = Severe

1. Sexual Drive/Preoccupation Scale	0	1	2
1. Prior Legally Charged Sex Offenses	0	1	2
2. Number of Sexual Abuse Victims	0	1	2
3. Male Child Victim	0	1	2
4. Duration of Sex Offense History	0	1	2
5. Degree of Planning in Sexual Offense(s)	0	1	2
6. Sexualized Aggression	0	1	2
7. Sexual Drive and Preoccupation	0	1	2
8. Sexual Victimization History	0	1	2
Sexual Drive/Preoccupation Scale Total			
2. Impulsive/Antisocial Behavior Scale			
9. Caregiver Consistency	0	1	2
10. Pervasive Anger	0	1	2
11. School Behavior Problems	0	1	2
12. History of Conduct Disorder	0	1	2
13. Juvenile Antisocial Behavior	0	1	2
14. Ever Charged or Arrested Before Age 16	0	1	2
15. Multiple Types of Offenses	0	1	2
16. History of Physical Assault and/or Exposure to Family Violence	0	1	2
Antisocial Behavior Scale Total			
3. Intervention Scale			
17. Accepting Responsibility for Offense(s)	0	1	2
18. Internal Motivation for Change	0	1	2
19. Understands Risk Factors	0	1	2
20. Empathy	0	1	2
21. Remorse and Guilt	0	1	2
22. Cognitive Distortions	0	1	2
23. Quality of Peer Relationships	0	1	2
Intervention Scale Total			
4. Community Stability/Adjustment Scale			
24. Management of Sexual Urges and Desire	0	1	2
25. Management of Anger	0	1	2
26. Stability of Current Living Situation	0	1	2
27. Stability in School	0	1	2
28. Evidence of Positive Support Systems	0	1	2
Community Stability Scale Total			

(continued)

Juvenile Sex Offender Assessment Protocol-II
Summary Form

Static/Historical Scales

1. Sexual Drive/Preoccupation Scale Score:
   (Add Items 1–8 [range: 0–16]) _____ /16 = _____
2. Impulsive-Antisocial Behavior Scale Score:
   (Add Items 9–16 [range: 0–16]) _____ /16 = _____

Dynamic Scales

3. Intervention Scale Score:
   (Add Items 17–23 [range 0–14]) _____ /14 = _____
4. Community Stability Scale Score:
   (Add Items 24–28 [range: 0–10]) _____ /10 = _____

Static Score

(Add Items 1–16) _____ /32 = _____

Dynamic Score

(Add Items 17–28) _____ /24 = _____

Total J-SOAP Score

(Add Items 1–28) _____ /56 = _____

Source: Adapted from Prentky and Righthand (2003).

However, these offenders are more difficult to assess also because they tend to possess more dynamic risk factors than typical offenders. This means that most groups of special needs offenders have risk factors that are subject to change and influence, depending on their environment. This also means that treatment with these offenders holds substantial promise but also has numerous potential consequences if not administered correctly.

Since we have determined that treatment is a necessary evil when trying to reduce recidivism and since it is clear that special needs offenders have more dynamic risk factors than most other offenders, it becomes clear that treatment must be a component to the processing of special needs offenders. Any failure to provide this component will simply result in recidivism for most special needs offenders. In Chapter 1, the distinctions between needs were discussed. Indeed, the entire issue of offender needs is presented as integral to the reduction of recidivism with these groups of offenders. Therefore, when discussing assessment, one final distinction must be presented. This distinction rests between the understanding of risk-principled assessment and the needs-principled assessment of special needs offenders.

With **risk-principled assessment**, the main concern revolves around the protection of society and/or the safe management of correctional institutions. This type of assessment is usually based mostly on static risk factors (Van Voorhis et al., 2000). However, the risk-principled assessment will ensure that dangerous offenders are separated from vulnerable inmates within facilities. However, within the treatment scheme, the risk-principled assessment system will ensure that hard-core offenders are not in the same treatment regimen as less serious offenders. This may seem to be a topical distinction, but it can be critical to long-term success. For instance, in an anger management program, an offender who has problems with verbal abuse and verbal explosiveness may not benefit from of being in an anger management group that has a majority of offenders who are severe domestic batterers. This would be even more true if these assaultive offenders had some form of personality disorder to further aggravate their success. In this case, it is likely that the success of the offender with verbal anger problems might actually be impaired by repeat exposure to these other offenders. These offenders could therefore ruin any positive prognosis for change that the offender might have. In essence, the treatment program could ironically make the offender worse than when he or she started. Although many students may be skeptical, this does frequently happen in many community health service provider agencies. The same could be true in various substance abuse treatment groups and programs and any other treatment regimen that mixes offenders at various levels of therapeutic recovery.

Further, research has shown that intensive correctional treatment programs are more successful with high-risk offenders than with low-risk offenders. Thus, it does not pay to place low-risk offenders in programs designed for high-risk offenders, and this could actually lower their likelihood of success because of negative influences from other high-risk members. Thus, treatment programs should distinguish between risk principles in their assessment and future placement of offender clients. Indeed, according to Van Voorhis et al. (2000), the risk principle notes that low-risk offenders tend to do more poorly as a group on intensive treatment than if they had not been assigned to an intensive correctional intervention. Van Voorhis et al. (2000) go on to add that the treatment implications of the risk-principled assessment are as follows:

1. Identify the high-, medium-, and low-risk offenders
2. Direct intensive treatment efforts (not just intensive security and supervision) to high-risk offenders
3. Think carefully about intensive treatment interventions for low-risk offenders

These three points clearly enunciate the importance of the risk-principled assessment and are specifically relevant to special needs offenders such as domestic batterers, differing types of sexual offenders (adult and juvenile, pedophile and rapist), substance abusers, mentally disordered offenders, and so on.

Needs-principled assessment, on the other hand, is concerned more with factors specific to the effective treatment and reintegration of the special needs offender. Thus, needs-principled assessment deals with the subjective and objective needs of the offender to maximize the potential for social reintegration and to reduce the likelihood of future recidivism. Needs-principled assessment takes into account factors such as substance addiction, medical assistance, mental health issues, job development, educational attainment, physical disabilities, and relationships with family and/or peers. The needs-principled assessment consists mostly of dynamic risk factors, but this assessment will assess offenders less on the basis of a certain risk factor and more on the severity of the specific need or the seriousness of the affliction. For instance, substance abusers whose primary addiction problem revolves around pain relievers may be substantially different from those who abuse to have an elevated mood. Though all are addicts, the type of drug and the type of addiction severity may again warrant differing levels and/or types of treatment for that offender.

Needs-principled assessment is also multifaceted and goes beyond looking at the main risk characteristic of concern. For instance, a substance-abusing offender may have a wide range of other needs, such as the settlement of legal issues, the maintenance of employment, and resolution of family-of-origin conflicts. Each of these issues is not specifically related to the offender's drug addiction, but each of these needs, if not properly addressed, can impair the offender's likelihood for further recovery. Rather, the failure to address one of these corollary needs can result in the likelihood of relapse since it is commonly known that drug offenders often resort to drug use during times of stress. Thus, the multifaceted nature of needs-principled assessment will examine the offender's global prognosis to optimize the likelihood of reintegration.

SPECIAL NEEDS OFFENDERS AND THE ASSESSMENT STAGE: SUBJECTIVE ASSESSMENT

Special needs offenders, because of their various challenges and unique subjective and objective needs, are difficult to assess. As mentioned before, these offenders are an extremely heterogeneous group with diverse concerns. This means that a "one-size-fits-all" approach is destined to failure with these specialized populations. Given the wide range of needs and security considerations involved with these offenders, proper assessment is absolutely critical. Many of these offenders have a wide range of mental health and physical health considerations that require some form of diagnosis, and if this diagnosis is not correct, the consequences could mean harm to someone in society. Thus, the wisest investment for any correctional system desiring to perfect its ability to ensure public safety will be in the arena of assessment. More money and resources in assessment means that the subsequent stages (diagnostic, recidivism prediction, and classification) in the equation will also operate better, resulting in increased public safety as the ultimate answer.

One method of assessment, the **subjective assessment process** of interviewing and observation, is an important yet less structured method of determining the security and treatment needs of the offender. This process entails the use of professionals who use their sense of judgment and experience to determine the offender's possible dangerousness, treatment needs, likelihood of responding to treatment, and likelihood of escaping. This is an important process that should not be overlooked. However, this process should not be the primary form of assessment, but it should serve as an integral part of a "two-pronged" assessment process. In some cases, clinicians may provide assessments but may not have seen the offender face-to-face. Rather, they may look through an offender's client file of information (such as the presentence investigation report file) to make their determination. This should never be allowed. Instead, each special needs offender should be seen, in person, by the practitioner who provides this subjective assessment.

There are some drawbacks to this process just as there are with any form of assessment. For one, the process is subjective, meaning that the determination is based on the impressions of an individual. Thus, these assessments are likely to vary from one professional to another. Second, these assessments can be lengthy and thus will not be useful for large facilities that do not have many well-qualified staff for such forms of assessment. Third, these forms of assessment require extensive skill from the staff administering them, and they are therefore only as good as those personnel. This means that these forms of assessment can be very costly since only highly educated and/or well-trained staff will be able to utilize this form of assessment.

To offset the potential capriciousness of a subjective assessment process, it is suggested that the use of a structured form of interview or observation process be utilized in all cases. A **subjective structured interview** is simply a process whereby an interviewer will ask a respondent a set of prearranged and open-ended questions so that the interview seems informal (as if a conversation), yet because of the prearranged questions, a structure evolves throughout the conversation that ensures that certain bits of desired data are gathered from the respondent. These forms of interviews are useful since they guide clinicians and other staff who may conduct intakes. Further, the structure of these interviews provides for consistency and uniformity in record keeping, meaning that agencies can ensure that similar criteria are considered despite the style and form of the individual interviewer. This provides a certain "baseline" of information against which all offenders are judged. Finally, this type of interview ensures that even less qualified staff can conduct an interview and that the interview will still contain that information that is considered critical for agency assessment.

It is the contention of this book that those special needs offenders who present with a multiplicity of issues should be provided with a thorough interview by a skilled clinician. This is absolutely imperative because special needs offenders, by virtue of the very term, are special and require specialized interventions. If programs are to be structured to meet these specialized conditions, it is necessary that specialized focus and attention be given to those cases that are identified as particularly problematic. These cases may be bizarre in some circumstances (and correspondingly rare) or may be quite common with a specified population. Some examples may illustrate this point:

1. A 57-year-old male offender has dementia and is also an opiate addict because of the need for relief from severe back and neck pain. On the recent death of his wife, he assaulted several family members who were arguing over where he would now stay.

2. A female prostitute with substance addiction has HIV and suffers from depression regarding her plight. She has a five-year-old son, and it is found that she was a victim of childhood sexual abuse.
3. A schizophrenic and paranoid-delusional offender has been homeless for most of his life. He is an alcoholic with cirrhosis of the liver.
4. A mentally handicapped 14-year-old boy molested his eight-year-old female cousin. He had found some pornography that his older brother had hidden under the couch, and he wanted to show his cousin how the pictures worked.

Each of these cases is somewhat unique, but it is clearly easy to see how each could (and likely does) occur every day in the criminal justice system. Because these cases are specialized (either a mental disorder, some kind of life course issue, or some form of social problem), the use of structured interview and observation processes must be employed. When conducting the initial observation, Drummond (1996) notes that practitioners should keep the following guidelines in mind:

1. Above all, be objective. Remain aware of personal biases and prejudices.
2. Be aware of what is called the "halo error," the tendency to be influenced by your first impression of an individual or by an exceptional trait. This influence can lead to bias in perception.
3. Recognize personal response tendencies, such as rating everyone on the higher or lower end or even a tendency to rate in the middle range.
4. Focus on relevant behaviors. Attend only to the assigned behaviors on the checklist or rating scale for the structured interview. Do not attend to other nonverbal or verbal cues despite the intuitive desire to do so. This is important because unlike an investigative interview, the structured interview seeks only limited data, and the determination, to be valid, must remain tightly focused on the specific data that are relevant to the point of the structured interview.
5. Be as unobtrusive as possible.
6. Observe the offender more than once if at all possible. The more observations, the better the chance of getting a complete and accurate picture of the client.

Standardized interviews are designed to collect the same type of information from all the respondents. If it is a structured interview, all offenders are asked the same questions in the same order, and the answers are recorded identically (Drummond, 1996). In unscheduled interviews, the interviewer sometimes varies the sequence of the questions and the order of the topics so that the data can be compared and summarized.

The following are some of the advantages of the interviewing process:

1. Clients can be guided to answer items completely (Drummond, 1996).
2. Additional information or understanding can be pursued (Drummond, 1996).

3. Nonverbal behavior and cues as well as affective behavior and voice tone and pitch can be observed and noted. Again, this information should be noted only when the nature of the interview allows the clinician to focus on these behaviors as relevant (see item 4 in the previous list).

The following are some of the disadvantages of the interviewing process:

1. Success often depends on the skill of the interviewer to ask the right questions with the right timing and to correctly interpret the observations (Drummond, 1996).
2. The communication of some individuals is inhibited, and clients may simply be unwilling to answer certain questions. They will then either refuse to answer or just provide a response that is a lie.
3. The personality of the interviewer can greatly influence the outcome (Drummond, 1996).

Drummond (1996) notes that even though the reliability and the validity of interviewing may be questionable, this is sometimes the only way possible to gather certain types of information. Further, the interviewer can reword questions, add questions, seek clarification of information provided, focus on topics of clinical interest, and so on. This means that information obtained from such a process will likely be much more relevant to the specific clinical focus, and it also means that helping professionals will have richer information to work with when consulting the client's case file.

SPECIAL NEEDS OFFENDERS AND THE DIAGNOSTIC STAGE

According to Carbonnell and Perkins (2000), mental health assessments attempt to answer questions about how and why people think, feel, and behave in the manner that they do. Issues pertaining to stress, emotional coping, ability to solve problems, and so on may be the focus in these types of assessment, ultimately leading to some form of diagnosis if the assessment finds suitable criteria for a diagnosis. While these forms of mental health assessment may seem to be specific to psychopathology, it should be noted that many diagnostic factors related to psychopathology arise when dealing with the criminal offender. Indeed, there is an inflated representation of mental illness among offenders in prison and on community supervision (Bartol, 2002). Further, it is estimated that close to 30 percent of all offenders in maximum-security institutions may have antisocial personality disorder (Ashford, Sales, & Reid, 2002). Likewise, conduct disorder, oppositional-defiant disorder, and attention-deficit/hyperactivity disorder are highly represented among child and juvenile offenders. Dementia is encountered among the elderly offender population. Various mood and substance abuse disorders are found among those offenders with communicable diseases. It is thought that the majority of inmate offenders have some form of substance abuse problem (Bureau of Justice Statistics, 1999). This is particularly true since over 50 percent of inmates report that they had used drugs or alcohol at the time of arrest for the sentence they were serving (Bureau of Justice Statistics, 1999). Further, approximately 73 percent of federal and 83 percent of state prison inmates noted that they had abused substances within the 12-month period prior to incarceration. Fully 70 to 80 percent of all prisoners are thought to have some form of substance abuse problem (Belenko, 1998; Reentry Media Outreach, 2005). Since substance abuse disorders are considered diagnosable disorders, this means that mental health again becomes central to the assessment and diagnosis of the offending population.

Each of the previously mentioned forms of disorders and/or mental health issues is included within the ***DSM-IV-TR***, which is the common vernacular for the ***Diagnostic and Statistical Manual of Mental Disorders*** (4th ed., text revision), published by the American Psychiatric Association (2000). This text is often referred to as the "bible" of mental health clinicians and diagnosticians. The *DSM-IV-TR* allows mental health practitioners to label, or diagnose, an individual (in this case an offender) so that they can be better categorized for further treatment interventions. This is a necessary process when attempting to match the right client with the correct treatment modality. Further, as will be seen in subsequent chapters, many special needs offenders will qualify for two, three, or more diagnoses, making them dual or comorbid in their diagnosis. This means that the proper diagnosis of special needs offenders can be quite complicated. In spite of this complexity, the *DSM-IV-TR* diagnostic categories provide important information when developing treatment plans for the offender.

It should be noted that the use of the *DSM-IV-TR* criteria is based on the judgments of the practicing clinician. This will therefore have a high degree of subjectivity that can be balanced only if the clinician is adequately trained to work with the offender population. But presuming that the clinician is adequately trained and experienced, this process of diagnosis can be effective. Naturally, this process of diagnosis also ties in to the previously discussed structured interviews and observations. The clinician should be skilled at this process, and ideally the same person conducting the initial subjective structured interview would also be responsible for applying any diagnoses from the *DSM-IV-TR*. This should be a requirement for any quality mental health provider.

In addition, this form of diagnosis should be used primarily for treatment rather than for security prediction. Moreover, the subjective determinations derived by practitioners should override other objective criteria when designing treatment plans. The experience of the clinician is much more important at this stage than any numerical pencil-and-paper form of detached and depersonalized assessment and diagnostic process. Thus, the MMPI-2, discussed later in this chapter, should be used only for classification purposes and should be used as a primary tool for augmenting security determinations from the Wisconsin Risk Assessment System and the Level of Supervision Inventory–Revised (also discussed later in this chapter). This is primarily for two key reasons. First, the MMPI-2 is a self-report instrument with information that is provided from the offenders themselves. Basing security or treatment considerations off these data is likely to result in failure since offenders may not themselves know what is functional or dysfunctional about themselves. Indeed, they may perceive themselves as quite functional. In addition, though the MMPI-2 has a variety of subscales designed to detect deceit, the clinician will still not necessarily know the underlying truth of the offender's motives or rationale for the deception; this is not a good foundation on which to base security decisions or treatment plans. Second, the clinician will be better able to detect exact points of discomfort for the offender during the interview and will be better able to probe those areas when determining how to approach treatment plans for the offender.

Although most correctional criminal justice personnel may not be full-blown clinicians, basic knowledge on the various diagnoses will prove useful in understanding the offending population on their caseloads. This knowledge will also allow criminal justice personnel (both correctional and law enforcement) to better understand mental health practitioners. In fact, some policing programs, such as the Crisis Intervention Teams established in Memphis, Tennessee (known commonly as the Memphis Model), train police in the basics pertaining to mental illness and the symptoms related to psychotropic medications so that police response to the mentally ill in the community can be improved.

The *DSM-IV-TR* is a multiaxial system that involves an assessment of the offender on several different "axes." Each axis refers to a different area of content information that can help a clinician plan treatment for an offender and can also aid in the prediction of the treatment outcome with that offender. There are five axes included in the *DSM-IV-TR* multiaxial classification:

Axis I	Clinical disorders and other conditions that may be a focus of clinical attention
Axis II	Personality disorders and mental retardation
Axis III	General medical conditions
Axis IV	Psychosocial and environmental problems
Axis V	Global assessment of functioning

The use of this multiaxial system facilitates comprehensive and systematic evaluation while paying attention to the various mental disorders and general medical conditions, psychosocial and environmental problems, and the offender's overall level of functioning. This approach thus examines various facets of the offender that might otherwise be overlooked if the focus were on assessing a single presenting problem.

This section of this chapter will provide a brief discussion of the various axes and their corresponding disorders. No discussion of each individual disorder will be provided. However, it should be pointed out that many of these disorders will be the topic of discussion in the chapters that follow. It is the purpose of this chapter simply to acquaint the student with the *DSM-IV-TR* and to demonstrate how this clinical guide is organized. The main point to presenting this is to give the student a clear and specific idea of how offenders with mental health issues are ultimately diagnosed.

Axis I consists of clinical disorders or conditions that may be the focus of clinical attention. The disorders included in this category are as follows:

1. Disorders diagnosed in infancy, childhood, or adolescence (excluding mental retardation)
2. Delirium, dementia, amnesia, and other cognitive disorders
3. Mental disorders due to a general medical condition
4. Substance-related disorders
5. Schizophrenia and other psychotic disorders
6. Mood disorders
7. Anxiety disorders
8. Somatoform disorders
9. Factitious disorders
10. Dissociative disorders
11. Sexual and gender identity disorders
12. Eating disorders
13. Sleep disorders
14. Impulse-control disorders not otherwise classified
15. Adjustment disorders

Axis II includes both personality disorders and mental retardation. This axis is also sometimes used to note maladaptive personality characteristics and defense mechanisms that the offender may use to avoid disclosure. These disorders are placed on a separate axis to ensure that symptoms from the personality disorders are not confused with the symptoms of those disorders in Axis I. Thus, such a structure ensures organization and accuracy of the clinical diagnosis. The disorders included in this category are as follows:

1. Paranoid personality disorder
2. Schizoid personality disorder
3. Schizotypical personality disorder
4. Antisocial personality disorder
5. Borderline personality disorder

6. Histrionic personality disorder
7. Narcissistic personality disorder
8. Avoidant personality disorder
9. Dependent personality disorder
10. Obsessive-compulsive personality disorder
11. Mental retardation

Axis III includes general medical conditions that are potentially relevant to the understanding or management of the individual's mental disorder. It should be noted that Axis III considerations are frequent among those offenders possessing communicable diseases (as covered in Chapter 4) and among geriatric offenders (see Chapter 13). A partial list of general medical conditions that are included in this axis is given here:

1. Infectious and parasitic diseases
2. Diseases of the nervous system and sensory organs
3. Immunity disorders
4. Diseases of skin, musculoskeletal, and connective tissue
5. Diseases of the digestive, circulatory, and respiratory systems

Axis IV includes psychosocial problems that can aggravate diagnosis, treatment, and prognosis of mental disorders possessed by an offender. A psychosocial or environmental problem may be a negative life event (financial problems or loss of employment), an environmental difficulty or deficiency (being in prison), familial or other interpersonal stress (divorce), inadequate social support (no family or reliable friends), or other problems that relate to the overall context in which the offender's problems have developed. The following individual problems listed here are key examples included within the Axis IV category:

1. Problems with primary support groups
2. Problems related to the social environment
3. Educational problems
4. Occupational problems
5. Housing problems
6. Economic problems
7. Problems with access to health care services
8. Problems related to interaction with the legal system/crime

Axis V deals with the overall functioning of the individual and is often referred to as the **Global Assessment of Functioning Scale** (hereafter GAF Scale), which is useful in tracking the clinical progress of an individual in global terms using a single measure. The GAF Scale must only be rated on psychological, social, and occupational functioning. The GAF Scale criteria are listed on Table 2.1.

The GAF Scale can be a useful mechanism for assessing the general functioning of an offender. This scale can be utilized as a supplemental screening device during structured interviews with practicing mental health professionals. While it is informal, it helps augment other objective forms of assessment, such as the Wisconsin Risk Assessment System. The GAF Scale likewise accounts for both static and dynamic risk factors that are likely to be important for both clinicians and security staff. Indeed, if security staff are trained to know the 10 general categories of the GAF Scale, they can then utilize the numerical score when making housing or job assignments within the institution or when making decisions with transitional housing and aftercare within the community corrections environment.

This is important because this scale helps tie together the informal and subjective interview and observation process into a format that is easy to understand and utilize by the layperson or general correctional worker. When combining both subjective and objective assessment tools, the offender can then be given a general GAF score that all parties can understand when making routine supervisory decisions with the special needs offender. The GAF Scale then provides some clarity to the overall functioning of a special needs offender who may have numerous problems (on multiple axes), such as HIV/AIDS (a general medical condition, Axis III), problems with their family of origin (primary support groups, Axis IV), and depression (a mood disorder, Axis I). Certainly, among those offenders presenting with HIV, there would likely be some depression, and it is likely that such an offender (e.g., a female prostitute who is a substance abuser and has recently contracted HIV) could perhaps either be in need of or have difficulties with his or her current support network of family and friends. Thus, the point is that it does not take a complicated special needs offender to qualify for a variety of axes on the GAF Scale. Relating all these factors to various practitioners may be easier to contextualize by also providing a simple, succinct synopsis of the offender's overall level of functioning. This is the precise purpose of this scale, and it is recommended that agencies adopt it as an "overlay" form of assessment and classification when dealing with offenders on their caseloads. Such an overlay will likely prove useful for both security and treatment purposes.

SPECIAL NEEDS OFFENDERS AND THE RECIDIVISM PREDICTION STAGE

The recidivism prediction stage is built off the information derived during assessment and diagnosis. It is at this stage that correctional personnel attempt to determine the risk involved with allowing the offender to be placed under community supervision. One key quasi-objective clinical inventory that is used to determine offender suitability is the **Level of Supervision Inventory–Revised (LSI-R)**. This inventory was created

Table 2.1. Global Assessment of Functioning Scale

Score	Narrative Level of Functioning
100–91	Superior functioning in a wide range of activities; life's problems never seem to get out of hand; is sought out by others because of his or her many positive qualities; no symptoms.
90–81	Absent or minimal symptoms (mild anxiety before an exam); good functioning in all areas; interested and involved in a wide range of activities; socially effective; generally satisfied with life; no more than everyday problems (an occasional argument with family members).
80–71	If symptoms are present, they are transient and expectable reactions to psychosocial stressors (difficulty concentrating after family argument); no more than slight impairment in social, occupational, or school functioning.
70–61	Some mild symptoms (depressed mood and insomnia) or some difficulty in social, occupational, or school functioning but generally functioning pretty well; has some meaningful interpersonal relationships.
60–51	Moderate symptoms (flat affect and/or occasional panic attacks) or moderate difficulty in social, occupational, or school functioning (has few friends and conflicts at work and/or school).
50–41	Serious symptoms (suicide ideation, severe obsessional rituals, or frequent shoplifting) or any serious impairment in social, occupational, or school functioning (no friends or unable to keep a job).
40–31	Some impairment in reality testing or communication or major impairment in several areas, such as work or school, family relations, judgment, thinking, or mood (depressed man avoids friends and neglects family or child frequently beats up younger children or is defiant at home and/or failing at school).
30–21	Behavior is considerably influenced by delusions or hallucinations or serious impairment in communication judgment or inability to function in almost all areas (stays in bed all day or has no job, home, or friends).
20–11	Some danger of hurting self or others (suicide attempts without clear expectation of death or frequently violent) or occasionally fails to maintain minimal personal hygiene or gross motor impairment in communication.
10–1	Persistent danger of severely hurting self or others (recurrent violence) or persistent inability to maintain minimal personal hygiene; serious suicidal act with clear expectation of death.
0	Inadequate information.

Source: Adapted from the *DSM-IV-TR* (American psychiatric Association, 2000).

by Don Andrews and James Bonta, and it has been found to be highly predictive of recidivism among a variety of correctional offender clients (Van Voorhis et al., 2000). The LSI-R is administered by case managers/counselors and/or mental health professionals. The assessment process includes a semistructured interview. As with the Wisconsin Risk Assessment System, the LSI-R provides for reassessments of an offender's risk score. Reassessment of risk scores can be useful when assessing program effectiveness as well as facilitating program release decisions. In fact, it was found that the LSI-R predecessor, the LSI, was a better predictor of parolee recidivism than the Wisconsin Risk Assessment System. A breakdown of initial classification levels based on the Wisconsin Risk assessment indicated that 98 percent of offenders scored in the maximum supervision range. This would suggest that the Wisconsin system is strongly influenced by raters and may lead to overclassification (O'Keefe, Klebe, & Hromas, 1998). With overclassification, there occurs a waste of money because more expensive security measures are used on offenders who do not require such extensive maintenance.

According to Andrews and Bonta (2003), the LSI-R inventory is a quantitative survey of attributes of offenders and their situations relevant to level of supervision and treatment decisions. The inventory was designed for offenders ages 16 and older and aids in predicting parole outcome, success with offenders in halfway houses and aftercare facilities, and probation recidivism. This inventory consists of 54 items that are based on legal requirements and include relevant factors needed for making decisions about security risk levels and the likelihood of treatment success (Andrews & Bonta, 2003). The LSI-R inventory is designed for probation and parole officers to assist them with decisions about probation and parole placement, security-level classifications, and possible treatment progress.

The LSI-R screening version (LSI-R:SV) consists of eight items selected from the full LSI-R. Like the full version, LSI-R:SV samples both risk and needs, and the item content reflects four key risk factors: criminal history, criminal attitudes, criminal associates, and antisocial personality pattern (Andrews & Bonta, 2003). In addition, the LSI-R:SV inventory examines other factors, such as employment, family, and substance abuse. The items included in the LSI-R:SV not only contribute to the predictive validity of the LSI-R:SV but also include information that is important to offender treatment planning (Andrews & Bonta, 2003). Each of these items is rated either "yes/no" or "0 to 3" (0, a very unsatisfactory situation with very clear and strong need for improvement, to 3, a satisfactory situation with no or little need for improvement).

It should be noted that the LSI-R is not intended to replace the professional judgment of the correctional worker: an objective risk–needs assessment enhances professional judgment, adds to the fairness of offender assessment, and alerts correctional staff to the need for a fuller offender risk–needs assessment (Andrews & Bonta, 2003). Research with the LSI-R shows that scores on the instrument have predicted a variety of outcomes important to offender management. Among probation samples, LSI-R scores have predicted violent recidivism and violations while under community supervision. Among incarcerated offenders, scores have predicted such varied outcomes as success in correctional halfway houses and institutional misconduct (Andrews & Bonta, 2003).

Andrews and Bonta (2003) make it clear that the LSI-R inventory is designed for use as a screening instrument in settings with high offender intakes where, because of time constraints and insufficient staff resources, a complete LSI-R assessment may not be feasible for everyone. Finally, the LSI-R also provides a summary of the static and dynamic risk factors that may require either further assessment or further intervention from agency personnel.

In addition, the LSI-R fits a rather specific type of treatment model. Attitudes, criminal history, and associates are strong correlates among the entire offending population (Van Voorhis et al., 2000). As a risk prediction inventory, the LSI-R fits best with programs that are based on clear cognitive-behavioral and social learning treatment modalities. This is not a problem, however, because most programs for special needs offenders are based on such orientations. But if clinicians desire an accurate assessment of the offender's likelihood of reforming, they must keep in mind that the LSI-R has limits that are grounded in cognitive-behavioral approaches. Van Voorhis et al. (2000) point out that most research on cognitive-behavioral and social learning approaches is showing that this modality is the most effective overall when dealing with the offender population. Thus, the LSI-R is ideally suited and designed for those programs that utilize the most effective modalities: cognitive-behavioral and social learning. The LSI-R therefore dovetails nicely with these programs and lends further validity to the nature and intent of the corresponding therapeutic treatment that will follow.

Beyond the use of specific instruments and inventories, it is important that the student understand the underlying presumptions behind risk prediction. These assumptions help ensure that agency decision makers understand the broader implications for their agency when making release decisions. Among these considerations are those related to **false negatives** and **false positives**. The chronic occurrence of these two mistakes in risk prediction can lead to tragic consequences for society and/or costly expenditures for correctional agencies.

When decision makers are making release decisions for offenders, they will ultimately have to decide if the offender will be allowed within the community or remain behind bars. There are some implications to these decisions that may not be readily apparent to the casual observer, and these implications, as well as the official professional terms associated with these implications, should be understood by the student.

First, when correctional decision makers predict that an inmate is not likely to reoffend (and thus is a good risk for community supervision), this is called a prediction in the negative. If the offender is released on community supervision and does not commit any future offense, this is referred to as a **true negative**. This is because the prediction turns out to be true. Thus, the true negative implies that the offender is predicted to not reoffend, and the prediction turns out to be true (see Table 2.2 for details). However, if the agency personnel predict that another offender is likewise not likely to offend and when on community supervision the offender commits some form of crime, this is referred to as a false negative. This is because the agency made the prediction in the negative (meaning that the agency thought the offender would not reoffend), yet it turned out that the prediction was false, or incorrect. Thus, the false negative implies that the offender is predicted to not reoffend, but the prediction turns out to be false.

On the other hand, if an offender is predicted to reoffend, this is referred to as a prediction in the positive. If the offender is predicted to reoffend but is allowed on community supervision because of the effectiveness of his or her legal representation or some other odd course of events and he or she later does in fact commit an offense, this is called a **true positive**. The true positive implies that the offender is predicted to

Table 2.2. True/False Positives and Negatives in Offender Prediction

	Offender Offends	Offender Does Not Offend
True Prediction	**True positive**	**True negative**
False Prediction	**False positive**	**False negative**

reoffend and that this prediction later turns out to be true. However, if another offender is likewise predicted to be likely to commit a crime but later the offender somehow is released onto community supervision and is found to never reoffend, this would be a false positive. The prediction was in the positive, indicating a risk of reoffending, yet it was false and thus not accurate.

Naturally, the true positives and true negatives are what agencies hope to obtain as often as possible. These are perfect predictions of offender behavior. However, things not being perfect, the false positive and false negative predictions are inevitable at some point. Because of this, there are a couple of key points that should be mentioned with false positives and false negatives. First of all, false positives are a "safe bet" for correctional prediction boards because if the offender is locked up, the offender simply cannot commit any further crimes in society. In this regard, it is prudent to simply incarcerate as many offenders as possible (optimally all of them) to ensure public safety. However, this would be very costly and can result in excessive expenditures on prison systems that have inmates who are neither dangerous nor likely to repeat their criminal behavior. This also can essentially "create" recidivism, as those who would normally refrain from further criminality are placed in an environment where they can learn and become socialized from other inmates, thereby increasing their incentive to reoffend in the future. Thus, overpredicting offender likelihood of recidivating is not a prudent long-term strategy, and this results in further overcrowding of prisons and even more costs to taxpayers. By the same token, false negatives result in dangers to public safety and also damage the public perception of community corrections. In addition, some correctional agencies may decide to deliberately make more false positives out of fear of committing a false negative. No criminal justice professional wants to see people in the community get hurt because they commit a false negative, and no agency wants its credibility at risk because of incorrect predictions. Thus, agencies find themselves in a dilemma between the risk of making a false negative and the short-term safety of a false positive.

CLASSIFICATION STAGE

As noted at the beginning of this chapter, the classification stage is tied largely to the previous recidivism prediction stage. Thus, once the general risk level of the inmate or offender on community supervision is known, the job of the correctional agency, whether institutional or community based, is to correctly match up the offender's treatment plan with the level of security determined by the LSI-SR and other risk prediction tests and procedures. One primary tool used in corrections is an instrument known as the **Minnesota Multiphasic Personality Inventory (MMPI-2)**, which is the most widely used objective test instrument used in corrections. The MMPI-2 is an objective personality adjustment inventory test that can be given to large numbers of offenders at the same time or individually as desired. The MMPI-2 has 567 true/false questions that require the offender to be able to read at the sixth-grade level. Further, the MMPI-2 has been restandardized and is on tape for blind, illiterate, semiliterate, and disabled individuals. It is important to stress that the MMPI-2 is primarily a clinical tool used for detecting mental health disorders among abnormal populations.

This test has a number of subscales within it. These subscales are a series of questions that are embedded and camouflaged within the remainder of the 567 total questions and are dispersed at random points within the test. All these questions are designed to measure specific points of interest to provide a multiprofile view of the offender's personality. However, the MMPI-2 is very effective with the manipulative offender population because of three specific subscales that are included: Lie (L), Infrequency (I), and Correction (K).

The Lie, or L, scale consists of 15 questions (out of 567 total questions) such as "I never get angry." The scale indicates whether the client is consciously or unconsciously presenting him- or herself as a perfectionist. The I scale consists of 64 questions (again out of 567 questions) but does not measure a trait. Because the items are answered in a deviant direction by less than 10 percent of those who take the test, a high score indicates that the offender has endorsed a large number of serious psychological items. For offenders, this may be an attempt to look bad on the test, or they may be confused or even having delusions (especially with mentally ill offenders). Finally, the correction, or K, scale measures defensiveness as a test-taking attitude. The scale has 30 items that cover a wide range of content areas. Low scores usually indicate a deliberate attempt to appear bad, but sometimes a self-critical offender (an addict, some pedophiles, or an offender who feels remorse) may endorse responses that indicate pathological tendencies.

Beyond this, the MMPI-2 is an effective instrument at determining underlying pathology within the offender. Table 2.3 provides the additional subscales that examine separate areas of mental health.

In addition to the MMPI-2, the **MMPI-2 Criminal Justice and Correctional Report (MMPI-2 CJCR)** is based on decades of research and is designed to more closely fit the outcome data from the MMPI-2 to a classification scheme (Megargee, 2005). The MMPI-2 CJCR is perfectly suited to match up the offender's treatment plan with the level of security and serves as an additional double-check when making security decisions from the LSI-SR. This report is used in conjunction with the MMPI-2 to provide information pertaining to the offender's needs assessment, risk assessment, and program planning within a correctional agency. The report is designed to identify those offenders who may suffer from thought disorders, serious depression, and alcohol and substance abuse and may need mental health treatment as well as those that are most likely to be hostile, predatory, bullied, or victimized while incarcerated. This report also includes predictor items related to self-injury and suicide.

Table 2.3. Clinical Scales of the Minnesota Multiphasic Personality Inventory-2

Scale	Item Total	Item Content
Hypochondriasis	32	Undue concern with physical health
Depression	57	Depression, denial of happiness and personal worth, lack of interest, withdrawal
Hysteria	60	Specific somatic complaints, discomfort in social situations
Psychopathic deviate	56	Activity/passivity, identification with culturally conventional masculine and feminine choices
Paranoia	40	Delusions of persecution, suspiciousness, moral self-righteousness
Psychasthenia	48	General dissatisfaction with life, indecisiveness, self-doubt, obsessional aspects
Schizophrenia	78	Feeling of being different, feelings of isolation, bizarre thought processes, tendency to withdraw, sexual identity concerns
Hypomania	46	Elevated energy level, flight of ideas, elevated mood, increased motor activity, expansiveness
Social introversion/ extroversion	69	Introversion/extroversion, social insecurity

Source: Adapted from Drummond (1996).

The MMPI-2 CJCR system was developed by Edwin Megargee and is fashioned around the well-regarded **Megargee Offender Classification System**. This system of classification is known to provide solid empirical support for classification and placement decisions. The Megargee System is especially effective in helping criminal justice practitioners deal with an offender population that is increasingly including the mentally ill or disordered within its ranks. Further, the Megargee System has been reported to effectively classify 90 to 95 percent of the MMPI-2 profiles encountered among most probation, parole, and institutional correctional settings. One federal institution used the system as a guide in providing offender cell assignments, and this process resulted in a 46 percent reduction in serious violence within that institution. The Megargee System is the basis for the MMPI-2 CJCR.

The results from the MMPI-2 CJCR can be used to support important management, treatment, and programming decisions. This includes the ability to do the following:

- Reliably classify offenders at initial intake of incarceration to support important supervision and treatment issues
- Identify offenders who may present less risk to the system, possibly allowing a downgrade in security level and improved placement on community supervision

- Better understand an offender's background, attitudes, and abilities to determine if the individual will benefit from substance abuse treatment, mental health programming, and other services
- Identify offenders who may do well in prison work programs based on their educational and vocational abilities
- Address the readiness of offenders to leave the institution and assist in developing effective aftercare programs
- Accurately evaluate and reclassify offenders over the course of their supervision to support programming or treatment decisions

The MMPI-2 CJCR also consists of nine behavioral dimensions. These behavioral dimensions compare offenders to other offenders rather than to the general outside population to ensure that results are correctly normed. The following is a list of the nine behavioral dimensions of the MMPI-2:

- Apparent need for further mental health assessment or programming
- Apparent leadership ability or dominance
- Indications of conflicts with or resentment of authorities
- Likelihood of positive or favorable response to academic programming
- Indications of socially deviant behavior or attitudes
- Apparent need for social participation or extroversion
- Likelihood of mature, responsible behavior or positive response to supervision
- Likelihood of positive favorable response to vocational programming
- Likelihood of hostile or antagonistic peer relations

Further, the MMPI-2 CJCR also identifies nine possible areas relevant to the offender. This provides treatment staff with indicators of difficulties that the offender may face. As with the other report components, the offender's problems are normed against a population of other offenders to ensure that comparisons are similar and that the test is valid for the offender population. The nine problem areas identified are as follows:

- Difficulties with alcohol or other substance abuse
- Manipulation or exploitation of others
- Thought disorders
- Overcontrolled hostility
- Family conflict or alienation from family
- Depressive affect or mood disorder

- Awkward or difficult interpersonal relationships
- Anger control problems
- Tendency to get sick/ill frequently

When taken together, the MMPI-2 and the MMPI-2 CJCR provide a comprehensive means of classifying offenders on the basis of both mental health and criminal justice categories of concern. The use of the LSI-R serves as an initial predictor of recidivism, and it is desirable to have one single instrument strictly for this purpose. Both the MMPI-2 and the MMPI-2 CJCR go beyond mere recidivism prediction and include mental health and security classification determinations. Because of the effectiveness of each of the tools presented (all have been shown to have better-than-average validity and reliability) and because of the manner in which each precisely fulfills the intended function within the assessment, diagnostic, recidivism prediction, and classification stages, these instruments are presented as a "Cadillac program" of providing for all four stages of special needs offender supervision. Indeed, the MMPI-2 serves to aid during the classification and diagnostic stages, and the MMPI-2 CJCR serves to aid during the recidivism prediction and classification stages. Thus, each instrument also provides a dual-purpose overlap in functions, ensuring that each stage and each instrument optimally complement one another.

The process described in this chapter would provide for optimal assessment, security, and treatment of special needs offenders and would ensure that special needs offenders are placed on the correct form of community supervision. Simultaneously, the offender would also be gaining excellent treatment programming from such a system that would address specific areas that are identified as possible "problem areas" in their effective reintegration. Thus, it is the contention of this chapter that the process outlined and the specific assessment instruments listed would be the ideal combination for providing comprehensive treatment and security services.

CONCLUSION

The process of offender supervision consists of four general stages: assessment, diagnostic, recidivism prediction, and classification. Each is fairly dynamic and fluid and should not be viewed as completely distinct from one another; rather, they are general guides to be used throughout the course and time of an offender's supervision. There may be substantial overlap between stages, and the assessment and classification instruments used in this four-stage model may actually serve to fulfill the purposes of two or more stages throughout the supervision process.

Both subjective and objective assessments should be used when making security and treatment decisions for special needs offenders. However, security decisions should be based solely on objective risk prediction criteria, while treatment decisions should be based more on subjective structured interviews and clinical diagnoses so as to capitalize on the expertise of the clinician. The Wisconsin Risk

Assessment System was presented as the recommended objective assessment scale for security-based decisions, while the use of subjective structured interviews based on the *DSM-IV-TR* diagnosis criteria was recommended for purposes of treatment. The LSI-R was presented as the preferred instrument at the recidivism prediction stage because of its utility with large populations, its quantitative aspect, the ease with which practitioners may use the instrument, and its ability to directly link with programs based on cognitive-behavioral treatment programs (most dealing with special needs offenders will use some variety of cognitive-behavioral intervention).

The problems and pitfalls associated with false positives and false negatives were noted to provide a general overview of the problems associated with inaccurate assessment in correctional systems. This demonstrates that it is assessment that provides the basic building block to the success of community corrections as a whole. The MMPI-2 and the MMPI-2 CJCR were presented as the premier tools for effective classification of offenders based on their self-reported pathology and a variety of behavioral dimensions and problem areas that were identified. The use of these tools is specifically designed to be consistent with the Megargee Offender Classification System, which is presented as a premier classification system that would ideally be utilized with any agency that has a substantial population of special needs offenders.

When taken together, each stage of the four-stage model works to complement the others and to provide an added verification of the effectiveness of the previous stage. The overlap between the stages is due to the interlocking nature of the various tools and instruments that serve to reinforce each other in assessing, diagnosing, predicting, and classifying special needs offenders. The added subjective components that are based on a working command of the *DSM-IV-TR* criteria ensure that the treatment process is both uniform and individualized between practicing clinicians and their offender-clients. This ensures that both perspectives work together in unison rather than in competition with each other. The end result is a process of supervision that builds on itself and provides multiple "cross-checks" and balances to ensure that both supervision and treatment are maximized.

KEY TERMS

Prognosis
Assessment stage
Diagnostic stage
Recidivism prediction stage
Classification stage
Presentence investigation report
Incapacitation
Treatment
Wisconsin Risk Assessment System
Static risk factors
Dynamic risk factors
Risk-principled assessment
Needs-principled assessment
Subjective assessment process
Subjective structured interview
Diagnostic and Statistical Manual of Mental Disorders (*DSM-IV-TR*)
Axes I, II, III, IV, and V

Global Assessment of Functioning Scale
Level of Supervision Inventory–Revised (LSI-R)
False negatives
False positives
True negatives
True positives
Minnesota Multiphasic Personality Inventory-2 (MMPI-2)
MMPI-2 Criminal Justice and Correctional Report (MMPI-2 CJCR)
Megargee Offender Classification System

REFERENCES

American Psychiatric Association. (2000). *Diagnostic and statistical manual of mental disorders* (4th ed., text revision). Arlington, VA: Author.

Andrews, D., & Bonta, J. (2003). Level of Supervision Inventory—Revised (LSI-R). Retrieved from http://www.mhs.com/LSI.htm

Ashford, J. B., Sales, B. D., & Reid, W. H. (2002). *Treating adult and juvenile offenders with special needs*. Washington, DC: American Psychological Association.

Bartol, C. R. (2002). *Criminal behavior: A psychological approach* (5th ed.). Upper Saddle River, NJ: Prentice Hall.

Belenko, S. (1998). *Behind bars: Substance abuse and America's prison population*. New York: National Center on Addiction and Substance Abuse at Columbia University.

Bureau of Justice Statistics. (1999). *Drug use and crime*. Washington, DC: U.S. Department of Justice, Office of Justice Programs.

Carbonell, J. L., & Perkins, R. (2000). Diagnosis and assessment of criminal offenders. In P. Van Voorhis, M. Braswell, & D. Lester (Eds.), *Correctional counseling and rehabilitation* (4th ed., pp. 63–80). Cincinnati: Anderson.

Clear, T. R., & Cole, G. F. (2003). *American corrections* (6th ed.). Belmont, CA: Wadsworth.

Drummond, R. J. (1996). *Appraisal procedures for counselors and helping professionals* (3rd ed.). Englewood Cliffs, NJ: Prentice Hall.

Megargee, E. I. (2005). *MMPI-2 criminal justice and correctional report*. Pearson Assessments. Retrieved from http://www.pearsonassessments.com/tests/megargee.htm

O'Keefe, M. L., Klebe, K., & Hromas, S. (1998). Supervision inventory (LSI) for community-based offenders in Colorado: Phase II. State of Colorado. Retrieved from http://www. doc.state.co.us/AlcoholDrug/pdfs/PHASE2.pdf

Prentky, R., & Righthand, S. (2003). *Juvenile sex offender protocol-II (J-SOAP-II) manual*. Washington, DC: Office of Juvenile Delinquency and Prevention. Retrieved from http://nicic.org/Library/019361

Reentry Media Outreach. (2005). *Health challenges of reentry: Briefing paper*. Indianapolis: Author. Retrieved from http://www.reentrymediaoutreach.org/pdfs/health_bp.pdf

Van Voorhis, P., Braswell, M., & Lester, D. (2000). *Correctional counseling and rehabilitation* (4th ed.). Cincinnati: Anderson.

LEARNING CHECK

1. With ________________, the main concern revolves around the protection of society and/or the safe management of correctional institutions.
   a. Objective assessments
   b. Subjective assessments
   c. Needs-principled assessment

d. Risk-principled assessment
e. None of the above

2. The ____________________ stage refers to the process of diagnosing offenders based on physical health or mental illness or the diagnosis of offenders based on the types of challenges they may face.
a. Assessment
b. Diagnostic
c. Recidivism prediction
d. Classification
e. None of the above

3. The GAF Scale is found on ___________ of the *DSM-IV-TR*.
a. Axis I
b. Axis II
c. Axis III
d. Axis IV
e. Axis V

4. ____________________ are those characteristics that can change and are more or less influenced or controlled by the offender, such as employment, motivation, drug use, and family relations.
a. Subjective assessments
b. Objective assessments
c. Static risk factors
d. Dynamic risk factors

5. ____________________ are characteristics that are inherent to the offender and are usually permanent.
a. Static risk factors
b. Dynamic risk factors
c. Objective needs
d. Subjective needs
e. None of the above

6. The ____________________ implies that the offender is predicted to not reoffend, and the prediction turns out to be true.
a. False positive
b. False negative
c. True positive
d. True negative

7. The ____________________ stage refers to both subjective methods of clinical interviews and observations as well as objective methods of test taking and mathematical models of offender profiling.
a. Assessment
b. Diagnostic

c. Recidivism prediction
d. Classification
e. None of the above

8. Staff members use this instrument to score probationers on the predictors contained on the list, and from this point they classify them into either high-, medium-, or low-risk categories.
a. *DSM-IV-TR*
b. LSI-R
c. Wisconsin Risk Assessment System
d. MMPI-2 CJCR

9. The MMPI-2 has a scale designed to detect lies from respondents taking the test.
a. True
b. False

10. The ______________________ category includes both personality disorders and mental retardation.
a. Axis I
b. Axis II
c. Axis III
d. Axis IV
e. Axis V

ESSAY DISCUSSION QUESTIONS

1. Discuss the underlying presumptions behind risk prediction. Define and explain false positives, false negatives, true positives, and true negatives. Provide an example for each one to clearly demonstrate your comprehension of these concepts.
2. Explain what the GAF Scale is and how it is used. Explain why this tool is a good instrument to bring the objective and subjective elements of assessment together.
3. Discuss the MMPI-2 and the MMPI-2 CJCR. Explain how these classification instruments are utilized with the offending population.

CHAPTER 3

SUBSTANCE ABUSERS AND SUBSTANCE ABUSE PROGRAMS

Chapter Objectives

1. Know the different demographic and psychological issues associated with the drug-abusing offender.
2. Know the forms of treatment employed within institutionalized settings, including jails, prisons, and therapeutic communities.
3. Identify the different types of drug treatment programs typically offered for substance-abusing offenders in the community; this specifically includes the development of drug courts.
4. Understand some basic treatment models and know about the effectiveness of these models.

INTRODUCTION

American culture is one that is given to a high consumption of drugs, whether they be legal or illegal. This high rate of drug use obviously factors into the rate of criminal behavior as well. To illustrate this fact, consider that in 1999 it was reported that at least 50 percent of adult male arrestees tested positive for at least one drug (Bartol, 2002). In fact, as much as 64 percent of all arrested adult males and 67 percent of all arrested adult females tested positive for the use of drugs (Bartol, 2002). It would appear that marijuana was the drug of choice among most male arrestees, with cocaine being the next-highest choice. With arrested adult females, cocaine, marijuana, and methamphetamines were found to be the most common, in that order (Bartol, 2002). The use of multiple drugs was also common, with more than one-quarter of the adult male arrestees testing positive for two or more drugs (Bartol, 2002).

Thus, with respect to the connection of drug use and criminal activity, three broad commonalities can be stated. First, drug abusers are more likely to commit crime than non–drug abusers. Second, many arrestees are under the influence while committing crimes. Third, drugs and violence tend to occur together in many reported violent incidents (Hanson, Venturelli, & Fleckenstein, 2002).

Other demographics on drug abusers are not always easy to determine. Of those that exist, most are based either on arrests or on admissions into detox or treatment programs. In 1995, there were an estimated 1.9 million admissions to publicly funded substance abuse treatment facilities (Bartol, 2002). Again, it should be noted that this number includes only publicly funded substance abuse programs and only those seeking treatment during that year. Of these admissions, about 54 percent were people seeking help for alcohol treatment with the remaining 46 percent seeking help for addiction to other drugs. Men made up the majority of those in treatment (approximately 70 percent), and women made up the other 30 percent. Racial demographics show that approximately 56 percent were Caucasian and that 26 percent were African American. Native Americans comprised 2.2 percent, and Asian Americans less than 1 percent of those in treatment (Bartol, 2002). Finally, the largest number of illicit drug treatment admissions was for cocaine (38.3 percent) followed by heroin (25.5 percent) and marijuana (19.1 percent).

The age of drug offenders likewise can shape the dynamics of their drug abuse, including the typical drug of choice. For children under the age of 12, experimentation is found with those who are neglected, abused, or isolated as well as those with undiagnosed behavioral or learning disorders (Myers & Salt, 2000). The abuse of inhalants and vapors from glues, paints, and solvents is of particular concern at this age (Myers & Salt, 2000). For adolescents, the individual risk factors of substance abuse are compounded by the confluence of developmental conflict and demands that occur during adolescence as well as a number of other risk factors toward general delinquency that may covary with the substance abuse risk factors (see Chapter 8). For middle-aged and elderly drug offenders, issues surrounding loss of body image, friends and family, and other normal life span losses may be pertinent. Further, elderly offenders may not necessarily have drug abuse problems with illegal drugs but are more likely to present with dependencies on prescription drugs that have resulted in usage levels that violate federal drug laws (Myers & Salt, 2000).

The gender of the drug offender is likewise an important consideration. When assessing female drug offenders, it is particularly important to explore relationships with significant others, support systems, and issues related to domestic abuse and prior childhood sexual abuse. Female drug abusers are prone to being involved with a male drug-abusing spouse or boyfriend. Female drug offenders tend to stay with their addicted partners, and the most important reason for their use and increase in use is the intimate relationship to which they belong (Myers & Salt, 2000). This is a particularly relevant issue when one considers that female offenders in general tend to become involved in crime with a romantic partner who is typically the primary active criminal. Thus, relationship dynamics are a critical factor with this type of drug offender, and this points to the potential that marriage and/or family therapy techniques can have for this group of offenders.

Further, cultural issues are often overlooked in drug assessment and treatment. There is considerable research that demonstrates that some social, racial, and/or cultural groups have general **drugs of choice** in their drug-using habits. A drug of choice is simply a drug that is consistently used with greater frequency than other types of drugs by a certain identifiable demographic group. For instance, crack cocaine is typically considered a drug of choice among the urban poor African American underclass, whereas heroin is more often associated with Latino Americans. Perhaps equally intriguing is the fact that the majority of drug offenders using methamphetamine and/or ecstasy tend to be Caucasians who are most often of middle class status (Hanson et al., 2002). Likewise, Latino American women are more likely than Latino American men to be shamed within their own cultures for substance abuse (Van Voorhis, Braswell, & Lester, 2000). In addition, while African American males do not seem to differ from other ethnic groups in their symptoms of drug abuse, black males convicted of drug offenses as a group experienced the largest increase in incarceration rates during the 1980s (Van Voorhis et al., 2000).

Regardless of public concern over hard drugs, it is the use of alcohol that is the most problematic for society. In fact, alcohol is responsible for more deaths and violence than all other drugs combined (Bartol, 2002; Hanson et al., 2002). Roughly one-third of all offenders who commit violent crime were drinking at the time of the offense, and many were highly intoxicated (Bartol, 2002). Despite the fact that alcohol is so debilitating and is the most common drug to be associated with violent crime, there is still widespread cultural support for the continued social use of alcohol (Hanson et al., 2002).

Finally, each year it is estimated that more than 16,000 Americans die from an overdose or the misuse of illegal drugs, and at least 500,000 drug-related emergencies occur in emergency rooms throughout the United States (FBI, 1999). Further, an estimated $82 billion is lost each year because of both alcohol and other drug abuse (Hanson et al., 2002). Regardless of whether the drug offender is caught by the criminal justice system, the cost to society, their families, and their friends is severe, causing both psychological and economic difficulty for all involved.

Hanson et al. (2002) provide an interesting description of drug users and abusers that is based on the offender's level of drug use. In their description, there are three basic patterns of drug usage: (1) **experimenters**, who are novel users;

(2) **floaters**, who vacillate between the need to seek pleasure and the need to relieve serious psychological problems; and (3) **compulsive users**, who are the truly addicted users of a drug or drugs.

According to Hanson et al. (2002), experimenters initially use drugs simply because of influence from the peer group. This is most frequently encountered with teens and young adults. However, this group of users will typically restrict their use to recreational settings that are "agreed-on" times of appropriate drug use. This group is usually capable of setting limits in their drug use (often in social situations), and they are able to regulate between their own light, moderate, and heavy drug use. In fact, this group may likewise monitor each other and share feedback on each member's condition, even going so far as to protect one another from contact with law enforcement and so forth. In essence, these are the "responsible" drug users, as it might be called, who can maintain some semblance of functionality in their daily operations despite their dabbling in the world of drug use.

Floaters may intermix with experimenters and will often frequent parties of known drug users. This group of drug user will usually focus more on using the drugs of other people and are more likely to maintain a moderate use of drugs. This group of drug abuser may vacillate between pleasure-seeking behavior and the desire to gain relief from environmental stressors and/or other problems with adjustment. As a result, this group is likely to go back and forth between experimental drug use to chronic use with more hard-core drug-abusing peers. These drug users are thought to be fairly marginal individuals (some may present with a variety of low-key adjustment or personality disorders) who do not strongly identify with experimenters or compulsive users (Hanson et al., 2002).

Compulsive users, on the other hand, are the true addicts. For these users, there is no such thing as having fun or enjoyment without drug use. Most compulsive users have difficulty assuming personal responsibility and suffer from low self-esteem. Many compulsive users come from dysfunctional families, have had problems with the law, and/or may have psychological problems that compound their substance-abusing behavior (Hanson et al., 2002). Other issues with childhood abuse, childhood behavioral disorders, family discord, or chronic bouts of depression may also make drug use more appealing as a coping mechanism for day-to-day stressors in their lives (Hanson et al., 2002).

Understanding the different patterns of drug use is important to prevent misguided use of criminal justice resources. The criminal justice system may find some types of abusers more amenable to treatment than others. By the same token, some forms of punitive sanctions, such as **drug courts**, may be effective with experimenters and floaters, but compulsive users may be in need of residential treatment services. The appropriate placement of these individuals has as much to do with the pattern of drug use as it does with the drug that is used (e.g., alcohol as opposed to crack cocaine). Such considerations are crucial during the screening process when determining placement of these individuals.

SCREENING AND PLACEMENT CRITERIA

Every form of treatment program involves some sort of screening. According to Myers and Salt (2000), screening serves two major purposes:

1. It attests to the presence of a condition that may go unrecognized if not detected.
2. It provides data to decide whether a client is appropriate for a specific treatment program and vice versa.

In the first use of screening, social, health, and criminal justice workers determine if there are sufficient grounds for referral of a client to a particular drug/alcohol treatment program. This screening is very important because the earlier the intervention takes place, the better the prognosis for the client. Obviously, the likelihood of reforming a drug experimenter (as described previously) is much better than when treating a compulsive user. The second use of screening is used to determine client appropriateness for a given treatment modality. It should be pointed out that the discretion in placement may not only consider the client's individual characteristics but also include the ability of a given agency to provide these services (e.g., fiscal constraints may be a factor despite the fact that the treatment program may be ideal for the client). In either case, it is this use of screening that provides the placement criteria for drug offenders in the criminal justice system.

Placement criteria are very important when processing drug offenders. The initial placement is important for both public safety and treatment-oriented concerns. When deciding on placement criteria, a match must be made between the severity of the addiction to the level of care needed, ranging from medical inpatient care, nonmedical inpatient care, and intensive outpatient care to outpatient care (Hanson et al., 2002). Further, matching the client's profile to a treatment modality is more likely to achieve lasting success, translating to a better evaluation of program effectiveness. For example, a client with attention-deficit/hyperactivity disorder might be unsuited for the regimentation of a therapeutic community. Conversely, a person with low self-esteem, insecurities, and a fragile sense of self-worth would not be appropriate for a highly confrontational style of intervention.

Goldberg (2003) notes the fact that different people have different learning styles. Further, as previously noted, different personalities respond to different types of treatment in ways that may be unique from one another. Thus, the matching of clients to the appropriate treatment is an important element to consider, as clients would not recover if the treatment were ill suited to their needs. In fact, it would be foolish to expect positive results from a program that is a poor match for the client. Goldberg (2003) states that many clients may drop out of treatment because the program is poorly defined in terms of content, goals, approach, and even duration. This lack of clarity can cause confusion and even aggravation among clients who are already challenged with their drug cravings, any withdrawal symptoms that they may experience, and the normal day-to-day stress that is exacerbated by the fact that they are drug abusers.

Goldberg (2003) notes that several questions should be asked before placing clients in treatment. Further, agencies should also consider these issues before they begin to go into operation or should at least consider changing their program to address these questions. According to Goldberg (2003, p. 297), prior to matching clients to specific treatments, the following questions must be addressed:

1. Which treatment produces the best outcome for a specific group or person?
2. Do members of certain ethnic or socioeconomic groups respond similarly to certain types of treatment?
3. Is the effectiveness of a specific program linked to the age of participants?
4. Do females and males differ in their response to treatment?

The matching of treatment to gender, culture, ethnicity, language, and even sexual orientation has been shown to improve the odds of achieving positive outcomes in a variety of treatment settings for a variety of treatment issues (Goldberg, 2003; Hanser, 2002; Jones & Hanser, 2004). In fact, the utilization of culturally competent programs for various racial/ethnic groups should be particularly addressed given the fact that minorities are highly prevalent within the correctional population.

Goldberg (2003) also points out the importance of addressing issues relevant to female drug offenders, among these being the need for prenatal care and treatment and the need for contact with their children. As will be seen in Chapter 13, a high proportion of female offenders on community supervision (72 percent) are the primary caretakers of children under 18 years of age (Bloom, Owen, & Covington, 2003). Thus, many female offenders may initially be motivated by the desire to reduce drug-related harm to their expected babies or to improve their relationship with and ability to attend to their children. This should not be overlooked, as this can be an effective source of motivation to encourage these offenders to complete their treatment, thereby improving their chances for long-term recovery.

Finally, the age of the client can be very important as well. Some research has shown that older clients are more successful in a variety of correctional treatment programs than are younger clients (Butzin, Saum, & Scarpitti, 2003). This is particularly true with adolescent drug abusers. Indeed, it has been found that many adolescent clients relapse before six months has elapsed since their completion of a treatment program (Goldberg, 2003). Much of the reason for this dismal outcome has to do with the youth's selection of friends who are again available upon leaving treatment. Thus, peer group attitudes have a strong effect on the likelihood of individual youth successfully overcoming their abuse of substances. This means that awareness of such factors as music, clothing, and youth media programming may be important elements for agency staff to possess if the treatment program is to be well suited to this population.

Thus, the main point is that treatments must be effectively matched to the specific client. Certain groups of clients may also have needs that are common to one another (e.g., those based on ethnicity, age, or gender), and they may have other, more individualistic factors (e.g., divorce, abuse trauma, and so on) that may significantly affect their likelihood of success in treatment. In either event, treatment programs will need to ensure that such factors are specifically taken into account within the structure of their programs, or they will run the risk of reaching some clients while completely failing to truly assist others.

DRUG OFFENDERS IN JAILS, PRISONS, AND INPATIENT TREATMENT FACILITIES

It is nearly impossible to discuss drug offenders in the United States without first acknowledging the impact that the War on Drugs has had on society, the criminal justice system, and racial minorities. Indeed, those convicted of drug offenses constitute the primary segment of the prison population, one that burgeoned in the 1990s. By 1994, 60 percent of all adults in federal prison had been convicted of drug offenses (Walker, 2006). Further, convictions for drug offenses were responsible for half the increase in the entire nation's prison population between 1980 and the mid-1990s (Walker, 2006).

Many offenders in state and federal prisons are convicted of violating drug laws (30 percent of the prison population increase from 1980 to 1995 is attributable to drug law violators), and others committed crimes while under the influence of drugs or alcohol or to facilitate their drug use (Inciardi, Rivers, & McBride, 1999). The problem is compounded by the fact that substance abuse is closely related to recidivism; inmates with prior convictions are significantly more likely than first-time offenders to be regular drug users (Inciardi, Rivers, & McBride, 1999). From this, it is clear that the War on Drugs has had a tremendous impact on U.S. society. Whether it has succeeded in reducing illegal drug use or serious crime associated with drug use is another question (Walker, 2006). Regardless, the issue quickly begins to revolve around what is going on with offenders once they are incarcerated. For most taxpayers, the issue is settled once drug offenders are locked behind bars, but, in reality, this is where the real problems for society can begin.

It has been estimated that perhaps roughly 65 to 80 percent of the inmate population in local jails and state or federal prisons are seriously involved with drug and alcohol abuse (Inciardi, Rivers, & McBride, 1999). Included in the 80 percent are inmates who used an illegal drug at least weekly for a period of at least one month, have been imprisoned for selling or possessing drugs, were under the influence of drugs or alcohol when they committed their crime, committed their offense to get money for drugs, or have a history of alcohol abuse. As stated before, drugs are commonly linked with crime, the issue not being if but how they are linked.

Table 3.1 provides an estimation of the percentage of jail inmates who have reported some form of a drug or alcohol problem. When noting such a problem, there are different types and definitions that may fit into this category, and it is important that the student and/or lay reader understand this fact. For instance, some offenders

Table 3.1. Prevalence of Substance Dependence or Abuse among Jail Inmates

		Percentage of Jail Inmates		
Diagnosis	**Estimated Number of Inmates**	**Alcohol**	**Drugs**	**Alcohol or Drugs**
Any substance dependence or abuse	415,242	46.6	53.5	69.0
Substance dependence and abuse	262,632	22.2	34.4	44.2
Substance dependence only	6,081	0.6	1.4	1.0
Substance abuse only	132,530	23.8	17.7	22.9
No dependence or abuse	195,054	53.4	46.5	32.0

Note: Definitions for dependence and abuse are based on the *Diagnostic and Statistical Manual of Mental Disorders* (*DSM-IV-TR*). This table also includes those inmates who did not use alcohol or drugs as well as 20,945 inmates for whom data are unknown.

Source: Adapted from Karberg and James (2003).

may have abused either drugs or alcohol at one or more points in their lives (particularly at the point of arrest), yet that does not mean that they are dependent on drugs or alcohol. Thus, it is important to distinguish between **substance abuse** and **substance dependence** (both physiological and psychological) when making decisions for treatment and for community release since dependence is naturally correlated with a higher likelihood of relapse and therefore requires more intensive intervention. For offenders who have simply abused drugs or alcohol, some treatment intervention is warranted, but it is more likely that intensive probation sanctions will keep such offenders correctly within the guidelines of appropriate social behavior since they do not have the full gamut of addiction symptoms to contend with.

The primary modality that is implemented in most jails is simple chemical **detoxification**. Detoxification is designed for persons dependent on narcotic drugs (e.g., heroin or opium) and is typically found in inpatient settings with programs that last for 7 to 21 days. The rationale for using detoxification as a treatment approach is grounded in two basic principles (Hanson et al., 2002; McNeece, Springer, & Arnold, 2000; Myers & Salt, 2000). The first is a conception of "addiction" as drug craving accompanied by physical dependence that motivates continued usage, resulting in a tolerance to the drug's effects and a syndrome of identifiable physical and psychological symptoms when the drug is abruptly withdrawn. The second is that the negative aspects of the abstinence syndrome discourage many addicts from attempting withdrawal, making them more likely to continue using drugs. The main objective of chemical detoxification is the elimination of **physiological dependence** through a medically supervised procedure. Naturally, the more the offender uses a given drug, the more **tolerance** the body builds to the drug, which then requires more of the drug to simply avoid the negative symptoms that occur after drug use (let alone obtaining a good sensation from the drug). This then means that the offender's dependence on the drug is ever more entrenched physiologically, generating a psychological dependence as well. Further, the seriousness of this **psychological dependence** should not be underestimated by clinicians or security staff since it can lead to other co-occurring disorders for the offender.

While many detoxoification programs address only the addict's physical dependence, some provide individual or group counseling in an attempt to address the problems associated with drug abuse. Many detoxification programs use medical drugs to ease the process of overcoming the physical symptoms of dependence that make the detoxification process so painful for the addicted substance abuser. For drug offenders in jails or prisons, the mechanism of detoxification varies by the client's major drug of addiction. For opiate users, methadone or chlonidine is preferred. For cocaine users, desipramine has been used to ease the **substance withdrawal** symptoms. Almost all narcotic addicts and many cocaine users have been in a chemical detoxification program at least once (Inciardi, Rivers, & McBride, 1999). However, studies show that in the absence of supportive psychotherapeutic services and community follow-up care, nearly all are certain to suffer from relapse (Ashford, Sales, & Reid, 2002). See Special Insert 3.1 for further details on abuse, tolerance, physiological and psychological dependence, and withdrawal.

In all detoxification programs, inmate success depends on following established protocols for drug administration and withdrawal. In a recent assessment of research literature on the effectiveness of detoxification, there appear to be promising rates

Special Insert 3.1. Common Terms Associated with Drug and Alcohol Addiction

Substance Abuse: Recurrent substance abuse resulting in failure to fulfill major role obligations at work, school, or home or when such use results in physically hazardous situations, recurrent legal problems, or recurrent social or interpersonal problems caused or exacerbated by the effects of the substance (as per *DSM-IV-TR*).

Tolerance: A need for markedly increased amounts of the substance to achieve intoxication or the desired effect (as per *DSM-IV-TR*).

Physiological Dependence: Dependence that results because a drug produces pleasant physical effects. The dependent person must also exhibit signs of both tolerance and withdrawal to truly be physiologically dependent.

Psychological Dependence: Dependence that results because a drug produces pleasant psychological effects. The dependent person must also exhibit signs of both tolerance and withdrawal to truly be psychologically dependent.

Substance Withdrawal: The development of a substance-specific maladaptive behavioral change, with physiological and cognitive impairments, that is due to the cessation of or reduction in heavy and prolonged substance use (as per *DSM-IV-TR*).

of program completion (McNeece et al., 2000). Yet many clinicians note that mere detoxification from a substance is not drug abuse "treatment" and does not help people stay off drugs. This in no way ensures that relapse will not occur, and thus it is important for any program to have much more than a simple detoxification process. This should instead be viewed as nothing more than an initial step after the intake process of a comprehensive treatment process. Thus, detoxification is a temporary regimen that gives addicts the opportunity to reduce their drug intake; for many, this means that the criminal activity associated with their drug taking and drug seeking is interrupted. Finally, given the association between injection drug use and HIV and AIDS, detoxification also provides counseling to reduce AIDS-related risk behaviors (McNeece et al., 2000). As will be seen in chapter 4, drug abuse elevates the risk of contracting a communicable disease. This is associated largely with those drug abusers who use intravenous drugs and those who engage in risky sex behaviors, particularly when prostitution and drug use are combined (as with female offenders; see Chapter 13).

THE THERAPEUTIC COMMUNITY

Beyond the detoxification phase of "treatment," the residential therapeutic community is the next full-service form of treatment that is given to substance abusers who are "behind bars." The therapeutic community is a total treatment environment in which the primary clinical staff are typically former substance abusers ("recovering addicts") who themselves were rehabilitated in therapeutic communities (Inciardi, Rivers, & McBride, 1999; Myers & Salt, 2000). The treatment perspective of the therapeutic community is that drug abuse is a disorder of the whole person—that the problem is the person and not the drug and that addiction is a symptom and not the essence of the disorder. In this view of recovery, the primary goal is to change the negative patterns of behavior, thinking, and feeling that predispose a person to drug use. As such, the overall goal is a responsible, drug-free lifestyle. Recovery through this form of treatment depends on positive and negative pressures to change. This pressure is brought about through a self-help process in which relationships of mutual responsibility to every resident in the program are built (Inciardi et al., 1999). In addition to individual and group counseling, this process has a system of explicit rewards that reinforce the value of earned achievement. As such, privileges are earned. In addition, therapeutic communities have their own rules and regulations that guide the behavior of residents and the management of their facilities. Their purposes are to maintain the safety and health of the community and to train and teach residents through the use of discipline. There are typically numerous rules and regulations within these facilities. Violation of the more important rules usually results in immediate expulsion from the facility (Inciardi, Rivers, & McBride, 1999).

The Federal Bureau of Prisons' Residential Drug Abuse Treatment Program attempts to identify, confront, and alter the attitudes, values, and thought patterns that lead to criminal behavior and drug or alcohol abuse. This model program consists of three stages. The first stage is a unit-based treatment program that exists within the confines of a prison where inmates undergo therapy for up to 12 months (Inciardi et al., 1999). In the second stage, on completion of the residential portion, inmates continue treatment for up to 12 months while in the general population of the prison through monthly group meetings with the drug abuse program staff. In the third stage, inmates are transferred to community-based facilities prior to release from custody and are provided with regularly scheduled group, individual, and family counseling sessions (Inciardi, Rivers, & McBride, 1999).

The designation of therapeutic community (TC) is known mostly as a demanding long-term, drug-free residential program run by recovering addicts. The TC model has its roots as far back as 1958 in California (Myers & Salt, 2000). During this time, a recovering alcoholic named Charles Dederich brought known drug addicts into an Alcoholics Anonymous (AA) group program. Shortly after starting this, he decided to create his own organization, which became known as Synanon (Myers & Salt, 2000). The development of Synanon was very different from AA in that it addressed nonalcoholic drug addiction, was fully residential, used confrontational methods of intervention, and completely abandoned the spiritual element found in AA programs.

This residential addict community was run totally by recovering addicts. Synanon developed a variety of harsh confrontational techniques that were designed to strip addicts of their abusing images and psychological defenses. These included confrontational groups, work therapy, and a hierarchy of rewards, privileges, and statuses up until graduation to resocialize the addict into responsible, mature behavior. The stratification system goes beyond graduation, as the TC graduate may return as a role model and often becomes part of the staff.

Social reactions to TCs have ranged from negative perceptions from the local community to highly supportive by various governmental programs. In fact, many communities frown on these types of treatment programs being in their locales because of the perceived threat that members pose and because of fluctuations in local real estate values. Despite this, some organizations have held that TCs hold an irrefutable value to society. For instance, the Ford Foundation's Drug Abuse Survey Project has held TCs in high regard. Further, there are hundreds of treatment programs that more or less follow the TC model (Myers & Salt, 2000). Therapeutic Communities of America, a national organization, has 58 affiliate programs (Myers & Salt, 2000). Many or most of the original, rather harsh practices have been modified considerably. The programs have seen the influence of social learning and cognitive psychology, and educational and occupational programs have been incorporated into many programs as intermediate sanctions and as sentencing to treatment (Myers & Salt, 2000).

Beyond the use of the therapeutic communities, other interventions typically fall within the category of being drug-free outpatient treatment programs. These usually encompass a variety of nonresidential programs that do not employ pharmacological interventions and instead provide a counseling/mental health perspective. In these forms of treatment programs, offenders are active in the community and report to their treatment providers during structured times throughout the week. Otherwise, they hold jobs and have lives very similar to the typical offender on probation or parole. Thus, we now turn our attention to those programs that are designed to divert offenders from secured facilities and other forms of incarceration.

DRUG OFFENDERS IN THE COMMUNITY: THE USE OF DRUG COURTS

Established as a result of court and prison overcrowding, special drug courts have proven popular. In 1989, a special drug court was established by judicial order in Miami. This high-volume court expanded on traditional drug-defendant diversion programs by offering a year or more of court-run treatment; defendants who complete this option have their criminal cases dismissed (Abidinsky, 2004). Between 1991 and 1993, Miami influenced officials in more than 20 other jurisdictions to establish drug courts (Abidinsky, 2004). Within a decade, drug courts moved from the experimental stage to being recognized as well-established programs. The government now lists over 325 drug courts in 43 states (Neubauer, 2002).

Although they vary widely, drug courts have some features in common, including a nonadversarial approach to integrating substance abuse treatment with criminal justice case processing. The focus is on early identification of eligible substance abusers and prompt placement in treatment, combined with frequent drug testing.

Drug courts vary widely in structure, target populations, and treatment programs. The primary goal is to speed up case dispositions of drug cases while freeing other judges to expedite their own dockets. Another type of drug court concentrates on defendants accused of serious crimes who also have major prior criminal records. Still other drug courts emphasize treatment. The assumption is that treatment will reduce the likelihood that convicted drug offenders will be rearrested.

In discussing the objectives of drug courts, McNeece et al. (2000) point out several points that have been clearly listed by the Drug Courts Program Office of the Office of Justice Programs (1997). From this discussion, eight key points emerge as particularly relevant to the point of this chapter:

1. Drug courts integrate alcohol and other drug treatment services with justice system case processing.
2. Using a nonadversarial approach, prosecution and defense counsel promote public safety while protecting participants' due process rights.
3. Eligible participants are identified early and promptly placed in the drug court program.
4. Drug courts provide access to a continuum of alcohol, drug, and other related treatment and rehabilitation services.
5. Abstinence is monitored by frequent alcohol and other drug testing.
6. A coordinated strategy governs drug court responses to participants' compliance.

7. Ongoing judicial interaction with each drug court participant is essential.
8. Monitoring and evaluation measure the achievement of program goals and gauge effectiveness.

These features are among those that are thought to constitute an "ideal" model of drug court, though few meet these requirements (McNeece et al., 2000). In general, an offender is placed in a drug court program for 9 to 12 months. On successfully completing that program, the offender will be continued on probation for another year. In some jurisdictions, the offender's criminal record may be expunged if all the court's conditions for treatment are satisfied (McNeece et al., 2000).

The role of the judge is crucial in a drug court. Judges are free to openly chastise or praise clients for their behavior during the courtroom proceedings. Beyond that, judges may issue court orders requiring that a client attend treatment, submit to urinalysis, seek employment, meet with a probation officer, avoid associations with drug-abusing friends, or any other condition that seems appropriate (McNeece et al., 2000). Failure to comply with these judicial determinations may place the offender in contempt of court or in jail or may transfer them to a regular criminal court. Judges are provided with continuous feedback on the offender's performance by the other drug court participants. Because of this, there is little room for the offender to evade accountability within the program.

Recently, drug courts have begun to acknowledge and address the needs of special populations and issues. Some examples are juvenile drug courts, drug courts for women (Drug Strategies, 1997), night drug courts, and the application of drug courts to judicial settings, such as family courts, where crack cocaine users who are involved in domestic violence and dependency cases are offered treatment. In addition, there is interest in expanding drug courts to the federal court system, where nearly 60 percent of all inmates are sentenced for drug offenses (Drug Strategies, 1997). Thus, while these forms of judicial and therapeutic intervention may be gaining popularity, it should be determined who is responsive to this type of drug intervention and, just as important, why they have responded positively to the program.

From the research on drug court treatment outcomes, some general trends in client outcomes can be determined. Butzin, Saum, and Scarpitti (2003) note in a comparison of the research that while there are often mixed findings in distinguishing the characteristics of clients likely to have successful outcomes, there are nevertheless some trends that can be noted among drug court clients. These general trends, drawn from this comparison of the research, are presented as follows:

- Compared to male clients, female clients who participate in drug court programs tend to be more heavily involved with drugs and thus tend to have a poorer prognosis for treatment.
- In general, older offenders have been found to be more successful in drug court treatment programs. Young drug offenders (adolescent and early adult) are

much more likely to drop out of drug court treatment programs and therefore have a poorer prognosis.

- While not definitive, it does appear that minority clients do not respond as well to drug court programs as do Caucasian clients.
- For the most part, it does appear that educational differences have a slight determining effect on a client's drug court treatment outcome. This is more often the case when comparing high school graduates (and persons with a general equivalency diploma) to non–diploma-holding clients.
- Overall, it would appear that income and employment are associated with drug court treatment outcomes.
- Marital status produces inconsistent results for both men and women in treatment, meaning that it does not appear that marriage provides a greater likelihood of program completion.
- The type, quantity, and frequency of drug use does seem to be important in determining both the completion of the drug court program and the achievement of long-term recovery.

Butzin et al. (2003) note that, in general, clients who tend to finish their treatment programs most often share a certain composite typology. A large proportion tend to be Caucasian, married (or at least once married), better educated, employed, and less frequent in their use of drugs. However, many of these aspects are interrelated (e.g., education may determine likelihood of employment, as a person with a degree may be more likely to have a job—and likely one with a decent wage—than would a person who has not finished high school), so it is difficult to tell if it is that particular item in question that affects the ultimate outcome for the client.

DRUG OFFENDERS IN THE COMMUNITY: COMMUNITY SUPERVISION

Probation is the main way of monitoring offenders who have been released to the community. Probation, in combination with therapy, support, and surveillance, is the most common type of treatment used as an alternative to incarceration (Champion, 2002; Chavaria, 1992). With regular probation, an offender lives at home and receives periodic monitoring. Many offenders with substance abuse problems are sentenced to intensive supervision probation (ISP), a more restrictive type of probation than traditional probation (as noted in Chapter 1). It is a method of monitoring that can be used as an alternative to incarceration and requires that the offender and probation officer keep in close contact, including random home visits to ensure compliance with the minimum criteria of the program (Champion, 2002).

In addition, the offender may have to perform community service, maintain employment, adhere to a curfew, and submit to urine testing for drugs. Compared to basic probation, ISP is more expensive and requires that probation officers have smaller caseloads to accommodate the increase in supervision of the offender. It may be more cost effective than basic probation in the long run when the alternative for offenders is prison or jail. In addition, ISP is less costly than incarceration even when the cost of supervision is included (Champion, 2002).

As mentioned previously, drug offenders on probation may be required to submit to drug screens to ensure compliance with treatment. Court and corrections officials will generally want to know if the offender is complying with treatment and is abstaining from drugs (Champion, 2002). In programs in which access to treatment may be limited by available space or funding, those who do not comply may be discharged from treatment. Those who do not successfully complete treatment and continue to have positive drug screens may be sent back to court for further sentencing (Champion, 2002). While drug testing does appear to serve a useful purpose in monitoring offenders with substance abuse problems, this testing alone is not sufficient to keep offenders from using drugs and reoffending. The best approach may be to combine random drug testing with forms of rehabilitative drug treatment to address the addiction and, it is hoped, minimize the likelihood that the individual will engage in future criminal behavior (Champion, 2002).

Drug offenders on probation are placed in what are termed "outpatient" treatment programs, which usually include individual and group therapy; some programs offer family therapy and relapse prevention support. An increasing number of drug-free outpatient treatment programs are including case management services as an adjunct to counseling. The basic case management approach is to assist clients in obtaining needed services in a timely, coordinated manner. The key components of the approach are assessing, planning, linking, monitoring, and advocating for clients within the existing nexus of treatment and social services (Myers & Salt, 2000).

Evaluating the effectiveness of drug-free outpatient treatment is difficult because programs vary widely from drop-in "talk" centers to highly structured arrangements that offer counseling or psychotherapy. Some include a strong "faith-based" element to their intervention that represents a blend between therapy and religious instruction. A number of studies have found that outpatient treatment has been moderately successful in reducing daily drug use and criminal activity. However, the approach appears to be inappropriate for the most troubled and the antisocial users.

The number of rigorously designed studies of corrections-based outpatient programs is quite small. One of the few examples involves a relatively well-funded and designed program known as Passages, an eight-hour-per-day, five-day-per-week, 12-week nonresidential program for women incarcerated in the Wisconsin correctional system. Although the treatment staff and correctional administrators agreed that the program improved clients' self-esteem, their subsequent reduced drug use and criminal activity was not reported (McNeece et al., 2000).

SELF-HELP GROUPS

Self-help groups, also known as 12-step programs, are composed of individuals who meet regularly to stabilize and facilitate their recovery from substance abuse. The best known is AA, in which sobriety is based on fellowship and adhering to the

12 steps to recovery (Hanson et al., 2002; Myers & Salt, 2000). The 12 steps stress faith, confession of wrongdoing, and passivity in the hands of a "higher power." The steps move group members from a statement of powerlessness over drugs and alcohol to a resolution that they will carry the message of help to others and will practice the AA principles in all affairs. Other popular self-help 12-step groups are Narcotics Anonymous, Cocaine Anonymous, and Drugs Anonymous (Hanson et al., 2002; Myers & Salt, 2000). All these organizations operate as stand-alone fellowship programs but are also used as adjuncts to other modalities. Although few evaluation studies of self-help groups have been carried out, the weight of clinical and observational data suggest that they are crucial to recovery.

Research has failed to demonstrate that anonymous fellowship meetings by themselves are effective with heavy drug users. According to Inciardi, Rivers, and McBride (1999), there are few known evaluations of prison-based self-help programs for a variety of reasons: prison administrators tend to prefer other types of programs, the model contains variables that are extremely difficult to operationalize and measure, members and leaders often view scientific studies of their groups as intrusive threats to anonymity and therapeutic processes, and evaluation research funding is more often available for innovative programming than for such well-established services. Nonetheless, self-help programs are widely used in community correctional agencies. There is a widely held belief that they work (Inciardi, Rivers, & McBride, 1999). The meetings are organized and run by volunteers at no cost to the prison authorities, and the meetings appear to help inmates make the transition from correctional to community-based settings (Inciardi, Rivers, & McBride, 1999).

The success of self-help programs in general and AA in particular may be explained by their comprehensive networks that support abstinence and recovery; the frequent attendance at AA meetings, where role modeling, confession, sharing, and support take place; and participation in the member network between meetings, including obtaining and relying on a senior member or sponsor (Myers & Salt, 2000). Al-Anon, a fellowship for relatives and significant others of alcoholics, was founded in 1951, although it did not take off as a movement until the 1960s. Narcotics Anonymous (NA), the third of the three major 12-step fellowships, was founded in 1953. It was relatively small throughout the 1950s and 1960s but obtained a great deal of popularity during the 1970s and 1980s. The atmosphere of NA meetings is more emotional than that of AA because many members attend drug treatment programs that emphasize interpersonal interaction in group sessions (Myers & Salt, 2000).

Outpatient treatment is the most common form of treatment with substance-abusing clients and offenders. These are organized nonresidential treatment services that the client visits at least once a week up to about 10 hours per week. Some of these programs are referred to as intensive outpatient programs (IOPs) or intensive outpatient treatment programs (McNeece et al., 2000). These programs consist of fully structured treatment settings in which the client participates for 10 to 30 hours per week. The broad category of intensive outpatient treatment may include programs called day treatment or, in a medical setting, partial hospitalization. Clients in IOPs may remain living at home, in a therapeutic or long-term residence of some sort, or in apartment dwellings as part of a special program of comprehensive treatment (McNeece et al., 2000). All thc components of rehabilitative treatment should be provided, including counseling (individual, group, and family), treatment planning, crisis management, medication management, client education, self-help education, and so on.

DRUG OFFENDERS AND CORRECTIONAL TREATMENT: COUNSELING MODELS

The styles of counseling for substance abusers vary from agency to agency. Regardless of theoretical orientation, most all programs rely primarily on group therapy that occurs augmented with individual therapy. Individual therapy is often used to address "comorbid" issues that are related yet corollary to the addiction issue. **Comorbidity** occurs when there are two or more potential diagnoses that may be involved with the drug offender's individual treatment situation. Because drug abuse and other forms of mental illness tend to occur together, most intervention professionals must deal with a multiplicity of issues rather than the drug abuse alone. Individual counseling might address areas such as depression, faulty cognitions, "using" behaviors, and sexual dysfunctions. This form of treatment involves the typical "talk therapy" between the client and the practitioner (McNeece et al., 2000; Myers & Salt, 2000; Van Voorhis et al., 2000).

Group therapy, on the other hand, is most often the preferred treatment by addiction intervention specialists. Such groups can be conducted in outpatient and inpatient settings. Working with group members in the criminal justice system takes on a different connotation than working with members in the community. In the criminal justice setting, the group worker is bound by structural constraints, policies, and laws.

One approach to chemical dependency counseling involves that of **behavioral-oriented approaches** (Van Voorhis et al., 2000). This type of approach incorporates learning modes of behavior that help the client meet personal needs through self-empowerment. In this approach, clients change negative thinking by learning behaviors and coping responses via "homework" assignments, sometimes referred to as bibliotherapy. Other behavioral change strategies include assertiveness training, which allows a direct, appropriate alternative to helpless, passive, aggressive, and passive-aggressive behavior. After several years of addiction, the individual is likely to have deficits in stability and responsibility. Behavioral approaches are useful in relapse prevention. These often involve identifying triggers of relapse and finding effective ways to deal with such situations (Van Voorhis et al., 2000).

Other approaches use social learning or cognitive-behavioral orientations. Through these methods, beliefs, attitudes, thoughts, categories, and self-statements act as lenses through which to view the world. Cognitive therapies use role models to model new cognitive skills, and social learning approaches often target cognitive patterns. However, with social learning approaches, the fundamental element for change within a social learning paradigm is the role model who can be imitated by others and offer feedback to those who are trying to defeat their addictive habits

(Van Voorhis et al., 2000). Members of AA and NA are encouraged to work with "sponsors." These are AA or NA members who have been in "recovery" for a significant period of time. Through their example, sponsors model skills of relationship building, responsibility, and support (Van Voorhis et al., 2000).

Another approach uses the family as the primary intervention component. It is well known that families can be critical to either the success or the failure of treatment. In many instances, family members have developed behaviors that have helped them cope with an addict but later proved to be dysfunctional when the addicted family member began to make progress in therapy (Van Voorhis et al., 2000). This may be referred to as codependency and/or enabling, where a family member makes excuses for the addict or protects them from others who discourage their drug usage.

Family systems therapy seeks to identify family routines, regulatory behaviors, rituals, or problem-solving strategies that have developed to deal with substance abuse within the family. When family matters become directed primarily toward coping with the drug abuse of a family member, other important family functions, such as parenting, financial responsibility, or physical health, may be impaired (Van Voorhis et al., 2000). Such processes also encourage the intergenerational transmission of substance abuse. In trying to correct this, family systems therapy often seeks to alter the family "structures" that sustain addiction. From this model, family therapy targets problem-solving strategies and dysfunctional family roles (such as when children must assume adult roles in the family or take care of the addictive parent) and appropriate boundaries to family relationships (Myers & Salt, 2000; Van Voorhis et al., 2000).

In recent years, there has been an increased emphasis on what are known as "faith-based" interventions. This has been the result of the recognition that clergy and other pastoral ministers have an array of opportunities to address problems of alcohol and drug dependence based on their own positions (e.g., small vs. large congregations or adult vs. youth ministries). Specifically, clergy and religious laypersons must utilize identified techniques to provide a general framework for a variety of pastoral situations. These programs and the techniques employed are in accordance with the spiritual and social goals of such a relationship.

The underlying thrust of **faith-based programs** is the notion that clients cannot defeat their addiction by simple willpower; if that were the case, then they would not be in their current position. Instead, they must give themselves over to their conviction and belief in the guidance of a higher spiritual power. While this is common in most AA programs, the faith-based program typically holds that the client's relationship with a spiritual guide is of primary concern and that addiction issues will be defeated largely by proxy of the client's faith, which provides him or her with the strength and courage to overcome the temptations of previous lifestyles. One such faith-based program that employs this outlook is demonstrated in Special Insert 3.2. This model program is an example of how the addiction is perceived as secondary to the client's need to correct faulty life choices.

Special Insert 3.2. Rays of Sonshine—A Faith-Based Program

Rays of Sonshine is a faith-based residential treatment facility that has developed a twelve lesson program with the objectives of helping clients to build self-worth, personal accountability, communication, and life management skills. These twelve lessons are all based on Christian Bible scripture and share the goal of directing the client toward a close spiritual relationship with God. The underlying premise behind the program is that a client that is fully devoted to living right spiritually according to Christian standards will ultimately cease their substance addiction. Clients who "fully give themselves over to God" ultimately relinquish their own personal control (or lack thereof) over their addiction or addictions (addictive issues tend to be comorbid, such as with sex addictions simultaneously existing with drug addiction) and rely on a power that is greater than themselves. It is through the power of faith, coupled with typical case management techniques, and a variety of life-skills training programs that clients are given a new lease on life. In essence, the client's old life is supplanted with a new life in Christ where addictions are essentially removed from the itinerary, so to speak. Rays of Sonshine is an intensive program where clients are kept busy in various lesson programs, chore activities, volunteer services, physical fitness regimens, and job training activities. Clients are given little, if any, unstructured time and are strongly encouraged to maintain a productive focus on structured and task-related activities. Any unstructured time is to be used on either "step-work" or Bible study. Rays of Sonshine has had a fair degree of success as reported by clients currently in the program and those who have since graduated from the program.

Recidivism rates are not yet clear for these clients, and not all of them are necessarily court-mandated. Nonetheless, probation officers express support for the program and do recommend clients to the facility. It is interesting to note that other state-based clinical facilities frequently send their unsuccessful cases to Rays of Sonshine for treatment, many of whom respond to the treatment program from Rays of Sonshine in a positive manner. While it is yet to be seen if this program is in fact a "success" in treating substance abuse, early interview and survey results seem promising. Also, the program has generated so much interest that a "sister program" is expected to be implemented abroad in the nation of South Africa. Comparative results of both programs are expected in the next couple of years and will provide a unique examination of the efficacy of faith-based programs in general, and the Rays of Sonshine program in particular.

Source: Rays of Sonshine, http://www.raysofsonshine.org

One last form of therapeutic intervention has to do with **relapse prevention**. These programs are based on the idea that high-risk situations either elicit effective coping responses or result in a lapse into drinking or drug use. The two situations, however, have different effects on a person's sense of self-efficacy (self-efficacy is a confidence level that the addict has in his or her coping skills). Ineffective coping decreases self-efficacy, increasing positive expectancies for the effects of the drug or alcohol and ultimately increasing the likelihood of a full relapse (Myers & Salt, 2000). Additional goals of relapse prevention include teaching clients to recognize and cope with high-risk situations and preventing deterioration of a lapse into more consistent use or relapse.

On recognizing the nature of the situations that are likely to lead to relapse, clients work to develop and rehearse plans for coping with each type of situation. In doing so, they develop an inventory of their existing strengths (e.g., a belief in self-discipline) and their support network (e.g., friends, family, therapists, and support groups). Discussion, role playing, and homework assignments are used to encourage clients to draw on these coping skills and to develop new skills (Myers & Salt, 2000). For each problem situation, clients and therapists work on a tentative plan of action for how they will deal with the event. Clients then plan ahead and rehearse alternative responses, become mentally prepared, and practice in increasingly difficult situations. The ultimate goal is to increase the client's self-efficacy over time. The entire process typically includes evaluations of the client's self-efficacy at different times throughout the relapse prevention therapy (Myers & Salt, 2000).

The effectiveness of substance abuse treatment programs has been well cited (Ashford et al., 2002). However, it should be pointed out that a growing body of literature suggests that some treatment orientations are better than others. For instance, Van Voorhis et al. (2000) note that cognitive-behavioral programs tend to be the most effective, especially those that include social skills training, community reinforcement, behavior contracting, relapse prevention, and motivational enhancement. Marital therapy has also been hailed as effective when behavioral and communication treatment techniques were emphasized. Among the least successful approaches are the general counseling programs, those based on psychotherapy, and those that employ strictly confrontational techniques.

CONCLUSION

Substance abuse offenders require numerous special services if the addiction is to be successfully overcome. Regardless of personal or professional viewpoints on treatment efficacy, it is clear that alcohol and drugs are strongly correlated with other criminal behavior. This correlation is so common that it could well be argued that substance abuse offenders are not "special" needs offenders but rather "common" needs offenders. Thus, any program that overlooks drugs or alcohol is overlooking a primary component behind most offenders' repertoires of behavior. Substance abuse programs have been shown to work among both court-mandated and voluntary clients. Finding the right treatment program to match the right offender with the right set of issues is the process that proves so difficult. Nonetheless, given the pervasiveness of the problem and the fact that such programs have frequently been found to be successful, further emphasis on drug interventions would appear to be not only desirable but also outright necessary in reducing the likelihood of recidivism among the offending population.

KEY TERMS

Drug of choice
Experimenters
Floaters
Compulsive users
Drug courts
Substance abuse
Substance dependence
Detoxification
Physiological dependence
Tolerance
Psychological dependence
Substance withdrawal
Self-help groups
12 steps to recovery
Comorbidity
Behavioral-oriented approaches
Family systems therapy
Faith-based programs
Relapse prevention

REFERENCES

Abidinsky, H. (1993). *Drug abuse: An introduction* (2nd ed.). Chicago: Nelson-Hall.

Ashford, J. B., Sales, B. D., & Reid, W. H. (2001). *Treating adult and juvenile offenders with special needs*. Washington, DC: American Psychological Association.

Bartol, C. R. (2002). *Criminal behavior: A psychological approach* (5th ed.). Upper Saddle River, NJ: Prentice Hall.

Bloom, B., Owen, B., & Covington, S. (2003). *Gender responsive strategies: Research, practice and guiding principles for women offenders*. Washington, DC: National Institute of Corrections. Retrived from http://www.nicic.org/Library/018017

Butzin, C. A., Saum, C. A., & Scarpitti, F. R. (2003). Factors associated with completion of a drug user treatment court diversion program. In L. Harrison, F. Scarpitti, M. Amir, & S. Einstein (Eds.), *Drug courts: Current issues and future perspectives* (pp. 153–168). Huntsville, TX: Office of International Criminal Justice.

Champion, D. (2002). *Probation, parole, and community corrections* (4th ed.). Upper Saddle River, NJ: Prentice Hall.

Chavaria, J. J. (1992). Successful drug treatment in a criminal justice setting: A case study. *Federal Probation, 56*(1), 48–52.

Drug Strategies. (1997). *Cutting crime: Drug courts in action*. Washington, DC: Author.

Federal Bureau of Investigation. (1999). *The FBI's national drug strategy*. Washington, DC: U.S. Department of Justice.

Goldberg, R. (2003). *Drugs across the spectrum* (4th ed.). Belmont, CA: Wadsworth.

Hanser, R. D. (2002). *Multicultural aspects in batterer intervention programs*. Dissertation for Doctor of Philosophy. Huntsville, TX: Sam Houston State University.

Hanson, G. R., Venturelli, P. J., & Fleckenstein, A. E. (2002). *Drugs and society* (7th ed.). Sudbury, MA: Jones and Bartlett.

Inciardi, J. A., Rivers, J. E., & McBride, D. C. (1999). Drug treatment behind bars. In P. M. Carslon & J. S. Garrett (Eds.), *Prison and jail administration: Practice and theory* (pp. 312–318). Gaithersberg, MD: Aspen Publications.

Jones, K. A., & Hanser, R. D. (2004). *Faith-based substance abuse treatment: Is it a better option for African American substance abusers?* NAAAS 2005 Monograph Series. Biddeford, ME: National Association of African American Studies.

Karberg, J. C., & James, D. J. (2003). *Substance dependence, abuse, and treatment of jail inmates, 2002.* Washington, DC: Bureau of Justice statistics. Retrieved from http://www.ojp.usdoj.gov/bjs/pubpdf/sdatji02.pdf

McNeece, C. A., Springer, D. W., & Arnold, E. M. (2000). Treating substance abuse disorders. In J. B. Ashford, B. D. Sales, & W. H. Reid (Eds.), *Treating adult and juvenile offenders with special needs* (pp. 131–170). Washington, DC: American Psychological Association.

Myers, P. L., & Salt, N. R. (2000). *Becoming an addictions counselor: A comprehensive text.* Sudbury, MA: Jones and Bartlett.

Neubauer, D. W. (2002). *America's courts and the criminal justice system* (7th ed.). Belmont, CA: Wadsworth.

Office of Justice Programs. (1997). *Defining drug courts: The key components.* Washington, DC: U.S. Department of Justice.

Van Voorhis, P., Braswell, M., & Lester, D. (2000). *Correctional counseling and rehabilitation* (4th ed.). Cincinnati: Anderson.

Walker, S. (2006). *Sense and non-sense about crime and drugs: A policy guide.* Belmont, CA: Wadsworth.

LEARNING CHECK

1. Which of the following are characteristics of a drug court?
   a. Integration of alcohol and other drug treatment services with justice system case processing
   b. Use of a nonadversarial approach
   c. Selection of participants after an observation period under criminal justice supervision
   d. Both a and b but not c
   e. Both b and c but not a

2. Which treatment model seeks to identify family routines, regulatory behaviors, rituals, or problem-solving strategies with substance abuse?
   a. Family services model
   b. Group therapy model
   c. Family systems model
   d. All of the above
   e. None of the above

3. A drug that is consistently used with greater frequency than other types of drugs by a certain identifiable demographic group is called a ______________.
   a. Primary drug
   b. Problem drug
   c. Drug typology
   d. Drug of choice
   e. None of the above

4. When deciding on placement criteria, which of the following are most important when deciding on treatment-related decisions?
   a. Getting the best match between the severity of the addiction and the level of care needed

b. Understanding the level of community supervision that should be involved
c. Both a and b
d. None of the above

5. The largest percentage of drug users was reported as being ______________.
a. Caucasian American
b. African American
c. Latino American
d. Asian American

6. When assessing female drug offenders, which of the following should be considered?
a. Relationships with significant others
b. Prior childhood sexual abuse
c. Indicators of antisocial personality disorder
d. Both a and b but not c
e. Both b and c but not a

7. This group of drug user will usually focus more on using the drugs of other people and are more likely to maintain a moderate use of drugs.
a. Experimenters
b. Floaters
c. Drifters
d. Chronic users
e. Social users

8. Which type of treatment is the most common form of treatment with substance abusing clients and offenders?
a. Jail facility detoxification
b. Prison-based group counseling
c. Therapeutic community interventions
d. Wilderness programs
e. Outpatient treatment

9. Which illegal drug or drugs appear to be the most commonly found among male and female arrestees?
a. Cocaine and methamphetamine
b. Oxycontin and heroin
c. Marijuana and heroin
d. Marijuana and cocaine
e. Alcohol and heroin

10. Which drug is responsible for more deaths and violence than all other drugs combined?
a. Alcohol
b. Cocaine
c. Crack cocaine

d. Heroin
e. Ecstasy

ESSAY DISCUSSION QUESTIONS

1. Provide a discussion on both AA and faith-based orientations of drug abuse intervention. Are the two likely to be effectively used together? Why or why not?
2. Identify and discuss the different types of drug treatment programs typically offered for substance-abusing offenders in the community. Be sure to thoroughly discuss drug courts.
3. Provide a discussion on race and gender characteristics of drug offenders. Be sure to include a discussion on the drug of choice for each type of offender as well.

CHAPTER 4

OFFENDERS WITH COMMUNICABLE DISEASES

Chapter Objectives

1. Become familiar with the more common types of sexually transmitted diseases, HIV/AIDS, tuberculosis, and the varieties of hepatitis that offenders may present to criminal justice personnel.
2. Identify the various communicable diseases that co-occur with risky behaviors that the offender population is prone to engage in.
3. Understand how prison subcultural dynamics will affect those inmates who are found to be HIV positive.
4. Understand the comorbid nature of communicable diseases with substance-abusing offenders. Also understand how substance abuse (and therefore communicable disease) correlates with sex industry offenders.
5. Understand how substance abuse, mental illness, homelessness, and communicable diseases have a tangled relationship that makes each difficult to separate from the others among a certain segment of the recidivating offender population.

INTRODUCTION

The offending population often has numerous lifestyle and developmental problems that compound their acts of criminal lawbreaking. Indeed, the tenet of this book is that offenders have numerous issues (some more complex than others) that surround and are intertwined with their propensity to commit crime. Many offenders, whether actually classified as special needs offenders or otherwise, have lived antisocial and/or unorthodox lifestyles that are characteristic of a criminal career. Their backgrounds are often dysfunctional, and the concurrent behaviors they have engaged in reflect a chaotic and imprudent form of coping with life stressors.

Risky sexual behaviors (whether this be from the type of sexual activity or having numerous sex partners, or from acts of sexual violence and aggression) may be associated with a drug habit. The problems associated with communicable diseases in the criminal justice system most often revolve initially around the risky sexual behaviors and/or intravenous drug use. Whether the offender engages in such practices or simply tends to come into contact with others who engage in these behaviors is the common denominator in explaining the heightened rate of infection among the offending population. And this is the point of this chapter: problems associated with communicable diseases are particularly pronounced among the offending population when compared to the nonoffending population. This creates a special set of needs and considerations that must be addressed in contemporary corrections, whether institutional or community based.

Therefore, this chapter begins with a brief introduction and overview of sexually transmitted diseases; tuberculosis; hepatitis A, B, and C; and HIV/AIDS. These infections, viruses, and/or diseases will be addressed because they have been most frequently identified as problematic among the offending population. The impact that these infectious agents have on jail and prison systems and the implications that follow on release into aftercare on community corrections is discussed. On completing this chapter, the reader will understand how these medical problems affect a substantial portion of the offending population and how this population tends to go back and forth between the jail/prison system and the surrounding community at large. This underscores the continual cycle of the problem and why it is important to address this problem as a public safety issue rather than as one restricted to the offender population.

SEXUALLY TRANSMITTED DISEASES

Simply put, **sexually transmitted diseases** (STDs) are those that are transmitted from one person to another through sexual contact. According to the Centers for Disease control, there are roughly 15 million cases of sexually transmitted disease reported each year. Those within the age range of 15 to 24 are most at risk, with at least 3 million cases a year being reported from within this demographic group (Epigee Foundation, 2004). It is interesting to note that this is also the age range that is most likely to be engaged in criminal activity in general. This once again shows how populations engaging in risky behaviors are also more likely to engage in behaviors that are correspondingly criminal, a point that seems to be intuitively obvious but clearly demonstrates that criminal offending may have a multiplicity of issues surrounding the simple act of offending. Most STDs are treatable. However, even the once easily cured gonorrhea has become resistant to many of the older traditional antibiotics. Other STDs, such as herpes, AIDS, and genital warts, all of which are caused by viruses, have no cure. Some of these infections are very uncomfortable, while others can be deadly. Syphilis, AIDS, genital warts, herpes, hepatitis, and even gonorrhea have all been known to cause death (Epigee Foundation, 2004).

The Epigee Foundation (2004) notes that "it is important to recognize that sexual contact includes more than just intercourse. Sexual contact includes kissing, oral-genital contact, and the use of sexual 'toys,' such as vibrators. There really is no such thing as 'safe' sex." This is important to note because many offenders simply may not know this or may not believe that they should have cause for concern. These individuals often believe that they are protecting themselves or are not armed with the information necessary to make prudent sexual choices. This is why offender education on these topics is a necessity.

The following discussion of STDs has been adapted from the Epigee Foundation (2004). These diseases are among those most commonly encountered within the offender population and those that are most problematic for correctional agencies.

Human papalloma virus is the most common STD; 33 percent of all women having an STD report with this virus, which can cause cervical (or penile in men) cancer and genital pain. Symptoms include cauliflower-like warts that develop on and inside the genitals, anus, and throat. It should be noted that condoms provide almost no protection against contracting the disease during sex, and even more disturbing is the fact that there is no known cure. The warts can be suppressed by chemicals, freezing, laser therapy, and surgery.

Syphilis, if left untreated, can lead to serious damage of the brain and heart. The most common way of contracting the disease is through vaginal, anal, or oral sex. However, it can be spread by nonsexual contact if the sores (cankers), rashes, or mucous patches caused by syphilis come in contact with the broken skin of a noninfected individual. If untreated, syphilis may cause serious damage to the heart, brain, eyes, nervous system, bones, and joints and can lead to death. A person with active syphilis has an increased risk that exposure to HIV will lead to infection because the sores provide an entry point for the AIDS virus. The disease can be cured with penicillin; however, damage done to body organs cannot be reversed. Latex condoms can reduce but not eliminate the risk of contracting the disease during sex. However, it is still possible to contract syphilis, even though using a condom, via sores in the genital area.

Chlamydia is a dangerous STD, as it usually has no symptoms; 75% of infected women and 25% of infected men have no symptoms at all. Infection can be cured with antibiotics. However, it cannot undo the damage done prior to treatment. Infected individuals are at greater risk of contracting HIV if exposed to the virus. Latex condoms can reduce but not eliminate the risk of contracting the disease during sex.

Gonorrhea is one of the most frequently reported STDs. Infection can be cured with antibiotics. However, it cannot undo the damage done prior to treatment. Latex condoms can reduce but not eliminate the risk of contracting the disease during sex. Untreated gonorrhea can infect the joints, heart valves, and brain and can cause sterility in men.

Herpes is a painful, episodic disease. It can be treated, but there's no cure. Herpes is spread by direct sexual skin-to-skin contact with the infected site during vaginal, anal, or oral sex. Abstaining from vaginal, anal, and oral sex with an infected person is the only effective means of preventing the sexual transmission of genital herpes. Latex condoms can reduce but not eliminate the risk of contracting the disease during sex.

From this discussion, it is clear that these diseases can easily be problematic to the correctional practitioner. Some of them (such as syphilis) do not even require sexual contact and can be transmitted simply by rubbing against the open sores. Thus, even though these diseases may not frequently be life threatening, it is still prudent that interventions and educational efforts be provided to offenders for their own safety and for the safety of staff who must interact with them.

HIV AND AIDS

AIDS came to the attention of medical authorities in the United States in 1981, when the Centers for Disease Control first formally recognized its existence. **HIV** (human immunodeficiency virus), the virus that leads to AIDS, was not detected or understood until 1983. Since 1981, roughly 750,000 cases of AIDS have been reported with approximately 83 percent being male and 17 percent being female in the outside population.

AIDS is caused by HIV. A person infected with HIV may not present with observable symptoms for several years. In fact, any indication will likely not be present until AIDS symptoms develop, and this could take up to 10 or even 20 years until it becomes evident to the infected person or to others. Although they may not have symptoms, those carrying the virus are still very contagious.

However, as HIV progresses over time, the infection becomes increasingly difficult to control, and severe opportunistic infections, such as tuberculosis, hepatitis, and pneumonia, are much more likely to lead to death. Offenders who are **intravenous drug users** are at increased risk of contracting these illnesses from sharing injection equipment contaminated with microorganisms that spread the infection. The proportion of AIDS cases among intravenous drug users has remained consistent and accounts for approximately 25 to 29 percent of recently diagnosed cases (Hanson, Venturelli, & Fleckenstein, 2002).

HIV is transmitted vaginally, orally, and especially through anal sex. HIV is also spread through infected blood or blood products and the sharing of drug needles with an infected person. Likewise, HIV can be transmitted from infected mother to infant in utero, during birth, or while breast-feeding. When symptoms are experienced, they typically include flu-like symptoms, including fever, loss of appetite, weight loss, fatigue, and enlarged lymph nodes. The symptoms usually disappear within a week to a month, and the virus can remain dormant for years. However, it continues to weaken the immune system, leaving the individual increasingly unable to fight opportunistic infections. It should be noted that virtually everyone who becomes infected with HIV will eventually develop AIDS and die of AIDS-related complications.

The best form of prevention is to abstain from sex with an infected person (especially anal sex), where body fluids, blood, semen, or vaginal secretions are likely to be exchanged. Latex condoms can reduce but not eliminate the risk of contracting the disease during sex. Naturally, individuals should avoid the use of intravenous drugs. With treatment, it should be noted that there is no known cure for HIV. Antiviral drugs of various sorts are used to prolong the life and health of the infected individual. Other antiviral treatments are designed to simply buffer against the invasion of opportunistic infections to the person. Any holistic treatment program will also include a wide array of vitamin supplementation and lifestyle modifications.

TUBERCULOSIS

Tuberculosis (TB) is a disease caused by bacteria that primarily affects the lungs, though it can affect any organ in the body. Tuberculosis is spread through the air from one person to another. The bacteria are put into the air when an infected person coughs or sneezes (Centers for Disease Control, 2004). But it is important to note that not everyone infected with TB becomes ill. This then requires a distinction between two types of TB: latent TB infection and active TB infection.

Most people breathing TB bacteria who become infected have immune systems that are able to effectively fight off the bacteria and thus keep the bacteria from further spreading. The bacteria then become inactive, though they do remain alive within the body and hold the ability to become active later. There are an estimated 10 to 15 million persons in the United States with latent TB infection. It should be noted that with inactive TB, carriers cannot spread the disease to others. Despite this, they should receive treatment as soon as possible to prevent them from developing active TB disease.

People with active TB, on the other hand, will feel ill and may experience symptoms such as fever, weight loss, and a bed cough that lasts longer than two weeks. They are also very contagious and will likely spread the disease. Further, active TB can be terminal if undiagnosed or untreated. Tuberculosis is a serious threat for HIV-infected persons. In fact, "worldwide TB is responsible for the deaths of one in three people living with HIV/AIDS—making it the leading cause of death among people infected with HIV" (Centers for Disease Control, 2004). Someone with latent TB infection and HIV infection is up to 800 times more likely to develop active TB during his or her lifetime than someone without HIV (Centers for Disease Control, 2004).

HEPATITIS A, B, AND C

Hepatitis A is a liver disease caused by the hepatitis A virus (HAV). Hepatitis A most frequently occurs through person-to-person transmission during community-wide outbreaks (Centers for Disease Control, 2003). Viral transmission can occur through close personal contact (e.g., household contact, sexual contact, drug use, or children playing) and contaminated food or water (e.g., infected food handlers).

The most frequently reported source of infection (12 to 26 percent) is household or sexual contact with a person with HAV infection (Centers for Disease Control, 2003). HAV infection is common among intravenous drug users. Intravenous drug use has been reported by 5 to 19 percent of hepatitis A patients. In certain communities, hepatitis A outbreaks involving users of injected and noninjected methamphetamine have accounted for approximately 30 percent of reported cases (Centers for Disease Control, 2003). Vaccines are also available for long-term prevention of HAV infection in persons two years of age and older. Generally, hepatitis A is not considered problematic among correctional agencies when compared to other infectious diseases (Hammett, Harmon, & Maruschak, 1999).

Sex is the predominant mode of **hepatitis B** transmission among adults and adolescents, accounting for more than half of newly acquired infections. Among reported cases of acute hepatitis B, approximately 40 percent reported heterosexual exposure to an infected partner or multiple partners. In addition, 14 percent of persons with acute hepatitis B reported intravenous drug use (Centers for Disease Control, 2003; Epigee Foundation, 2004). A vaccine exists, but there is no cure. Hepatitis B can cause cancer of the liver. Abstaining from sex with an infected person, especially anal sex, where body fluids, blood, semen, or vaginal secretions are likely to be exchanged, is the only effective means of preventing the sexual transmission of hepatitis B. Latex condoms can reduce but not eliminate the risk of contracting the disease during sex. Avoid illicit intravenous drug use and the sharing of drug needles (Centers for Disease Control, 2003; Epigee Foundation, 2004).

Hepatitis C is not a disease that causes many symptoms (Jones, 2003). When first infected, approximately 75 percent of individuals have no symptoms at all. When symptoms do occur, they tend to be general and are usually not detected as symptoms of a more serious illness by the individual (Jones, 2003). Indeed, roughly 80 percent of those individuals with hepatitis C experience only bouts of fatigue and will not be aware that they are carrying the infection in their blood and liver (Jones, 2003). Hepatitis C infection is acquired more rapidly after the initiation of intravenous drug use than either hepatitis B or HIV infection. Recent studies report the rate of hepatitis C at around 30 percent for intravenous drug users who have two or more years of such drug use (Centers for Disease Control, 2003).

BEHIND THE BARS IN JAILS AND PRISONS

When discussing the problems associated with communicable diseases in the criminal justice system, it should first be noted that the inmate population is not representative of the broader community in general. In fact, it is because of the risky lifestyles and behaviors of the offending population that they are more at risk of contracting such diseases. Among individuals in prison, it is their behavior that is outside the norm for legal constraints that lands them in these environments. Many of these same behaviors are also those that put one at risk of contracting some form of communicable disease.

In most communities in the United States, the use of illicit drugs, buying and selling them, or engaging in the sundry activities associated with supplying a drug habit are the same behaviors that result in imprisonment. Further, it is evident that the majority of intravenous drug users serve at least some brief period of incarceration. This high-risk group places the inmate population in even greater peril of contracting some form of debilitating illness.

In 1999, roughly 34,372 inmates in prisons and jails throughout the United States were HIV positive, and 9,723 of these inmates had full-blown AIDS (Kantor, 2004). This essentially means that in 1999, about 2.3 percent of all state prison inmates, almost 1 percent of federal prison inmates, and 1.7 percent of all jail inmates were infected with HIV (Kantor, 2004). In fact, this percentage continues to increase, with the federal prison system having had 1.1 percent of its inmate population test HIV positive during 2002 (see Table 4.1 for a detailed state-by-state count of HIV cases in prison systems in the United States). This rate of infection is reportedly about five to seven times that of the general population (Ross, 2001). The rate of AIDS in correctional systems throughout the United States is about five times that of the outside population throughout the country.

It should be noted that roughly half of all the HIV-positive inmates are located within the state systems of Texas, New York, and Florida. This is not surprising since these three states and the state of California have the four largest and most prominent correctional systems in the United States, lending them the nickname "**The Big Four**" among correctional system scholars (Clear & Cole, 2003). During 1999, New York had 7,000 HIV-infected inmates, Florida had 2,633, and Texas had 2,520. These numbers are fairly consistent with the relative prevalence of HIV among intravenous drug users in each of these states.

This is important because this substantiates the previously discussed notion that these offenders make up a group of individuals who lead high-risk lifestyles, be they in or out of prison. Essentially, then, this group lives a high-risk lifestyle within the broader community and are simply circulated and recirculated through the criminal justice system, as these high-risk behaviors are most often illegal. Thus, this confluence of high-risk individuals becomes a population that has a revolving relationship with correctional agencies in their locales.

However, when talking about communicable diseases, one cannot overlook the fact that other diseases also threaten correctional systems and the personnel within them. The existence of hepatitis B and C has been noted to be of serious concern in many state-level prison systems (see Table 4.2). Studies of prison populations in California, Texas, and Virginia have found hepatitis infection ranging anywhere from 29 to 42 percent (Ross, 2001; Centers for Disease Control, 2002). Nationally, the rate of hepatitis infection for the inmate population is estimated to be around 15 to 30 percent, with some researchers noting that some exceptional jail/prison systems may have rates closer to 40 percent (Jones, 2003). In California in particular, a survey found that roughly half of all incoming female inmates and about a third of all male inmates tested positive for hepatitis.

Table 4.1. Inmates in Custody of State or Federal Prison Authorities and Known to Be Positive for HIV, 2000–2002

	Total Known to Be HIV Positive			HIV/AIDS Cases as a Percentage of Total Custody Population		
Jurisdiction	**2002**	**2001**	**2000**	**2002**	**2001**	**2000**
U.S. total reported	23,864	24,147	25,333	1.9	1.9	2.0
Federal	1,547	1,520	1,302	1.1	1.2	1.0
State	22,317	22,627	24,031	2.0	2.0	2.2
Northeast	7,620	8,136	8,721	4.6	4.9	5.2
Connecticut	666	604	593	3.6	3.5	3.6
Maine	—	15	11	—	0.9	0.7
Massachusetts	290	307	313	2.9	3.0	3.0
New Hampshire	16	17	23	0.6	0.7	1.0
New Jersey	756	804	771	3.2	3.4	3.2
New York	5,000	5,500	6,000	7.5	8.1	8.5
Pennsylvania	800	735	900	2.0	2.0	2.4
Rhode Island	86	148	90	2.5	4.4	2.6
Vermont	6	6	20	0.4	0.4	1.5
Midwest	2,133	2,135	2,252	1.0	1.0	1.1
Illinois	570	593	619	1.3	1.3	1.4
Indiana	—	—	—	—	—	—
Iowa	33	27	27	0.4	0.3	0.3
Kansas	48	41	49	0.5	0.5	0.6
Michigan	591	584	585	1.2	1.2	1.2
Minnesota	37	33	42	0.5	0.5	0.7
Missouri	262	262	267	0.9	0.9	1.0
Nebraska	24	24	18	0.6	0.6	0.5
North Dakota	4	4	2	0.4	0.4	0.2
Ohio	417	398	478	1.0	0.9	1.1
South Dakota	6	5	4	0.2	0.2	0.2
Wisconsin	141	164	161	0.8	0.9	1.0
South	10,656	10,392	10,767	2.2	2.2	2.3
Alabama	276	302	419	1.1	1.2	1.8
Arkansas	100	108	101	0.8	0.9	0.9
Delaware	128	143	127	1.9	2.1	1.9
Florida	2,848	2,602	2,640	3.8	3.6	3.7
Georgia	1,123	1,150	938	2.4	2.5	2.1
Kentucky	—	105	124	—	1.1	1.3

Table 4.1. (Continued)

	Total Known to Be HIV Positive			HIV/AIDS Cases as a Percentage of Total Custody Population		
Jurisdiction	**2002**	**2001**	**2000**	**2002**	**2001**	**2000**
Louisiana	503	514	500	2.5	2.6	2.6
Maryland	967	830	998	4.0	3.5	4.3
Mississippi	224	234	230	1.9	2.0	2.1
North Carolina	602	573	588	1.8	1.8	1.9
Oklahoma	146	130	145	0.9	0.9	1.0
South Carolina	544	559	560	2.4	2.6	2.7
Tennessee	218	231	215	1.5	1.7	1.6
Texas	2,528	2,388	2,492	1.9	1.8	1.8
Virginia	425	507	550	1.4	1.7	1.9
West Virginia	24	16	14	0.7	0.5	0.5
West	1,908	1,964	2,291	0.7	0.8	0.9
Alaska	16	16	—	0.5	0.5	—
Arizona	130	122	110	0.4	0.4	0.4
California	1,181	1,305	1,638	0.7	0.8	1.0
Colorado	182	173	146	1.1	1.2	1.0
Hawaii	22	13	19	0.6	0.3	0.5
Idaho	18	14	14	0.4	0.4	0.3
Montana	8	11	11	0.4	0.6	0.7
Nevada	113	127	151	1.2	1.4	1.6
New Mexico	30	27	28	0.5	0.5	0.5
Oregon	42	30	41	0.4	0.3	0.4
Utah	58	34	37	1.4	0.8	0.9
Washington	101	88	90	0.6	0.6	0.6
Wyoming	7	4	6	0.6	0.4	0.5

Source: Adapted from Maruschak (2002).

As with HIV/AIDS, intravenous drug use and high-risk sexual behaviors are the main methods of transmission for hepatitis. Often, new inmates may have chronic hepatitis when they first enter the correctional system. But because symptoms may go undetected by infected offenders, they may not even realize that they are infected and may unwittingly spread the virus to other inmates via intravenous drug use, consensual sex, rape, and tattooing with infected needles and equipment. Transmission of the virus is even possible from the sharing of items such as razors or toothbrushes. As with the HIV/AIDS problem, this health problem is then recirculated through the

Table 4.2. States That Test 500 or More Inmates for Hepatitis C

	Inmates in Facilities Reporting		Percentage Positive	
State	Number of Tests	Positive Test Result	Inmates Tested	All Inmates
California	15,549	7,178	46.2	5.4
New York	5,278	367	7.0	0.7
Georgia	5,206	1,314	25.2	3.1
Virginia	2,046	782	38.2	2.9
Arizona	2,898	405	14.0	1.4
Idaho	2,565	68	2.7	2.4
Massachusetts	2,393	941	39.3	9.6
North Carolina	1,713	368	21.5	1.5
Illinois	1,753	190	10.8	0.4
Indiana	1,416	302	21.3	1.7
Oklahoma	1,271	276	21.7	1.4
New Mexico	1,213	498	41.1	16.0
Louisiana	897	347	38.7	3.9
Ohio	1,082	366	33.8	1.1
Missouri	1,112	354	31.8	1.3
Connecticut	1,029	725	70.5	6.1
Washington	971	409	42.1	2.8
New Jersey	699	324	46.4	1.6
Texas	858	324	37.8	1.7
Maryland	839	264	31.5	1.4
Wisconsin	732	417	57.0	4.1
Montana	682	199	29.2	9.6
Kentucky	611	178	29.1	1.4
All states	57,018	17,911	31.4	2.5

Source: Adapted from Beck and Maruschak (2004).

community (and then back through the correctional system) if an offender continues to practice (and many do continue) high-risk drug use and/or sexual behaviors on release. This is frequently the case, as parolees tend to return to their original community origins and have been noted to have a high recidivism rate.

In an article on the problems with hepatitis C in correctional agencies, Jones (2003) notes that a minority of the cases of hepatitis C transmission occur within the jail or prison setting. It is clear that the majority of offenders having hepatitis C became infected "on the streets." Further, Jones (2003) notes that it is simply impossible for correctional agencies to treat every infected inmate in a given state because of budgetary concerns alone, not to mention that some simply will not place value on a treatment program. Although not everyone can be treated with antiviral therapies (the medical treatment of choice and the most expensive), all offenders should be educated about the disease and how to not contract or spread the infection.

One fact that pertains to all communicable diseases (including STDs, TB, and HIV/AIDS) is that antiviral treatment is not the only treatment available for offenders (Jones, 2003). Other strategies, such as avoidance of alcohol and other illicit drugs, good nutrition, rest, and exercise, are all important considerations. The cessation of smoking is also a good step, and limiting the number of medications processed by the liver will also help the prognosis of an offender with hepatitis C. Making lifestyle changes is difficult but should be emphasized with these offenders (Jones, 2003). Consideration for substance abuse treatment must also be a component if inmates are to avoid getting reinfected. The importance of integrating substance abuse treatments with communicable disease therapies (and further integrating education on communicable disease into current substance abuse treatments) will be elaborated on later in this chapter since this lack of interweaving within treatment programs undermines the overall effectiveness of each program individually.

Another point to note is prison sexuality. The prevalence of homosexual activity within male prisons should not be underestimated. Whether consensual or due to coercion by other inmates, a substantial number of this population engage in what would typically be considered high-risk sexual activity in the outside society. Further, among those inmates who are forcefully coerced into such activity, these inmates are likely to be forced into literal servitude in which they must service numerous other inmates with sexual favors (Hanser & Moran, 2004). Frequently, a young and fairly powerless inmate may be intimidated into engaging in what might be considered "quasi-consensual" sexual activity that he may cope with by further drug use within the prison. This drug use places this inmate in further jeopardy, and if there is intravenous drug use, needle sharing is likely. In further support of this concern is the consistent finding that HIV-infected (or hepatitis-infected) prisoners are more likely to have injected themselves when they were in prison than noninfected inmates (Dolan, Donoghoe, & Stimson, 1990).

Inmates with HIV often have other medical and psychological problems that co-occur with their infections. As a result of this, a growing number of prison and jail facilities are incorporating new forms of therapy into a range of services that deal comprehensively with the problems associated with HIV within the offender population. According to the Centers for Disease Control (2001a, 2001b), these improved programs are likely to include the following:

- Screening to identify medical as well as psychological problems
- Substance abuse treatment needs
- Case management in which one person is assigned the inmate's file and is responsible for overseeing the inmate's coordinated service delivery
- Psychosocial services such as one-on-one counseling or support groups

- Hospice care for terminally ill inmates
- Discharge planning that helps inmates return to their communities without spreading infection
- Systems of aftercare that are interlinked with parole agencies in the community

However, it should be noted that correctional agencies are often strapped for spare financial resources. Medication costs for communicable diseases (HIV/AIDS in particular) are high. Inmates may also be reluctant to seek testing and treatment because of denial or mistrust of prison officials. Likewise, the competence of medical staff in correctional facilities may be marginal, and this may also be a cause of concern. Patient characteristics and facility factors must be considered before implementing a therapeutic program. According to the Centers for Disease Control (2001b, 2001c), factors to consider might include the following:

- The offender's willingness to adhere to the program
- The severity of the offender's drug addiction and whether this is likely to impair successful participation in HIV/AIDS treatment
- The presence of other illnesses, such as hepatitis, mental illness, and so on, along with HIV/AIDS, in which case the offender may not be suitable for the program

In addition, correctional staff must understand that the inmate may have difficulty trusting that staff will keep the inmate's health and security as a concern. But if treatment programs are to be successful (and this is the only way to improve long-term safety from the virus for both inmates and staff) a solid relationship must exist between the inmate client and medical staff or clinicians. Facilities and clinicians must do the following:

- Deal with the inmate's mistrust of authority and unfamiliarity with health care providers and services
- Be clear and open about the limits to and likely success of various interventions

HIV counseling and testing includes HIV antibody testing and individual, client-centered risk reduction counseling (Centers for Disease Control, 2001b, 2001c). These types of programs are designed to help the individual decide whether he or she will get further help. These programs may take place in different forms (e.g., during and following the initial intake medical screening, during or following education and prevention sessions, and so on). The counseling and psychoeducational programs should also be available to noninfected inmates.

By counseling noninfected inmates on how to avoid infection, these programs can reduce further infection and can save both correctional agencies and society an enormous amount of money and future grief and misery. It should be noted that the estimated lifetime treatment costs for an inmate with HIV vary from $165,000 to

$267,000 for correctional agencies that must foot the bill. Thus, HIV prevention and psychoeducational interventions can save a great deal of money, even if just a handful of cases are prevented.

According to the U.S. Department of Health and Human Services (DHHS, 2001), all 50 states and the Federal Bureau of Prisons (BOP) follow a varying system of HIV test policies. As of 1999, the DHHS reported the following:

- The BOP and all 50 states test inmates if they have HIV-related symptoms or if the inmate requests a test.
- Thirty-nine states test inmates after they have been in an altercation that leads to open bleeding.
- Sixteen states test inmates belonging to certain high-risk groups, such as intravenous drug users, commercial sex workers, or those with prior STDs.
- Only 19 states test all entering inmates.
- The BOP and three states test inmates on release.

Just as with the broader population outside the prison environment, the **confidentiality** of HIV test results is a crucial concern when providing effective services. This is because the fear of disclosure may cause a person to avoid or refuse testing. Confidentiality in the correctional setting can be difficult because privacy is harder to maintain. This is particularly true when one considers that everyone within the prison may know when and where appointments for HIV-positive inmates occur. Information may spread rapidly through inmate orderlies, and inmates visiting prison infirmaries during the allocated time and/or place may quickly be identified by other inmates and/or staff as being HIV positive.

This can have serious, damaging consequences for individuals who seek medical services for their infections, and these consequences can prevent other inmates from seeking testing. This then simply aggravates the problem with HIV/AIDS in the prison setting since the virus is left unchecked because of social concerns. It should be noted that this simply places both inmates and staff in potential jeopardy and at risk of becoming infected in the future.

The point regarding prison staff and inmate identification of other inmates that are suspected of having HIV is important when one considers the effects of the informal subculture within many state prison systems. Hanser and Moran (2004) discuss at length the effects of the **prison subculture** on sex and sexuality identification within the prison setting. Inmates who are at risk or identified as such may be targeted by inmate perpetrators who are sexually assaultive (and are also HIV positive) since the newly diagnosed inmate is considered to be already infected. This places the inmate as "fair game" among HIV-positive sexually assaultive inmates and among the inmate subculture that is not HIV positive. Inmates who are not HIV positive are likely to condone this victimization since this prevents spreading the infection to other inmates who are not HIV positive and since the subculture will see the inmate as a "punk" and therefore deserving of further victimization. Thus, whether the inmate is or is not positive becomes a moot point as he or she becomes singled out among the already HIV-positive perpetrators as a likely target.

On the other hand, even if inmates are not subjected to a label or stereotype related to homosexuality within the prison, they still can suffer other consequences. For instance, many staff may be hesitant to provide the same level of service to inmates suspected of HIV because of a misguided fear of the contagious nature of the infection. Further, staff may be in fear because of the potential danger the inmate could present were he or she to become assaultive. This can be a reasonable fear in some cases. Inmates who are despondent or depressed may mask their depression with anger and hostility. This is a common occurrence with the male inmate population. Because of this, it could be likely that an HIV-infected inmate, in a state of depression turned to hostility, might decide to simply turn that hostility toward a staff member, particularly one who has had prior difficulty with that particular inmate. Thus, staff members may see these inmates as potential "loose canons" who have little or nothing to lose in spreading their infection through unruly and assaultive behavior.

Likewise, the inmate suspected of potentially being HIV positive will likely be shunned by many other inmates who desire to avoid infection. This inmate will find his or her standard of living and social inclusion to be very limited. Opportunities to recreate and engage in other activities may be substantially impaired because of social pressure from other inmates who seek to eliminate HIV-positive inmates from mutually participating in group functions. In fact, in some prison systems, HIV-positive inmates may be segregated from the remainder of the prison population.

The segregation of HIV-positive inmates has drawn substantial debate in recent years. The correctional system in Alabama is regarded as one of the toughest in the nation with regard to HIV-positive inmates. Alabama's prison populations are tested on entry into the Department of Corrections, and HIV-positive inmates are segregated and placed in separate dormitories. Some correctional experts consider this to be a more practical and effective manner of delivering services to the HIV-positive prison population. This argument for segregation may be very sound regardless of the social penalty that inmates may perceive with this type of intervention.

Indeed, it is thought that the use of segregation allows agencies to extend their resources by identifying gaps in services and filling those gaps during incarceration all the way through reentry into society. The Alabama Department of Corrections does address prevention and in-house care that continues with effective aftercare while on community release. The program's aftercare, titled "Be Free Stay Free—Life Enrichment Model Program," has leveraged the assistance of community-based organizations to provide primary and secondary education about HIV and the treatment of the virus. These programs include numerous classes and services, both inside the prison and during aftercare, including classes on addiction, TB, and the method of obtaining and using medications when on community supervision. The intent is to empower these offenders to do things for themselves on release, being less of a burden and/or health risk to society.

The use of these comprehensive types of programs is of interest to professionals who wish to truly confine and limit the spread of communicable diseases within the broader society. It is also because the offending population is much more likely to carry and transmit these diseases that these services cannot be ignored. Failure to provide prevention and intervention programs is essentially more costly to society than simply "punishing" the offender and hoping that the virus will go away. With the HIV-positive offender, treatment is not a luxury, but it is a necessity for public safety. Both lay citizens and correctional staff must mutually understand that there is simply no alternative if we wish to make sure that the public is safe. Arguing over whether the offender population deserves effective treatment is fruitless since in the midst of the argument the virus will continue to spread to both offending and nonoffending populations. HIV, AIDS, and other communicable diseases do not discriminate, nor should we when attempting to correct this social ill. It is with this in mind that we next discuss programs for offenders that exist outside the prison within the context of probation and parole services.

OFFENDERS WITH HIV/AIDS AND/OR OTHER COMMUNICABLE DISEASES IN THE COMMUNITY

As discussed in the previous section, the prevalence of HIV infection among the incarcerated population is much higher than that within society outside the prison. Further, approximately 13 to 19 percent of people living with HIV in the general population of the United States have been incarcerated at some previous time (Centers for Disease Control, 2001a, 2001b). This demonstrates that the high-risk population within the prison is simply a subsample of the high-risk population within the broader society. Likewise, the student may recall from Chapter 1 that the National Institute of Corrections indicates that roughly 97 percent of the 1.3 million inmates now in prison eventually will be released and will return to communities. This percentage naturally includes those offenders with HIV and other communicable diseases. From this, it can be determined that these groups tend to recycle through the respective state prison systems, and these offenders often come into frequent contact with those individuals who are recycled through the system simply because both infected and noninfected offenders tend to have similar behaviors that are common to one another given the lifestyle that is associated with substance abuse and risky sexual practices.

One document in particular illustrates this connection between this group of individuals who stand at the center of the HIV/AIDS problem. A report titled *The Health Status of Soon-to-Be-Released Inmates—A Report to Congress* was released to Congress in July 2002. This report identified high rates of HIV infection among the incarcerated and substantial barriers, including a lack of resources, to address HIV and AIDS within correctional facilities. These findings demonstrate a clear need for better collaboration between correctional institutions and community-based agencies. Thus, HIV prevention programs should consider the needs of the incarcerated and soon-to-be-released population.

The need to consider the incarcerated and those inmates who are scheduled for community supervision underscores the many ties that connect the community with correctional institutions. Millions of offenders circulate in and out of the nation's correctional systems annually. As of 2000, the occupancy of the combined state and federal correctional systems exceeded 2 million people. But this number does not reflect the total amount of individuals who have been incarcerated throughout the span of that year. It is estimated that roughly five times this number (about 11 million offenders) were released from prisons and jails during this time. About half these individuals who are booked at police stations are released into the community within 24 to 48 hours (Academy for Educational Development, 2003). However, they are still at heightened risk of exposure to HIV/AIDS, hepatitis, and/or TB. Likewise, among individuals serving longer sentences in prison, many are most likely to eventually return to their respective communities at some point.

The lack of prevention programs within many prisons contributes to the transmission of communicable diseases within the community that surrounds the prison itself. Few prisons or jail systems have implemented comprehensive and effective prevention and intervention programs. Because of this, HIV-positive offenders are often released back into communities without the required knowledge or access to resources to stop the transmission of the virus. Thus, if a community's correctional facilities are overlooked as a venue for fostering HIV prevention skills among individuals, the risk of infection being introduced back into the community will continue (Academy for Educational Development, 2003).

While most offenders will be infected prior to their incarceration, their period of confinement offers the opportunity to provide needed health services for offenders. Unfortunately, such opportunities are not fully realized because of a lack of effective prevention programs in prisons. As previously noted, the rate of HIV and AIDS is much higher in the prison than in the general U.S. population. The same is even more true with TB. Although TB has declined throughout the United States, the rate among offenders in correctional systems tends to be 4 to 17 times higher than for persons not either within institutional custody or on community supervision (Centers for Disease Control, 2001a). Inmates who return to their communities (and again many do so) must continue to follow their treatment program in order to avoid infecting others. This is a particularly relevant point when one considers that one in three persons with HIV/AIDS dies from contracting TB. Thus, the two communicable diseases are interlaced within the same subgroup of offenders.

Because prevention programs within prisons and jail systems are often woefully inadequate, community supervision agencies must implement preventive measures of their own. Craig and York (2003) note that there should be more utilization of effective and comprehensive immunization programs. The use of these immunizations should ideally be utilized within the jail setting and on entry into aftercare as a requirement of successfully meeting probation requirements. While at a cursory level it might appear that offering immunizations to offenders in local jails would have no benefit to the institution because of rapid turnover, this is not true since offenders tend to circulate through the facility and into the community, only to recirculate back within the jail facility.

It is suggested that state-level public health departments be tasked with providing vaccination materials and supplies at no cost to the correctional medical staff (Craig & York, 2003). Access to immunization education programs for offenders and staff should also be provided by state health departments. Offering immunizations to the incarcerated population allows public health practitioners to access a segment of the population that normally does not have the money or insurance to afford these services (Craig & York, 2003). This will result in decreasing communicable diseases both inside the correctional facility and in the surrounding community, including those offenders on probation departmental caseloads.

THE IMPORTANCE OF COMMUNITY AND FAMILY

Offenders who have been behind bars for even a short period of time find their relationships strained with other family members, particularly spouses and children. Their relationships with employers will also likely be strained, if not severed, and this in turn further intensifies the strain within their own family system because of economic stressors. These strains severely diminish the likelihood of the offender being successfully reintegrated into the community. In fact, research has shown that inmates with family ties during the period of incarceration do better when released than those without such ties (Champion, 2002). Comprehensive programs that work collaboratively between health agencies and correctional agencies are needed, along with the inclusion of any community outreach programs that might be available.

While it is fairly well known that family integration is an important factor in offender rehabilitation (this book makes this clear in several chapters) the exact function of the family and/or supportive personnel is even more critical with offenders who have communicable diseases. There are a few reasons for this that should be discussed.

First, offenders and their families have commonalities that are similar to any other family that is dealing with a member who has an infectious disease. A family of nonoffenders that has a member with TB, hepatitis, or HIV/AIDS must interact with one another in a manner that ensures that the group is not placed at further risk of infection (Centers for Disease Control, 2001c). Since offenders who are paroled tend to return to their communities (and families) of origin, they will come into contact with these individuals, and the same precautions as with any other family must be taken. For families that find themselves with a member who has some communicable disease, they must gain training and knowledge on how to protect themselves and others from further infection (Centers for Disease Control, 2003).

This training is certainly necessary if the offender is returning to a less-than-functional family system, which often is the case. Further, it can sometimes be the case that the offender's family of origin may have other members who have a communicable disease, and it could even be that the offender does not have such a disease but will be returning to a spouse or extended relative who does. In each of these cases, the need for family system intervention is necessary, and this is most frequently provided through community agencies.

Second, the family may need to act as caretaker to some extent. This is an important role that someone must play if the offender needs assistance with health concerns. Indeed, even transportation issues to obtain medication can be a major hurdle for an offender (Centers for Disease Control, 2001c). Having family or friends who are willing to assist can increase the likelihood of treatment being successful just on a practical level. Likewise, an offender who is ill with potentially terminal results will need assistance from those who care about him or her. In many cases, the offender may go to jail or prison, but the family may not lose contact with the offender. This may particularly be true with younger, first-time offenders whose parents or siblings may still hold hope of the offender's reintegration. If the offender presents with a communicable disease, these primary and extended family members may be the most direct source of assistance for the offender's treatment.

Third, for female offenders in particular, the issue of children and child care may be a major impediment to successful treatment. In addition, the child's welfare is a consideration that is paramount when dealing with an offender-parent who may present with a communicable disease. If the mother is released and has some form of communicable disease, there will undoubtedly be precautions that must be taken to ensure that infection is not spread from mother to child. Most female offenders seem to respond well to programs that unite them with their children (Crawford, 2003). While many community supervision treatment programs for female offenders tend to have a variety of parenting programs, it is important that services related to communicability of certain diseases be included. This is particularly true for two reasons: (1) the female population is at a much greater risk of having a communicable disease, and (2) the female offender is frequently the primary caretaker for her children at the point of arrest. Given these two considerations, the need for family-centered interventions with female offenders becomes clear.

FEMALE OFFENDERS, COMMUNICABLE DISEASES, AND PERIPHERAL ISSUES

The female offender population has continued to rise at a rate that is almost twice that of the male offending population. Female offenders account for roughly 7 percent of all offenders in state and federal correctional facilities (Clear & Cole, 2004). This is important because it is the female offender population that is most at risk of having HIV/AIDS or STDs. This higher risk is due to the fact that a high number of female offenders engage or have engaged in various forms of prostitution or sex industry activity. Further, drug use is commonly associated with prostitution, and this further exacerbates the likelihood of this offender group using needles and therefore having yet another avenue of transmitting infection. Because heterosexual prostitution is much more frequently demanded in the community, female offenders are more at risk, and this is particularly pronounced if they use prostitution as a means of supporting their drug habit. The high rates of STDs, mental illness, and substance abuse make this population particularly vulnerable and difficult to treat.

Aside from the family involvement and child-rearing issues that are pertinent to many female offenders, some agencies note that there are substantial challenges when dealing with communicable diseases among the female offending population. In particular, the onset of STDs seems to be especially problematic with female offenders, mainly younger offenders who find themselves active in prostitution or other sex industry activity. In one program, medical staff noted a high rate of STDs as well as a need for increased gynecological services. To address this need, this agency worked with its local health department to provide free culture media for the girls and women as well as free medication for STDs. This allowed the agency to diagnose and treat the women more quickly, as it eliminated the need to send them to off-site locations for testing and also eliminated the waiting period involved with obtaining results of the medical exams. Other tests included glucometers, pregnancy tests, strep throat tests, and urine dipsticks (Craig & York, 2003).

In addition, it is very likely that the female offender is likely to need relationship counseling of some sort or another. This is important because many of these offenders have themselves been victims of domestic violence and/or sexual abuse. In fact, it is the sexual violence in particular that is of primary concern when discussing communicable diseases. As will be discussed in subsequent chapters, female offenders have a commonality in that they tend to have histories of abusive relationships, most frequently at the hands of male partners. Further, their criminal involvement often occurs while connected with a male accomplice or counterpart, with the female acting more as either a "mule" (carrying drugs for the dealer) or a "trick" for a male who prostitutes them out (Drug Policy Alliance, 2004). This is in addition to other forms of involvement that very often occur in a relationship with a male offender. Because this becomes normalized, female offenders are more inclined to be involved with "high-risk" males who are likely to transmit infectious diseases to their female sexual and/or drug partners. The female offender must break this cycle and engage in pro-social relations with persons. Counseling and psychoeducation should be specifically tailored for this population to encourage more healthy relationships so that fewer women will find themselves behind bars and on community supervision.

SUBSTANCE ABUSE AND MENTAL HEALTH COMORBIDITY

Many of these offenders have comorbid problems that extend beyond just having a communicable disease. Most will still have some form of substance abuse issue that they must address, and many may have mental illness. Indeed, the mental illness may be what contributes to the drug use, or the drug addiction may eventually induce the mental illness over time and put the offender at risk of disease if he or she is an intravenous drug user.

To further aggravate the matter, fewer than one-third of exiting inmates who are in need of assistance receive substance abuse or mental health treatment while within the confines of prison. While the majority of prison inmates enter prison with substance abuse problems, only about 10 percent of state inmates report receiving professional substance abuse treatment. It should be noted that since HIV/AIDS is directly linked to intravenous drug use, drug counseling services and interventions should be integrated within the treatment scheme for any community-based treatment for communicable diseases.

Indeed, it would perhaps be helpful for drug treatment programs to specifically solicit drug offenders whose addiction has resulted in infection with HIV/AIDS to serve as co-leaders of group counseling services for addicted persons. This can have several benefits. First is the fact that substance abusers who are required to sit face-to-face with someone dealing with the dire consequences of a painful and terminal illness may engage in introspective analysis. This would, it is hoped, serve as somewhat of a deterrent for future use, or at least it might serve as incentive to remain in drug treatment. This is particularly true among intravenous drug users. Second, for those drug abusers who are already dealing with infectious diseases, this approach would provide them with a contact who is facing similar difficulties in their recovery process. Finally, the offender who is HIV-positive may gain psychological rewards from acting as co-leader and providing a service to others who may still be able to avoid infection.

This sense of positive contribution to society can create a sense of well-being that can substantially improve the overall prognosis of the offender. It is commonly the case that medical factors are improved by positive social conditions that surround the patient who is attempting to fight an affliction. Thus, the sense of involvement could be beneficial in keeping the offender from recidivating and from getting progressively more ill. Similarly, these individuals could also educate family members involved in Al-Anon programs so that they are not only equipped with addressing the addiction issues within their own family but also better able to lend assistance to a loved one who suffers from a debilitating communicable disease that results from an addiction problem.

As discussed in Chapter 3 pertaining to substance abuse issues, there is a tendency for mental illness to develop as a result of drug addiction and a similar tendency for mental illness to result in drug use to medicate the mood effects of the mental illness. All the intertwining factors between communicable disease, addiction, and mental illness demonstrate the multivaried nature of the problems associated with communicable diseases in the offender population. These factors often cannot be completely untangled from one another, and because of this, treatments for each must be interwoven whenever the client presents with the entire range of problems. This is yet again what makes special needs offenders so complicated to service and difficult to treat.

OTHER GENERAL POINTS FOR EFFECTIVENESS

Identifying resources to help family members support the offender on community supervision in overcoming substance abuse problems, addressing health problems, and meeting the requirements of their supervision and their individualized treatment plan will likely improve the overall prognosis. According to the Centers for Disease Control (2004), open and frequent lines of communication between community corrections and community public health resources are essential to an effective public health strategy. Thus, probation and parole must have frequent contact with hospitals and service agencies if such programs are to be effective.

Informal and formal meetings, perhaps luncheons, should be arranged where contacts from each agency gather on at least a quarterly basis to ensure that persons from each agency know each other on a first-name basis and to ensure that a "face can be put to the name" when they are talking and coordinating by phone. This would ideally be coordinated by some municipal, county, or state-level office but could also be informally started by the probation and/or parole agency. These groups should include sheriffs and probation chiefs along with public health officers, correctional health administrators, and any other personnel. This would result in a better working relationship and should improve access to community resources such as HIV education programs and TB skin testing and communicable disease training for staff (Craig and York, 2003). Further, such meetings would not need to be extravagant in terms of budget or human resources. In fact, churches and other civic organizations may be willing to donate their facilities and even volunteer human resources to assist such a gathering. Likewise, these collaborative arrangements should avoid bureaucratic complexity so that communication lines remain clear (Potter, 2003). The main point is that agencies are made to come together on at least a semifrequent basis.

Likewise, just as noted with offenders in the prison or jail setting, the same concerns with confidentiality of information will be critical. Indeed, as more collaboration occurs, the confidentiality issue becomes more problematic (Centers for Disease Control, 2004). This cannot be underestimated because medical records and screening are protected by law, and hospitals and medical practitioners can be made liable if sufficient precautions are not taken. This may be reason for the reluctance among medical care workers to collaborate with other community agencies. Thus, agencies will have to ensure that training on the confidentiality of medical records is provided to staff and that this is honored to avoid impairing community relations with the community supervision agency.

Offenders returning to the community require immediate access to services, but there is often a waiting list. Any collaborative program needs to do as much as possible to ensure that priority medical conditions are treated in the most prompt manner possible. Further, offenders who are newly released may find the agencies, facilities, and bureaucratic "red tape" associated with these services too daunting. This is understandable given the fact that the newly released offender will likely be going through a psychological readjustment that may impair effective decision making and the ability to process day-to-day stresses in the world outside prison. Thus, staff may find that overall success is more readily achieved if they are willing to initially give a "kick start" by making the initial appointments for the offender to receive health services within the community during the initial postrelease period rather than simply pointing them in a general direction with information on a pamphlet and instructions to place a call to the medical facility. Such clarity and follow-up may seem labor intensive initially, but the ultimate result is likely to be an ex-offender who learns all the steps correctly, the first time around, so that he or she is able to function independently on subsequent visits. Failure to learn correctly the first time simply sets a bad precedent and a poor foundation for the offender to build on. It also makes the probation or parole agency appear to have failed at reintegration.

CONCLUSION

Problems associated with communicable diseases are common to the general offending population. The various sexually transmitted diseases that occur in society are disproportionately represented among the offender population given the range of risky behaviors that are associated with a criminogenic lifestyle. These diseases tend to be recycled through the offender population as infected persons come into contact with one another through a variety of illicit activities. For some groups of offenders this is even more pronounced than would typically be found in the offender population. Female offenders and intravenous drug users are particularly susceptible to these diseases.

Likewise, the correctional institution, namely the prison, serves to exacerbate problems associated with these diseases. The physical living conditions of such facilities place these individuals within close proximity of one another. Further, the subcultures within many prison systems tend to create a social environment that compounds the problems associated with contracting these diseases. Both inmates and staff may deliberately or unwittingly engage in acts that serve to make the entire matter worse. Ultimately, the release of these offenders back into society simply serves to increase the threat to society as whole.

Lastly, these problems associated with communicable diseases are embedded within a wide array of problematic issues inherent to the offender population. For many special needs offenders, substance abuse, homelessness, mental illness, and other factors contribute to an increased likelihood of contracting these diseases. Special needs offenders with communicable diseases then become a health hazard for the broader public, regardless of whether they engage in further criminality. It is for this reason that society would be well served to ensure that these offenders receive the appropriate care that is necessary for anyone contending with these health concerns.

KEY TERMS

Sexually transmitted diseases
Human papalloma virus
Syphilis
Chlamydia
Gonorrhea
Herpes
AIDS
HIV
Intravenous drug users
Tuberculosis
Hepatitus A, B, and C
"The Big Four"
Confidentiality
Prison subculture

REFERENCES

Academy for Educational Development. (2003). *HIV prevention community planning groups and correctional institutions: A collaboration for all*. Washington, DC: Center for Community-Based Health Strategies. Retrieved from http://www.healthstrategies.org

Beck, A. J., & Maruschak, L. M. (2004). *Hepatitis testing and treatment in state prisons*. Washington, DC: U.S. Department of Justice.

Centers for Disease Control. (2001a). *Providing services to inmates living with HIV*. Retrieved from http://www.cdc.gov/idu

Centers for Disease Control. (2001b). *Helping inmates return to the community*. Retrieved from http://www.cdc.gov/idu

Centers for Disease Control. (2001c). *Working with the criminal justice system*. Retrieved from http://www.cdc.gov/idu

Centers for Disease Control. (2003). *Morbidity and mortality weekly report*. Retrieved from http://www.cdc.gov/mmwr/PDF/rr/rr5201.pdf

Centers for Disease Control. (2004). TB and HIV coinfection. Retrieved from http://www.cdc.gov/nchstp/tb

Champion, D. (2002). Probation, parole, and community corrections (4th ed.). Upper Saddle River, NJ: Prentice Hall.

Clear, T. R., & Cole, G. F. (2003). *American corrections* (6th ed.). Belmont, CA: Wadsworth.

Craig, R., & York, J. G. (2003). The shared responsibilities of corrections and public health. *Corrections Today, 65*(6), 64–66.

Crawford, J. (2003). Alternative sentencing necessary for female inmates with children. *Corrections Today*. Retrieved from http://www.aca.org/publications/ctarchivespdf/june03/commentary-june.pdf

Dolan, K., Donoghoe, M., & Stinson, G. (1990). Drug injecting and syringe sharing in custody and in the community: An exploratory survey of HIV risk behaviour. *The Howard Journal, 29*, 177–186.

Drug Policy Alliance. (2004). Affected communities: Women of color. New York: Office of Public Policy. Retrieved from http://www.drugpolicy.org/communities/race/womenofcolor

Epigee Foundation. (2004). *Birth control guide on sexually transmitted diseases*. Author. Retrieved from http://www.epigee.org/guide/stds.html

Fehr, L. M. (2004). Washington female offender re-entry programs combine transitional services with residential parenting. *Corrections Today, 66*(6), 82–85.

Hammett, T. M., Harmon, P., & Maruschak, L. M. (1999). *1996–1997 update: HIV/AIDS, STDs, and TB in correctional facilities*. Washington, DC: U.S. Department of Justice, National Institute of Justice. Retrieved from http://www.ncjrs.org/pdffiles1/176344.pdf

Hanser, R. D., & Moran, N. R. (2004). Labeling theory as an etiological paradigm for prison rape. In F. P. Reddington & B. W. Kreisel (Eds.), *Sexual assault: The victims, the perpetrators, and the criminal justice system* (pp. 163–169). Durham, NC: Carolina Academic Press.

Hanson, G. R., Venturelli, P. J., & Fleckenstein, A. E. (2002). *Drugs and society* (7th ed.). Sudbury, MA: Jones and Bartlett.

Jones, R. D. (2003). Hepatitis C—Not just corrections' problem. *Corrections Today, 65*(6), 78.

Kantor, E. (2004). *HIV transmission and prevention in prisons*. Retrieved from http://hivinsite.ucsf.edu/InSite?page=kb-07&doc=kb-07-04-13

Maruschak, L. M. (2002). *HIV in prisons, 2000.* Washington, DC: Bureau of Justice Statistics. Retrieved from http://www.ojp.usdoj.gov/bjs/pub/pdf/hivp00.pdf

Potter, R. H. (2003). Discharge planning and community case management for HIV-infected inmates: Collaboration enhances public health and safety. *Corrections Today, 66*(6), 80–85.

Ross, H. (2001). *HIV in prisons in five times the rate of the general population: Public health efforts coordinate with corrections*. Washington, DC: U.S. Department of Health and Human Services.

LEARNING CHECK

1. Roughly half of all the HIV-positive inmates are located within the state systems of Texas, New York, and Florida.
   a. True
   b. False
2. The rate of HIV infection for incarcerated offenders is reportedly about ______________ times that of the broader general population.
   a. 2 to 3
   b. 4 to 5
   c. 5 to 7
   d. 6 to 8
   e. None of the above
3. This is one of the most frequently reported STDs. Infection can be cured with antibiotics.
   a. Syphilis
   b. Gonorrhea
   c. Chlamydia
   d. None of the above
4. In the United States, offenders tend to contract TB at a rate that is roughly ______________ times higher than for persons not either within institutional custody or on community supervision.
   a. 2 to 5
   b. 3 to 7
   c. 4 to 8
   d. 4 to 17
   e. None of the above

5. Sex is the predominant mode of transmission for this type of hepatitis.
   a. Hepatitis A
   b. Hepatitis B
   c. Hepatitis C
   d. None of the above

6. This is a very dangerous STD, as it usually has no symptoms; 75 percent of infected women and 25 percent of infected men have no symptoms at all.
   a. Syphilis
   b. Gonorrhea
   c. Chlamydia
   d. None of the above

7. An inmate recently rumored to be HIV positive may be seen as "fair game" among HIV-positive sexually assaultive inmates and among the inmate subculture that is not HIV positive.
   a. True
   b. False

8. The majority of the 50 states test inmates for HIV/AIDS and/or other communicable diseases on initial entry of the state prison system.
   a. True
   b. False

9. The female offender population is most at risk of having HIV/AIDS or STDs because a high number of female offenders engage or have engaged in various forms of prostitution or sex industry activity.
   a. True
   b. False

10. The estimated lifetime treatment costs for an inmate with HIV vary from ______________ for correctional agencies that must foot the bill.
    a. $165,000 to over $250,000
    b. $155,000 to $250,000
    c. $125,000 to about $200,000
    d. $125,000 to roughly $175,000
    e. None of the above

ESSAY DISCUSSION QUESTIONS

1. Identify and discuss the various strains of hepatitis. Explain which strain is most detrimental to institutional safety and which one is least dangerous.
2. Discuss the comorbid nature of communicable diseases with substance-abusing inmates. Also understand how substance abuse (and therefore communicable

disease) correlates with sex industry offenders. Be sure to address the female offender as being particularly at risk.

3. Provide a discussion on the likely experiences that an HIV-positive inmate might face while in a prison facility.
4. Demonstrate how substance abuse, mental illness, homelessness, and communicable diseases tend to be collectively possessed among a certain segment of the recidivating offender population. Provide some suggestions on what community-based agencies should do to address this problem.

CHAPTER 5

MENTALLY DISORDERED OFFENDERS

NATHAN MORAN AND ROB HANSER

Chapter Objectives

1. Identify and discuss the common types of mental disorders encountered by criminal justice professionals.
2. Distinguish between myth and fact when determining if a mentally ill offender is likely to be violent.
3. Understand the challenges in dealing with the mentally ill in prison facilities.
4. Know and discuss the various jurisprudence alternatives used throughout the nation when addressing the mentally ill offender in the community.

INTRODUCTION

This chapter will address the challenges involved when addressing mental disorders within the offender population. As will be seen, the problems associated with mentally disordered offenders may have less to do with their actual threat to society and more to do with the bizarre nature of their behavior. Indeed, most mentally ill do not commit crimes, especially when intent is considered. However, many mentally ill may act strange by public standards or may act in a manner that would be considered "irresponsible" from a common citizen's standpoint. However, the behavior of a mentally ill person, regardless of how unorthodox it may be (e.g., a catatonic person falling asleep in the middle of a retail store, a person with Tourette's syndrome making unusual noises, or a bipolar person's extreme mood swings), does not necessarily mean that he or she is more prone to criminal behavior.

Bartol (2002) notes that the media have portrayed the mentally ill as not only criminal but also outright violent. This is often the case on television and in newsprint. Too often, violent criminals are portrayed as having diagnosable disorders when in fact they are not necessarily mentally ill; they are simply criminal and uncaring about their impact on their victims. Further, most violent crime (particularly murder) is impulsive, being committed by non–mentally disordered persons who are simply stressed to the point of using violence among their repertoire of behavioral responses. Further, violence (e.g., drug smuggling, gang violence, organized crime, arson, robbery, and so on) committed for utilitarian purposes is obviously not the result of mental illness.

Mental disorders are manifested in a variety of behaviors, ranging in severity from what many might refer to as "crazy behavior" to conduct that is simply unusual. Crazy behavior is that which is obviously strange and cannot be logically explained (Bartol, 2002). The concept of mental disorder includes behaviors that are bizarre, dramatic, harmful, or mildly unusual behaviors, and the classifications for individuals exhibiting these behaviors can be found in the *Diagnostic and Statistical Manual of Mental Disorders* (4th ed., text revision) (*DSM-IV-TR*). This manual, published by The American Psychiatric Association (2000), is formed by gatherings of psychiatrists and psychologists from around the world, and it sets forth the specific guidelines in applying a specific diagnosis to a person presenting with a mental disorder. For the purposes of this chapter, **mental illness** will be defined as any diagnosed disorder contained within the *DSM-IV-TR*. Mental illness causes severe disturbances in thought, emotions, and ability to cope with the demands of daily life. Mental illness, like physiological forms of illness, can be acute, chronic, or under control and in remission.

COMMON TYPES OF MENTAL DISORDERS IN THE CRIMINAL JUSTICE SYSTEM

Specific types of disorders have been found to be more problematic than others among the offending population. Among these are **mood disorders**, **schizophrenic disorders**, and **personality disorders**. Along with these disorders is the reality that many offenders also have addiction or substance abuse disorders that are comorbid with the primary diagnosis (Sacks, Sacks, & Stommel, 2003). This is commonly referred to as **dual diagnosis** within the treatment community and simply denotes the fact that the offender has two or more disorders. In most cases, when an offender is said to have a dual diagnosis, the clinician is referring to a primary disorder accompanied by a substance abuse–related disorder as well. The frequency of the dual diagnosis among the offending population was the reason for the eventual development of mental health courts.

Mood disorders are those disorders such as **major depressive disorder**, **bipolar disorder**, and **dystymic disorder**. Major depressive disorder is characterized by one or more major depressive episodes (i.e., at least two weeks of depressed mood or loss of interest accompanied by at least four additional symptoms of depression). Major depressive disorder is the most common mood disorder associated with the offender population and will thus be the focus of this section. Bipolar disorder is characterized by one or more manic episodes, usually accompanied by major depressive episodes. The individual afflicted with bipolar disorder will have mood swings that go back and forth between manic and depressive states. Dystymic disorder is characterized by at least two years of depressed mood for more days than not, accompanied by additional depressive symptoms that do not meet the criteria for a major depressive disorder.

According to the *DSM-IV-TR*, the degree of impairment associated with major depressive disorder varies, but even in mild cases there must be either clinically significant distress or some interference in social, occupational, or other important areas of functioning. The afflicted person will likely have decreased energy, tiredness, and fatigue without physical exertion. Even the smallest tasks may seem to require substantial effort. Further, these individuals often have a sense of worthlessness or guilt that may include unrealistic negative evaluations of one's worth or guilty preoccupations or ruminations over minor past failings. Such individuals often misinterpret neutral or trivial day-to-day events as evidence of personal defects and have an exaggerated sense of responsibility for untoward events.

There are multiple designations for depression within the *DSM-IV-TR*, and these various subcategories of diagnosis can be confusing and somewhat overly complicated for the layperson. Many of the differences in these categories have to do with the factors that led to the onset of depression, such as life course events, the use of toxic substances, or even physiological factors. Providing a complete overview of each of these types of depression would go well beyond the scope of this chapter. However, the following symptoms are included since they are the most frequently encountered among the gamut of depression categories of diagnosis. Specifically, the National Institute of Mental Health (2002) notes that a person experiencing major depression is likely to present with the following:

- Persistent sad, anxious, or "empty" mood
- Feelings of hopelessness or pessimism
- Feelings of guilt, worthlessness, or helplessness
- Loss of interest or pleasure in hobbies and activities that were once enjoyed, including sex
- Decreased energy, fatigue, or being "slowed down"
- Difficulty concentrating, remembering, or making decisions
- Insomnia, early morning awakening, or oversleeping
- Appetite and/or weight loss or overeating and weight gain
- Thoughts of death or suicide or suicide attempts
- Restlessness or irritability
- Persistent physical symptoms that do not respond to treatment, such as headaches, digestive disorders, and chronic pain

Among those persons presenting with bipolar depression, manic symptoms will also typically occur, with a cycle between bouts of depressive symptoms and manic symptoms that occur back and forth. These manic symptoms are taken from the National Institute of Mental Health (2002) and are listed here:

- Abnormal or excessive elation
- Unusual irritability
- Decreased need for sleep
- Grandiose notions
- Increased talking
- Racing thoughts
- Increased sexual desire
- Markedly increased energy
- Poor judgment
- Inappropriate social behavior

Schizophrenic disorders, according to the *DSM-IV-TR*, have five characteristic symptoms, and at least two must be present before the diagnosis can be given to an individual: (1) delusions, (2) hallucinations, (3) disorganized speech, (4) grossly disorganized behavior, and (5) inappropriate affect. Further, the social, self-care, and/or occupational life of the individual must show signs of being well below the level achieved prior to the onset of the illness. Finally, these symptoms must have existed for six months or longer.

There are five specific subtypes of schizophrenia that are listed in the *DSM-IV-TR*:

1. Disorganized—The essential features of this type of schizophrenia are disorganized speech, disorganized behavior, and flat or inappropriate affect.
2. Catatonic—The essential feature of this type of schizophrenia is a marked psychomotor disturbance that may involve motoric immobility (stupor), excessive motor activity, or mutism. These individuals may also display the pathological, parrot-like, senseless repetition of a word or phrase just spoken by another person. During severe catatonic stupor or excitement, the individual may need careful supervision to avoid self-harm or harming others.
3. Paranoid—The essential feature of this type of schizophrenia is the presence of prominent delusions or auditory hallucination in the context of a relative preservation of cognitive functioning and affect. Delusions are typically persecutory or grandiose.
4. Undifferentiated—Simply put, this type of schizophrenia is the "standard" type of schizophrenia. The individual possesses two of the following symptoms during

a significant portion of time for at least one month: delusions, hallucinations, disorganized speech, grossly disorganized behavior, and/or negative or flat affect. The individual does not meet the criteria for disorganized, catatonic, or paranoid schizophrenia.

5. Residual—This diagnosis is used only when there has been at least one episode of schizophrenia but the current clinical picture is without prominent psychotic symptoms.

Schizophrenic disorders are the second most frequent types of disorders. Only the cluster of personality disorders (discussed immediately hereafter) are found more frequently among the offending population. It should also be noted that schizophrenia is greatly compounded when offenders are locked in isolation for long periods of time. Offenders who are placed in administrative segregation or those housed in so-called supermaximum facilities either present with progressively worse cases of schizophrenia or may begin to develop schizophrenic "breaks" with reality. Thus, the occurrence of schizophrenia within the offending population is both the result of inherent disorder possessed prior to criminal involvement and frequently a product of the offender's intensive contact with institutional seclusion from typical social stimuli and support.

Personality disorders are disorders that are characterized by an enduring pattern of behavior that deviates markedly from the expectations of the individual's culture, is pervasive and inflexible, has an onset in adolescence or early adulthood, is stable over time, and leads to distress or impairment. The focus of this section will be on specific personality disorders that are most frequently seen as problematic within the offender population. The following list contains these disorders, with the exception of antisocial personality disorder, which is so problematic and is encountered so frequently among the offender population that an entire section is devoted to this disorder and its link with violent actions by offenders so that it can be given the full attention it deserves.

Borderline personality disorder is a pervasive pattern of instability in interpersonal relationships, self-image, and affects and marked impulsivity beginning by early adulthood and is present in a variety of contexts as indicated by five or more of the following:

1. Frantic efforts to avoid real or imagined abandonment
2. A pattern of unstable and intense interpersonal relationships characterized by alternating between extremes of idealization and devaluation
3. Identity disturbance: markedly and persistently unstable self-image or sense of self
4. Impulsivity in at least two areas that are potentially self-damaging (e.g., spending, sex, substance abuse, reckless driving, or binge eating)
5. Recurrent suicidal behavior, gestures, or threats, or self-mutilating behavior
6. Affective instability due to a marked reactivity of mood

7. Chronic feelings of emptiness
8. Inappropriate, intense anger, or difficulty controlling anger
9. Transient, stress-related paranoid ideation or severe dissociative symptoms

One key group of offenders who have been purported to present with this disorder would be perpetrators of spousal abuse. Dutton (1995) presents a psychological profile of batterers in which he contends that these men have a fear of abandonment coupled with inappropriate and intense anger that makes them susceptible to presenting with borderline personality disorder. Consider that many of these batterers reportedly suffer from the following:

- Jealousy (manifesting as paranoid ideation with women and their spouse)
- A tendency to abuse substances (substance abuse correlates strongly with domestic violence)
- The cycle of violence that goes from the classic "honeymoon" period to the ultimate explosive eruption (similar to symptom 2 in the previous list) where idealization and devaluation of others is common among borderline-disordered individuals
- The classic manipulative ploy of some abusers to use the threat of suicide to control their victims (identical to symptom 4 in the previous list)

With this in mind, the connection between borderline personality disorder and battering becomes much more clear. While this is not to imply that all batterers present with this disorder, it is meant to imply that this disorder is frequently found among the population of domestic batterers who have been screened for psychopathology.

Histrionic personality disorder is a pervasive pattern of excessive emotionality and attention seeking, beginning by early adulthood and present in a variety of contexts, as indicated by five or more of the following:

1. Is uncomfortable in situations in which he or she is not the center of attention
2. Interacts inappropriately with others in ways often characterized as sexually seductive or provocative
3. Displays rapidly shifting and shallow expression of emotions
4. Consistently uses physical appearance to draw attention to self
5. Has a style of speech that is excessively impressionistic and lacking in detail
6. Shows self-dramatization, theatrically, and exaggerated expression of emotion
7. Is suggestible (i.e., easily influenced by others or circumstances)
8. Considers relationships to be more intimate than they actually are

Among the offending population, this disorder is seen among female offenders most frequently. This is not surprising because female offenders often engage in criminality while under the guidance or because of the influence of a male partner. Because of the "codependent" nature of their relationship and the often-noted low self-esteem found among female offenders, this disorder seems to develop in the need to have attention. Likewise, these offenders are easily suggestible. This works well for male counterparts, such as drug runners using the female to carry drugs, the pimp involving the female offender in prostitution, or the male offender implicating the female by asking for assistance or for help with alibis and other peripheral support.

Narcissistic personality disorder is a pervasive pattern of grandiosity (in fantasy or behavior), need for admiration, and lack of empathy, beginning by early adulthood and present in a variety of contexts, as indicated by five or more of the following:

1. Has a grandiose sense of self-importance (e.g., exaggerates achievements and talents or expects to be recognized as superior without commensurate achievements)
2. Is preoccupied with fantasies of unlimited success, power, brilliance, beauty, or ideal love
3. Believes that he or she is "special" and unique and can be understood only by, or should associate with, other special or high-status persons or institutions
4. Requires excessive admiration
5. Has a sense of entitlement (i.e., unreasonable expectations of especially favorable treatment or automatic compliance with his or her expectations)
6. Is interpersonally exploitative (i.e., takes advantage of others to achieve his or her own ends)
7. Lacks empathy: is unwilling to recognize or identify with the feelings and needs of others
8. Is often envious of others or believes that others are envious of him or her
9. Shows arrogant, haughty behaviors or attitudes

Prevalence rates of this disorder within the clinical population range from 2 to 16 percent. Since most offenders are given clinical screening and are more frequently diagnosed than the general population (whose prevalence is only 1 percent), the expectation is that the offender population will present with higher percentages of this disorder. Indeed, possession of this disorder will result in a person who is likely to be tough-minded, glib, superficial, exploitative, and unempathetic. However, such a person is not likely to have characteristics of impulsivity, aggression, and/or deceit that is associated with antisocial personality–disordered individuals. The *DSM-IV-TR* notes that vulnerability in self-esteem makes the disordered individual very sensitive to "injury" from any form of criticism or defeat. Such experiences may not be apparent outwardly, but they are likely to feel humiliated, degraded, hollow, and empty. Reactions may range from disdain to rage and to defiant counterattack. Violent offenders occasionally present with this disorder and make note that their violence was sparked by a display of insult from the other party. Family violence batterers also have a tendency to present with this disorder.

ANXIETY AND STRESS-RELATED DISORDERS

Generalized anxiety disorder is characterized by excessive anxiety and worry (apprehensive expectation), occurring more days than not for at least six months, about a number of events or activities. The individual also must report that it is difficult to control the worry to the point that it causes clinically significant distress or impairment in social, occupational, or other areas of functioning. The anxiety and worry are associated with three or more of the following six symptoms (with at least some symptoms present for more days than not for the past six months):

1. Restlessness or feeling keyed up or on edge
2. Being easily fatigued
3. Difficulty concentrating or mind going blank
4. Irritability
5. Muscle tension
6. Sleep disturbance (difficulty falling or staying asleep) or restless unsatisfying sleep

A number of offenders may present with this disorder, though it may be difficult to determine because many of them will have objectively sound reasons for their anxiety. The hallmark of this disorder is when the individual worries when there is no specific reason for this worry. This is not necessarily a common disorder among offenders but is for those who have particularly difficult backgrounds (e.g., abuse) or for those who had difficulty adjusting to their experiences within the criminal justice system. This disorder is most prevalent in female offenders, as it is more prevalent among females in the general population.

The primary reason that this disorder is presented is because it tends to coexist with mood disorders (often precipitating depression) or to be comorbid with addiction disorders. Often, the addiction disorder may be a direct attempt to medicate the sense of anxiety.

Posttraumatic stress disorder (PTSD) is a reaction that can occur when a person has been exposed to a traumatic event in which both of the following were present:

1. The person experienced, witnessed, or was confronted with an event or events that involved actual or threatened death or serious injury or a threat to the physical integrity of self or others.
2. The person's response involved intense fear, helplessness, or horror.

Further, the individual must present with the following symptoms for a period that is longer than one month. The individual will have PTSD if the traumatic event is persistently reexperienced in one or more of the following ways:

1. Recurrent and intrusive distressing recollections of the event, including images, thoughts, or perceptions
2. Recurrent distressing dreams of the event
3. Acting or feeling as if the traumatic event were recurring
4. Intense psychological distress at exposure to internal or external cues that resemble the traumatic event
5. Physiological reactivity to the exposure to the internal or external cues that resemble the event

Other factors that may indicate PTSD are persistent avoidance of stimuli that are associated with the trauma and numbing of general responsiveness as indicated by three or more of the following:

1. Efforts to avoid thoughts, feelings, or conversations associated with the trauma
2. Efforts to avoid activities, places, or people that arouse recollections of the trauma
3. Inability to recall an important aspect of the trauma
4. Markedly diminished interest or participation in significant activities
5. Feeling of detachment or estrangement from others
6. Restricted range of affect
7. Sense of a foreshortened future

Persistent symptoms of increased arousal (not present before the traumatic event) are indicated by two or more of the following:

1. Difficulty falling or staying asleep
2. Irritability or outbursts of anger
3. Difficulty concentrating
4. Hypervigilance
5. Exaggerated startle responses

This disorder is commonly found among female offenders because of prior childhood and adult sexual abuse. Often, the female offender (particularly those involved in the sex trade and/or having addiction problems) will have at least mild levels of this disorder. Likewise, as odd as it may seem, many juvenile and adult sex offenders may present with this disorder because of similar childhood sexual abuse, which is also consistent with the research that indicates that many sex offenders are themselves victims of prior childhood sexual abuse. The connection between the prior childhood sexual trauma and future sex offending by perpetrators is discussed at length in Chapters 9 and 10 dealing with juvenile and adult sex offenders, respectively.

This disorder is also found among men who have been victimized (especially sexually) while incarcerated. Male and female offenders who have been victimized in the jail or prison setting often present with this disorder, which is then further magnified because of the poor psychological surrounding of the prison. This disorder can originate from any number of factors, and it is important to remember that even criminal offenders are often victims (e.g., in a gang fight), and even though they may have willingly engaged in the activity, it can still leave traumatic scars on the psyche of that individual. Similarly, some offenders may present with this disorder because of their experiences in other activities, such as military combat. This can be particularly common among older offenders.

ANTISOCIAL PERSONALITY DISORDER, PSYCHOPATHY, AND OTHER MENTALLY DISORDERED OFFENDERS WHO HAVE HEIGHTENED RISKS OF VIOLENCE

The offender with **antisocial personality disorder** presents the most concern to the criminal justice system and to the public at large. This is the offender who is likely to be violently dangerous and likely to be a true recidivist. It is these offenders who make it hard to plead mercy and leniency for other offenders presenting with other forms of mental disorder. The essential feature of antisocial personality disorder is a pervasive pattern of disregard for and violation of the rights of others that begins in childhood or early adolescence (originating with conduct disorder; see Chapters 7 and 8) and continues into adulthood. Diagnosis with this disorder occurs if the individual presents with three or more of the following symptoms:

1. Failure to conform to social norms with respect to lawful behaviors as indicated by repeatedly performing acts that are grounds for arrest
2. Deceitfulness, as indicated by repeated lying, use of aliases, or conning others for personal profit or pleasure
3. Impulsivity or failure to plan ahead
4. Irritability and aggressiveness, as indicated by repeated physical fights or assaults
5. Reckless disregard for safety of self or others

6. Consistent irresponsibility, as indicated by repeated failure to sustain consistent work behavior or honor financial obligations
7. Lack of remorse, as indicated by being indifferent to or rationalizing having hurt, mistreated, or stolen from another

It should also be noted that the individual must be at least 18 years of age and that the occurrence of conduct disorder must have been noted prior to age 15. This criterion is to ensure that behaviors of the "rebellious teen phase" are not confused with the possession of a full-blown disorder. Many of the symptoms indicated are common to adolescents who are testing their sense of autonomy. Indeed, many adolescents will engage in delinquency and may exhibit the previously listed symptoms. However, this is a far cry from having full conduct disorder (a youthful disorder) or antisocial personality disorder.

Additional symptoms, as outlined in the *DSM-IV-TR*, include stealing, fighting, truancy, and resisting authority, which are typical childhood symptoms. Those with antisocial personality disorder lack empathy and tend to be callous, cynical, and contemptuous of the feelings, rights, and sufferings of others (Bartol, 2002). Further, they frequently engage in precocious and aggressive sexual behavior, excessive drinking, and the use of illicit drugs. These individuals also seem to lack the ability to maintain lasting and meaningful relationships with family, friends, or intimate partners.

For the most part, those with antisocial personality disorder rarely become independent and responsible adults. They spend much of their lives in one form of institutional setting or another (juvenile or adult correctional facilities, secure rehabilitation facilities, and so on), or they may remain dependent on family members. It should be noted that this disorder is much more prevalent in males than females with base rates in the community being roughly 3 percent for males and 1 percent for females (Gacono, Nieberding, Owen, Rubel, & Bodholdt, 2001). However, it is estimated that up to 30 percent of all males in secure correctional facilities have this disorder, with more such inmates being progressively found as the level of institutional security increases (Gacono et al., 2001).

It is from this group that another even more dangerous (but more rare) group of offenders emerges. These are the "psychopaths" among the offender population. While offenders with antisocial personality disorder tend to decrease the frequency and severity of their criminal and substance abusing behaviors by their mid-40s, the psychopath tends to continue on a chronic course of criminal—and particularly violent—offending (Gacono et al., 2001). In fact, it is very difficult to distinguish antisocial personality disorder from **psychopathy**, and even clinicians themselves have been misled by the criteria (Gacono et al., 2001). However, the severity of the crime and the persistence of offending throughout the life span are prime indicators of psychopathy.

Robert Hare (1970) was the originator of the term "psychopathy," which he proposed as a scheme to outline three categories of individuals: the primary, the secondary, and the dissocial psychopath. The **primary psychopath** is the "pure" psychopath in the sense of the word that is commonly meant in the general public. The other two categories are simply distinctions between antisocial personality–disordered offenders (making it completely understandable as to why confusion abounds when distinguishing between psychopaths and individuals with antisocial personality disorder). **Secondary psychopaths** commit antisocial or violent acts, but this is largely because of severe emotional problems or mental disorders. Many of these disorders may be anxiety related in origin and represent the offender's "acting out" against the neurotic sense of anxiety that they may experience. The **dyssocial psychopath** exhibits aggressive antisocial behavior, but this behavior is simply the result of prior social learning from his or her subculture, family, or other significant models of behavior. There is nothing inherent in the psychopath to explain the behavior; it is simply learned and thus seems somewhat rational given the learning circumstances involved.

Psychopathy in general tends to predict higher reoffense rates and a higher risk for violence, even after the age when this behavior typically decreases in nonpsychopathic offenders (Gacono et al., 2001). Psychopathy seems to be especially high among convicted rapists, with research showing psychopathy among roughly 35 to 43 percent of all serial rapists or rapists who killed their victims (Hare, 1996). Likewise, Bartol (2002) notes a report cited by Hare (1996) from the FBI (1992) where it was "found that nearly half of the law enforcement officers who died in the line of duty were killed by individuals who closely matched the personality profile of the psychopath" (p. 85). Criminal psychopaths frequently engage in violence as a form of revenge or retribution or during excessive inebriation. Bartol (2002) notes that rapists who have psychopathic characteristics are more likely to have nonsexual motivations that revolve around anger, vindictiveness, and sadism.

Psychopathic individuals are pathologically narcissistic, experience deficits in anxiety and affect, exhibit impaired empathy and remorse, are often impulsive, are unable or unwilling to tolerate frustration, do not trust, and exhibit high rates of all types of misbehavior within the institutional setting (Gacono et al., 2001). Secondary and dyssocial psychopaths may have some hope of treatment, depending on the degree of mental disorder and/or the ability to unlearn negative behaviors. However, the primary psychopath has severe neurological and nervous system deficits that are inherent in their physiology. The primary psychopath is unique, being neither neurotic, psychotic, nor emotionally disturbed, as is commonly portrayed. Further, primary psychopaths are not given to explosive behavior but instead will exhibit a great degree of patience when necessary to gain their desired outcome. Primary psychopaths are not afflicted with mental disorders, and they are also not affected by symptoms of excessive worry, irrational thinking, delusions, depression, or hallucinations (Bartol, 2002). Even when under pressure with stressful situations, they tend to remain calm and collected. Likewise, the primary psychopath tends to be selfish and has an inability to love or give affection to others (Bartol, 2002). Because of these factors, it is generally held that the primary psychopath is truly beyond successful treatment (Gacono et al., 2001; Hare, 1996).

It should be noted that pscyhopathy is not a true diagnosis in the technical sense of the term, as there is no such category or diagnostic code for psychopathy within the *DSM-IV-TR*. It is instead a guide for clinicians (and the criminal justice system) in identifying certain individuals who have certain factors and traits that tend to cluster among a given group of individuals. This is important because the diagnosis for antisocial personality disorder is based solely on behavioral indicators. Psychopathy, on the other hand, is based on both behavioral and emotional elements.

The most widely cited measuring instrument of criminal psychopathy is the Psychopathy Checklist developed by Robert Hare. The Psychopathy Checklist has been shown to be both reliable and valid (Bartol, 2002). According to this checklist, psychopathy contains two stable, oblique factors characterized by egocentricity, callousness, and remorselessness (factor 1) and an irresponsible, impulsive, thrill-seeking, and antisocial lifestyle (factor 2). The two factors and their trait and behavioral criteria are listed here:

Factor 1	**Factor 2**
1. Glibness	1. Proneness to boredom
2. Superficial charm	2. Impulsivity
3. Grandiosity	3. Irresponsibility
4. Pathological lying	4. Correlates with criminality
5. Conning and/or manipulation	5. Correlates with low IQ
6. Shallow affect	6. Correlates with low education
7. Lack of empathy and remorse	7. Correlates with low socioeconomic status
8. Low anxiety	
9. Correlates with histrionic and/or narcissistic personality disorders	

Finally, it should be noted that while most criminal psychopaths meet the criteria for antisocial personality disorder, most individuals with this disorder are not psychopaths.

For the most part, the research in the field of crime and mental illness shows that the mentally ill offenders tend to be no more violent than nondisordered offenders (Bartol, 2002). However, there are some exceptions in which it has been found that currently mentally disordered patients are involved in violent behavior far more often than the nondisordered members of the general population. Furthermore, this difference persists even when demographic and social factors are taken into account. Monahan (1992) notes two important points about this research connecting mentally ill offenders to violent actions. First, the relationship refers only to individuals who are currently experiencing a serious mental disorder. This means that individuals who have experienced a serious mental disorder in the past but are not showing current symptoms are not any more likely to engage in violent behavior than nondisordered offenders (Bartol, 2002; Monahan, 1992). Second, over 90 percent of the currently mentally disordered do not present with violent behavior (Bartol, 2002). This then contradicts media portrayals of psychotic killers suffering from delusions that compel them to rape and/or murder. This is the common portrayal by Hollywood, but such occurrences are rare.

It should also be noted that it has been found that arrest rates for discharged mental patients are much greater than those for nondisordered offenders (Bartol, 2002). However, the disproportionate arrest rates are due mainly to those discharged patients who had been dually diagnosed with alcoholism or substance addiction or to those who possessed some form of personality disorder. Further, alcoholism and substance addiction are on the periphery of traditional diagnoses because they do not represent what are considered serious or typical mental disorders (Bartol, 2002).

Research from the MacArthur Research Network on Mental Health and the Law confirms this contention. This group conducted the *Violence Risk Assessment Study* to determine which former psychiatric hospital patients would be considered dangerous. This study followed 1,000 people between the ages of 18 and 40 for one year after discharge, interviewing the subject and at least one other person who was most familiar with their behavior in the community every 10 weeks. Researchers also examined police and hospital records. The study classified approximately three-quarters of the patients they assessed into one of two risk categories: "high-risk" patients were defined as being at least twice as likely as the average patient to commit a violent act within the first 20 weeks following hospital discharge, and "low-risk" patients were defined as being, at most, half as likely as the average patient to commit a violent act within the first 20 weeks following hospital discharge. Over a year's time, researchers estimated the occurrence of violence to others in the community on the basis of patients' self-reports, reports of family members, arrest records, and mental hospital records. The MacArthur Research Network found that dual-diagnosis offenders (who were not psychopathic) were much more prone to violent behavior than were mentally ill offenders who lacked a substance abuse problem. Consider the following:

1. People diagnosed with a major mental disorder and without a substance abuse diagnosis are involved in significantly less community violence than people with a co-occurring substance abuse diagnosis.
2. The prevalence of violence is higher among people—discharged psychiatric patients or nonpatients—who have symptoms of substance abuse. People who have been discharged from a psychiatric hospital are more likely than other people living in their communities to have symptoms of substance abuse.
3. The prevalence of violence among people who have been discharged from a psychiatric hospital and who have symptoms of substance abuse is significantly higher than the prevalence of violence among other people living in their communities who have symptoms of substance abuse for the first several months after discharge.

In another piece of research using a sample of 1,195 criminal defendants who were referred for psychiatric assessment, it was found that the most frequent type of diagnoses were those falling within the category of personality disorders (Bartol, 2002; Henn, Herjanic, & Vanderpearl, 1976). Personality disorders accounted for nearly 40 percent of all the diagnoses. Even more telling was the fact that roughly two-thirds of these personality disorders were specifically diagnosed with antisocial personality disorder. Further, it was found that alcoholism tended to be present across all the disorders, but the combination of alcoholism and drug addiction as a secondary diagnosis was extremely common in persons diagnosed with antisocial personality disorder (Bartol, 2002; Henn, Herjanic, & Vanderpearl, 1976). This clearly demonstrates that this group of offenders is the one most troubled and the least likely to reform. Therefore, those offenders who have a dual diagnosis of antisocial personality disorder and substance abuse addiction are most at risk of recidivating. This single group is the most problematic for criminal justice personnel and is the primary group that should be closely supervised.

Because of the public concern pertaining to the violently mentally ill, some states have enacted specific legislation and/or correctional polices to address these offenders. The state of Washington is one example. The state has enacted the Dangerous Mentally Ill Offender Program to address the concerns surrounding these rare but publicity-generating offenders. Because of a stated increase in the number of mentally ill persons entering the criminal justice system, the state of Washington notes that this increase of mentally ill and seriously mentally ill persons incarcerated in jails and prisons has stretched the resources available not only to identify them but also to provide adequate treatment within the Washington prison system. In addition, the transitioning and release of mentally ill offenders to the community has met with daunting obstacles historically.

In 1997, a tragic event occurred in Washington that triggered legislation and extensive changes in practices in identifying and transitioning **dangerous mentally ill offenders** (DMIOs) from prisons (see Special Insert 5.1). This incident involved the slaying of a man who was attending a baseball game with his family in Seattle. The man was attacked and killed at knifepoint by a mentally ill perpetrator. The incident generated substantial public concern over mentally ill persons who had histories of violence and who were not adequately addressed in the criminal justice or mental health systems (Washington State Department of Corrections, 2004). In an effort to address this public concern, the Washington state legislature passed a law in 1999 that required improvement in the process of identifying and providing additional mental health treatment for mentally ill offenders who pose a threat to public safety on being released from the state prison system (Washington State Department of Corrections). This legislation contains a two-part definition for DMIOs stating that these offenders are (1) reasonably believed to be dangerous to self or other and (2) also have a mental disorder (Washington State Department of Corrections).

The legislation specifically mandated the following requirements:

1. The Department of Corrections will identify offenders in confinement who meet the above two criteria and will consider all behavior known to the Department of Corrections and behavior indicated by research to be linked with increased

likelihood of dangerousness. This can and should include the offender's chemical dependency or abuse.

2. The development of a plan for delivery of support services and treatment for the offender prior to and on release by a planning team composed of representatives from such agencies as the Department of Corrections, the state mental health division, substance abuse division, community mental health treatment providers and Regional Support Networks, law enforcement, and other individuals as indicated by the needs of the offender.

The DMIO program was initiated in March 2000 beginning with the identification process of offenders who would qualify for the program. Any offender who is committed to a Washington state prison facility is eligible for consideration if he or she meets the conditions described in the legislation. The legislature's intent was to provide additional mental health and other necessary treatment services and resources that would not otherwise be available on release from prison, thereby decreasing the risk to public safety. The DMIO program provides additional funding for those services ($10,000 per year for five years for each DMIO). This funding is provided to the designated mental health agency to pay for these extra services. This may include not only additional case management and mental health treatment services but also fulfilling such needs as chemical dependency treatment, vocational and educational services, living skills, sex offender treatment, and housing.

Special Insert 5.1. The Tragic Case That Led to the Implementation of Mental Health Courts for Mentally Ill Offenders (MIOs) in the State of Washington

The process that formed the King County Mental Health Court was catalyzed by the brutal, random murder of Fire Department Captain Stanley Stevenson by a mentally ill offender in a Seattle park in August 1997. The assailant was a misdemeanor defendant who had been found incompetent by the Seattle Municipal Court. The defendant was released into the community by the court just prior to the homicide. The shocking incident prompted King County executive Ron Sims to convene a task force including broad representation of mental health and justice system professionals to review how mentally ill offenders were handled by the justice system. The Mentally Ill Offenders Task Force, chaired by the Honorable Robert Utter, retired chief justice of the Washington Supreme Court, was given the responsibility of making recommendations for improving the handling of mentally ill persons in the criminal justice system. Among many other suggestions, including reevaluation and reform of competency law, the Task Force recommended the establishment of a mental health court in the King County District Court on a pilot basis.

Source: Bureau of Justice Assistance (2000).

Similar to the developments that have occurred in Washington, there has been nationwide recognition of the need to provide enhanced interventions for the mentally ill offender. In November 2004, the **Mentally Ill Offender Treatment and Crime Reduction Act** (S. 1194) was passed and signed into law (American Psychological Association, 2004). This law is designed to improve access to mental health services for adult and juvenile nonviolent offenders. This law is designed to improve collaboration among various practitioners in the criminal justice and mental health systems (Newman, 2004). This law is also intended to ensure that nonviolent offenders with mental health disorders are accurately screened and identified and that they receive comprehensive treatment both within the institutional setting and on release into aftercare while on probation or parole (Newman, 2004). The specific objective is to eliminate the trend of "recycling" the mentally ill offender through the criminal justice system (American Psychological Association, 2004).

MENTALLY ILL OFFENDERS AND THE INSANITY DEFENSE

First, it should be made abundantly clear that the insanity defense is used only very rarely (Ogloff, Schweighofer, Turnbull, & Whittemore, 1992). Further, it should be noted that the "insanity defense" is a legal term and not a mental health term. Therefore, the student will find no reference to an "insanity" diagnosis within the *DSM-IV-TR*. In fact, the term "insanity" is less a mental health term than is the term "psychopath" (even though "psychopath" is not a diagnostic criterion in the *DSM-IV-TR* either). Although both refer to behavioral characteristics, "psychopathy" is designed to explain behavioral and emotional traits, whereas "insanity" is used to simply determine the level of the offender's culpability during the exact moment that the crime was committed. Further, it is well beyond the scope or intent of this chapter (and this book) to provide the student with a discussion on the various forms of determining insanity or whether the defense should be invoked.

Rather, this section of the chapter simply addresses this very small group of offenders since many students will naturally desire an explanation about this group within the context of mental health and special needs. Likewise, it should be noted that most of the contemporary research literature refers to this defense as **not guilty by reason of insanity** (NGRI). It has been found that roughly 34 to 46 percent of those individuals evoking the insanity defense had a previous mental hospitalization or criminal conviction (Ogloff et al., 1992). The most frequent diagnoses at the point of admission were psychosis (68 percent) and personality disorder (25 percent). Further, the crimes for offenders employing the insanity defense were more violent than average, and this was especially true for female offenders (though these offenders are a small minority of the offender population). Among some researchers, it has been found that the most frequently possessed personality disorder is antisocial personality disorder. This demonstrates that the population claiming the insanity defense often have some form of mental illness that helps impair their ability to function.

Interestingly, it should be noted who those offenders who are found NGRI do not have higher recidivism rates than other offenders who commit comparable crimes. Of those who do recidivate, it has been found that their crimes are usually much less violent than those with comparable crimes who do not use the NGRI defense. In fact, there is substantial evidence that those who "fail" when on community supervision do so more as a result of a mental disorder rather than because of criminogenic factors (Ogloff et al., 1992). Thus, community mental health support and maintenance may be effective in reducing arrest rates among this small segment of the offending population (Ogloff et al., 1992). The main point is that the majority of these offenders have several commonalities with the mentally ill offenders discussed previously. Whether their ability to appreciate the wrongfulness of their act exists is more a question for lawyers and courthouse officials to determine. But the fact that this category of offenders has a substantial amount of mentally ill members within its ranks makes it an area of specific interest when discussing the topic of special needs offenders.

MENTALLY ILL OFFENDERS BEHIND BARS

In 1997, roughly 42,000 inmates in the United States were assigned to programs specifically designed to address mental illness in prisons. This means that almost 5 percent of the entire nation's inmate population were given intensive mental health assistance (Johnson, 1999). Further, when diagnoses of major depression and manic depression are included, the number inflates to roughly 300,000 inmates throughout the nation who suffer from some form of mental health challenge (Clear & Cole, 2003). With the current trend toward increased sentence length, it is clear that this number will continue to rise. In fact, the proportion of inmates seeking mental health assistance will most assuredly continue to rise from the current 5 percent to nearly 7 percent or more as the correctional population continues to age behind bars. Problems with dementia and other cognitive disorders are steadily increasing as a natural consequence of mandatory sentencing, habitual offender, and three-strikes laws that are in place.

The adequacy of mental health services has been a substantial concern to researchers, mental health practitioners, and correctional administrators alike (Hafemeister, Hall, & Dvoskin, 2000). The burden placed on institutional corrections is compounded by the significant number of inmates who have a dual diagnosis of both mental illness and substance abuse (as discussed earlier in this chapter). Further, there are numerous inmates who have marginal levels of mental health problems but find these problems worsened by conditions of incarceration that cause their condition to deteriorate to a more severe state of mental illness. Because of this, it is mandatory that facilities screen for mental health problems at intake, and it is necessary to identify any inmate who may be at risk of inmate suicide. Staff must not simply consider suicide data with respect to "profiles" of suicidal potentiality but must ensure that they meet the legal objective criteria required (Hanser, 2002). This is important for the welfare of the offender but is also a necessity to evade liability if nothing else.

Correctional facility administrators are legally required to implement an adequate health care delivery system that can ensure inmate access to health care and health care providers (Johnson, 1999). This legal requirement for adequate health care also extends to mental health care (Hanser, 2002). An adequate care delivery system for mental health services in a correctional facility must address a range of specialized needs. In the U.S. Supreme Court case of ***Ruiz v. Estelle***, the Court focused on several issues required to meet minimally adequate standards for mental health care in a correctional environment (see Special Insert 5.2).

The following requirements articulated by the *Ruiz* Court are pertinent to this chapter:

1. Correctional administrators must provide an adequate system to ensure mental health screening for inmates.
2. Correctional facilities must provide access to mental health treatment while inmates are in segregation or special housing units.
3. Correctional facilities must adequately monitor the appropriate use of psychotropic medication.
4. A suicide prevention program must be implemented.

These **four standards of mental health care** are common to all jail and prison systems in the United States. The case of *Ruiz v. Estelle* was instrumental in laying much of the groundwork for correctional responsibilities to provide adequate mental health care. Other cases would soon follow that would clarify various fine points of law regarding liability issues, involuntary confinement, and so on, but the four standards of mental health care for prison systems are generally considered to have evolved from the decisions in the case of *Ruiz v. Estelle*.

SCREENING, TREATMENT, AND MEDICATION

Mental health care services begin at the screening stage. Given the volume of patients entering the correctional environment and the fact that the presentation of these individuals is often unplanned, it is important that a good initial screening system be in place. Inmates should be screened on a routine basis before they are placed on a cell block or in a dormitory. Such measures are good for the inmate's own mental health, but they are also good for the security and safety of institutional staff in the long term. Further, effective screening at the beginning is likely to prevent future problems and headaches for administrators. Thus, good screening practices will aid in the smooth running of the institution.

The primary goal of screening is to quickly identify emergency situations and inmates who might require more extensive intervention prior to placement in the prison population (Johnson, 1999). The persons conducting the screening should note the inmate's hygiene and whether the inmate coherently understands the situation.

Special Insert 5.2. The Case of *Ruiz v. Estelle*

In 1972, David Ruiz sued the director of the Texas Department of Corrections (William J. Estelle) over dangerous and inhumane living conditions. This was a long battled suit that ended in 1982 with a final consent decree that the Texas prison system was resolved to obey. In this class-action suit, it was held that the Texas prison system constituted "cruel and unusual punishment," which is prohibited by the Eighth Amendment to the U.S. Constitution. Some of the specific problems noted from this case are as follows:

1. Overcrowding—The prison system had been placing two or three inmates within a single cell designed for only one inmate.
2. Inadequate security—The prison system utilized a system of security that incorporated selected inmates as guards. This practice led to numerous injustices and civil rights violations.
3. Inadequate health care—The prison system did not have an adequate number of medical personnel and also used the services of nonprofessional personnel (including inmate "surgeons" and orderlies) to deliver medical care. Likewise, the therapy for psychiatric patients was deficient.
4. Unsafe working conditions—Unsafe conditions and procedures were the norm for inmate laborers.

Ultimately, all these complaints were rectified within the Texas prison system. However, this case held further stipulations that would affect the future of all mentally ill and mentally challenged inmates in Texas and throughout the entire nation. In this case, it was further ruled that it was also cruel and unusual punishment to confine mentally ill inmates in solitary confinement. In response to this ruling, the prison administration in Texas developed the Administrative Segregation Maintenance Psychiatric Program to provide intensive counseling to inmates with serious mental illness in need of high-security housing as well as a program to transition these inmates back to the general prison population. Correction officials also increased mental health training for security staff and established oversight through regular onsite audits by various outside review bodies.

Source: *Ruiz v. Estelle*, 503 F. Supp. 1265 (SD Tex. 1980). Retrieved from http://www.correctionalassociation.org/PVP/publications/Out%20of%20State%20Models.pdf.

Further, proper mental health intake screening will determine the type and immediacy of mental health needs.

Inmates requiring further assessment should be housed in an area with staff availability and observation appropriate to their needs. The assessment should be assigned to a specific mental health staff member and should consist of interviews, a review of prior records and clinical history, a physical examination, observation, and, when necessary, psychological testing. The types of mental health problems and the types of services needed to address these problems are similar throughout each phase of the correctional system's process (i.e., jail detention, imprisonment, and community supervision). As noted earlier, offenders may enter the system with a certain degree of mental illness that is further aggravated, or they may present new symptomology once incarcerated (Johnson, 1999).

The stress of being involved in the criminal justice process can itself serve as a causal factor for some mental illness. Stressors might include those induced by the legal system, separation from community and/or family support systems, or interactional problems with other offenders within the correctional facility. Indeed, if mental illness is already present, these offenders are more subject to victimization from the remainder of the inmate population (Hanser & Moran, 2004). In fact, those who present with mental illness (particularly along the spectrum of mood disorders and/or anxiety disorders) are at an inflated risk of sexual assault within the prison environment (Hanser & Moran, 2004). Further, several documented cases exist that link this victimization with later suicidal ideation and completion among the inmate population (Hanser, 2002).

Problems with sleeping and eating may be experienced, as access to anxiety-reducing activities such as television, exercise, socialization, and smoking are much more limited (Johnson, 1999). All this is compounded by a lack of control over one's environment and the diminished sense of autonomy that is experienced. Thus, inmates first appearing in the correctional facility must be closely watched and screened on initial entry and during the first 90 to 180 days so that their integration into the institution can be appropriately monitored.

The correctional institution has an obligation to maintain security and control over the day-to-day routine for the welfare of staff and inmates involved. This means that inmates who present with psychological problems in coping must be kept "in check" so that they do not create a breach in institutional security. This is important and will likely be the primary (if not only) concern among security staff personnel. When disruptions do occur, it is common practice for security personnel to utilize methods of seclusion and/or restraint that are not necessarily consistent with clinical considerations. This can sometimes pit security staff against mental health staff. However, these same mechanisms of control may be used as part of the treatment regimen when acutely disturbed psychiatric patients are involved (Johnson, 1999). A closely monitored review system must be implemented to ensure that these special security procedures are used only when necessary.

Limited reasons for the use of these special treatment procedures exist and are generally restricted to (1) the imminent risk of harm to self or others and (2) imminent likelihood of serious damage to property. Inmates in seclusion require enhanced monitoring, and this may mean continuous observation by line staff. This is especially true if self-injury is a potential risk. Inmates kept in restraints must be routinely assessed to ensure that they are not injured as a result of restraining procedures and to ensure that they are able to maintain hygiene and nutritional requirements (Johnson, 1999).

Medication prescription, just like the use of restraint, is considered another high-risk form of inmate control within the correctional facility. **Psychotropic drugs** are those prescribed for mental health issues, and their effective use requires mental health practitioners to use the right dose of the right drug for the correct period of time. The use of psychotropic drug medications is both a boon and a bane to correctional administrators. On the one hand, these medications can help stabilize the behavior of those who have serious mental illness, thereby assisting in the smooth flow of the institution when such medications are determined to be necessary. On the other hand, these medications may be sought after by numerous inmates, and trafficking and trading of these drugs may develop within the institution.

Further, Johnson (1999) notes that the use of **malingering** may occur within institutions. Malingering is when inmates falsely claim and consciously fake symptoms of an illness. Inmates may malinger to avoid the consequences of being responsible for their behavior or to gain certain privileges. Malingering may result in an inmate being referred for mental health evaluation or treatment. However, it is important that security staff do not attempt to discern between inmates who are malingering and those with a true mental illness. Security staff may be prone to do this when the inmate in question tends to be manipulative or the security staff have had previous disciplinary problems with the inmate. However, failure to assess correctly can simply compound the problems for the mentally ill offender, and this will ultimately lead to further problems for the institution as a whole, including security staff. Thus, this determination should be made during the assessment period only by qualified mental health professionals who have an objective eye.

Aside from the problems associated with the potential trafficking of psychotropic drug medications and/or possible malingering, problems with the abuse of the medication system may arise from inmates experiencing chronic pain or insomnia or inmates who were prior substance abusers but are now cut off from their previous drug of choice. Because of the problems associated with psychotropic drug medications, Johnson (1999) provides the following list of recommendations when administering medications to the inmate population:

1. Medication prescription should be held to the minimum amount necessary for the affliction at issue.
2. Sleep medication should be avoided except in acute situations and even then should be limited to no more than three days of use. This is important because sleeping problems are a common symptom of depression. Instead, clinicians should attempt to address the underlying causes of the likely depression rather than encourage a sleep medication addiction.
3. Medication compliance should be closely followed.

Finally, it should be noted that some distinctions between a disorder and true psychiatric mental illness may be more serious than one simple disorder from the *DSM-IV-TR*. The issue of mental health nonetheless requires the inclusion of the broad range of personality, mood, adjustment, and anxiety-related disorders since each is a precursor to further lapses in mental stability and overall functioning. With this in mind, it should again be noted that the prevalence of antisocial personality disorder is a frequent problem in institutional corrections. Indeed, it is a central issue as the level of institutional security becomes higher. Thus, in maximum-security, supersegregation, or supermax facilities, there will be many offenders with this treatment-resistant disorder. While not every inmate in maximum-security facilities will have this disorder, the disorder is often comorbid with other disorders among the inmate population. Possession of this disorder within higher-security facilities means that the treatment effectiveness of inmates in these facilities may be poor.

This is important to point out because treatment rates in security-minded facilities are often much more dismal than those in less security-oriented facilities and/or programs. However, it should be made clear to the reader that this is simply a reality that cannot be avoided for the most part since it is the offender's behavior that necessitates the heightened security in the first place rather than the heightened security being the initial cause of the offender's behavior. It is in situations such as these that the "causal order" between illness and incarceration must be maintained if institutional security and staff liability are to be kept at reasonable levels along the risk-management continuum of correctional supervision.

SUICIDE PREVENTION

It has been found that suicide rates among mentally ill inmates who have made previous attempts are more than 100 times higher than the rate in the general population (Sentencing Project, 2002). Over 50 percent of jail suicides are committed within the first 24 hours in jail. According to the Sentencing Project (2002), more than 95 percent of those who commit suicide in correctional facilities have a treatable psychiatric illness. Suicide prevention in jail depends on the ability of corrections and mental health staff to cooperate in identifying inmates at risk and providing the treatment and monitoring necessary to ensure their safety.

The need for crisis intervention or suicide prevention may arise with inmates at any level of treatment as well as those not identified as in need of treatment. Crisis intervention can be defined as short-term care for acute mental distress (Johnson, 1999). This level of distress can vary from acute anxiety or anger to that associated with psychosis (Johnson, 1999). Most frequently, the crisis entails suicidal ideation or a previous attempt of suicide. In addition, suicidal inmates typically do inform others of their intent at some point prior to commission. This is naturally the classic "cry for help," but it may fall on deaf ears among other inmates, or, even more dangerously, the staff may be indifferent to the inmate's suicidal ideation (Hanser, 2002).

The frequency of occurrence for suicidal thinking or behavior requires that all correctional staff be familiar with suicide prevention. The correctional administration must ensure that an adequate suicide prevention program is in place within the institution (Hanser, 2002). A suicide prevention program should provide adequate training to staff in identifying the precursor events and/or symptoms of potential suicide. Agencies that fail to train employees in proper suicide prevention or to place proactive policies in writing cannot automatically escape liability (Hanser, 2002). Because of the relapsing nature of those with mental disorders, discharge planning and follow-up are critical both when returning inmates to the general institutional population and when releasing them from the institution to community supervision. Assessment of dangerousness to self and others must be reviewed to ensure that discharge is the correct decision.

TRANSFERS AND INVOLUNTARY COMMITMENT

As mentioned earlier, some offenders may exhibit behaviors that become progressively worse over their term of incarceration. Because of this, it is somewhat common that some of these offenders will be deemed more suitable for psychiatric hospitalization. Indeed, roughly 54 percent of all persons in secure mental hospitals were transferred from a prison system (Steadman, Fabisiak, Dvoskin, & Holobean, 1987). Although a substantial number of persons committed to psychiatric hospitals come from prisons, the reverse is not true. Few prison inmates actually end up being committed to psychiatric facilities. Thus, prisons have become the essential "catchall" or "dumping ground" for much of society's mentally ill. In 1980, the Supreme Court held in *Vitek v. Jones* that a transfer of any inmate to a mental health hospital required, at a minimum, an administrative hearing to determine the appropriateness of such confinement. While this is generally not a difficult process to comply with, the reality is that most hospitals are at maximum capacity just like prison systems. Thus, the option of mental hospitalization holds limited utility for correctional administrators.

LACK OF PRERELEASE PLANNING AND SYSTEM INTEGRATION

Finally, there is a noted lack of coordination between police, courts, prisons, and community supervision. This lack of coordination is even more pronounced when other community agencies are brought into the picture. This lack of coordination results in offenders leaving jail or prison without any connection to support services. Once the mentally ill are placed within the criminal justice process, their conditions are likely to worsen on release. Unless prison systems intend to keep the mentally ill offender within their confines for an indefinite period of time (essentially an "until-death-do-us-part" relationship between the prison and the mentally ill offender), it will be necessary to ensure that adequate aftercare is provided. This is an absolute necessity if recidivism among these offenders is to be kept in balance. Otherwise, offenders will again recycle through the correctional system, resulting in a never-ending cyclic relationship between the state correctional system and mentally ill offenders throughout the entire course of their life spans. Such thoughtless processing can create a "cradle-to-grave" situation for the criminal justice system and the mentally ill offender. With the need for effective aftercare and community involvement, we now turn our attention to community-based concerns with the mentally ill offender.

MENTALLY ILL OFFENDERS IN THE COMMUNITY

Long-term inpatient or hospitalization of the mentally disordered has largely ceased. As a result, the mentally disordered individual has become more prevalent within society. This trend from hospitalization to community release was first set in motion in 1959, when nearly 559,000 mentally ill patients who were housed in state mental hospitals were progressively released over time because of a shift to "deinstitutionalize" mentally ill persons (National Institute of Corrections, 2004). By the late 1990s, the total number of persons housed in public psychiatric hospitals dropped to approximately 70,000. This is despite the fact that the U.S. population (and the mentally ill population as well) has grown considerably since 1959. Thus, more people are mentally ill, but fewer of them are placed in secure facilities. Rather, these individuals are returned to the community. Some mentally ill persons experience difficulty adjusting to life in the community and as a result may come into increasing contact with the criminal justice system. This points out the true need for alternative forms of case disposition, as discussed in Chapter 14. Programs that emphasize restorative justice elements and other less punitive strategies will likely be much more effective with this population given that these offenders are most likely to end up in the community because of the nuisance-like nature of most crimes committed by the mentally ill.

Indeed, homelessness is often a co-occurring problem with the mentally ill who are released on probation and/or parole (Connelly & Larivee, 2004). Because the mentally ill tend to recycle through the criminal justice system, they may have repetitive contact with the same local police agency over a period of years. Indeed, if their offenses are minor, they are likely to come into contact and receive only brief periods of incarceration before they are again released into the community. This means that police officers may become familiar with the same offender over time. Such familiarity means that individual officers may find themselves exercising substantial discretion because of their keen contextual knowledge surrounding the offender and their life course situation. This frequently occurs among seasoned veteran police officers who learn the futility of repetitively filling out reports for arrests that lead to brief punishments with a person who may not even truly gain appreciable insight from the consequences of his or her misdemeanant offending. This means that the police agency and the individual officer can have a substantial impact on the daily effectiveness of a mentally ill offender's reintegration into the community, particularly if the police agency is so inclined to assist in the process.

POLICE CONTACT

When discussing the mentally ill in the community, it is important to note that these offenders are encountered by the police on a fairly frequent basis. Often, police who patrol urban jurisdictions will come to know certain individuals on their "beat" who are mentally ill and transient. Indeed, these individuals may be generally nonaggressive but may be prone to petty crimes or may often simply be a nuisance within the community. In addition, during winter months some of these offenders may even deliberately commit some minor offense so that they can reside within the warmer jail facility. This is a somewhat sad state of existence but also demonstrates how truly challenged these individuals are.

Because police are usually the first responders to a disturbance involving a mentally ill offender, they have some degree of discretion when deciding on the course of events that will take place (Sentencing Project, 2002). A number of options may exist, such as arrest, hospitalization, or some form of warning or informal disposition, and the choice depends on the police's own analysis of the seriousness of the disturbance and the behavior of the offender being questioned.

Many jurisdictions allow their police officers to initiate emergency hospitalization for people who are a danger to themselves or others. In reality, this discretionary authority is restricted by legal considerations involved with involuntary commitment, the lack of community-based treatment options, the unwillingness or inability of mental health facilities or emergency rooms to accept additional persons, and so on. It should be noted that the appropriate use of discretion also requires police officers to understand the problem they are faced with and how best to react. Because of this, the following suggestions are provided (Sentencing Project, 2002) for police agencies that must deal with the challenge of the mentally ill offender within their community:

1. Police agencies should provide in-service training to enable officers to recognize the signs and symptoms of serious mental illness.
2. Specialized police units can provide an immediate response to a crisis involving mentally ill people. Officers in these units who have been trained to interact with the mentally ill focus on defusing potentially volatile situations by gathering relevant history, assessing medication information, and evaluating the individual's social support system.
3. Whenever possible, the mentally ill should be diverted from the criminal justice system on initial contact with law enforcement officers. Prior to booking, diversion should take place, but this will require that police have realistic options other than placing the arrestee in jail. If no such option exists, then police simply have no choice but to place the mentally ill offender in jail.

It should be noted that programs such as these do exist. Select police agencies in Tennessee, Oregon, Pennsylvania, Florida, and Washington have training programs to train their officers on how to handle calls involving individuals with mental health or substance abuse issues (Sentencing Project, 2002). Further, these and other police departments throughout the nation are utilizing a variety of **mental health diversion programs** with a "no-refusal" policy so that the mentally ill are not jailed unless necessary for public safety. Such programs provide the screening that determines whether diversion or adjudication is necessary and determine the prognosis and treatment services of the mentally ill offender.

As a general rule, diversion from jail and reintegration into the community should be the primary goal for nonviolent and nondangerous mentally ill offenders. These individuals should be diverted from jails that are often already overcrowded and be placed in community-based mental health programs. This will help society in two respects. First, the jail system will operate much more smoothly and will not be as crowded. This will reduce the costs to the police agency and to the taxpayers of the community. Second, the long-term prognosis for the mentally ill offender will be much improved since these offenders are in need more of assistance than of punishment. In addition, it should be noted that, as indicated in Chapters 1 and 2, the ability to correctly assess the dangerous from the nondangerous mentally ill offender is critical to the success of these programs. When making this determination, the assessment cannot be made on the basis of the current offense and/or even simply on previous arrests or convictions. Rather, these programs for diversion will need to consider data from prior school records (particularly if the offender is roughly 18 to 25 years of age), information from family and/or friends, supervisors (if the offender is employed), or civic organizations (such as churches).

Such a comprehensive assessment of violence is important for two additional reasons. First, such an assessment ensures accuracy of the offender's placement in jail and/or treatment. Second, as has been discussed, the public is wary of mentally ill offenders who are seen as a danger, and any mistakes in assessment that lead to a later violent incident against a community member will undermine the entire diversion process for these offenders. Thus, public safety must remain paramount for mental health diversion programs, or community support for the program might disappear (Washington State Department of Corrections, 2004).

Likewise, the diversion program must be tasked with this comprehensive assessment because police will be unable to make such an assessment. However, the police agency should provide the diversionary crisis center with its full support, including investigative resources if necessary, so that the crisis center's personnel can obtain all the information they need with ease. In other words, legal issues arising with school systems, family members who may need convincing to visit the crisis center, and so on may prevent the crisis center's employees from conducting the full assessment, and police should be willing to aid the program employees in any way possible to ensure that they are given access to people and/or records that they need, even if a subpoena becomes necessary. In either event, such occurrences should be rare but nonetheless are important if the screening of potentially violent offenders is to be correctly conducted.

Further, if the mentally ill offender is dangerous or the offense is serious enough to warrant further adjudication (detention in jail being necessary), then the jail system should be tasked to provide early screening, classification, and referral whenever reasonable. The Sentencing Project (2002) notes that in Summit County, Ohio, a three-tiered screening system is used that consists of an initial evaluation of mental status by the booking officer, a cognitive function examination by a mental health worker, and a psychological evaluation by a clinical psychologist.

One other recommendation for police departments and local courthouses is to modify bail decision procedures so that defendants can spend their pretrial time in an approved community setting or mental health facility, presuming that such a facility is available. In rural areas, this may be difficult to find because of a lack of facilities. By the same token, jail space may not exist in the local area, but approved family or other community forms of informal supervision of nonviolent offenders may be good alternatives to holding the person in jail. Many mentally ill offenders may lack family or friends who are willing to take them into their homes for even a short period of time. Because of this, agencies can consider the use of designated volunteers in these special cases. Many police departments may have auxiliary or "reserve" police officers who are community volunteers who complete the standard police training but simply are not on the formal police agency payroll. Those individuals who take this work seriously are often well trained with good knowledge of policing and the liabilities involved. These individuals may be good informal candidates to establish a "volunteer corps" for some form of **alternative mental health pretrial supervision** program. In these cases, the agency would need to ensure that appropriate training was given and that the situation (including physical facilities) was appropriate. Likewise, participation would need to be from those individuals who expressly noted an interest in such a program.

Such alternative mental health pretrial supervision programs can be of great benefit to the community, the offender, and even the volunteer. First, the community is alleviated of the additional expense of using more jail space, and the community is ensured that the offender is given quality supervision by someone trained and capable of addressing all criminal justice concerns. Second, the offender is helped because he or she will be relieved of the stressful environmental effects of incarceration and will likewise have the opportunity to develop a more personalized "point of contact" with the supervising volunteer officer. Finally, the volunteer will have the opportunity to truly provide extended service to the agency and to the community in a manner that can be personally rewarding. The volunteer essentially plays an important and specialized role within the department and thus becomes an integral component of the police agency and the agency's community outreach and public relations. This can be an important function for the police agency, and volunteers who participate should receive substantial recognition for their services.

It almost goes without saying that supervised pretrial release programs should include involvement of all potentially relevant agencies, including mental health and criminal justice practitioners, prosecutors, and defense counsel and the courts as well as community service providers, the individual with mental illness, and his or her family. Further, a postbooking diversion program should screen offenders to evaluate their eligibility for a disposition outside the jail rather than prosecution or as some condition in the plea-bargaining process (Sentencing Project, 2002). One model program is the Maryland Community Criminal Justice Treatment Program, where the case manager works with mentally ill offenders who are diverted to develop a treatment plan that works well with the court and mental health services. The plan is discussed with the assistant state attorney, the public defender, and the judge assigned to the case. When all parties agree that diversion is appropriate, the judge places the case on the "stet" docket, which leaves it open for one year (Sentencing Project, 2002). The defendant is then released to the community to complete his or her treatment program. This program and others like it are increasingly being referred to as **mental health courts** (discussed in the following section) and are reflective of the trend toward therapeutic jurisprudence, as noted in Chapter 14.

Because the problems associated with mentally ill offenders and community safety have received substantial attention, some communities have generated alternative methods of dealing with this population that are even more comprehensive than the program discussed in Maryland. The concepts utilize many techniques associated with restorative justice and are much like the drug courts discussed in Chapter 3 except that the central focus is on mental illness rather than addiction illness. In fact, as we will see in the next section, the commonalities between mental health courts and drug courts are not necessarily by happenstance, as the two often work in tandem with one another. We now turn our attention to the recent emergence of mental health courts.

MENTAL HEALTH COURTS

According to Watson, Hanrahan, Luchins, and Lurigio (2001), "The mental health court movement emerged out of recognition of inequities in the experiences of mentally ill offenders and two converging developments in the legal arena: therapeutic jurisprudence and the drug court movement" (p. 3). As will be seen in Chapter 14, the term **therapeutic jurisprudence** initially appeared in legal research literature during the late 1980s, when mental health law was going through substantial modification (Schma & Rosenthal, 1999). Therapeutic jurisprudence is "the study of the extent to which substantive rules, legal procedures, and the roles of lawyers and judges produce therapeutic or anti-therapeutic consequences for individuals involved in the legal process" (Schma & Rosenthal, 1999, p. 460). Since the 1980s, therapeutic jurisprudence has developed into an approach for examining a wide range of legal issues pertaining to mental health and the criminal court process. At its heart is the notion that the two systems—psychotherapeutic and criminal court services—can work hand in hand to achieve a common interest that is best for both systems, the offender, the victim, and society.

However, another movement was forming in the late 1980s as well. The general basis of this movement was academically similar to that of therapeutic jurisprudence. Starting in 1989, the first drug treatment court introduced drug treatment principles into the criminal justice process for addicted criminal defendants (Watson et al., 2001). Within less than 10 years, a total of 325 courts were operating in 48 states (Watson et al., 2001). This innovative movement reflected the growing recognition and frustration among all parties in the system that traditional methods had failed to significantly reduce drug use among criminals (Watson et al., 2001).

The drug treatment court concept synthesizes therapeutic treatment and judicial process (Watson et al., 2001). This means that drug possession is viewed not only as a problem solely within the domain of the criminal justice system but also as a problem that affects the health of society (see Chapter 4). Current evaluations of drug courts have found promising results in the reduction of drug use, criminal behavior, and costs (Schma & Rosenthal, 1999). As the number of drug courts has increased, so has the influx of individuals with mental health problems. In response, several jurisdictions in several states have developed mental health tracks within the drug treatment courts themselves (Watson et al., 2001). These and similar court developments have been seen in California, Hawaii, New York, and Oregon, among others. Some jurisdictions have separate drug courts and mental health courts but with the same judge presiding over both. Other jurisdictions have created mental health courts that are independent of the drug courts.

In Ohio and Florida, mental health courts are emerging to help local courts handle the growing number of disturbed persons in their criminal justice systems. Judges in these two states have specifically noted their desire to have these types of courts as they find themselves loaded with revolving-door dockets of minor offenders in their courthouses (McNutt, 1999). Butler County, Ohio, and Broward County, Florida, have prepared specific budgets for nonviolent, mentally ill, petty offenders that seem to overwhelm the court docket. In addition to modifications in court processing of the mentally ill, a coordinated police response has been established with specific training on handling the mentally ill to improve police response. Prior to this, most police agencies simply jailed the mentally ill if they presented a community nuisance. The problem for police as well as traditional court systems is that there has not been any specific legal agency that could have legal jurisdiction over offenders and yet also be adequately suited to address their specific needs if they are expected to not recidivate. The established mental health courts have provided this jurisdiction and integrate both therapeutic and criminal justice strategies through techniques such as the use of a computer link between the jail facility and a mental health provider so that mental health workers can check the names of defendants against client rosters. If a client's name appears on the list, then the caseworker is able to visit the jail and intervene (McNutt, 1999).

King County, Washington, followed the Broward County model and developed a multidisciplinary task force of judges, public defenders, prosecutors, police, mental health professionals, and family advocates. According to Watson et al. (2001), "This court differs from conventional courts in three ways: cases are heard on a separate calendar by the same core team of professionals, there is more emphasis on linkage between the criminal justice and mental health systems, and participants in the program receive greater court supervision" (p. 7). The initial experience of the court suggests that more is needed in certain areas of service, such as in the treatment of offenders with dual diagnoses and the lack of transitional housing (this again exemplifies earlier discussions regarding the correlation between substance abuse and homelessness among the mentally ill in the community). Despite the shortcomings, participants still hold that the new type of court is much improved over the previous manner of processing cases involving the mentally ill misdemeanant population (Watson et al., 2001).

TRIAL AND SENTENCING

More specific to the court process is the issue of trial and sentencing. Jurisdictions utilizing either mental health courts or their own hybrid system should ensure that certain factors are taken into account within the court system. Specifically, judges and other parties involved in the court process should be cognizant of the effects that mental illness can have on a person's behavior, particularly when criminal behavior is at issue. Such an understanding should go beyond merely determining competency to stand trial and should consider other factors as well. The Sentencing Project (2002) makes note of several factors to consider when promoting such awareness among courthouse parties involved in the sentencing process:

1. The defense bar needs training on mental health issues, including the following:
   - Interviewing techniques
   - Use of social worker and staff trained in mental health issues
   - Practice of obtaining records and tracking down discharge summaries or physician's evaluations for a client with a mental health history
   - Staff with familiarity with treatment issues, especially medications and their various impacts
2. Mentally ill individuals should be given timely access to counsel, preferably with attorneys who have experience in working with individuals with mental illnesses.
3. Judges must have information on offenders' mental health status available to them so that they can make a determination regarding the defendant's competence to stand trial, whether medication is needed in order to achieve competency, and the viability of developing specific plans to address offenders' mental health needs and establish referral mechanisms.
4. State criminal codes should authorize or permit judges to divert nonviolent offenders with mental illness away from incarceration to appropriate treatment, including the authority for judges to defer entries of judgment pending completion of treatment programs and to dismiss charges and expunge records of individuals who successfully complete treatment programs.

PROBATION AND PAROLE

Services for mentally ill probationers can be most effective when they are provided through special programs staffed by officers with specialized training and experience (Sentencing Project, 2002). For probation services to be successful with the mentally ill, they must address the broad range of offenders' needs and work in collaboration with other agencies and services to ensure that those needs are met. Specifically, community service agencies should do the following:

1. Increase access to mental health professionals.
2. Provide specialized cross-training to parole and probation officers pertaining to characteristics of mental illness, the effects that these illnesses have on daily functioning, and the goals of treatment programs. In addition, core functions of the therapeutic process, such as crisis intervention, screening, counseling, discharge planning, and community follow-up in case management, are very helpful.
3. Fully understand the requirements of confidentially statutes and mental health law.
4. Ensure increased communication between community supervision and other provider agencies. This should result in a collaborative effort between the therapist/treatment facilitator and the client's probation officer. Each should know each other on a first-name basis.
5. Provide training for culturally competent community corrections services.
6. Ensure that caseloads for individual probation officers are reasonable.

The last recommendation is critical since this is one of the primary complaints of probation officers. Indeed, Lurigio (1996) notes that probation officers struggling with large caseloads are likely to avoid mentally disordered probationers because of their problematic or bizarre behavior. Further, officers often do not feel equipped to address the problems associated with emotional instability. Because of this, specialization among probation and parole officers is becoming a common strategy for handling probationers and parolees with particular needs or elevated risk for continued criminality (Lurigio, 1996).

Officers with educational backgrounds and experience in the mental health arena can be chosen to staff special units for mentally ill offenders. Specialized units should monitor smaller caseloads, something that is crucial when servicing mentally ill offenders who need more time and attention than non–mentally ill offenders. Mentally ill offenders are typically individuals with a multiplicity of problems: comorbidity with substance abuse disorders and developmental disabilities, poor health, housing and financial difficulties, homelessness, joblessness, and lack of social support mechanisms. Thus, probation and/or parole officers with in-depth training and lighter caseloads will be better able to address this population. Further, continuing experience with the same types of cases allows specialized officers to gain greater expertise in handling mentally ill offenders and to cultivate closer, more productive working relationships with mental health professionals. They also gain more knowledge of referrals and a better understanding of how to access and use community mental health services.

In most agencies, probation and parole officers will not be frontline caregivers or service providers for mentally ill offenders. In addition, they will become increasingly dependent on mental health professionals as they become more adept at recognizing the mental illnesses afflicting their clients. Therefore, community corrections staff need to become more informed about the activities of the mental health staff who deal with their cases. Mental health and criminal justice personnel are disparate in backgrounds, education, philosophies, responsibilities, and goals when working with cases. Community corrections staff are driven by their role as agents of the courts or prison authorities. Their goals are to monitor the conditions of probation or parole and to file court petitions to individuals who violate those rules. Ultimately, enforcing rules and protecting community safety supersede any considerations of the mental health and well-being of the individuals under their supervision. In contrast, mental health staff focus on the clinical features of cases and may not understand the actions of community corrections staff that may appear to mental health professionals as arbitrary or overly harsh.

Cross-training for mental health and correctional staff would go a long way toward increasing their mutual understanding and respect and will greatly improve the working relationship between the two groups. They can learn about each other's roles, lexicons, job descriptions, primary responsibilities, practices, and competing interests in their work with mentally ill offenders. Most important, cross training encourages a team approach to working with the same cases. Community corrections and mental health staff who agree on case management strategies can better serve their own professional interests and those of mentally ill offenders.

It is recommended that probation officers have a strong connection with case managers assigned over the mentally ill offender. The roles of case managers are to integrate services by facilitating communication and cooperation among the various agencies, convene meetings with representatives of agencies to coordinate roles and services, and act as advocates for mentally ill clients (Davidson, 1996). Support is strengthened with community agencies through interagency agreements or memoranda of understanding (Davidson, 1996). Often, these case managers are employed with non–criminal justice agencies that provide blanket mental health services to the mentally challenged in the community. The effective link between the case manager and the community supervision officer is imperative and means that the case manager in such an agency should also be somewhat of a specialist, being trained to understand what the community supervision department holds as important for the offender's recovery. The case manager and the probation officer must monitor the offender-client on a frequent, ongoing basis, not only when illegal behaviors or symptoms are present. Further, these case managers must have lighter-than-average caseloads if the entire process is to be reasonably implemented. It should be noted that there is no shortcut around this; any failure to reduce caseloads of these mental health workers constitutes deliberate and tacit impairment of the agency's willingness to provide services that will ensure effectiveness for the offender and for public safety. Probation and/or parole officers make up the critical link in ensuring that a comprehensive case management model is effective. Thus, it is imperative that community supervision officers also have reasonable caseloads so that they can devote adequate time and attention to their collaborative duties with other personnel, such as case managers.

THE NEED FOR INTERAGENCY COLLABORATION

As has been noted throughout this chapter, one single agency cannot single-handedly provide the entire range of necessary services for this group of offenders. Rather, it will take efforts from a combination of agencies if a reduction in recidivism is to be achieved among this population. When arranging such collaborative efforts, an organizing body should be created (if one does not already exist) that is designed to bring the numerous agencies together. This body should coordinate these efforts so that "double work" is eliminated and so that resources from each agency are maximized. Such an organizing body would essentially consist of what is known as a "steering committee" where a group of officials (ideally from each of the participating agencies) come together and plan and organize such a collaborative program (Davidson, 1996).

Steering committees tasked with the goal of establishing care for offenders with mental illness should consist of corrections professionals from law enforcement, jails, prisons, and community correction agencies who have direct contact with the mentally ill, deliver services to them, and have to deal with safety and liability issues relating to their care (Davidson, 1996). Such a committee should also involve mental health professionals and service providers from mental health centers, hospitals, and residential programs since these professionals have direct contact with and provide direct treatment to the mentally ill and are knowledgeable about interventions that work (Davidson, 1996). It should include substance abuse treatment providers, as this is perhaps the most common denominator for all categories of mentally ill offenders.

Likewise, universities should also be included in the committee process. This is especially true for the fields of social work, psychology, counseling, and criminal justice since these disciplines are directly associated with issues pertinent to mentally ill offenders (Davidson, 1996). Their ability to access and conduct research can be critical to tracking the success of intervention programs, recidivism rates, and the process of obtaining grant funding. Likewise, they can play a role as facilitators or consultants to the group (Davidson, 1996).

Because most community and state-level criminal justice systems are so bureaucratic and because such a collaborative undertaking will involve numerous personnel from diverse areas of the community, the use of joint training sessions is perhaps the best method to simplify and integrate various systems. As the members of the steering committee gain an understanding of the various systems involved, communication between representatives and members of each organization should become more clear if committee members ensure that information is disseminated within their agency (Davidson, 1996). Committee members should ensure that their own agencies are up to date on developments by scheduling specific training activities that address the specific issues decided on by the committee. Attendance should be mandatory for any personnel in the agency who are selected to work with mentally ill offenders. This ensures that techniques, interventions, and programs are exchanged both between and within member agencies.

The inclusion of community members should not be overlooked. This is consistent with restorative justice elements that are increasingly associated with the therapeutic jurisprudence movement. Members of local churches and civic organizations can be helpful in providing assistance. In addition, a subcommittee that targets the families of both special needs offenders and their victims should be included. These persons can provide firsthand examples of living with the mentally ill and trying to address their unique challenges. Family members of any victims who may be involved can also gain an appreciation for these challenges while ensuring that the rights of the victim are given full consideration. This also sends a message to the community that public safety is still the main concern and that the rights of individual community members will not be ignored in the pursuit of services for the mentally ill offender.

CONCLUSION

From this chapter, it should become clear that the concerns about mentally ill offenders are somewhat misunderstood by the general public, particularly when the effects of the media on public perception are considered. For the most part, those offenders who are mentally ill either have bizarre behaviors (if they have some form of psychosis) or present with extremes in mood or personality development. Still, a select group of offenders, those with antisocial personality disorder, do seem to pose an elevated risk to society and are particularly resistant to treatment. Other diagnoses present themselves more frequently than others within the offender population (e.g., personality disorders, schizophrenia, and mood disorders). Further, with all mentally ill offenders, the dual diagnosis of substance abuse exacerbates the illness, and it is this duality in diagnosis that creates the truly dangerous mentally ill offender.

The ability to distinguish between those mentally ill offenders who are violent and dangerous and those who are simple nuisances and nondangerous is critical both for public safety and when planning methods of intervention within the institution and the community. Various jurisdictions around the country are becoming more aware of this need within the criminal justice and mental health systems and are thus retailoring various criminal justice responses to better address the specialized needs of the mentally ill offender. It becomes clear that these offenders have a multiplicity of problems and that a "one-size-fits-all" approach to mental illness is not appropriate for treatment or effective for public safety. With this in mind, institutional and community corrections have generated a wide array of programs that address these complex issues. The philosophical underpinnings of these programs are grounded in the restorative justice and community justice movements and utilize techniques commonly associated with therapeutic jurisprudence. These unorthodox methods of dealing with mentally ill offenders have become necessary since it is clear that conventional programs have been found wanting in the wake of recent criminal offending patterns and subsequent recidivism rates among the mentally ill offender.

KEY TERMS

Mental illness
Mood disorders
Schizophrenic disorders
Personality disorders
Dual diagnosis
Major depressive disorder
Bipolar disorder
Dystymic disorder
Histrionic personality disorder
Narcissistic personality disorder
Antisocial personality disorder
Psychopathy
Primary psychopath
Secondary psychopath
Dyssocial psychopath
Dangerous mentally ill offenders
Mentally Ill Offender Treatment and Crime Reduction Act
Not guilty by reason of insanity
Ruiz v. Estelle
Four standards of mental health care
Psychotropic drugs
Malingering
Mental health diversion programs
Alternative mental health pretrial supervision
Mental health courts
Therapeutic jurisprudence

ABOUT THE CONTRIBUTORS

Nathan Moran is chair of criminal justice at Midwestern State University. His specialty areas include offender mental illness and trauma.

Rob Hanser is director of the Institute of Law Enforcement at the University of Louisiana at Monroe. His specialty areas include ethics in policing, community policing, corrections, multiculturalism, and treatment interventions for victims and perpetrators.

REFERENCES

American Psychiatric Association. (2000). *Diagnostic and statistical manual of mental disorders* (4th ed., text revision). Arlington, VA: Author.

American Psychological Association. (2004). *Mentally ill offender treatment and crime reduction act becomes law*. Washington, DC: Author. Retrieved from http://www.apa.org/releases/S1194_law.html

Bartol, C. R. (2002). *Criminal behavior: A psychological approach* (5th ed.). Upper Saddle River, NJ: Prentice Hall.

Bureau of Justice Assistance. (2000). *Emerging judicial strategies for the mentally ill in the criminal caseload: Mental health courts in Fort Lauderdale, Seattle, San Bernardino, and Anchorage.* Washington, DC: U.S. Department of Justice. Retrieved from http://www.nejrs.org/html/bja/mentalhealth/contentsc.html

Connelly, L., & Larivee, L. (2004). Community-based treatment for homeless parolees. *Corrections Today, 66*(6), pp. 100–104.

Davidson, C. (1996). From territoriality to collaboration: A multisystem response to offenders with mental illness. In A. J. Lurigio (Ed.), *Community corrections in America: New directions and sounder investments for persons with mental illness and codisorders* (pp. 166–171). Washington, DC: National Institute of Corrections.

Dutton, D., & Golant, S. (1995). *The batterer: A psychological profile*. New York: Basic Books.

Federal Bureau of Investigation. (1992). *Killed in the line of duty: A study of selected felonious killings of law enforcement officers*. Washington, DC: U.S. Department of Justice.

Gacono, C. B., Nieberding, R. J., Owen, A., Rubel, J., & Bodholdt, R. (2001). Treating conduct disorder, antisocial, and psychopathic personalities. In J. B. Ashford, B. D. Sales, & W. H. Reid (Eds.), *Treating adults and juvenile offenders with special needs* (pp. 99–130). Washington, DC: American Psychological Association.

Hafemeister, T. L., Hall, S.R., & Dvoskin, J. A. (2000). Administrative concerns associated with the treatment of offenders with mental illness. In J. B. Ashford, B. D. Sales, & W. H. Reid (Eds.), *Treating adult and juvenile offenders with special needs* (pp. 131–170). Washington, DC: American Psychological Association.

Hanser, R. D. (2002). Inmate suicide in prisons: An analysis of legal liability under Section 1983. *Prison Journal, 82*(4), 459–477.

Hanser, R. D., & Moran, N. R. (2004). Labeling theory as an etiological paradigm for prison rape. In F. P. Reddington & B. W. Kreisel (Eds.), *Sexual assault: The victims, the perpetrators and the criminal justice system* (pp. 163–169). Durham, NC: Carolina Academic Press.

Hare, R. (1976). *Psychopathy: Theory and research*. New York: Wiley.

Henn, F. A., Herjanic, M., & Vanderpearl, R. H. (1976). Forensic psychiatry: Diagnosis and criminal responsibility. *Journal of Nervous and Mental Disease, 162*, 423–429.

Johnson, S. C. (1999). Mental health services in a correctional setting. In P. M. Carslon & J. S. Garrett (Eds.), *Prison and jail administration: Practice and theory.* Gaithersberg, MD: Aspen.

Lurigio, A. J. (1996). Responding to the mentally ill on probation and parole: Recommendations and action plans. In A. J. Lurigio (Ed.), *Community corrections in America: New directions and sounder investments for persons with mental illness and codisorders* (pp. 166–171). Washington, DC: National Institute of Corrections.

McNutt, R. (1999). Court for mentally ill offenders advocated: Judicial officials at seminar told that treatment is lacking. *Cincinnati Enquirer*. Retrieved from http://www.enquirer.com/editions/1999/11/10/loc_court_for_mentally.html

Monahan, J. (1992). Mental disorder and violent behavior: Perceptions and evidence. *American Psychologist, 47*, 511–521.

National Institute of Corrections. (2004). *Mentally ill persons in correctional settings*. Retrieved from http://www.nicic.org/resources/topics/MentallyIll.aspx

National Institute of Mental Health. (2002). Depression. Bethesda, MD: Author. Retrieved from http://www.nimh.nih.gov/publicat/nimhdepression.pdf

Newman, R. (2004). *Mentally ill offender treatment and crime reduction act becomes law*. Washington, DC: American Psychological Association Practice Organization. Retrieved from http://www.apa.org/releases/S1194_law.html

Ogloff, J. R. P., Schweighofer, A., Turnbull, S., & Whittemore, K. (1992). Empirical research regarding the insanity defense: How much do we really know? In J. R. P. Ogloff (Ed.)., *Law and psychology: The broadening of the discipline* (pp. 171–210). Durham, NC: Carolina Academic Press.

Sacks, S., Sacks, J. Y., & Stommel, J. (2003). Modified therapeutic community programs: For inmates with mental illness and chemical abuse disorders. *Corrections Today, 65*(6), 90–100.

Schma, H. P., & Rosenthal, W. (1999). Therapeutic jurisprudence and the drug court movement: Revolutionizing the criminal justice system's response to drug abuse and crime in America. *Notre Dame Law Review, 74*, 439–555.

Sentencing Project. (2002). *Mentally ill offenders in the criminal justice system: An analysis and prescription*. Washington, DC: Author.

Steadman, H. J., Fabisiak, S., Dvoskin, J., & Holobean, E. (1987). A survey of mental disability among state prison inmates. *Hospital and Community Psychiatry, 38*, 1086–1090.

Washington State Department of Corrections. (2004). Dangerous mentally ill offender program. Retrieved from http://www.doc.wa.gov/CPU/dmio_index.htm

Watson, A., Luchins, D., Hanrahan, M., & Lurigio, A. (2001). Mental health courts and the complex issue of mentally ill offenders. *Psychiatric Sevices, 52*(4), 477–481.

LEARNING CHECK

1. Which of the following is a common diagnosis for offenders who are violent?
   a. Antisocial personality disorder
   b. Bipolar personality disorder
   c. Conduct disorder
   d. All of the above
   e. None of the above
2. Which of the following are symptoms of antisocial personality disorder?
   a. Deceitfulness, as indicated by repeated lying
   b. Failure to conform to social norms with respect to lawful behaviors
   c. Lack of remorse
   d. All of the above
   e. None of the above
3. Which of the following are symptoms of posttraumatic stress disorder?
   a. Inability to recall an important aspect of the trauma
   b. Feeling of detachment or estrangement from others
   c. Recurrent distressing dreams of the event
   d. Restricted range of affect
   e. All of the above
4. Borderline personality disorder is a pervasive pattern of grandiosity (in fantasy or behavior), need for admiration, and lack of empathy, beginning by early adulthood.
   a. True
   b. False
5. Correctional facility administrators are legally required to implement an adequate health care delivery system that also extends to mental health care.
   a. True
   b. False
6. Mental health diversion programs should have which of the following?
   a. Adequate jail space since most mentally ill will need to be detained for indefinite periods of time
   b. A "no-refusal" policy regarding the admission of mentally ill offenders
   c. At least one psychiatrist that is available for emergency duty at all times during the week

d. All of the above
e. None of the above

7. Mental illness is defined as ______________.
   a. Any diagnosed disorder contained within the *DSM-IV-TR*
   b. Any aberrant behavior that causes impairment in normal day-to-day functioning
   c. Any maladaptive behavior that is harmful to self or to others
   d. All of the above
   e. None of the above
8. Which factors that should be considered when promoting effective responses to mental illness among courthouse parties?
   a. Police should note mental illness whenever filing their official report.
   b. Mental illness should be an admissible defense against guilt.
   c. Defense attorneys should have more flexibility in using defenses of guilty by reason of insanity.
   d. State criminal codes should authorize judges to divert nonviolent offenders with mental illness away from incarceration.
   e. None of the above
9. The mentally ill are often victims of crime within prison facilities.
   a. True
   b. False
10. The rate of suicide for the mentally ill who are incarcerated is up to 100 times higher than that for people in broader society.
    a. True
    b. False

ESSAY DISCUSSION QUESTIONS

1. Identify, define, and discuss mood disorders. Next explain how mood disorders might affect the outcome of a treatment program for a given offender. Also be sure to discuss whether normal punitive sanctions would be likely to deter an offender with some form of depression or other negative mood disorder.
2. Discuss the difference between offenders diagnosed with antisocial personality disorder and offenders who are likely psychopaths.
3. Provide a discussion on the symptoms related to schizophrenic disorders. Explain how these offenders might be at risk of victimization within a prison facility.

CHAPTER 6

MENTALLY RETARDED AND LEARNING-DISABLED OFFENDERS

Chapter Objectives

1. Know the different levels of mental retardation. Understand how each level of retardation may affect the offender's likelihood to offend.
2. Identify and define the different types of learning disabilities. Understand how the offender population is disproportionately affected by learning disabilities.
3. Understand the need for special educational programs for mentally retarded and/or learning-disabled offenders.
4. Be familiar with treatment programs for mentally retarded and/or learning-disabled offenders.

INTRODUCTION

At every stage of the criminal justice process, mentally retarded and severely learning-disabled inmates experience more problems than usual for offenders. Some of their problems are directly related to their handicaps, but others are a result of a lack of training on the part of criminal justice personnel, a lack of material resources, and a lack of interagency cooperation with the system itself. The problems associated with the mentally retarded and learning disabled offender include some specific concerns.

First, they are more likely to get caught in the act and arrested, frequently escalating the situation by strange, panicky, or assaultive behavior. Without adequate training, police officers are also unlikely to identify the arrestees as handicapped or to know how to deal with them. Further, handicapped arrestees may not understand their rights (thus conflicting with Miranda requirements). These arrestees often will waive their rights because of a lack of understanding, and they also have a lesser ability than the average offender to obtain bail or to be released on their own recognizance. During court proceedings, mentally retarded and learning-disabled offenders are inadequate in their own case preparation, they frequently make self-incriminating statements, and they have a difficult time speaking in their own defense. As a result, they are at higher risk of standing trial and of being found guilty.

The worst problem for mentally challenged offenders is associated with that period of pretrial incarceration in jail or after conviction during prison. These offenders are often highly susceptible to victimization from other inmates because of their inability to mentally safeguard themselves. This has been found true with both male and female inmates. Examples of this victimization include theft of commissary items to verbal and physical abuse. These offenders are highly vulnerable to physical and sexual assault among the incarcerated population, and this trauma simply compounds their mental deficiencies with resultant mental illness that may not have existed prior to their incarceration. Further, mentally challenged inmates are often fooled or coerced into committing institutional infractions and/or because of their inadequate understanding of the institution's rules may commit frequent infractions more by accident rather than with intent. In either case, this means that these offenders are disciplined more frequently than the typical offender in custodial environments. Naturally, this negatively affects their likelihood of reform.

BACKGROUND OF OFFENDERS WITH MENTAL RETARDATION

The mentally retarded offender's background is often characterized by a poor urban environment and a family of limited ability. He or she is likely to have suffered significant psychosocial deprivation, to have exhibited a range of behavioral problems during childhood and adolescence, and to have spent substantial periods in some form of residential care or schooling (Day & Berney, 2000). The mentally retarded adolescent has difficulty attaining a place in a normal peer group and becomes the willing follower of a more able, delinquent gang or of criminal family members, ready to be used by them and to accept "dares" in a search for status and acceptance. Further, the mentally retarded offender's lack of mental savvy makes him or her the most likely to be apprehended when engaging in illegal behavior. The majority of these offenders are first arrested during their adolescent years.

Delinquency, vandalism, and property offenses are usually noted in faulty upbringing, poor parenting models, and delinquent exposure, to which mentally retarded youth are particularly vulnerable. Occasionally, solitary delinquent acts occur as a consequence of poor self-control or frustration (Day, 1990). Offenses involving physical violence are uncommon, but a substantial number of mentally retarded offenders show a low tolerance for frustration, often in association with organic brain damage and sometimes epilepsy (Day & Berney, 2000).

OFFENDERS WITH MENTAL RETARDATION

Defining **mental retardation** has been something of a controversial issue. However, the definition provided by the American Association on Mental Retardation (AAMR) is the definition of choice among the courts of the United States. According to this definition, "mental retardation refers to significantly subaverage general intellectual functioning existing concurrently with deficits in adaptive behavior and manifested during the developmental period."

Usually, to be considered mentally retarded, the individual must have an IQ of less than 70. Further, the person must also demonstrate impairments in adaptive behavior as well. These impairments may come in many forms, such as slow overall emotional maturation, poor personal responsibility, or low social skills that are below those normally expected of a person their age. Moreover, the individual must present with the disorder during the formative years, typically well before the age of 18.

According to the *Diagnostic and Statistical Manual of Mental Disorders* (4th ed., text revision; *DSM-IV-TR*) (American Psychiatric Association, 2000), mental retardation is divided into four categories reflecting the severity of the retardation. The ranges of mental retardation, as noted by the American Psychiatric Association (2000), are listed here:

Severity	IQ	Percentage of Mentally Retarded Population
Mild	51–69	89.0
Moderate	36–50	6.0
Severe	21–35	3.5
Profound	Under 20	1.5

Generally, it is estimated that mental retardation has a prevalence of 3 percent in society with roughly 89 percent having mild retardation. Similar percentages have been found to exist in the correctional population as well. Offenders with severe or profound retardation are often either unlikely to commit crime or diverted in the early stages of processing through the criminal justice system.

It should be noted that it is often difficult to identify mildly retarded offenders since their handicap is not especially pronounced so as to be easily identified. This is further compounded among the offender population when one considers that the offender population tends to have intellectual scores (IQs) that are slightly lower than the majority of the nonoffending population (much of this is due to lower socioeconomic status and lack of education among the majority of the lower-income offending population within the correctional system).

Moderately retarded offenders are more easily identifiable. Their deficits usually manifest in early childhood and exhibit some delayed muscular-motor development. These persons can usually learn to take care of themselves and can do simple tasks. However, they often have difficulty with more complex tasks. They can usually progress to a third- or fourth-grade academic level. These offenders do require fairly extensive training for community living and often need some form of structured employment setting.

Offenders with severe retardation often show marked delays in motor development early in life and are extremely hindered from functioning independently. These offenders need constant supervision simply to function and communicate. These individuals often need constant nursing care and often have other existing physical and/or mental impairments beyond their mental retardation. These individuals need extensive training for the simplest of basic skills. Because of this, they are seldom kept in the institutional or community correctional systems. Offenders with this level of impairment are extremely rare.

It is important to provide a clear distinction between mental retardation and mental illness. In technical terms, mental illness is a disease, whether temporary, periodic, or chronic. Mental retardation, on the other hand, is a developmental disability and therefore not considered a disease. A person suffering from mental illness may recover; however, the state of mental retardation is a permanent characteristic that will limit the individual's ability to learn indefinitely.

Distinguishing between the two impairments is further confounded when one considers that these two handicaps are not necessarily exclusive of one another. There are offenders in the correctional system who are dually diagnosed. This dual diagnosis means that the offender may both have a mental illness and be mentally retarded. For instance, these offenders may have mild retardation and may also suffer from some form of personality, mood, or adjustment disorder (see Chapter 2 for further information on types of disorders). These offenders do not often receive the specialized services they need because of the plethora of needs they may have and the difficulty in providing the needed services for this severely challenged group of offenders.

BACKGROUND OF EDUCATIONAL DISABILITIES IN THE JUSTICE SYSTEM

Estimates of the prevalence of persons 21 years of age and younger in correctional facilities who are in need of special education vary widely. The reasons for this are many but have to do mostly with inadequate screening and assessment procedures, problems with implementing special education programs in correctional settings, and institutional polices pertaining to security that cause educational considerations to take a backseat in priority.

Another problem in identifying these types of offenders has to do with the overlap of disabilities that is likely to occur. For instance, an individual may be diagnosed with both learning disabilities and emotional disturbance or with learning disabilities and **attention deficit disorder** (ADD) or **attention-deficit/hyperactivity disorder** (ADHD). In fact, considerable overlap exists between learning disabilities and ADHD. Further, roughly 50 to 70 percent of youth with learning disabilities or emotional disturbance have ADD (Rutherford, Griller-Clark, & Anderson, 2001).

In addition to the inconsistencies in defining disabilities, there are inconsistencies in the legal age for differentiating delinquent and adult criminal behavior. The lack of standard procedures for defining individuals with disabilities in juvenile and adult corrections, policies that place security above education, and the overall lack of reliable prevalence research in juvenile correction special education contribute to the discrepancies in prevalence estimates.

OFFENDERS WITH LEARNING DISABILITIES

Learning disabilities are difficult to define, and there is no single all-encompassing definition of the term (see Special Insert 6.1). Learning disabilities constitute a set of problems that result from difficulties in the way that information is received and processed by the brain. Learning disabilities are usually associated with neurological disorders, such as physical disorders of the brain or nervous system. Learning-disabled persons are almost always born with their disabilities, although most of these disabilities do not become obvious until the individual reaches school age and has to learn to read, write, or compute. Learning disabilities tend to be permanent conditions. However, individuals can develop strategies that allow them to compensate and work around the disability.

The distinction between mental retardation and specific learning disabilities should be noted. Mental retardation is the result of an overall intellectual slowness; learning disabilities are a result of an impediment that causes learning problems despite normal intelligence. Learning disabilities are suspected when a person with an IQ in the normal-or-above range functions two or more grade levels below the norm for that person's age and social environment.

Since learning disabilities cover such a broad array of handicaps, the characteristics are varied. It should be noted that learning disabilities are caused more from the inability to process types of information correctly than from impaired intellectual functioning (as with mental retardation). The following characteristics are among those most frequently encountered with the learning disabled:

1. Hyperactivity
2. Perceptual motor impairment
3. Lack of emotional control
4. Poor general coordination

5. Disorders in attention
6. Impulsivity
7. Poor memory
8. Difficulty in specific areas of reading, writing, spelling, or arithmetic
9. Other neurological symptoms

Special Insert 6.1. Types of Learning Disabilities

According to the *DSM-IV-TR*, learning disorders are diagnosed when the individual's achievement on individually administered, standardized tests in reading, mathematics, or written expression is substantially below that expected for age, schooling, and level of intelligence.

Estimates of the prevalence of learning disorders range from 2 to 10 percent, depending on the nature of ascertainment and the definitions applied. Approximately 5 percent of students in public schools in the United States are identified as having a learning disorder. It should be noted that these disorders should be differentiated from normal variations in academic attainment and from scholastic difficulties due to a lack of opportunity, poor teaching, cultural factors, or impaired vision and/or hearing. The following are some of the more common categories of learning disorders:

Reading disorder, consisting of the following:

1. Reading achievement, as measured by individually administered standardized test of reading accuracy or comprehension, is substantially below that expected given the person's chronological age, measured intelligence, and age-appropriate education.
2. The disturbance in criterion 1 significantly interferes with academic achievement or activities of daily living that require reading skills.
3. If a sensory deficit is present, the reading difficulties are in excess of those usually associated with it.

Mathematics disorder, consisting of the following:

1. Mathematical ability, as measured by individually administered standardized tests, is substantially below that expected given the person's chronological age, measured intelligence, and age-appropriate education.
2. The disturbance in criterion 1 significantly interferes with academic achievement or activities of daily living that require mathematical ability.
3. If a sensory deficit is present, the difficulties in mathematical ability are in excess of those usually associated with it.

Disorder of written expression, consisting of the following:

1. Writing skills, as measured by individually administered standardized test, are substantially below those expected given the person's chronological age, measured intelligence, and age-appropriate education.

2. The disturbance in criterion 1 significantly interferes with academic achievement or activities of daily living that require the composition of written texts.
3. If a sensory deficit is present, the difficulties in writing skills are in excess of those usually associated with it.

Motor skills disorder, consisting of the following:

1. Performance in daily activities that require motor coordination is substantially below that expected given the person's chronological age and measured intelligence. This may be manifested by marked delays in achieving motor milestones.
2. The disturbance in criterion 1 significantly interferes with academic achievement or activities of daily living.
3. The disturbance is not due to a general medical condition and does not meet the criteria for a pervasive developmental disorder.
4. If mental retardation is present, the motor difficulties are in excess of those usually associated with it.

As stated in the section titled "Background of Educational Disabilities in the Justice System," there is substantial overlap between the learning disorders noted here and ADD and ADHD. Although ADD and ADHD are not considered learning disorders, the tendency for ADD and ADHD to be comorbid with learning disorders is the justification for including them in this insert as well. These two disorders are described next:

A. Either (1) or (2):

Indicates Inattention

1. Six or more of the following symptoms of inattention that have persisted for at least six months to a degree that is maladaptive and inconsistent with developmental level:
   a. Often fails to give close attention to details or makes careless mistakes in schoolwork, work, or other activities
   b. Often has difficulty sustaining attention in tasks or play activities
   c. Often does not seem to listen when spoken to directly
   d. Often does not follow through on instructions and fails to finish school work, chores, or duties in the workplace (not because of opposition or lack of understanding)
   e. Often has difficulty organizing tasks and activities
   f. Often avoids, dislikes, or is reluctant to engage in tasks that require sustained mental effort
   g. Often loses things necessary for tasks or activities
   h. Is often easily distracted by extraneous stimuli
   i. Is often forgetful in daily activities

(continued)

Indicates Hyperactivity

2. Six or more of the following symptoms of hyperactivity-impulsivity that have persisted for at least six months to a degree that is maladaptive and inconsistent with developmental level:
    a. Often fidgets with hands or feet or squirms in seat
    b. Often leaves seat in classroom or in other situations in which remaining seated is expected
    c. Often runs about or climbs excessively in situations in which it is inappropriate
    d. Often has difficulty playing or engaging in leisure activities quietly
    e. Is often "on the go" or often acts as if "driven by a motor"
    f. Often talks excessively

Indicates Impulsivity

    g. Often blurts out answers before questions have been completed
    h. Often has difficulty awaiting turn
    i. Often interrupts or intrudes on others

B. Some hyperactive-impulsive or inattentive symptoms that caused impairment were present before age seven years.

C. Some impairment from the symptoms is present in two or more settings.

D. There must be clear evidence of clinically significant impairment in social, academic, or occupational functioning.

E. The symptoms are not the product of some other more appropriate disorder and are not only present when possessing some other simultaneously occurring disorder.

LINKS BETWEEN MENTAL RETARDATION, LEARNING DISABILITIES, AND DELINQUENCY

It has been stated that learning disabilities lead to school failure and that this school failure results in a negative self-image, in turn producing the likelihood of school dropout and delinquency. This line of thought naturally presupposes that school suspension and dropout necessarily increase the likelihood of delinquent behavior. The negative labeling associated with being a "school dropout" may encourage the student to associate with other students who are not adept at school. This does make sense, as such youth are not as likely to associate with children who actively participate in school and school-associated activities simply because these children will not be in proximity of one another. This is known as "school failure theory" because it is thought that failing at school leads to the negative self-image that results in delinquent behavior.

It has also been suggested that learning-disabled children possess certain cognitive and personality characteristics that predispose them to delinquent (and future criminal) behavior. This contention holds that disabilities are frequently associated with numerous problematic personality characteristics. These characteristics include such behaviors as an inability to anticipate the consequences of one's behavior, lack of impulse control, poor perception of social cues, and tendencies toward aggressive behavior (Murray, 1976; Rutherford et al., 2001). This is known as "susceptibility theory" because these youth are more susceptible to delinquent behavior.

Another notion regarding the link between learning disabilities and delinquency proposes that differential treatment occurs between non–learning-disabled and learning-disabled delinquent youth. According to this notion, teachers, social workers, and other juvenile justice officials treat these youth differently (and unfairly), increasing the likelihood of arrest and adjudication of learning-disabled youth. The differential arrests are purported to occur because learning-disabled youth are more likely to be apprehended by the police because they lack the abilities to plan strategies, avoid detention, interact appropriately in encounters with the police, or comprehend the justice system process (Rutherford et al., 2001).

BEHIND BARS: MENTALLY RETARDED AND LEARNING-DISABLED OFFENDERS IN JAIL AND PRISON

Institutional treatment is necessary if the offense is serious; the offender is deemed to pose a significant danger to the public; there is general need for care, training, supervision, or control that cannot be properly provided in the community; an in-depth assessment is required; and persistent multiple offenders have proven unresponsive to other treatment approaches (Day & Berney, 2001).

The total number of people with mental retardation in prisons and residential programs (26,500 to 32,500) underestimates the extent of the problem since the number of those who are on probation, in local jails, or placed in programs for people with mental illness remains unknown. While those in the criminal justice system constitute a small portion of all people with this disability, the number is significant enough to warrant the attention and concern of self-advocates, parents, criminal justice personnel, and policymakers. Standardized procedures that gather data nationwide are necessary before a more accurate number of people with mental retardation involved in the criminal justice system can be determined (Noble & Conley, 1992).

Treatment programs for mentally retarded offenders were initially developed within the institution, while most interventions for the learning disabled were often developed in primary and secondary educational systems. The programs for the most profoundly disabled and for those with mental retardation usually make up a comprehensive package of personal, occupational, and social skills training (Day & Berney, 2001). These programs are often based on a **token economy** of rewards aiming to link behavior with its consequences by the systematic issuance of tokens or points contingent on behavior that is deemed appropriate and desirable by institutional staff. In most programs, inappropriate behavior is punished with the corresponding loss of a set number of tokens. If offenders engage in violent behavior, they will typically suffer the loss of tokens and will also be placed in some form of solitary confinement. Privileges that the inmates may seek are "purchased" with their accumulated tokens for good behavior.

With mentally retarded inmates, token economy schemes are effective frameworks for the general operation of the institution and when facilitating individual counseling about problem behavior. Such schemes are able to operate with a high degree of structure because the whole group is subject to the same living and working environment and they provide an excellent basis for social learning. Institutional programs that use this form of treatment may be somewhat uniform in their approach, but there have been examples of programs that also allow for individualized treatment plans for offenders.

For the mentally retarded offender, learning occupational skills and/or a trade can be critical to successful integration into society. The ability to provide a productive contribution can be an excellent esteem builder for these types of offenders. This is important to mention because, as stated previously, these offenders often engage in their aberrant behaviors because of a desire to be accepted by others. Their naive trust and their desire to please others for acceptance allows them to be exploited through trickery and motivation. Programs that instill a sense of self-efficacy, particularly through concrete "skill-building" activities, are likely to address many of these concerns. One such program is discussed in Special Insert 6.2.

Pretrial centers and jails are designed to confine juvenile and adult offenders who have been arrested and are awaiting preliminary or dispositional court hearings. This confinement can seriously interfere with the continuity of educational programming for learning-disabled offenders who are adjudicated for indefinite periods of time in these facilities.

Rutherford et al. (2001) note that although few jails offer educational programs, most detention centers provide some level of school programming for youthful detainees. But because the placement and length of stay for delinquent youth in detention centers are determined by juvenile courts rather than by educators, appropriate, comprehensive educational services seldom are provided. This is particularly difficult given the high level of student rotation within any detention facility.

For the learning-disabled offender in adult correctional institutions, some general education classrooms may exist, but special educational programming is still in the developmental phases in many respects. As Rutherford et al. (2001) note, adult correctional institutions usually are overcrowded, and the number of youthful offenders is rising. Although youthful offenders make up approximately 20 to 30 percent of the population of adult correctional facilities, there has been a reported reluctance on the part of many correctional administrators to embrace the special educational services available to youth (Rutherford et al., 2001).

To demonstrate the impact of learning disabilities on the offender population, consider the following points by Haigler, Harlow, O'Connor, and Campbell (2004):

- Thirty-six percent of prisoners reported having at least one disability, compared with 26 percent of the household population. Significantly more inmates than

Special Insert 6.2. Mentally Retarded Reintegration

BURGAW—Mentally retarded inmates at Pender Correctional Institution are learning landscaping, horticulture, commercial sewing and woodworking skills in a six-month training program.

"The inmates adjust well," said Prison Psychologist Russell Smith. "A full performance appraisal is completed for each inmate. Those who meet the program's objectives and display good behavior graduate. Those who don't remain in the program."

Designed to teach basic work and social skills, the training program runs five days a week. It started in 1993. Each of the 66 inmates in the program is assigned two of the skill activities by prison staff. Inmates working in the landscape and design learn to measure lawn areas and to decide where to place plants or trees. They get experience in clearing an area, grading, filling, leveling and tilling. Inmates learn to take care of trees and install lawn borders of wood, stone, brick or plastic. Inmates can also master hand planting and laying walkways or patios.

At the prison's greenhouse, inmates learn about watering, lighting, fertilizer, seed germination, transplanting, pruning and recognizing different pests.

"Staff members are actually therapists in work situations," said Smith. "Therapeutic interaction is what this program is all about. Staff teach inmates about life and living during routine work activities by responding to the inmate's behavior and conversations. We try to build on the positive."

"This is clearly a strong, worthwhile program," said Correction Secretary Franklin Freeman. "The training program provides mentally retarded inmates with important social and work skills that could keep them from returning to prison after their release."

Source: Retrieved from http://www.doc.state.nc.us/NEWS/1996/96news/Pender.htm.

householders reported having a learning disability or a mental or emotional condition. The proficiencies of inmates with a learning disability are significantly lower than those of inmates reporting most other disabilities and are also lower than those of householders reporting a learning disability.

- The racial/ethnic composition and educational attainment of the prison population differ from those of the household population. About 65 percent of prisoners are minorities versus 24 percent of the household population. About 51 percent of prisoners have completed at least high school or its equivalent, compared with 76 percent of the household population. These differences in demographic composition help explain the lower average performance of inmates as compared with householders.
- Inmates do not appear to have as high an opinion of their reading, writing, and arithmetic skills as do householders. Slightly over half the inmates reported that they read or write English very well compared with 71 and 64 percent of householders who said they read or write English very well. Forty percent of inmates, compared with 53 percent of householders, said they can do arithmetic

very well. The proficiencies of inmates who said they read, write, or do arithmetic very well or well are lower than those of their counterparts in the household population.

COMMUNITY SUPERVISION: MENTALLY RETARDED AND LEARNING-DISABLED OFFENDERS IN THE COMMUNITY

Most offenders with mental retardation can be managed in the community supported by social, probation, and specialist psychiatric services. Many continue to live with their families while attending local programs, but some require an out-of-home placement because, as noted in Special Insert 6.3, these offenders lack appropriate reasoning and judgment and therefore require more structure and support.

The same principles of treatment and care apply in the community corrections setting as in the institution system. The key to success often has more to do with effective interagency coordination within the community. Obviously, probation personnel and any peripheral treatment personnel must be well versed in the needs of these types of offenders. One successful community-based program is the Special Offenders Service in Lancaster County, Pennsylvania (Day & Berney, 2001). This program provides services to both juvenile and adult offenders suffering from mental retardation. It emphasizes personal responsibility and accountability, increasing self-esteem, and improving social competence. The team sees clients, at first on a daily basis and then on a weekly basis, for counseling services and other forms of support. This program is intensive and includes work orientation, social skills training, time management, and, where appropriate, involvement of the family. This program is considered highly successful since it has a recidivism rate of only 5 percent as compared with the national average of 60 percent with this type of offender (Day & Berney, 2001).

Special Insert 6.3. The Mentally Retarded and Capital Punishment

In June 2002, the U.S. Supreme Court abolished the execution of mentally retarded offenders in the landmark case of *Atkins v. Virginia* (536 U.S. 304). The Court passed its ruling with a 6 to 3 vote and used the fact that 18 out of 38 death penalty states specifically banned the practice of executing the mentally retarded offender. Such punishment was held to be "cruel and unusual" in violation of the Eighth Amendment. Justice Stevens wrote in a majority opinion that "because of their disabilities in areas of reasoning, judgment and control of their impulses . . . they do not act with the level of moral culpability that characterizes the most serious adult criminal conduct." From this ruling, it has since been determined that punishment objectives grounded in deterrence and obtaining retribution are not legally valid when the offender is of an intelligence level that is so far below average as to be considered mentally retarded Generally, this is typically an offender who has an IQ of 70 or less (*DSM-IV-TR*).

GENERAL TREATMENT CONSIDERATIONS FOR MENTALLY RETARDED AND LEARNING-DISABLED OFFENDERS

The Americans with Disabilities Act

The Americans with Disabilities Act (ADA) of 1990 is an act that prevents government agencies and/or employees from discriminating against persons with disabilities. The ADA requires that all public agencies (i.e., jails, prisons, community corrections agencies, and other organizations) with 50 or more employees conduct a self-evaluation of their programs, services, and activities to ensure that they are fully accessible, that barriers are removed in a timely manner, and that the institution's policies and procedures do not result in discriminatory behavior, whether intended or accidental. This act provides a basis for the legal obligations that correctional agencies may have to mentally retarded and learning-disabled offenders in their custody.

DEVELOPING AND IMPLEMENTING A SPECIAL EDUCATION PROGRAM

From the discussion so far, it is clear that offenders with learning disabilities and/or mental retardation need specialized services similar to individuals who are not offenders but possess similar deficits. This is imperative if these offenders are to be effectively absorbed into the community without further recidivism and financial burden to the criminal justice system and the individual taxpayer.

With this in mind, it should be noted that the special education program in a prison or community supervision system must begin with the offender's entry into the system. According to Coffey, Procopiow, and Miller (1989), the process continues with the following:

1. Referral for screening of individuals suspected of having a learning disability
2. Evaluation of inmates suspected of being handicapped
3. Eligibility decision if special education placement is needed
4. Development of an individualized education program (IEP)
5. Implementing the IEP

Referral is when an offender is recommended for participation in a special education program and usually occurs during the intake process or shortly after that (Coffey et al., 1989). The referral is made to the multidisciplinary team that meets to determine whether an inmate needs a special education program. Screening for a handicapping condition is accomplished by collecting the following information:

1. Every attempt should be made to obtain previous **education and family history** records. When educational records are obtained, they may provide information such as history of dropout, truancy, or deficiencies in intellectual development (Coffey et al., 1989).

2. In **preintake identification**, during pretrial, detention, or sentencing, law enforcement personnel might observe that the offender has characteristics of retardation, learning disabilities, or other handicapping conditions. Written documentation of observed poor motor abilities, expressive language problems, speech difficulties, unusual emotional behaviors, or difficulty following instructions can assist in identifying these offenders. The probation officer's presentence investigation report may be especially useful in this area (Coffey et al., 1989).
3. An interview should be conducted with the offender to obtain a personal account of school attendance, educational level obtained, difficulties in school, and any special services received in school that may indicate previous placement in special education. Information as to medical problems, previous counseling, or other social services received can be useful in screening for learning handicaps. Such information, coupled with the interviewer's professional observations, should be written down and retained in the inmate's **interview file** (Coffey et al., 1989).
4. **Hearing, vision, and medical screening** should be conducted. It is best to have this initial screening done in the diagnostic and classification process so that by the time the individual is assigned to a specific facility, education staff will be aware of a potentially handicapping condition (Coffey et al., 1989).

Evaluation is the process by which the agency will determine suitability of an offender to a special education program (Coffey et al., 1989). All offenders must be given written consent to be evaluated before any evaluation is conducted prior to their placement in a special education program. An evaluation must comply with two important stipulations that ensure protection from discrimination. First, evaluation procedures must not be racially or culturally discriminatory, and all materials and procedures should be provided in the individual's native language or primary means of communication. Second, no one single test or any one single examiner is allowed to make the determination of special education eligibility unto themselves. Rather, a team of multidisciplinary individuals using several tests would be most appropriate. According to Coffey et al. (1989), examples of the types of tests that might be used include:

1. Psychological tests to measure general mental ability as well as specific areas of strengths and weaknesses
2. Educational tests to provide information about a person's skills and achievement levels in academic areas
3. Tests to assess auditory and visual perception and memory, motor skills, and vocational interest
4. Speech and language tests to evaluate articulation, auditory processing, and expressive and receptive language development
5. Behavioral or personality measurements to describe the individual's responses to himself or herself, others, and work responsibilities

Eligibility is determined from the evaluation data, including any information from previous educational records, observations of staff, and interviews with the offender to determine whether special education is needed (Coffey et al., 1989). If it is determined that the offender is in need of special educational services, the specific handicapping condition must be clearly articulated.

Development of the IEP is a process that is individualized to the objective and subjective needs of the offender, according to his or her specific area of deficit (Coffey et al., 1989). The process occurs with a group of professionals who will develop the IEP, which must include several components. A statement of the offender's present level of educational performance and a statement of annual goals, including short-term instructional objectives, must be included. A statement of the specific education and related services to be provided to the offender, along with an explanation of the offender's ability to participate in routine educational programs, should be included as well. Further, the projected dates of initiation of the service and the expected length of time that these educational services will be rendered should be clearly noted. Finally, appropriate objective criteria and evaluation procedures and schedules for determining whether the short-term objectives are being achieved must also be included.

Implementation of the IEP refers to the process by which educational services are specifically administered and includes aspects such as predictability, supportiveness, and feedback (Coffey et al., 1989). Predictability enables offenders to develop expectations and a sense of security from knowing what to expect. Routines for completing and grading work, consistency of response to offenders, recognition of achievement, and management of daily tasks should be established. Support is demonstrated through encouraging offenders to do their best and fostering an environment that emphasizes learning rather than punitive elements of being an offender. Feedback is given to the offender on progress academically as well as progress behaviorally. Indeed, the two aspects of integrating the offender with society can often be paired in the learning environment through various points of managing the offender's behavior in the classroom. The most effective feedback is prompt, to the point (yet respectful, not the "brutally honest" approach often used as a disguise for spiteful intentions), and sincere.

TREATMENT PERSONNEL AND PROGRAMS IN COMMUNITY CORRECTIONS

Treatment programs and the staff involved within them must be specifically suited for this population if the offender is to be integrated within the community. Coffey, Procopiow, and Miller (1989) note that the key components of a comprehensive community-based program include the following:

1. Appropriately trained and experienced staff
2. Specialist treatment programs

3. Specialist community-based services for assessment, treatment, aftercare, and continuing care, including support personnel and a range of residential and day facilities
4. Open inpatient assessment and treatment units with varying levels of community supervision (i.e., house arrest with family supervision, electronic monitoring, and so on) security for the more dangerous offenders
5. Inpatient assessment and treatment units with varying levels of security for the more dangerous offenders

TREATMENT ISSUES WITH THE MENTALLY RETARDED AND/OR LEARNING-DISABLED OFFENDER

Attempts should be made to diagnose mental retardation as early as possible. If discovered early enough, some cases of mental retardation and their progression can be arrested, slowed, or partially reversed. Obviously, this option would be available only to childhood and perhaps adolescent offenders. With adult offenders, it may be their commission of aggressive or violent offenses that has drawn the most attention from the public and the media. Rifkin (2000) states the following:

> Aggression, which is rarely a diagnostic symptom of most mental disorders as defined in the *DSM*, constitutes the most common symptom that brings mentally retarded individuals to psychiatric attention. We must also consider whether the aggressive symptoms represent psychopathology or a normal response to abnormal conditions. Many adults with mental retardation live under unpleasant circumstances. They have much less autonomy than other adults. Most have family members and/or caregivers constantly telling them what to do. They observe that non-retarded adults around them have many more privileges than they do. Their desire for physical intimacy is usually thwarted. To some extent, anger and frustration seem appropriate and normal. The patient's intellectual disability may make it difficult to express that frustration in non-aggressive ways, such as putting it into words, seeking out other companions, or moving to a different living situation or location. (p. 201)

It is for these reasons that these offenders are more vulnerable to abuse, especially within a correctional institution that holds other, nonimpaired inmates. These abusive interactions (whether at home or in the correctional institution) are another reason for anger among these offenders. Further, since they typically lack the ability to provide any coherent form of complaint (especially in grievance systems of correctional institutions), the sense of injustice can exacerbate their display of negative behaviors (Rifkin, 2000).

Sedating antipsychotics probably have been overused in mentally retarded children for behavioral control. Specific accompanying diagnoses, such as ADHD, seizures, and mood disorders, should be specifically addressed as well. It should be noted that those individuals with mild retardation often respond better than those with more serious forms of retardation. Two drugs—clomipramine and selective serotonin reuptake inhibitors—may be helpful in reducing anxious, obsessional, or self-injurious behavior (Maxmen & Ward, 2002). These medications are used in some correctional institutions when mentally retarded inmates become unmanageable. Rifkin (2000) notes that mentally retarded patients very often receive psychotropic drugs, perhaps at a higher rate than any other diagnostic group. One survey found a rate of use of 57 percent in institutions, 41 percent in community-based programs, and 22 percent in school-based settings (Baumeister, Todd, & Sevin, 1993). Since these patients receive close supervision, they have a high level of compliance. Most commonly, they receive antipsychotic medication for the symptoms of aggression. Further, Rifkin (2000) points out that because self-injurious behavior is a common symptom in mentally retarded patients, Naltrexone (ReVia) is sometimes used, and this drug shows a mixed picture of efficacy in anecdotal reports (Aman, 1993).

It should be pointed out that mental health clinicians are not necessarily qualified to address the needs of learning-disabled offenders. The disorders are complex and often fall better under the forte of an educational specialist. This is reflected in the descriptors pertaining to each learning disability. However, mental health clinicians are often useful in handling issues such as depression, low self-esteem, dysfunctional socialization, substance abuse, or behavioral shaping. These issues often are experienced with offenders who have learning disabilities. When addressing these corollary mental health issues, Reiss, Goldberg, and Ryan (1993) recommend the following psychotherapeutic treatment strategies:

- Psychopharmacology—There are many disorders that can be controlled or alleviated with medication. However, there has been a tendency in the past to overmedicate people with mental retardation and not to carefully monitor the behavioral effects of medications. Even when used appropriately, medications are only part of an effective total treatment program.
- Counseling/psychotherapy—People with mild mental retardation can benefit from counseling. Many individuals cope better when another person listens to their problems and provides social support and understanding.
- Cognitive therapy—This treatment teaches people with mild mental retardation to recognize the situations in which they get into trouble and to develop alternative behavior and solutions to their problems. Although widely used with the general population, cognitive therapy has been adapted only recently for use with people with mental retardation (Benson, 1992).
- Behavior management—This approach is widely used with people with mental retardation, especially to control behavior problems. The approach often leads to significant behavioral improvements, at least during the time period when the treatment is in effect. Many advocates have called for the complete elimination of aversive (punishment) behavior management techniques and the reliance instead on positive behavioral techniques.
- Social skills training—This is a cost-effective, time-limited approach that often produces noticeable improvements in quality of life and interpersonal behavior.

Individuals are gradually taught effective social interactions and appropriate social behavior.

- Activity, music, and art therapy—These are relatively cost-effective services that help build positive experiences and self-confidence. Some individuals with mental retardation have considerable artistic skills. Occupational and physical therapy can be helpful for some individuals.

As noted earlier, the comorbid occurrence of ADD or ADHD necessitates that the clinician address this potential issue in any treatment program with these types of offenders. If ADD or ADHD occurs often in conjunction with other conditions, such as IQ impairments, mental retardation, learning disabilities, speech and language deficits, or psychiatric deficits, referrals should be made as soon as other possible diagnoses are suspected. Restlessness can also be caused by chronically used medications, including obviously stimulating medications (e.g., antiasthmatics). Medication, individual tutoring, family counseling, behavior therapy, and educational training are all critical to mentally retarded and learning-disabled offenders, particularly those with ADD or ADHD.

FAMILIES, SUPPORT SYSTEMS, AND OTHER CAREGIVERS

Families and caregivers often need help understanding and adjusting to the situation as well as advice on handling a whole range of other practical problems. Their support and cooperation can be critical to the success of treatment. Family therapy, whether conjoint or separate, can be effective in many cases. Of course, this presumes that the family system itself is fairly functional. In those cases where the family is grossly dysfunctional, the emphasis might have to be on insulating the offender against the adverse influences of his or her family. An important element of many residential programs is the removal of the person from the exploitative relationships they have had with the family and/or peer group.

CONCLUSION

The mentally retarded offender is one who has been largely misportrayed in the public media. There are definitely cases in which the mentally retarded have committed terrible crimes, but these are isolated and tend to receive a vastly disproportionate amount of media attention compared to other violent crimes. For the most part, the mentally retarded should be considered treatable and should also be given some form of intervention within the community since they are so susceptible to victimization within a prison facility. Placement and intervention should be conducted by qualified professionals, but this is often lacking.

Offenders with learning disabilities are fairly common both within the institutional and community-based offending population. Because of their poor ability to read, complete mathematics, and so on, these offenders have a diminished likelihood of integrating into society and are therefore more likely to recidivate. These offenders should be given IEPs and must be provided services that remedy the deficiency if they are to be expected to maintain adequate employment. As is widely known, the ability to obtain and maintain employment is a strong correlate with an offender's successful and permanent reintegration. Unless this is fully realized, society will continue to pay for prison bed space when such space is not even needed.

KEY TERMS

Mental retardation
Attention deficit disorder
Attention-deficit/hyperactivity disorder
Learning disabilities
Reading disorder
Mathematics disorder
Disorder of written expression
Motor skills disorder
Token economy
Referral
Education and family history
Preintake identification
Interview files
Hearing, vision, and medical screening
Evaluation
Eligibility
Development of the IEP
Implementation of the IEP

REFERENCES

Aman, M. G. (1993). Efficacy of psychotropic drugs for reducing self-injurious behavior in the developmental disabilities. *Annals of Clinical Psychiatry, 5*(3), 171–188.

American Psychiatric Association. (2000). *Diagnostic and statistical manual of mental disorders* (4th ed., text revision). Arlington, VA: Author.

Baumeister, A. A., Todd, M. E., & Sevin, J. (1993). Efficacy and specificity of pharmacological therapies for behavioral disorders in persons with mental retardation. *Clinical Neuropharmacology, 16*(4), 271–294.

Benson, B. A. (1992). *Teaching anger management to persons with mental retardation*. Worthington, OH: IDS Publications.

Coffey, O. D., Procopiow, N., & Miller, N. (1989). *Programming for mentally retarded and learning disabled inmates: A guide for correctional administrators*. Washington, DC: National Institute of Corrections.

Day, K. (1990). Mental retardation: Clinical aspects and management. In R. Bluglass & P. Bowden (Eds.), *Principles and practice of forensic psychiatry* (pp. 399–418). Edinburgh: Churchill Livingstone.

Day, K., & Berney, T. (2000). Treatment and care for offenders with mental retardation. In J. B. Ashford, B. D. Sales, & W. H. Reid (Eds.), *Treating adult and juvenile offenders with special needs* (pp. 131–170). Washington, DC: American Psychological Association.

Haigler, K. O., Harlow, C., O'Connor, P., & Campbell, A. (2004). *Executive summary of literacy behind prison walls: Profiles of the prison population from the national adult literacy survey*. Washington, DC: National Center for Education Statistics. Retrieved from: http://nces.ed.gov/naal/resources/execsummprison.asp

Maxmen, J. S., & Ward, N. G. (1995). *Essential psychopathology and its treatment*. New York: Norton.

Murray, C. (1976). *The link between learning disabilities and juvenile delinquents: Current theory and knowledge* (Publication No. 241-093-2134). Washington, DC: U.S. Government Printing Office.

Noble, J., & Conley, R. (1992). Toward an epidemiology of relevant attributes. In R. W. Conley, R. Luckasson, & G. N. Bouthilet (Eds.), *The criminal justice system and mental retardation* (pp. 17–53). Baltimore: Paul H. Brookes.

Reiss, S., Goldberg, B., & Ryan, R. (1993). *Mental illness in persons with mental retardation.* Retrieved from htttp://www.thearc.org/faqs/mimrqa.html

Rifkin, A. (2000). Diagnosing and treating mentally retarded adults. *Psychiatric Times, 17*(12). Retrieved from http://www.psychiatrictimes.com/p001225.html

Rutherford, R. B., Griller-Clark, H. M., & Anderson, C. W. (2001). Treating offenders with educational disabilities. In J. B. Ashford, B. D. Sales, & W. H. Reid (Eds.), *Treating adult and juvenile offenders with special needs* (pp. 221–246). Washington, DC: American Psychological Association.

LEARNING CHECK

1. What are the key components of a comprehensive community-based treatment program?
   a. Inpatient assessment and treatment units with varying levels of security for the more dangerous offenders
   b. Specialist treatment programs
   c. Appropriately trained and experienced staff
   d. All of the above
   e. None of the above

2. What approach is widely used with people with mental retardation, especially to control behavior problems?
   a. Social skills training
   b. Cognitive therapy
   c. Activity therapy
   d. Behavior management
   e. None of the above

3. Which of the following are examples of learning disabilities?
   a. Reading disorder
   b. Mathematics disorder
   c. Motor skills disorder
   d. All of the above
   e. None of the above

4. The offender population tends to have a higher proportion of learning-disabled members than that found in the broader population.
   a. True
   b. False

5. Mentally retarded offenders are often highly susceptible to victimization from other inmates.
   a. True
   b. False

6. The special education program in a prison or community supervision system must begin with the offender's entry into the system. What should such a program include?
   a. Evaluation of inmates suspected of being handicapped
   b. Development of the individualized education program
   c. Separate educational facilities from mainstream offenders
   d. Both a and b but not c
   e. Both b and c but not a
7. Mental health clinicians are not necessarily qualified to address the needs of learning-disabled offenders. Instead, these disorders are considered the forte of an educational specialist.
   a. True
   b. False
8. The vast majority of mentally retarded offenders have which of the following level/severity of retardation?
   a. Mild
   b. Moderate
   c. Severe
   d. Profound
   e. None of the above
9. Which of the following categories has an IQ range of 36 to 50?
   a. Mild
   b. Moderate
   c. Severe
   d. Profound
   e. None of the above
10. Which disorder tends to frequently be found among offenders with learning disabilities?
    a. Antisocial personality disorder
    b. Mental retardation
    c. ADD/ADHD
    d. Split personality
    e. Schizophrenia

ESSAY DISCUSSION QUESTIONS

1. Explain some of the dynamics that often lead to the mentally retarded acting out in aggressive or violent behavior. How does this compare with those occurrences in the media where the mentally retarded do commit heinously violent crimes?
2. If an offender has a learning disability, how is this likely to affect his or her ability to obtain a job in the community? Provide at least two specific examples. In

your opinion, if the offender is not able to obtain employment, how is this likely to affect his or her ability to reform in the community?

3. Provide your opinion as to whether those who are mentally retarded and are violent should be provided treatment or whether these offenders are even treatable. Remember that these offenders will ultimately return to society. Consider the concepts provided in Chapter 2 when you form your answer.

CHAPTER 7

EARLY CHILDHOOD OFFENDERS

PAULETTE CAPPEL AND ROB HANSER

Chapter Objectives

1. Understand the various aspects of childhood aggression.
2. Identify and discuss risk factors associated with childhood aggression and be familiar with the childhood diagnosis of conduct disorder.
3. Understand the dynamics involved with violence at school, including problems with bullying, classroom management, and the potential use of gun violence.
4. Understand the various aspects of childhood crimes of arson, including risk factors and typologies.
5. Know and discuss the types of sex crimes that are most commonly perpetrated by early childhood sex offenders.

INTRODUCTION

Recently, the media have generated substantial hype pertaining to childhood violence and criminality. Because of this sensationalism, it is no longer suitable to consider the "child" to be beyond culpability for his or her actions. In reaction to the media attention, children are being sentenced at younger ages for crimes that seem to be getting more serious. With this in mind, it is the focus of this chapter to provide an overview of some common theories and diagnoses associated with childhood violence and misbehavior. This chapter will likewise provide a few examples of some of the more common crimes that are encountered by early childhood offenders who are of the preteen and early teen age ranges. From this point, it is expected that the student will be better informed about early childhood crime and able to distinguish the myths from the facts of these sensationalized offenders.

In 1997, there were an estimated 253,000 children ages 12 years or younger who were arrested. This represents 9 percent of all juvenile arrests (University of Pittsburgh, 2002). At first glance, these numbers do not appear to be that dramatic. However, juvenile courts have seen a significant change in the characteristics of childhood delinquents and the crimes with which they are charged. For instance, in 1997, only 10 percent of the arrests of children were for status offenses, such as curfew violations, running away from home, or violating liquor laws (University of Pittsburgh, 2002). However, from 1988 to 1997, the arrests of children for violent crimes increased 45 percent. Drug abuse violations among childhood offenders also soared by 156 percent (University of Pittsburgh, 2002). Thus, preteen children who are delinquents are being charged with drug offenses, weapons violations, or violent crimes much more frequently than in years past. Further, the rate at which they are being charged for both serious and less serious charges continues to increase at rates that would be expected of children in this age range.

To further illustrate the seriousness of childhood delinquency, consider the 33 percent rise in juvenile court cases involving child offenders from 1988 to 1997. This gain has far exceeded the rate of *arrests* for childhood offenders (though arrest rates have increased as well), meaning that police have referred more children to court rather than handling these calls informally. It is thought that this is probably due to the increased seriousness of crimes committed by childhood offenders (University of Pittsburgh, 2002). From 1988 to 1997, cases that resulted in formal court-ordered probation for preteen childhood delinquents increased 73 percent, and residential placements rose 49 percent (Cohen, 1998). These early childhood delinquents are two to three times more likely to become serious, violent, and chronic offenders in adult life. Although difficult to precisely measure, the cost of a criminal career should include the effects of ruined lives, lost life course potential, and the dollars that are involved in the entire process. Indeed, it is estimated that a single criminal career spanning from childhood to adulthood costs society anywhere between $1.7 million and $2.3 million (Cohen, 1998).

CHILDHOOD AGGRESSION

Researchers of childhood aggression have come to a consensus on how these children perceive their own aggressive actions. Following an information-processing model, they have been able to identify the ways in which the information processing of aggressive children differs from more adaptive and less aggressive children. Indeed, Dodge (1991) breaks down the cognitive tasks of problem solving into the following stages: (1) encoding, (2) mental representation, (3) response access, (4) response evaluation and selection, and (5) enactment. Problems at each of these stages have been found in aggressive children, although not all these children have problems at each stage. Further, these children exhibit the following tendencies:

1. Often fail to encode all relevant environmental cues
2. Are biased to assign hostile intentions to their social partners
3. Generate fewer and less effective solutions for problematic situations
4. Pursue inappropriate social goals
5. Experience deficits in the enactment of many social behaviors
6. May display a degree of egocentrism in evaluating the social environment's response to their behavior

In terms of encoding relevant environmental cues, aggressive children have been found to attend more to hostile acts directed toward themselves. While this pattern may have arisen as an adaptive defensive reaction, it serves to increase the likelihood that the child will misidentify situations as hostile when they are not.

Dodge (1991) includes in the heading of "mental representation" a variety of functions, including attributions of causation and intent, social perspective taking, and moral reasoning with the meaning of an event on the child's sense of self-worth. Research has shown that aggressive children are more likely to assign hostile intent to another's actions than nonaggressive children. Because these children are more likely to perceive hostile intent, they are then predisposed to exhibit aggressive behavior.

It is interesting to note that aggressive children are more likely to interpret hostile intentions only when they are directly involved in an incident rather than when they are simply observing an incident. Thus, hostile attribution is associated more with reactive aggression than proactive aggression (Dodge, 1991). This is often described as "intention-cue detection deficit," which is simply a term for the child's ability to accurately understand and perceive the correct intent of a person's behavior. This intention-cue detection deficit has been shown to exist among both intelligent and lower-IQ children; however, depressed children seem to have an even more serious deficit in this ability but also tend to experience more "self-blame" for their hostile actions rather than blame directed at another person (Dodge, 1991).

Response access includes the ability of the child to generate effective and adaptive responses to different situations. Aggressive children tend to generate more atypical responses to difficult situations and to be more inflexible in their ability to generate alternative responses. The research shows this to be resoundingly true with these children. For example, in response to friendship or peer group acceptance dilemmas, aggressive children are more likely to generate responses that are "verbally coercive, physically aggressive, or bizarrely irrelevant to the task" (Dodge, 1991, p. 568).

Aggressive children and adolescents have been found to consider a smaller range of potential intentions from others, to value aggressive behavioral responses more than other children, and to underestimate the level of disapproval that their actions will generate. They tend to expect more positive outcomes from aggressive behavior than nonaggressive children. Whereas reactive anger was found to be associated more with the mental ability to process overtaxing stressors, proactive (or instrumental aggressive) behavior was found to correlate more with the characteristics of the aggressive individual's repertoires in handling problem scenarios. Although aggressive children engage in behaviors that are deviant, it is not clear if these result purely from a deficit in knowledge or if the behaviors reflect some other deficit (Huesmann, 1988).

Many of these children possess what are referred to as "aggressive scripts" that are learned in early childhood. The child may learn these scripts from direct experience or from witnessing the aggressive behaviors of others. Cues related to the event are then likely to elicit the previously learned scripts for aggressive behaviors. According to Huesmann (1988), the likelihood that a child will access a script for specific aggressive behaviors is dependent on the relevant cues that are present in the environment at the time of recall. In theory, the most important cues are those from the environment that are identical with those present when the script was originally encoded in memory (Huesmann, 1988). The child may not even be consciously aware of the script or that the cues are necessarily generating the scripted behavior. Rather, the child may simply react, almost instinctively, to the scenario presented because of the power of conditioning between prior cues and scripted reactions. Dodge (1991) also notes that children who have aggressive constructs in thinking tend to get into more fights in school than those who do not have such thought constructs.

When determining aggressive behavior in children, Lochman and Lenhart (1993) note that a definition of aggression should include the following:

1. Causing or threatening to cause physical harm to others
2. Exhibiting actions directed toward others or toward objects with some intent to injure or destroy

Aggression is not a psychiatric diagnosis in and of itself but is frequently associated with the behavioral disorders first diagnosed in childhood and adolescence. These disorders are characterized by socially unacceptable or potentially harmful behaviors. These behaviors include hyperactivity, impulsivity, inattention, oppositional-defiance, deceitfulness, disruptiveness, and violation of societal norms or rules (Fauman, 1994).

THEORETICAL CAUSES OF AGGRESSION

There are a number of factors that can explain the development of aggression. These are discussed in the following sections.

PARENTING STYLES

Two types or styles of parenting have been associated with behavior problems and child/adolescent aggressiveness. **Authoritarian parenting** is characterized as unrealistic and highly demanding. Frequently, parents of this style have little knowledge of childhood developmental stages and often make demands that are beyond children at a given age range. Parents of this style may become physically or verbally abusive when the child does not respond adequately to the parent's demands. **Permissive parenting** is characterized as nonresponsive to a child's needs. Parents of this style may be neglectful not only of the child's basic physical needs but also of his or her emotional needs. In both styles of parenting, a lack of warm and supportive responsiveness is associated with the development of aggressiveness (Baumrind, 1997).

While parents are not likely to have just one style of parenting that they never deviate from, they do tend to have typical habits or tendencies when raising children. (For more detail, see Table 7.1.) Other than parenting styles, additional parental

Table 7.1. Four Styles of Parenting and Their Effects on Children

Parental Style	Method of Parenting	Typical Effect on Child
Indulgent parents (also referred to as permissive or nondirective)	Generally, these parents "are more responsive than they are demanding. They are nontraditional and lenient, do not require mature behavior, allow considerable self-regulation, and avoid confrontation" (Baumrind, 1991, p. 62).	Children and adolescents from indulgent homes (high in responsiveness and low in behavioral demand) are more likely to be involved in problem behavior and perform less well in school, but they have higher self-esteem, better social skills, and lower levels of depression (Baumrind, 1991; Weiss & Scwarz, 1996).
Authoritarian parents	These parents are highly demanding and directive but not responsive. "They are obedience- and status-oriented, and expect their orders to be obeyed without explanation" (Baumrind, 1991, p. 62).	Children and adolescents from authoritarian families (high in behavioral demand but low in responsiveness) tend to perform moderately well in school and free of problem behavior, but they have poorer social skills, lower self-esteem, and higher levels of depression (Baumrind, 1991; Weiss & Scwarz, 1996).
Authoritative parents	These parents are both demanding and responsive. "They monitor and impart clear standards for their children's conduct. They are assertive, but not intrusive and restrictive. Their disciplinary methods are supportive, rather than punitive. They want their children to be assertive as well as socially responsible, and self-regulated as well as cooperative" (Baumrind, 1991, p. 62).	Children and adolescents whose parents are authoritative rate themselves and are rated by objective measures as more socially and instrumentally competent than those whose parents are nonauthoritative (Baumrind, 1991; Weiss & Scwarz, 1996).

(continued)

Table 7.1 (Continued)

Parental Style	Method of Parenting	Typical Effect on Child
Uninvolved parents	These parents are low in both responsiveness and demandingness. In extreme cases, this parenting style might encompass both rejecting/neglecting and neglectful parents, although most parents of this type fall within the normal range (Baumrind, 1991).	Children and adolescents whose parents are uninvolved perform most poorly in all domains (Baumrind, 1991; Weiss & Scwarz, 1996).

factors associated with child/adolescent aggression include poor problem-solving abilities, marital discord, parental depression or other emotional disturbance, lack of follow-through, and delay between child misbehavior and appropriate discipline (Patterson, Capaldi, & Bank, 1991). Baumrind (1997) cited a lack of parental responsiveness and parent–child communication as a more important factor in the development of childhood aggression than whether physical punishment is used.

BIOLOGY AND GENETICS

Adoption studies have shown that children with biological fathers who were criminals were at higher risk of criminal behavior (Brennan, Mednick, & Kandel, 1991). Violent criminality among boys is more likely if one parent has been convicted and the other diagnosed and treated for antisocial personality disorder (Moffit, 1993). Moffitt (1993) and Golden (1996) suggested a "neuropsychological correlation" with aggression. Neuropsy deficits as a result of heredity and perinatal complications may predispose a child to problems with temperament, cognitive deficits, and motor delays that leave the child susceptible to later aggressive behavior. Moreover, children with neuropsychological deficits have been shown to experience a lack of fear of punishment and thus do not learn to control aggressive behavior (Brennan et al., 1991).

FAMILY AND SOCIAL ENVIRONMENT

Moffitt (1993) explained why some children develop life course–persistent antisocial behavior. Children with neuropsychological and temperament difficulties often live in negative environments (e.g., parental neglect or abuse) where parents offer limited socially appropriate role modeling. Thus, the child becomes "ensnared" in lifelong, antisocial behaviors. Children who have both neuropsychological deficits and negative social environmental factors have been shown to score four times higher on aggression scales (Moffitt, 1993). In a related study of juvenile delinquency, children with a history of family violence in conjunction with neurological problems were predicted to be at greater risk of arrest for violent crimes (Lewis et al., 1989).

BELIEFS, PERCEPTIONS, AND RESPONSES

Many aggressive children are suspicious of the motivations of others and see hostile intent in them. These children typically exhibit difficulty with problem solving and overlook nonviolent solutions to conflict. They frequently respond to conflict impulsively with aggression, believing that this solution will work best. This lack of impulse control in aggressive children may prevent them from conceptualizing and implementing alternative solutions to conflicts.

RISK FACTORS ASSOCIATED WITH CHILDHOOD AGGRESSION

The first five years of life are the most important regarding risk factors for child delinquency. These early years are closely dependent on a child's individual characteristics and the family dynamics that exist. Risk factors at home include antisocial parents, a mother suffering from depression, family poverty, marital strife, a large family, a history of family violence, and parents who abuse drugs or alcohol, discipline harshly and erratically, and rely on poor parenting practices.

In these cases, children who have persistent adjustment problems may present with a childhood disorder known as **conduct disorder**. This diagnosis can be found in the *Diagnostic and Statistical Manual of Mental Disorders* (4th ed., text revision) (*DSM-IV-TR*), published by the American Psychiatric Association (2000). Certain characteristics of a child, such as a difficult temperament as an infant and depressed moods as a child, are risk factors for conduct disorder and/or future delinquency. If the child has been a victim of violence or has been exposed to a steady dose of violence on television, in movies, and/or in video games, the child may be at increased risk of developing conduct disorder. Some factors stand out more than others, but aggression seems to be the best predictor of conduct disorder. Thus, many factors can contribute to a child's developing conduct disorder, including brain damage or trauma, child abuse, genetic vulnerability, school failure, or other traumatic life experiences.

Essentially, conduct disorder is a complex group of behavioral and emotional problems that are experienced by some children. Children and adolescents with this disorder have great difficulty following rules and behaving in a socially acceptable way. They are often viewed by other children, adults, and social agencies as "bad" or delinquent rather than disordered. According to the *DSM-IV-TR*, children with conduct disorder may exhibit a repetitive and persistent pattern of behavior in which the basic rights of others are violated. This is often manifested by the presence of three or more of the following criteria (all taken from the *DSM-IV-TR*) in the past 12 months, with at least one criterion present in the past six months:

Aggression to People and Animals

- Bullies, threatens, or intimidates others
- Often initiates physical fights
- Has used a weapon that could cause serious physical harm to others (e.g., a bat, brick, broken bottle, knife, or gun)
- Is physically cruel to people or animals
- Steals from a victim while confronting them (e.g., assault)
- Forces someone into sexual activity

Destruction of Property

- Deliberately engages in fire setting with the intention to cause damage
- Deliberately destroys others' property

Deceitfulness, Lying, or Stealing

- Has broken into someone else's building, house, or car
- Lies to obtain goods or favors or to avoid obligations
- Steals items without confronting a victim (e.g., shoplifting but without breaking and entering)

Serious Violations of Rules

- Often stays out at night despite parental objections
- Runs away from home
- Often is truant from school

Children who exhibit these behaviors should receive a comprehensive assessment. Many children with conduct disorder may have coexisting conditions as well, such as attention-deficit/hyperactivity disorder (ADHD), learning disorders, or posttraumatic stress disorder. Research shows that children with conduct disorder are more likely to have ongoing problems if they and their families do not receive early comprehensive treatment. Many children with conduct disorder are unable to adapt to the demands of adulthood and thus have repetitive problems with relationships, job performance, and legal issues. These children are at high risk of becoming adult offenders.

In addition, antisocial behavior in children is associated with several school factors, including low job satisfaction among teachers, poor cooperation among teachers, poor teacher–student relationships, poorly defined rules and expectations for conduct, weak rule enforcement, and norms that tend to support antisocial behavior. Because of this, it is important to include a discussion in this chapter on the effects of primary school teachers and their maintenance of classroom management. This is a relevant issue for teachers who have disruptive students in large classes who impair the ability to teach other students. Teachers are under enormous pressure not only to impart information but also to ensure that students do well on grade-specific standardized tests as an indicator of teaching effectiveness. A disruptive child in the classroom adds challenges to this and can make it appear as if the teacher is not able to adequately teach the material.

Finally, the association between juvenile offending and friendships with deviant peers is another commonly held social fact within the field of criminology. Children who count deviant peers among their friends are more likely to be arrested than those who do not associate with such youths (Crick, 1996). A delinquent sibling can also encourage a brother or sister to become delinquent, especially when the siblings are of a similar age and have a close relationship. Peer rejection at school is another factor. Research has shown that aggressive behavior and rejection by peers in the first grade predicted later delinquency (Crick, 1996).

COPING WITH AGGRESSIVE CHILDREN IN THE CLASSROOM

Because primary and secondary schooling is such a central issue for children, it would be an oversight if this chapter did not address the issue of childhood behavior on the school ground and in the classroom. Managing aggressive students has become a daily reality for schoolteachers, and there is a need for professionals working with the teachers to provide support and guidance to teachers who must maintain control of aggressive students in the classroom.

Since teaching involves more than simply providing students with information, the class environment requires management skills because of the many different levels and types of activity that occur. Teacher characteristics that lead to sound decision making when coping with aggression in the classroom are the following:

1. Remaining calm in the face of a crisis
2. Listening actively without becoming defensive and authoritarian
3. Avoiding win-lose situations
4. Maintaining a problem-solving approach

Effective teacher supervision is likewise important on the playground and during other recreational programs. The effects of aggressive children in school can be detrimental to other kids, especially when the aggression is repetitive and targeted at a single victim. This bullying is common among this group of children with aggressive characteristics. While these behaviors are not necessarily criminal, they can lead to victimization and trauma for the victim and thus to lifelong effects on children's self-esteem. These effects can reinforce the bullying child's behavior, leading to further (and more serious) acts of aggression in adolescence or adulthood.

There has been recent recognition of the seriousness of bullying in various school systems. The American Counseling Association has gone so far as to designate bullying a form of child abuse (Duncan, 2004). This is important because it underscores the seriousness of this behavior and, at least for the purposes of this book, places this behavior within the context of an assault on a person. In fact, the only thing that separates this behavior from being criminal is the age of the perpetrator; this then seems to be grounds for at least declaring that bullying is a status offense if nothing else. However, the effects of the bullying child may have more long-term involvement with the criminal justice system since the development of the childhood bully into the adulthood perpetrator is becoming clear. Current research shows that adult perpetrators begin their violent activities during their childhood development (Duncan, 2004).

One primary point to understand about abuse is that it often revolves around the desire to have absolute power and control over another person (Duncan, 2004). If no adult steps in to stop bully abuse, the cycle of power and control on the school yard will continue to flourish, causing harm to other children as well. According to Duncan (2004), the school counselor can be instrumental in preventing the perpetuation of bullying by setting up antibullying programs within the school. Teachers should likewise be alert to potential victimization at the hands of bullies. Most important, the behavior must be detected, and school officials should not ever turn a blind eye to the behavior, as this lends tacit approval for the behavior.

When addressing bullying, three parties should be considered: the bully, any bystanders, and the victim. Duncan (2004) provides several clear guidelines on how to approach all three parties involved. With the bully, it is important that staff instruct the detected bully to write a description of how the behavior constituted bully abuse, how he or she probably made the other person feel, and how he or she felt during the bullying (Duncan, 2004). This process is then followed by a letter of apology. This ensures accountability by the bully-offender, putting him or her in a position where being receptive to the feelings of others is required. Bystanders during the incident should also be instructed to write down what they witnessed and how it constituted abuse, how their behavior served to encourage the abuse, and what they can and should do in the future to discourage or prevent such abuse (Duncan, 2004). Finally and most important, the victim of this abuse should be assured that they are not in trouble, and they should be asked if they feel safe (Duncan, 2004). Staff should follow up within a week to ensure that further bullying is not taking place on a covert level. Table 7.2 outlines the effects, indicators, myths, consequences, and possible outcomes associated with bullying (see also Special Insert 7.1).

Indeed, overt aggressive behavior, particularly physically aggressive behavior, is thought to be a hallmark feature of life course–persistent delinquency and future adult criminality (Moffitt & Caspi, 2001), as discussed later in this book (see Chapter 8).

Table 7.2. Bullying

Bully Indicators	**Bully Victim Consequences**
Intimidates and pokes fun	Missing school and/or poor grades
Incessant teasing that is hurtful	Decline in self-confidence
Embarrasses and ridicules	Depression
Loss of anger control	Anxiety
Pushes and shoves	Suicidal thoughts
Interrupts others	Sleep disorders
Center of attention with peers	Nervous habits
Always blames others	Stress headaches
Discourteous language and behavior	Loss of appetite
Lack of empathy toward others	Inability to concentrate or stay on task
Inability to apologize	Building of rage
Makes excuses for their behavior	
Myths about Bullying	**Where Bullying Can Lead**
It is harmless	Juvenile crime and delinquency
It toughens kids up	Violence and assault
It is just "kids being kids"	Alcohol and drug use
It is a stage of life; kids go through it	Low achievement in life
It is not to be taken seriously	
Overview of Strategies to Prevent Bullying	**Methods of Identifying Bully Abuse and Developing Awareness**
Include component in existing child abuse prevention program	Student posters, essays, art stories, and/or poems
Adult intervention required	Teachers promote awareness in the classroom
Zero tolerance needed within the school	One day a month is awareness day
	Posters that promote an antibullying campaign

Source: Adapted from Duncan (2004).

Persistent offenders are prone to fighting in childhood much more often than adolescents who engage in delinquency and then "age-out" of such behavior. These same aggressive children also tend to commit more violent and other serious offenses than incidental offenders during adolescence. Thus, overt behavior from early childhood is strongly associated with persistent and violent adult offenders.

Special Insert 7.1. Bullying: A Comparative Perspective

Bullying has been noted as a problem within the Japanese school systems. In fact, it has sometimes been contended that this is because of the intense pressure that this school system places on its children in the home and at school. Japan, like the United States, has been slow to develop an overall plan to thwart the harmful effects of bullying in public schools. In a search for an effective antibullying policy, the United States may indeed be well served to look toward other countries that have already grappled with this issue.

For instance, in Norway, all schools now have a proven antibullying program. In England, since 1999 schools have been required to have antibullying policies. Other countries with this kind of policy include Sweden and Wales (as well as some U.S. states). Since much of the problem seems to be that parents and teachers as well as peers tend to look the other way or to not intervene enough when a child is being bullied, antibullying programs work from various angles, trying to change the attitudes of children, teachers, and parents to protect the victims. It is presumed that bullying not only affects children immediately, but also has long-term debilitating effects on the psychological health of children. The anxiety, depression, fear, and withdrawal may permanently impair a child's social growth and rate of maturity. This may even lead to self-esteem issues that continue into adulthood.

Source: Adapted from Omori (2001).

With this in mind, aggression in the school system should not be taken lightly, as it could be the precursor to adult criminal offending. School systems and educational personnel may find themselves already swamped with activities and simply may not have time to monitor more effectively. This means that families must be perceptive to the possibility of victimization in school, and such schools may find it useful to implement a form of "community policing" on the playground and in school whereby designated students "patrol" for bullying. If this is given peer group support among class members (e.g., parents support and encourage this at home, kids bond together, and teachers and school administrators give credibility to the program), then more proactive work on the part of already busy primary teachers may not be as necessary as it may seem. Still, regardless of the logistics of antibullying programming, failure to acknowledge this aspect of early-to-middle-childhood aggression will likely carry long-term consequences.

YOUTH AND SCHOOL GUN VIOLENCE

Research on the dynamics of children who bring guns to school and shoot students and teachers is limited because of the low base rate of this behavior. Verlinden, Hersen, and Thomas (2000) studied students who used firearms at schools across the nation and found that the most common factors associated with the perpetrators

Special Insert 7.2. Juvenile School Shooting Rampage

On April 20th of 1999, Dylan Klebold and Eric Harris entered the Columbine High School during the lunch hour. These two attended the school and had been making plans for roughly a year prior to this day, which proved to be like no other. The two youth walked into the school and within a period of 15 minutes they killed 13 people and injured 21 others before killing themselves. This has been held as the most devastating school shooting to occur in the United States.

Source: Wikipedia (2004).

were uncontrolled anger, depression, blaming others for problems, threatening violence, and having a detailed plan to commit violent acts. More than half these child offenders had produced violent drawings or writings, and half had also threatened suicide. Cruelty to animals was found in about half these childhood offenders as well (Verlinden et al., 2000).

Children who use lethal violence in school settings are often isolated and rejected by their peer group. Often, they are reported to have keen interests in guns and explosives. Their ruminations may dwell on notions of revenge or obtaining justice for the perceived wrongs or for achieving fame. Further, it is disturbing to know that their violent intentions were usually clearly communicated to others, often with the details of the time and place of the attacks, but that the warnings were not taken seriously in the past—though this has changed as a result of the Columbine shootings (see Special Insert 7.2).

The prediction of violence has been considered a problem area by psychologists for some time because of the inherent difficulty of predicting low base rate behavior and the potential for falsely labeling certain youth as "at risk." Risk for violence is also a dynamic process rather than a static one. The variables associated with risk also change with the type of risk, such as being at risk for killing a parent, conducting a shooting to mimic observed behavior, being bullied at school, or being a member of a gang. Despite these differences, there are five indicators that Kaser-Boyd (2002) notes as potential warning signs of possible child/juvenile gun violence:

1. Exposure to violence, either in the home or in the community. Although exposure to television violence is not commonly cited, it is a factor in a number of homicides. Further, the preoccupation with violent images is a definite warning sign. This preoccupation is often stimulated by media exposure to violent acts.
2. A lack of success with the normal tasks of adolescence, such as failing in school, having no extracurricular involvement, and so on.
3. Social rejection and poor social supports. Alienation and lack of empathy develop in large part from social deprivation. Many children and adolescents who commit homicide report intense feelings of aloneness.

4. Intense anger that has built up from previous events. Often this anger is due to relationship issues (e.g., abuse, rejection, or narcissistic wounds).
5. An inability to express or resolve intense feelings in adaptive ways and a proclivity for externalizing defenses or acting out.

It should be noted that children often give indicators through artwork or other imagery that can provide clues for likely future behavior. This is certainly true with children who may be likely to commit homicide. Teachers, parents, and other child care workers may be hard pressed to identify usual fantasy drawings from those that are warning signs. But among younger children (10 years and under), the more vivid the artwork or the behavioral description, the more problematic it is likely to be. With children in the older age ranges (including the teens), drawings are not as likely to correlate with intent for homicide. However, it should again be stated that many older youth will provide verbal references and warnings that are often dismissed by adults who could prevent such tragedies from occurring. Despite this, few variables can provide school administrators any certainty in prediction. The FBI's National Center for the Analysis of Violent Crime has explored variables associated with numerous school shootings and has concluded that there are no variables that are effective in distinguishing school firearms offenders from other students (Kaser-Boyd, 2002).

ARSONISTS

The scope of the juvenile fire-setting problem in the United States is clear from the simple number of fires that are reported to various fire departments. In 1997, children playing with fire started over 110,000 fires (Snyder, 1999). This underscores the fact that roughly 50 percent of all arrests for arson involve a juvenile offender (Snyder, 1999). Much of the information describing fires set by children has been collected in the context of fire-setting screening evaluations at various community-based programs. Several reports have included descriptions for different motives that these children may have for starting fires. In one survey by Cotterall et al. (1999), the three most frequent reasons given for fire setting were (1) just for fun, (2) to see what would happen, and (3) because of boredom. These responses were similar for both boys and girls. Other reasons cited by a minority of the respondents indicated that they were angry or that they wanted to hurt someone (Cotterall et al., 1999).

In studies comparing children who do set fires with those who do not, structured rating scales and diagnostic interviews show that fire-setting children have been found to be more likely to suffer from various forms of child dysfunction, such as heightened aggression, and that they are more likely to engage in covert behaviors, such as lying, stealing, or running away (Kolko, 2002). Fire setting has also been associated with conduct disorder or other disorders that are characterized by impulsivity, elevated emotionality, or hostility (Kolko, 2002).

Regarding demographics of juvenile fire setters, it should be noted that roughly 89 percent of all juvenile arsonists are male (Snyder, 1999). In addition, nearly 77 percent involved Caucasian males with almost 22 percent being African American (FBI, 2002). Further, an estimated 35 percent of all juvenile arsonists are under the age of 12 years (Snyder, 1999). Roughly more than half are processed informally, and only a rare minority (less than 1 percent) are transferred to criminal court (Snyder, 1999). Roughly 60 percent of these formally processed cases result in probation, nearly 30 percent result in placement within a residential facility, and the remainder are made to simply pay restitution (Snyder, 1999).

Some studies have used **projective assessment** (see Chapter 2) tests with youth in residential treatment programs and have identified an array of psychological characteristics that were more common among fire setters than non–fire setters. The characteristics include greater problems with sexual excitement, anger at the mother and/or father, rage and fantasies of revenge, sexual conflicts or dysfunction, poor social judgment, difficulty verbalizing anger, and a diagnosis of conduct disorder. Other types of psychopathology have distinguished fire setters from non–fire setters in one study conducted with an adolescent inpatient sample (Moore, Thompson-Pope, & Whited, 1996). When compared to non–fire setters, fire setters were more likely to have had some form of prior childhood sexual abuse and also more likely to use inhalant drugs. Interestingly, this group also tended to score higher on the schizophrenia and mania scales of the **Minnesota Multiphasic Personality Inventory (MMPI)** (Moore et al., 1996).

Specific parental factors also seem to correlate with a child's likelihood of starting fires. For example, parents of fire setters have reported higher levels of personal or relationship problems (e.g., psychiatric distress, marital discord, and less child acceptance) and/or greater difficulties in parenting practices (e.g., less parental supervision, lax discipline practices, and low involvement in prosocial activities). At the family level, children who set fires indicate through subjective self-report measures that their parents had higher levels of hostility and difficulty with parenting (Kolko, 2002). Objective measures of life experiences and events also indicate that these children tend to have more family and life course trauma (Kolko, 2002).

The descriptive characteristics provide only a general overview of the characteristics of children who set fires. Further, the family and life course variables presented may have little to do with the cause of the behavior and more to do with the individual child's interest or attraction to fire, exposure or access to fire-building materials, personality quirks, or simple incompetence when exploring with fire (Kolko, 2002; Porth, Periera, & Lapsansky, 2002). This means that there is considerable difficulty creating typologies of youthful fire starters because the behavior has multiple motives, antecedent conditions, and consequences. Therefore, the student should keep in mind that these offenders vary significantly in level of personal dysfunction, parental effectiveness, family integrity, and exposure to fire-related factors. Because of this, this chapter will examine fire setters from the perspective of the offender's underlying motivation and dangerousness. Using the motivation and likely risk of fire setting as a guide, this chapter will classify children who engage in fire setting into three basic categories: curiosity fire starters, reactionary fire starters, and extreme concern fire starters.

Curiosity fire starter refers to a child's fire setting that will most likely be resolved through educational intervention. These youth are considered type 1: **low-risk arson offenders**. The child's fire-setting behavior is typically a result of a lack of information about fire and its consequences (Gaynor, 2002; Porth et al., 2002).

Reactionary fire starter describes the fire-setting behavior as a reaction to some type of stress or crisis occurring in the life of the child and/or family. These youth are considered **definite risk arson offenders.** Educational intervention alone, while important, will not likely resolve the fire-setting behavior. For this book's purposes, this group should be divided into two subgroups: type 2: troubled reactionary fire starter and type 3: delinquent reactionary fire starter. Some type of behavior modification is often necessary, such as mental health intervention, medical treatment, parental intervention/training, or other such assistance (Gaynor, 2002; Porth et al., 2002).

Extreme concern fire starter includes children who have an immediate need for some type of intervention beyond education. These youth are classified in the category type 4: **extreme risk arson offenders**. A child who presents a behavior profile that, coupled with the fire-setting behavior, makes it appear likely that the fire-setting behavior will continue before the family can access qualified assistance is categorized as being at extreme risk of future fire setting. It is imperative that such children get help as soon as possible (Gaynor, 2002; Porth et al., 2002).

Students who are interested in this specialized population of youthful offenders should read the work by Gaynor (2002). This work provides detailed information on the typologies and interventions that should be utilized with juvenile arsonists. The typologies provided on the following pages are from this work and serve to provide the student with an understanding of the individual traits and social situations that are common to each type of juvenile arsonist.

Type 1: Low Risk—Curiosity Fire Starter

Factor	**Profile**
Individual traits	The majority are young boys coming from a variety of social and economic backgrounds. Girls are involved less frequently. Physical, cognitive, and emotional development is normal. There is no evidence of psychiatric disturbance.
Social circumstances	There is a functional family providing support and guidance. Peer relationships are adequate. School performance and behavior are well within the normal range.
Fire-setting scenario	Fire setting is unplanned and usually a single episode motivated by curiosity or experimentation. Resulting fires may be accidental. Available matches or lighters are used, and there is no specific material or target ignited with the intention to destroy or harm. Attempts are made to extinguish the fire or call for help. Feelings of guilt or remorse occur after the incident.

Type 2: Definite Risk—Troubled Reactionary Fire Starter

Factor	Profile
Individual traits	The majority are boys coming from a variety of social and economic backgrounds. One or more of the following problems exist: a greater number of physical illnesses, histories of physical or sexual abuse, poor impulse control, and overwhelming feelings of anger. For adolescent boys there may be gender confusion, higher levels of sexual conflict, lack of emotional depth, and greater risk-taking behavior.
Social circumstances	Many live in single-parent households, with an absent father. There is little adult supervision and inconsistent methods of discipline. One or more parents may carry a psychiatric diagnosis. There are difficulties establishing and maintaining friendships. Learning difficulties are common, and attention deficit disorder with or without hyperactivity may be diagnosed. School performance and behavior are below average.
Fire-setting scenario	Recent or chronic stressful events trigger emotional reactions that result in fire starting. The fire represents the release of displaced emotions, such as frustration or anger. The fire also has the reinforcing properties of effect and attention. No attempt is made to extinguish the fire. There is no consideration of the negative consequences of the potential destruction.

Type 3: Definite Risk—Delinquent Reactionary Fire Starter

Factor	Profile
Individual traits	Most are boys, many of whom live in low-income households. These young boys tend to be impulsive, stubborn, mischievous, and disobedient. Preteens are generally defiant and frequently involved in lying and stealing. Teens are angry and aggressive and usually are involved in other antisocial activities, such as substance abuse, petty theft, and vandalism.
Social circumstances	Many live in single-parent households, with an absent father. There is no formal supervision or discipline. Physical abuse and other violent patterns of family interaction are common. One or more parents may carry a psychiatric diagnosis; the most frequent is alcoholism. There is a small but influential peer group that supports participation in antisocial activities. School truancy is typical. When school is attended, performance is poor and behavior argumentative and defiant.
Fire-setting scenario	Supported by their peer group, repeated, intentional fire setting occurs. Feelings of excitement and defiance are reported. Fire starting often is accompanied by other antisocial activities, such as drug or alcohol use, petty theft, or vandalism. No attempts are made to extinguish the fire. Feelings of guilt or remorse are rare. There is little fear of the consequences or punishment.

Type 4: Extreme Risk—Extreme Concern Fire Starter

Factor	Profile
Individual traits	Depending on the diagnosed mental disorder, there can be a number of problems, including extreme mood swings, uncontrolled anger, bizarre thoughts and speech, poor judgment, an inability to care for themselves, and potential harm to themselves or others.
Social circumstances	Family background will vary according to the diagnosed mental disturbance. Often it will be difficult for these youngsters to live at home because of their impairment. They may be hospitalized or live in a residential treatment facility. Peer relationships usually are poor. School performance is severely impeded by mental dysfunction.
Fire-setting scenario	Fire as a fixation may be a part of their mental disorder; therefore the reinforcing properties of the fires cause frequent fire starts. Reinforcing properties can be the sensory aspects of the fire or sensual or sexual arousal. Fire setting also may be a part of a delusional thought process. There is no rational or purposeful aspect to the fire setting, and the willingness to harm is difficult to predict.

Intake is the first step in the treatment process when providing interventions for juvenile arsonists. Juveniles are identified and referred to the program by a variety of sources (Porth et al., 2002). All intake information should be confirmed with the parent or caregiver of the juvenile involved. This process can be done over the phone or in person and may take from 10 to 30 minutes (Porth et al., 2002). Confirming this information with parents is important in preventing the child from lying about his or her involvement with the fire-starting incident. After the initial discussion with the child and his or her parental caretakers, an interview is usually scheduled with a trained intervention specialist. If a family refuses to participate, the investigator or the treatment provider should document any efforts that have been made in the youth's file at the agency tasked with addressing the situation (Porth et al., 2002). If the child is then referred again to the agency at a later date, the prior refusal will be documented. This is important because it can tell a lot about the family's motivation for help (Porth et al., 2002). This process is intended to help the treatment provider determine the motivation behind the fire-setting behavior and determine the ultimate needs of the child and family.

The main goal of an intervention is to determine the child's motivation for the inappropriate use of fire. For children whose motivation falls into the category of curiosity, education is the most appropriate intervention. When children are identified as engaging in reactionary fire-setting behaviors, the required intervention is probably beyond the limits of what most treatment programs can offer. Extreme concern fire starters urgently need intervention beyond the scope of the program (Porth et al., 2002). For children with reactionary or extreme concern behaviors, an intervention program should assist the family in finding a program or agency best suited to the family's needs. This may range from inpatient hospitalization for the child to family counseling. Parenting classes may be another recommended intervention plan (Porth et al., 2002).

Families commonly exhibit extreme denial that a child was involved in fire-setting activity (Porth et al., 2002). Some parents also claim that the incident was isolated and that discipline provided by the family will remedy the situation. In these cases, the family may be correct. However, the common consensus among many arson interventionists is that psychoeducation cannot harm the situation, and thus the family should be persuaded to actively participate in the educational process regardless of the remedies they may propose (Porth et al., 2002). Rather, the psychoeducational process will most likely improve the understanding and emphasis of what the parents should teach the children (Porth et al., 2002).

Education is the most critical part of any arson intervention program. When children have had an experience with fire, it is crucial that they gain an understanding of why their behavior was inappropriate (Porth et al., 2002). This involves pointing out their mistakes and identifying appropriate corrective action. Many times, parents may think they have offered direction to their child. According to Porth et al. (2002), parents visiting the program have usually attempted to educate their children about proper fire use by applying one or more of the following approaches:

- Instilling fear in the child
- Using punitive measures only
- Ignoring the problem, fearing that ideas will be put into the child's head
- Explaining unrealistic outcomes of fire-setting behavior (e.g., if you play with fire, you will be killed or will go to jail and so on)

A treatment program should provide fire safety education as an integral part of the interview/screening process. The interviewer begins by establishing a positive, friendly rapport with the family, particularly the child. Each interviewer may use any variety of education and rapport-building techniques. However, throughout the interview, messages about the proper use of matches and lighters should be provided. The basic fire survival skills (e.g., stop, drop, and roll and crawl low in smoke) are also discussed, but emphasis is placed on understanding the appropriate use of and rules about fire.

For the most part, therapeutic interventions have sought to modify children's cognitive-behavioral repertoire, parental practices, and family functioning in cases presenting with significant clinical challenges. Some programs also utilize individualized negative practice of fire starting (e.g., repeatedly lighting matches to the point that it becomes boring) to satiate and extinguish the child's curiosity with fire. Contingency management procedures (i.e., rewards for appropriate behavior and punishment for undesired behavior) have been used to discourage involvement with fire and to reinforce contact with non–fire materials (Kolko, 2002). Visual aids such as still photos, videotapes, and personal experiences should be used with caution as part of the interview to depict the damaging effects of fire (Porth et al., 2002).

At the conclusion of the treatment session, the interviewer may assign fire safety homework that is designed to build accountability in the child. This is an especially relevant form of intervention for children who are 10 years of age or older. The child may be asked to show proof of completion, or the parent may be given the responsibility to see that the assignment is completed. Occasionally, a "non–fire use contract" is established between the treatment provider and the child (Porth et al., 2002).

Referrals are typically made when treatment requires intensive and multi-modal interventions. Referrals are often administered from a wide range of agencies throughout the community. Several issues may occur simultaneously for the child, and each may need to be appropriately addressed (Porth et al., 2002). Typical referral sources include the following:

- Mental health professional
- Child protective services
- School counselor
- Inpatient hospitalization
- Physician for medical evaluation
- Parenting classes (for parents)
- ADHD screening
- Juvenile justice authorities
- Attorneys

SIBLING INCEST

Assessing a potential case of sibling incest involves a careful critique of the family dynamics surrounding the children involved in the incident (Pesciallo, 1998). After conducting a family assessment, noting the family dynamics surrounding the occurrence, and the cognitive-behavioral factors of the offender, this assessment is further evaluated for motivational factors that may be present. It will likely be important to consider the type of incest that has occurred in relation to its context and the broad intrafamilial dynamics that may be present (Pesciallo, 1998). While a case may have several contributing factors that are in common with other sibling abuse cases, no single factor alone can provide adequate explanation for the abuse (Pesciallo, 1998). The incident is often further complicated by the reactions of other family members: father, mother, other siblings, extended family members, and friends (Pesciallo, 1998). Their role within the family can have an important impact on the offending sibling.

When assessing a family for a potential occurrence of sibling incest, a common risk factor may be overlooked. Although this may seem to be common knowledge, an unhappy family life is a significant risk factor. Finkelhor (1990) found that among those (1) who lived without a natural parent, (2) had few friends, or (3) possessed inadequate sex education, having had an "unhappy family life" was the most prevalent risk factor for both men (35 percent victimized) and women (60 percent victimized) for the occurrence of childhood sexual abuse. Such a simple need is often neglected in these families (Finkelhor, 1990; Pesciallo, 1998).

In a study by Worling (1995) of 90 adolescent male sex offenders committing physical acts, it was found that children who live with abusive and rejecting parents may turn to each other for comfort, nurturance, and support. Although this is often viewed as somewhat normal, the onset of puberty places the children at risk. This then suggests that when male children begin puberty and have unmet needs for comfort, nurturance, and support, they may turn to a female sibling to meet these needs. The sibling may be a willing partner so that she can get her needs met. This occurs because both live with the same pair of dysfunctional parents (Pesciallo, 1998; Worling, 1995).

Worling (1995) also noted that the comparison group of nonsibling incest adolescent offenders and those of the sibling incest group did not differ substantively in terms of depression, self-esteem, hostility, peer popularity, aggression, or physical parental punishment and negative family relationships. However, the parents of the sibling incest offenders were reported to be significantly more dysfunctional and abusive (Pesciallo, 1998; Worling, 1995). It would appear that dysfunctional and abusive parents place the children at risk for sibling incest in brother–sister families (Pesciallo, 1998). It is therefore important to consider parental factors when screening for sibling abuse. Worling's conclusion was that verbal, emotional, and physical violence, combined with a history of sexual victimization, places the children at risk for sibling incest (Pesciallo, 1998; Worling, 1995).

When working with children victimized by sibling incest, it is important to exercise caution when screening incident reports in order to gather data effectively. Persons investigating or interviewing victims of sibling incest should have a working knowledge of what are normal and what are abnormal acts of sexual exploration for children. There are three main categories for evaluating sibling incest: (1) incest experimentation, (2) incest exploitation, and (3) incest sexual abuse (Abrams, 1993; Pesciallo, 1998). An act considered to be more or less **incest experimentation** might be when young children close in age, size, and cognitive level engage in sexual acts that are more exploratory than gratifying. An act of **incest exploitation** might be if their behavior has been repudiated but the frequency of the behavior not reduced (Pesciallo, 1998). On the other hand, an example of **incest sexual abuse** might be a sex act where there is a considerable age or developmental difference between the two children. Before ending the interview of the victim, the investigator should ask if the child has been victimized by other persons as well as the primary perpetrator. This is important because these children may have been abused by more than one perpetrator and may not disclose this unless asked (Pesciallo, 1998).

It is likewise important to ask the perpetrator how he or she learned the behavior, but investigators should understand that disclosure may be unlikely since the child, in all probability, has learned the behavior from others as a form of sexual exploration, exploitation, or sexual abuse. In fact, such child offenders are likely to become juvenile sex offenders (and subsequently adult sex offenders) unless they receive the appropriate treatment. It is at this point that the **sexual abuse cycle** can first be detected and stopped. The sexual abuse cycle is where older-generation family members sexually abuse children who in turn eventually become sex abusers themselves. Since childhood sexual abuse is common among juvenile and adult sex offenders, the investigator could be saving numerous potential future victims from trauma by ensuring that the current childhood incest sex offender is provided effective treatment. This is perhaps one of the most important aspects to preventing the intergenerational transmission of sexual abuse that is reflective of the sexual abuse cycle.

Sibling incest cases can be multifaceted, meaning that more than one or two factors have occurred that contribute to the abuse. Therefore, it is important to have a comprehensive protocol to use when screening or assessing sibling incest cases. Pesciallo (1998) points out one such protocol developed by Smith and Israel (1987). This protocol lists specific considerations when collecting data during the investigative intake process. This list of considerations (Pesciallo, 1998) is provided below.

1. Nature and duration of sexual contact
2. Where sexual contact occurred
3. Finding out who may know about the sibling sexual contact
4. Knowing who the victim told
5. History of prior sexual abuse of either victim or perpetrator
6. Prior history of sexual abuse of parents
7. Possible sexual activity between parent and child
8. Significant role reassignment in family
9. Quality of the parental marital relationship
10. Parenting responsibilities
11. Sexual boundaries in the home; restrictive or flexible
12. Ability of parents to protect children in the future

CHILDHOOD MURDERERS

It is important to understand the dynamics that lead children to commit the unusual act of murder or intentional killing (see Special Inserts 7.3 and 7.4). This area of childhood offending is most rare and has few typological methods for describing these young offenders. However, this type of offending is becoming more prevalent among the child offending population. It should be noted that the number of juveniles arrested for homicide in the mid-1990s was almost three times the number of two decades earlier and cannot be attributed solely to increases in population (Heide, 1997). In the mid-1990s, about 16.7 percent of those arrested for homicide were juveniles (FBI, 1995). In raw numbers, this equals about 1,000 to 1,700 homicides per year

Special Insert 7.3. Childhood Violence Turns to Murder

In 2001, Lionel Tate, a 12-year-old boy who weighed close to 180 pounds, said he was imitating professional World Wide Federation wrestlers when he killed Tiffany Eunick, a 48-pound six-year-old. The injuries that were found demonstrated severe beatings to the six-year-old victim and were numerous and severe enough to rule out any chance for an accidental killing. Tate received a first-degree murder conviction that was later remanded to life in prison.

Special Insert 7.4. Unexplained Childhood Murder

On February 12, 1993, in Liverpool, England, Robert Thompson (age 10) and John Venables (age 10) grotesquely murdered a two-year-old boy named James Bulger. The two 10-year-old perpetrators found Bulger in a shopping center and led the child along a series of streets to disorient and exhaust the toddler. They took the toddler to some local railroad tracks and splashed paint on him. While the toddler was crying, confused, scared, and unable to see clearly, they hurled bricks at him, then beat him with an iron bar. Amazingly, the toddler survived this abuse, and Thompson and Venebles then proceeded to tie James to the railroad tracks and went so far as to build a decorative "tomb" of bricks around his head. Later that day a train passed over James's body, cutting the toddler's already beaten body in half.

(Kaser-Boyd, 2002). It should be made clear that most children who commit murder are 15, 16, or 17 years old; fewer than 1 percent of these types of offenders are under the age of 15 (Kaser-Boyd, 2002).

The dynamics of homicide committed by very young children (preadolescents) often differ substantially from those of homicides by adolescents and often vary according to the victim's relationship with the killer. One example would be the dynamics associated with a child killing a parent as opposed to a school shooting. Further, young children often have a limited understanding of death, and thus their behavior is much more likely to occur for impulsive reasons. Patricide and matricide account for only about 1.5 percent to 2.5 percent of all homicides, which amounts to no more than 300 to 400 cases per year in the United States (Kaser-Boyd, 2002).

Most studies of homicide by juveniles and young children were published prior to 1990 and were restricted to the analysis of individual and family characteristics. More recently, Heide (1997) has proposed a five-factor model for explaining juvenile homicide:

1. Situational factors: child abuse, child neglect, and absence of positive male role models

2. Societal influences: crisis in leadership, lack of heroes, and witnessing violence
3. Resource availability: access to guns, involvement in alcohol and drugs, and poverty and lack of resources
4. Personality characteristics: low self-esteem, inability to deal with strong negative feelings, boredom and nothing constructive to do, poor judgment, prejudice and hatred, little or nothing left to lose, and biological disorders
5. Combinations of the previous four factors.

One of the most common findings in the histories of children who kill parents is child abuse. In some studies, this is defined as witnessing domestic violence, but more commonly the child has been a victim of abuse. Sometimes children kill to protect their battered mother, typically after years of severe violence. More often, the child kills to escape what is a physically and psychologically intolerable situation. Special Insert 7.5 provides an example of this kind of preteen offender. Some interesting research has focused exclusively on abused children who kill a parent or parents (Mones, 1991). These cases follow a fairly predictable pattern in which one parent, usually the father, is the primary abuser, in which case the mother is frequently a coconspirator. Mones (1991) further notes that in the worst cases the mother visits her own brand of mistreatment on her children, most often by abusing her children by actively condoning the father's mistreatment or even assisting in the father's or stepfather's mistreatment.

Regardless of these circumstances, childhood violence can be seemingly unpredictable and can occur in situations that you might least expect. Further, the violence may be against parents or adults who might seem the least likely to be targeted (see the example in Special Insert 7.6).

ASSESSMENT OF CHILDHOOD AGGRESSION, VIOLENCE, AND IMPAIRMENT

When evaluating the child's mental state at the time of the homicide or homicide attempt, there are several factors that should be considered. These may be helpful in determining how to process the child offender and may explain the reason for the behavior. Kaser-Boyd (2002) notes five specific areas of **subjective assessment** that can be helpful in assessing the childhood offender who kills:

1. School records to assess the presence of learning disabilities or other cognitive or neurological impairments
2. Children's services records to see whether there were incidents of abuse that offer a window into the home life of the youth
3. Medical records to identify or rule out traumatic medical conditions or other accidents or medical conditions that could affect cognitive and emotional functioning (such as head trauma or previous serious childhood illness)

Special Insert 7.5. Boy Shoots Father during Custodial Visitation; Unfounded Allegations of Abuse an Issue

In August of 2004, in Houston, Texas, a 10-year-old boy shot and killed his father by causing numerous gunshot wounds. The father and mother of the boy had divorced approximately a year before and the divorce had been bitter. Unproven allegations of physical and sexual abuse had been made by the mother against the father. When the father came to pick up his 10-year-old son and his younger seven-year-old brother, the older sibling obtained a gun from his mother's bedroom and went to the vehicle where his father was located. The boy then entered the vehicle and fired numerous rounds from the back seat and shot his father. The boy then left the vehicle and fired again at the father's vehicle. The boy was kept in custody and tried as a juvenile because he was too young to be waived to adult court though some speculative consideration for murder charges have been considered. A closed court hearing was in progress at the time that this book was written.

Source: Retrieved from Halifax Live News Source, http://www.halifaxlive.com/shooting_08292004_3923.php.

Special Insert 7.6. Eleven-Year-Old Shoots His Father because of an Argument over Chores

In June of 2003 in the town of Fountain, Colorado, an 11-year-old boy was arrested for firing five rounds from a .357 revolver at his father, hitting his father once in the chest. The boy and his father had argued over assigned chores and the father eventually left the house to attend to some errands. When the father returned, the boy fired at his father twice from the living room hitting his father once. The boy fired three more times as he fled the scene of the crime. The boy was held at a juvenile facility and was charged with attempted murder and possession of a handgun by a juvenile.

Source: Retrieved from *New Zealand Herald*, http://www.hypocrites.com/article12932.html.

4. Interviews with family members (both immediate and extended family members) to learn about the minor's home life
5. Interviews with other people (teachers, neighbors, or scout leaders) having contact with the child to corroborate information from other sources

Finally, numerous tools may be used to assess this type of offender. **Objective assessment** tests may include the MMPI or the Millon Adolescent Personality Inventory. There is a complete lack of research in using these instruments to assess children who kill. Children who are abused will also typically have higher scores on indicators of anger, alienation, and paranoia. Thus, results of these objective assessment tests must factor the subjective information into the final assessment so that the scores are considered in the correct context.

Projective assessment tests, however, are considered much more useful forensic tools than objective and/or subjective tools, though all three should be used together if at all possible. Projective assessments do not rely on the child's self-report. Rather, they try to get a "behind-the-scenes" reading of the child's mental state that is often safeguarded by a variety of defense mechanisms. Two types of projective assessments are most often used with children who commit homicide: the **Rorschach Test** and the **Thematic Apperception Test** (TAT). Both the Rorschach and the TAT explore for trauma in the child and are useful since many children and teens who murder report some form of prior trauma.

TREATMENT ISSUES IN BRIEF

Research shows that childhood offenders in general and those diagnosed with conduct disorder specifically are likely to have persisting problems if they and their families do not receive early and comprehensive treatment. To be successful, early intervention strategies designed to reduce aggressive and disruptive behaviors must take into account the age of the child. Treatment of these children can be complicated, and the age appropriateness of the treatment is therefore important. Age-appropriate cognitive and behavioral approaches, including coping skills and problem-solving training, have proven useful. Anger control training and counseling on antecedents to anger are likewise paramount. Treatment can be provided in a variety of different settings, depending on the severity of the behavior.

Family therapy may be required in order to fully implement the strategies throughout the duration of the week. In developing any thorough treatment plan, information and assistance from the family, teachers, and medical specialists should be elicited. In addition, it is important to remember that ADHD is a dual diagnosis in roughly 30 to 40 percent of children who have conduct disorder. Moreover, special education may be needed for those youth who have learning disabilities. Thus, treatment programs must deal with corollary issues as well. Behavior therapy is usually necessary to help the child learn to appropriately perceive intent from other persons and to learn to express frustration and anger in a more adaptable manner. Treatment may also include medication in some youth, such as those with attention deficits and poor impulse control and those who report with depression.

CONCLUSION

When considering juvenile delinquency, we normally think of teenagers as the primary type of offender. Although preteen children are a small proportion of the delinquent population, their numbers are increasing at a faster rate than those noted for teens. Further, it has been noted that the types of crime committed by children are becoming more serious and are happening with more frequency, so researchers have begun to examine youth aggression with a careful eye.

Youth aggression is caused by a wide range of factors, both physiological and social. Children who offend are engaged in some common types of aggression from sibling incest to gun violence in schools and at home. Specific types of crime that are of concern in the United States today were discussed in detail. Further, these youth may present with a diagnostic criteria known as conduct disorder. This disorder and its antecedents may be primary indicators for the likelihood of further offending in adulthood. It is because serious offending in childhood tends to be a precursor to future offending in adulthood that we must pay close attention to the prediction, prevention, and treatment of childhood offenders.

Assessment scales are utilized to predict those youth most at risk, and these scales guide practitioners in forming interventions for these children. These interventions could be the likely key to stopping serious future criminality and could be instrumental in reducing future crime since these targeted youth are most at risk of becoming long-term adult criminals. With this in mind, society must be more careful with early childhood offenders, and we should fully consider any approaches used when processing this unique type of special needs offender.

KEY TERMS

Authoritarian parenting
Permissive parenting
Conduct disorder
Projective assessment
Minnesota Multiphasic Personality Inventory (MMPI)
Curiosity fire starters
Low/Definite/Extreme risk arson offenders
Reactionary fire starters
Extreme concern fire starters
Incest experimentation
Incest exploitation
Incest sexual abuse
Sexual abuse cycle
Subjective assessment
Objective assessment
Rorschach Test
Thematic Apperception Test

ABOUT THE CONTRIBUTORS

Paulette Cappel is assistant professor of social work at the University of Louisiana at Monroe. Her specialties include child and adolescent populations, aggression, and clients who present with conduct disorder and antisocial personality disorder.

Rob Hanser is director of the Institute of Law Enforcement at the University of Louisiana at Monroe. His specialty areas include ethics in policing, community policing, corrections, multiculturalism, and treatment interventions for victims and perpetrators.

REFERENCES

Abrams, H. (1993). *Evaluating sibling incest.* Walla Walla, WA: Child Services District, Walla Walla College.

American Psychiatric Association. (2000). *Diagnostic and statistical manual of mental disorders.* (4th ed., text revision). Arlington, VA: Author.

Baumrind, D. (1991). The influence of parenting style on adolescent competence and substance use. *Journal of Early Adolescence, 11*(1), 56–95.

Baumrind, D. (1997). The discipline encounter: Contemporary issues. *Aggression and Violent Behavior, 2*, 321–335.

Brennan, P., Mednick, S., & Kandel, E. (1991). Congenital determinants of violent and property offending. In D. J. Pepler & K. H. Rubin (Eds.)., *The development and treatment of childhood aggression* (pp. 81–92). Hillsdale, NJ: Lawrence Erlbaum Associates.

Cohen, M. A. (1998). The monetary value of saving a high-risk youth. *Journal of Quantitative Criminology, 14*(1), 5–33.

Cotterall, A., McPhee, B., & Plecas, D. (1999). *Fireplay report—A survey of school-aged youth in grades 1 to 12.* British Columbia: University College of the Fraser Valley.

Crick, N. R. (1996). The role of overt aggression, relational aggression, and prosocial behavior in the prediction of children's future social adjustment. *Child Development, 67*, 2317–2327.

Dodge, K. A. (1991) The structure and function of reactive and proactive aggression. In D. J. Pepler & K. H. Rubin (Eds.), *The development and treatment of childhood aggression* (pp. 201–218). Mahwah, NJ: Lawrence Erlbaum Associates.

Duncan, K. A. (2004, November). *Bullying as child abuse: Intervention strategies schools can employ.* Alexandria, VA: American Counseling Association. Retrieved from http://www.counseling.org/Content/NavigationMenu/PUBLICATIONS/COUNSELINGTODAYONLINE/NOVEMBER2004/Reader_Viewpoint.htm

Fauman, M. A. (1994). *Study guide to DSM-IV.* Washington, DC: American Psychiatric Association.

FBI. (1995). *Crime in the United States series for the years 1975–1994.* Washington, DC: Government Printing Office.

FBI. (2002). Crime index offense reports—Arson. Retrieved from http://www.fbi.gov/ucr/cius_02/html/web/offreported/02-narson11.html

Finkelhor, D. (1990). Early and long-term effects of child sexual abuse: An update. *Professional Psychology: Research and Practice, 21*(5), 325–330.

Gaynor, J. (2002). *Juvenile fire-setter intervention handbook.* Washington, DC: United States Fire Administration, Federal Emergency Management Administration. Retrieved from http://www.millersafetycenter.org/Documents/2AToc2001.pdf

Heide, K. M. (1997). Juvenile homicide in America: How can we stop the killing? *Behavioral Sciences and the Law, 15*, 203–220.

Huesmann, L. R. (1988). An information processing model for the development of aggression. *Aggressive Behavior, 14*, 13–24.

Kaser-Boyd, N. (2002). Children who kill. In N. G. Ribner (Ed.), *Handbook of juvenile forensic psychology* (pp. 195–229). San Francisco: Jossey-Bass.

Kolko, D. (2002). *Handbook on fire setting in children and youth.* Boston: Academic Press.

Lewis D., Lovely, R., Yaeger, C., & Della Femina, D. (1989). Toward a theory of the genesis of violence: A follow-up study of delinquents. *Journal of American Academy of Child and Adolescent Psychiatry, 28*(3), 431–436.

Lochman, J. E., & Lehart, L. A. (1993). Anger coping intervention for aggressive children: Conceptual model and outcome effects. *Clinical Psychology Review, 13*, 785–805.

Moffitt, T. E. (1993). Adolescent limited and life-course-persistent antisocial behavior: A developmental taxonomy. *Psychological Review, 100*, 647–701.

Moffitt, T., & Caspi, A. (2001). Childhood predictors differentiate life-course persistent and adolescent-limited antisocial pathways among males and females. *Development and Psychopathology, 13*, 355–375.

Moore, J., Jr., Thompson-Pope, S. K., & Whited, R. M. (1996). MMPI-A profiles of adolescent boys with a history of firesetting. *Journal of Personality Assessment, 67*(1), 116–126.

Mones, P. (1991). *When a child kills: Abused children who kill their parents*. New York: Pocket Books.

Omori, M. (2001). Bullying: A new sense of need in the U.S. educational system. Child Research Net. Retrieved from http://www.childresearch.net/cgi-bin/topics/column.pl?no=00106&page=1

Patterson, G. R., Capaldi, D., & Bank, L. (1991). An early starter model for predicting delinquency. In D. J. Pepler & K. H. Rubin (Eds.), *The development and treatment of childhood aggression* (pp. 139–168). Hillsdale, NJ: Lawrence Erlbaum Associates.

Pesciallo, J. (1998). Understanding sibling incest. Walla Walla, WA: Walla Walla College. Retrieved from http://www.bmi.net/jgp/USI.htm

Porth, D., Periera, N., & Lapsansky, L. (2002). Developing and managing youth fire-setting intervention programs. Gresham, OR: SOS Fires, Youth Intervention Program. Retrieved from http://sosfires.com/Program%20development%20article.pdf

Smith, H., & Israel, E. (1987). Sibling incest: A study of the dynamics of 25 cases. *Child Abuse and Neglect, 11*(1), 101–108.

Synder, H. (1999). *Juvenile arrests 1998*. Juvenile Justice Bulletin (NCJ No. 179064). Washington, DC: U.S. Department of Justice, Office of Juvenile Justice and Delinquency Prevention.

University of Pittsburgh. (2002). The youngest offenders: Understanding and preventing child delinquency. University of Pittsburgh Office of Child Development. Retrieved from http://www.education.pitt.edu/ocd/publications/sr2002-03.pdf

Verlinden, S., Hersen, M., & Thomas, J. (2000). Risk factors in school shootings. *Clinical Psychology Review, 20*, 3–56.

Wikipedia. (2004). Columbine high school massacre. Retrieved from http://en.wikipedia.org/wiki/Columbine_High_School_massacre

Worling, J. (1995). Adolescent sibling-incest offenders: Differences in family and individual functioning when compared to adolescent non-sibling sex offenders. *Child Abuse and Neglect, 19*(5), 633–643.

LEARNING CHECK

1. Which of the following is a common diagnosis for children who display excessive levels of aggression or who are otherwise difficult to manage?
   a. Antisocial personality disorder
   b. Bipolar personality disorder
   c. Conduct disorder
   d. All of the above
   e. None of the above

2. Which of the following is not one of the five factors used in predicting juvenile homicide?
   a. Situational factors
   b. Resource availability
   c. Personality characteristics
   d. a and c but not b
   e. All of the above

3. Research shows that many aggressive children have a tendency to interpret a hostile intent when interacting with others.
   a. True
   b. False
4. Which of the following is not one of the categories to consider when investigating childhood offender incest?
   a. Incest experimentation
   b. Incest exploitation
   c. Incest sexual abuse
   d. All of the above
   e. None of the above
5. In Cotterall's 1999 study of juvenile arsonists, which was one of the three most frequent reasons that juveniles reported for setting fires?
   a. To see what would happen
   b. To get "even" with another person
   c. Peer pressure
   d. All of the above
   e. None of the above
6. One reason that aggressive children often react to others in an aggressive manner is due to intention-cue detection deficit.
   a. True
   b. False
7. What disorder is commonly associated with children who commit aggressive or criminal actions?
   a. Antisocial personality disorder
   b. Oppositional defiant disorder
   c. Conduct disorder
   d. Schizophrenia
   e. None of the above
8. Approximately what percentage of arsonists are juveniles?
   a. 30
   b. 40
   c. 50
   d. 60
   e. 70
9. What are some common indicators associated with the possibility of a youth resorting to lethal violence in school?
   a. Drawings and writings from the child
   b. Social rejection among peer groups
   c. Threats of suicide
   d. All of the above
   e. None of the above

10. The types of crime among childhood offenders have become more serious in the past decade or so.
    a. True
    b. False

ESSAY DISCUSSION QUESTIONS

1. Discuss how an effective arson intervention program might deal with a child that has recently exhibited fire-setting behavior.
2. Explain how conduct disorder might be relevant to children who exhibit bullying, fire-setting, or sexually assaultive behaviors.
3. Fully discuss two theoretical causes of childhood aggression.

CHAPTER

THE CHILD AND ADOLESCENT OFFENDER

8

Chapter Objectives

1. Understand the differences between typical adolescent misbehavior and such behavior that is likely to become a lifelong crime problem.
2. Understand the various risk factors that are likely to contribute to juvenile delinquency.
3. Understand the diathesis-stress model for explaining why some adolescents may have predispositions to continue into a life of crime and why others do not.
4. Know about various treatment and supervision modalities within the institutional and community setting.

INTRODUCTION

As with any treatment program, the groundwork for success begins with appropriate assessment. This is especially true when it is difficult to identify individuals who are in need of intervention services. Since many juvenile justice systems are overburdened and have limited resources, it is important to effectively target the most at-risk youth. Failure to apply juvenile justice resources toward reaching the most at-risk youths will result in poor delivery of services to those who are in need of appropriate intervention. Without adequate assessment, any intervention or prevention program is destined to either become an absolute failure or achieve mixed results at best.

This need for adequate assessment will be emphasized throughout this chapter. Briefly, **assessment** is the process that mental health practitioners use to gain information about an offender. As the student may recall from Chapter 2, the assessment stage refers to both subjective methods of clinical interviews and observations as well as objective methods of test taking and mathematical models of offender profiling (see Chapter 2 for additional details on subjective and objective forms of assessment). It is during this stage that the clinician is often interested in diagnosing the problem of a client and will desire to describe the client's behavior, predict future behavior, or evaluate therapeutic interventions (Drummond, 1992). A wide variety of assessment techniques are often used, including aptitude tests, ability tests, personality tests, checklists, rating scales, and behavioral observation in natural or created settings.

Assessment can be divided into two forms: psychodiagnostic and psychometric. The **psychodiagnostic method** is a model of clinical assessment that is holistic and is intended to describe the client in a variety of ways (Drummond, 1992). The model calls for the use of a number of procedures (e.g., self-disclosure surveys, observation, and questioning of parents and teachers), the measurement of various areas of psychological functioning, the assessment of conscious as well as unconscious behavioral and cognitive characteristics, the use of projective techniques as well as objective personality instruments, and descriptions that are tailored to the individual tested. The psychodiagnostic method may employ any number of subjective and objective forms of assessment, typically determined by the clinician's expert judgment. The **psychometric method** of assessment, on the other hand, tends to utilize tests and assessment instruments that are more objective (Drummond, 1992). These tests must be reliable (producing similar results when repeatedly given) and valid (testing the concept that is needed to be tested) for the purposes that are identified. These tests do not rely on clinical judgment of the test giver but are based solely on the responses given by the client.

The use of appropriate assessment instruments is paramount to addressing the special needs of juvenile offenders who are either young children or adolescents. While Chapter 2 discusses the importance of assessment with special needs offenders, this is especially important with juvenile offenders because of temporal considerations in the youth's development. Indeed, it is at this point that the criminal justice system makes its first determination of a juvenile offender, and this determination is likely to have a long-range outcome. All types of treatment and intervention given to these offenders will be based entirely on the results of the assessment(s) given. Thus, it is at this point that the trajectory for future offending or future reformation begins. It is at this point that a juvenile's delinquency may be short- or long term, depending on the intervention that is provided. The wrong intervention can increase the likelihood of their becoming an adult criminal. We refer to the two types of adolescent offenders as **adolescent-limited offenders** (meaning that they cease delinquency at some point in adulthood) and **life course–persistent offenders** (their delinquency carries through to criminal acts throughout adulthood). This type of division is commonly referred to as a dual taxonomy of delinquency (Moffitt, 1993).

ADOLESCENT-LIMITED VERSUS LIFE COURSE–PERSISTENT JUVENILE DELINQUENTS

The most well-established developmental taxonomy in the study of youth aggression revolves around the previously mentioned distinctions between life course–persistent and adolescent-limited antisocial behavior (Moffitt, 1993). There is a significant difference between adolescent-limited and life course–persistent offenders. However, during the adolescent period, it is difficult to distinguish the difference between these two offenders because their delinquent behaviors are so similar (Moffitt, 1993).

The majority of individuals who are delinquents during childhood and adolescence stop offending before they reach adulthood. According to Moffitt (1993), those adolescents who desist from delinquency are referred to as adolescent-limited juvenile delinquents. Many adolescents may be inclined to mimic their antisocial peers who appear to have attained adult status in many ways. Through antisocial conduct, the adolescent rejects the ties of childhood and demonstrates that he or she can act independently. Under Moffitt's theory, youthful antisocial and risk-prone acts are personal statements of independence. For example, these youth may engage in underage drinking or cigarette smoking, particularly with their peers, as a means of displaying "adult-like" behaviors. Another common form of delinquency for this group might be minor vandalism that is often perceived more as a gag than as an act of victimization (actions such as the defacing of road signs, the destruction of residential mailboxes, and other petty forms of destruction). Shoplifting in various stores may also be encouraged among some members of this group for the occasional "five-finger discount" in chosen music and/or clothing stores that are frequented by the adolescent peer group—displaying bravado among one's peers and incidentally obtaining an item that is valued by the individual and the peer group. Finally, some of these individuals may engage in occasional truancy from school, particularly if they are able to hide their absence. These adolescents typically commit acts of defiance or nonconformity simply as a means of expressing their developing sense of autonomy. However, these adolescents are not likely to continue their activities into late adulthood.

It should be noted that self-report studies indicate that most teenage males engage in some criminal conduct, leading criminologists to conclude that participation in delinquency is a normal part of teen life (Scott & Grisso, 1997). Thus, adolescent-limited delinquents are likely to engage in crimes that are profitable or rewarding, but they also have the ability to abandon these actions when pro-social styles become more rewarding (Bartol, 1999). Adolescent-limited youths are relatively free from personality disorders or poor decision making based on life skills deficiencies. Because of this, this group usually has adequate social skills to both compete and cooperate within the strictures of day-to-day society.

Some adolescents, however, continue their delinquent behavior into and throughout adulthood; these are the life course–persistent juvenile delinquents. Unlike the adolescent-limited delinquent, these adolescents lack many of the necessary social skills and opportunities possessed by the adolescent-limited delinquent.

The reason for this difference in development is startling but nonetheless is a common phenomenon in this group. For these offenders, the clue to their difference in conformative ability lies less in their adolescent years and more in their early childhood development.

Indeed, it has been found that many life course–persistent delinquents are children with inherited or acquired physiological deficiencies that develop either prenatally or in early childhood. To compound this problem, many of these same children often come from high-risk social environments as well, reflecting the parental deficiencies that are thought to be genetically transmitted intergenerationally from parent to child (Moffitt, 1993). This combination of the difficult child with an adverse child-rearing context serves to place the child at risk for future delinquent behavior, setting the initial groundwork for a life course–persistent pattern of antisocial behavior during years when the child is usually most impressionable (Moffitt, 1993). Moffitt also found that early aggressive behavior is an important predictor of later delinquency and could possibly be a marker for the life course–persistent offender.

In the early-onset-trajectory, life course–persistent offender, problem behavior that begins in early childhood gradually escalates to more violent behavior, culminating in serious violence before adolescence (Surgeon General, 2002). A child's first serious violent act may have been officially recorded, or it may have been reported by the child to researchers in a confidential survey (Martin, 2004). The early-onset group, in contrast to the late-onset group, is characterized by higher rates of offending and more serious offenses in adolescence as well as greater persistence of violence from adolescence into adulthood (reviewed in Stattin & Magnusson, 1996; Tolan & Gorman-Smith, 1998). The National Youth Survey shows that nearly 13 percent of male adolescents in the early-onset trajectory engaged in violence for two or more years, compared to only 2.5 percent in the late-onset trajectory (Tolan & Gorman-Smith, 1998).

Research shows that between 20 and 45 percent of all boys who are serious violent offenders by age 17 have violent histories that go back to their early childhood (D'Unger et al., 1998; Elliott et al., 1986; Huizinga et al., 1995; Nagin & Tremblay, 1999; Patterson & Yoerger, 1997; Stattin & Magnusson, 1996). An even higher percentage of girls who were serious violent offenders by age 17 (45 to 69 percent) were violent in childhood (Elliott et al., 1986; Huizinga et al., 1995). This means that most violent youths begin their violent behavior during adolescence. However, of those youth who commit the most serious violent acts and who continue their violent behavior beyond adolescence, their violent natures can frequently be traced back to early childhood (Loeber et al., 1998; Moffitt, 1993; Tolan, 1987; Tolan & Gorman-Smith, 1998).

This demonstrates that the greater prevalence of late-onset youth violence refutes the myth that all serious violent offenders can be identified in early childhood. In fact, the majority of young people who become violent show little or no evidence of childhood behavioral disorders, high levels of aggression, or problem behaviors—all predictors of later violence. However, it is still noteworthy to find that even though early predictors may not accurately assess the most *numerous* pool of violent offenders, this process is more likely to correctly identify the most *dangerous* juvenile offenders (Surgeon General, 2002). It is for this reason alone that appropriate assessment is so critical; it may not necessarily lower overall delinquency rates significantly (a phenomenon considered "normal" among American adolescents), but it is likely to reduce violent crimes against members of society. Certainly, this is the category of crime that concerns the public most.

Thus, this distinction is important from an assessment point of view. Knowledge of these early indicators can allow the appropriate specialists an advantage in identifying those children most at risk for delinquency. This knowledge then translates to an enhanced ability to provide effective interventions during an age when the child is likely to be more receptive. During early childhood, negative behaviors such as aggression have not been as clearly reinforced as they are by the time the child reaches adolescence (Martin, 2004). Thus, the earlier the intervention, the better the chance of saving the potential life course–persistent offender from a life of misery and trouble. Although all this may seem obvious, there often are discontinuities in networking between schools and the criminal justice system or, more commonly, a lack of connection between parents and school systems. Because of this, most interventions are applied only after the juvenile has been caught, at which point the juvenile's delinquent activities may have been fully reinforced as valid options in his or her behavioral repertoire. Even worse is when the need for intervention is never adequately noted by anyone in contact with the juvenile because of a lack of awareness of the youth's activities. This lack of interconnected supervision greatly increases the likelihood that delinquency will occur. Thus, it is imperative that partnerships be employed between criminal justice, social service, and educational agencies if treatments are to provide optimal service delivery for those youth who are most at risk of committing serious offenses. See Special Insert 8.1 for an example of effective collaborative partnerships.

RISK FACTORS

The **risk factors** that lead to juvenile delinquency must be understood in order to determine the types of interventions that are necessary for each individual. Risk factors may be found in the individual, the environment, or the individual's ability to respond to the demands of the environment. Research has indicated a number of factors that have a high likelihood of leading to delinquent behavior (McCall, 1994; Moffitt, 1993). Further, each of these factors, when added together, can have a cumulative effect on the likelihood of future delinquency (McCall, 1994). For instance, while poor parenting is a risk factor, this becomes more pronounced when it is coupled with a child's poor academic performance. Further, the environment can serve to compound this, such as when a child attends a school where rules of conduct are lax and teachers are dissatisfied. In these cases, the chances of the child engaging in delinquency increase (McCall, 1994).

Special Insert 8.1. Issues in Juvenile Probation: Community Partnerships in Community Supervision Interventions for Juvenile Offenders

One example of a successful partnership between community agencies that provide juvenile interventions would be the programs administered by the juvenile division of Ohio's Court of Common Pleas in Lucas County. This program has created a community cluster group that was created to address issues affecting youths who are involved in multiple systems. The Lucas County Cluster, as it is called, is a multidisciplinary team staffed by various agencies throughout Lucas County. These agencies work together to develop treatment plans and oversee the case management of those plans. This jurisdiction has also developed a police/probation team. This collaborative effort involves not only the court and the Toledo Police Department but also a community mental health agency in the county. The result is assessment and services at the community level that maximize collaboration, thus eliminating much of the disjointed intervention services that are typically administered to at-risk youth. As just mentioned, this particular partnership includes members of the local police department. These police/probation teams have gained increased popularity in the past decade or so and serve to provide enhanced supervision of offenders in the community. Public safety is thus improved, and services to juveniles with special needs are reinforced by involvement of the police. Such partnerships reinforce a seamless flow of service delivery, ensure community safety, and provide increased incentive for offender compliance with both treatment and community supervision requirements.

Source: Adapted from Townsend (2003).

The risk factors are many and occur along a continuum within the child's development. Table 8.1 shows some risk factors that could be used to predict the onset of juvenile violence and delinquency. Also included are many factors that might help reduce the likelihood of juvenile delinquency. However, it should be pointed out that these risk factors simply serve to increase the likelihood of future delinquency and do not cause delinquency. But, as stated previously, it is the early physiological characteristics, coupled with the presentation of these risk factors, that tend to create the life course–persistent offender. Those adolescents who lack such early childhood characteristics are less likely to suffer from these risk factors, and if they do, these factors tend to have diminished effects as the adolescent achieves adulthood.

Thus, while the risk factors in Table 8.1 play a significant role in producing delinquent behavior, they are not necessarily factors that produce the more violent delinquent. Rather, the numerous physiological and biological precursors set the stage for how adversely these risk factors will impact the adolescent. Such precursors include problems at birth such as low birth weight and prematurity, neuropsychological problems, and various hormonal and neurotransmitter abnormalities. It is suggested that the reader envision this interplay between physiological precursors and

Table 8.1. Risk Factors for Delinquency

	Risk Factor		
Domain	**Early Onset (ages 6–11)**	**Late Onset (ages 12–14)**	**Protective Factors**
Individual	1. General offenses 2. Substance use 3. Male gender 4. Hyperactivity 5. Antisocial (problem) behavior 6. Exposure to television violence 7. Low IQ 8. Dishonesty	1. General offenses 2. Risk taking 3. Aggression 4. Being male 5. Antisocial attitudes 6. Crimes against persons 7. Low IQ 8. Substance abuse	1. Intolerant attitude to criminality 2. High IQ 3. Female gender 4. Positive social orientation 5. Perceptions of sanctions
Family	1. Low socioeconomic status 2. Antisocial parents 3. Harsh, lax, or inconsistent discipline 4. Separation from parents 5. Abusive home 6. Neglectful home	1. Harsh or lax discipline 2. Poor adult supervision 3. Low parental involvement 4. Low socioeconomic status 5. Abusive home	1. Warm relationship with adult caretaker 2. Peer group accepted by parents 3. Parental monitoring
School	1. Poor attitude or performance	1. Poor attitude or performance 2. Academic failure	1. Commitment to school 2. Recognition for conventional activities
Peer group	1. Weak social ties 2. Antisocial peer group	1. Weak social ties 2. Antisocial peer group	1. Friends who engage in conventional behavior
Community	1. Neighborhood crime and drugs	1. Neighborhood crime and drugs	1. Crime, delinquency, and drug-free neighborhood

Source: Adapted from Surgeon General (2002).

risk factors (as presented in Table 8.1) along the lines of what is often referred to as the **diathesis-stress model**. In the medical field, "diathesis" refers to a predisposition to develop a particular disease (Morris, 1990). In the same way, some people are more likely than others to develop various kinds of maladaptive behaviors or disorders when exposed to stress (Morris, 1990). In some cases, this diathesis can even be hereditary, while in other cases it seems to reflect prior experiences.

Whatever the cause, these people have a weakness that leaves them susceptible to certain kinds of maladaptive behaviors when experiencing stress in their lives

(Morris, 1990). This does not mean that everyone with such a diathesis will develop a particular kind of psychological disorder under stress. Rather, they are simply more likely to display the disorder than are most others faced with the same stressful situation (Morris, 1990). In this case, we will equate "disorder" with criminal activity, "diathesis" with physiological precursors, and "stress" with risk factors to explain differences in juvenile delinquency among life course–persistent and adolescent-limited offenders. Thus, those children who present with early physiological precursors (e.g., brain anomalies, fetal alcohol syndrome, **attention-deficit/hyperactivity disorder** [ADHD], and nervous system disorders) have a diathesis that, when presented with certain risk factors (those listed in Table 8.1), makes them more likely than others to respond to stress by engaging in criminal activity. Not only does it increase the likelihood of delinquency, but it also serves to increase the severity and continued persistence of future delinquency. This is precisely what separates the life course–persistent offender from the adolescent-limited offender. Given this, we must now turn our attention to those physiological factors that are likely to produce a diathesis toward lifelong criminality, as is the case with life course–persistent offenders.

PHYSIOLOGICAL FACTORS: SOURCES CONTRIBUTING TO A DIATHESIS TOWARD CRIMINAL BEHAVIOR

Hormone levels, neurological dysfunction, brain damage, and learning disabilities are widely cited mechanisms involved in the development of psychosocial disorders and violence among youth (Rutter & Casaer, 2001). It has been noted that antisocial behavior peaks in the teenage years because hormonal activity is greatest during this time of individual development. It has been argued that the increased level of the male androgen testosterone is the main causal factor for excessive levels of violence among teenage boys (Buchanan, Eccles, & Becker, 1992; Siegel, Welsh, & Senna, 2003). Adolescents who experience more intense moods, mood swings, anxiety, and restlessness than their peers who do not suffer from these symptoms tend to engage in more pervasive and more serious delinquency (Buchanan et al., 1992).

Siegel et al. (2003) note that neurological dysfunction has been measured with electroencephalograms, computerized arial tomography, and observation of performance indicators (e.g., gross motor, visual and auditory, and language functioning) to examine whether the roots of conflict and aggression have a neurological basis. Accordingly, it has been found that children who manifest behavior disturbances may have neurological deficits, such as damage to one or both hemispheres of the brain (Voeller, 1986). This may sometimes be described as "minimal brain dysfunction," which Siegel et al. (2003) define as "an abnormality in the cerebral or brain structure that causes behavior injurious to a person's lifestyle and social adjustment" (p. 77). Moffitt (1993) has noted that this impairment is thought to be brought about by factors such as low birth weight, brain injury, birth complications, and inherited abnormality. Siegel et al. (2003) note that children displaying neurological impairment are also at increased risk for having a wide range of developmental problems, including low IQ scores and cognitive impairment, each of which has also been found to correlate with delinquency.

Finally, learning disabilities seem to be correlated with delinquency. As this topic was covered in Chapter 6, no lengthy discussion on learning disabilities is required at this point. Nevertheless, it should be pointed out that among arrested and incarcerated youth, there is a much higher rate of learning disabilities than among those who have never been arrested or incarcerated. Siegel et al. (2003) point out that while roughly 10 percent of youth in the United States may present with some form of learning disability, adjudicated youth have a much higher likelihood of having a learning disability. While it is not certain if learning disabilities are a leading cause of delinquency, it is undeniable that both tend to correlate with one another (Siegel et al., 2003; see Chapter 6 for more details). See Special Insert 8.2 for a discussion on the importance of psychological screening with adolescent offenders.

THE ADHD CONNECTION

ADHD is a disorder that is commonly linked with childhood antisocial and future teenage delinquent behavior. Data suggest that youths with ADHD and delinquent behavior are at a very high risk of developing lengthy and serious future adult criminal careers (Moffitt, 1990; Satterfield, Swanson, Schell, & Lee, 1994). ADHD has three central behavioral characteristics: (1) inattention (does not listen or is easily distracted), (2) impulsivity (acts before thinking, and shifts quickly from one activity to another), and (3) excessive motor activity (cannot sit still, fidgets, runs about, and is talkative and noisy) (Bartol, 1999). The American Psychiatric Association's (2000) *Diagnostic and Statistical Manual of Mental Disorders* (4th ed., text revision) defines a person as having ADHD if there is a persistent pattern of inattention and/or hyperactivity-impulsivity that is more frequent and severe than is typically observed in individuals at a comparable level of development. ADHD is one of the most common mental disorders among children, affecting 3 to 5 percent of all children. The ability to learn, retain, and recall new information, especially in the verbal domain, is critical for a person's success in school. It has been shown that children with ADHD can exhibit unexpected weaknesses in learning even without a formal learning disability (Cutting, Koth, Mahone, & Denckla, 2003). This is important because poor school performance often correlates with juvenile delinquency.

According to one study, parents reported more symptoms of aggression with an earlier estimated age of onset for ADHD (Turgay & Morgan, 2002). Canadian researchers reported that ADHD is commonly associated with chronic and serious aggressive behavior in children and adolescents (Turgay & Morgan, 2002). One hundred and twenty-nine children and adolescents were included in a study that revealed that 82.4 percent of ADHD cases demonstrated verbal aggression and 72.1 percent presented with physically aggressive acts (Turgay & Morgan, 2002). An article in *Child Psychiatry and Human Development* by Weiss and Hechtman (1993)

Special Insert 8.2. Adolescents with Mental Health Needs

In an effort to improve services to this specialized population, the Texas Juvenile Probation Commission (TJPC) was tasked with creating a mental health screening instrument to be used by all departments. TJPC has developed a comprehensive array of mental health services to this population. The project was named the Special Needs Diversionary Project and consists of juveniles with mental health issues who are supervised by juvenile probation officers who, in turn, work closely with mental health practitioners (eliminating the "organizational cracks" in the intervention process that are discussed in this chapter), guaranteeing the delivery of the necessary mental health services. The goals of the project are to keep the offenders at home within the community, reduce recidivism of those in the project, and have juvenile probation work closely with local mental health providers to ensure both proper assessment and interventions for those juvenile probationers in the program. Some of the elements contained in this project's package of interventions are the following:

1. Coordinated service delivery and planning between probation and mental health staff
2. Provision and monitoring of medication
3. Individual and/or group therapy
4. Skills training
5. In-home services such as multisystemic or functional family services
6. Family focus support services
7. Co-location of supervision and treatment services

Youth participation is determined by indicators on the mental health screening instrument and the availability of a caretaker/guardian willing to work with the mental health and probation departments. At this point, an additional clinical assessment is made to determine the child's ability to function in society. As a side note, it was found that 22 percent all these youth suffered from depression, 19 percent qualified for the diagnosis of oppositional defiant disorder, 18 percent had the diagnosis of conduct disorder (a precursor to antisocial personality disorder), and 9 percent had ADHD.

The Special Needs Diversionary Project illustrates how important assessment can be to both community supervision and mental health services. This program also demonstrates how public safety and offender needs can be better served when disparate community agencies create partnerships in providing service to special needs populations. Such partnerships, when coupled with accurate assessment instruments and procedures, can provide better interventions that are tailored for the offender. Interventions then will be more likely to have a better "goodness of fit" with the needs of the juvenile offender and will be better able to target those most at risk of recidivating when released on community supervision.

Source: Adapted from Spriggs (2003).

found that during interviews for a study of ADHD adolescents more than half reported that they were restless, impatient, irritable, and impulsive. Forty percent of the subjects had more than three of the following symptoms: chronic lying, frequent fighting, being difficult to raise, and swearing and being defiant; 31 percent reported that they were stealing (Weiss & Hechtman, 1993). Research such as this demonstrates a connection between ADHD and childhood delinquency in general as well as a more direct link to future aggressive and violent delinquent behavior during the later teenage years.

CHILD AND ADOLESCENT OFFENDERS BEHIND BARS

Roughly one-fifth of all juvenile arrestees are detained (Clear & Cole, 2003). This detention is usually for only one or two days until an initial appearance can be arranged. While most child and adolescent offenders (CAOs) are returned to their families after this period of time, some are kept in a detention facility for longer periods of time. According to Clear and Cole (2003), roughly 18 percent of juveniles who are in detention are found to either be a danger to society or unlikely to reappear in court and are thus kept in detention for longer periods of time until adjudication can be arranged (essentially one-fifth of all juveniles are placed in detention, and roughly one-fifth of those are kept in detention, meaning that only about 4 percent of all CAO offenders are kept in detention for more than a handful of days).

Correctional facilities for CAOs range from places that look similar to adult prison to places that are more like a residential treatment facility (Godwin & Helms, 2002). However, it is estimated that among these facilities, nearly two-thirds are privately run operations that tend to be smaller than state-based public facilities. Among the youth who are in long-term incarceration, roughly 75 percent are held in public facilities (Martin, 2004).

Typically, CAOs in public facilities are around 15 to 16 years of age, are Caucasian, and remain in such facilities for approximately five to six months. The CAO in private facilities tends to be younger than one in public facilities. Public institutions provide custodial care for CAOs, including that small segment that is between the ages of 18 and 21; CAO offenders are most often incarcerated for personal, property, or drug-related offenses (Godwin & Helms, 2002). The rate of incarceration in the United States is approximately 368 out of every 100,000 CAOs showing that few juveniles are actually incarcerated for prolonged periods of time (the national total being no more than 110,000).

Male delinquents constitute the majority of incarcerated youth. Recently, attention has focused on the fact that minority juveniles are overrepresented in the institutionalized juvenile population. This is particularly true with the African American population, but similar outcomes with Latino American youth are found in areas of the United States where the Latino population is higher. In fact, minority juveniles are incarcerated at a rate anywhere from two to five times that of Caucasian youth.

Further, minority youth are more likely to be placed in a public facility (where treatment services are not as well funded) than in a private facility (where treatment services are better funded and presumably more effective). This then creates a situation where the prognosis (likelihood for rehabilitation) for minority youth is often much poorer than for Caucasian youth. While researchers, policymakers, and the general public are becoming more aware of this disparity within the juvenile justice system, the simple fact remains that over 60 percent of juveniles in custody belong to a racial or ethnic minority group.

One interesting form of institutional juvenile corrections is the use of boot camps. Juvenile boot camps vary from state to state but tend to be highly structured residential programs that include military-style regimens (drills and physical training) with some rehabilitative elements, such as drug counseling and educational programs. These programs are usually designed with the nonserious juvenile offender in mind and have a duration of three to six months. Thus, while these forms of incarceration are more intensive, they do not necessarily last longer than typical forms of institutionalization for juvenile offenders. In general, it has been found that these programs do not adequately protect the public, nor do they appear to help the confined youth appreciably (Brown, Borduin, & Henggeler, 2003). Further, several cost analyses have concluded that juvenile boot camps are more costly than the usual routine of services. To make matters worse, there is evidence that those youth given boot camp interventions have no improvement in their recidivism rates. Overall, there are consistent findings that indicate that boot camp programs do not effectively serve treatment functions for juvenile offenders and that they are not at all cost effective (Brown et al., 2003; Clear & Cole, 2003).

For those child and adolescent offenders who are incarcerated for violent crimes, a special form of incarceration may be employed. This occurs when the juvenile case is transferred to adult court and results in what is commonly known as juvenile waiver. Waiver to adult court can theoretically be utilized for any offense, but this process is usually reserved for serious, violent felonies or for property crimes with which juveniles are repeat offenders (Godwin & Helms, 2003). Child and adolescent offenders who are tried in adult criminal court are most often kept in a juvenile facility or separate wing until they are of sufficient age to be transferred to the adult population. Those who are placed in an adult prison are usually separated from the adult population.

The disposition of a CAO who has been tried and sentenced in an adult court varies from state to state. The usual procedure is that younger offenders who are found guilty are sent to a juvenile detention facility until they are at least 16 to 18 years of age. Their treatment there is basically the same as that of juveniles who are tried under the juvenile justice system. However, if the crime and the circumstances are severe enough, the adolescent can be sent to an adult prison if over 16 years of age (Neubauer, 2002).

Neubauer (2002) points to the advantages and disadvantages involved with the controversial process of juvenile waiver. The public sends a strong message to CAOs that violence will not be tolerated. This approach also ensures that juvenile court and correctional resources are not disproportionately allocated to violent offenders, particularly with repeat CAO offenders who seem unlikely to reform.

The chief disadvantage to this process is that it sends a message of hopelessness to the youth and society regarding the likelihood of reformation. Further, there is the possibility that this approach will only increase the criminality of juveniles as they are exposed to the adult criminal population. The adult prison system's mission is primarily the punishment of offenders, and this naturally would include those juveniles included within its confines as well. It is perhaps that these offenders are best considered to be targeted by a form of legal "selective incapacitation" where the most severe of offenders are removed from society for no other reason than to protect society from further harm. However, this automatically translates to an admission by the justice system regarding its ability to reform the youth, something that can be disturbing considering the number of years left to transpire for a young offender of, say, 14 or 15 years of age.

It should be noted that CAOs who are given brief periods of incarceration are no more likely to recidivate than are adults who are subject to incarceration. However, it is likely that those individuals who are given incarceration are life course–persistent offenders waiting to mature. Thus, it is important to provide effective interventions during the juvenile's incarceration, as this may prevent criminality in adulthood. Naturally, these same interventions are equally crucial once the juvenile is released into the community, which invariably occurs at some point. It is here that last-ditch efforts to prevent adulthood criminality occur, and failure to stem this trajectory can easily lead to more serious violations of the law. Still, the likelihood of developing into life course–persistent offenders will have much to do with the individual disposition of the child and/or adolescent offender. It is precisely because of this that treatment plans must be specialized to the individual offender. However, this specialization is seldom if ever provided in most institutional settings. This makes the community-based response that follows all the more important in the long-term picture of the child and/or adolescent offender.

CAOs IN THE COMMUNITY

Juvenile probation is the most common form of sanction given to CAO offenders. In fact, roughly 53 percent of all juvenile cases result in the juvenile being placed on probation and being released to the care of a parent or a guardian. In most cases, the juvenile court judge will add specialized requirements, such as counseling, or some enhanced penalty, such as restitution. The primary point to juvenile probation has traditionally been the reintegration of the CAO offender into the community. However, there has been a gradual shift in juvenile probation toward more punitive approaches. In fact, this sanction alone, given after the previously mentioned brief detention period, is increasingly considered insufficient among many juvenile courts.

Instead, the use of intensive supervision programs (ISPs) has found increasing popularity within the juvenile justice system. The only real difference between these types of supervision and standard probation is the intensity and frequency with which program requirements are mandated. Although ISPs tend to vary by the type of offender and by the offender's aggravating or mitigating circumstances, extremely high-risk CAOs tend to be excluded from participation in ISPs (Brown et al., 2003).

According to Brown et al. (2003), ISPs are community-based correctional alternatives to incarceration and regular probation that are designed to both punish and control juveniles in the community. They are considered favorable to the public because they reduce the need for institutionalizing the juvenile, enhance regular probation, and are less costly than institutionally based sentences.

Components of ISPs include frequent contact between the juvenile offender and the juvenile probation officer, home confinement, curfew requirements, random drug testing, work-related community service, payment of restitution, and sometimes even electronic monitoring. Further, boot camps and other residential placements may be used in conjunction with ISPs. Although this offsets the cost-effectiveness of these programs, they are still considered much more viable alternatives to boot camp programs or other less restrictive forms of institutionalization.

Those CAOs who are awarded with institutionalized forms of sentencing are eventually released back into the community as well. As stated previously, most will be incarcerated for only five to six months, meaning that must juvenile offenders will end up on community supervision for the majority of their sentence. For those who are released from their short stint in the institution, a process of aftercare is implemented that largely resembles ISPs.

Aftercare is often likened to adult parole. This system receives juveniles who have been under some form of custody, whether it be a state training school, a residential treatment facility, or another such institution. The aftercare system then provides supervision and support during the period of readjustment to the community. The importance of aftercare rests on the notion that young offenders face significant obstacles to readjustment after they have been away from their homes and that the chances of failure in readjustment are high for these individuals.

Aftercare workers are highly aware of the difficulties these youths face. Because these youths have been incarcerated, their offenses will often be on the more serious end of the spectrum or ones they have engaged in repeatedly. This alone lowers the prognosis for such youth. Further, these youth have been a source of discord for their own family, neighbors, and schools and thus may not be given a warm or welcoming return home. Further, the family of origin may itself may be dysfunctional and may have been a source of the juvenile's initial maladjustment in the community. If this is the case and if the juvenile is returned to the family, aftercare workers must monitor the family system carefully. Likewise, the juvenile's peer group may have also been a primary source of maladaptive activity. In this case, it is important that the aftercare worker watch for further negative peer group effects on the juvenile. In this case, the juvenile should be dissuaded from continuing relations with this group unless parameters are appropriately set in place. However, this is often easier said than done.

CAOs IN CORRECTIONAL TREATMENT

Any intervention program must be capable of distinguishing between life course–persistent and adolescent-limited delinquent offenders. In addition, particular attention should be paid to the life course–persistent offender because of the chronic and repetitive nature of his or her delinquent and, ultimately, criminal career. Again, however, these delinquents are hard to identify among their peer group, as their behaviors will be fairly normalized by the acts of independence and autonomy associated with teen offenders in general (Harman, 1990).

In particular, both intervention and prevention programs should seek to identify factors that are most frequently associated with life course–persistent delinquents. In accordance with the diathesis-stress model, some youth are predisposed to develop delinquent behavior when exposed to certain types of stressors (Morris, 1990). The diathesis-stress formula is an integral component of the successful treatment of both life course–persistent and adolescent-limited delinquents. However, the life course–persistent offender requires early intervention so that future delinquency can be prevented or at least minimized in frequency and severity. Therefore, prevention is the best method for dealing with the life course–persistent offender. At very young ages, certain factors can be identified, such as prenatal deficiencies, maternal substance abuse, injury to the embryo, neural anomalies, and so on. When such characteristics are reported, specific attention should be given to decrease the likelihood of future delinquent conduct.

A program aimed at detecting such risk factors would need to provide a satisfactory network between the maternity wards of regional hospitals, the child's family of origin, local preschool programs, and the local public school system. In fact, each of these will be crucial to the successful prevention of long-term delinquency among those at risk for becoming life course–persistent offenders. Early identification of mothers who are substance abusers, who fail to seek adequate prenatal care, and so on can be achieved with appropriate cooperation with hospital facilities that track these records. Newborns determined to be at significant risk should be given particular attention with adequate nutrition and material needs provided. Mothers must likewise be assisted, and cooperation must be made mandatory for those youth most at risk. Although this mandatory participation might be controversial, it is imperative if prevention is to be attained. While some programs such as these do currently exist, many do not specifically target potential delinquency as an objective, and many fail to appropriately network with one another. Because of this, prevention programs can become haphazard constructions with each addressing a limited portion of the larger picture and collectively failing to address the problem as a whole. Such gaps in preventive programs essentially produce cracks in the organizational network through which many life course–persistent offenders can slip, falling into increasingly severe acts of misbehavior.

Beyond the initial medical identification of risk at birth, children can be found to be at risk in early childhood as well. In addition, these children may not necessarily provide at-risk indicators during prenatal and early birth periods. For instance, children with attention default disorder or ADHD often show no symptoms of this disorder until around ages three to five (Slap-Shelton, 1994). Even in this case, it may be difficult to sort out ADHD from developmentally normal behavior for children in this age range (Slap-Shelton, 1994). Thus, assessment procedures must likewise be in place in the early formative years following birth with the preschool environment being ideally suited. Once these children who are at risk are identified, parent education and/or training should be considered essential. This can often mimic programs such as Head Start.

The point to these preventive programs is to accurately identify those children likely to be at an increased risk of delinquency by noting various risk factors that demonstrate a likely diathesis, or predisposition, toward future delinquency. Beyond basic survival needs (e.g., nutrition and proper medical care), programs should address other factors that are important in determining future delinquency. The stressors that are encountered by the child are often increased because of the child's frequently difficult temperaments. Parents can and often do feel overwhelmed when dealing with such children and as a result find themselves in a downward spiral of continued negative interactions. These negative interactions between the child and the environment (i.e., parents, school, and peers) tend to reinforce the negative behavior of at-risk youth, creating a direct path toward antisocial and future delinquent behavior.

Thus, the crucial objective beyond assessment and medical/nutritional intervention is to specifically address those environmental stressors that aggravate the predisposition toward delinquent behavior. Such stressors are common to many underprivileged homes and are also a common factor in homes that experience neglect and/or abuse. The Office of Juvenile Justice and Delinquency Prevention has targeted several "nurturing" parenting programs that help these at-risk youth who are likewise members of at-risk family systems (Bavolek, 2000). These programs teach parents how parenting patterns are learned; both effective and ineffective patterns are learned behaviors that can assuage or aggravate, respectively, the likelihood of future delinquency.

In particular, these programs educate parents on appropriate expectations of children. Parents must understand the predispositions of their children and know how to appropriately deal with these issues. Specifically, parents must not be allowed to "discount" their child's predisposition, nor should they be allowed to avoid dealing with this hereditarily based temperament. Further, the effect of inappropriate parental expectations on children can best be characterized as a stressful environment that negatively impacts the children's self-worth (Bavolek, 2000). A lack of critical experiences and persisting traumatic stress leads to negative effects on neural modulation and regulation capacities (Bavolek, 2000). This often results in an overdevelopment of brain stem and midbrain neurophysiology and functioning (e.g., anxiety, impulsivity, poor affect regulation, and motor hyperactivity) and an underdevelopment of limbic and cortical functions, resulting in deficits of empathy and problem-solving skills (Perry, 1997). It is easy to see how these factors and their resulting symptoms can serve to increase the likelihood of future delinquent behavior. Those youth who already possess neural deficiencies, nervous system imbalances, and so on are more likely to be adversely affected by these factors than are children who do not experience such deficiencies. Therefore, targeting those children who possess both predispositions and corresponding environmental characteristics that contribute to potential delinquency is imperative to a successful assessment procedure. Similarly, an effective assessment procedure is critical to any successful delinquency prevention program. Finally, a preventive-based program is more likely to have success with life course–persistent delinquents than is an intervention-based program because of the inherent predisposition that these children possess beginning in the womb itself.

Beyond this, however, is the reality that prevention will not work perfectly and that there is still a need for intervention programs to address those youth who are currently involved in delinquent behavior. Thus, any delinquency program must likewise possess an intervention component as well. It is at this point that community and school factors (from Table 8.1) must be incorporated fully into any delinquency intervention program. Youth at risk of adolescent delinquency often come from stressed and socially isolated families (McDonald, 1999). Indeed, both affluent and low-income families struggle with the same issues concerning how to raise their children successfully (McDonald, 1999). Thus, while many of the material issues such as poor parental care, poor nutrition, and so on may be represented more among low-income families, the challenge of raising children who resist delinquent activity is a struggle shared by all families regardless of socioeconomic status.

With respect to intervention, many of these programs should have similar techniques in dealing with both life course–persistent and adolescent-limited offenders. This is because the behaviors are nearly identical for both groups. However, the life course–persistent offender is likely to fare worse in interventions because of a failure to capitalize on pro-social opportunities in earlier childhood. For such youth, successful interventions will require that programs provide instruction and life skills so that they can "catch up" with their cohorts. Because of this, it will be necessary for these programs to place much more emphasis on individual risk factors (see Table 8.1) than would be likely with their adolescent-limited counterparts. Failure to address these deficiencies originating from an early childhood cycle of negative interactions will produce adverse results for these youth who participate in such a treatment program. Because of this, assessment is again important in the intervention stage just as it is in the prevention stage. Beyond addressing these deficits, interventions will take on a flavor that resembles forms of family therapy and will need to involve the regional school system if they are to be successful. Both are particularly important for the potential life course–persistent offender since it is the "gaps" between these organizations that have led to a discontinuous form of preventive effort. This involvement in a multipronged intervention will compensate for **protective factors** that can serve to reverse or hold in check many of the risk factors that the youth has been exposed to. Again, the earlier the intervention, the better, with prevention being the goal.

One such program, known as **Families and Schools Together (FAST)**, has obtained some statistically significant positive results in impacting at-risk children and families (McDonald, 1999). This program is based on family therapy techniques and pays particular heed to delinquency-based research. It employs protective factors for youth and increases both parental and school-based involvement. This program brings at-risk children and their families together into multifamily groups to strengthen families and increase the likelihood that children will succeed at home, at school, and in the community (McDonald, 1999).

The FAST program purports to have several goals within its agenda. The first of these is to enhance family functioning by strengthening the parent–child relationship and empowering parents to be the primary prevention agents for their children. Equally important is the prevention of school failure among at-risk children. In doing so, the program seeks to improve the child's short- and long-term behavior and performance in school. This program likewise empowers parents to be partners in the educational process (McDonald, 1999). The program also targets substance abuse prevention by the child and family, linking the family to appropriate assessment and treatment services when needed. Finally, and perhaps more important, this program acknowledges and seeks to reduce the stress that parents and children experience from daily situations (McDonald, 1999).

The FAST program assumes that participants are at risk and that families are under stress and need social support. Six research-based strategies are used to build protective factors for youth in the FAST program. These strategies address each child's interpersonal bonds, the family system, parent-to-parent support, parent self-help support groups, parent empowerment training, and school–community affiliation (McDonald, 1999). Positive bonds and relationships on multiple levels counteract many youth risk factors and reduce behavior problems correlated with later violence, delinquency, substance abuse, and school failure (McDonald, 1999). Further, in an attempt to provide more accurate assessment, the school principal, teachers, and student services teams screen youth for indicators of risk to identify children who could most benefit from the FAST program.

The introduction of this program (or others similar to it) is relevant to our previous discussion of life course–persistent and adolescent-limited offenders. First, this model of treatment emphasizes protective factors that guard against future delinquency. This has been specifically noted as crucial to circumventing delinquency by Moffitt (1993) in explaining why some youth never engage in delinquency. These protective factors likewise fit perfectly within the schema of the diathesis-stress model of explaining persistent delinquency. Indeed, these factors serve to provide a coping buffer against the "stressor" component of the model discussed earlier. Thus, the FAST program serves to deal directly with protective factors in an attempt to first prevent and then intervene in the likelihood of future delinquent behavior. Further, this model places a unique point of interest on the assessment component, utilizing the feedback of school officials and educators. This is important because these professionals have frequent access to the adolescent and, being outside the family, provide the best glimpse into the behavior of the adolescent. For the life course–persistent offender, this is important, as youths require selective attention and support to prevent their delinquent trajectory from progressing further into adulthood. Unlike the adolescent-limited offender, this group runs the risk of continued criminality into their adult years, and thus the ramifications—and the corresponding intervention needs—are much more complex and serious.

For the adolescent-limited offender, however, such concerns are not as severe. Instead, concerns revolving around these offenders tend to be limited, as their forms of delinquency tend to be transient and limited to those periods where expressions of autonomy and independence are considered part of the "normal" adolescent journey to adulthood. Intervention programs for these offenders are nonetheless important so as to prevent the likelihood of these youth from inadvertently slipping into circumstances that can significantly alter their "trajectory" through the life cycle (Sampson & Laub, 1993). However, most of these delinquents will adequately find their way back into mainstream societal roles, having acquired the variety of prosocial skills necessary to operate successfully within the larger society. Interventions for these youth will typically be temporary and will deal frequently with the normal day-to-day concerns of adolescents rather than the true dysfunctions likely to be encountered with life course–persistent offenders.

What is important about these intervention programs is the fact that they dovetail nicely with the diathesis-stress model discussed previously. These programs are applicable to both life course–persistent and adolescent-limited delinquents. This fits snugly with the theory presented by Moffitt (1993). This is significant because it demonstrates that this theory can be adapted toward both explaining and treating delinquency. Insight that does not translate into some form of constructive action becomes useless. This treatment approach utilizes the insight provided by Moffitt (1993) and translates this into potential action in both preventing and treating delinquency among youth. Finally, it must be noted that in either case, it is inevitable that some youth will engage in at least some minor forms of delinquency and that some youth will fall through the cracks simply because of the imperfect nature of any subjective treatment program. Despite this, a treatment model that emphasizes accurate assessment coupled with prevention programs targeted for those youth most in need will serve to significantly minimize the long-term effects of delinquency in society. These long-term effects are the most devastating and debilitating to society, the family, and the delinquent. Simply identifying these distinctions can serve to avoid therapeutic betrayals to both society and its youth, maintaining ethical honesty in attempting to unravel the delinquency puzzle that is presented to researchers, practitioners, and parents alike.

CONCLUSION

This chapter demonstrates that a wide range of factors can place an adolescent at risk of committing delinquent acts. In fact, to at least some extent, such behavior is to be expected. However, some adolescents go on to lead crime-free lives, while a certain segment will go on to lead a life plagued by crime and turmoil. The premise of this chapter is that practitioners can distinguish between these two groups if they use sound, effective assessment techniques.

The diathesis-stress model helps explain why some adolescents fall into a lifelong association with crime and why others do not. With this knowledge as the background and with adequate tools of assessment, practitioners can identify risk factors and provide interventions that can prevent these youth from continuing further into criminal behavior. Because of their age, these youth are characterized as special needs offenders. However, once they turn majority age, this status may no longer apply, and it is then that they may find themselves in a life wrought with the pains associated with long-term incarceration. Effective assessments, particularly objective assessments, are perhaps the best line of prevention and are also the most consistent tools that we have to attempt to prevent such life course outcomes from occurring.

KEY TERMS

Assessment
Psychodiagnostic method
Psychometric method
Adolescent-limited offenders
Life course–persistent offenders
Risk factors
Diathesis-stress model
Attention-deficit/hyperactivity disorder
Protective factors
Families and School Together (FAST)

REFERENCES

American Psychiatric Association. (2000). *Diagnostic and statistical manual of mental disorders* (4th ed., text revision). Arlington, VA: Author.

Bartol, C. R. (1999). *Criminal behavior: A psychological approach*. Englewood Cliffs, NJ: Prentice Hall.

Bavolek, S. J. (2000). The nurturing parenting programs. *Juvenile Justice Bulletin, NCJ 172848*, 1–12.

Brown, T. L., Borduin, C. M., & Henggeler, S. W. (2003). Treating juvenile offenders in community settings. In J. B. Ashford, B. D. Sales, & W. H. Reid (Eds.), *Treating adult and juvenile offenders with special needs* (pp. 445–464). Washington, DC: American Psychological Association.

Buchanan, C. M., Eccles, J., & Becker, J. (1992). Are adolescents the victims of raging hormones? Evidence for activational effects of hormones on moods and behavior at adolescence. *Psychological Bulletin, 111*, 62–107.

Cadoret, R. J., Yates, W. R., Troughton, E., Woodworth, G., & Stewart, M. A. (1995). Adoption study demonstrating two genetic pathways to drug abuse. *Archives of General Psychiatry, 52,* 42–52.

Clear, T. R., & Cole, G. F. (2003). *American corrections* (6th ed.). Belmont, CA: Wadsworth/Thomson Learning.

Cutting, L., Koth, C., Mahone, M., & Denckla, M. (2003). Evidence for unexpected weaknesses in learning in children with attention-deficit/hyperactivity disorder without reading disabilities. *Journal of Learning Disabilities, 36*(3), 259–270.

David, H. B. (2000). Peer group, families, and school failure among urban children: Elements of risk and successful interventions. *Preventing School Failure, 44*(3), 97–98.

Dishion, T. J., Capaldi, D., Spracklen, K. M., & Li, F. (1995). Peer ecology of male adolescent drug use. *Development and Psychopathology*, 7, 803–824.

Drummond, R. J. (1992). *Appraisal procedures for counselors and helping professionals* (3rd ed.). Englewood Cliffs, NJ: Prentice Hall.

D'Unger A.V., Land, K. C., McCall, P. L., & Nagan, D. S. (1998). How many latent classes of delinquent/criminal careers? Result from mixed poisson regression analysis. *American Journal of Sociology, 103*, 1593–1620.

Elliott, D. S., Huizinga, D., & Morse, B. J. (1986). Self-reported violent offending: A descriptive analysis of juvenile violent offenders and their offending careers. *Journal of Interpersonal Violence, 1*, 472–514.

Godwin, C. D., & Helms, J. L. (2002). Violence risk assessment of youth. In N. G. Ribner (Ed.), *The handbook of juvenile forensic psychology* (pp. 318–342). San Francisco: Jossey-Bass.

Harman, L. D. (1990). Acceptable deviance as social control: The case of fashion and slang. In C. D. Bryant (Ed.), *Deviant behavior: Readings in the sociology of norm violations* (pp. 62–77). New York: Hemisphere.

Huizinga, D., Loeber, R., & Thornberry, T. P. (1995). *Recent findings from the program of research on the causes and correlates of delinquency.* U.S. Department of Justice, Office of Justice Programs, Office of Juvenile Justice and Delinquency Prevention, NCJ 159042. Washington, DC: U.S. Government Printing Office.

Martin, A. (2004). *Causal factors associated with juvenile delinquency* (unpublished manuscript). Monroe, LA: University of Louisiana.

McCall, N. (1994). *Makes me wanna holler*. New York; Random House.

McDonald, L. (1999) Families and schools together: Building relationships. *Juvenile Justice Bulletin, NCJ 173423*, 1–19.

Moffitt, T. E. (1990). The neuropsychology of juvenile delinquency: A critical review. In M. Tonry & N. Morris (Eds.), *Crime and justice: A review of research* (pp. 156–178). Chicago: University of Chicago Press.

Moffitt, T. E. (1993). Adolescence-limited and life-course persistent antisocial behavior: A developmental taxonomy. *Psychological Review, 100*, 674–701.

Morris, C. G. (1990). *Contemporary psychology and effective behavior* (7th ed.). Glenview, IL: Scott Foresman.

Nagin, D., & Termblay, R. E. (1999). Trajectories of boys' physical agression, opposition, and hyperactivity on the path to physically violent and nonviolent juvenile delinquency. *Child Development, 70*, 1181–1196.

Nebauer, D. W. (2002). *America's court and the criminal justice system* (7th ed.). Belmont, CA: Wadsworth.

Patterson, G. R., & Yoerger, K. (1997). A developmental model for late-onset delinquency. In D. W. Osgood (Ed.), *Motivation and delinquency* (vol. 44, pp. 121–177). Lincoln, NE: Nebraska Symposium on Motivation.

Perry, B. (1997). Incubated in terror: Neurodevelopmental factors in the cycle of violence. In J. D. Osofsky (Ed.), *Children, youth and violence: Searching for solutions* (pp. 124–149). New York: Guilford Press.

Rutter, M., & Casaer, P. (2001). *Biological risk factors for psychosocial disorders*. Cambridge: Cambridge University Press.

Sampson, R. J., & Laub, J. H. (1993). *Crime in the making: Pathways and turning points through life*. Cambridge, MA: Harvard University Press.

Satterfield, J. H., Swanson, J., Schell, A., & Lee, F. (1994). Prediction of antisocial behavior in attention-hyperactivity disorder boys from aggression/defiance scores. *Journal of the American Academy of Child and Adolescent Psychiatry, 33*, 185–191.

Scott, E. S., & Grisso, T. (1997). The evolution of adolescence: A developmental perspective on juvenile justice reform. *Journal of Criminal Law and Criminology, 88*(1), 137–189.

Siegel, L. J., Welsh, B. C., & Senna, J. J. (2003). *Juvenile delinquency: Theory, practice, and law*. Belmont, CA: Thomson/Wadsworth.

Slap-Shelton, L. (1994). *Child therapy today: Volume I of the child therapy news*. King of Prussia, PA: Center for Applied Psychology.

Spriggs, V. (2003). Identifying and providing services to Texas: Juvenile offenders with mental health needs. *Corrections Today, 65*(1), 64–66.

Stattin, H., & Magnusson, D. (1996). Antisocial development: A holistic approach. *Development and Psychopathyology, 8,* 617–645.

Surgeon General. (2002). Youth violence: A report of the surgeon general. Retrieved from http://www.mentalhealth.org/youthviolence/surgeongeneral/SG_Site/chapter4/sec1.asp

Tolan, P. H., & Gorman-Smith, D. (1998). Development of serious and violent offending careers. In R. Loeber & D. P. Farrington (Eds.), *Serious and violent juvenile offenders: Risk factors and successful interventions* (pp. 68–85). Thousand Oaks, CA: Sage.

Turgay, A., & Morgan, E. (2002). Aggressive behavior commonly linked to ADHD. *Brown University Child and Adolescent Behavior, 12*(18), 4–5.

Voeller, K. (1986). Right hemisphere deficit syndrome in children. *American Journal of Psychiatry, 143*, 1004–1009.

Weiss, G., & Hechtman, L. (1993). *Hyperactive children grown up: ADHD in children, adolescents, and adults*. New York: Guilford Press.

LEARNING CHECK

1. Some research has found that delinquency is related to individual risk factors such as impulsivity and even IQ.
   a. True
   b. False

2. In the diathesis-stress model, stress is equated to a ______________.
   a. Disorder
   b. Diathesis
   c. Behavioral condition
   d. Risk factor
   e. All of the above

3. Being female is considered a protective factor against delinquency.
   a. True
   b. False

4. An offender who is predicted to offend late in life is a ______________.
   a. Chronic recidivist
   b. Adolescent-limited offender
   c. Life course–persistent offender
   d. None of the above

5. During adolescence, it may be difficult to distinguish life course–persistent offenders from adolescent-limited offenders because their behavior is likely to be similar.
   a. True
   b. False

6. A preventive-based program is more likely to have success with life course–persistent delinquents than is an intervention-based program.
   a. True
   b. False

7. Roughly _______________ of all juvenile offenders are kept in detention beyond a handful of days.
   a. 20%
   b. 16%
   c. 12%
   d. 8%
   e. 4%

8. Both harsh and lax or lenient parental discipline are considered risk factors for delinquency.
   a. True
   b. False

9. In the diathesis-stress model, physiological precursors are equated to a _______________.
   a. Disorder
   b. Diathesis
   c. Behavioral condition
   d. Risk factor
   e. All of the above

10. In the diathesis-stress model, criminal activity is equated to a _______________.
    a. Disorder
    b. Diathesis
    c. Behavioral condition
    d. Risk factor
    e. All of the above

ESSAY DISCUSSION QUESTIONS

1. Provide a discussion of the various individual risk factors that affect the likelihood of a child being delinquent. Then compare these with the various protective factors that might offset the likelihood of a child turning delinquent.
2. Explain in detail how the diathesis-stress model can be applied to determining the likelihood of future delinquency among youth. From this model, explain what interventions we would expect to use to prevent future delinquency.
3. Discuss the FAST program and provide your opinion on whether this is a good program or whether it is a faulty program. Explain your answer. What might you change about the program (if anything) to improve it?

CHAPTER 9

GANG MEMBERS AS SPECIAL NEEDS OFFENDERS

JEFF RUSH AND ROB HANSER

Chapter Objectives

1. Understand the importance of effectively defining a gang problem within a given community.
2. Understand the interplay between gangs and gang members outside the prison facility and those within the prison facility (the concept of cross pollination).
3. Know, discuss, and apply the four stages of the problem-solving model for gang problems in the community.
4. Identify the characteristics of a full-service gang unit.
5. Understand the complexities involved when supervising prior gang-related offenders who are on community supervision.

INTRODUCTION

Working with gangs in the community is hampered significantly by what Sliwa (1987) refers to as the **DID syndrome**. The DID syndrome involves (1) **d**enying that a gang problem exists, (2) **i**gnoring the problem when it arrives, and (3) **d**elaying a response to the problem. Communities involved in this syndrome are simply not willing to accept the fact that a gang problem exists. Political considerations may be the basis for a community's leaders denying that a gang problem exists (Curry, 1995). All too often, denial is based on ignorance. Such leaders seem to think that since their gang problems are not "like" those in Los Angeles or Chicago, it is not a gang problem. In fact, gang problems in many cities are so entrenched because they too operated by the DID syndrome, and thus their problems may never go away. Further, it is sometimes noted that once gangs have arrived (and become entrenched), it is next to impossible to get rid of them (McBride, 1990). This is not to say that a community and its agencies (including the police) should necessarily assume that gangs are on the horizon. It is to say that when the outward signs begin to appear (e.g., graffiti and colors) the existence of a gang problem should be assumed, and then, like every other criminal problem, a plan needs to be developed to address it. An increase in certain crime rates may also forewarn a community that it is time to plan for and create a gang unit:

> Certain types of crimes are especially likely to involve gang members, and a sudden increase in those crimes may be viewed as a potential "distant early warning signal" that crime in the community may be increasingly gang-related. Crimes that may be especially worth monitoring closely are assaults involving rival groups; auto theft and credit card theft; carrying concealed weapons; taking weapons to school; assault/intimidation of victims, witnesses, and shoppers; drug trafficking; driveby shootings, and homicide, all of which frequently involve gang members and may serve as reasonably accurate "gang markers" in some communities at some points in time. (Huff, 2000, p. 403)

Moreno (2003) notes that gangs are "a bad thing. They are bad for business, bad for the real estate market, bad for tourism, bad for a school district, bad for politicians and bad for the community" (p. 152). So if gangs are so bad, why not acknowledge them and move to prevent or suppress them? The answer is that many politicians believe that acknowledging gangs suggests that the city has lost control or that visitors will no longer come for a visit. So they assume that the visitors are blind or dumb when they are in the city and see gangsters (or at least those who appear to be gangsters). However, "the people" often are far more intelligent than politicians give them credit for and would be far more accepting of acknowledging the problem than denying it, for, in the end, denying the problem only makes it significantly more difficult to address. Moreno (2003) states, "If there is a potential or emerging gang problem in your jurisdiction, no amount of wishful thinking, denial or creative branding will make it go away" (p. 153). But what does this mean for those who see the problem?

Regardless of the response or commitment of the community, any police officer, teacher, probation or parole officer, or community leader who believes a gang problem exists must begin to take steps to document such a problem. Thus, the next step is defining the problem and assessing whether it exists within the community.

DEFINING THE GANG PROBLEM

For many, particularly academics, defining a gang is the most important element of dealing with the gang problem. There is little consensus on the definition of the term "gang" by either practitioners or researchers who evaluate gang activity (Wilson, 2000). Some narrow their definition of gangs to being interchangeable with the term "street gangs" (Howell, 2000). Others define "gang" as synonymous with "organized crime group" and treat such terms as one would "Mafia" or "Triads" (Orvis, 1996). The following characteristics have been used to identify the existence of a gang (Wilson, 1994):

1. Formal organization structure (not a syndicate)
2. Identifiable leadership
3. Identified with a territory
4. Recurrent interaction
5. Engaging in serious or violent behavior

The thought is that we must define the problem before we can address the problem. While there is certainly some truth to this, we cannot let such a procedure paralyze us. In the most simplistic form, *"gangs are what gangs do"* (Ryan, personal communication, 1998; emphasis added), and what they do is crime, in many cases violent crime. Whether the state provides a definition or not, police, probation and district attorney agencies must have a working definition of their own. Such a definition is important if criminal justice professionals are to effectively work together and share gang-related intelligence across jurisdictions (National Alliance of Gang Investigators Associations [NAGIA], 2000). Spergel (1995) notes that we do not know much about gangs in the aggregate because of differences in reporting across jurisdictions. Some of this is due in part to the lack of a common definition. Clearly, the National Youth Gang Survey helps alleviate this problem, although it continues to focus on the "youth" aspect of gangsterism, specifically excluding motorcycle gangs, **prison gangs**, hate or ideology groups, and gangs with an exclusively adult membership (Egley, 2000). The NAGIA has put together a definition to facilitate a national discussion. We adopt their definition in this chapter as the definition of a gang. Generally, a gang is a group or association of three or more persons who may have a common identifying sign, symbol, or name and who individually or collectively engage or have engaged in criminal activity that creates an atmosphere of fear and intimidation. Criminal activity includes juvenile acts that, if committed by an adult, would be a crime (NAGIA, 2000).

A benefit to the NAGIA definition is that it is applicable within and across the criminal justice spectrum, putting everyone on the same page. It can also be used by non–criminal justice agencies (e.g., education). Being on the same page is important as the gang problem is being assessed and the question of whether a gang problem exists is being answered, which is the first question that should be asked. The answer lies in the existence of graffiti (on walls, school books, bathrooms, and so on) and of the gangsters themselves (who "dress" the part and have the tattoos, paraphernalia, photos, and so on). Thus, regardless of the "official" recognition of gangs, the officer must take it on him- or herself to learn as much as possible about the gangs that do exist and prepare for "the big one, because something of significance will eventually happen" (Moreno, 2003, p. 157).

GANG OFFENDERS BEHIND BARS

One serious problem in jails and prisons is gang activity. In modern corrections, jail and prison gangs are frequently referred to as **security threat groups**. According to the Florida Department of Corrections (2004), a security threat group is a "formal or informal ongoing group, gang, organization or association consisting of three or more members who have a common name or common identifying signs, colors, or symbols" (p. 3). This term encompasses gangs in jail or prison but is also useful since it accurately describes any group that presents a challenge to the smooth running of a correctional facility.

In 1990, the American Correctional Association conducted a groundbreaking survey of gangs in institutions, and it was found that nearly all prison systems faced challenges with gang activity. Further, problems with staff assault were reported, as was frequent inmate assault due to gang rivalry. The subversive nature of jail and prison gangs made them particularly difficult to challenge. As a result, many prison systems eventually developed different forms of gang intelligence units within their facilities. These units were tasked with collecting paraphernalia associated with gang operations. For instance, many gangs may communicate in writing through some form of coded alphabet. The gang intelligence unit is tasked with deciphering this code and intervening with the gang's communication.

Once a gang member is identified within the prison facility, he or she is given an affiliation and marking through the classification committee. Active members (determined by staff, not by the inmate's version of his or her activity in the gang) are often placed in some form of single-cell lockdown, typically referred to as "ad seg," which is short for "administrative segregation." While in administrative segregation, the inmate will be locked down for 24 hours a day with few amenities. Recreation is carried out alone in segregation yards. Likewise, food is served to the inmate in the cell, and all other services are provided within the inmate's administrative segregation cell block. This is the most common form of gang inmate management within most prison systems throughout the United States.

It should be noted that many prison gang members were prior street gang members, and because of this, researchers can vaguely determine likely gang growth both inside and outside the prison. In 1998, there were an estimated 780,000 gang members across the nation. A large proportion of these gang members also served time behind bars at some point in their criminal careers. In fact, in some prison systems, such as in Texas, gangs nearly controlled the prison system and had even controlled many of the prison staff through various forms of friendships or occasional intimidation, all designed to manipulate staff within the organization.

Thus, prison gangs in some state systems were both persuasive and very powerful (Buentello, 2001). Potential recruits for existing prison gangs enter prison with natural feelings of anxiety and quickly learn the value of having some form of affiliation. Indeed, inmates without the protection of affiliation are likely to be the target of other inmates who are members of a gang. Likewise, this affiliation tends to be based along racial allegiances. In fact, most prison gang membership is strictly defined by the race of the member.

Traditional prison gangs include but are not limited to the Aryan Brotherhood, the Mexican Mafia, La Nuestra Familia, the Black Guerilla Family, the Texas Syndicate, and the Mexikanemi. Further, there is a confluence of street gangs that have permeated several prison systems, particularly in California, Illinois, New York, Texas, and Florida. Common street gangs that are found in prisons are the Crips and the Bloods. In the Chicago area, most street gangs are aligned with either the Folks or the People nation. The Folks include notorious street gangs such as the Gangster Disciples and the Two-Sixers (Fleisher & Rison, 1999). The People include groups such as the Latin Kings and the Vice Lords (Fleisher & Rison, 1999). Historically, the main distinction between prison gangs and street gangs has been the internal structure and leadership styles (Fleisher & Rison, 1999). However, over time this distinction has become so blurred as to be meaningless in the offender world (Fleisher & Rison, 1999). In the correctional environment of today, the Gangster Disciples and Latin Kings, classic street gangs, are just as influential and powerful as the Mexican Mafia and the Texas Syndicate (Fleisher & Rison, 1999). More telling is the fact that the Mexican Mafia, the Aryan Brotherhood, and even emerging local groups such as the Barrio Aztecas have become just as formidable in their respective ethnic and/or culturally based neighborhoods or regions. Thus, both types of gangs have become "cross-pollinated" and are fully operational in both sectors of the criminal world. Indeed, it is sometimes common for leaders of the gang to be incarcerated, all the while giving orders for various actions to members who are still outside the prison operating within the community. In this book, this will be called **gang cross-pollination**, whereby the gang has developed such power and influence as to be equally effective regardless of whether its leadership is inside or outside the prison walls.

When discussing gangs that are cross-pollinated, this book will use the term **disruptive offender group** to describe a gang that possesses the following high functioning group and organizational characteristics:

1. Prison and street affiliation is based on race, ethnicity, geography, ideology, or any combination of these or other similar factors (Fleisher & Rison, 1999).
2. Members seek protection from other gang members inside and outside the prison, as well as insulation from law enforcement detection (use of safe houses when wanted).
3. Members will mutually take care of one another's family members, at least minimally, while the member is locked up since this is an expected overhead cost in the organization.
4. The groups mission integrates an economic objective and uses some form of illicit industry such as drug trafficking to fulfill the economic necessities to carry forward other stated objectives (Fleisher & Rison, 1999). The use of violence or the threat of violence is a common tool in meeting these economic objectives.

Regardless of whether these groups are cross-pollinated to the point of being a disruptive offender group, there are other characteristics that are common to prison gangs that go beyond racial lines of membership. These characteristics are common to most any gang within jail and/or prison, though not necessarily common to those based primarily on the street. First, prison gangs tend to have highly formal rules and a written constitution. The constitution and the rules are adhered to by all members who value their affiliation, and sanctions are taken against those who violate the rules. Second, prison gangs tend to be structured along a semimilitary organizational scheme. Thus, authority and responsibility are clearly defined within these groups. Third, membership in a prison gang is usually for life. This has often been referred to as "blood in, blood out" among the popular subculture. This lifelong affiliation is also one of the root causes of parolees continuing their affiliation beyond the prison walls, and this lifelong membership is enforced against those who attempt to exit the prison gang. Thus, when a gang member leaves the prison environment, he or she is expected to perform various "favors" for the members who are still incarcerated. Finally, as members circulate in and out of prison, they are involved in gang activities both inside and outside the penal institution. Thus, the criminal enterprise continues to be an active business, and prison simply becomes part of the overhead involved in running that business.

GANG OFFENDERS IN THE COMMUNITY

According to the Bureau of Justice Assistance (1999), gang problems can be addressed using a comprehensive problem-solving model that encompasses the four stages of the problem-solving process: scanning, analysis, response, and assessment (SARA). This process is designed to solve a problem by clearly identifying it, using numerous sources of information to investigate the problem with different levels of detail, developing a variety of solutions, and conducting an evaluation (Bureau of Justice Assistance, 1999). Each of these stages is discussed in the following paragraphs. The presentation of each of these stages comes from the Bureau of Justice Assistance (1999).

The initial stage is the **scanning stage**, which involves looking for and identifying problems. A problem exists when the following parenthetical terms can be replaced with specific examples: (victims) are (harmed) by the (behaviors) of (offenders) at or in (places) at (times). Completing this problem statement is an important first step in problem solving; it achieves consensus on the kind of problem being addressed and provides guidance to further understand the problem.

The objective of the **analysis stage** is to develop a thorough understanding of a problem. Although often overlooked, analysis is perhaps the most important part of the problem-solving model because it provides valuable information that can be used to craft appropriate responses to a problem. Analysis is also useful for assessing the effectiveness of responses because it often provides a baseline for simple before-and-after measurements of a response's impact. Analysis consists of straightforward investigation of concrete problems. The best analysis involves creative information collection. After a problem has been thoroughly analyzed, goals should be established for the problem-solving effort.

The **response stage** has three objectives: developing response options that are consistent with the information analyzed, selecting responses, and implementing the responses. Responses should focus on offenders, victims, third parties, places, and/or tools used to create the harm. The information collected during the analysis stage facilitates the selection of the most effective responses—those responses that take into account community values and often contain input from individuals directly affected by the problem. When implementing a response, programs need clear and consistent leadership, even in the most collaborative efforts.

The **assessment stage** provides useful feedback on how well the response is working. This information can be used to change the response, improve the analysis, or even redefine the nature of the problem. Information gathered through assessment can also be used to plan strategies for classes of problems and to revise the problem-solving process. The assessment should focus on the problem statement rather than on the response. An assessment plan should link the implemented response with the problem that was identified during the scanning stage. The true impact of a response is measured by its effect on the harm suffered. While there are no definite rules for assessing gang problems, assessment programs do not have to be complex; rather, the methods of information collection used in the analysis stage should, for the most part, simply be replicated during the assessment.

While the police may have (and should have) the primary responsibility for addressing the gang problem, they cannot do it alone. As Los Angeles County retired sheriff's Sergeant Wes McBride has said, "We can't police ourselves out of this." The sociopsychological and sociological ramifications of the gang problem are too immense. Coalitions must be built, and agencies with complementary missions must be active members of the team. This must be something that is recognized by everyone involved in the community. However, nearly all gang task forces involve only criminal justice agencies (Wilson, 2000). An extreme example of the opposite approach is the Aurora Gang Task Force (AGTF), which won the 1992 City Livability Award from the National Conference of Mayors for its efforts to mobilize an effective response to the gang problem. Formed in 1989 in Aurora, Colorado, the AGTF's members come from government agencies, social services, churches, volunteer organizations, businesses, the military, and the media. The most amazing fact about the AGTF is that all its members volunteered for the task force (Howell, 2000). On a GANGINFO e-mail list, a private security agent with a major department store was inquiring whether there existed gang units in her area, as she wanted to become a member. She saw this as important to her security assignment and to the safety and security of the stores under her purview. This is just one example of reaching out beyond public criminal justice to staff the gang unit.

Gangs and gangsters cut across a variety of criminal and community lines. The importance of knowing and understanding what is happening and then communicating that information to others is of paramount importance. The bad guys do not stay in one place anymore, so law enforcement must account for and be able to explain the movements. This requires being proactive and having a good working (or at least a good communicative) relationship with a variety of agencies. Information cannot be kept by a single individual; it must be shared with any and all parties that might be affected by gangs and their members. Where information sharing is difficult, law enforcement must take the lead in smoothing out the rough spots, calling on the "bosses" and "suits" when necessary to intervene.

The importance of sharing information cannot be overemphasized. Everyone affected by the gang problem must be appraised. This includes the media when necessary. However, there are two schools of thought on this matter. On the one hand, publicity enhances the gang's image among those in their "turf" and among rival gangsters, and it might induce the gang to greater feats of criminality in order to get more publicity. On the other hand, media attention on gangs increases public awareness and often creates public pressure on government officials to increase resources to deal with the gang problem, thus benefiting the gang unit (Jackson & McBride, 1992).

All too often, specialized units keep to themselves, not willing to let others know what they know. While this is never good for any unit, it is especially bad for the gang unit. Gangs themselves change to meet the demands "of the street" or the pressures from law enforcement; they are on the Internet, are using schools and prisons as places of recruitment, are traveling from city to city, and are collaborating in ways previously unheard of. If information is not shared between and among those who fight gangs, policing can be assured of always being one step behind the gangsters.

It is also important to open communications with law enforcement agencies in other communities:

> Since gangs do not exist solely within city or county boundaries, and since gang clashes all too frequently involve more than one jurisdiction, it helps to know what gangs are active or reside in adjacent areas or jurisdictions.... To keep informed it is necessary to maintain a good working relationship and have an effective information exchange arrangement with gang units of other law enforcement agencies. (Jackson & McBride, 1992, p. 97)

To be effective in responding to the problem, law enforcement generally and the gang unit specifically must change their old ways of doing business, and this includes hoarding of information. Egos must be put aside, and collaborations must take place. The department's "brass" must make information sharing and dissemination a priority both within and across agencies. This idea of shared information, communication, and unorthodox approaches is readily seen with Operation Night Light in Boston (see also Special Insert 9.1):

> The success of Night Light depends on a number of key operating principles. First, intensive communication and a unified sense of mission among all the partners [including ministers, social workers, parents, and so on] are crucial.... Night Light is committed to a broad strategy characterized by prevention, intervention and enforcement. (Jordan, 1998, pp. 2–3)

Special Insert 9.1. Operation Night Light

Operation Night Light is an excellent example of how community supervision and local police officers can work together for a common good: improving public safety. Initiated in 1992, this collaborative program began in Boston due to an increase in gang violence that had led to a rise in the number of juvenile homicide victims. The Boston police department's Anti-Gang Violence Unit implemented procedures to work in tandem with community supervision officers to assist in enforcing probation requirements related to curfews and other restrictions on gang-related youth. Without knowledge of probation caseloads, police found themselves in a legal "limbo" when determining whether the person was bound by added restrictions on their liberty. With this in mind, the project initially paired one probation officer with two police officers as backup so that surprise visits could be safely made at the homes, schools, and places of employment associated with high-risk youth on probation. These visits traditionally have included nontraditional hours from 7:00 P.M. until midnight with the goal being improved detection of the probationer's behavior.

As noted by Reichert (2002), "Operation Night Light, and other similar programs, focus their limited resources on high-risk offenders, the relatively small percentage of probationers who pose a threat to public safety" (p. 2). But it should be noted that the police and community supervision officer teams make a specific point to avoid the use of heavy-handed approaches to their surveillance and response. This has been prudent since many of these youth do have family within the community, and while most of these family members may wish to have their kids out of the gangs, they do not want to see their child penalized more than is proportionally necessary. The approach used in Operation Night Light has thus maintained effective community relations within the city and surrounding area while simultaneously "cracking down" on gang-related crime. Currently, all new probation officers are expected to commit to spending at least a fifth of their time in the community during evening and weekend hours. This program has also been subsumed within a broader community policing program within the department, providing yet another critical link in effective offender supervision through inclusion of community members.

Source: Reichert (2002).

Regardless of which approach or combination thereof is taken by the unit, the most important function of the gang unit is information/intelligence. Officers in the unit must be on the streets, working the gangsters, and being approachable and visible not only to gangsters but also to other citizens who may have information the gang unit needs. The gathering of intelligence fuels all the other goals of the unit (and the department). Without up-to-date information, the ability to solve cases diminishes. Street gangs are street criminals, and information sharing must be a priority within and among all agencies involved with these criminals.

It is best for the unit to use a combination of all three approaches: intelligence, investigation, and suppression. To do this, the unit should take the lead in liaison with the prosecutor's office and the probation/parole office (both juvenile and adult) to ensure a coordinated approach to gangs and gangsters. If the gang unit is going to take the lead in combating gangs, the unit's personnel become very important.

SPECIAL PROBLEMS

Gang units are unique among elite units and therefore have unique problems. Unlike most other specialized units, a gang unit's problems are often different from those of even other gang units. Thus, gang units may need special training to deal with these problems, although not all gang units need the same training. Howell (2000) recommends a centralized federal approach to training: "Training and technical assistance for police and other local community agencies should be expanded, primarily through the addition of technical training teams, which would provide a broader range of gang diagnosis and program development expertise" (p. 313). Some examples of such training and technical assistance are those provided by the National Youth Gang Center, the California Gang Investigators Association, and the National Gang Crime Research Center.

As noted earlier, the mission and composition of gang units vary. The goal or goals of the unit (e.g., gang suppression, prevention, intelligence, investigation, intervention, or some combination of these) can create problems unique to that unit. Too many goals or not enough resources allocated to a single goal can create financial problems for the unit's managers. Part-time personnel can create a division of loyalty and attention, distracting gang unit members from fulfilling their mission. A lack of a centralized unit authority or too broad a span of control for unit supervisors can create management problems as well. These logistical problems vary from gang unit to gang unit but are similar in that they are solved if planning and support are adequate from the beginning.

Not all gangs have the same dynamics, and often this is due to the culture the gang originates from. At the turn of the twentieth century, most American gangs were white and with various European backgrounds. By the 1970s, four-fifths of gang members were either Hispanic or African American. Asian gangs are spreading quickly today (Howell, 1994). It was found in a recent survey that only 12 percent of all youth gang members are Caucasian, with 46 percent being Hispanic, 34 percent African American, and 6 percent Asian. Furthermore, two-thirds of all gangs are dominated by members from a single racial or ethnic group (Wilson, 2000). Law enforcement agencies estimate that more than 90 percent of gang members are male (Esbensen, 2000). However, female gang members and even all-female gangs are increasing in number but not to a significant extent (less than 3 percent). Needless to say, the low social class of gang members has remained constant over the years (Howell, 1994). Gang unit members must be prepared to deal with the cultural diversity or uniqueness of the gangs in their jurisdiction.

Further, gangs in the community tend to have one of two different forms of organizational structure: the vertical/hierarchical organization and the horizontal organizational structure (Bureau of Justice Assistance, 1999). Gangs with a vertical/hierarchical organizational structures are likely to indulge in group as opposed to individual violence; however, these gangs generally avoid using violence at all. This type of gang tends to focus on making money, which typically overrides individualistic acts of violence. In addition, these gangs are able to exert greater control over their members. On the other hand, gangs that have a horizontal structure tend to have less control over their members (Bureau of Justice Assistance, 1999). While some of these gangs may include cliques or subgroups that are well organized and able to control their members, the gang as a whole is a loose collection of factions with limited organizational coordination (Bureau of Justice Assistance, 1999).

The gang unit must also be aware of the culture of the neighborhoods in which the gangs operates (each gang's "turf"). Some neighborhoods are continually terrorized and intimidated by gangs and therefore are afraid to cooperate with police because of gang retaliation (Jackson & McBride, 1992). However, recent immigrants from countries whose police are oppressive may fear police because of their past experiences. Further, English may not be the predominant language in some neighborhoods, so a language barrier between gang units and the citizens they seek to protect may have to be overcome. Gang units must be able to adapt to these contingencies, and therefore some unit members must be skilled in the languages and aware of the cultures of the neighborhoods whose cooperation they need to be successful. Gang units engaging in a strategy of "community policing" in those neighborhoods may find it easier to overcome cultural barriers:

> Among agencies that had implemented community policing for at least 1 year, 99 percent reported improved cooperation between citizens and police, 80 percent reported reduced citizens' fear of crime, and 62 percent reported fewer crimes against persons.... Citizens in community policing jurisdictions were more likely to participate in a Neighborhood Watch Program, serve as volunteers within the agency and on agency-coordinated citizen patrols, and attend a citizen police academy. (Travis, 1995, pp. 1–2)

Studying the culture of the gang's turf is important for prevention as well as suppression programs, especially for youth gangs. The city of Westminster, California, studied youth of Vietnamese descent from a neighborhood where Vietnamese youth gangs dominated in order to develop successful programs to divert the youths from joining gangs in the future (Wyrick, 2000).

THE FULL-SERVICE GANG UNIT

Spergel (1995) notes that a community problem-solving approach to gangs seems to be slowly emerging. This is based on the idea that "an arrest and lock-em-up strategy is not sufficient" (p. 199). Sergeant Wes McBride of the Los Angeles County Sheriff's Department, an author, a trainer, and one of the foremost gang experts in the country, notes that a person working with gang members must understand the gang ethic, customs, and practices of the gangs in their area. Knowing these things helps the officer develop rapport with the gangsters, makes dealing with them easier, and allows for more and better communication with the gang and the gangster (Valdez, 2000). McBride (1993) notes that when "firm but fair law enforcement [is coupled] with personal knowledge of the gang members backed by a demonstrated humanitarian concern for the status of the individual, violence within targeted gangs began to decline" (p. 413).

Father Greg Boyle, who runs the Delores Mission in Los Angeles, has noted that "gang members need hope to help make it in life" (Valdez, 2000, p. 543). Father Boyle suggests that many gang members have no hope and "don't want to look in a mirror and accept what they see" (p. 543). Dealing with gangs and gangsters requires both a Wes McBride and a Father Boyle (and the many other types of people who work with gangs and gangsters). Dealing with gangsters needs what McBride refers to as **full-service gang units**.

A full-service gang unit has responsibility for suppression, intervention, and prevention. It "kicks butt" and makes arrests when necessary, and it refers gangsters to a wide array of programs depending on the need of the gangster. A full-service gang unit is a collaborative program using resources already in existence while being open to new resources that become available. The key element is that all members are working toward the same goal: increasing the quality of life for the people they serve. Each member works collaboratively but independently (depending on his or her specific expertise and perspective) toward the same goal under the auspices of a program manager.

The program manager coordinates the efforts of the various agencies involved in the full-service gang unit. They also know what each agency is doing and ensure that all agencies are "on the same page." The full-service gang unit allows for immediate action depending on the need. When working with gangs and gangsters, all too often one cannot wait until tomorrow. When a gang crime is committed, immediate action must take place. "When a gangster comes to you and says, 'I want to change,' that is a totally different scenario and should be acted on immediately" (Valdez, 2000, p. 544). Young children need the tools and information to handle the pressures of living in gang neighborhoods and avoiding gang membership. In addition, they need the tools sooner rather than later. This requires involving schools in the full-service gang unit.

Full-service gang units do not reinvent the wheel. They simply take the multitude of agencies working with gangs and gangsters and put them together in a collaborative program, sharing costs, expertise, knowledge, and intelligence. The full-service gang unit is a model that can be adopted by any agency and one that can be regionalized depending on the city or county. Just as gangs share some characteristics, they also regionalize many practices. The full-service gang unit has the flexibility to address this. The issues are time, cooperation, and commitment. Egos, rivalries, biases, and other negative influences or thoughts must be set aside (Valdez, 2000). The goal is simple: improving the quality of life of the communities that are served.

GANG MEMBERS ON COMMUNITY SUPERVISION

For community supervision officers, it is important to determine whether their clients are affiliated with gangs. These officers must learn gang recognition signals and familiarize themselves with gang turf and the areas of the community in which an offender resides. Gangs in the community are therefore treated as community threat groups (Champion, 2002). Champion (2002) notes that many states and the U.S. Probation Office have created specialized threat group programs that attempt to coordinate resources in the community to combat those gang members on probation or parole who pose a serious threat to the community that they are in. Some community supervision departments may have supervision officers who have special expertise with offenders who are gang members. This harkens back to the specialized needs caseload model (discussed in Chapter 1), which pertains to community supervision officer assignments to offenders who share common specialized needs, of which gang affiliation should be one to consider. Officers specifically trained and knowledgeable about local gang culture should be assigned to hard-core gang members. These officers are likely to be much more in tune with the pressures placed on former gang members who are on community supervision. Indeed, it may even become necessary at some point to protect this offender from potential retaliatory violence from his or her former gang members. These community supervision officers should also be skilled at detecting the indicators of an offender's possible gang activity while on community supervision (Champion, 2002).

Champion (2002) notes that increasing numbers of parolees are affiliated with gangs. Indeed, if the convicted offender was not a gang member prior to incarceration, there is a strong likelihood that he or she will become one while in prison. This is problematic because gang membership increases an offender's likelihood to reoffend. This is due to the need to do "favors" for gang members inside prison or to the need to assist gang members outside prison who may be running organized criminal activities such as drug trafficking.

Community supervision officers often find supervising parolees challenging because these offenders may hide their gang affiliation. Likewise, it is difficult to prescribe treatments or needed community services for offenders who are affiliated with gangs because these offenders tend to offer strong resistance to most types of community-based intervention. The gang culture tends to isolate the offender from other elements of society and to undermine the ability of treatment providers to address problems that the offender is facing. In fact, research shows that parolee failure is strongly linked with prior records and belonging to gangs prior to being sent to prison (Champion, 2002).

Overcoming gang influence is difficult, and despite the best efforts of community supervision personnel, there will always be a hard-core group of members who will prove to be unstable and not adhere to their supervision or treatment program. In fact, it is noted that roughly 10 percent of these members account for 55 percent of the criminal activity that gang members may engage in. The other members tend to vary more in their degree of involvement. Champion (2002) points out that greater police presence in gang-dominated neighborhoods tends to assist supervision officers in their attempts to keep parolees from engaging in further criminal activity due to gang influence.

As can be seen, for offenders on community supervision, gangs have a strong influence on whether these individuals will be able to remain law abiding and conform their behavior to the constraints of community supervision. Given the connection between prison and street gang membership, this means that pulls come from behind bars as well as in the community. For some offenders, there may seem to be no way out. Because of this, the use of an effective **gang exit strategy** should be adopted by community supervision agencies that have a substantial number of gang members on their caseloads.

ESTABLISHING A YOUTH GANG EXIT PROGRAM

According to Evans and Sawdon (2005), antigang programs should include not only law enforcement sweeps and gang suppression efforts but also community advocacy to facilitate cohesive neighborhoods that are not intimidated by gang threats and activity. In Toronto, Canada, a program does just that and is targeted toward young gang members. This gang exit program strategy has three components: (1) assessment and intake, (2) intensive training and personal development, and (3) case management process.

Gang member assessment and intake is the phase that identifies interest and motivation of the gang member, the amount of gang involvement, and the member's family and social history (Evans & Sawdon, 2005). During this phase, members are provided with an orientation to the program. The next phase is that of **gang member intensive training and personal development**. This phase implements two separate curricula, one for the male gang member and another for the female gang member. Each curriculum involves up to 60 hours of intensive training. Topics during this training include anger management, aggression, sexism, racism, homophobia, and bullying. Communication skills training is also given during this phase. The last phase, **gang member case management**, involves both individual support for the member and ongoing group meetings for the ex–gang member. The intent is to reinforce what was learned at intake and to provide a proactive intervention when life takes some unforeseen turn for the former gang member.

This program utilizes former members who successfully complete the exit program as future facilitators with future members of the program. These former gang members are tasked with being active in establishing community contacts and outreach. Participants visit local community centers and other youth services to provide information about the program. From this point, many former members will engage in community presentations to help generate support (financial and otherwise) for the antigang program. This program trains these former members who are "passing the word" with leadership skills training, empathy building, counseling, and the development of their own "personal stories" that explain how they became involved in gangs and why they have chosen to cease involvement with the gang. This story is told in schools and other areas where the ex–gang member tries to warn against joining the gang life.

If it is possible to extract youth from the gang-oriented environment, then this option should be given priority. Indeed, youth are much less likely to recidivate when away from adverse peer groups. In the absence of such an intervention, the next-best strategy is to inoculate him or her from the effects of the gang world and to also replace the former peer group with a new pro-social peer group. This is specifically what the gang exit program attempts to do, all the while working against the backdrop of the former gang family's pressure to return. What makes the task so difficult for the offender and the community supervision officer is the strong tug of a subculture that eschews any attempt at reform made by the former member.

CONCLUSION

This chapter provides a general overview of the difficulties in addressing gang-related crime in the community. The fact that many communities overlook gang problems within their jurisdiction demonstrates the secretive and subversive nature of gangs. The use of the SARA system in fighting gang activity in the community provides a good operational framework from which communities can address gang problems. Community collaboration is important with this group of special needs offender, and the police must assist and coordinate their preventive efforts with local community supervision. Such collaboration is the best bet in fighting any gang problem.

A "revolving-door" effect has been noted between incarceration and community release with gang offenders. This is because gang membership is often lifelong and because offenders who are released from prison are still tied by bonds of allegiance to those members still behind bars. Further, other members are often present in the community and will serve as reinforcement for further gang activity once outside. Thus, offenders who are gang members have a variety of pushes and pulls that serve to keep them in their gang and involved in gang activity, and this naturally undermines most treatment regimens that they are assigned.

KEY TERMS

DID syndrome
Prison gangs
Security threat groups
Gang cross-pollination
Disruptive offender group
Scanning stage
Analysis stage
Response stage
Assessment stage
Full-service gang units
Gang exit strategy
Gang member assessment and intake
Gang member intensive training and personal development
Gang member case management

ABOUT THE CONTRIBUTORS

Jeff Rush is assistant professor of criminal justice at the University of Louisiana at Monroe. His specialty areas include gangs and gang violence, juvenile crime, and extremist group activity.

Rob Hanser is director of the Institute of Law Enforcement at the University of Louisiana at Monroe. His specialty areas include ethics in policing, community policing, corrections, multiculturalism, and treatment interventions for victims and perpetrators.

REFERENCES

Buentello, S. (2001). *Personal interview at TDCJ-ID Administrative Annex*. Huntsville: Texas Department of Criminal Justice Institutional Division.

Bureau of Justice Assistance. (1999). *Addressing community gang problems: A model for problem solving*. Washington, DC: Office of Justice Programs. Retrieved from http://www.ojp.usdoj.gov

Champion, D. (2002). *Probation, parole, and community corrections* (4th ed.). Upper Saddle River, NJ: Prentice Hall.

Curry, G. D. (1995). *National youth gang surveys: A review of methods and findings*. Washington, DC: U.S. Department of Justice.

Egley, A. (2000). *Highlights of the l999 National Youth Gang Survey: OJJDP fact sheet*. Washington, DC: U.S. Department of Justice.

Esbensen, F. (2000). *OJJDP Juvenile Justice Bulletin: Preventing adolescent gang involvement*. Washington, DC: U.S. Department of Justice.

Evans, D. G., & Sawdon, J. (2004, October). The development of a gang exit strategy. *Corrections Today, 66*(6), 78–81.

Fleisher, M. S., & Rison, R. H. (1999). Gang management in corrections. In P. M. Carlson & J. S. Garrett (Eds.), *Prison and jail administration: Practice and theory* (pp. 232–238). Gaithersburg, MD: Aspen.

Florida Department of Corrections. (2004). *Gang and security threat group awareness*. Tallahassee: Author. Retrieved from http://www.dc.state.fl.us/pub/gangs/faq.html

Howell, J. C. (1994). *Gangs: OJJDP fact sheet*. Washington, DC: U.S. Department of Justice.

Howell, J. C. (2000). *Youth gangs: Programs and strategies. OJJDP summary*. Washington, DC: Office of Juvenile Justice and Delinquency Prevention.

Huff, C. R. (2000). Youth gangs and public policy. In B. W. Hancock & P. M. Sharp (Eds.), *Public policy, crime, and criminal justice* (pp. 302–348). Upper Saddle River, NJ: Prentice Hall.

Jackson, R. K., & McBride, W. D. (1992). *Understanding street gangs*. Placerville, CA: Copperhouse.

Jordan, J. T. (1998). Boston's Operation Night Light. *FBI Law Enforcement Bulletin, 67*(8), 1–8.

McBride, W. (1990, Summer). Speech given in Gulf Shores, AL.

McBride, W. (1993). Part II—Police departments and gang intervention: The Operation Safe Streets concept. In A. P. Goldstein & C. R. Huff (Eds.), *The gang intervention handbook* (pp. 411–415). Champaign, IL: Research Press.

Moreno, T. (2003). *Lessons from a gang cop*. Richmond Hill, Ontario: Astwood.

National Alliance of Gang Investigators Associations. (2000). *National Alliance of Gang Investigators—Section V: Recommendations*. Retrieved from http://www.nagia.org/nagia_recommends.htm#GangDefinitions

Orvis, G. P. (1996). Innovative prosecution of youth gangs by treating them as organized crime groups. In J. M. Miller & J. P. Rush (Eds.), *Gangs: A criminal justice approach* (pp. 112–138). Cincinnati: Anderson.

Reichart, K. (2002). *Police probation partnerships: Boston's Operation Night Light*. Washington, DC: Jerry Lee Center of Criminology. Retrieved from http://www.sas.upenn.edu/jerrylee/programs/fjc/paper_mar02.pdf

Sliwa, C. (1987, May). Speech given in Birmingham, AL.

Spergel, I. (1995). *The youth gang problem.* New York: Oxford University Press.

Travis, J. (1995). *Community policing strategies*. Washington, DC: National Institute of Justice.

Valdez, A. (2000). *Gangs: A guide to understanding street gangs* (3rd ed.). San Clemente, CA: LawTech Publishing.

Wilson, J. J. (2000). *1998 National Youth Gang Survey: Summary*. Washington, DC: U.S. Department of Justice.

Wyrick, P. A. (2000). *Vietnamese youth gang involvement: OJJDP fact sheet*. Washington, DC: U.S. Department of Justice.

LEARNING CHECK

1. Which of the following is not one of the components of the DID syndrome?
   a. Denying
   b. Investigating
   c. Delaying
   d. Ignoring
   e. None of the above

2. Gangs have often been defined by which of the following characteristics?
   a. Leadership
   b. Religion
   c. Organization
   d. a and b but not c
   e. a and c but not b

3. Gang member case management is a component of which of the following?
   a. DID
   b. Full-service gang unit
   c. STG response team
   d. Gang exit program
   e. Gang problem-solving model

4. The response phase is a component of which of the following?
   a. DID
   b. Full-service gang unit
   c. STG response team
   d. Gang exit program
   e. Gang problem-solving model

5. What is the phase that addresses topics such as anger management, aggression, sexism, racism, homophobia, and bullying?
   a. Intensive training and personal development phase
   b. Belief systems transition phase
   c. Cognitive restructuring phase
   d. None of the above

6. In 1998, there were an estimated ________ gang members across the nation.
   a. 980,000
   b. 880,000
   c. 780,000
   d. 680,000
   e. None of the above

7. Which of the following are characteristic of a disruptive offender group?
   a. Prison and street affiliation is based on race, ethnicity, geography, ideology, or any combination of these or other similar factors.
   b. Members seek protection from other gang members inside and outside the prison as well as insulation from law enforcement detection.
   c. Members will mutually take care of one another's family members while a member is locked up.
   d. The groups mission integrates an economic objective and uses some form of illicit industry such as drug trafficking to fulfill the economic necessities.
   e. All of the above

8. The organization of gangs in the community tends to follow which type of organizational structure?
   a. Vertical/hierarchical
   b. Horizontal
   c. Horizontal/lateral
   d. Both a and b but not c
   e. Both a and c but not b

9. Membership in prison gangs tends to be transient, with members joining and dropping out of the gang with some degree of frequency.
   a. True
   b. False

10. The scanning phase is part of which of the following?
    a. DID
    b. Full-service gang unit
    c. STG response team
    d. Gang exit program
    e. Gang problem-solving model

ESSAY DISCUSSION QUESTIONS

1. Explain why it might be important for police and/or community supervision agencies to train gang unit staff on multicultural issues.
2. Provide a discussion on some of the collaborative partnerships that agencies would need to develop when trying to remedy a gang problem in their community.
3. What are some potential problems that should be considered when an offender is trying to remove him- or herself from gang membership? What should community supervision officers do to assist the offender in breaking out of the gang?

CHAPTER 10

JUVENILE SEX OFFENDERS AS SPECIAL NEEDS OFFENDERS

Chapter Objectives

1. Understand the unique characteristics of juvenile sex offenders. Be especially cognizant of the probability of their own victimization at an earlier point in their childhoods.
2. Identify and define Prendergast's seven juvenile sex offender typologies.
3. Understand the various types of therapy used with juvenile sex offenders and how these therapies are implemented.

INTRODUCTION

Sexually assaultive behavior has typically been a crime that is associated mainly with adult male offenders. However, in the past 15 years, sexual assault perpetrated by juvenile sexual offenders has received increased public and media attention. Conservative estimates show that at least 20 percent of all sex offenses are committed by youth younger than 18 and that 50 percent of all molestations may be committed by youth younger than 18. As if these statistics were not alarming enough, it is thought that anywhere from 50 to 90 percent of all adult sex offenders (particularly pedophiles) are victims of prior childhood sexual abuse (Prendergast, 2004; Zolonder, Abel, Northey, & Jordan, 2001).

Researchers have tried in vain to find commonalities among this offending population, but ultimately all of them seem to agree to disagree, the only definite conclusion being that this is a very heterogeneous group of offenders (Zolonder et al., 2001). However, the modal age of juvenile sex offenders tends to be around 14 to 15 years, with their first offense having happened around 12 to 13 years of age (Zolonder et al., 2001). Further, one-quarter of all juvenile sex offenders are thought to have committed their first offense prior to age 12.

From the literature, it can be concluded that it is fairly rare for juvenile molesters of children to have both male and female victims. Victims are most likely to be female acquaintances or siblings; rarely are they strangers. In fact, it is in roughly 50 percent of all cases that the victim and offender know each other, with the likelihood being as high as 75 percent in cases where juvenile perpetrators molest child victims. It has been found that nearly 40 percent of all juvenile sex offenders were blood relatives of their victims. This naturally ties in with earlier discussions on the prevalence of sibling incest among early childhood offenders in Chapter 7 and explains where some of the breeding ground for the juvenile sex offender has been.

THE NOTION OF SPECIAL NEEDS OFFENDERS

Most incidents of juvenile sexual aggression involve male perpetrators (Sickmund et al., 1997). However, a number of clinical studies also point to prepubescent youths and females engaging in sexually abusive behaviors. Although racial and socioeconomic differences may be overrepresented in certain settings (e.g., juvenile justice), juveniles referred for treatment in a variety of environments reflect the same racial, religious, and socioeconomic distribution as the general population of the United States (Ryan et al., 1996).

The manner in which victims respond to sexual victimization is important since most juvenile sex offenders are thought to be victims of prior sexual abuse. Understanding victim reactions can assist in identifying the etiology of juvenile sex offending and can also lay the foundation for accurate screening of their likelihood of future recidivism. Prendergast (2004) provides an explanation that includes three patterns of adaptation for children who experience sexual abuse: (1) **denyers**, who tend to repress the event; (2) **adjusters**, who tend to not show any symptoms for a variety of reasons; and (3) **accepters**, who believe that the abuse is deserved and is their fault. Prendergast likewise demonstrates the differences in adaptation and the resulting symptoms of such adaptation between both male and female victims turned perpetrators. Table 10.1 illustrates this paradigm in a succinct manner.

Another point that should be noted is that most offenses committed by juvenile sex offenders are verbally coercive rather than physically aggressive. Only a small fraction of these criminal incidents results in physical injury to the victim. Most

Table 10.1. Negative Reactions of Survivors of Sexual Abuse

Denyers: Tend to repress the event. Their behavior abruptly changes, but the true results of the trauma do not surface until later in life, usually due to some triggering event (marriage, lost of employment, sexual dysfunction, death of a loved one, etc.).

Boys	**Girls**
Often become satyrs to prove their manhood.	Develop problems in their adult sex lives, especially frigidity.
If the behavior becomes pathological, they become sexually assaultive persons, especially if they were forcibly sodomized and interpreted this as being a girl.	See sex as dirty or disgusting; may become physically abusive parents without knowing why. Nudity is embarrassing, and any arousal produces shame/guilt.

Adjusters: Usually have no negative effects because they

- put all blame and responsibility on the abuser,
- vent appropriate anger onto the abuser who molested them,
- discuss what happened with their parents and friends,
- want the abuse reported to the authorities, and
- ask for counseling or therapy if the feel they need it.

Accepters: Accept the abuse as deserved and their fault. As a result, self-image is damaged, and the effects are long lasting and sometimes permanent.

Boys	**Girls**
Repeat their own abuse on a same-age child, almost ritualistically in order to reverse roles with the abuser.	Tend to prostitute, become promiscuous, or develop other self-punishing behaviors. This is an attempt to undo the abuse.
They feel that they are the adult aggressor in control rather than the victim being controlled.	If they marry, they tend to marry an aggressive, battering type (dominant) husband.
They may show no other visible signs or problems in their employment or in their social lives.	They tend to lose all goal motivation and isolate socially.

Source: Adapted from Prendergast (2004).

offenders use bribes or coercion to gain compliance from their victims, and if force is used, it is usually only the minimum necessary to complete the act.

As with most problematic juvenile offenders, juvenile molesters are disposed toward a diagnosis of conduct disorder, often qualifying according to the criteria in the *Diagnostic and Statistical Manual of Mental Disorders* (4th ed., text revision), published by the American Psychiatric Association (2000). One factor that contributes to this is the observation of aggressive male role models. Studies show that male child witnesses to domestic violence tend to engage in externalizing behaviors (the acting out of psychological conflict or tension), including acts of interpersonal aggression, more than their female counterparts (Stagg et al., 1989). Exposure to family violence is linked to the likelihood of sexually offending as an adolescent as well as the severity of psychosexual disturbance (Fagan & Wexler, 1988). The effects of exposure may be cumulative as well as interactive with other developmental experiences, such as child abuse and neglect (O'Keefe, 1994). Recent studies suggest that exposure to severe community violence (e.g., murders) may also increase the likelihood of engaging in violent and antisocial behavior (Johnson-Reid, 1998).

Substance abuse is likewise common among those juvenile sex offenders who are in their mid- to late teens but not among those who are younger than 14 years of age. While there is strong research to support the association between violent crime and alcohol use, the association between sexual offending and substance abuse is not fully established. Estimates of the extent of substance abuse vary widely for the population of youth who sexually offend (Lightfoot & Barbaree, 1993; Prendergast, 2004). Prendergast (2004) estimates that over 90 percent of adolescent-aged juvenile sex offenders have at least a marginal problem with drug abuse. The ramifications of this for those treating this type of offender are noted in Table 10.2.

According to the Center for Sex Offender Management (1999), other influences that tend to aggravate the likelihood of juvenile sex offending include pornographic material, particularly that pairing violence/aggression with sexuality. The influence of pornography on the developing male's potential for sexual offending is an issue of similar controversy. One study found that sexually abusive youth were exposed to pornographic material at younger ages on the average and to "harder-core" pornography than either status offenders or violent non–sex offending youths (Ford & Linney, 1995). Research in these areas is lacking, and clearly juvenile sexual offending is far more complex than simple exposure to pornography or substance abuse.

Table 10.2. Substance Abuse in Adolescent Sex Offenders, Including Food, Alcohol, and Drugs

1. Ninety to 95 percent of all adolescent sex offenders have a substance abuse problem to some degree.
2. This abuse should be treated separately in a group setting, preferably a self-help drug group (see Chapter 4).
3. The relevance/importance of the substance abuse may be and, at times, should be also part of the sex therapy.
4. Counselors/therapists should not allow the client to use the substance abuse as an excuse/alibi for his or her deviant behavior.
5. Self-image issues are usually involved in substance abuse in adolescents.
6. Group conformity issues are also usually involved where alcohol and drugs are concerned.

Source: Adapted from Prendergast (2004).

The Center for Sex Offender Management (1999) also adds that sexually abusive youth share other common characteristics, including the following:

1. High rates of learning disabilities and academic dysfunction (Epps, 1994)
2. The presence of other behavioral health problems, including substance abuse and conduct disorders (up to 80 percent have the same diagnosable psychiatric disorder) (Prendergast, 2004)
3. Observed difficulties with impulse control and judgment (Epps, 1994)

Before proceeding to the corresponding sections on juvenile sex offenders in confinement, on community supervision, and in treatment, some distinctions in the types of juvenile sex offenders should be further illustrated so that the true heterogeneity of this type of offender can be better appreciated. According to Prendergast (2004), there are roughly seven types of adolescent sex offenders who are likely to come into contact with the juvenile justice or criminal justice system:

Type 1: Naive experimenters tend to be young (11 to 14 years of age), with little history of acting-out behavior. They are sexually naive and engage in one or just a few sexually exploratory acts with a younger child (typically two to six years old), using no force or threats.

An example of this might be when an older sibling or cousin (perhaps a preteen around age 10 to 12) suggests that the group play "doctor" together. During this game, the kids witness different parts of genitalia and/or engage in nonintrusive acts of touching.

Type 2: Undersocialized **child exploiters** evidence chronic social isolation and social incompetence. Their abusive behavior is likely to be chronic and includes manipulation, rewards, or other enticement. They are motivated to offend by a desire for greater self-importance and for intimacy.

This might be a typically reserved youth who keeps to him- or herself. The victim is likely to be much younger and is likely to be tricked or bribed into the sexual activity by this type of abuser. The abuser is not often likely to have any degree of sophistication in the approach but rather will tend to use somewhat overt forms of manipulation and/or bribery. This also tends to put this youth in a position of power and importance in the relationship. The youth may use any number of enticements (e. g., a type of toy for a very young kid, promises to take the kid to a movie or other event, and so on).

Type 3: Pseudosocialized child exploiters have good social skills and little acting-out history and are likely to seem self-confident. They may be a victim of some form of abuse, which is likely to have occurred repetitively for a number of years. The tend to be motivated by a desire for sexual pleasure via exploitation. They tend to rationalize their behavior and feel little remorse or guilt.

These types of youth will tend to be teens with a strong preoccupation with sex and are likely to encourage their victims that the activity is both normal and fun. As noted, the fact that the victim is younger than them will be of no consequence, and they may even find a way to make the victim feel guilty if the victim does not comply with their requests.

Type 4: Sexual aggressives come from an abusive, chaotic family. They are more likely to have a long history of antisocial acts, poor impulse control, and substance abuse. Their sexual assaults involve force, and they are motivated by desires for power and control. Humiliation of the victim is common with this perpetrator.

These types of teens will have behavioral problems that are easily identified among friends and the school system. They are just as likely to select a stranger as they are to select an acquaintance for the victim. When assaulting their victim, they are likely to make threats should the victim disclose the victimization, and they will tend to use derogatory terms and language with the victim.

Type 5: Sexual compulsives have families that are usually emotionally repressive and whose members are rigidly enmeshed with one another. These offenders are likely to commit repetitive acts that are often compulsive and are more likely to engage in acts such as voyeurism or exposing than the assault of the victim.

This might include a youth who has grown up in an overprotective environment (e.g., the stereotypical "overprotective mother" or in a household where the parents have a strong authoritarian approach to parenting; see Chapter 7 for more details on styles of parenting).

Type 6: Disturbed impulsives are likely to have a history of previous delinquent behavior and/or to be psychologically disordered. They frequently come from dysfunctional families, have substance abuse issues, and possess learning deficits. Their offenses are impulsive.

An example of this type of offender might be a youth who has dropped out of school or who is in school and is part of the delinquent and/or drug abusing peer group. This youth may commit this act with a stranger but will more likely do so in some form of acquaintance rape.

Type 7: Group influenced offenders are likely to be younger teens with previously detected delinquent activity. They tend to engage in assault when with the peer group and do so for peer group approval.

An example of this would be a juvenile gang member who engages in gang rape activity or a member of a group of boys who dare each other to sexually assault a chosen female victim.

JUVENILE SEX OFFENDERS IN JAIL AND PRISON CONFINEMENT

Out of the population of juvenile offenders, the adolescent sex offender is considered likely to require some form of treatment while in residential care. Although it should be pointed out that most juvenile sex offenders do not use violent force to complete their acts, some may represent too high a risk or danger to society to be released to community supervision. Thus, it is crucial that communities have a continuum of sanctions that include the typical community supervision and outpatient treatment at one end of the spectrum and the inclusion of secure residential facility placement on the other (Becker & Johnson, 2001).

Treatment of juveniles who sexually offend is usually court ordered or provided on a mandatory basis in correctional settings. Historically, juvenile courts have prescribed mental health care for youths with an emphasis on rehabilitation. In contrast, adult courts have typically ordered involuntary treatment on the grounds that the youth represents an imminent danger to public safety. Given the shift of juvenile courts to a more adult-like criminal justice model and the increasing frequency with which juveniles are being adjudicated and tried as adults, the issue of involuntary treatment may need to be reexamined. Judicial decisions are no longer made with a consistent emphasis on rehabilitation rather than punishment as a means of ensuring public safety. However, many sexually abusive youth may not meet the legal criteria for involuntary treatment based on criteria of imminence of danger.

The confinement of juvenile sex offenders is similar to that described earlier for other child and adolescent offenders (see Chapter 7). While many juvenile sex offenders will be within that category that gets some form of institutionalized sanction, this is likely to last for only about six months.

It would seem that the majority of juvenile sexual offender treatment programs have generally adhered to a traditional adult sex offender model (Jordan Institute for Families, 2002). In these types of programs, interventions typically include the teaching of relapse prevention and the sexual abuse cycle, empathy training, anger management, social and interpersonal skills training, cognitive restructuring, assertiveness training, journaling, and sex education (Jordan Institute for Families, 2002).

Juvenile sex offenders are occasionally kept in medium-security correctional facilities. Such facilities are typically reserved for those offenders who commit acts of fondling or penetration rather than noncontact acts such as voyeurism or exhibitionism (Becker & Johnson, 2001). Treatment issues that are often addressed in these types of facilities include techniques of breaking through denial, addressing the offender's own history of victimization, confronting attitudes that support victimization, teaching social skills, and recognizing deviant arousal patterns (Becker & Johnson, 2001).

One belief that has not turned out to be true is the notion that juvenile sex offenders are more likely to reoffend than are adult sex offenders. In fact, most juveniles who engage in sexual assault cease this behavior by the time they are adults (Hunter, 2000; Jordan Institute for Families, 2002). It has been found that juveniles who participate in treatment programs have sexual recidivism rates that range between 7 and 13 percent over follow-up periods of two to five years (Jordan Institute for Families, 2002). Interestingly, some research indicates that recidivism for nonsexual offenses is higher than for sex-related offenses among juveniles (Hunter, 2000; Jordan Institute for Families, 2002). Validating the efficacy of treatment is the fact that youths participating in treatment have lower recidivism rates than either adult sex offenders or untreated juvenile sex offenders (Jordan Institute for Families, 2002).

JUVENILE SEX OFFENDERS IN THE COMMUNITY

Clinical experience has demonstrated that the suspension of the youth's sentence contingent on his or her successful completion of a treatment program is a particularly effective motivator. Under collaborative arrangements, the treatment specialist provides ongoing progress reports to the courts. Those youth who fail to comply with program expectations can be brought back before the court for review.

In many programs, parole and probation officers play an important function in assisting treatment providers by addressing critical issues and supervising youth activities in the home and community. Parole and probation officers help evaluate the extent to which clients are productively participating in the treatment program and complying with court and therapeutic directives. They provide an additional link between the provider and the youths' families and often assist therapists in ensuring that families are actively involved in the juvenile's rehabilitative programming. While there is little consensus among the treatment community about the proper role of supervision officers in the treatment of young sexual abusers, community supervision officers should at least be kept up to date on the progress that treatment providers are having with the offender (Center for Sex Offender Management, 1999).

Typically, parole and probation officers provide an essential case management function. This includes an analysis of the appropriateness of youth receiving in-home treatment and of the need for supplemental community programming, such as community service projects (Center for Sex Offender Management, 1999). Functioning as case managers, parole/probation officers also facilitate appropriate communications between treatment providers and other community agencies, such as school officials involved in the youths' overall care. Thus, the probation officer may be the primary link between the offender, the criminal justice system, and numerous agencies in the community and is likely to be the primary expert on the juvenile's case history and development.

Assessments of the juvenile's appropriateness for community-based programming should include a thorough review of his or her living arrangements as well as a determination as to whether his or her family is capable of providing adequate supervision and oversight. Proper assessment requires evaluation of whether the living environment affords the level of structure and supervision necessary for the youth while providing for the safety of others in the home and the community. Special consideration must be given to the needs and concerns of individuals living in the home who may have been victimized by the youth (Center for Sex Offender Management, 1999). Because of this, it may be necessary to place a juvenile who sexually offends against family members temporarily outside the home. These youth should not be returned home until sufficient clinical progress is attained and issues of safety and psychological comfort of family members are resolved (Center for Sex Offender Management, 1999). Ultimately this decision is typically made by the presiding judge of the case with corresponding input from the probation officer or aftercare worker, any social service providers, the youth's treatment provider, the victim services provider, and the youth's family (Center for Sex Offender Management, 1999).

Assessment is an important factor when placing juvenile sex offenders under community supervision. The assessment of juvenile sex offenders provides a prediction of the juvenile's continued risk to the community and will be used to determine sanctions added under intensive supervision probation (discussed in Chapter 7). The assessment phase is also used to recommend the appropriate treatment plan and program for the juvenile sex offender. Many factors complicate the assessment of juvenile sex offenders. Some of these stem directly from the legal system, and some factors may come from the juvenile's family of origin, which may be reluctant to acknowledge the offenses committed by the child or to participate in the assessment process (Center for Sex Offender Management, 1999).

According to Flitton and Brager (2002), the most widely used method of assessing juvenile sex offenders is a review of records (e.g., academic, juvenile justice, and mental health) and a clinical interview with the offender, the family, and other collateral sources who have knowledge of the offender. Information gained from this initial assessment can help practitioners form diagnostic impressions of the offender, begin to develop appropriate levels of treatment modalities, and assess risk in an effort to protect the community.

Risk assessment should examine the number of victims; the type of victim (e.g., male or female, family member, friend or acquaintance, or stranger), the specific nature of the offense; the number and range of offenses; and escalation in the number, frequency, and severity of offenses, including the degree of intimidation, threat, and physical harm or violence involved (Flitton & Brager, 2002). Assessment staff should also obtain information about the degree of the offender's obsessive ideation, paraphiliac arousal, deviant arousal patterns, concern for the victim, and capacity for empathy (Flitton & Brager, 2002).

The offender's degree or denial of responsibility, values, or attitudes that support or condone offenses and attitudes toward treatment, intervention, and supervision are also essential components of a comprehensive assessment protocol. According to Flitton and Brager (2002), some specific factors that are important to consider in assessing sexual offenders include the following:

1. Types of sexual offenses—The nature and severity of the sexual offenses are also used to determine the appropriate setting for the offender.
2. Coercion—Coercion and intimidation are significant aspects of the sexual offense and must be considered during the assessment phase. Discovering the level and type of coercion can help evaluators determine the level of treatment that is necessary as well as the potential risk the offender presents to the

community. As was noted previously, the majority of juvenile sex offenders do not use violent force to commit their crimes.

3. Psychological and emotional functioning—Factors such as faulty cognitive processes, low intellectual functioning, poor impulse control, poor social skills, poor self-awareness and self-image, and limited coping resources are often found in juvenile sex offenders. An evaluation of the level of severity of each of these factors is paramount in designing a comprehensive treatment plan; such a comprehensive orientation is necessary if the specific sex-related issue is to be effectively counteracted.
4. Social environment—When using interviews, personal histories, and formal testing as assessment aids, clinicians must also consider the offender's social environment prior to constructing any treatment plan. This would include both the family at home and the peer group members in their neighborhood or community.
5. Cognitive and intellectual functioning—Deficits in cognitive and intellectual functioning have been found to have causal links with juvenile sex offending. As a result of their cognitive and intellectual deficits (coupled with disorders such as conduct disorder or a variety of emotional disorders), offenders may develop rationales that justify their sexually offending behavior.
6. Understanding of sex and sexuality—Many cognitive distortions are the product of deviant sexual fantasies and may be developed over time as the offender masturbates to these fantasies. Many offenders disclose elaborate sexual fantasies and plans prior to enacting their offenses (these are sometimes the product of observed pornography or exposure to sexual practices from older children or perpetrators who victimized the offender during his or her earlier childhood). These powerful fantasies, when paired with the intensive stimuli of the sexual response cycle, can create an addictive compulsion that resembles obsessive-compulsive disorder and draws the offender to their type of criminal offending (Slap-Shelton, 1994).
7. Affect—High rates of emotional problems, low rates of emotional bonding with peers, and problems with anger control have been associated with juvenile sexual offenders. Likewise, depression is often found in a high number of juvenile sex offenders (Prendergast, 2004). Many of these offenders are unable to accurately empathize with others and thus have distorted views on the "voluntariness" of their victims during the sex act.

JUVENILE SEX OFFENDERS AND CORRECTIONAL TREATMENT

Most important among treatment goals is achieving the offender's complete acknowledgment and acceptance of responsibility, establishing and ensuring personal and community safety, and helping offenders understand their cycle of abuse

(Prendergast, 2004). In fact, some treatment specialists make the claim that no true progress can be made with these offenders until this point is reached (Prendergast, 2004).

Similar to Moffitt's theory on adolescent-limited and life course–persistent juvenile offenders (see Chapter 8), this chapter will likewise contend that there are some identifiable characteristics that distinguish between single and repeat juvenile sex offenders. These characteristics are drawn from the research of the New South Wales Department of Juvenile Justice (Kenny, Keogh, Seidler, & Blaszczynski, 2004). According to this group of researchers, the most significant and distinctive differences among these two types of offenders lies in the following areas:

1. Poor social skills
2. Learning problems
3. Deviant sexual experiences
4. Deviant sexual fantasies, and
5. Cognitive distortions

What is important to note is that these offenders differ not so much on possession of each of these characteristics but rather on the severity by which each is possessed or has occurred in the juvenile's past childhood (Kenny et al., 2004). In particular, their predictive model indicated that social skills and cognitive distortions have a direct link to future recidivism in these offenders. On the other hand, learning problems, deviant sexual experiences, and deviant sexual fantasies are thought to be aggravating factors that indirectly affect the likelihood of recidivism among juvenile sex offenders. This may be because therapeutic interventions are most suited in changing a client's perception, and these factors may thus be amenable to such changes in perception, particularly the way prior deviant sexual experiences may be interpreted by the offender as well as the manner by which these offenders perceive their recurring sexual fantasies.

Based on their predictive information, Kenny et al. (2004) conclude that individual treatment needs of juvenile sex offenders should be tailored to the individual juvenile's profile and that they should, at a minimum, include the following:

1. The teaching of social skills
2. Challenging and modifying deviant sexual fantasies
3. Challenging and modifying cognitive distortions
4. The reduction of learning problems

Further, these researchers note the importance of community involvement in this process and suggest the following added components:

1. Added training of the judiciary
2. Risk management approach to prison and juvenile detention administration, particularly when aftercare is approaching the juvenile's sentence

3. A multisystemic view of the problem and of treatment, incorporating psychotherapy, educational tutoring, a functional family system, and community integration

The ideas presented by Kenny et al. (2004) are important because they point toward the fact that no offender lives in a social vacuum. This is particularly true with juvenile sex offenders. The specific factors that place this group at risk of recidivism are both individual and systemic. Total attention to individual issues with a corresponding failure to address systemic issues is likely to result in failure. Further, a failure to target and identify those issues that place the juvenile at risk of future recidivism will ensure future offending once social controls are no longer in place and the juvenile must make his or her own discretionary judgments on behavior. Therefore, the interplay between individual and community factors (e.g., school system, parents, and churches) is critical to complete an effective overall case management of these offenders. This will improve the likelihood of their completing probation and their ultimate recovery from sex-offending behaviors. We now turn our attention to specific forms of intervention techniques that address both the individual and the community-oriented aspects of treatment for juvenile sex offenders.

INDIVIDUALIZED FACTORS IN TREATMENT

As noted previously in the research by Kenny et al. (2004), therapists need to directly address, challenge, and modify inappropriate deviant sexual fantasies and thoughts that juvenile sex offenders may possess. However, treatment success can be impaired if forceful techniques are utilized. This point is important because many criminal justice agencies will be fond of overly forceful, direct, and confrontational methods because they meet the punitive and the measurable outcomes desired by probation agencies and the public they serve. According to Prendergast (2004), "Attempting to force change through threat, success motivation techniques, or through classical behavior modification techniques…simply does not work (p. 97). All that this approach accomplishes is frustration and the loss of confidence in treatment with the juvenile offender. However, it is equally important to understand that sex offenders in general, including juvenile sex offenders, lack honesty in most cases and are manipulative.

Because of these factors, therapists need to directly address juvenile offender fantasies and paraphilias in a nonthreatening manner and should assess the juvenile's knowledge on sexual issues. This is important because with younger offenders the intention behind the act committed might have been more exploratory than violative of the individual victim. Further, as discussed earlier, pornography may be a culprit in leading to juvenile sex offending. Therapists need to ask about issues pertaining to pornography, heterosexual and homosexual fantasies, and fantasies of assault, torture, control, or killing (especially with so-called snuff pornography). The key is that the therapist should look for motivators that may not be immediately apparent and that may not necessarily show up in any formal assessment method. Paying close attention to attitudes toward violence, movie depictions of violence and sex, and so on may give the therapist a great deal of useful information.

Along this same line of thought, the treatment specialist should attempt to get disclosure regarding fantasies during masturbation, such as with the existence of inappropriate sexual thoughts, the mixing of aggression, and sexual excitation. There is some indication in the literature (Slap-Shelton, 1994) that paraphilias may be related to obsessive-compulsive disorders or characteristics. If overwhelming thoughts and attention are placed on anatomy or sexually oriented material or if masturbation or sexual self-touching is persistent or repetitive behaviors are overly modest, indication of obssesive-compulsive disorder that is related to sexual preoccupation could be present. Treatment should consist of an internal self-management system where juveniles identify and discuss their risk factors and learn coping strategies to use when faced with a stressor or risk factor. Further, these teens must have no access to pornographic material, and the family system should be willing to ensure that the juvenile avoids media that depict violence and/or abuse with sexuality. It is also a good idea to have juveniles keep a log of the times that they fantasize, particularly when coupled with television.

Sex offender therapy is highly confrontive, and many juvenile sex offenders will either deny or minimize their actions. However, the therapist must be insistent since the point is for the juvenile to ultimately accept responsibility for his or her behavior. Therapists will note that with external community, family, and social approaches, the juvenile sex offender is likely to be quite skilled at paying "lip service" to the treatment program. The therapist, on the other hand, must address the individualized process (which includes building a rapport with the offender) so that an accurate determination can be made regarding the juvenile's true progress.

Beyond this, therapists may use role plays for pro-social peer relations. This is particularly effective since these offenders often have had little actual experience communicating with the opposite sex or communicating about sex. In either case, the juvenile sex offender must learn to have conversations and relationships with age-appropriate peers rather than younger peers. Juveniles are also provided psychoeducation regarding the nature of sexual perpetration, and the traumatic effects on the victim are provided as part of this education. But if the juvenile is a sadistic rapist, then this will be all the more difficult, even impossible. This is particularly true if the juvenile also presents with conduct disorder.

Finally, cognitive-behavioral forms of therapy are most frequently employed with "cognitive restructuring" for the subject to gain understanding about his or her own thoughts and feelings and to learn how to change or modify these feelings. These types of interventions will focus on faulty beliefs (e.g., females usually like to be raped, children need to learn and like it once they try it, if they do not resist then they approve, and so on). It should be noted that group therapy allows for more extensive confrontation with these faulty belief systems.

Specific individualized techniques often include safety plans, supporting age-appropriate relationships, supplying appropriate sex education, reducing or eliminating conditioned deviant arousal patterns, encouraging the development and application of empathy, and the clarification of personal values (Flitton & Brager, 2002). Strategies for managing anger include the ability to refrain from impulsive choices and actions, sound and appropriate judgment abilities, and social skills. Treatment programs should also address issues related to substance abuse, depression, and the potential sexual abuse that may have occurred in the offender's past childhood (Becker & Johnson, 2001; Flitton & Brager, 2002; Prendergast, 2004). Also important are treatment efforts aimed at building the offender's self-esteem; resolving his personal shame, humiliation, and guilt; allowing him an opportunity to be self-forgiving; and establishing trustworthiness in the eyes of family and others (Flitton & Brager, 2002; Prendergast, 2004). When it is feasible and no further harm will befall the victim, the offender, or the respective families, involving each of these parties in any restorative justice or victim-offender dialogue can produce tremendous healing for all the participants (Flitton & Brager, 2002). Helping the offender use the events as a therapeutic tool to develop empathy, compassion, and respect for self and others is highly beneficial, as it is this lack of empathy that is a central concern with these types of offenders, particularly those who present with conduct disorder (Becker & Johnson, 2001; Flitton & Brager, 2002).

COMMUNITY, SOCIAL, AND FAMILY FACTORS IN TREATMENT

As mentioned earlier, another critical aspect of treatment for juvenile sex offenders is the involvement of the parents in the treatment process. In fact, to some extent, the family should be seen as an extension of the probation office within the offender's own home. Effective family supervision is likely to reduce the risk of reoffending behavior. Those offenders who have families that are involved not only successfully comply with the conditions of their probation but also tend to be more successful in treatment (Flitton & Brager, 2002). It has also been found that these same offenders have lower rates of future recidivism, thus showing that the family can have a lasting impact on the offender's ultimate life trajectory. When parents are involved in treatment, they must be given clear guidance on how to maintain consistent expectations, structure, and supervision. When the offender has been removed from the home and is placed in a residential, foster, or group home setting, treatment still is tailored with the eventual return of the juvenile offender to his or her family of origin.

This external supervision component will be a network between the therapist and community members as well as the family. The central objective is to prevent the offender from relapsing by providing support and early intervention. Parental involvement, teacher and other adult observations, and the insight of other close relatives and friends are all critical (Prendergast, 2004). Note that while many of these juveniles will feel "spied on," this process will simply ensure that the juvenile stays on the treatment program, which is the ultimate priority of the criminal justice system. Making a true internal change within, however, is something that can be accomplished only individually and at the will of the juvenile. Without family/social system support and persuasion, a positive internal dialogue is less likely.

CONCLUSION

Juvenile sex offenders make up a heterogeneous group that display a wide degree of characteristics. Most of these offenders tend to have been victims of prior childhood sexual abuse. Other attempts to "typologize" this group of offenders turn out to be difficult, with large lists of differing groups and types that likewise have numerous exceptions. While juvenile sex offenders frequently do not use force, their offenses are serious and can lead to recidivism in their sexually assaultive behavior. Certain risk factors place them at higher risk for continued offending. Treatment plans need to focus on these risk factors and must include interventions tailored for that individual that include family and social components of supervision. Only a comprehensive, multisystemic treatment plan is likely to prove effective with this population of offenders, and it would appear that it takes collaborative action between the criminal justice system, the family of origin, and the community to ensure that these offenders overcome relapse.

KEY TERMS

Denyers
Adjusters
Accepters
Naive experimenters
Child exploiters
Sexual aggressives
Sexual compulsives
Disturbed impulsives
Group influenced

REFERENCES

American Psychiatric Association. (2000). *Diagnostic and statistical manual of mental disorders* (4th ed., text revision). Arlington, VA: Author.

Becker, J. V., & Johnson, B. R. (2001). Treating juvenile sex offenders. In J. B. Ashford, B. D. Sales, & W. H. Reid (Eds.), *Treating adult and juvenile offenders with special needs* (pp. 131–170). Washington, DC: American Psychological Association.

Center for Sex Offender Management. (1999). Understanding juvenile sexual offending behavior: Emerging research, treatment approaches, and management practices. Silver Spring, MD: Author. Retrieved from http://www.csom.org

Epps, K. (1994). Treating adolescent sex offenders in secure conditions: The experience at Glenthorne Centre. *Journal of Adolescence, 17*, 105–122.

Fagan, J., & Wexler, S. (1988). Explanations of sexual assault among violent delinquents. *Journal of Adolescent Research, 3*, 363–385.

Flitton, A. R., & Brager, R. C. (2002). Juvenile sex offenders: Assessment and treatment. In N. G. Ribner (Ed.), *Handbook of juvenile forensic psychology*. San Francisco: Jossey-Bass.

Ford, M. E., & Linney, J. A. (1995). Comparative analysis of juvenile sexual offenders, violent nonsexual offenders, and status offenders. *Journal of Interpersonal Violence, 10*, 56–70.

Hunter, J. A. (2000). Understanding juvenile sex offenders: Research findings and guidelines for effective management and treatment. *Juvenile Justice Fact Sheet*. Charlottesville: Institute of Law, Psychiatry, and Public Policy, University of Virginia.

Johnson-Reid, M. (1998). Youth violence and exposure to violence in childhood: An ecological review. *Aggression and Violent Behavior, 3*, 159–179.

Jordan Institute for Families. (2002). Understanding juvenile sex offenders. Asheville: North Carolina Division of Social Services. Retrieved from http://sswnt7.sowo.unc.edu/fcrp/Cspn/vol7_no2/understand_jso.htm

Kenny, D., Keogh, T., Seidler, K., & Blaszczynski, A. (2004). *Juvenile sex offenders in the NSW Department of Juvenile Justice: Can we distinguish single from multiple offenders and what are the implications for the treatment?* New South Wales, Australia: Department of Juvenile Justice.

Lightfoot, L. O., & Barbaree, H. E. (1993). The relationship between substance use and abuse and sexual offending in adolescents. In H. E. Barbaree, W. L. Marshall, & S. W. Hudson (Eds.), *The juvenile sex offender* (pp. 203–224). New York: Guilford Press.

O'Keefe, M. (1994). Linking marital violence, mother–child/father–child aggression, and child behavior problems. *Journal of Family Violence, 9*, 63–78.

Prendergast, W. E. (2004). *Treating sex offenders: A guide to clinical practice with adults, clerics, children, and adolescents* (2nd ed.). New York: Haworth Press.

Ryan, G., Miyoshi, T. J., Metzner, J. L., Krugman, R. D., & Fryer, G. E. (1996). Trends in a national sample of sexually abusive youths. *Journal of the American Academy of Child and Adolescent Psychiatry, 35*(1), 17–25.

Sickmund, M., Snyder, H. N., & Poe-Yamagata, E. (1997). *Juvenile offenders and victims: 1997 update on violence*. Washington, DC: U.S. Department of Justice, Office of Juvenile Justice and Delinquency Prevention.

Slap-Shelton, L. (1994). *Child therapy today: Volume I of the child therapy news*. King of Prussia, PA: Center for Applied Psychology.

Stagg, V., Wills, G. D., & Howell, M. (1989). Psychopathy in early child witnesses of family violence. *Topics in Early Childhood Special Education, 9*, 73–87.

Zolonder, S. C., Abel, G. G., Northey, W. F., & Jordan, A. D. (2001). The self-reported behaviors of juvenile sexual offenders. *Journal of Interpersonal Violence, 16*(1), 73–85.

LEARNING CHECK

1. The juvenile offender tends to be a fairly heterogeneous type of offender.
   a. True
   b. False
2. According to Prendergast, ______________ of all adolescent sex offenders have a substance abuse problem to some degree.
   a. 60 to 65%
   b. 70 to 75%
   c. 80 to 85%
   d. 90 to 95%
   e. None of the above

3. Treatment programs for juveniles should include, at a minimum, which of the following?
   a. Challenging and modifying of deviant sexual fantasies
   b. Challenging and modifying cognitive distortions
   c. Peer group training
   d. Both a and b but not c
   e. Both b and c but not a
4. Which type of juvenile sex offender tends to come from a family that is usually emotionally repressive and whose members are rigidly enmeshed with one another?
   a. Sexual compulsive
   b. Sexual aggressive
   c. Group influenced
   d. Disturbed impulsive
5. According to Prendergast, this group's self-image is damaged, and the effects are long lasting and sometimes permanent.
   a. Accepters
   b. Denyers
   c. Adjusters
   d. None of the above
6. Which type of juvenile sex offender is likely to have a history of previous delinquent behavior and/or to be psychologically disordered?
   a. Sexual compulsive
   b. Sexual aggressive
   c. Group influenced
   d. Disturbed impulsive
7. Intense sexual fantasies may lead to symptoms of obsessive-compulsive disorder if the fantasies persist long enough.
   a. True
   b. False
8. Which of the following characteristics have been found to differ considerably between single-incident and repeat juvenile sex offenders?
   a. Deviant sexual experiences
   b. Deviant sexual fantasies
   c. The intensity of cognitive distortions
   d. All of the above
   e. None of the above
9. Therapists need to directly address juvenile offender fantasies and paraphilias in a nonthreatening manner and should assess the juvenile's knowledge on sexual issues.
   a. True
   b. False

10. Which of the following tends to correlate with juvenile sex offending?
    a. Diagnosis of conduct disorder
    b. Exposure to domestic violence
    c. Substance abuse
    d. All of the above

ESSAY DISCUSSION QUESTIONS

1. Explain how prior sexual abuse is a concern with many juvenile sex offenders. Be sure to include a discussion on sibling incest from Chapter 7 and explain how both Chapters 7 and 10 may explain the cause of juvenile sex offending.
2. List, identify, and define each of Prendergast's typologies for juvenile sex offenders.
3. Describe some of the common techniques used and methods employed when treating juvenile sex offenders.

CHAPTER 11

ADULT SEX OFFENDERS

Chapter Objectives

1. Identify, define, and discuss the various types of sexual assault that are perpetrated against adult victims.
2. Know and understand the commonalities among adult sex offenders that victimize primarily adult victims. Be able to distinguish between various adult sex offenders who choose adult victims.
3. Know and discuss the commonalities among sex offenders who victimize children.
4. Know and understand the commonalities among the various typologies for child molesters/pedophiles.
5. Identify and understand common treatment techniques for sex offender programs within the institutional and community corrections setting.

INTRODUCTION

To understand the various types of sex offenders, it is first necessary to understand the various types of sexual assault and/or sexual offending. Thus, this chapter is divided into five sections. The first section provides a discussion of the various types of sexual assault commonly perpetrated against adult victims. The second section is divided into two parts. The first part discusses the commonalities among sexual offenders who victimize adults, followed by a presentation of various typologies among sex offenders who assault adults. The second part discusses some commonalities among sex offenders who victimize children, followed by a presentation of the various typologies among child molesters/pedophiles. The third section addresses sex offenders who are incarcerated. The fourth section addresses issues pertaining to sex offenders within the community. The fifth section addresses common treatment techniques for sex offender programs within the institutional and community corrections setting.

TYPES OF SEXUAL ASSAULT COMMONLY PERPETRATED AGAINST ADULT VICTIMS

As implied, this section addresses the issue of **sexual assault** against adult (not child) victims. However, the reader should understand that the term "sexual assault" is used as a blanket term that refers to a number of sexually related forms of victimization. This term includes all types of sexual offenses that involve touching or penetration of an intimate part of a person's body without consent (LeBeau & Mozayani, 2001). Thus, sexual assault includes sexual assault, forced sodomy, forced oral copulation, child molestation, and any form of undesired sexually related touching (LeBeau & Mozayani, 2001). For purposes of this chapter, sexual assault is the act of forced penetration of any bodily orifice (vaginally, anally, or orally) or forced cunnilingus or felatio involving violation of the survivor's body and psychological well-being. The assault is accomplished by the use of force, the threat of force, or without force when the survivor is unable to physically or mentally give consent.

STRANGER SEXUAL ASSAULT: A STEREOTYPICAL DEFINITION

For the purposes of this discussion, **stranger sexual assault** is defined as nonconsensual or forced sex on a person who does not know the attacker. According to Boumil, Friedman, and Taylor (1993), this type of sexual assault is what people usually think of when they think of sexual assault. Most people envision a rapist as an unknown man who ambushes his victim at night armed with some type of weapon that is used to force compliance from the victim (Boumil et al., 1993). The victim is caught by surprise and may or may not resist the attack, depending on how terrified she is and whether she perceives that it may save her from further attack and/or injury (Boumil et al., 1993). This type of stranger sexual assault can occur in any place where a potential victim can be found, including the victim's home, car, or anywhere outside (Boumil et al., 1993). However, stranger assaults are more likely to occur in open public areas than sexual assaults among nonstrangers (Laufersweiler-Dwyer & Dwyer, 2004).

This is the stereotypical sexual assault that common law definitions originally recognized. As such, most people have no problems defining this type of sexual assault, and empathy for victims of this type of sexual assault is usually readily extended. Because this definition of sexual assault is so well accepted and straightforward, there is little need for extensive discussion in explaining its definition. The occurrence of stranger sexual assault, in this society, is more widely accepted than acquaintance sexual assault.

ACQUAINTANCE RAPE

Acquaintance rape is any rape in which the parties know each other but are not and have not been involved in any form of romantic activity with one another. The word "acquaintance" is sometimes used to describe a person who is known but is not close to the person. The word can also be used to describe any person who is known to the victim. This would include anyone and everyone who is not a stranger (Parrot & Bechhofer, 1991). Thus, this would include neighbors, coworkers, friends, and so on. Often this is a person whom the victim knows but is not a close friend. The amount of force used and the usual time of commission are often different from stranger rape. In acquaintance rape, the amount of force used often has more subtle types of coercion.

INTIMATE (DATE) RAPE

While "acquaintance rape" and "date rape" are often used interchangeably, they are not the same phenomenon for the purposes of this chapter. Rather, **date rape** is a narrower term referring to nonconsensual sex between people who are dating or on a date (Parrot & Bechhofer, 1991). Therefore, date rape is only one form of acquaintance sexual assault.

The classic "real" sexual assault for many people is one similar to that described earlier as stranger sexual assault. The rapist is commonly thought to be a stranger who attacks at night and uses a weapon, and the victim resists but is overpowered. However, a high number of sexual assaults do not fit this criteria (Parrot & Bechhofer, 1991). Thus, the classic sexual assault scenario does not leave room for acquaintance rape or date rape. Most date or acquaintance rapes (as will be discussed later), even most group sexual assaults, do not use a weapon in committing the assault. Further, the victim often has engaged in some type of voluntary communication with the perpetrator that can be as brief as a few leisure conversations to fully intimate discussions among dating or married couples. The problem here is in determining exactly when the voluntary interaction between the two ended and the coercion and/or force began (Parrot & Bechhofer, 1991). Since many people have a difficult time explaining these disparities between their definition of sexual assault and the circumstances that surround a sexual assault, they create mechanisms that help justify their ability to disqualify a sexual assault incident from their idea of real sexual assault (Parrot & Bechhofer, 1991).

These offenders have a number of characteristics in common with one another. They are more aggressive, more likely to view pornographic material, more likely to use alcohol, hold hostile attitudes toward women, and seek out peer groups that reinforce stereotypical views of women (Laufersweiler-Dwyer & Dwyer, 2004). In addition, other research has found that these offenders are more likely to condone rape and violence. Further, they tend to hold stereotypical views of women in society. As will be seen in subsequent sections, these characteristics are similar to a variety of rapist typologies.

SPOUSAL RAPE

Marital rape is any sexual activity by a legal spouse that is performed or caused to be performed without the consent of the other spouse (Wiehe & Richards, 1995). These activities, as with acquaintance rape, include fondling, oral sex, anal sex, intercourse, or any other unwanted sexual activity. There is a lack of public awareness of marital rape that can be attributed to the secrecy that surrounds the problem (Finkelhor & Yllo, 1985). This secrecy is maintained by most parties familiar with the situation, such as the victim, the rapist, and even extended family members who wish to protect the rapist or who believe that marriage problems should be handled between the two involved (Finkelhor & Yllo, 1985). In this case, the marital rapist is nothing less than a marital abuser since in fact sexual assault is an assault (Finkelhor & Yllo, 1985). These abusers may keep the victim quiet through intimidation, threats, emotional blackmail, and even manipulative forms of "turning the tables," making it seem as if the incident was somehow the victim's fault. In discussing these similarities between standard marital violence and rape, Finkelhor and Yllo (1985) have created some distinctions with marital sexual assault. Two of these categories, the battering marital rapist and the force-only marital rapist, will be presented to demonstrate the differences in force and rationales presented to explain that use of force.

The battering marital sexual assault is a phenomenon in which marital sexual assault victims experience all the typical trauma from abuse, assault, entrapment, and terror as part of being a battered wife (Finkelhor & Yllo, 1985). In these types of marital sexual assault occurrences, the sexual violence is just one aspect of the general abuse that the victim must suffer. Thus, just as other researchers contend, sexual assault in this case is more an assault to exploit, humiliate, and degrade than one to simply gratify sexual needs. The force-only marital sexual assault, according to Finkelhor and Yllo (1985), is when marital sexual assault also occurs in relationships where sexual assault is largely the only type of violence utilized. In these cases, the amount of force used is usually the minimum amount necessary for the rapist to accomplish his goal (Finkelhor & Yllo, 1985). Although these assaults are just as humiliating and create a sense of powerlessness, the use of other types of force in these cases is limited to just enough to accomplish the sex act.

GROUP SEXUAL ASSAULT AND GANG SEXUAL ASSAULT: SEXUAL ASSAULT DEFINED BY NUMBER OF PERPETRATORS

Brownmiller (1975) defines **group sexual assault** as any situation in which two or more offenders sexually assault one female victim. In many cases, victims of sexual assault have suffered at the hands of two or more assailants (Brownmiller, 1975; MacDonald, 1995). This definition may seem objectionable since some researchers (MacDonald, 1995) make a distinction between pair sexual assault and group sexual assault. For the purposes of this chapter, such a distinction will be avoided since the dynamics of both types of sexual assault are essentially the same. With both types, there is a sought-after advantage through sheer numbers. The increased numerical odds of multiple assailants acting in methodical unison is proof of brutal intention and the desire to humiliate the victim beyond the act of general sexual assault through a process of mass assault (Brownmiller, 1975). The act of group sexual assault forges an alliance among the perpetrators against the victim (Brownmiller, 1975). This sense of alliance creates a sense of group anonymity among these offenders. This anonymity exists whether the sexual assault occurs among a group by chance, such as at a nightclub, or is the product of a group acting with deliberation, such as a violent youth gang.

MacDonald (1995) discusses group sexual assault that occurs among men by chance, giving scenarios that have been commonly experienced by victims. An example might be a young woman at a drinking party who remains after the other women have left. The woman may find that the men take advantage of the situation, encouraging and even coercing her to drink while "gently" convincing the woman to have sex with one or even all of them (MacDonald, 1995). Although the exact point at which consent can be truly given may vary, the amount of "coercion" and the deliberation to drug the victim can result in nothing less than overt sexual assault.

Further, group sexual assault can often be perpetrated against a victim who is already involved or associated with the group. MacDonald (1995) describes one such pattern among group rapists in which a man who has had prior sexual relations with a woman may deliberately place her in a social situation to get sexually assaulted. The supposed "boyfriend" will invite the woman to a party, and on arriving the woman may notice that no other women are present. If concern is expressed, the men will explain that other women are on the way. After some drinking and idle conversation, the woman is forcibly sexual assaulted by all present except her supposed boyfriend. The other men go through the motions of threatening the boyfriend with some sort of weapon to prevent intervention on behalf of the victim, who often has no idea that her boyfriend was part of the scheme to begin with. This example clearly demonstrates the level of duplicity that may go into group schemes to commit an act of sexual assault (MacDonald, 1995).

To expound on this sense of alliance, it should be noted that group sexual assaults can and often do occur with perpetrators who share an initial bond that leads to their acting together in a sexual assault. While this is widely recognized as a behavior among gang members, there are other socially accepted and supported groups that, perhaps unbeknownst to the supportive public, also have a propensity toward sexual assault (MacDonald, 1995). One type of group, the college fraternity, has developed a notorious reputation for engaging in acts that demean women, including sexual assault (Martin & Hummer, 1995). Some researchers demonstrate that groupthink and notions of in-group superiority, coupled with group reinforcement of masculine behavior, are the base elements that encourage group sexual assault among fraternity members (Boumil, Friedman, & Taylor, 1993).

Another type of group that is likely to be implicated in group sexual assault is sports teams (Benedict, 1998). When looking at the wider question of sexual assaults and sexual assaults of all types, various researchers agree on the basic notion that there is a social problem with male athletes sexually victimizing women (Benedict, 1998). Many of the same factors that affect fraternities are important with athletes as well (Benedict, 1998; MacDonald, 1995; Schwartz & DeKeseredy, 1997). Much of the heightened propensity toward sexual assault among athletic groups is centered around values of hypermasculinity that devalue men who are weak, equating them with being women (Benedict, 1998). In this case, women are essentially spurned, and toughness is idealized as the prime concern for being a winner. The use of degrading language describing women, whether from coaches or among athletes in the locker room, are thought to create an environment that is charged with sexual assault overtones (Benedict, 1998).

The last type of sexual assault to be discussed within this category is the phenomenon of **gang sexual assault**. MacDonald (1995) points out that informal rituals of adolescent gangs are somewhat similar to puberty rites in primitive societies. In many primitive societies, puberty rites may require the male youth to commit sexual assault to prove his manhood (MacDonald, 1995). This idea of gender identification through sexual assault has been cited in various public incidents of gang sexual assault. "Gang bangs" or "trains" are a part of the social life of street gangs and serve as initiation rites and confirmation of loyalty and bonding to the gang (Chancer, 1994; MacDonald, 1995; Ullman, 1999). The attack and gang sexual assault of a young female jogger in New York City's Central Park in April 1989 is discussed by Chancer (1994) and demonstrates the manner in which such gangs may execute such sexual assaults. It is important to note that gang sexual assaults have been found to be characterized by fewer weapons, more night attacks, less victim resistance, and more severe sexual assault outcomes when compared with sexual assaults committed by individuals (Ullman, 1999). The distinction between gang sexual assault and group sexual assault may in fact be a bit blurred, but the term "gang sexual assault" is typically reserved for sexual assaults committed by street gangs who are criminally oriented rather than formal or professional groups who are typically created for purposes outside the criminal enterprise.

SEX OFFENDER TYPOLOGIES I: VICTIM CHOSEN IS ADULT

Throughout North America, sex offenders make up an increasing proportion of persons who are convicted and later incarcerated. In some states, it has been found that the largest group of offenders are sex offenders (Morris & Tonry, 1990). The most common demographic is that rapists tend to be young. Data from the Uniform Crime Reports show that half of those arrested are under 25 years of age, and a full 80 percent are under the age of 30. Further, the National Crime Survey estimates that roughly one-fourth of all combined rapes and attempted rapes that occur at any point in the year are committed by offenders who are between the ages of 12 and 20. Further, it has been shown that a high number of rapes of adult victims have been committed by juvenile offenders. This underscores the finding that roughly half of all adult sex offenders report that their first sexual offense occurred during their teens (Bartol, 2002).

Bartol (2002) notes that roughly half of all men arrested for rape tend to come from working-class occupations, with another approximate third being unemployed. Of the convicted rapists, only 20 percent had a high school education, and the overwhelming majority came from labor-oriented occupations (Bartol, 2002). Thus, few white-collar or professional workers are convicted of rape. There is substantial evidence that most charges of rape are dropped or pleaded out of court to a lesser charge for those men who are more affluent.

The majority of these offenders are not under correctional supervision before their initial arrest for their sex offense, and most have some establishment within the community. Further, it has been found that sex offenders do not share the same tendency to "age out" of their crimes as do offenders who are fond of committing other types of offenses (Able & Rouleau, 1990). Thus, one can deduce that sex offenders start their offending at a young age and they are likely to continue offending throughout their lifespan if some form of intervention is not successful.

It should also be noted that most sex offenders do not present with a serious mental illness, though a couple of subgroups do frequently present with the typical personality disorders. Although a diagnosis of antisocial personality disorder is common among sex offenders, it is generally not considered sufficient criteria to dub the offender a "mentally disordered" offender in and of itself (Rice, Harris, & Quinsey, 2002). But despite sensationalism from the media, most sex offenders do not have a major mental disorder such as schizophrenia or some other psychoses (Sturgeon & Taylor, 1980).

Many researchers have attempted to classify various kinds of rapists (Holmes & Holmes, 2002). However, the chosen typology used in this book and this chapter was originally devised by Knight and Prentky (1990). This typology divides rapists into four categories: power reassurance, power assertive, anger retaliation, and sadistic. In addition, two additional categories have been provided to more adequately discuss the various types of adult-on-adult sex offenders and their motives for committing their crimes. These two additional categories are the opportunistic rapist and the sexual gratification rapist.

POWER REASSURANCE RAPIST

The **power reassurance rapist** is probably the least violent of the types considered here. These offenders are typically not socially competent and may be quite introverted in thought and behavior. These individuals typically have a low sense of self-esteem and suffer from profound feelings of inadequacy both socially and sexually. With this group of sex offenders, aggression is not a key factor of motivation; instead, these offenders seek to prove their sexual prowess and adequacy. These offenders are likely to have fantasies in which they imagine eagerly yielding victims who succumb to their sexual coercion, enjoying the experience so much that they actually begin to desire further sexual intercourse. Such fantasies are soothing to their sense of insecurity and incompetence and thus are self-reinforcing the longer the offender ruminates over them.

Knight and Prentky (1990) point out that many of these offenders come from single-parent homes. They also do not tend to do well in school and have an average educational level of tenth grade. They are themselves typically single and may be adults who continue to live with their parents. This offender is not likely to be athletic, is likely to be passive, and will generally have few if any friends. He is, however, likely to be a stable and reliable worker but is likely to be employed in a menial occupation because of his lack of desire of achievement.

These offenders are not likely to be mentally ill, but they may have other sex disorders, such as transvestism or fetishism. They may engage in exhibitionism, voyeurism, and so on, as this may be part of the method by which they select victims in their own neighborhoods for future sexual assaults. These offenders may watch their victim intensely over time until they feel secure in their decision to assault. They will likely case the home of most of their victims and are most likely to commit the act within the home of the victim when it appears that the opportunity is best available.

The main purpose of rape for this type of offender is to simply improve his own sense of self-respect. The primary aim is sexual, and this is an important distinction that should be made. This offender does not necessarily desire power over his victim, nor does he necessarily desire to control his victim. This runs counter to much of the conventional wisdom on sexual offenders. Rather, this offender might be perfectly content if the victim were willing at the onset, as long as it turned out that the victim felt the experience was good and provided complimentary feedback to the offender. Thus, the sexual assault for this type of rapist has more to do with getting self-desired validation from a sex partner as a means of simply overcoming insecurity. The control over the victim is only the minimum amount necessary to ensure that the sex act takes place.

It is important to remember that this offender's behavior during the crime is actually just an expression of his sexual fantasies. Thus, he does not desire to hurt his victim since he believes that this is an experience that his victim will ultimately come to enjoy. This offender may request that his victim talk in a vulgar or provocative manner that demonstrates her desire for him to have intercourse with her (Holmes & Holmes, 2002). The fact that the victim is vulgar makes her deserving and for the offender presents the appearance of her intense arousal and desire for the sexual violation. It should be noted that this offender may even go so far as to show "respect" to the victim by asking her politely to remove her clothing (Holmes & Holmes, 2002). He may even go so far as to ensure the victim that she will be okay throughout the experience, and he might attempt to show concern for her comfort throughout the experience.

The power reassurance rapist usually will choose victims from his own age cohort and within his own racial group, and he usually rapes within his own community or near the location of employment since this offender most frequently travels on foot. The power reassurance rapist is the only type of rapist who may later contact his victims to inquire about their general well-being, particularly after the sexual assault (Bartol, 2002; Holmes & Holmes, 2002). This type of offender may also desire to talk with the victim to set up another "date" since in his mind the victim enjoyed the encounter and since he views the rape as a form of "ice breaker" to what are hoped to be a series of possible interludes in the future. Naturally, as one would guess, this can make this type of offender easy to apprehend, presuming that the behavior is reported by the victim.

SEXUAL GRATIFICATION RAPIST

For the **sexual gratification rapist**, aggression is simply instrumental and designed to gain compliance. However, unlike the power reassurance rapist, this offender is not necessarily withdrawn or reclusive. Rather, this offender may simply desire sex and may be in a situation where he feels that force or coercion may successfully get the sexual intercourse that he desires. This type of rape is most reflective of date rape and similar forms of sexual assault. It may or may not be a repetitive behavior, depending on how any previous attempts at coercion have ended. It is unlikely that this type of offender will allow the coercion and/or aggression to escalate to the point of serious injury of the victim.

This type of offender may have a high degree of social and interpersonal competence, and the sexual offense is likely to reflect more sexualization in both activity and interaction. Further, the offender is likely to express his interest in the victim as a sex object. However, he may use any means of cajoling, flattery, or pleading while using the gentlest of force necessary to encourage the victim to submit to his desire. Within this group of offenders are those who drug their victims (e.g., rohypnol, excessive alcohol, or Ecstasy), and there is often no use of physical violence against the victim. The offender simply has sex with the victim against her consent. This is still clearly rape, but it is also clearly not based on attempting to cause pain to the victim as much as it is designed to gratify the sexual urges of the offender.

The offender who is successful in this type of rape is likely to repeat the act with other victims as well. Further, it should be noted that many victims will fail to report the act because they know the offender (perhaps very well) or because there may be a sense of guilt or shame from the victim. Further, the intoxicated state of the victim does not help her sense of credibility, in her mind if nothing else. Thus, the act tends to go undetected. This is a primary tactic that is used on many college campuses and among individual students and among student groups that may rape, such as fraternities and/or athletic groups.

OPPORTUNISTIC RAPIST

The **opportunistic rapist** demonstrates neither strong sexual nor aggressive features but engages in spontaneous rape when there appears an opportunity that makes the possibility look easy. This form of rape is usually conducted during the commission of another crime, such as robbery or burglary (Bartol, 2002; Holmes & Holmes, 2002). The victim simply happens to be at the scene and available, or the victim of the crime resists, and this provokes the idea of assaulting the victim. In most cases, this offender is likely to have a history of criminal offenses (not necessarily all of the crime being detected by police, however) besides rape. In fact, the offender may have never committed a prior rape and may not even rape again after the isolated opportunity that had presented itself. In order to fall within this category, the offender must both show callous indifference to the welfare and comfort of the victim and use no more force than would be necessary to obtain compliance from the victim (Bartol, 2002; Holmes & Holmes, 2002).

POWER ASSERTIVE RAPIST

With the **power assertive rapist**, rape is an attempt to express virility and sense of dominance over the victim (Holmes & Holmes, 2002). This offender has a sense of superiority that is based on "hypermasculinity" in which he believes he is entitled to sexual access simply because he is a man. For this offender, rape is simply an impulsive act of predatory victimization that the female deserves simply because she is female and is fair game for subjugation (Holmes & Holmes, 2002). The aggression exhibited in the rape is intended to secure the compliance of the victim rather than necessarily cause harm to the victim. To be sure, the power assertive rapist is not concerned with whether the victim is injured in the process, but this is not his primary motivation when using force against his victim (Holmes & Holmes, 2002). His primary motivation is to simply obtain and maintain control over the victim. Thus, unlike the power reassurance rapist, this rapist is indifferent to the comfort of his victim; he is simply concerned with ensuring compliance from the victim (Holmes & Holmes, 2002). The power assertive rapist commits sexual assault simply to feel a sense of dominance and control over a female victim because of heightened beliefs regarding the roles and rights of men and women (Holmes & Holmes, 2002).

Holmes and Holmes (2002) note that about 70 percent of these rapists have been raised in single-parent households and that roughly a third of these offenders have stayed in foster homes. In addition, the majority of these offenders (three-fourths) have suffered prior abuse as children (Holmes & Holmes, 2002; Knight & Prentky, 1987). This type of rapist generally has many domestic problems and has often been involved in numerous failed marriages. Obviously, these marriages are replete with negative incidents, including (some might say especially including) domestic violence.

This type of offender is likely to frequent bars and nightclubs designed for meeting singles (Holmes & Holmes, 2002). He might do this regardless of whether or not he is married at the time (Holmes & Holmes, 2002). When visiting such places, it will be clear that he is attempting to elicit attention from the opposite sex. That is, this offender will usually be very clear about his desire to find a female who is interested in intercourse. Further, this offender is very "image conscious" and goes to great lengths to "primp" and present a debonair demeanor targeted at soliciting sexual attraction from females (Holmes & Holmes, 2002). In keeping with his macho sense of self-identity, the power assertive rapist is likely to have an occupation that is traditionally held by male workers (similar to the anger retaliation rapist, and the selection of occupations will tend to be similar for both types of rapists).

The attack of the power assertive rapist consists of a mixture of verbal and physical violence (Holmes & Holmes, 2002). If he is resisted, he will physically overpower his victim. The level of aggression of these rapists tends to escalate as their raping continues (Holmes & Holmes, 2002). This is very similar to many of the characteristics of category 3 batterers (discussed in Chapter 12). Category 3 batterers are also likely to have serial marriages, with nearly all of them having abusive qualities. The batterers are not typically considered amenable to treatment. The same is true with the power assertive rapist. In fact, Holmes and Holmes (2002) clearly point out that the power assertive rapist is likely to be the most difficult of rapists to interview and interrogate. These rapists are simply unlikely to provide any cooperation even when intimidation, pleas for aid, and/or appeals for the victim's welfare are used.

Holmes and Holmes (2002) note that "the power assertive rapist... may be considered to be close to the clinical evaluation of having a character disorder" (p. 153). In fact, these authors state that this category of rapist is likely to be psychopathic. It is equally true that the category 3 batterer commonly has some form of personality disorder as well. Antisocial, borderline, and narcissistic personality disorders are frequently found among both category 3 batterers and power assertive rapists. Thus, their psychological profiles are likely to be similar and have a high degree of overlap. Further, both the category 3 batterer and the power assertive rapist feel absolutely no remorse for their actions (reflective of their common underlying disorders of antisocial personality disorder, narcissism, and tendencies toward psychopathy) or the victim's welfare (Holmes & Holmes, 2002). They simply care about having power over the victim and/or the situation. The fact that they have information that is desired by investigators itself becomes a form of power that they are likely to relish.

It should be noted that the beliefs held by power assertive rapists regarding men and women are identical to those of category 3 batterers. Groestch (1996) notes that category 3 batterers often present patterns of abuse that are centered around their internal belief system regarding the rights of men in relationships with women. Naturally, these views on male and female roles are similar to the views of the power assertive rapist. Further, it has been found that the category 3 batterer is the most likely to commit marital rape.

Because of these consistencies in the profiles, it is clear that this group may be one and the same and that the result is a rapist who is power assertive when between marriage and when single but may also be a category 3 batterer who also rapes his spouse during periods of marriage. Although there is not always a precise clinical match, these two groups do tend to be one and the same. In fact, the power assertive rapist may very well be married but also a philanderer (after all, what would deter them from promiscuity outside the marriage if they were a rapist and a batterer presenting with underlying psychopathic personality tendencies?) who frequents nightclubs. He will likely have a steady sex partner, either consensually or through marital rape, all the while being a batterer and a likely rapist when there is opportunity. Again, though it is clear that not every power assertive rapist will present with these coalescing factors, there is a group that is most problematic and fits the bill for the categories of marital rapist, power assertive rapist, and category 3 batterer. This group of sex offenders who present with all three of these criteria are referred to as the **power assertive marital battering rapist** (also discussed in Chapter 12). It should be noted that the power assertive marital battering rapist should not be considered suitable for therapeutic intervention because of the complexity and nearly impossible prognosis associated with this multiplicity of dangerous disorders and consequent beliefs surrounding gender interactions.

ANGER RETALIATION RAPIST

This offender is considerably different from the power reassurance rapist and even the power assertive rapist typologies previously discussed. The **anger retaliation rapist** strongly desires to harm women and has personal problems with women. This offender seeks to "get even" with women who have embarrassed or humiliated him in his past. These causes for embarrassment or humiliation may be real or imagined, but this type of offender essentially views women as bad, even evil, and thus deserving of harm. Unlike the power reassurance rapist, the anger retaliation rapist is socially competent (Holmes & Holmes, 2002). The anger retaliation rapist usually has come from a noxious family of origin where abuse and/or neglect are fairly common. Indeed, there is a high likelihood that male role models were themselves abusive to the mother of the offender, and there is also a high likelihood that the mother was in turn abusive to the offender when he was a child (Holmes & Holmes, 2002). These abusive mother–child interactions may be a substantial part of why this type of offender harbors resentment for women. It is thought that over half of these offenders suffered some form of abuse as children and that over 80 percent of them came from homes in which the parents had divorced (Holmes & Holmes, 2002). It is also estimated that roughly half of this category of offender has been raised, at least partially, in a foster home. In addition, a high percentage have been raised by a single female parent. Because of this rapist's experiences with females throughout his life, he has developed a position of negative and hostile feelings toward women in general.

The self-perception of this offender is very important, and Holmes and Holmes (2002) note that this type of offender may see himself as athletic and masculine. Thus, this rapist may seek recreation that centers on sports (especially contact sports). When younger in age (late teens and early 20s), this may be the type of offender who engages in group sexual assault, particularly if this offender attends college. This offender profile may fit well for members who spontaneously initiate group rape among athletic team members or among fraternity members (Holmes & Holmes, 2002). Note, however, that these rapists do not necessarily plan their assaults well in advance, but they are likely to be much more willing than average to consider rape since they have such a negative view of women. Since many individuals who participate in group rapes themselves do this as a form of obtaining both masculine excitement and a sense of belonging, their participation in group sexual assault confirms their masculinity not just to themselves but to others in the group as well. Thus, group rape activity can help reinforce the masculine self-image for the anger retaliation rapist.

When such offenders mature or are not the stereotypical "college student" (later 20s), they are most likely to act on their own and will not have partners in the rape. In addition, when choosing careers, they may be drawn toward "action-oriented" occupations such as the military, firefighting, and so on, or they may engage in action-oriented hobbies, such as car racing. Further, they are likely to ultimately be married, and they will not likely be assaultive to their mates (Holmes & Holmes, 2002). Thus, spousal rape will never be likely to occur among this group of offenders. However, those who are close to such offenders are likely to not have violent tempers, and the tendency to rape will be more of an urge or a spontaneous behavior that is sparked by events or problems that occur with a wife, a mother, or some other significant female.

For this type of offender, the act of rape is meant to humiliate the offender and again may be consistent with some of the groupthink that is associated with group rape where a victim is chosen because she seems to be particularly promiscuous or because she is seen as deserving of the abuse (Holmes & Holmes, 2002). When acting alone, this type of offender is likely to use verbal insults toward the victim and is likely to rip off her clothing in a demonstration of force. This rapist will also be likely to use weapons of opportunity to assault the victim. This rapist will tend to commit his crimes near home and will likely stalk victims who are of his own race and near his own age. It should also be noted that this type of offender is not likely to attempt further contact with the victim after the assault is over (Holmes & Holmes, 2002).

SADISTIC RAPIST

Among all rapists, the **sadistic rapist** is the most dangerous and the most likely to kill or permanently maim his victim. The primary desire of this offender is to simply cause pain to the victim. The infliction of pain is gratifying to this group of offenders, and there is simply no hope for the victim unless the sadistic rapist is either caught unaware and stopped or if, by some small miracle, becomes bored or distracted. This offender will seek to express sexual aggressive fantasies that have formed from an extended history of the classically conditioned pairing of sexual excitement and violence. Indeed, graphic pairings such as that presented in "snuff" pornographic films are a mainstay component of their lifestyle in many cases. This offender's main desire is to inflict intense and excruciating physical pain and psychological torment on his victim.

It should not be surprising that most of these offenders present with some form of personality disorder, with antisocial personality disorder being the most frequent diagnosis. Further, all almost automatically have the co-occurring disorder of **sexual sadism** as well (see Special Insert 11.1). The individuals will be given to sadistic fantasies involving dominance over the victim and may often use restraint, blindfolding, paddling, spanking, whipping, pinching, beating, burning, electrical shock, cutting, strangulation, mutilation, and any other imaginable act of torture and abuse to their rape victim (*DSM-IV-TR*). Among this group of offenders are a high number that present with the classic traits for psychopathy. It cannot be understated that this

Special Insert 11.1. Diagnostic Criteria for Sexual Sadism

A. Over a period of at least 6 months, recurrent, intense sexually arousing fantasies, sexual urges, or behaviors involving acts (real, not simulated) in which the psychological or physical suffering (including humiliation) of the victim is sexually exciting to the offender.

B. The person has acted on these sexual urges with a non-consenting person, or the sexual urges or fantasies cause marked distress or interpersonal difficulty.

Source: Taken from the *Diagnostic and Statistical Manual of Mental Disorders* (4th ed., text revision [*DSM-IV-TR*]) by permission of the American Psychiatric Association (2000).

offender has so strongly paired aggression and sexual gratification that he has eroticized it, and this type of offender is likely to be incapable of having sex that does not have violent overtones.

A little more than half of these offenders come from single homes, the majority suffered some form of childhood abuse, and many come from homes in which there has been evidence of sexual deviance (Holmes & Holmes, 2002). As youngsters, these offenders may have themselves presented with pathologies such as voyeurism, indiscriminant sex, and excessive masturbation. Further, their sadistic sexual fantasies (as discussed previously) are likely to present during childhood.

According to Holmes and Holmes (2002), this offender is likely to be fairly intelligent and probably has no previous police record. This type of offender carefully plans out his acts and will tend to be methodical in his approach. His intelligence, knowledge of police work, and care in the planning and implementation of his rapes make him especially difficult to apprehend (Holmes & Holmes, 2002).

This type of rapist is very ritualistic. In order to instill terror in his victim, he may use gags, handcuffs, and blindfolds when such are not even necessary for control of the victim (Bartol, 2002; Holmes & Holmes, 2002). He is also likely to tell his victim what he has in store for her so as to further terrify her. Because this rapist is so ritualistic, he will wish for each rape to go according to plan if he is to experience the feelings that he believes are necessary (Bartol, 2002). In addition, he may require his victims to say certain phrases or to talk in a manner that will arouse him. This rapist is prone to having collected a "rape kit" of materials that he has carefully selected as tools to assist in his planned rapes (Holmes & Holmes, 2002).

As this offender continues his rapes (and there are likely to be several), he will learn better methods of completing them and will also learn more effective methods of body disposal (Bartol, 2002; Holmes & Holmes, 2002). The need to learn techniques of body disposal will become increasingly likely because the severity of sadistic acts increase over time (Bartol, 2002; Holmes & Holmes, 2002). When sexual sadism is severe and especially when it is associated with antisocial personality disorder, these individuals are likely to kill their victims. Because it is unlikely that this type of crime can go unreported by the victim because of the nonsexual injuries that would require hospitalization, this offender is more likely than any other to murder his victim so that she will be silenced. Similar to the power assertive rapist, the prognosis for this group of offenders is extremely poor.

SEX OFFENDER TYPOLOGIES II: CHILD AS VICTIM

According to the *DSM-IV-TR*, **pedophilia** involves sexual activity with a prepubescent child (generally age 13 and younger) (see Special Insert 11.2). The individual with pedophilia must be at least 16 years of age and at least five years older than the child who was the victim. For individuals in late adolescence with pedophilia, no precise age difference is specified, and clinical judgment must be used. Accordingly, the sexual maturity of the child and the age difference must be taken into account.

Special Insert 11.2. Diagnostic Criteria for Pedophilia, as Found in the *DSM-IV-TR*

A. Over a period of at least 6 months, recurrent, intense sexually arousing fantasies, sexual urges, or behaviors involving sexual activity with a prebuscent child or children (generally age 13 years or younger).

B. The person has acted on these sexual urges, or the sexual urges or fantasies cause marked distress or interpersonal difficulty.

C. The person is at least age 16 years and at least 5 years older than the child or children in Criterion A.

Note: Do not include an individual in late adolescence involved in an ongoing sexual relationship with a 12- to 13-year-old.

The clinician should specify if the offender is:

Sexually attracted to males
Sexually attracted to females
Sexually attracted to both
Limited to incest

The clinician should also indicate if the offender is attracted only to children (termed exclusive) or if they are attracted to both children and adults (termed nonexclusive).

Pedophiles most often report a stronger attraction to children within a certain age range. Those most attracted to females usually prefer 8- to 10-year-olds. Those attracted to males usually prefer slightly older children. Pedophilia involving female victims is reported more often than pedophilia involving male victims.

Individuals may limit their activities to their own children, stepchildren, or relatives, or they may victimize children outside their families. Some individuals with pedophilia threaten the child to prevent disclosure. Others, particularly those who routinely victimize children, develop complex techniques for obtaining access to children, which may include winning the trust of a child's mother, marrying a woman with an attractive child, trading children with other individuals with pedophilia, or, in rare cases, taking foster children from underdeveloped countries or even abducting the children from strangers.

The pedophile may be attentive to the child's needs in order to gain the child's affection, interest, and loyalty and to prevent the child from reporting the sexual assault. Pedophiles start to notice their urges in adolescence in most cases, but some do report that they did not become aroused by children until middle age. The recidivism rate for those involving a preference for males is roughly twice that for those who prefer females (*DSM-IV-TR*).

While there is considerable variability in age for child molesters, most convicted child molesters are between the ages of 36 and 40 (Bartol, 2002). This is in stark contrast to the common rapist where about 75 percent are under age 30. Despite the statistical finding that child molesters tend to be older than most other sex offenders, there seems to be a pattern of victim preference that is based on the age of the pedophile (Bartol, 2002). It has been found that older pedophiles (over the age of 50) seek immature children who are 10 years old or younger. On the other hand, younger pedophiles (under the age of 40) tend to select girls who are between the ages of 12 to 15 years of age (Bartol, 2002). These latter pedophiles are referred to as hebophiles, which simply denotes a type of pedophile who prefers preteen and teenage rather than prepubescent children. Most child molesters do not present with mental illness of any sort other than the pedophilia disorder as listed in the *DSM-IV-TR*. Pedophiles typically do not finish high school, and most have poor work histories in unskilled employment backgrounds. When providing more specific typologies of pedophiles, this chapter and this book will adopt that presented by the Massachusetts Treatment Center (MTC), which has been widely cited in other forms of literature on pedophiles (Bartol, 2002; Holmes & Holmes, 2002; Laufersweiler-Dwyer & Dwyer, 2004). From the MTC model, four types of pedophiles have been identified: (1) the fixated type, (2) the regressed type, (3) the exploitative type, and (4) the aggressive or sadistic type.

FIXATED PEDOPHILES

The **fixated pedophile** presents with a long-standing, exclusive preference for children as both sexual and social companions (Bartol, 2002; Holmes & Holmes, 2002). This type of offender has probably not had a mature relationship with his adult peers, whether they be male or female. This type of offender would likely be considered timid, passive, and reclusive by most people (Bartol, 2002; Holmes & Holmes, 2002). This offender feels most comfortable and at ease when relating to children because he is intimidated by adults, particularly in intimate relationships. Sexual contact between the offender and the child is likely only after the two have become quite acquainted with one another. Such offenders rarely use physical force or aggression; however, they see absolutely nothing wrong with their activity with children. Although they know that others in society view it as wrong, they do not understand why this is the case and simply cannot identify with the idea that their behavior is inappropriate. Because of this entrenched view, this type of pedophile is very difficult to treat and is at a high risk of recidivism (Bartol, 2002; Holmes & Holmes, 2002).

REGRESSED PEDOPHILES

The **regressed pedophile** most likely had a fairly normal adolescence and good peer relations (Bartol, 2002; Holmes & Holmes, 2002). This includes heterosexual relations that probably included romantic involvement. However, at some point later in their personality development, these offenders have typically developed feelings of masculine inadequacy and self-doubt. This type of offender typically has a history of alcohol abuse, failed marriages, and poor employment. This offender usually commits acts of pedophilia after some stressful occurrence (Bartol, 2002; Holmes & Holmes, 2002). Unlike the fixated pedophile, this offender typically prefers victims who are strangers and who live outside their neighborhood. The victims of this offender are most often female. It should be noted that this offender often expresses remorse for his actions and often is willing to go through the necessary steps to reform and make restitution. Thus, there is a possibility for treatment with this group of offenders. Bartol (2002) contends that as long as stress-inducing events are limited and if he learns to cope adequately with those events that do emerge, he is not likely to recidivate.

EXPLOITATIVE PEDOPHILES

The **exploitative pedophile** seeks children primarily to satisfy his sexual needs. This offender will gain compliance from the child in any way that he can and will try any number of techniques to get the child to agree to his desires. The offender is typically not known to the child, and this prompts the offender to attempt to lure the child from the proximity of family and friends in the area. If it become necessary, this offender will use aggression and physical force to get the child to comply with his wishes. The exploitative offender cares not at all for the welfare of the child and simply desires to sexually abuse the child. This offender's primary desire is simply sexual gratification, not to hurt the child, though he will hurt the child if his demands are not met. This offender tends to be irascible and impulsive. His interactions in other aspects of his life reflect a foul mood and temper. Because of this underlying characteristic, this offender is not likely to have a good prognosis for treatment.

SADISTIC PEDOPHILE

The **sadistic pedophile** is motivated by sex and aggression and selects children because of their sense of vulnerability. This offender is similar to the sadistic rapist when discussing offenders that victimize adults. These offenders are likely to have a long history of antisocial behavior and likewise are prone to present with antisocial personality disorder and/or sexual sadism. The offenders tend to prefer victims of the same sex, making them homosexual pedophiles. Since the primary connection for gratification is dominance through aggression and sexual manipulation, this offender usually assaults the child viciously and sadistically. The more harm and pain inflicted, the more this offender becomes sexually excited. Such offenders are those most likely to commit child abductions and murders. While this type of offender is rare, they commit an unimaginable amount of damage and tragedy to families who have one of their members victimized. They also invoke unbridled fear within society. Finally, for purposes of this book, this type of pedophile is simply unable to be successfully treated because of the extreme reinforcement that has been experienced in maintaining the behavior. Such reinforcement is nearly impossible to reverse or unlearn, and clinicians in prison systems are seldom effective in reversing any substantial part of the learning. The possibility of releasing these offenders to community supervision should not be considered.

ADULT SEX OFFENDERS BEHIND BARS

Generally, most sex offenders are housed within the general population of the correctional institution unless they are selected for some form of specialized program, such as a residential therapeutic community. In 2001, about 108,500 individuals were in state or federal prisons for rape or other sexual assault. Rape and sexual assault offenders accounted for roughly 5 to 6 percent of the entire state-level correctional population (Bureau of Justice Statistics, 1997). The total number of sex offenders under correctional supervision was about 234,000 in 2001, and over 64 percent of these offenders are under community supervision at any given time (Bureau of Justice Statistics, 1997).

Roughly two-thirds of convicted rape defendants do receive a prison sentence (with about 2 percent receiving a life sentence). Another fifth of these offenders receive jail sentences, while the remaining 13 percent or so tend to receive a sentence in the community of probation (Bureau of Justice Statistics, 1997). The average sentence for rape defendants sent to prison is usually around 14 years, and the average jail term given averages around eight months. Probation sentences average around six years for most offenders who are not given a period of incarceration. Likewise, the length of incarceration has increased for sex offenders across the nation. For example, from 1985 to 1993, the average time served by a convicted rapist increased from three and a half years to about five years. During this same period, the average time served by offenders committing sexual crimes other than rape increased by six months to almost three years.

However, while it has been a general trend for sex offenders to spend more time in prison, it is clear that they are not spending the majority of their sentences behind bars. In fact, most sex offenders eventually end up in the community. Because of this, this section of the chapter will briefly discuss the characteristics of sex offenders in prison. More in-depth discussion will be given to those offenders who are under community supervision. Further, the topics related to treatment programs and types of interventions used will be provided in their own sections, as the techniques often are very similar between institutional and community programs, aside from some obvious differences due to differences in types of supervision. Nonetheless, the underlying method of treatment and rationale for that treatment tend to have similar overtones.

Imprisoned violent sex offenders have been found to be Caucasian more often than other violent offenders (Bureau of Justice Statistics, 1997). Offenders serving time for sexual assault, in contrast to those incarcerated for rape, were substantially more likely to be Caucasian (see Table 11.1), and they were nearly three years older, on average, at the time of their arrest for the offense. While about half of incarcerated rapists were white, about three out of four prisoners serving time for sexual assault were Caucasian (Bureau of Justice Statistics, 1997). Likewise, age differences show that 5 percent of incarcerated violent offenders are at least age 50 but that about 7 percent of rapists and 12 percent of sexual assaulters are 50 or older. The average age at arrest of violent offenders serving time in state prisons was 29 years, compared to rapists at 31 years and sexual assaulters at 34 years (Bureau of Justice Statistics, 1997).

Further, it is clear that the majority of sex offenders given prison sentences were or had been married at the time of or prior to their prison sentence. This fits the profiles presented in the previous section for many of these offenders. This is particularly true for those offenders who were pedophiles (a substantial part of the prison population). Table 11.2 provides specific statistics on the marital statuses of incarcerated sex offenders in the United States.

Among offenders in prison systems of different states, assessment processes will determine whether the offender is most amenable to treatment. Most will be provided treatment if they are willing; however, those determined to be most motivated will likely be given a special form of incarceration through a therapeutic community. For instance, the state of Texas implements a three-phase program where the last two phases utilize the therapeutic community approach. The first phase

Table 11.1. Race of Sex Offenders in Prisons around the United States

Sex Offense Category	Caucasian	African American	Other
Rape	52.2%	43.7%	3.7%
Sexual assault	73.9%	22.8%	3.3%

Source: Bureau of Justice Statistics (1997).

Table 11.2. Marital Status of Sex Offenders in Prisons around the United States

Sex Offense Category	Married	Divorced or Separated	Never Married
Rape	22.1%	34.7%	42.0%
Sexual assault	21.8%	39.9%	36.6%

Source: Bureau of Justice Statistics (1997).

most often lasts three to six months and occurs within the standard institutional environment. The second and third phases involve intensive treatment that lasts approximately 9 to 12 months. This is a highly structured and intensive phase that restructures patterns through various forms of confrontive and reflective psychological interventions. The therapeutic community provides necessary behavior modifiers in the form of sanctions and privileges that allow offenders immediate feedback about their behavior and treatment progress. This is important to note because these types of programs occur while offenders are theoretically "behind bars," yet eventually these types of treatments are utilized to reintegrate the offender into the community.

On the other hand, when sex offenders are deemed high risk, they may be subjected to intensely oriented programs with tight levels of security. Public safety is the paramount concern with these programs. The state of Minnesota has one such program at its Willow River/Moose Lake facility. The Minnesota Department of Corrections has worked in collaboration with the Minnesota Department of Human Services to develop this treatment program aimed specifically at the highest-risk sex offenders. These are those offenders who might likely be referred to civil commitment as a sexually dangerous person or sexual psychopathic personality at the end of their prison sentence. These offenders are screened on intake into prison. After an extensive clinical interview and committee discussion as well as a file review, the highest-risk incarcerated offenders are selected for this program. Note that this program is not necessarily voluntary, as the Minnesota Department of Corrections retains the right to subject offenders to up to another 30 months of extended incarceration if they refuse to participate in the program or if they fail to complete the program. For more details on this unique form of incarceration for dangerous sex offenders, see Special Insert 11.3.

ADULT SEX OFFENDERS IN THE COMMUNITY

When addressing the notion of sex offenders on community supervision, the first concern that often comes to mind is public safety. This concern is the overriding and understandable priority when considering the suitability of community supervision for sex offenders. One thing should be clear from the discussion in the preceding section: most of them will ultimately end up on community supervision at one point or

Special Insert 11.3. Civil Commitment of Sex Offenders

Unlike other crimes, when a sex offender has done his time, that offender is not automatically entitled to his or her liberty. In 16 states, there now exist laws that allow for the civil commitment of sex offenders after their prison sentence has been successfully served!

These laws have been upheld by the U.S. Supreme Court. In the case of *Kansas v. Hendricks* (1997), the Court upheld Kansas's Sexually Violent Predator Act, which permitted the state to keep sexual offenders in a mental institution after they complete their criminal sentence. The premise behind this was that the offender was being kept for treatment purposes, not punishment, and therefore the loss of liberty was not different than if the offender had been civilly committed from the free world without having had any form of conviction. Thus, the civil commitment is in the offender's best interest as well as society's.

Since 1997, these states conduct yearly review hearings where these men are judged by their sexual tastes and fantasies, which are determined by psychiatrists of the state. Objective standards, such as performances on psychological tests, their attitudes toward authority, and their accountability for their crimes, also affect the ultimate decision. In 1998, New Jersey maximized the boundaries of this legal precedent to authorize the commitment of any offender convicted who has served time for a sex crime and is found to have a "mental abnormality or personality disorder" that makes him likely to commit another crime. The offenders are to be given treatment until they are finally judged to no longer be dangerous. Given their complicated disorders, entrenched belief systems, and poor prognoses for treatment, it is then likely that the vast majority of those sex offenders who are committed will never return to society. This is perhaps the most pragmatic of options for sadistic rapists and sadistic pedophiles.

another. Thus, understanding the true recidivism rates for sex offenders and the recidivism rates for different types of sex offenders is critical if an agency is to make effective, safe decisions about early release. In 2003, the U.S. Department of Justice published a study that examined recidivism among sex offenders released in 1994 and tracked their reoffending rates during the subsequent three years to 1997. This study examined prison systems in 15 states that released a total of 9,691 male sex offenders. These 9,691 offenders constituted two-thirds of all the male sex offenders released from state prison systems throughout the United States in 1994 (Bureau of Justice Statistics, 2003). These offenders were divided by type of sex offender and consisted of the following breakdown:

- 3,115 released rapists
- 4,295 released child molesters
- 6,576 released sexual assaulters
- 443 released statutory rapists

It should be noted that the study included the "Big Four" among state correctional systems (California, New York, Texas, and Florida). The other states were selected because of their representativeness of the overall U.S. correctional population. These states released a total of 272,111 prisoners in 1994, meaning that the 9,691 sex offenders consisted of about 3.6 percent of all those released on community supervision (Bureau of Justice Statistics, 2003). On average, the 9,691 sex offenders served three and a half years of an average eight-year sentence before being released in 1994 (Bureau of Justice Statistics, 2003).

This study found that within the first three years following their release from prison in 1994, 5.3 percent (517 of the 9,691) of released sex offenders were rearrested for a sex crime. The rate for the 262,420 released non–sex offenders was lower at 1.3 percent. The first 12 months following their release from a state prison accounted for roughly 40 percent of the sex offender recidivism cases. On the other hand, an average of 4,295 child molesters were released after serving about three years of an approximate seven-year sentence. With child molesters, the first three years following release from prison resulted in 3.3 percent (141 of 4,295) of released child molesters being rearrested for another sex crime against a child (Bureau of Justice Statistics, 2003).

While recidivism studies typically find that the older the prisoner when released, the lower the rate of recidivism, this was not the case with sex offenders. Overall, of the 9,691 released sex offenders, 3.5 percent (339 of the 9,691) were reconvicted for a sex crime during the three-year follow-up period. From these results, it can be seen that sex offenders have a higher likelihood of recidivism (3.5 percent) than do non–sex offenders (1.3 percent). Although one can therefore say that sex offenders are essentially more than twice as likely to reoffend than are non–sex offenders, this can be misleading when presented to the public. Although the thought of having someone sexually victimized is terrible and no one wishes to see this occur, it becomes clear that the recidivism rates for sex offenders can make community supervision a potentially viable option. It is because of this that sex offenders are ultimately returned to the community. However, the quality of supervision is greatly enhanced for this type of offender when compared to most other offenders on community supervision.

Thus, many community supervision programs utilize what is referred to as the containment approach, which has been publicized by the American Probation and Parole Association. The **containment approach** is based on the idea that multiple dimensions of supervision are necessary to optimize public safety, and this requires numerous actors within the criminal justice and community setting. When utilizing the containment approach, the supervision team will consist of at least three persons, each with his or her own specific role in the process (Hunt County Community Supervision and Corrections Department, 2004). The community supervision team in Hunt County, Texas, provides an excellent overview on the containment approach and a well-organized glimpse of an effective sex offender supervision program on its

Web site. According to the Hunt County Community Supervision and Corrections Department, the personnel involved with this containment approach are tasked to work closely together so that the offender's activity is closely monitored throughout the week. Members of the typical supervision team would be as follows:

1. Community supervision officer—This officer will monitor the offender's behavior in the community and assess compliance with court mandates. These officers of the court will maintain regular contact with the offender (usually through some form of intensive supervision coupled with electronic monitoring) and routine conversations with the treatment therapist. Through this process, the officer is aware of the offender's offense cycle and will be informed of his likelihood of relapse at critical points in his supervision. This agent represents the cognizant authority of the court and is responsible for initiating court action if the offender does not comply with the terms of his supervision.
2. Sex offender therapist—The therapist will usually see the offender once a week in a group counseling setting. These therapists will be highly trained and experienced in working with the sex offender population. Advanced training is usually required in most states before a therapist can provide services. The therapist will maintain close contact with the community supervision officer, and both work collaboratively to identify potential problems in the offender's compliance with his community supervision requirements. When the sex offender therapist and the community supervision officer work together, the offender is less able to hide relevant issues from the therapist or the treatment group.
3. Polygraph examiner—Sex offenders are generally manipulative and superficially compliant. Sex offenders are adept at withholding information and keeping secrets. The expertise of the polygraph examiner is useful in detecting deception in sex offenders. The information gained from polygraph examinations is forwarded to the therapist and community supervision officer.

Thus, these three supervising agents work together to "contain" the offender's risk to the community. In addition to the three-pronged supervision, there are a number of other supervision requirements that are likely to be mandated to ensure compliance. For instance, the sex offender will usually be required to submit to routine polygraph testing, and the offender will be made to pay for this testing. The polygraph is usually given every 3, 6, or 12 months, depending on the jurisdiction.

Further, depending on the type of sex offender, there may be conditions with his potential contact with children. Most offenders are initially restricted from having contact with children. This is often the case with pedophiles. However, some offenders may be allowed to have supervised contact with their own children if they had not been victims and if the offender does not seem to be a risk to the children. As the offender's progress in treatment continues, the conditions of this restriction may be modified as seems practical with that offender. Further, these offenders are almost always restricted from residing near a school or day care center and cannot go to places commonly known to have children. Finally, it is common that sex offenders are restricted from purchasing pornography or frequenting sexually oriented businesses. Restrictions on Internet use is also becoming a common condition as well.

Hunt County, Texas, utilizes an approach that is known as the Sex Offender Accountability Program. This program is a good example of what a community supervision program should entail when sex offenders are the primary client caseload. This program utilizes the treatment team approach for supervision of sex offenders endorsed by the American Probation and Parole Association. Offenders in this program are required to attend sex offender treatment. This treatment is cognitive-behavioral in orientation, and offenders often have their views and beliefs challenged with intense confrontation. Group therapy is utilized most frequently because offenders are expected to challenge one another as well while under the guidance of the group facilitator. Offenders are taught such things as predictable indicators in their offense cycle, victim empathy, and relapse prevention. Further, offenders are required to state and behaviorally model their accountability for their offense. Finally, to ensure public safety and as a backup to ensure their compliance with the treatment program, this program uses the polygraph, the penile plethysmograph, random field visits, and electronic monitoring to ensure that offenders are committed to the treatment regimen and that they are adequately supervised.

Many of the instruments mentioned in this program of supervision are common to most treatment programs throughout the nation. Our current discussion has entailed some recently published research on recidivism rates of sex offenders released from prison and has also presented a number of characteristics that are common to community supervision programs around the nation. From our example chosen from the Hunt County Community Supervision and Corrections Department, it is clear that supervision and treatment become almost one and the same to a large extent. In fact, it seems difficult to talk about one without including the other dimension. With this in mind, we now turn our attention to some treatment techniques and orientations beyond those that we have already discussed.

TREATMENT STRATEGIES FOR SEX OFFENDERS

While most students (particularly students of criminal justice) are aware that a variety of offenders may be given treatment, they are not typically aware of how these treatment techniques are utilized. This section is intended to simply provide a brief overview of some of the techniques used in sex offender treatment. Specifically, the student will be given a list of various methods of intervention that are used with the sex-offending population to ensure that a more direct understanding is imparted to the student in determining how interventions are applied. The primary type of treatments discussed in this section fall under one of three categories: cognitive-behavioral, interrogation oriented, and drug administrative. We now turn to each of these categories.

COGNITIVE-BEHAVIORAL TECHNIQUES

These treatments are geared toward reducing and/or eliminating the deviant sexual arousal. Many techniques are commonly used by clinicians, each with a different rationale to its use. One group of interventions teaches impulse control, another teaches arousal reduction, and yet another teaches empathy to the offender. Impulse-control forms of cognitive-behavioral techniques include the following:

1. **Thought stopping** is used to disrupt a deviant thinking pattern. The offender is given pictures of arousing images and is forced to stop his thoughts when the image is seen. The use of group confrontation, observation, and journaling assist in ensuring that this is accomplished (Knopp, 1989).
2. **Thought shifting** requires that the offender shift his thoughts to aversive imagery. The sex offender may be allowed to view or think about some arousing image but then is trained to think about something aversive, like an approaching police officer. Again, the use of group confrontation, observation, and journaling assist in ensuring that this is accomplished (Knopp, 1989).
3. **Impulse charting** is a method used to track points and times when certain thoughts and or desires seem more intense. The time of day, location, and number of times per week are all important. The offender will usually also be required to report the level of intensity of the impulse (i.e., on a 1-to-10 scale), and this will be tracked through a journaling process with the therapist (Knopp, 1989).

Arousal reduction forms of cognitive-behavioral techniques include the following:

1. **Scheduled overmasturbation** requires that the client routinely masturbate on a progressively more frequent schedule throughout the week. This is intended to reduce sexual drive and make control easier for the offender. This exercise also teaches that the client does have some measure of control over his sexual arousal and use of sexual energy (Knopp, 1989).
2. **Masturbatory reconditioning** involves having the client masturbate to an appropriate fantasy until he has an ejaculation (Knopp, 1989).
3. **Aversion therapy** is often used in varying degrees within several sex offender programs. The aim of aversive techniques is to teach offenders to associate unpleasant stimuli with presently desirable yet unacceptable behaviors (Van Voorhis, Braswell, & Lester, 2000). A wide range of physical or overt aversive

stimuli have been used to treat sex offenders. Most notable are electric shock, foul odors and tastes, drugs that temporarily paralyze, and drugs that induce vomiting. Because of ethical and constitutional considerations, some of the more extreme forms of aversive stimuli are not used as frequently as they were some 20 to 30 years ago.

4. **Spouse monitoring** involves supervision on the part of the spouse (if and when available, though other family members may be able to assist) or significant other to complete a daily checklist on the offender's compliance with the treatment and to ensure that any therapeutic homework given to the client is being completed at the prescribed times in the week. This increases the overall supervision that the offender has (Knopp, 1989).
5. **Environmental manipulation** helps get the offender out of situations that are high risk for him and his potential victims. The offender should train himself to move out of the house, not the victim (Knopp, 1989).

Empathy training forms of cognitive-behavioral techniques include the following:

1. The use of **victim counselors** involves inviting victims to attend the group meeting. In fact, the victim may colead the group. Offenders may be required to visit a victim advocate center and, at their own expense, ask a victim counselor to explain their feelings on sex crimes.
2. In **cognitive restructuring**, the offender constructs scenes that cast him or significant others in the role of the victim. The client then focuses on typical rationalizations he uses to justify the assault (Knopp, 1989). Scenes are constructed where he utilizes and internalizes the rationalization. These scenes are then paired with aversive imagery. Finally, alternate scenes are constructed where the offender catches himself in the distortion and counters with a reality-grounded message in which it is acknowledged that these actions do not end in the way that the offender hopes (Knopp, 1989).
3. In **role playing**, the offender reenacts his own crime scene(s) with another offender, and they take turns playing the role of their victim. The remaining group offenders observe and later critique the role play and allow for group processing of the effects on the victim.

INTERROGATION-ORIENTED TECHNIQUES

The next group of techniques used are designed to ensure that the offender is being honest in his feedback that he is providing program treatment staff. This is important and necessary since sex offenders are notorious for lying and manipulating. These tools assist the therapist and community supervision staff in determining whether progress is earnestly being made in the program. The two techniques presented require the use of mechanical instruments to ensure compliance with the program. They are as follows:

1. A **polygraph** is the standard lie detector used to measure biological responses to deception. The polygraph is used in sex offender supervision for three primary reasons: (1) to break through offender denial of the offense, (2) to assess honesty in sexual history, and (3) to monitor the offender's compliance with probation conditions (Hunt County Community Supervision and Corrections Department, 2004).
2. The **penile plethysmograph** uses a cup or band that is placed around the penis while the offender is in a private room. The offender is shown nonpornographic pictures of different categories of stimuli, and auditory stimuli are also provided. A computer records the degree of arousal experienced by the offender (Hunt County Community Supervision and Corrections Department, 2004).

DRUG-ADMINISTERED TECHNIQUES

Drug-administered techniques include **chemical castration**, by which sex offenders are injected with drugs (most commonly Depo-Provera) to reduce the amount of testosterone in the offender's body. This achieves the sex drive reduction of surgical castration but does not require the controversial surgery. Some side effects include fatigue, weight gain, loss of body hair, and depression. Drug offenders typically regard this as the least-preferred intervention (Rice et al., 2002).

The use of these drugs has been found to work generally but only if the offender dutifully maintains his schedule of intake. Programs can monitor this by having the offender report to a clinic that works with the community supervision agency to receive his injection. Nonetheless, this drug will not be effective for all sex offenders. For instance, sadistic rapists and pedophiles are not necessarily motivated by sex alone. Rather, the infliction of pain is their primary source of arousal. Thus, this treatment would not be effective with this group of offenders.

CONCLUSION

Sex offenders can be classified by numerous typologies. In this chapter, we have examined the various types of sex offenses to illustrate the numerous methods by with these offenses are perpetrated. Indeed, the method of perpetration is important, as this can tell us a great deal about the offender and his motivation. Likewise, the sex offender varies by motivation, and typologies for offenders who victimize adults and those who victimize children vary considerably. Nonetheless, these typologies are important for both public safety and treatment purposes.

From recent research, it can be seen that sex offenders have a higher recidivism rate when compared to other types of offenders, but this rate has not been determined to be high enough to preclude their ultimate release into the community. However, some sex offenders (those with sadistic sexual disorders and/or psychopathic characteristics) are perhaps untreatable, and it is recommended that they be incarcerated indefinitely. Finally, methods of supervision in the community need to be collaborative to ensure compliance from these offenders. The confluence between community supervision personnel and treatment providers is a necessity if public safety is to be ensured.

KEY TERMS

Sexual assault
Stranger sexual assault
Acquaintance rape
Date rape
Marital rape
Group sexual assault
Gang sexual assault
Power reassurance rapist
Sexual gratification rapist
Opportunistic rapist
Power assertive rapist
Power assertive marital battering rapist
Anger retaliation rapist
Sadistic rapist
Sexual sadism
Pedophilia
Fixated pedophile
Regressed pedophile
Exploitative pedophile
Sadistic pedophile
Containment approach
Thought stopping
Thought shifting
Impulse charting
Scheduled overmasturbation
Masturbatory reconditioning
Aversion therapy
Spouse monitoring
Environmental manipulation
Victim counselors
Cognitive restructuring
Role playing
Polygraph
Penile plethysmograph
Chemical castration

REFERENCES

Abel, G. G., & Rouleau, J. L. (1990). The nature and extent of sexual assault. In W. L. Marshall, D. R. Laws, & H. L. Barbaree (Eds.), *Handbook of sexual assault: Issues, theories, and treatment of the offender* (pp. 9–20). New York: Plenum.

American Psychiatric Association. (2000). *Diagnostic and statistical manual of mental disorders* (4th ed., text revision). Washington, DC: Author.

Bartol, C. R. (2002). *Criminal behavior: A psychosocial approach* (6th ed.). Upper Saddle River, NJ: Prentice Hall.

Benedict, J. R. (1998). *Athletes and acquaintance rape*. Thousand Oaks, CA: Sage.

Boumil, M., Friedman, J., & Taylor, B. (1993). *Date rape: The secret epidemic*. New York: Lexington Books.

Brownmiller, S. (1975). *Against our will: Men, women and rape*. New York: Simon and Schuster.

Bureau of Justice Statistics. (1997). *Sex offenses and sex offenders*. Washington, DC: U.S. Department of Justice.

Bureau of Justice Statistics. (2003). *Recidivism of sex offenders released from prison in 1994*. Washington, DC: U.S. Department of Justice.

Chancer, L., & Donovan, P. (1994). A mass psychology of punishment: Crime and the futility of rationally based approaches. *Social Justice, 21*, 50–72.

Finkelhor, D., & Yllo, K. (1985). *License to rape: Sexual abuse of wives.* New York: Holt, Rinehart, & Winston.

Groetsch, M. (1996). *The battering syndrome: Why men beat women and the professional's guide to intervention*. Brookfield, WI: CPI.

Holmes, R. M., & Holmes, S. T. (2002). *Profiling violent crimes* (3rd ed.). Thousand Oaks, CA: Sage.

Hunt County Community Supervision and Corrections Department. (2004). Why sex offenders on probation? Retrieved from http://www.koyote.com/users/hunt/page9.html

Knight, R. A., & Prentky, R. A. (1990). Classifying sexual offenders: The development and corroboration of taxonomic models. In W. L. Marshall, D. R. Laws, & H. E. Barbaree (Eds.), *Handbook of sexual assault: Issues, theories, and treatment of the offender* (pp. 23–52). New York: Plenum.

Knopp, F. H. (1989). Northwest treatment associates: A comprehensive community-based evaluation and treatment program for adult sex offenders. In P. C. Kratcoski (Ed.), *Correctional counseling and treatment* (2nd ed., pp. 364–380). Prospect Heights, IL: Waveland Press.

Laufersweiler-Dwyer, D. L., & Dwyer, G. (2004). Rapists. In F. P. Reddington & B. W. Kreisel (Eds.), *Sexual assault: The victims, the perpetrators and the criminal justice system* (pp. 205–227). Durham, NC: Carolina Academic Press.

LeBeau, M., & Mozayani, A. (2001). *Drug-facilitated sexual assault*. San Diego: Academic Press.

MacDonald, D. (1995). *Rape: Controversial issues*. Springfield, IL: Charles C Thomas.

Morris, N., & Tonry, M. (1990). *Between prison and probation: Intermediate punishments in a rational sentencing system*. Oxford: Oxford University Press.

Parrot, A., & Bechofer, L. (1991). *Acquaintance rape: The hidden crime.* New York: Wiley.

Rice, M. E., Harris, G. T., & Quinsey, V. L. (2002). Research on the treatment of adult sex offenders. In J. B. Ashford, B. D. Sales, & W. H. Reid (Eds.), *Treating adult and juvenile offenders with special needs* (pp. 291–312). Washington, DC: American Psychological Association.

Schwartz, M., & DeKeseredy, W. (1997). *Sexual assault on the college campus: The role of male peer support*. Thousand Oaks, CA: Sage.

Sturgeon V. H., & Taylor, J. (1980). Report of a five-year follow-up study of mentally disordered sex offenders released from Atascadero State Hospital in 1973. *Criminal Justice Journal, 4*, 31–63.

Ullman, S. E. (1999). Social support and recovery from sexual assault: A review. *Aggression and Violent Behavior, 4*(3), 343–358.

Van Voorhis, P., Braswell, M., & Lester, D. (2000). *Correctional counseling and rehabilitation* (4th ed.). Cincinnati, OH: Anderson.

Wiehe, V. R., & Richards, A. L. (1995). *Intimate betrayal: Understanding and responding to the trauma of acquaintance rape*. Thousand Oaks, CA: Sage.

LEARNING CHECK

1. Which type of pedophile most likely had a fairly normal adolescence and good peer relations?
   a. Exploitative pedophile
   b. Sadistic pedophile
   c. Fixated pedophile
   d. Regressed pedophile

2. Which of the following is required for a diagnosis of pedophilia?
   a. The person is at least 16 years old and at least five years older than the child victim.
   b. Over a period of at least six months, recurrent, intense, sexually arousing fantasies, sexual urges, or behaviors involving sexual activity with a prebuscent child or children have existed.
   c. The person has acted on these sexual urges, or the sexual urges or fantasies cause marked distress or interpersonal difficulty.
   d. All of the above
   e. Both b and c but not a.
3. Acquaintance rape would include which of the following?
   a. Marital rape
   b. Gang rape
   c. Date rape
   d. All of the above
   e. Both a and c but not b
4. The majority of sex offenders given prison sentences were or had been married at the time of or prior to their conviction.
   a. True
   b. False
5. Which of the following is probably the least violent of the types that were considered?
   a. Power reassurance rapist
   b. Anger retaliation rapist
   c. Power assertive rapist
   d. Sadistic rapist
6. ______________________ is the idea that multiple dimensions of supervision are necessary to optimize public safety and that this requires numerous actors within the criminal justice and community setting.
   a. Intensive supervised probation
   b. Human supervision model
   c. The community supervision model
   d. Containment approach
7. Recidivism studies typically find that the older the prisoner when released, the lower the rate of recidivism. This tends to be true with sex offenders as well.
   a. True
   b. False
8. The aim of this type of technique is to teach sex offenders to associate unpleasant stimuli with presently desirable yet unacceptable behaviors.
   a. Aversion therapy
   b. Cognitive restructuring

c. Punishment
d. Negative reinforcement

9. Beliefs held by power assertive rapists regarding men and women are identical to those who are category 3 batterers.
a. True
b. False

10. Depo-Provera is sometimes used with sex offenders for the purposes of ______________.
a. Treatment of depression
b. Chemical castration
c. Treatment for aggressive behavior
d. All of the above
e. None of the above

ESSAY DISCUSSION QUESTIONS

1. List and describe the three forms of cognitive-behavioral empathy training techniques. Next, describe the techniques used to ensure that the offender is being honest in his feedback that he is providing program treatment staff. Explain how both of these techniques are used to augment one another in addressing the sex offender.
2. Fully define, compare, and contrast the different typologies for pedophiles.
3. Fully define, compare, and contrast power reassurance rapists with sadistic rapists.
4. Define and discuss group rape and group assault. What are the differences? What are the similarities? When considering these dynamics, explain whether you believe that common treatment techniques discussed in this chapter would work with this type of offender.

CHAPTER 12

DOMESTIC BATTERERS AS SPECIAL NEEDS OFFENDERS

Chapter Objectives

1. Understand the differences between category 1, category 2, and category 3 batterers.
2. Know the various personality and anxiety disorders that are purported to be found among batterers.
3. Identify and discuss the various treatment modalities used with batterers and be able to connect the correct treatment modality with the correct category of batterer.
4. Understand the difficulties involved with community supervision of the battering offender. Also be aware of liability concerns for therapists under the *Tarasoff* ruling.

INTRODUCTION

Domestic batterers are offenders who are a unique class unto themselves. While being violent, these offenders are selective with whom and how their violence will be utilized (Groestch, 1996). This is important because the distinction between batterers and generally violent offenders is that their choice of victim is one who is close to them. Further, the reasons for their use of violence usually involve control and manipulation of an emotionally based relationship with the victim. While much attention has been given to the issue of domestic violence, it is the domestic batterer who is frequently misunderstood among both the general population and the body of criminal justice practitioners.

One of these misunderstandings is the fact that there are stark differences between batterers themselves. These differences can often be observed in the reported reasons for such abuse and the various levels of lethality of the abusive incident(s). Indeed, batterers should be envisioned as falling on a continuum (Groetsch, 1996) along which three categories of domestic batterers can be identified. For this chapter's purposes, these categories are based on the work of Groetsch (1996), who proposes the potential danger from the abuser as the standard by which categorization should occur.

The approach of using categories is useful in determining which batterers are treatable from those who are simply beyond the scope of successful rehabilitation. In general, **category 1 batterers** are the least dangerous and most treatable. **Category 2 batterers** fall between category 1 and **category 3 batterers** (the latter being very dangerous and not likely to complete treatment), with prognoses that are the least predictable. Note that these categories are for the most part artificial and are simply a method by which classification and identification of likely prevention and treatment outcomes can be identified.

Category 1 batterers are often the "ordinary guy" who is caught in abnormal circumstances, such as a in child custody dispute. Their abuse tends to be situational and isolated with much of the cause for the incident being generated from what are referred to as "external" environmental factors rather than internal thoughts or belief system issues (Groetsch, 1996). These offenders will typically have had no previous violent relationships with intimates and are the least likely to use weapons during their abuse. These offenders are also the least likely to present with any mental health or life development issues. What is perhaps most important is that these offenders do actually feel and express remorse over their actions. It is this last characteristic that makes this group treatable and truly separates them from the other two groups categorized in this chapter.

Category 2 batterers, on the other hand, often display several character defects, including substance abuse/addiction, nondomestic violent activity, and problems related to moral turpitude. Abuse by these batterers is not situational and is not isolated (Groestch, 1996). However, abuse by these batterers is likely to be unpredictable, sometimes with little or no apparent provocation. Interestingly, it is difficult to determine causal factors that weigh most in their abusiveness, with both external environmental and internal belief system factors having nearly equal effects and thus explaining, at least in part, their unpredictable use of violence (Groestch, 1996). These batterers may have had previously violent relationships with other partners and may have inflicted premarital abuse on their current partner (Groestch, 1996). These abusers may use weapons, though they are not prone to lethal levels of weapon use. Instead, weapons are often used to threaten the victim rather than to inflict actual harm. Further, these offenders feel and express little remorse and are not necessarily amenable to treatment. This makes their treatment as unpredictable as the onset of their violence.

Category 3 batterers are high risk and often possess true personality disorders. These batterers often present ongoing and chronic patterns of abuse. Causal factors of abuse among this population are due largely to internal belief system issues regarding the rights of men in relationships with women (Groestch, 1996). For this group, most all previous relationships with partners have been violent. Further, these batterers are likely to have exhibited some form of premarital violence toward their current partner. These abusers are likely to present and use dangerous weapons (Groestch, 1996). In addition, these batterers demonstrate no remorse for their actions and seem to lack a conscience. These batterers are generally not considered to be amenable to treatment. In fact, it is most likely that a program of selective incapacitation would be the most pragmatic "intervention" when considering their extremely poor prognosis.

According to Groestch (1996), these batterers frequently present with one or more personality disorders listed in the *Diagnostic and Statistical Manual of Mental Disorders* (4th ed., text revision) (*DSM-IV-TR*; American Pyschiatric Association, 2000), including narcissistic, antisocial, borderline, histrionic, paranoid, and obsessive-compulsive personality disorders. Of course, these disorders may occur in conjunction with numerous other *DSM-IV-TR* disorders, such as substance abuse or depression. Sadly, this group is in the most dire need for treatment, yet the comorbid nature of disorders among this population makes them the most difficult to treat. While it is true that many people who have one psychological disorder experience other disorders at the same time, this occurrence is particularly pronounced among the category 3 battering population. The simultaneous occurrence of disorders, or comorbidity (Davis & Palladino, 2002), increases the difficulty associated with making appropriate diagnoses and developing effective treatment plans for these batterers.

In discussing typologies of batterers, it is important to clarify some of the differences that current research has outlined. Johnson (1995) has categorized spousal abusers into two main groups: those based on "common couple violence" and those based on "patriarchal terrorism." The origins, motivations, and patterns are quite different even if they do have the similar theme of physical aggression in an intimate relationship. Again, the heart of the difference between these two types of family violence lies in the motivation. **Common couple violence** is an intermittent response to the occasional conflicts of everyday life, motivated by a need to control a specific situation. In this case, the complexities of family life produce conflicts that occasionally get out of hand and sometimes escalate to a violent yet isolated incident (Johnson, 1995). This form of violence is no more likely to be enacted by men than by women (Groestch, 1996; Johnson, 1995). This type of violence is not usually a part of a pattern in which one partner is trying to exert control over the other. It is this common couple violence that is most typical of the category 1 abuser that is discussed later in this chapter.

On the other hand, **patriarchal terrorism** consists of men who commit acts of spousal abuse because of a need to be in charge of the relationship and to control the woman by any means necessary. This type of abuse is sexist based, being rooted in notions of male privilege in a typical heterosexual relationship (Russell, 1995). The males in these relationships are determined to maintain a structure of power and control, utilizing the various abusive strategies of physical violence, threats and intimidation, sexual abuse, emotional abuse, economic control, and social isolation (Johnson, 1995). This type of abuse is common to category 2 and especially category 3 abusers and is also discussed later in this chapter.

Beyond this, it is important to note that researchers cannot exactly agree on the typologies of men who commit acts of domestic violence (Wexler, 2000). To attempt to cover this entire body of literature would be beyond the scope of this chapter. However, several different leading researchers have developed basic categories many of which often overlap. While numerous theorists and researchers (Dutton & Golant, 1995; Gondolf & Hannekenn, 1987; Holtzworth-Munroe & Stuart, 1994) have developed a variety of psychological typologies to aid in classifying and treating domestic batterers, our discussion will continue to revolve around the three categories of domestic batterers previously mentioned. The reason for this is that regardless of the psychological typology, most fit within a category very similar to one of these three categories. This is particularly true when considering the most dangerous batterers, who are often distinguished by their psychological disorder(s), which are considered to be partial causal determinants of their abusive behavior. Further, while most psychological typologies are interesting from a theoretical standpoint, they provide little assistance to the criminal justice system because of the in-depth assessment needed to identify personality characteristics and because of the lack of typology-based interventions available (Healey, Smith, & O'Sullivan, 1998). Thus, a simple three-category method of classification is presented in this chapter to demonstrate differences in etiology, lethality, and treatment that should be addressed among the battering population. In developing these typologies, significant contributions were derived from the research of Holtzworth-Munroe and Stuart (1994) as well as that outlined by Groetsch (1996).

BATTERING OFFENDERS IN JAIL AND IN PRISON

There has been much legislation in the past few years that has advocated for increased jail and/or prison terms for domestic batterers (Durand, 1995). Much of the reason for this legislation has to do with two key issues. First, prior to the 1980s and 1990s, there was very little consensus or even general understanding of the dynamic of domestic violence. While the women's movement had articulated concerns surrounding such issues, widespread society had not necessarily adopted similar concerns for women and/or the violence inflicted against them. Second, it was becoming increasingly more evident that batterers were a group of recidivists who seemed to take up an enormous amount of police and court docket time. Further, the police became fond of the fact that certain households on their beat were "repeat customers."

Thus, the issue of jailing domestic batterers became a common concern. Indeed, this ultimately became the "treatment" of choice. And when risk assessment was accurate, this was a fairly effective method of reducing the likelihood of future recidivism. However, the difficulty lies in the very assessment of the offender (Hanson & Wallace-Capretta, 2000). Social policy that is aimed at controlling male battering has drawn much inspiration from deterrence theory. By requiring police to arrest offenders and by imposing stiff penalties, it was hoped that potential recidivists would fear punishment and therefore be motivated to desist.

But again, the effective use of this deterrence methodology hinged on understanding the offender population that one was dealing with. As has been the contention throughout much of this book, no "one-size-fits-all" approach is likely to work with any group of offenders, including the battering population. Table 12.1 shows the demographic characteristics of all domestic batterers in the United States between 1998 and 2002. From this table, it can be seen that of the nearly 32.2 million total violent crimes during this period, roughly 11 percent included domestic battering. The remaining instances were nonfamily violence.

From Table 12.1, it is also clear that Caucasians are most likely to commit domestic battering. Indeed, though they commit roughly 62 percent of all nonfatal violent crime, the percentage likelihood of victimizing a family member exceeds this, meaning that Caucasian violent offenders are more likely to victimize a family member than a stranger. Further, Caucasian males are more likely to commit an assault against their spouse or children than with another, more distant family member (82 percent likely with spouse or children versus roughly 73 percent likely with a family relative).

For African Americans, this trend is exactly the opposite. African American violent offenders committed nearly 25 percent of the overall nonfatal assaults but

Table 12.1. Demographic Characteristics of Domestic Battering Offenders between the Years 1998 and 2002

		Percentage of Crime in Which the Victim Was the Offender's Family Member			
Offender Characteristics	**All Nonfatal Violent Crimes**	**Total**	**Spouse**	**Son or Daughter**	**Other Relative**
Gender					
Male	79.9	75.6	86.1	68.2	64.9
Female	17.0	22.6	13.0	29.6	32.4
Both	3.1	1.8	0.9	2.2	2.6
Race					
Caucasian	62.0	78.5	82.5	82.0	72.8
African American	24.6	14.9	11.5	14.3	19.3
Other	13.4	6.6	6.0	3.8	8.0
Age					
Under 18	22.4	10.7	0.8	2.2	25.2
18–29	34.3	25.5	25.5	2.5	31.5
30 or older	34.2	62.4	73.0	93.9	40.9
Mixed age-group (multiple offenders)	9.1	1.4	0.6	1.4	2.4
Total offenses	32,116,920	3,534,150	1,729,360	369,220	1,435,570

Source: Adapted from Durose et al. (2005).

only about 15 percent of all domestic batterings. Further, while the order of victim likelihood for Caucasian offenders goes from spouse (82.5 percent) to child (82 percent) and then to relative family member (72.8 percent), for African American offenders the opposite is true. African American offenders are more likely to assault a relative family member (19.3 percent), followed by one of their children (14.3 percent), and finally their spouse (11.5 percent).

Data on other racial groups do not distinguish between Latino American, Native American, and Asian American racial groups. But when taken together, it is clear that these groups do not exhibit the same likelihood for domestic battering as does the Caucasian offender. However, the common literature does often note the high rate of domestic violence within the Native American community, and it is likely that this is simply not detected when the groups are collectively demonstrated.

Finally, it should also be noted that domestic battering does tend to be an issue associated with adult offenders. Although this crime does occur among youthful offenders, nearly 70 percent occur at the hands of offenders who are at least 18 years of age, with a trend toward more perpetration of family violence at or around age 30 and beyond. Likewise, it is clear that only a small percentage of domestic batteries include two or more offenders. Thus, domestic batterers tend to commit their crimes individually.

Generally, it was presumed that a token amount of jail time would allow offenders to "cool down" and consider the consequences of their actions. From this, it was presumed that the majority would be deterred from engaging in further abusive behavior that is assaultive. However, it should again be stated that category 1 batterers are the "ordinary guy" types of offender and that their violent incidents are often truly isolated to one occurrence. Further, these offenders do express remorse over their actions, and this separates them from other types of batterers. Whether jail time is even advisable with this group is questionable. But when they are given jail time, brief stints behind bars seem to be very effective, particularly if their significant others desire to continue a relationship as long as the abusive behavior does not persist.

Most jail facilities do not have a domestic abuser intervention program. This is not really a concern when dealing with category 1 batterers if they are simply kept in jail for a brief period for added shock value. These offenders (and most of those in jail) will ultimately receive some form of treatment on their release from jail. Typically, jail is used either to provide for the victim's safety or to give the offender a sense of the reality of their consequences.

However, the support for a deterrence effect of arrest in Sherman and Berk's (1984) groundbreaking study was eventually undermined by inconsistent findings in five other jurisdictions (see Garner, Fagan, & Maxwell, 1995). Maxwell, Garner, and Fagan's (2001) reanalysis of the information from all five of these jurisdictions found a deterrence effect of arrest that was consistent across all five jurisdictions but much smaller than that originally reported by reported by Sherman and Berk. For category 1 batterers, this issue is probably irrelevant because these offenders may not even need jail time to begin with. If in fact they do get jail time, they tend to have enough sincere consideration for the welfare of their significant other that they participate in treatment soon after their short period in jail and are the least likely to recidivate. Thus, deterrence is not a key area of concern with this group.

However, this is the opposite with category 2 offenders, whose probability of risk is much less easy to predict. This group of offenders is also much more likely to be given jail sentences that may be three months to a year, depending on the specific state laws involved, the severity of the assault, the plea bargain agreement, and so on. The problem with this is that these offenders are ultimately released, meaning that they often return to their previous victims, and while they are in jail, few of them will ever receive treatment-related interventions for their battering behavior. Thus, the common criticism of simply jailing offenders is that they are not provided with consequences that are serious enough to deter them and that they are not given the interventions needed to identify and stop their abusive behavior. It should also be noted that most of these batterers are more likely to be category 2 or 3 batterers than category 1 batterers because category 1 and 2 batterers are most likely to repeat their offenses and also are more likely to commit more severe forms of violence. Thus, the very offenders who have the most likely rate of recidivism also need intervention skills the most. The irony is that they are the least likely to receive it in the short term because they will be confined in jail settings that do not typically provide such intervention. Special Insert 12.1 provides a clear example of the difficulties associated with simple jail terms with batterers.

Special Insert 12.1. Problems Associated with Incarcerated Batterers

More men are being sent to county jails on domestic violence charges, but little or no money is being spent by authorities to treat those inmates once they're locked up.

The Plymouth County House of Corrections spent $23,000 to treat violent inmates—about 20 who were jailed for domestic violence—while the Bristol County jail spent nothing.

"The ideal would be to have every inmate enrolled in a good treatment program, but that doesn't happen," said Carol Charpentier, director of the Southeast Human Resource Associates in Plymouth, which runs a 10-week program at the Plymouth County Jail. But that isn't likely to happen soon.

The state and county aren't providing any money to treat jailed batterers, Plymouth and Bristol County jail officials say, and the jails don't have enough cash to run the programs.

This comes at a time when the numbers of prisoners jailed for domestic violence offenders are creeping up as more judges put offenders behind bars.

Plymouth County Jail officials estimate about $2 million was spent last year incarcerating batterers—about $68 a day for each inmate—a figure that will continue to grow with the rising population.

But experts said jailing abusers won't stop the violence—or solve the domestic violence problem in the community. Experts note that, without treatment, abusers will

(continued)

continue the cycle of violence and probably wind up back behind bars. But the jails aren't taking enough steps to break that cycle, one expert said.

For example, Bristol County spends about $1 million each year to treat those jailed on alcohol offenses and nothing specifically targeting batterers, said Robert Sisson, who runs a treatment program at the Bristol County Jail.

Dr. Sisson said the state and county must address the problem of battering the same way it looks at alcohol abuse. Although there is no program designed for batterers, Dr. Sisson runs a group session for about 20 inmates on how to control tempers. Dr. Sisson estimates half of those in the sessions are batterers.

But Bristol County is not alone in its lack of treatment programs for jailed batterers. Only Plymouth and Barnstable counties are starting to incorporate batterer treatment programs.

"The first question that should be asked is what is the most effective program to change the batterers' behavior. Usually that is one of the last questions many prison officials ask—if at all," said Thomas Stewart, a state Department of Mental Health social worker who has been treating violent men for 16 years.

But even if there were enough programs, most often the jails can't force prisoners to participate. "The law prohibits us from forcing someone into a program. That's for every inmate, even drug abusers," said Roy Lyons, spokesman for the Plymouth County sheriff. "When these guys come in, they can sit in their cell all day if they want," Dr. Sisson said. Few corrections officials seem interested in even knowing what happens to the offender. Rather, many prison officials see the inmates as being "out of sight—out of mind" once they leave their facilities.

Source: Adapted from the Standard Times News Article. Retrieved from http://www.s-t.com/projects/DomVio/jailsstop.html

For general offenders, the severity of criminal justice sanctions (e.g., prison and sentence length) appears to have no relationship to recidivism (Gendreau, Goggin, & Cullen, 1999). The severity of criminal justice sanctions also appears to have no influence on domestic violence offenders (Davis, Smith, & Nickles, 1998). Thistlethwaite, Wooldredge, and Gibbs (1998) reported a small deterrence effect for the type of sentence imposed on domestic violence offenders (jail combined with probation appeared more effective than probation, jail, or fine imposed individually). Tolman, Edleson, and Fendrich (1996) found no relationship between expectations of negative consequences for continued abuse and recidivism; however, their study did not separate social and criminal justice consequences. Fear of official consequences (e.g., arrest) may have little deterrent effect, but some men may inhibit violent impulses for fear of losing their partner.

Research on the sentencing of domestic batterers demonstrates that most will get simple jail time at best (Durose et al., 2005). As seen in Table 12.2, only about 28 percent of all offenders convicted of family assault actually go to prison. Rather, most of these offenders (roughly 59 percent) go to a local jail facility. Only a small percentage are given probation-only sentences—about 14 percent of all family assault offenders in the research conducted by Durose et al. (2005) on behalf of the U.S. Department of Justice. Likewise, the most frequent amount of months that these

Table 12.2. Most Severe Sentence Received by Domestic Batterers Compared to General Assault Offenders in State Courts of 11 Large Counties

Sentence Type	Percentage Incarcerated When Convicted of		
Incarceration	**All Assaults**	**Family Assaults**	**Nonfamily Assaults**
Prison	41.9	27.4	50.7
Jail	41.2	58.9	30.6
Nonincarceration	16.9	13.7	18.7
Probation	16.5	13.7	18.2
Fine	0.4	0	0.5
Total convicted of felony assault	675	237	438

Source: Adapted from Durose et al. (2005).

offenders are likely to receive if sent to prison is fairly light, as shown by the median sentence of 24 months for these offenders in Table 12.3. Indeed, fully 88 percent of these offenders receive less than four years of prison time for their offense. Likewise, Table 12.3 demonstrates that a total of almost 67 percent of all domestic assault offenders sent to jail will receive only six months or less. Thus, from Table 12.2, it is clear that most of these offenders will receive simple jail time and that, out of these offenders, most are likely to receive six months or less of actual incarceration. Thus, many of these offenders are ultimately released on community supervision since they are likely to have short stints within a jail facility. The offender will ultimately be in the vicinity of the victim once again since many offenders do tend to return to their locale of origin prior to their incarceration.

Because of this, the notion of achieving deterrence by developing a fear of consequences leaves much to be desired. Further, the fear of negative consequences is only one mechanism to motivate behavior change. While this may work for category 1 and 2 offenders, it is not as likely to work for category 3 batterers. Even if there is some support for deterrence theory, motivation to change may nevertheless play an important role in preventing recidivism. Offenders who acknowledge their abusive behavior and express intentions to change should be lower risk than offenders who deny their misbehavior and resist treatment. Motivational factors are frequently considered in clinical assessments (and court proceedings), but there is little evidence directly linking motivation to recidivism. Court-mandated clients (an indirect measure of motivation) show similar recidivism rates to voluntary clients in most studies (Hemberger & Hastings, 1990). It does appear, however, that offenders who fail to complete treatment are at increased risk for recidivism (Hamberger & Hastings, 1988).

The point to this is simply that category 1 domestic abusers are unlikely to spend long periods of time in jail; they simply are not a substantial concern in jail and prison settings on a long-term basis. Rather, these offenders will most often be

Table 12.3. Length of Prison and Jail Sentences Received by Defendants of Family Assault Compared to Nonfamily Assault in State Courts of 11 Large Counties

	Percent of Defendants Convicted of		
Maximum Sentence Length	**All Assaults**	**Family Assault**	**Nonfamily Assault**
Sentenced to prison			
1–24 months	31.1%	55.0%	23.4%
25–48 months	28.7	33.3	27.2
49–72 months	15.2	1.7	19.6
73–120 months	14.3	10.0	15.8
10 years	4.9	0	6.5
Life	5.7	0	7.6
Average number of months			
Mean	83.4	38.3	98.1
Median	48.0	24.0	48.0
Sentenced to jail			
1 month or less	1.7%	3.1%	0
2–3 months	9.7	13.2	5.6
4–6 months	45.3	50.4	39.3
7–9 months	10.2	9.3	11.2
10–12 months	33.1	24	43.9
Average number of months			
Mean	7.5	6.8	8.4
Median	6.0	6.0	9.0
Total sentenced to jail	274	140	134

Source: Adapted from Durose et al. (2005).

on community supervision and will obtain treatment through a community-based response. Category 2 batterers, on the other hand, are likely to be the types who spend long periods in jail and are likewise more apt to reoffend.

However, it is at this time that criminal justice treatment specialists have a literal "captive audience" with whom to work. In fact, if treatment is intensive enough and if the appropriate follow-through is given, this can be an ideal time to teach nonviolence, anger management, and gender role socialization. If the institutional treatment regimen is structured to reinforce the specific intervention program on a daily basis, this may be the ideal treatment setting for this group. Such an approach, if implemented correctly, could result in the safety of victims not only during the offender's stint in jail but also well beyond when the offender is released in the community. Thus, such an approach may hold more long-term promise for victims and society (one example is given in Special Insert 12.2). Yet jails, for the most part,

Special Insert 12.2. Batterer Interventions behind Bars

The staff at Dauphin County Prison in Harrisburg, Pennsylvania, have developed an educational program for batterers, Men Establishing New Directions (MENDS), which focuses on changing attitudes and violent behavior toward women. MENDS is a two-phase program. In the first phase the men attend one two-hour group session per week for six weeks. The second phase is an open-ended group session conducted weekly for men who have successfully completed phase 1.

It is important that cofacilitators who run the groups keep the men focused on their abusive behavior, challenge the behavior, and never accept their excuses for abusing women. We found that a man and a woman as cofacilitators prevents any inadvertent sympathy for the abusive behaviors the men describe. The men tend to look to the male cofacilitator as the leader, and in many instances it is a valuable experience for the men to be forced to recognize the woman as the group leader.

The MENDS format is based on the premise that abusive men can change their behavior. The first phase of the program concentrates on overcoming the resistance the men have to taking responsibility for their violent actions against women. We define domestic violence as any physical, emotional, or sexual abuse used to control a woman in an intimate relationship. Since the men are incarcerated, they are not able to practice nonabusive behavior in the domestic setting.

One measure of success has been the number of men who have completed phase 1 and accepted the invitation to join phase 2. Out of a group of 20 men, we usually have 18 who are eligible and want to continue with the program. Some of the men have told other inmates about the group, and we now receive requests from inmates to join phase 1 of MENDS. This is surprising because most men do not want other inmates to know they abuse women. However, we have found that when men are shown what domestic violence is, the pain it causes, and the impossibility of sharing true intimacy with women they are abusing, they will, in most cases, take the responsibility for changing their attitudes and their behavior.

Source: Adapted from Baugh (1994).

simply house these offenders for their proscribed periods of time, and the offender is funneled through with the other sundry offenders, essentially becoming lost and unidentifiable in the jail population until the time of their release.

It should be noted that domestic batterers seldom go to state-level prisons for a long-term basis. In either case, those who do are most likely to be category 3 offenders. Further, many of them will have a list of other crimes as well. This group is also the most prone to having some form of diagnosable personality disorder (to be discussed later in this chapter). Thus, the group of batterers in prison as opposed to jail will likely be either career criminals (violent or combined with nonviolent crimes) or those who commit some form of stalking, sexual assault, or other such crime often associated with battering that serves to lengthen their sentence. Many of these are likely to be category 3 batterers, and it is unlikely that any treatment program is likely to work with this group of batterers. Rather, the use of selective incapacitation is probably the best suggestion for this group.

Selective incapacitation, in this case, refers to the process of identifying certain offenders and providing them with prison sentences that are simply designed to "incapacitate" them from committing further crimes against society. Thus, it is recommended that these types of offenders be restricted from society once they are clinically identified by the criminal justice system. The hope for treating these types of offenders is bleak at best, and in this case the offender should simply have his civil liberties restricted as much as is necessary to ensure the protection of society's law-abiding members.

THE BATTERER IN THE COMMUNITY

Community supervision officers should expect high levels of recidivism among the battering population. In a 30-month follow-up of court-mandated batterers in four cities across the United States, Gondolf (2000) found that 42 percent of the men reassaulted their initial or new partners sometime during the 30 months following treatment. While numerous evaluations of batterer interventions have been conducted, domestic violence researchers concur that findings from most of these studies are inconclusive because of methodological problems (Healey et al., 1998). But among those studies considered methodologically sound, most have found modest but statistically significant reductions in recidivism among men participating in batterer interventions. Frustration with the lack of empirical evidence favoring one curriculum has led some researchers to look at batterers as a diverse group for whom specially tailored interventions may be the only effective approach. As a result, current research is shifting toward studying which subgroups of batterers respond to which specialized interventions.

At the same time, the question of how to evaluate batterer interventions may need to include the broader context of criminal justice support. While the simplest answer to the problem of domestic battering is to arrest the offender, there have been conflicting results in determining whether this approach truly works (Riedel & Welsh, 2002; Sherman & Berk, 1984). As a case in point, most research shows that arrest alone is not as effective in reducing recidivism as is arrest coupled with other multiagency responses to domestic violence. Even if the research can identify the perfect match between interventions and offenders, it seems unlikely that criminal justice agencies will have a crucial impact on the success of matching programs to appropriate clients because of public pressure to place emphasis on public safety. But a continuous confluence between the criminal justice system and the intervention staff is exactly what is needed to prevent future harm to the victim. Sufficient oversight is imperative if one considers that the batterer's victim is even more likely to stay in the relationship if the batterer seeks treatment. Because of this, batterer interventions should be seen as a public safety program rather than a pure treatment program. See Special Insert 12.3 for an example of a community-based public safety program.

Special Insert 12.3. Police and Community Collaborative Responses to Domestic Violence Offenders

In 1997, the Brockton Police Department worked in connection with the Brockton Family and Community Resources Domestic Violence Action Program to develop a task force approach to domestic violence. The result of this collaboration produced the Teaching, Education, and Mediation (TEaM) program, which not only involved the entire police department but also integrated all other agencies in the community and the criminal justice system. The TEaM was tasked with ensuring that opportunities existed for all agencies to spend time with police officers in police cruisers, in the police station, and in the streets and homes of the community. Police officers, in turn, were provided training through an informal setting in their normal work environment, and the training provided them with skill and/or knowledge that was relevant to their day-to-day experiences. On the other hand, the community was tasked to take responsibility by responding effectively to end domestic violence. Neighborhood Watch members were trained in current laws and were provided with appropriate material to disseminate to neighbors.

This demonstration of action was accomplished through the collaboration of schools, media, health organizations, business, police, courts, the fire department, battered women's programs, mental health agencies, and neighborhood watch programs. This program demonstrates how an entire community can become active in monitoring a given social ill and, incidentally, a certain type of special needs offender. Through a combination of police and community efforts, domestic abusers are given more "human supervision" (as opposed to electronic supervision) than would normally be possible if left simply to the area probation department.

Programs such as TEaM demonstrate how police can be incorporated into overall program success in meeting intervention objectives for certain special needs offenders. Indeed, the police should be viewed as a "relapse prevention" effort that will serve to ensure compliance among domestic abusers whether or not they are on community supervision. Further, adding the police into the treatment schema provides community supervision with an enhanced ability to provide for public safety, an obligation that probation departments have to the public. The use of other community agencies just serves to further reinforce the treatment goals and provides a multilayered response to domestic abusers. One theme throughout this book has been the illustration of potential police/probation teams, which give community supervision personnel and police certain benefits in maintaining public safety. Such teams also provide domestic abusers with added coercive incentive to successfully complete their programs, a goal that would be considered desirable by any criminal justice or treatment-related program.

Source: Adapted from Davis (1998).

However, the old adage "you can bring a horse to water, but you can't make him drink" should perhaps be held as a prime directive in treating the battering population. This is because one factor that has been found to be crucial in successful treatment is the supposed "stake-in-conformity" hypothesis. The stake-in-conformity hypothesis suggests that the deterrent effect of arrests is more likely to work if there is a social cost associated with arrest, such as loss of a job, relationships, and children and loss of status in the neighborhood. A study by Riedel and Welsh (2002) supported this notion by finding that arrest or the threat of arrest was more likely to have a deterrent effect if the offender was employed or married. Thus, a criminal justice sanction is effective if it also means the person will lose something he or she values highly, such as a job. Thus, while legal sanctions have only limited effect, legal sanctions are effective when they are reinforced by informal social controls. The difficulty with this hypothesis is that offenders may have nothing to lose as a result of arrests. Another point is that there are relatively few prosecutions of domestic violence, which may also serve to explain why arrest is not very effective (Riedel & Welsh, 2002).

Further, the deterrence logic as applied to battering assumes that the perpetrator is a rational actor—someone who weighs the costs of violence in the form of legal sanctions. But in a study of batterers, Dutton and Golant (1995) suggested that batterers may have impaired cognition or mental disorders. This may be a problem with offenders who pursue their intimate partners after they have left the relationship. The behavior may be purposeful but not rational, undermining the logic from which sanctions against batterers are derived.

REINTEGRATING THE FAMILY

As noted earlier in this chapter, the use of conjoint therapy (having both the perpetrator and the victim present in couple's counseling) is typically not considered acceptable. In no case should this form of treatment be considered the primary form of intervention. However, such an outlook can be somewhat idealistic and ignores the fact that many victims do maintain or rejoin a relationship with the offender. Further, with category 1 batterers, there may be hope in conducting therapy that involves the couple, presuming the victim is willing to participate.

It should be stated that in this type of therapy, therapeutic "alliances" are always an issue but are perhaps more prominent when working with violent couples. While the therapist must ensure the safety of the victim, it is also critical that therapists working with violent men be able to accept them as human beings fully deserving of respect (Holtzworth-Munroe, Beatty, & Anglin, 1995). Batterers may enter therapy anticipating rejection or punishment from therapists and thus adopt a resistant posture. Therapists can circumvent this dynamic by emphasizing their acceptance of the batterer and their concurrent rejection of his violent behavior (Holtzworth-Munroe et al., 1995). This nonjudgmental status regarding the batterer's worth as a person must be balanced against a condemnation of his violence.

In marital or couple's therapy, the therapist often serves as an advocate for the couple's relationship rather than for the individual interests of either spouse (Holtzworth-Munroe et al., 1995). However, in the case of violent couples, a marital therapist must reconsider this assumption. For example, at what point is it better for a marital relationship to be dissolved? And can one be an advocate for the relationship, for the victim, and for the offender?

As noted earlier, advocates of couple reintegration note that many violent couples would like to remain together and that there may be positive aspects to the relationship that counseling can build on (Healey et al., 1998). However, while some observers report that over half of domestic violence couples remain together, a study of abused wives whose husbands did become nonviolent found that most of the women subsequently terminated the marriage because of other marital problems that became apparent after the violence ended (Healey et al., 1998).

Further, when attempting to reintegrate the family of a batterer, therapists must keep in mind the legal, ethical, and moral responsibilities involved in working with violent couples. In fact, legal rulings regarding the duty to warn and protect potential victims already exist and are directly applicable to abusive couples. In *Tarasoff v. Regents of the University of California* (1976), the California Supreme Court ruled that the therapist had a duty to use "reasonable care" to protect an intended victim; this might include warning the victim, hospitalizing the patient, or warning the police (see Special Insert 12.4). This duty to protect potential victims was defined to include cases where the client communicates a serious threat of violence against a reasonably identifiable victim. The exact specifics of this duty are not specifically stated but are often thought to include the communication of these threats to the victim and the respective local law enforcement agency (Holtzworth-Munroe et al., 1995).

Special Insert 12.4. *Tarasoff v. Regents of the University of California* (1976)

The *Tarasoff* case, as it is commonly called, is a landmark case known by most therapists and mental health workers. This case involved a client by the name of Prosenjit Poddar, who was a student at the University of California at Berkeley. Poddar was seeing a psychologist because of depression related to his relationship with another student named Tanya Tarasoff. Poddar's psychologist ultimately found that Poddar suffered from a paranoid schizophrenic reaction to his difficulty in coping with his broken relationship with Tanya. This diagnosis was also validated among other mental health professionals at the facility that Poddar had visited. During this time, Poddar revealed his intention to get a gun and shoot Tanya Tarasoff. Poddar's psychologist sent a letter to the campus police requesting that they take Poddar to a psychiatric hospital. The campus police interviewed Mr. Poddar, but he convinced them that he was not dangerous and released him on the promise that he would stay away from Tanya Tarasoff. Later Poddar did pursue contact with Tanya, and he eventually stalked her and stabbed her to death. The parents of Tanya Tarasoff sued the campus police, Health Service employees, and Regents of the University of California for failing to warn them that their daughter was in danger. The case sustained a long and fought-out history but was ultimately heard by the California Supreme Court. The California Supreme court, because of the controversial nature and reactions to the case, heard the case twice

(continued)

(once in 1974 and then again in 1976). The court did eventually hold that when a therapist determines that a client presents a serious danger of violence to another, there exists a professional obligation to use reasonable care to protect the intended victim against such danger.

The court did note that therapists are not expected to be perfect in their assessment of client dangerousness. The court noted in its opinion that "...obviously we do not require that the therapist, in making that determination, render a perfect performance; the therapist need only exercise that reasonable degree of skill, knowledge and care ordinarily possessed and exercised by members of that professional specialty under similar circumstances." Further it was determined that the discharge of this duty may require the therapist to warn the intended victim, to notify the police, or to take whatever steps are reasonably necessary under the circumstances.

Since this ruling in 1976 numerous states (nearly all of them) have adopted some or all of the basic views noted in the *Tarasoff* case. Buckner and Firestone (2000) perhaps sum up this ruling for therapists most appropriately by noting that

> therapists must attend to this issue with greater sensitivity and detail. Past medical records, where applicable, must be thoroughly reviewed; past therapists and referral sources must be queried where appropriate. Consultations and second opinions must be sought when threats of violence occur or when there is question about competence to drive, as part of outpatient management, as well as in-patient discharge planning. A wide array of options must be considered in managing the risks considered, including hospitalization, warnings, more frequent therapy sessions, starting or increasing medication, and/or close monitoring. The approach should be similar to management of an acutely suicidal patient, regarding the handling of the concern for the patient's acting out the threat. If such a careful and reasonable approach is taken, including documentation of the assessment of the pertinent issues and treatment plan, then the therapist should not be held liable, even if harm should occur to a third party. (p. 5)

While the ***Tarasoff* case** dealt with a perpetrator who stalked and ultimately murdered his victim, the legal rulings of this case and the resulting guidelines are applicable to virtually all cases of marital violence (Holtzworth-Munroe et al., 1995). Given the data demonstrating the continuation and escalation of marital violence, continued violence in such cases is predictable without a specific verbal threat. Thus, it is recommended that therapists conducting conjoint therapy with an abuser and a victim make a point to warn the couple that there is a high probability of continued violence (Sonkin, 1986). Many marital therapists are unaccustomed to working with the legal system. However, such cooperation is often required in marital violence cases (such as when the abuser has been court-ordered to seek therapy). Therapists lacking such experience may wish to seek consultation regarding such issues as confidentiality, reports to probation officers, and court appearances (Holtzworth-Munroe et al., 1995).

For criminal justice community service practitioners, legal issues, court appearances, and balancing risks with needs assessments are all simply "part of a day's work." This is precisely one reason for increased collaboration among clinicians and community supervision personnel. Both entities seek to protect the public from further victimization regardless of client needs. Tragedies such as the *Tarasoff* case make clear the severity involved when dealing with offenders who are released into the community. Because of this, clinicians and community supervision personnel may find themselves skeptical and even pessimistic when providing services to many special needs offenders. However, such pessimism can lead to an excess of wasted resources and can serve to ironically increase recidivism among offenders who might otherwise have reformed. Because of this, the balancing act between providing for specialized needs of batterers and providing for public safety concerns becomes necessary. It is the use of appropriate assessment scales (a recurring theme throughout this book) that emerge as the fulcrum in this balancing act between offender needs and public safety. The better the assessment, the more accurate the prediction, leading to a more balanced application of treatment services and community supervision sanctions. It is at this fulcrum point that the challenges involved with special needs offenders becomes most pronounced, it is here that criminal justice and treatment personnel find themselves making decisions with potentially lethal and potentially lifesaving consequences. See Special Insert 12.5 for an example of how such offenders can be supervised in the community.

Special Insert 12.5. Domestic Abusers and Community Supervision Issues

In 1997, the St. Louis City Circuit Attorney's Office and the St. Louis Circuit Court created a partnership to establish the St. Louis City Domestic Violence Intervention Project. In this program, offenders proceed through a three-phase program based on their compliance with their probation conditions. Phase 1 includes weekly office visits, employment verification, participation in a domestic violence program, urinalysis testing, and home visits. Failure to comply with the program results in the offender being stuck in phase 1 with even more intensive restrictions, such as increased office visits or electronic monitoring or house arrest. Electronic monitoring is used to provide structure and limit the offender's movements within the community so that public safety is enhanced.

If offenders comply with the phase 1 requirements, they may progress to phase 2. Phase 1 and phase 2 are each roughly 90 days in duration. During phase 2, offenders must report to their probation officer every two weeks, and they are still monitored by the probation department. Once offenders enter phase 3, restrictions and supervision are relaxed, with mandatory reporting occurring on a monthly basis, but all treatment and restitution requirements remain intact. On completion of the intervention program and all community supervision requirements, each case is then reviewed by the court for early discharge consideration.

(continued)

While each domestic abuse intervention program varies in length, offenders must attend for a minimum of 90 minutes per week for at least 32 weeks. It is important to note that these programs consist of much more than simple anger management. Indeed, they focus on the offender's interpersonal relationships with significant others, children, extended family, and other household members.

One unique aspect of this treatment plan is the inclusion of the victim(s). The probation officer will attempt to contact victims to obtain impact statements. The victim impact statement includes any information victims wish to share with the court as well as the victim's description of the offense. Information provided by victims is used to ensure that offenders meet treatment (and community supervision) goals. It is not shared with offenders for safety reasons. Likewise, the probation officer maintains contact with the victim(s) to ensure that the offenders do not continue their abusive behavior.

When verifiable information is received by the probation officer that the offender has reoffended or has attempted to reoffend, immediate action is taken. The offender may be placed in a residential facility or electronically monitored to closely supervise his or her behavior. In addition, the probation officer can revoke the offender's probation. If documented physical abuse is found, a warrant is immediately issued, and the offender is taken into custody. This will lead to an additional and separate legal charge. Working closely with victims allows for immediate response to be taken rather than having to go through all the bureaucratic channels if a violation occurs.

This program has experienced some optimistic results. It is thought that the involvement of the probation officer greatly enhances the positive outcomes received by this program. Further, the involvement of probation officers also enhances the public safety aspect of this treatment program. The Domestic Violence Unit started as a partnership with the community to better supervise domestic violence offenders and to increase the level of safety for victims and their families. By supervising these offenders with an enhanced level of intensity and by working closely with community agencies, this intervention program has delivered responsible services to the victim and the community at large.

Source: Adapted from Duffy, Nolan, and Scruggs (2003).

THE BATTERER AND CORRECTIONAL TREATMENT: CATEGORY 1 BATTERERS

Category 1 batterers rarely appear in the criminal justice system. When they do, these types of batterers are likely to be receptive to both the punitive/deterrent effects of punishment and the treatment-related aspects of their criminal sanction (Groestch, 1996). These batterers are often described as "family-only" abusers (Wexler, 2000). These abusers are often dependent on the affection from their significant others and they often express jealousy if it appears that this affection is not centered around them (i.e., if it is also given to the woman's children). As a manner of coping, they tend to suppress emotions and withdraw, later erupting into violence only after long periods of unexpressed negative emotions (Groestch, 1996; Wexler, 2000). They tend to commit acts of abuse only in the family. Their acts of abuse are generally less severe than those of batterers, and they are generally less aggressive (Groestch, 1996). They also frequently express remorse for their abusive actions. Because these batterers often present voluntarily for treatment and because they are the least assaultive among court-mandated batterers, treatment modalities for this group can vary greatly, especially from those recommended for category 3 batterers (Groestch, 1996). Indeed, for these batterers, the focus of the intervention might in fact include reconciliation. According to Groestch (1996), the following treatment modalities should be considered with category 1 batterers:

1. Individual counseling—One-on-one counseling should focus on the external issues or trauma that brought the offender's aggression to the surface. Naturally, other issues, such as grief, substance abuse, stress, or other precursors to the aggression, should be addressed.
2. Marriage counseling—It should be noted that this type of intervention is typically *not* recommended for batterers. This is often due to concerns for the victim. But many category 1 batterers are voluntary participants who report for treatment to repair the damage that they have done in their relationships with their partners. Further, many victims of these abusers are likely to continue in the relationship with this type of batterer, particularly if the onset of physical assault is perceived by the victim to be generated by outside stressors.
3. Support groups—One-on-one counseling and marriage counseling are limited in the time that a client spends in therapy. Support groups that focus on the specific issues or trauma that caused the batterer's violence are excellent means of reducing isolation, giving him exposure to others who understand his trauma and providing him with an opportunity to establish peer relationships and fellowship. Support groups that address issues of stress, grief, substance abuse, and so on and that employ a 12-step program modality are excellent resources for such clients. If alcoholism is a concern, then victims should be simultaneously referred to Al-Anon.
4. Spiritual needs—In efforts to utilize a holistic approach in treatment, the batterer's spiritual orientation should be appropriately addressed. In fact, if possible, these beliefs and sources of pro-social support should be integrated into the treatment process. This is also an important consideration for those offenders who identify with a religious belief system or are members of a cultural group that holds a given set of spiritual tenets. For example, programs such as the Duluth Model of batterer intervention incorporate spiritual concepts that are tailored to the Native American battering client. In fact, an entire curriculum has been designed to accommodate this group. Further, it is important to understand that some religious institutions may provide a certain view of marital violence that may or may not be conducive to therapy. This should likewise

be addressed, particularly if the religious institution provides support for the husband's (provided the couple is married) "discipline" of his wife.

5. Boundary setting—The category 1 abuser responds well to spouse- and court-imposed mandates. A spouse who is ready to end the relationship with her abuser and a court that is ready to prosecute him can create significant levels of motivation relative to clinical intervention for this batterer.

CATEGORY 2 BATTERERS

Category 2 batterers are more severe in the type of violence they employ and the frequency with which they employ that violence when compared to category 1 batterers. Further, they are likely to be much more devious and methodical in their modus operandi than are category 3 batterers. While category 2 batterers are not as lethal as category 3 batterers, they are much more effective at hiding their abuse and evading law enforcement detection. Thus, extreme caution must be taken with the category 2 batterer. As a case in point, many experienced intervention providers report very low success rates with these individuals.

According to Wexler (2000), this type of batterer is occasionally referred to as "emotionally volatile." This group tends to be violent mostly within their family, but they are often more socially isolated and socially incompetent than category 1 batterers. They exhibit higher levels of anger, depression, and jealousy (Wexler, 2000). Further, they find ways of misinterpreting their partners and blaming their partners for their own mood states. Depression and feelings of inadequacy are prominent among abusers of this category (Groestch, 1996; Holtzworth-Munroe & Stuart, 1994; Wexler, 2000). Further, this category may have borderline or other personality disorders, though personality disorders are much more prevalent among the category 3 batterer. Such batterers typically have a poor likelihood of successful treatment. Since this batterer's violence is based more on internal issues and defective character traits than external trauma, the treatment for a category 2 batterer should be of a different format than that of a category 1 batterer. Unless a holistic approach is taken with the category 2 batterer wherein most of the following approaches are employed, there is little chance for a positive change. Groestch (1996) discusses the basic approaches to counseling intervention as presented here:

1. Individual counseling—One-on-one counseling should focus on the many defective character traits and internal issues of the category 2 batterer (Groestch, 1996).
2. Group counseling—This type of counseling is often used because it is more economical than individual counseling. However, another benefit to this type of counseling is that other batterers who know and recognize manipulation from their cohorts are able to assist in holding the batterer accountable for his behavior. This "group pressure" has been shown to be very effective with this

population (Groestch, 1996). However, it is not uncommon for members of such a group to get into behavioral collusion with one another whereby negative traits are actually reinforced. A trained therapist should be aware of such a possibility and should counter peer collusion appropriately.

3. Educational groups–Since much of the violence of the category 2 assailant is associated with learned behavior, an educational component to a group can be essential. This type of group will seek to modify elements of the batterer's socialization and will reeducate the batterer on matters involving gender roles, control, and sexism.
4. Support groups—As with the category 1 batterer client, individual and group counseling time is very limited and expensive. While the therapist may spend one or two hours weekly with this client, the reality is that there are innumerable daily interactions throughout the week that can trigger relapse in this client. Support groups can serve as an excellent "backup" to therapy and also can help build rapport among other group members who are in the support group. These groups likewise can be more readily available at the time of crisis rather than during a rigidly scheduled point throughout the week.
5. Spiritual needs—Just as with category 1 batterers, this area of batterer development can be of huge benefit in motivating the batterer toward change. As noted with category 1 batterers, this is an important consideration for those offenders who identify with a religious belief system or are members of a cultural group that holds a given set of spiritual tenets.
6. Boundary setting—This type of batterer responds only moderately well to court- and spouse-imposed restrictions. A spouse who temporarily leaves her assailant and a court which is poised to prosecute him can provide enough leverage to motivate him into a treatment program (Groestch, 1996).

CATEGORY 3 BATTERERS

It is important to understand that category 3 batterers are not only lethal but manipulative as well, being able to escape the detection of even the most seasoned therapists. This type of batterer is generally antisocial and more likely to engage in instrumental violence. By instrumental, it is meant that this violence is designed to gain a specific end or material outcome. In this case, violence "works" more successfully for such batterers in getting what they want (Holtzworth-Munroe & Stuart, 1994). They are limited in their capacity for empathy and attachment, and they hold the most rigid and conservative attitudes about women (Groestch, 1996; Holtzworth-Munroe & Stuart, 1994; Wexler, 2000). They tend to be violent across situations and across different victims. They are generally more belligerent, more likely to abuse substances, and more likely to have a criminal history. This group is also unlikely to show remorse (Groestch, 1996; Holtzworth-Munroe & Stuart, 1994; Wexler, 2000).

Within this category, there is a certain population of battering men that could be best described as **vagal reactor batterers** or "cobras" (Jacobson & Gottman, 1998) or, in a more general sense, psychopaths (Hare, 1993). Psychophysiologically oriented studies have identified an unusual pattern among a subgroup of the most severe batterers (Gottman et al., 1995; Wexler, 2000). Such batterers have actually shown reductions in measures of arousal during aggressive interactions with their partners—completely contrary to expectations and typical patterns during aggressive interactions (Gottman et al., 1995; Wexler, 2000). These batterers have been dubbed "vagal reactors" because their nervous system arousal is strangely disconnected from their behavior (Gottman et al., 1995; Wexler, 2000). These batterers deliberately and manipulatively control what goes on in the marital relationship (Wexler, 2000). Jacobson and Gottman (1998) call these men "cobras" because of their ability to become still and focused before striking their victim—this is in contrast to the more typical category 2 and category 3 **pit bull batterers**, who slowly burn in frustration and resentment before finally exploding (Wexler, 2000). Men who operate in this cold, calculating manner are not at all likely to be successfully treated (Groestch, 1996; Wexler, 2000). In fact, the best intervention for this group is most likely simple incapacitation. They display many of the characteristics of classic psychopathic behavior—not necessarily typical of all category 2 and category 3 abusers (Hare, 1993; Wexler, 2000). In short, these are the worst of the worst among the battering population.

Obviously, a healthy degree of skepticism must be utilized with this specific group of batterers and with category 3 batterers in general. Category 3 assailants who enter treatment generally do so in an effort to avoid criminal prosecution or in an attempt to lure their victims back into relationships. With category 3 batterers, Groestch (1996) recommends that treatment specialists follow these guidelines:

- Instead of promoting treatment for the category 3 batterer, promote boundaries such as court mandates, restraining orders, and restrictions that serve to protect the victim.
- Recognize that the criminal justice system refers batterers to treatment programs indiscriminately.
- Recognize that the chronic batterer has extensive levels of denial. This batterer will minimize, externalize, and rationalize all his behaviors and violence.
- If you do provide treatment to the chronic batterer, never allow him to portray himself as a victim. While in some cases it may be true that he had a terrible childhood, he is now the perpetrator and should be confronted as such.
- Never consider the alcoholism or drug addiction of the category 3 batterer as the reason for his aggression. Substance abuse is not a direct causative factor for the violence. For chronic batterers, it is just one of the many symptoms of the personality-disordered batterer.
- Remember, it is very common that this group of batterers will often present with separate personality disorders that aggravate the battering personality.

These other disorders must be treated as well. See the following discussion for a listing of the common personality disorders found among this population.

Personality disorders common to category 3 batterers include the following:

1. Narcissistic—Exhibits a grandiose sense of worth and self-importance. On the surface, he seems self-confident, but below the surface his self-esteem is very fragile; he is easily impacted by the remarks of others (Groestch, 1996).
2. Antisocial—The violence of this batterer is blatant even in public. He displays a lack of impulse control and is completely unconcerned about the future consequences of his behavior (Groestch, 1996).
3. Borderline—This batterer has weak and unstable self-identity. He will use manipulation, especially threat of suicide, to gain compliance from his spouse. He also has rapid mood swings because of feelings of abandonment, rejection, and intense fears of being alone (Groestch, 1996).
4. Histrionic—Exaggeration of emotional expression is common. He seeks to be the center of attention and often portrays himself as a victim.
5. Paranoid—This batterer is pathologically jealous and is obsessed with the issue of infidelity. He constantly suspects his significant other of engaging in acts of infidelity. He believes that others know but are hiding the truth. He views the world as hostile and finds hidden meaning in what others say and do (Groestch, 1996).
6. Obsessive-compulsive—This batterer is obsessed with structure, order, and trivial detail. He often acts as a military instructor within the family. He is overly rigid and preoccupied with rules, order, and regulations. This is often to hide his insecurity of facing the unknown variables in life (Groesttch, 1996).

ADDITIONAL NOTES ON TREATMENT APPROACHES FOR ALL THREE CATEGORIES OF BATTERERS

For all batterers, it is important to address all substance abuse issues first for other treatments to have any chance of success. Without such primary interventions being established, the therapist will simply be reaching the "chemical" rather than the batterer's actual personality and belief system. This explains why it is common practice for batterers to continue drug counseling as an adjunct to their batterer's group counseling. This tactic naturally helps prevent drug-induced relapse of domestic abuse. This is important to keep in mind because substance abuse correlates strongly with aggressive behavior among batterers. This correlation has been found to be especially true with alcohol, which overwhelmingly emerges as a primary predictor of marital violence (Hanson, Venturelli, & Fleckenstein, 2002). In fact, one study found that rates of domestic violence were as much as 15 times higher in households where the husband was described as "often" being drunk rather than "never" being drunk (Collins & Messerschmidt, 1993; Hanson et al., 2002).

Research consistently shows that spouse abusers have numerous alcohol-related problems (Barnett, Miller-Perrin, & Perrin, 1997). Because drunkenness can precipitate domestic battering and can be used as an excuse, clinicians must address alcohol treatment and not allow the batterer to evade responsibility by blaming the alcohol for the behavior. Further, the mere treatment of alcohol or substance abuse problems is not thought to be sufficient unto itself to rectify abusiveness among any category of batterer (Barnett et al., 1997; Zuretsky & Digirolamo, 1994). In fact, it could likely be that a batterer is more prone to abusiveness when he stops drinking because of the stressful and unpleasant effects of withdrawal during his newfound sobriety (Barnett et al., 1997). On the other hand, treatments that combine behavioral marital therapy with treatment of alcoholism have been found to reduce abusiveness (Barnett et al., 1997; O'Farrell & Murphy, 1995). Findings such as these demonstrate the complexities involved in addressing the alcohol–violence correlation. Further, as discussed earlier in this chapter, substance abuse/addiction disorders tend to be comorbid with other disorders (e.g., depression and other mood disorders, emotional disorders, and the various personality disorders), providing a treatment picture that is convoluted at best.

Regardless of corollary issues in treatment, it is important to remember that in distinguishing between the three categories of batterers the main difference lies in the degree of the violence, how often it occurs, and the level at which the violence is sustained. This is crucial from a community supervision standpoint, as frequency and lethality of violence should be the primary concern in public safety risk-prediction decisions. Remember that while the category 1 abuser's violence is isolated, the category 2 batterer's abuse is sporadic and reoccurring. The abuse of the category 3 offender, on the other hand, is always ongoing and chronic. Making matters even more complicated is the fact that batterers will not always exhibit a perfect profile of category 1, 2, and 3 types of offenders. They frequently may fall somewhere between categories, making the diagnosis and corresponding risk-prediction of these offenders very difficult.

Likewise important in batterer treatment is the selection of therapeutic styles employed. This was of course a primary point in Chapter 1, and this chapter will reemphasize this since it is critical for the victim's safety as well as the batterer's prognosis. Thus, it is not only important to understand distinctions between types of batterers, but to also understand the theoretical underpinnings to a variety of treatment modes. In this way, the correct treatment plan can be fitted to the correct type of batterer. This helps agencies that provide these interventions to operate at higher levels of treatment success. While there are a variety of treatment programs, most all of them can be generally categorized within the following schemes: confrontational, client centered, psychoeducational, cognitive-behavioral, and solution focused.

With confrontational approaches to treatment, the focus is always on gender and power issues. All attempts to rationalize the problem are considered to be forms of denial or avoidance of self-responsibility. In this view, the perpetrator should consistently be confronted on rationalization, denial, and victim blaming (Wexler, 2000). Group members are pushed to admit that they have committed violent and abusive acts and to describe these acts in detail without minimization, rationalization, or denial. However, Wexler (2000) notes that even if this approach applied to all cases of domestic abuse (which it does not), insisting that men recognize that they are representing a male patriarchal culture, that they are engaged in power and control tactics with their partners, and that their partners' violence toward them was strictly an act of self-defense will alienate many of them. Thus, these forms of treatment have come under scrutiny by many researchers who find such techniques counterproductive in reducing battering behavior and in protecting victims.

Client-centered approaches are much different from confrontational approaches. In fact, they should be viewed as the diametric opposite of confrontational approaches. This approach emphasizes the use of reflections, or mirroring the feedback of the client, to demonstrate understanding of their perspective. This approach employs the use of empathy building to build a rapport with the client. The therapist–client relationship is considered paramount to this approach, and clinicians using this approach accept the client but reject the behavior (Wexler, 2000).

Cognitive-behavioral approaches focus on cognitive restructuring of the client's basic thoughts and the use of basic skill building. Clinicians focus on identifying the chain of events that lead each batterer to violence (Healey et al., 1998), starting with beliefs and "self-talk," or the way we talk to ourselves in our minds. These programs hold that men batter because (1) they are imitating examples of abuse they have witnessed during childhood or in the media, (2) abuse is rewarded, (3) it enables the batterer to get what he wants, and (4) abuse is reinforced through victim compliance and submission (Healey et al., 1998). These programs teach nonviolent alternative behaviors, such as conflict resolution tactics, relaxation techniques, and communication skills.

Solution-focused approaches emphasize the strengths and potential of the individual rather that the problems and dysfunctions. Proponents of this approach believe that lasting, positive changes can occur by focusing on current client strengths, competencies, and solution-building abilities rather than deficiencies. The language is one of "solution and strengths" rather than deficits and blame (Wexler, 2000). Clinicians focus on key questions to "reframe" the person's reactions and the nature of the problem. For instance, they may use exception questions, such as "What is different about the times when you do *not* blow up?" In addition, they might use coping questions, such as "How exactly do you manage to cope with the stresses in your marriage and family?" (Wexler, 2000). Many other techniques exist, but the key is that without denying the aggressive or violent nature of the behaviors, group leaders avoid confronting clients and provoking defensiveness to hold the batterers as capable and willing to control their violence—by finding evidence through investigating past successes at avoiding abusive behavior (Wexler, 2000). In short, rather than focusing on the violence, the emphasis is on the exceptions to the violence.

CONCLUSION

The battering offender has drawn considerable attention in the past two decades. Because of their propensity for violence and because of their tendency to recidivate, these offenders have had increased sanctions put into effect in an attempt to dissuade them from further battering. While this is understandable, it does not acknowledge the reality of battering or the batterer: one size does not fit all. This chapter presents three different categories of batterers in an attempt to distinguish between the different motivations between each type of batterer. This chapter also provides the likely prognosis for each category of batterer, demonstrating that some are more likely to benefit from treatment than others, with some being completely inappropriate for treatment.

A variety of personality disorders have been presented, as these are purported to frequently occur among the battering population. Further, numerous treatment considerations are discussed to provide the most practical methods for addressing this population. It should be noted that this is in the best interest of the public in general and the victim in particular. It is foolish for treatment and criminal justice personnel to ignore the fact that many victims do return to the batterer and remain in a relationship with the batterer. Not that this is the best decision or one that should be encouraged, but in reality, it may be most prudent for us to determine which offenders may be salvageable and which must be incarcerated so that in both ways the safety of adult and childhood victims can be optimized.

KEY TERMS

Category 1 batterers
Category 2 batterers
Category 3 batterers
Common couple violence
Patriarchal terrorism
Tarasoff case
Vagal reactor batterers
Pit bull batterers

REFERENCES

American Psychiatric Association. (2000). *Diagnostic and statistical manual of mental disorders* (4th ed., text revision). Arlington, VA: Author.

Barnett, O. W., Miller-Perrin, C. L., & Perrin, R. D. (1997). *Family violence across the lifespan: An introduction*. Thousand Oaks, CA: Sage.

Baugh, S. (1994). County prison combats domestic violence with Mends program contributors. *Corrections Today, 56*(5), 84.

Buckner, F., & Firestone, M. (2000). Where the peril begins: 25 years after *Tarasoff. Journal of legal Medicine, 21*(2), 2–6. Retrieved from http://www.adoctorm.com/docs/tarasoff.htm

Collins, J. J., & Messerschmidt, M. A. (1993). Epidemiology of alcohol-related violence. *Alcohol, Health, and Research World, 17*, 93–100.

Davis, R. C., Smith, B. E., & Nickles, L. B. (1998). The deterrent effect of prosecuting domestic violence misdemeanors. *Crime and Delinquency, 44*, 434–442.

Davis, R. L. (1998). *Domestic violence: Facts and fallacies*. Westport, CT: Praeger.

Davis, S. F., & Palladino, J. J. (2002). *Psychology* (3rd ed.). Upper Saddle River, NJ: Prentice Hall.

Duffy, M., Nolan, A., & Scruggs, D. (2003). Addressing issues of domestic violence through community supervision of offenders. *Corrections Today, 65*(1), 50–53.

Durand, D. (1995). Jail stops violence, but only temporarily. Standard-Times Newspaper. Retrieved from http://www.s-t.com/projects/DomVio/jailsstop.html

Durose, M. R., Harlow, C. W., Lanjan, P. A., Motivans, M., Rantala, R. R., & Smith, E. L. (2005). *Family violence statistics*. Washington, DC: Bureau of Justice Statistics. Retrieved from http://www.ojp. usdoj.gov/bjs/pub/pdf/fvs.pdf

Dutton, D., & Golant, S. (1995). *The batterer: A psychological profile*. New York: Basic Books.

Garner, J., Fagan, J., & Maxwell, C. (1995). Published findings from the Spouse Assault Replication Program: A critical review. *Journal of Quantitative Criminology, 11*, 3–28.

Gendreau, P., Goggin, C., & Cullen, F. T. (1999). *The effects of prison sentences on recidivism. User Report 1999–03*. Ottawa: Department of the Solicitor General of Canada.

Gondolf, E. W. (2000). A 30-month follow-up of court-referred batterers in four cities. *International Journal of Offender Therapy and Comparative Criminology, 44*(1), 11–18.

Gottman, J., Jacobson, N., Rushe, R., Shortt, J., Babcock, J., La Taillade, J., & Waltz, J. (1995). The relationship between heart rate activity, emotionally aggressive behavior, and general violence in batterers. *Journal of Family Psychology, 9*, 227–248.

Groetsch, M. (1996). *The battering syndrome: Why men beat women and the professional's guide to intervention*. Brookfield, WI: CPI.

Hamberger, L. K., & Hastings, J. E. (1988). Skills training for treatment of spouse abusers: An outcome study. *Journal of Family Violence, 3*, 121–130.

Hamberger, L. K., & Hastings, J. E. (1990). Recidivism following spouse abuse abatement counselling: Treatment program implications. *Violence and Victims, 5*, 157–170.

Hanson, G. R., Venturelli, P. J., & Fleckenstein, A. E. (2002). *Drugs and society* (7th ed.). Sudbury, MA: Jones and Bartlett.

Hanson, R. K., & Wallace-Capretta, S. (2000). *Predicting recidivism among male batterers*. Department of the Solicitor General Canada, Montreal. Retrieved from http://www.sgc.gc.ca

Hare, R. (1993). *Without conscience*. New York: Pocket Books.

Healey, K., Smith, C., & O'Sullivan, C. (1998). *Batterer intervention: Program approaches and criminal justice strategies*. Washington, DC: U.S. Department of Justice.

Holtzworth-Munroe, A., Beatty, S. B., & Anglin, K. (1995). The assessment and treatment of marital violence: An introduction for the marital therapist. In N. S. Jacobson & A. S. Gurman (Eds.), *Clinical handbook of couple therapy* (pp. 317–339). Spring Street, NY: Guilford Press.

Holtzworth-Munroe, A., & Stuart, G. L. (1994). Typology of male batterers: Three subtypes and the differences among them. *Psychological Bulletin, 116*(3), 476–497.

Jacobson, N., & Gottman, J. (1998). *When men batter women*. New York: Simon and Schuster.

Johnson, M. (1995). Patriarchal terrorism and common couple violence: Two forms of violence against women. *Journal of Marriage and the Family, 57*, 283–294.

Maxwell, C. D., Garner, J. H., & Fagan, J. A. (2001, July). *The effects of arrest on intimate partner violence: New evidence from the spouse assault replication program.* Washington, DC: National Institute of Justice.

O'Farrell, T. J., & Murphy, C. M. (1995). Marital violence before and after alcoholism treatment. *Journal of Consulting and Clinical Pscyhology, 63*, 256–262.

Riedel, M., & Welsh, W. (2002). *Criminal violence: Patterns, causes, and prevention*. Los Angeles: Roxbury Publishing.

Russell, M. N. (1995). *Confronting abusive beliefs: Group treatment for abusive men.* Thousand Oaks, CA: Sage.
Sherman, L. W., & Berk, R. A. (1984). The specified deterrent effects of arrest for domestic assault. *American Sociological Review, 49*, 261–272.
Sonkin, D. (1986). Clairvoyance vs. common sense: Therapist's duty to warn and protect. *Violence and Victims, 1*, 7–22.
Thistlethwaite, A., Wooldredge, J., & Gibbs, D. (1998). Severity of dispositions and domestic violence recidivism. *Crime and Delinquency, 44*, 388–398.
Tolman, R. M., Edleson, J. L., & Fendrich, M. (1996). The applicability of the theory of planned behavior to abusive men's cessation of violent behavior. *Violence and Victims, 11*, 341–354.
Wexler, D. B. (2000). *Domestic violence 2000: An integrated skills program for men.* San Diego, CA: Norton & Company.
Zubretsky, T. M., & Digirolamo, K. M. (1994). Adult domestic violence: The alcohol connection. *Violence Update, 4*(7), 1–2, 4, 8.

LEARNING CHECK

1. What is the primary drug that most strongly correlates with chronic battering?
   a. Crack cocaine
   b. Crystal methamphetamine
   c. PCP
   d. Alcohol
   e. Heroin

2. The violence of this batterer is blatant, even in public. He displays a lack of impulse control and is completely unconcerned about the future consequences of his behavior.
   a. Histrionic
   b. Borderline
   c. Narcissistic
   d. Schizoid
   e. Antisocial

3. Brief periods of jail time are probably most effective with ______________ offenders.
   a. Category 1
   b. Category 2
   c. Category 3
   d. Vagal reactors
   e. All of the above

4. With category 1 and category 2 batterers, it may be important to address spiritual issues.
   a. True
   b. False

5. This category of batterer is the most likely to present with some form of personality disorder.
   a. Category 1
   b. Category 2
   c. Category 3
   d. None of the above

6. Depression and feelings of inadequacy are prominent among abusers of this category.
   a. Category 1
   b. Category 2
   c. Category 3
   d. None of the above

7. Which of the following types of treatment are suggested with the battering population?
   a. Confrontational
   b. Psychoeducational
   c. Cognitive-behavioral
   d. Solution focused
   e. All of the above

8. Of all the groups of batterers, these are the least predictable.
   a. Category 1
   b. Category 2
   c. Category 3
   d. None of the above

9. Which type of disorder is reflective of exaggeration of emotional expression, seeking to be the center of attention, and often portraying oneself as a victim?
   a. Borderline
   b. Paranoid
   c. Narcissistic
   d. Histrionic
   e. None of the above

10. Although not typically recommended, if marital counseling were going to be used when one partner is known to be a batterer, which type of batterer would be most able to benefit from this?
    a. Category 1
    b. Category 2
    c. Category 3
    d. None of the above

ESSAY DISCUSSION QUESTIONS

1. Discuss some of the common concerns with the community supervision of the battering offender. Next, explain the basic outcome of the *Tarasoff* ruling and explain how this might be relevant to therapists providing clinical interventions to batterers on community supervision.

2. Identify and discuss the various treatment modalities used with batterers. Next, explain which category of batterer is appropriate for each of these treatment modalities.

3. Briefly compare category 1 with category 3 batterers and discuss the types of community supervision and/or institutional supervision that is most appropriate to each one.

4. Compare and contrast common couple violence with patriarchal terrorism. Which one is more of a long-term problem? What type of interventions are most appropriate for each type?

CHAPTER 13

FEMALE OFFENDERS

Chapter Objectives

1. Know and understand the various demographic and background characteristics of female offenders.
2. Understand the unique conditions associated with female offenders as primary caretakers for their children.
3. Demonstrate awareness of the unique dynamics associated with female offenders in prison, including services for female offenders, the informal subculture, and the problems with sexual abuse of female offenders.
4. Know and discuss the full range of treatment considerations pertinent to female offenders.

INTRODUCTION

This chapter will familiarize the student with the common problems associated with the female offending population. As will be seen in subsequent pages, women have several physiological and psychological characteristics that set them apart from the male offending population. Some of these characteristics are often unique to the female population in broader society, whereas others are unique to females who find themselves involved in the criminal process. Of the offending population, no more than 8 to 10 percent are women, depending on whether one is talking about jails, prisons, community supervision, or a combination of these. This number is small enough to appropriately categorize them as a "special needs" offender, particularly since it will become clear that female offenders have numerous considerations that are not important for the remaining nine-tenths of the offending population. On the other hand, the number of female offenders in the United States correctional system and the higher rate of growth of this offending population (as compared to male offenders) ensures that we cannot overlook this population. Indeed, considerations for the female offending population will become an increasingly important variable for the police, courts, corrections, and treatment specialists for some time to come.

When discussing female offenders, it becomes clear that most female offenders are minority members. Further, it is likewise the case that these women typically have few options and few economic resources. Thus, many of these offenders are marginalized in multiple ways from the access to success and stability commonly attributed to broader society. As of 2003, roughly 176,300 women were incarcerated in a state prison, federal prison, or local jail. Of these female inmates, about 76,100, or 44 percent, were Caucasian; 66,800, or 38 percent, were African American; and 28,300, or 16 percent, were Latino American (Harrison & Beck, 2003). Of those women who are incarcerated, approximately 44 percent have no high school diploma or general equivalency diploma (GED), and 61 percent were unemployed at the point of incarceration (Bloom, Owen, & Covington, 2003). In addition, roughly 47 percent were single prior to incarceration, while an approximate 65 to 70 percent of these women were the primary caretakers of minor children at the point that they were incarcerated (Bloom et al., 2003). Finally, over one-third of those incarcerated can be found within the jurisdictions of the federal prison system or the state prison systems of Texas and California (Harrison & Karberg, 2004).

With respect to community supervision, roughly 844,697 female offenders are on probation with another 87,063 on parole (Bloom et al., 2003). Of those women on community supervision (both probation and parole combined), about 62 percent are Caucasian, 27 percent are African American, and roughly 10 percent are Latino American (Bloom et al., 2003). Of those women on community supervision, roughly 40 percent have no high school diploma or GED, 42 percent are single while under supervision, and 72 percent are the primary caretakers of children under 18 years of age (Bloom et al., 2003).

With these demographic characteristics in mind, we now turn our attention to several subcharacteristics that have been found to be common among the female offending population. We will consider each subcategory in an attempt to demonstrate the multitude of difficult problems that confound effective intervention for many female offenders.

DOMESTIC VIOLENCE

The research on the prevalence of **domestic violence** and its impact on women in the United States is so abundant that it goes beyond the scope of this chapter to discuss as a whole. However, when limiting the discussion to female offenders and their experiences with domestic violence, it appears that they are at greater risk for physical abuse than those in the general population. One survey of female offenders shows that incarcerated women are very likely to have histories of physical abuse (American Correctional Association, 1990). This study indicated that 53 percent of adult women and nearly 62 percent of juvenile girls had been victims of physical abuse. Nearly half of both these groups (49 percent of adults and 47 percent of juveniles) reported experiencing multiple episodes of physical abuse. Further, this study found that this violence is most likely to have been perpetrated by a boyfriend or husband in the case of adult women offenders (50 percent) or by a parent in the case of juvenile girls (43 percent).

For juvenile girls, most of the cases of domestic violence occur between the ages of 10 and 14 years (Bloom et al., 2003). Adult incarcerated women report being subjected to the most violence at ages 15 to 24 (Bloom et al., 2003). This means that this abuse tends to follow the female offender throughout her life span, indicating that these offenders return to a lifestyle that is self-damaging. Because the women on probation and parole are likely to be somewhat socially isolated from common social circles, their peer networks are likely to be limited (Bloom et al., 2003). At best, such groups will include other women in a similar situation or perhaps persons from employment (keep in mind the educational level, unemployment rate, and vocational skills of these women). More likely, these women are likely to continue to associate within the subculture of origin, meaning that many of the friends and family to whom they return are likely to be or have been criminal offenders themselves. This may be much more common since many women who offend tend to do so as secondary accomplices with a male primary offender. Thus, these women are not likely to have many resources to rely on and may find themselves dependent on a man, including an abusive man.

There has long been a noted relationship between substance abuse and domestic violence. For example, Miller et al. (1990) argue that female alcoholics are at significantly higher risk for becoming victims of domestic abuse. According to the same study, male parolees are at high risk for involvement as perpetrators of spousal abuse. Although Miller et al. (1990) do not address whether spouses or partners of male parolees are themselves former offenders, these findings clearly show that many women released on community supervision may be in abusive relationships. Further, since it is the case that many female offenders commit their crimes while acting in tandem with a primary male offender (e.g., acting as a "mule" for drug smugglers, having a pimp with whom they may associate, or providing alibis and resources for the male offender during periods of crime commission), many of them may simply be returning to their criminal significant others who are more likely to be abusive than otherwise noncriminal men. There is an added danger with this because these women already tend to be marginalized, and with the added stigma of being an offender on community supervision, along with worries of maintaining custody of any children who are likely to exist, the female offender may simply consign herself to such a dangerous and damaging lifestyle because of the lack of available options.

PHYSICAL AND SEXUAL ABUSE

A study on the self-reported prior abuse conducted by the Bureau of Justice Statistics in 1999 found that female offenders are abused more frequently than male offenders. State prison inmates reported both physical and sexual abuse experiences prior to their being sentenced. The results found that 57.2 percent of females had experienced abusive treatment compared to 16.1 percent of males. Of this same group, 36.7 percent of the female offenders and 14.4 percent of the male offenders reported that the abuse occurred during their childhood or teenage years. Other findings from this study were the following:

1. Males tend to be mistreated as children, but females are mistreated as both children and adults.
2. Both genders reported much more abuse if they had lived in a foster home or other structured institution.
3. Higher levels of abuse were reported among offenders who had a family member who was incarcerated.
4. Offenders reporting prior abuse had higher levels of drug and alcohol abuse than those who did not report abuse. Further, female offenders who were abused did abuse drugs or alcohol more frequently than did male offenders.

SEX INDUSTRY ACTIVITY AND SEXUALLY TRANSMITTED DISEASES

A large body of research shows that female criminals often have some sort of history of prostitution, although the causal factor(s) and the order of causal factors are not very clear. A debate (indeed a schism) exists among researchers as to whether this is the case because of economic necessities or whether prior sexual victimization is at the root of this common form of female offense (see Special Insert 13.1). Many researchers contend that prior victimization (especially sexual) is at root, pointing toward the high rate of incidence of sexual abuse among female criminals and the high rate of their involvement in prostitution.

Special Insert 13.1. Community Solutions to Prostitution

In St. Paul, Minnesota, an informal jail administration study of female inmates who had been repetitively arrested for engaging in prostitution found that each inmate had served four to six cumulative years of jail time through these repetitive commitments for prostitution. Further, chemical dependency was found in almost every case. Likewise, histories of prior sexual abuse were reported among the majority of the women, with most of them experiencing trauma from physical violence, sexual violence, and incest. In fact, 70 to 75 percent were reportedly diagnosed preliminarily with post-traumatic stress disorder. Women interviewed tended to express a desire to leave prostitution.

With this information, Volunteers of America began the process of establishing the development of a residential recovery center to serve as a court diversion option or a voluntary postrelease option. Various agencies such as the police department (which assisted with referral issues at the point of detection), faith-based organizations, social service agencies, mental health services, and so on helped to arrange comprehensive services to these offenders. The program was named the Women's Recovery Center. Given the dynamics of female offenders and of prostitution, three ingredients were considered paramount to the Women's Recovery Center program structure: (1) gender-specific chemical dependency treatment, (2) mental health treatment with emphasis on sexual trauma and, (3) a cognitive teaching program of expanded life choices.

Because it is common knowledge among criminal justice practitioners and researchers that the female offender typically engages in crime with male guidance (i.e., assisting the male in drug smuggling, taking the "rap" for a male partner, providing alibis, and so on), it was considered an important dimension to the treatment modality that would be used. The relational nature of the female offender has typically been likened to a form of mental pathology, but it was the view of the Women's Recovery Center that relationships were a central (and important) component to successful recovery for female offenders. Thus, the program's central focus is more directed to topics like relationships with the mother, sexuality and addiction, self-esteem, and spirituality.

In addition, the program provides counseling services for mental health issues and specializes in issues and disorders common to sexual assault and trauma victims. The program focus revolves around concepts such as connectedness/disconnectedness with a focus on trauma/recovery within a relational framework. This program is a great example of how neighborhoods, law enforcement, social service delivery systems, and community volunteers can work collaboratively to reduce social ills that develop within their respective communities.

Source: Adapted from Nelson (2004).

The rate of HIV infection is higher for female offenders than for male offenders. According to the Bureau of Justice Statistics (Snell, 1994), among state prisoners tested for HIV, women were more likely to test positive. An estimated 3.3 percent of the women reported being HIV positive, compared to 2.1 percent of the men. Among prisoners who had shared needles to inject drugs, more women than men were likely to be HIV positive (10 percent versus 6.7 percent).

DRUGS

Drug use is a major contributor to female criminality. Female offenders use drugs more often than male offenders, though differences are not extreme, and research focuses most on arrested and incarcerated subjects. Between 1985 and 1994, women's drug arrests increased 100 percent, whereas men's drug arrests increased only by about 50 percent. Regardless, the point is that when dealing with female offenders, addressing drug use is critical in preventing recidivism.

Further, female offenders engage in riskier drug habits than male offenders, as they report higher levels of needle usage and needle sharing (Snell, 1994). This social problem is further compounded because a high number of female offenders who are intravenous drug users likewise engage in prostitution and sex industry activity to support their habits.

VIOLENT CRIME

It is important to note that when it comes to violent crime, there is a huge disparity between male and female offenders. Simply put, female offenders do not commit violent crimes with great frequency. Most crimes revolve around larceny, theft, and fraud. Of those women who do commit homicides, most involve the killing of intimates, usually in self-defense or in retaliatory response to long-term abusive relationships (Bloom, Brown, & Chesney-Lind, 1996). Female chronic offenders are similar to male chronic offenders in that they are likely to be a minority group member, single, and a substance abuser and have a history of spouse abuse. But they differ in that they show differences in years of education (women typically have more), are more likely to come from homes of divorce, and are more likely to come from criminogenic families (Bloom et al., 2003). When both genders are compared, men are likely to be sentenced to prison for violent, property, and drug offenses, while women are likely to be sentenced to prison for drug offenses and property crimes. Only about one-fifth of all prison sentences for female offenders are due to violent offenses.

Given the high rates of abuse that the female offending population experiences (in both childhood and adulthood), the female offender is commonly referred to as the **victim turned offender**. The prior victimization of female victims, particularly with domestic violence, is held as a primary causal factor in predicting female criminal behavior.

MENTAL HEALTH ISSUES

As noted in Chapter 5, the experience of prison can exacerbate the prevalence and/or severity of mental illness. The experience of incarceration can deteriorate existing mental conditions and can lead to the breakdown in mental health among otherwise well-adjusted individuals. The mental health issues for female offenders are often tied to stages in their life cycle and development, such as with puberty, adolescence, and phases of reproductive development (Seiden, 1989). However, because a disturbing number of women are sexually and physically abused as girls and as adult women, attention has been focused on the anxiety, depression, and other psychological illnesses resulting from these events (Seiden, 1989). The trauma of early sexual and physical abuse may be manifested in borderline personality disorder and multiple personality disorders as well as the more common posttraumatic stress disorders and alcoholism (Seiden, 1989). As with most forms of mental illness, these disorders develop largely in response to stressors that push an already overtaxed psyche. Indeed, because of their higher rates of abuse and victimization, coupled with their drug offending, female offenders may have numerous "predispositions" that make them prone to mental illness when the stressor of incarceration is presented as a life experience.

Depression is a very common mental illness among the incarcerated (see Chapter 4) and is even more pronounced among the female offending population because this is a disorder that tends to have higher prevalence rates among females in general society. Further, depression is a common symptom and dual diagnosis among drug abusers, so when the numerous problem variables are taken together, female offenders are very susceptible to bouts of depression and to the full array of mood disorders. Male offenders tend to mask their depression with anger and aggressive reactions that serve as defensive "fronts" or displays of force that mask their underlying depression. Much of this is due to socialization, but for women their socialization tends to ensure that their symptoms of depression are recognized for what they are. Thus, men who are incarcerated may simply be diagnostically labeled as aggressive, and, when in a prison environment, this can go one step further into a classification of being assaultive. Although from the view of institutional security this is accurate, it nonetheless fails to detect the sense of depression that the male inmate may be experiencing. On the other hand, for female inmates, socialization provides a ready tolerance for acts of depression and the expression of emotional sorrow; thus, prevalence rates among female and male inmates in prison may be compounded by social expectations and norms that prison staff are accustomed to. Further, as would be expected, prior abuse plays a role in addiction and depression, further cementing these two variables together as correlates among female offenders. Likewise, when it is considered that female victims of battering tend to present with depressive disorders and posttraumatic stress disorders and given the fact that domestic battering is targeted at female victims much more frequently than male victims, it is not surprising that this variable also aggravates rates of depression among the female offending population.

FEMALE OFFENDERS AS MOTHERS

In 1998, female offenders in the criminal justice system were mothers to approximately 1.3 million children. Many female offenders under criminal justice supervision face losing custody of their children. Some female offenders do have relatives or friends who will care for their children while they are incarcerated, but many do not. For those who are able to arrange placement with relatives, the likelihood of permanent separation between mother and child is significantly reduced. It has been observed that maternal grandmothers most often care for the children of female prison inmates (Bloom, Brown, & Chesney-Lind, 1996). If a mother is unable to place her children with relatives or friends, the local child welfare agency will most likely place the child in foster care. When children of imprisoned, mothers are placed in foster care, and caseworkers are expected to make concerted efforts to sustain family ties and to encourage family reunification (Bloom et al., 1996). Most incarcerated mothers, particularly those who are mentally ill, do not have access to the resources they need to meet other reunification requirements imposed by the court, such as parent education, counseling, drug treatment, and job training. On release from custody to community corrections, mothers face numerous obstacles in reunifying with their children. They must navigate through a number of complex government and social service agencies in order to regain custody of their children. Although differences may exist across jurisdictions, in many cases it is considered beyond the purview of probation and parole agencies to intervene in child custody cases.

When fathers are incarcerated, there is usually a mother left at home to care for the children. However, when mothers are incarcerated, there usually is not a father in the home. This situation is further exacerbated by the fact that there are fewer women's prisons, so female offenders tend to be incarcerated a great distance from the location in which they lived prior to incarceration. Because of this, there is a greater risk that female offenders will be incarcerated at a greater distance from their children than males (Bloom et al., 1996). Indeed, an average female inmate is more than 160 miles farther from her family than a male inmate, and at least half the children of imprisoned mothers have either not seen or not visited their mothers since they were incarcerated (Bloom et al., 1996). This low rate of contact between mother and child tends to weaken family bonds, causing psychological and emotional damage both to the child and to the incarcerated mother. This low rate of contact also has a negative effect on the female offenders themselves, as recidivism rates tend to go up when inmate mothers have diminished contact with their children (Bloom et al., 1996).

This separation between mother and child causes what has been called **collateral damage** to children and society by the current incarceration trends of female offenders who typically commit property and/or drug crimes (Crawford, 2003). Although female offenders separated from their children are at an increased risk of later recidivism, the damage done to the children is probably more serious than to the adult when a parent is incarcerated (Bloom et al., 1996; Crawford, 2003). A number of children display symptoms of posttraumatic stress disorder, namely, depression, feelings of anger and guilt, flashbacks about their mother's crimes or arrests, and the experience of hearing their mother's voice.

Children of incarcerated mothers display other negative effects, such as school-related difficulties, depression, low self-esteem, aggressive behavior, and general emotional dysfunction (Bloom et al., 1996). These effects can be very pronounced and show how an "intergenerational transmission" of criminality can occur if interventions are not provided. For instance, some studies on children of incarcerated mothers have found that 40 percent of the boys ages 12 to 17 were delinquent, while the rate of teenage pregnancy among female children of incarcerated mothers was 60 percent (Bloom et al., 1996). Frequently, the children are left with a caregiving arrangement that is inadequate, unreliable, or irregular, and this causes further long-term damage to the development of the child. Because of these deprivations and traumas, children of incarcerated parents may be six times more likely than their counterparts to become incarcerated themselves (Bloom et al., 1996).

The practice of incarcerating women who are mothers of minor children is extremely damaging and costly for society (Crawford, 2003). It damages both the children during their developmental stages and their parents. The children are more likely to enter into the criminal justice system than their peers who do not have incarcerated parents, and the mother who is separated from her child is more likely to recidivate herself. This form of intervention is likely to cost society untold billions within the next generation, again resulting in even more collateral damage (Crawford, 2003). Women are pushing perhaps 8 percent of the entire U.S. prison population (Clear & Cole, 2002). To ensure that the numbers are kept in perspective, consider that at the end of 2003, U.S. prisons held 1,368,866 men, which equates to an increase of 2 percent compared to 2002. This means that in 2003, one in every 109 men was in prison. For women, the figure was one in every 1,613. It should be noted that because of the War on Drugs and the extended sentences associated with that era, many women were incarcerated for lengthier sentences, and this has helped fuel the growth in the female inmate population. Given the rates of drug use among female offenders, the growth in their numbers behind bars is not surprising.

Special Insert 13.2. Female Offenders as Mothers: "Thinking Out of the Box"

In an attempt to alleviate some of the pains of imprisonment for female offenders who are mothers and for children who have mothers in prison, the use of child nurseries has developed in some prison systems. Child nurseries are an excellent concept for both the female offender and the child. These programs help female offenders "learn to become effective mothers" with a focus on meeting the mental health needs of both the mother and the child.

Health care for pregnant inmates is provided by the Women and Infants At-Risk Program, a residential rehabilitation program in Detroit that facilitates the natural relationship between mother and child. Inmates enter the program prenatally after 28 weeks and stay in the program up to six months postpartum.

Motheread Programs, such as in North Carolina, simultaneously improve literacy of female inmates and create stronger bonds between mother and child. Mothers read to their children and write stories to improve their own literacy.

Girl Scouts Beyond Bars, in conjunction with the National Institute of Justice, allows girls ages 5 to 13 to join their mothers two Saturdays a month for a Girl Scout troop meeting in prison or jail. These are two-hour sessions where troop projects are carried out.

Special Insert 13.3. Female Transitional Services and Residential Parenting

This chapter has clearly noted how important mother–child dynamics are for female offenders and their children. However, for those mothers who were not able to maintain contact or for those who had state intervention with the child custody arangements, the issue is no less important. One program in the state of Washington provides such transitional assistance for female offenders who are leaving incarceration and returning to the community. Two facilities, the Ratcliff House in downtown Seattle and Chase House in Spokane, utilize collaboration between state staff and private contract staff in providing transitional services for female offenders.

When the mothers arrive, they are connected with state social services and the Early Head Start program. A nurse visits the facility for routine medical treatment with the children. Once day care is arranged, the mother is responsible for obtaining and maintaining full-time employment. Naturally, the mother will pay restitution and restoration fees once employed, which is the appeal for community supervision over institutionalized supervision. The mother is responsible for getting the child to day care and for getting to work.

When transitioning these women back into motherhood, there is a separate Child Visit Program that female offenders can participate in provided they pass a Child Protective Services background check, enroll in prescribed parenting classes, and meet with the resident counselor. After completing three supervised visits and three unsupervised visits, the mother is allowed to participate in the Overnight Visitation Program with her child or children. The child is allowed to stay overnight at the facility (which is structured much like a communal home), and staff monitor the interactions between the child and the mother during this process, working closely with the mother if any issues develop. These staff also assist with the overall reunification process. Overall, this program has been shown to be effective at achieving the reentry and family reunification process while preventing recidivism and family disintegration.

Source: Adapted from Fehr (2004).

According to numbers from the U.S. Department of Justice, the number of women in prison has grown 48 percent since 1995, when the figure was 68,468. The male prison population has grown 29 percent over that time, from 1,057,406. Over the years, the number of women incarcerated grew an average of 5 percent compared with an average annual increase of 3.3 percent for men. However, it should be noted that the prison statistics do not fully reflect the number of people behind bars. About 80,000 women were in local jails in 2003, along with more than 600,000 men. The federal prison system held a large share of female prisoners, with a population of 11,635 at the close of 2003. The state of Texas held even more female offenders, with 13,487 women. California, which is the nation's largest prison system, held 10,656 women. The conditions for women in the California prison system have likewise become a recent source of attention as noted by a watchdog group known as the

Little Hoover Commission, where an improvement of services was clearly communicated to the California governor and legislature. This development will be discussed in more detail later in this chapter.

It should be noted that women incarcerated in state prisons are less likely than men in state prisons to have a prior conviction record. Finally, similar to the population of men who are incarcerated, the demographic characteristics of female inmates show them to be largely minority in composition. Roughly five out of every 1,000 white women, 15 out of every 1,000 Hispanic women, and 35 out of every 1,000 black women will be sentenced to prison during their lifetime (Bloom et al., 1996).

CLASSIFICATION, IDENTIFICATION, AND DIAGNOSIS

It is considered a general fact that female prison institutions do not meet the inmate's needs as effectively as do male prisons. As a testament to the poor services that tend to be delivered to female inmates, consider the case of *Glover v. Johnson.* This case involved the Michigan Department of Corrections and the issue of parity in service programming between female and male offenders. A class-action lawsuit filed on behalf of all female inmates in the state of Michigan alleged that the constitutional rights of female inmates throughout the state had been violated because these inmates were being denied educational and vocational rehabilitation opportunities that were being provided to male inmates. Ultimately, the Michigan Department of Corrections was found liable, and a decree was issued for the department to provide the following to female inmates within its jurisdiction:

1. Two-year college programming
2. Paralegal training and access to an attorney to remedy past inadequacies in law library facilities
3. A revision of the wage policy for female inmates to ensure parity with male inmate wage compensation policies
4. Access to programming that had previously been provided only to male inmates
5. Prison industries that previously existed only at male facilities

It would appear that despite such legal precedents, more recent practices have not improved substantially in other parts of the nation. For instance, in California the Little Hoover Commission (2004) was tasked with providing recommendations to the state governor and legislature. This commission found that the correctional system was not doing well and that conditions were particularly bleak for female offenders (Vesely, 2004). In California, the number of women in prison has increased fivefold during the past 20 years with a total number of around 10,000 women in 2004. This means that roughly 10 percent of the state's prison population consists of female offenders. Further, an additional 12,000 women are on parole in California.

Two-thirds of these offenders are serving time for nonviolent offenses, and close to 70 percent are single mothers.

Further, there has been a noted need for substance abuse treatment programs among female inmates in California as well as victim services for these offenders, who have often been prior victims of domestic violence and sexual assault in the past. Indeed, it was found by the Little Hoover Commission that roughly 40 percent of the female offenders in California had been physically or sexually abused prior to turning 18 years of age. Most of these female inmates were not found to be a threat to the safety of the public. Indeed, more of these offenders were found to have themselves been victims of violent crimes than were those who had been convicted of violent crimes. This also underscores the fact that many female offenders commit violent acts in defense from or retaliation to domestic abuse at the hands of a significant other. Further, an estimated 80 percent of female inmates have some form of documented substance abuse problem.

Among many of the recommendations from the Little Hoover Commission, some of the more pertinent ones to female facilities were the following:

1. Revise classification procedures so that they are tailored to better make housing assignments and programming decisions for female inmates. The classification tool should be validated to ensure that it accurately assesses the risks female offenders pose to public safety while simultaneously considering the needed services to successfully transition from prison to the community.
2. Develop a continuum of incarceration options to match female inmates with the facility that best achieves the goals of public protection and public reentry within a cost-effective budgetary framework. The commission specifically noted that "the continuum should include community correctional facilities to house inmates closer to their communities; halfway back facilities to support the transition from prison to the community; and, facilities specifically designed to address the needs of parole violators who are inappropriate for less restrictive sanctions" (p. vii). In addition, this continuum should include more mother–child programs.
3. Partner with communities to plan, develop, and operate facilities focused on reentry. The commission specifically noted the problems with the rural and distant location of many female prison facilities under this recommendation. As will be seen, the need to partner with the community will be a constant theme for many special needs offenders. Further discussion on community involvement will be discussed in Chapter 14.

The Little Hoover Commission provides a recent indication of the state of affairs for female offenders in both the state of California and throughout the nation. This demonstrates the need for improved services for female inmates in the nation's largest state facility, meaning that a substantial if not an all-inclusive amount of the female inmate population is in dire need of greatly improved services.

To improve services for female inmates in prisons, several modifications should be considered. First, on intake, the prison staff should have clearly established gender-specific inmate needs so that classification programs will be accurate and meaningful when processing female offenders. This means that one cannot simply use an "add water and stir" approach with general classification programs. Those typical programs (discussed in Chapters 1 and 2) that are designed for institutions with male inmates will need to be greatly modified to be of any practical value in the institution. Needs related to children, histories of spousal and child sexual abuse, underlying beliefs about sex and sexuality for those involved in the sex industry, and improved vocational training are all critical for female offenders. Many of these issues are not even a minor concern for male inmates (aside from vocational training).

Further, it is commonly understood that women are much more in touch with their emotional framework, and, as such, prison management should be adjusted so that differences in behavioral patterns among females are not overlooked. Female offenders tend to emphasize more social relationships in prison and are not typically based on "power and dominance" themes like in male institutions. Moreover, female inmates tend to present with emotional and mental health problems more frequently than male inmates, and prison facilities need to be prepared to address these psychological variables. It is less a problem of institutional security than an issue of simple institutional harmony. Facilities that are most effective include a combination of substance abuse programs, work training programs, parenting classes, child visitation programs, work release, and a variety of transition, aftercare, education, and health programs.

THE FEMALE INMATE SUBCULTURE AND COPING IN PRISON

The conditioning of women in the United States regarding the traditional social role of motherhood and the forced separation from their families has a considerable effect on women in prison. A significant aspect of the female coping mechanism inside prisons is their development of family-like environments with the other female prisoners. These fictional family atmospheres, or kinship structures, enable women to create a type of caring, nurturing environment inside prison (Bartollas, 2002; Engelbert, 2001). Associating with a prison family provides a woman with a feeling of belonging and social identity. Many of these relationships are formed on the basis of friendships and develop into the companionship roles of "sister-to-sister" and "mother-to-daughter" bonds. These relationships can become intimate and include touching and hugging without having sexual overtones (Bartollas, 2002). However, sexual relationships in prison do exist and are not uncommon. In some instances, a prison family will consist of "married" couples, with specific male and female roles. These relationships may last only while the women are incarcerated and do not necessarily signify homosexuality.

Some women who are in prison for an extended period of time may find that in order to have their needs for love and companionship filled, they become involved with other women. The female acting in the male role will take on the stereotypical male mannerisms. She may walk and talk like a man, cut or shave her hair, and attempt to dress in a masculine fashion. In contrast, the female partner will behave in a traditional feminine manner. There are women who become involved in these relationships only while in prison and therefore do not feel that they are lesbians in the strictest sense of the word. Similar to male prison settings, sexuality inside the walls is considered separate from sexual identity outside of the walls. These women become involved in a relationship only to fulfill their need to be "loved" and desired and to feel special and attractive, just as they would outside prison. There are other additional advantages associated with belonging to a prison family structure. These family structures are sometimes called kinship networks (Brown, 2003). Bartollas (2002) explains that the meanings of the kinship relationships within the prison are many and varied. They provide protection and a common support system, and they may be encouraged by the prison administration because of the social control aspect of keeping the female inmates out of trouble. Bartollas (2002) further states, "Above all, they [relationships] create situations for fun and laughter" (p. 358). This may be the most powerful aspect of the kinship relationship because it provides not only a feeling of belonging but also feelings of joy and harmony.

On the television series *Primetime Live*, Diane Sawyer spent a day and a night inside a women's prison as a mock inmate to witness firsthand the female inmate subculture, a culture that is very different from everyday society. The process of relationship development is one of the most uniquely affected components of the female prison experience. Kept apart from men for years at a time, the women of Metro State Prison in Atlanta, Georgia, have evolved a different approach to romance and family (*Primetime Live,* 2004). From this newscast, it could be seen that the hierarchy of desire in prison follows a guideline by which women develop lesbian relationships: the most desirable partners are the ones who are most masculine. These female offenders are referred to as "studs," while those who are submissive are referred to as "femmes." Unlike in male prisons where sex is used as a tool of violence and intimidation, sex in the female inmate subculture tends to be more or less genuinely consensual rather than coerced. In fact, most violence in women's prisons is often based on jealousy or possessiveness rather than violence.

There is some controversy over the extent of these kinship networks within the prison system. While it is clear that women do form ties of affection in prison much more frequently than men, it is doubtful that the relationships follow strict definitions of kinship in most facilities. Thus, any categorization is not necessarily to be taken literally in the strictest sense but instead gives a general idea of how the relationships between female inmates are arranged while in prison. On release, nearly all female inmates return to traditional heterosexual roles where they most often play a feminine role. Regardless of whether the kinship relationships are as defined as some believe, there is no doubt that studies have revealed interesting information pertaining to the female subculture within the prison system. Women, just like male inmates, are faced with surviving the term of their sentence inside the prison walls. Doing so requires that they create some type of acceptable social environment in which to cope with the situation.

PROBLEMS WITH CUSTODIAL SEXUAL MISCONDUCT IN FEMALE FACILITIES

During the 1990s, roughly 23 correctional departments were involved in class-action or individual lawsuits related to staff sexual misconduct with female inmates. One notorious case in particular (*Cason v. Seckinger*) occurred in Georgia and included staff throughout the entire institution and at all levels of supervision. The U.S. Department of Justice filed civil lawsuits in two states (Arizona and Michigan) alleging systematic sexual misconduct by male correctional staff in women's prisons (Human Rights Watch, 1996).

Much of the **custodial sexual misconduct** included the use of force or the threat of force that was targeted toward female offenders in at least 11 different state correctional systems. Correctional staff also used their authority and ability to procure goods and services for the female inmates to encourage the inmates to engage in an exchange for sexual favors. Further, some of the misconduct was "consensual" between inmate and staff, but this is nonetheless abuse on the part of correctional staff. It must again be noted that many of the female offending population were themselves abused prior to incarceration, both as children (in abusive families of origin) and/or as adults (as with domestic abusers or through involvement in the sex industry). Because of this, the dysfunctional exchange and confusion between sex and a mature emotionally intimate relationship is normalized for many of these women. Any sense of ethics pertaining to such arrangements may simply be beyond their ability to grasp given the prior learning and socialization that they may have been exposed to. In either event, it is the obligation of staff to ensure that appropriate boundaries are set and to ensure that these are not violated.

FEMALE OFFENDERS IN THE COMMUNITY

In 1999, female offenders accounted for nearly 18 percent of all probationers and 10 percent of all parolees in community correctional systems throughout the nation (Pastore & Maguire, 2002). Most female offenders were involved in some form of property offense, with roughly 40 percent being convicted of some form of fraud and another 24 percent being convicted of larceny. On the average, women are sentenced to probation more often than men, and this is largely thought to be true because of the differences in offense patterns. With respect to parole, female offenders tend to be found in numbers that are proportionate with their offending patterns, and this tends to be true at both the state and the federal level. Thus, most female offenders on parole are drug or property offenders. Further, it should be noted that female parolees have a lower recidivism rate than men, making them much more ideal for most forms of community supervision (Latessa & Allen, 1999).

The realization that community supervision and alternative sentencing were highly suited to female offenders was made in the state of Missouri, where House Bill SB720 was passed in 1998 to establish the **Children of Incarcerated Parents Task Force** in 1999. This task force noted that while Missouri is the seventeenth most populous state in the United States, it was among the top 10 for the number of persons behind bars. Further, in 2001 there were 2,077 female inmates in the state, which led the Midwest in the number of incarcerated female offenders. It was noted that approximately 61 percent of the female inmate population committed nonviolent convictions and that nearly 50 percent had no previous criminal history. This stands in stark contrast to most male inmates who typically have prior convictions before a prison sentence (Clear & Cole, 2002). More alarming is the fact that over 78 percent of the female inmate population had dependent children. Between the daily cost of incarcerating the female offender ($36 per day) and the cost to the Missouri Department of Family Services for the foster care of the children in 2002 (between $227 and $307 per month per child), it was found that incarcerating women was both counterproductive to the appropriate sentencing (when considering the offense) and rehabilitation and too costly to be of much utility to the state. This was further compounded by the fact that female offenders on probation and parole have been found to be an equal (probation) or better (parole) risk for recidivism when compared with male inmates.

The Children of Incarcerated Parents Task Force specifically noted many alternatives to incarceration because alternative services were found to be the best approach to breaking the generational cycle of incarceration. Added to this was the fact that most incarcerated women were found to be the primary custodian of at least one child under the age of 18, and the task force's desire was to keep the family intact if this proved to be in the best interest of the child. The task force's specific recommendations were similar to alternative community sanctions noted in this book (see Chapters 3 to 5). Among these recommendations were the following:

1. The use of drug courts as an effective alternative to incarceration—Offenders in Missouri are offered a stay of prosecution if they agree to participate in a court-supervised treatment program. On successful completion of the program, the participant may be discharged without a criminal record; failure to complete the program results in the filing of criminal charges. Under this program, mothers who are charged with drug offenses would be able to maintain the caregiver role while receiving treatment for their addictions.
2. The use of mental health courts to serve offenders with co-occurring disorders (mental disorder and substance abuse disorder), developmental disabilities, or head injury in the criminal justice system—The goal of the mental health court program is to reduce the number of offenders with co-occurring disorders

committed to the Department of Corrections while still providing for public safety. Successful completion of the program may result in deferred prosecution for the offender.

3. The use of restorative justice to address offenses (particularly property offenses that are common to female offenders) through direct restitution to the victim (financially or through services provided by the offender) or indirect restitution via community service—The use of victim-offender mediation in particular was noted because this has been shown to be an effective approach for dealing with crime and for reviving the community. More important, this form of intervention allows the female offender to make amends while at the same time keeping the family intact within the community. This ultimately relieves the community of much of the previously mentioned "collateral damage."

FEMALE OFFENDERS AND TREATMENT IMPLICATIONS

In a study of 110 programs that deal with female offenders, Bloom, Owen, and Covington (2003) found that programs conducive to treatment success of female offenders should use female role models and pay particular attention to gender-specific concerns not common to male offenders. Treatment for female offenders requires a heightened need to respond to expressions of emotions and an ability to communicate openly with offenders. Much of this has to do with socialization to be open and nurturing, emphasizing reciprocity and so on.

Based on the research presented and on the specific specialized needs of female offenders, it becomes clear that treatment considerations for female offenders can be quite complicated. Indeed, it is plausible that a female offender could have the sundry challenges outlined in this chapter as well as numerous others included in various other chapters of this book. Thus, many female offenders can be viewed as being "special needs plus" when considering the various issues that may be present. With this in mind, specific recommendations from this book regarding treatment programs for female offenders are outlined as follows:

1. Treatment plans must be individualized in structure, including the following:
   a. Clear and measurable goals
   b. Intensive programming with effective duration
   c. Appropriate screening and assessment

2. Female offenders must be able to acquire needed life skills:
   a. Parenting and life skills are taught. Both are critical.
   b. Anger management must be addressed.
   c. Marketable job skills are important because female offenders typically have few job skills and, unlike male offenders, have more difficulty obtaining jobs

in the manual labor sectors that pay higher (e.g., construction, plant work, and so on).

3. Programs must address victimization issues:
   a. Programs should address self-esteem, which is typically tied into previous abuse issues, which in turn increase the likelihood of substance abuse and prostitution, two main segments of female crime.
   b. Programs must address domestic violence issues. These are highly common among female offenders both from the family of origin and between previous boyfriends and/or spouses. Often this is intergenerationally transmitted.

Dolan, Kolthoff, Schreck, Smilanch, and Todd (2003) discuss the importance of having gender-specific treatment programs for correctional clients with co-occurring disorders. Their insights are important for a couple of key reasons that should be emphasized in this chapter. First, it is becoming increasingly clear within the treatment literature that therapists, caseworkers, and the curriculum that they use must be able to address diverse populations. Many law persons do not consider that women, the elderly, and the disabled are part of most diversity programs just as are ethnic and racial groups. This is important because it is also becoming clear that correctional programs must address these issues as well. Indeed, this is the basis of this entire book. Second, special needs offenders are a complicated group with a multiplicity of issues (in most cases), but the problems associated with co-occurring disorders have been extensively illustrated in prior chapters of this book. The issue of co-occurring or dual diagnoses is not simply restricted to special needs offenders but is also a current theme in much of the treatment literature, particularly within the fields of counseling, psychology, and social work. Thus, programs such as those suggested by Dolan et al. (2003) are important because they "fit the bill" on several levels.

In Iowa, the First Judicial Department of Correctional Services established a community-based treatment program in its correctional facility (incidentally, this also demonstrates how both correctional facilities and community supervision programs can successfully interface with one another). This program established a gender-specific female program to provide integration of treatment services designed to focus on dual diagnosis of female offenders. This is important since it is clear that female offenders may be at heightened risk of having dual-diagnoses given their frequent prior abuse trauma, maternal concerns for their children, and the high rate of substance abuse.

The key concept of this program was to ensure that treatment for multiple issues was comprehensively provided simultaneously within the same facility rather than being made available in a piecemeal fashion within a patchwork system of agencies that were only loosely connected. Thus, contractors from local mental health providers, community caseworkers, probation/parole officers, and so on all operated from within the facility and were able to have eye-to-eye contact with one another.

The program addresses physical and sexual abuse issues, substance abuse, mental disorders, family-based counseling, and parenting issues. The program is founded on the notion that most of these clients have grown up in dysfunctional families, so it is difficult for these clients to even be able to conceive how a functional family operates on a routine basis. Further, this program specifically strives to include the children in the treatment process since it has been found that this increases likelihood of client program completion and helps the client's recovery from various other issues. Thus, treatment is optimized because the offender's role as a parent is used as a therapeutic tool to enhance the relevance of the treatment to the client.

Specific issues pertaining to physical health care, adult sexuality, preventive pregnancy education, education on sexually transmitted diseases, and grief/loss issues pertaining to the woman's role as a parent are included within this program. A consortium of individuals and agencies are involved, including staff from the local Planned Parenthood, the local police force, community supervision, private therapists, and so on. The topics covered by these individuals are also discussed in the group therapy sessions throughout the daily routine to reinforce the learning process. Specifically, Dolan et al. (2003) note that treatment for women with dual diagnoses and histories of violence is optimized when it does the following:

1. Focuses on a woman's strengths
2. Acknowledges a woman's role as a parent
3. Improves interactions between the parent and child
4. Provides comprehensive, coordinated services for a mother and her children

The program by Dolan et al. (2003) is an excellent example of how most programs for female offenders should be structured and should be considered a model program. The reasons for this are because it is comprehensive and demonstrates how the multitude of issues pertinent to female offenders can be addressed within a single facility while utilizing a wide array of services within the community. This program falls well within the theme of this book, demonstrating how integration of community resources and public and private agencies can be combined to address complicated social ills in cost-effective ways. Because of this, it is the contention of this book that other areas of the nation should look toward this program when designing treatments for their female offending client population.

CONCLUSION

While female offenders are a small proportion of the offending population, they are a rapidly growing group of offenders. It is becoming increasingly clear that services for female offenders are inadequate within both institutional and community intervention programs. There is a need to address specific social ills that are fairly unique to female offenders since this population is likely to continue to grow in numbers. Among these social ills are domestic violence, sexual abuse, drug use, prostitution, sexually transmitted diseases, and child custody issues. Many of the problems associated with female offenders have hidden costs that affect the rest of society in a multifaceted manner. Any failure to improve services to this offending population will simply ensure that future generations likewise adopt criminogenic patterns of social coping. This is specifically the case given the "collateral damage" that emanates from the impairment of children whose mother (and likely sole caretaker) is incarcerated. When thinking long term, it becomes both socially and economically sound practice to work to improve services and ensure that accommodations are made for the special needs of the female offender.

KEY TERMS

Domestic violence
Victim turned offender
Collateral damage
Little Hoover Commission
Custodial sexual misconduct
Children of Incarcerated Parents Task Force

REFERENCES

American Correctional Association. (1990). *The female offender: What does the future hold?* Washington, DC: St. Mary's Press.

Bartollas, C. (2002). *Invitation to corrections.* Boston: Allyn & Bacon.

Bloom, B., Brown, M., & Chesney-Lind, M. (1996). Women on probation and parole. In A. J. Lurigio (Ed.), *Community corrections in America: New directions and sounder investments for persons with mental illness and codisorders* (pp. 51–76). Washington, DC: National Institute of Corrections.

Bloom, B., Owen, B., & Covington, S. (2003). *Gender responsive strategies: Research, practice and guiding principles for women offenders*. Washington, DC: National Institute of Corrections. Retrieved from http://www.nicic.org/Library/018017

Brown, J. W. (2003). The female inmate. *International Encyclopedia of Justice Studies*. Retrieved from http://www.eijs.com/Corrections/female_inmate.htm

Clear, T. R., & Cole, G. F. (2003). *American Corrections* (6th ed.). Belmont, CA: Wadsworth.

Crawford, J. (2003). Alternative sentencing necessary for female inmates with children. *Corrections Today*. Retrieved from: http://www.aca.org/publications/ctarchivespdf/june03/commentary_june.pdf

Dolan, L., Kolthoff, K., Schreck, M., Smilanch, P., & Todd, R. (2003). Gender-specific treatment for clients with co-occurring disorders. *Corrections Today, 65*(6), 100–107.

Engelbert, P. (2001, July/August). Women in prison. *Agenda Magazine*. Retrieved from http://www-personal.umich.edu/~lormand/agenda/0107/womenprison.htm

Fehr, L. M. (2004). Washington female offender re-entry programs combine transitional services with residential parenting. *Corrections Today, 66*(6), 82–83.

Harrison, P. M., & Beck, A. J. (2003). *Prisoners in 2002*. Washington, DC: Bureau of Justice Statistics. Retrieved from http://www.ojp.usdoj.gov/bjs/pub/pdf/p02.pdf

Harrison, P. M., & Karberg, J. C. (2004). *Prison and jail inmates at midyear 2003*. Washington, DC: Bureau of Justice Statistics. Retrieved from http://www.ojp.usdoj.gov/bjs/pub/pdf/pjim03.pdf

Human Rights Watch. (1996). *All too familiar, sexual abuse of women in U.S. state prisons*. New Haven, CT: Yale University Press.

Human Rights Watch. (1999). Nowhere to hide: Retaliation against women in Michigan state prisons. Retrieved from http://www.hrw.org/reports98/women/Mich.htm

Latessa, E. J., & Allen, H. E. (1999). *Corrections in the community* (2nd ed.). Cincinnati: Anderson.

Little Hoover Commission. (2004). *Breaking the barriers for women on parole*. Retrieved from http://www.lhc.ca.gov/lhcdir/177/execsum177.pdf

Miller, B. A., Nochajski, T. H., Leonard, K. E., Blane, H. T., Gondoii, D. M., & Bowers, P. M. (1990). Spousal violence and alcohol/drug problems among parolees and their spouses. *Women and Criminal Justice, 2*, 55–72.

Nelson, W. F. (2004). Prostitution: A community solution alternative. *Corrections Today, 66*(6), 88–91.

Pastore, A. L., & Maguire, K. (2002). *Sourcebook of criminal justice statistics, 2001*. Washington, DC: U.S. Bureau of Justice Statistics.

Primetime Live. (2004, December 10). Retrieved from http://abcnews.go.com/Primetime/story?id=227295&page=1

Seiden, A. M. (1989). Psychological issues affecting women throughout the life cycle. In B. L. Parry (Ed.), *The psychiatric clinics of North America* (pp. 1–24). Philadelphia: W. B. Saunders.

Snell, T. (1994). *Women in prison*. Washington, DC: Bureau of Justice Statistics.

Vesely, R. (2004). *California rebuked on female inmates*. Retrieved from http://www.womensenews.org/article.cfm/dyn/aid/2122/context/archive

LEARNING CHECK

1. Roughly ______________ amount of all prison sentences for female offenders are due to violent crimes.
   a. One-fourth
   b. One-half
   c. One-fifth
   d. Three-fourths
   e. Three-fifths

2. Among those women who do commit homicides, most involve the killing of intimates, usually in self-defense or in retaliatory response to long-term abusive relationships.
   a. True
   b. False

3. What does the term "collateral damage" refer to?
   a. The damage done to children when separated from their mothers
   b. The double abuse women suffer—first from their prior life, then when in prison
   c. Damages addressed only in civil court
   d. All of the above
   e. None of the above

4. Which of the following disorders were specifically noted to be more common with female offenders?
   a. Borderline personality disorder
   b. Posttraumatic stress disorder

c. Antisocial personality disorder
d. Both a and b but not c
e. Both b and c but not a

5. Unlike the male offending population, the female offending population is mostly Caucasian.
   a. True
   b. False

6. The War on Drugs greatly contributed to the sharp rise in incarcerated female offenders.
   a. True
   b. False

7. Nearly ______________ of female offenders have dependent children at the time of incarceration.
   a. 40%
   b. 50%
   c. 60%
   d. 70%
   e. 80%

8. Services in female prisons have typically met the needs of female inmates much better than those for male offenders.
   a. True
   b. False

9. The phrase ______________ refers to the high rates of abuse that the female offending population experiences.
   a. Mistreated and abused
   b. Forgotten victims
   c. Victim turned offender
   d. None of the above

10. When is treatment optimized for women who suffer trauma from victimization or for those with dual diagnoses and histories of violence?
    a. When it acknowledges the female offender's role as a parent
    b. When it provides comprehensive services for the female offender and her child
    c. When it addresses prior victimization of the female offender, when relevant
    d. All of the above
    e. Both a and b but not c

ESSAY DISCUSSION QUESTIONS

1. Discuss the findings of the Little Hoover Commission. Next, list and discuss the recommendations by the commission for improving services for female offenders.

2. Discuss the recommendations made by the Children of Incarcerated Parents Task Force to improve criminal justice interventions for female offenders.
3. Provide a discussion on how the victim-turned-offender hypothesis applies to female offenders. Use specific examples from the chapter to illustrate your point.

CHAPTER 14

GERIATRIC OFFENDERS

Chapter Objectives

1. Distinguish between the elderly first-time offender and the habitual elderly offender. Understand the different supervision and treatment standards that are associated with each type of offender.
2. Understand the difficulties and challenges involved with elderly offenders who are in prison. This includes issues associated with dementia, chronic illness, and terminal illness.
3. Know the methods of classifying elderly offenders and be able to identify class 1 through class 4 elderly offenders.
4. Understand the challenges and requirements for supervising elderly offenders in the community.

INTRODUCTION

The issue of elderly offenders has become a concern for criminal justice personnel only in the past 20 years or so. In fact, when discussing crime, justice, and the elderly, topics typically revolve around the victimization of the elderly. However, our topic in this chapter deals with offenders who are in the elderly age range. Elderly offenders who have aged while serving lengthy prison sentences, particularly habitual offenders who have aged while serving enhanced penalties in prison, will be distinguished from those who were otherwise noncriminal during their young and early adulthood but offended later in life. This distinction is important because the mind-set of each of these types of offenders can be substantially different. Likewise, the different concerns for elderly supervision in prisons and those on community supervision will also be presented. It is this confluence between the type of elderly offender (habitual or first offense while elderly) and the type of supervision (prison or community supervision) that generates debate on processing the elderly offender through the criminal justice system. It is this confluence that will be the central focus of this chapter.

It is often cited that the age demographic of the elderly population in the United States is growing. Those who are 65 and older are the fastest-growing age-group in the United States (Morton, 1992). It is estimated that roughly one-third of the United States will be over the age of 50 in the year 2010. This group made up only about a quarter of the U.S. population during the early 1990s. Because of this, it is only natural that one would expect the number of older offenders to increase as well. Further, it would appear that the rate of offending is rising slowly. This is in addition to the aging and graying of prisoners who committed crimes earlier in their lives but are still in the justice system's supervision because of their lengthy sentences.

While the numbers are low and the typical types of offenses are minor, it is true that more senior citizens are committing more violent crimes, particularly with firearms. Indeed, crime committed by the elderly is increasing (Price, 2000). In fact, this trend is expected to continue as prior generations present with Alzheimer's disease at continually higher rates. Because of such dementia and a host of other factors, it is expected that more violent crime from elderly offenders will be observed (Price, 2000).

However, it should be made clear that this trend is not meant to be presented as a source of "sensational" news. No rapid crime problem is expected from this population, but it is not expected that crime within the ranks of senior citizens will decrease. It is expected that elderly offenders, particularly first-time offenders, will continue to be a small minority of the criminal population. Still, it is clear that elderly offending is increasing, a trend that was noted during the 1990s. For instance, in 1989 a total of 3,347 persons age 65 and older were arrested for committing violent crimes; in 1995 this figure rose to 4,043. This amounted to an approximate 21 percent increase, which is about 6 percent higher than arrests among offenders from other age-groups (Price, 2000).

However, it is clear that the majority of offenses involving elders are minor. Nevertheless, elderly offenders have been the fastest-growing age-group in prison during the past 10 years. Elderly inmates for the purpose of this chapter will include all inmates 50 years old and older (Morton, 1992). Inmates falling within this age-group have grown from 4.9 percent of the national prison population in 1990 to about 6.8 percent in 1997. This is roughly a 38 percent increase within just seven years.

To make things even more complicated, consider that the nation's population of Alzheimer's patients is skyrocketing (see Special Insert 14.1). In 1980, an estimated 2.9 million seniors had the disease. Today, the total is about 4 million, according to the Chicago-based Alzheimer's Association. The disease strikes about one in 10 who are older than 65 and nearly half of those older than 85. The association anticipates that the number of Americans suffering from Alzheimer's will double by

Special Insert 14.1. Diagnostic Criteria for Dementia of the Alzheimer's Type

A. The development of multiple cognitive deficits manifested by both
   1. Memory impairment (impaired ability to learn new information or to recall previously learned information)
   2. One (or more) of the following cognitive disturbances:
      a. aphasia (language disturbance)
      b. apraxia (impaired ability to carry out motor activities despite intact motor function)
      c. anosia (failure to recognize or identify objects despite intact sensory function)
      d. disturbance in excecutive functioning (i.e., planning, organizing, sequencing, abstracting)

B. The cognitive deficits in Criteria A1 and A2 each cause significant impairment in social or occupational functioning and represent a significant decline from a previous level of functioning.

C. The course is characterized by gradual onset and continuing cognitive decline.

D. The cognitive deficits in Criteria A1 and A2 are not due to any of the following:
   1. Other central nervous system conditions that cause progressive deficits in memory and cognition
   2. Systemic conditions that are known to cause dementia
   3. Substance-induced conditions

E. The deficits do not occur exclusively during the course of delirium.

F. The disturbance is not better accounted for by another Axis I disorder.

Source: Diagnostic and Statistical Manual of Mental Disorders (4th ed., text revision) (American Psychiatric Association, 2000).

2030 and reach 14 million by 2050. Although some advocates may contend that violence among Alzheimer's patients is rare, it is more likely that this rarity is due to the fact that the violence is simply not reported. Given the likely family dynamics, the seriousness of the offense, and the overall contextual view of elderly commiting crime, it is likely that the rate of violence among those inflicted with Alzheimer's is underreported. Further, if individuals with Alzheimer's are widowed or living alone, their mental disorders may simply evade detection and diagnosis. The symptoms of Alzheimer's—paranoia, hallucinations, and delusions—can work to predispose these individuals to violence. According to Price (2000), as many as 70 percent of those diagnosed with dementia develop significant behavioral problems in the first six or seven years of their illness.

It is also predicted that other factors will become important in dealing with the elderly offender. Family dynamics and racial/ethnic diversity among this group are likely to become increasingly important. In general, the elderly are more heterogeneous than any other age-group (Morton, 1992). This fact makes it even more difficult on correctional agencies because more attention must be given to individualized assessment, programming, planning, and monitoring to meet the needs of this diversified and growing group of offenders (Morton, 1992).

Likewise, as has been often cited with the gamut of other special needs offenders, problems with alochol and drug abuse treatment are likely to emerge as a primary concern with elderly offenders. This is particularly true with both alcohol and prescription durgs, and some elderly offenders may ignore the interaction effects of alcohol with prescription drugs because of pain or other problems they are experiencing. In fact, in 1990 it was found that among 179 "nonjustifiable" homicides committed by people age 60 and older, 44 percent had consumed alcohol before killing. Further, 46 percent of these inmates had some kind of extended history of alcohol abuse (Price, 2000).

Morton (1992, 2001) notes that the complexity of the relationship among the various inherited and environmental factors results in wide variations among individuals relative to aging. In other words, some individuals might be physically or mentally "old" at age 50, while others might be active and "young" at age 70. Morton (1992, 2001) notes that in today's society, whether people are considered old increasingly depends on their individual, physical, emotional, social, and economic level of functioning. Indeed, Fabelo (1999) notes how a given set of lifestyle choices among offenders, coupled with the poor health experiences of incarceration, tends to make the offending population (and the incarcerated population in particular) much older in health terms than the nonoffending population of a similar age.

It should be noted that there is some difference in the definition of the term "old" when referring to elderly people. Some agencies, such as the Texas prison system, define this as being roughly 55 years in age. Other agencies, such as the Florida prison system, have adopted the age of 50 as qualifying as an elderly offender. Other states have been found to use 60 and even 65 as the criteria in determining elderly status with inmates under their supervision.

In this chapter and throughout this book, we will stay consistent with the age selected by most correctional systems and will thus follow Morton's (1992) recommendation that "in order to have a uniform reference point, correctional agencies nationwide adopt age 50 as the chronological starting point to define older offenders" (p. 4). Thus, the age of 50 will be the criterion in this book to determine when an offender is elderly. Therefore, the definition of an **elderly offender** is any offender who is convicted and is at least 50 years of age or older, as determined by a comprehensive consideration of factors that include prior lifestyle, medical health, mental health, and the effects of prior incarceration on that individual's overall functioning.

It is important that correctional agency administrators avoid stereotyping elderly offenders. Gross generalizations can negatively affect the effective planning and programming of various services for these offenders. Staff stereotypes and presumptions about health care needs, emotional and mental health, learning deficits, and other characteristics of elderly offenders can essentially lead to staff not recognizing that most elderly offenders can act independently in the community for the most part.

Understanding the normal aging process is essential to planning and programming efforts for these offenders. When designing new or existing policies and practices that encourage healthy lifestyles and optimal functioning of older inmates, this understanding is important because mistakes in programming can prove to be costly in the long run. For instance, changes that affect the immune system of the elderly make these offenders more susceptible to illness and require them to be immunized or reimmunized against certain illnesses (Morton, 1992). This means that older inmates are vulnerable to tuberculosis and other contagious diseases and that they may need additional immunization.

As you may recall from Chapter 4, communicable diseases are a serious problem in many correctional agencies. Further, many agencies may not utilize widespread immunization because of cost factors. However, those agencies that have tight budgets should still consider using a form of "selective immunization" where the most at-risk offenders are identified and immunized. Failure to do this will simply ensure that prison medical bills for inmates with communicable diseases continue to rise beyond the already exorbitant costs that now exist. And the elderly inmate will be more at risk of getting and spreading any viruses passed throughout the institution, making the failure to immunize even more costly to the agency on a long-term basis. Thus, immunization of the elderly could save the agency substantial resources in the future.

Morton (1992) also points out that because of the physical aging process, prison systems need to survey facilities and see that precautions are taken to minimize the potential for falls. Contrasting colors between stair steps and risers can improve visibility and accommodate the needs of this population. Finally, things as simple as ensuring the availability of eye examinations and obtaining glasses that correctly fit can prevent the likelihood of future falls that will require expensive medical care to treat. Thus, having some form of medical prevention program can easily pay for itself in the reduction of projected losses due to injuries among elderly offenders.

In the area of mental health, one study found that roughly 15 to 25 percent of the elderly suffer from mental illness (Morton, 1992). This has been found to be true in research both in the United States and in other countries like Canada and the United Kingdom. In fact, some of the international research contends that mental illness may be as high as 50 percent for those over 60 and in custody of the criminal justice system (BBC News, 1999). This demonstrates that dealing with the elderly offender is a complicated, multifaceted issue that will require correctional systems (both institutional and community based) to provide some form of treatment since these offenders are not necessarily safe to be left on their own within society.

Among the forms of mental disorder or mental illness, depression has been found to be the most common mental disorder reported. The second most reported illness was dementia, which is associated with confusion, memory loss, and disorientation. The most serious form of dementia is Alzheimer's disease. **Dementia of the Alzheimer's type** is a serious concern for correctional systems because of its debilitating nature and the costs associated with treating it. The third most problematic disorder is associated with substance abuse, particularly relating to alcohol abuse. Since many of these offenders have a history of substance abuse, correctional systems will need to be prepared to address mental health problems in this area with the elderly offender.

As has been noted in previous chapters (Chapter 3 on substance abusers, Chapter 4 on communicable diseases, and Chapter 5 on mentally ill offenders), the substance abuse problem is often comorbid with a number of related disorders, each of which serves to debilitate the offender's ability to contend with other disorders. Add to this the problems associated with age (e.g., dementia), and you have a group of offenders with a cluster of interrelated problems that become ever more challenging because of deficits related to aging. Thus, correctional agencies will have a substantial challenge to contend with when dealing with their elderly population that is drawn from their career criminals.

Because of these challenges and because offenders tend to age out of crime, some may contend that it would simply be more logical to release many elderly offenders. This possibility has been considered in the states of California and Georgia (Jonsson, 2003). California has rejected the possibility of an early medical reprieve, but Georgia has released 49 already with plans to release more, depending on the circumstances (Jonsson, 2003). Within the state prison system of Georgia, it is estimated that the elderly population will exceed 6,000 by 2006 (Jonsson, 2003). Prison officials are increasingly concerned about the expenditures within the legal requirements to provide health care to inmates. A California study found that the cost of younger inmates was about $21,000 annually (Jonsson, 2003). This is compared to a price tag of about $60,000 for inmates over the age of 60 (Jonsson, 2003). In essence, the elderly population costs roughly three times that of the rest of the offender population to incarcerate (Jonsson, 2003).

However, despite the costs associated with elder offenders, prison officials are also worried about the accurate assessment of these inmates. In Georgia an inmate faked an infirmity that classified him as "wheelchair bound," only to leap out of his chair and sprint away when being wheeled to an appointment in the surrounding community (Jonsson, 2003). The inmate was apprehended within a short time with no incident, but risks such as these are what scare most correctional officials. In determining whether inmates should be released early in the community to alleviate the costliness of incarceration, a type of "functional assessment" has been suggested. This assessment generally determines whether infirm inmates are capable and likely of reoffending. But again, skepticism reigns among prison administrators in many state systems.

The worry associated with the potential dangerousness of elderly offenders is well founded given that some research shows that sex offenders are disproportionately at risk of having dementia. Indeed, it is thought that elderly sex offenders may have a form of dementia, called frontal lobe dementia, that affects their decision making. The offenders become reckless and sexually disinhibited, exposing themselves and approaching small children (BBC News, 1999). Given the public fears and outrage surrounding sex offending (and pedophilia in particular), it is understandable why correctional administrators are hesitant to release elderly offenders. This is especially true with those offenders who have been repetitive and/or violent violators of the law. Meanwhile, enhanced-penalty laws for habitual offenders and for offenders of specifically targeted crimes continue to incarcerate at an all-time high, resulting in the continued aging and crowding of the prison population in Georgia and throughout the United States.

When discussing elderly inmates, it becomes apparent that a "one-size-fits-all" approach will not adequately address the entire population. Indeed, the elderly offender population has different levels and types of criminal history that are important when making assessments related to public safety risks. From the offending patterns of elderly offenders, three basic typologies emerge: the elderly first-time offender, the habitual elderly offender, and the offender turned elderly in prison.

The rise in numbers of the **habitual elderly offender** and the **offender turned elderly in prison** has to do largely with the advent of "three-strikes" felony sentencing in many states (Anno, Graham, Lawrence, & Shansky, 2004). These sentences require that third-time felony offenders serve mandatory sentences of at least 25 years up to life. It should be noted that the felony does not necessarily mean that the offender is violent. Also adding to these statistics are the punitive sentencing measures associated with the War on Drugs of the 1980s and the 1990s where drug-using offenders were locked up at an all-time high regardless of whether the crime involved violence or any form of drug trafficking (Anno et al., 2004). Finally, 14 states and the Federal Bureau of Prisons have eliminated parole, and state laws have increasingly required "truth in sentencing" so that inmates are sure to serve at least 85 percent of their prison terms (Anno et al., 2004).

Thus, the habitual elderly offender and the offender turned elderly in prison are the result of a confluence of social factors and criminal justice policies. These offenders, for various reasons, have been given enhanced penalties that preclude their release in the community. This greatly distinguishes them from the **elderly first-time offender**, who does not share a similar criminogenic background. Although they may look the same while in inmate clothes in the prison facility, they are usually quite different from one another, and the public would be well served to keep this squarely in mind. States that have abolished parole and other community outlets may be well served to establish specialized court interventions for this type of offender. It is at this point that we turn our attention to the three typologies of elderly offenders.

ELDERLY FIRST-TIME OFFENDERS

It is estimated that approximately 50 percent of elderly inmates are first-time offenders, incarcerated when they were age 60 or older. New elderly offenders frequently commit crimes of passion. Conflicts in primary relationships appear to increase as social interactions diminish with age. Older first-time offenders often commit their offenses in a spontaneous manner that shows little planning but is instead an emotional reaction to perceived slights or disloyalties. These offenders do not typically view themselves as criminal per se but instead see their situation as unique and isolated from their primary identity. Elderly first-time offenders are those who commit their offense later in life. For those who commit violent crimes, these are usually crimes of passion rather than being premeditated.

It should be noted that many of these offenses may unfortunately be the simple product of biological factors associated with the aging process. The higher rates of dementia among the elderly population are thought to be a contributory causal explanation for acts that were otherwise nonexistent for the individual throughout one's earlier life. Rather, some forms of dementia are associated with a loss of inhibitory mechanisms (perhaps in the reticular activating system) in the brain. These losses of inhibitory ability mean that brain functions that regulated behavior cease to function correctly. The resulting behavior is often manifested in odd and illegal forms of sexual behavior, inflexibility, paranoia, and even aggression.

It should be noted that first-time offenders are more likely to be sentenced for violent offenses. These offenses will usually be directed at a family member because of proximity if nothing else. Some experience crises of one sort or another because of disparity regarding the aging process; this is also thought to instill a sense of abandonment and resentfulness that may lead to aberrant forms of coping. In addition, sexual offenses involving children are common among the first-time offending elderly. It should be noted that in the Tennessee prison system, nearly a third of older inmates were incarcerated for sex crimes. For persons over the age of 65, aggravated assault is the violent offense most often committed, followed by murder (Aday, 1994).

The new elderly inmate probably was already maladjusted in society and was probably not good at changing with environmental demands. Other characteristics include a volatile personality and the propensity for suicide. These individuals were probably likely to have had mental health problems earlier in life, and they are probably the type to withdraw when possible (Aday, 1994). These offenders are also the most likely to be victimized in prison, as their irascible behavior and demeanor is likely to draw the attention of younger inmates rather than providing any form of deterrence from victimization within the institutional setting (Aday, 1994). These offenders are the most likely to have strong community ties and therefore are usually the most amenable to community supervision.

HABITUAL ELDERLY OFFENDERS

Habitual elderly offenders have a long history of crime and also have a prior record of imprisonment throughout their lives. These offenders are usually able to adjust well to prison life because they have been in and out of the environment throughout a substantial part of their lives. Thus, they are well suited and adjusted to prison life. They are also a good source of support for first-time offenders and, if administrators are wise enough to implement this, are able to act as mentors for these first-time offenders. These offenders typically have substance abuse problems and other chronic problems that make coping with life on the outside difficult. Some of these inmates are not considered violent but instead serve several shorter sentences for lesser types of property crimes. Such offenders are the most likely to end up as geriatric inmates who die in prison.

OFFENDER TURNED ELDERLY IN PRISON

Offenders turned elderly in prison have grown old in prison, have long histories in the system, and are the least likely to be discipline problems. Long-term offenders are very difficult to place on release because they have few ties in the community and limited vocational background from which to earn a living. These offenders are often afraid to leave the prison and go back to the outside world because they have become so institutionalized within the predictable schedule of the prison. This also means that suicide may be considered among these individuals, particularly prior to release or even within a short time after release. This phenomenon is no different from that noted in the classic movie *The Shawshank Redemption*, which portrays a released inmate who cannot cope with life on the outside, choosing instead to end his life prematurely by a self-hanging suicide.

GENERAL CHARACTERISTICS OF ELDERLY OFFENDERS

Elderly offenders are a special population in terms of their criminal patterns, health care needs, individual adjustment to institutional living, and difficulties within their own families of origin. On the average, elderly inmates tend to score lower on IQ tests. It is not clear whether there is something unique to this population since the offending population tends to score lower on IQ tests than nonoffending persons or whether the aging process has simply caused deficits in IQ for this population. Among habitual elderly offenders and offenders turned elderly in prison, there tends to be history of part-time employment or unemployment and an unstable family life due to alcohol abuse. The combination of joblessness, lack of family ties, and alcohol abuse increases the likelihood of criminal behavior. This is more true among the elderly than it is among younger offenders.

Older offenders who commit violent crimes are likely to be unmarried males and non-Caucasian with lower socioeconomic status and fewer dependents. Most of the characteristics of elderly inmates are similar to those of inmates in general. However, elderly offenders tend to withdraw into themselves because of the lack of privacy in most prisons. Aging inmates may feel frightened, may be ridiculed, and may be anxious. They become more dependent on and cooperative with the prison staff for protection because they can no longer compete physically with younger inmates. Indeed, these offenders may be singled out by younger inmates and may indeed find themselves substantially threatened by younger inmates. Morton (2000) notes that in

Florida, elderly inmates experienced more interpersonal problems with other inmates than they had with staff. While these offenders do eventually adapt to prison life, they do present with high levels of stress and feelings of hopelessness about their future. Death and loss are very real fears that must be dealt with routinely, and they are doubly hard to assuage given the environment in which they are placed.

GERIATRIC OFFENDERS BEHIND BARS

During the past decade, the number of elderly and infirm inmates in state prison systems has increased substantially (Anno et al., 2004). During the eight-year period between 1992 and January 1, 2001, the number of state and federal inmates age 50 and older has increased from 41,586 to 113,358, equaling an amazing 172.6 percent increase (Anno et al., 2004). It is important to again reiterate that this population had nearly tripled in just eight years (see Special Insert 14.2).

Special Insert 14.2. Facts on Aging Prison Populations in Various States

- There were over 5,000 inmates in California over the age of 55 in 1999.
- In Florida, the elderly inmate population over 50 years of age was 5,873 in 2000.
- Louisiana reported 2,099 inmates over the age of 50 in 2000. This amounts to about 14. 1 percent of that state's inmate population, meaning that this state had the highest percentage of elderly inmates in the nation.
- In New York, there were 4,369 inmates over the age of 50 representing 12 percent of the entire state inmate population.
- Kentucky reported 1,106 inmates in 2000. This was approximately 8.4 percent of its entire inmate population.
- Ohio reported 3,346 inmates who were 50 or older in 2000. This was about 7 percent of the prison population.
- In Texas, there were 4,790 inmates over 55 years of age in 1998, representing roughly 3.7 percent of that state's inmate population. It is projected to increase by 121 percent between 1998 and 2008, growing to over 10,601 inmates, representing approximately 8.2 percent of the overall inmate population in 2008.
- The Federal Bureau of Prisons had 13,833 inmates who were 50 years of age or older in 1999. This amounts to almost 12 percent of the inmate population being classified as elderly.
- In Canada, the elderly offender population doubled between 1990 and 1998. There were approximately 3,752 offenders aged 50 or over in 2000.

Source: Adapted from State of Maryland Commission on Criminal Sentencing (2001).

According to Anno et al. (2004), in 1992 inmates who were 50 years of age and older accounted for 5.7 percent of the total national prison population. By 2001, elderly inmates accounted for 7.9 percent of the national population. Such growth is both phenomenal and a source of serious concern for correctional administrators who are concerned about the cost that elderly inmates incur on their facilities. Further, this concern is compounded by the fact that while in the prison, these offenders are the least problematic with regard to behavior management.

Research on the disciplinary behavior of elderly offenders seems to indicate that elderly offenders tend to have fewer problems with conflict or disruption than offenders who are in the early stages of life (Vito & Wilson, 1985). However, elderly offenders do tend to present with more emotional problems than younger offenders, which implies that their state of mental health is much more impaired than younger offenders. However, it has been found that elderly offenders are less socially deviant, less impulsive, and less hostile than young offenders. This was especially true for those elderly offenders who had first been incarcerated at a young age (Teller & Howell, 1981).

It should be noted that the amount of time elderly offenders have to serve substantially affects their ability to maintain contacts within the outside community. This can then affect the manner in which they socialize with inmate groups within the prison. Indeed, the longer the length of incarceration, the more distance that will develop between them and their contacts in the community. This typically results in elderly offenders becoming much more dependent on the correctional agency since they lack the family support network that exists for many elderly persons. When the length of sentence impairs their previous view of themselves, they will go through a period of dissonance as they become familiar with their new social groups, their new role within these groups, and their own sense of identity within the prison setting.

Many older offenders who serve prolonged sentences behind bars begin to develop a form of **institutional dependency**. Such dependency is defined as the process whereby the elderly inmate exchanges his or her prior life identity with a prison-based identity with reference groups changing from outside friends and family to those persons within the institution. More institutional dependency has been observed among unmarried older offenders, those incarcerated earlier in their lives, and chronic recidivists. This is not surprising since these groups spend the most total time in prison and therefore have the best opportunity to normalize the prison environment (Aday & Webster, 1979). Some researchers have examined elderly offenders and their adjustment to prison and have found some degree of satisfaction among older offenders who have become institutionally dependent. These offenders appear to develop strategies of coping that allow them to deal with the pains of imprisonment with little distress (Wooden & Parker, 1980).

The tendency to develop institutional dependency is understandable, but it likewise creates numerous management problems, as correctional administrators must address issues concerning the elderly inmate's vulnerability to abuse and predation and their difficulty in establishing social relationships with younger inmates (Anno et al., 2004). These social factors tend to aggravate the already difficult process of meeting the needs for special physical accommodations in a fairly rigid environment (Anno et al., 2004). In addition, the elderly offender has a greater need for peace, quiet, and privacy, which are rare commodities in prison life. This puts them in further conflict with the prison regimen and creates more specialized needs for correctional administrators to accommodate if they desire a smooth-running facility. The elderly inmate requires assistance in coping with the fast pace, noise, and confusion of modern life itself regardless of whether they are in a prison or in the community (Anno et al., 2004). These offenders also often feel intimidated and vulnerable around the younger offender population, and conflict between the young and old is increasing within many prison systems (Anno et al., 2004).

It has been speculated that victimization and the fear of victimization have become serious problems for elderly offenders. These offenders are more susceptible to being coerced into compliance than are more robust, younger offenders. While these offenders may cope with the pains of the imprisonment process itself, they may be unable to defend themselves effectively from the brutality of other inmates. The susceptibility to victimization can cause substantial difficulty for prison administrators, so questions regarding the most suitable form of accommodation often begin to emerge with this group. Thus, debates on age segregation as opposed to age integration have developed among experts on elderly offenders. **Age segregation** is the view that elderly offenders should be incarcerated separately from younger offenders. On the other hand, **age integration** is the view that all inmates should be incarcerated in mixed environments with no concern over the age of the offenders who are incarcerated together. It has been reported that most older offenders find living with younger offenders stressful because younger offenders are often loud and assaultive (Uzoaba, 1998).

Advocates of the age segregation of elderly inmates do not necessarily stop with concerns over physical safety. Those in favor of age segregation often seek to improve the situation for elderly offenders in other areas of general well-being as well. These advocates contend that age-specific groups by the older offenders may increase self-esteem for the elderly offender and may also decrease feelings of depression for these offenders (Uzoaba, 1998). Overall, it is expected that if these inmates are free of concerns over their general physical welfare and safety, their mental health will improve as well. This is not surprising since other theorists on human motivation and well-being have made similar contentions. The contentions of Abraham Maslow would agree with the notion that basic physiological needs for these offenders must be met if they are to have a sense of belonging during incarceration. It is thought that if elderly inmates have a general sense of well-being, then they will be less prone to have costly physical and mental health problems for the administration.

Naturally, if the facility were safe from assault from the remaining inmate population, then medical expenses would be less costly. Likewise, facilities that have adequate adjustments in lighting, stairways, and other features for the disabled will also prevent injury that can cost the agency an enormous amount of money. In addition, if the elderly inmate's mental health is kept stable, they are less likely to be problematic for administrators as possible disciplinary problems. Thus, preventing their ill health and providing for adequate services to this population can save problems for correctional agencies in the long term. Regardless of whether the elderly inmate is placed in a specific age-segregated facility or whether they are dispersed throughout the prison system, it is important that facilities meet the various special needs of the elderly inmate both in the interest of conserving financial resources and in the interest of prison security. So that correctional agencies are better able to meet these needs, an adequate method of classifying these offenders on the basis of need must be implemented. Although this may sound obvious, it is often underestimated within the overstuffed world of corrections that currently exists in the United States.

CLASSIFICATION OF ELDERLY OFFENDERS

Perhaps the first step in ensuring than any offender's needs are appropriately met is through the process of assessment. This assessment then must classify the elderly offender into categories that will ensure that the right standard of care is given to the correct inmate. This accomplishes three goals: (1) it ensures that the inmate receives adequate care, (2) it ensures that precious resources are not wasted on inmates not needing more intensive care, and (3) it provides a guide when deciding on housing and security levels for offenders to protect them and others from possible harm. The Ohio Department of Rehabilitation and Correction uses a screening process in which a nurse performs a complete medical and mental health check within 14 days of intake. This screening includes the following:

1. An overall medical history
2. A physical exam
3. Numerous diagnostic tests
4. Tests for communicable diseases
5. Hearing and vision checks
6. Substance use and abuse history
7. Mental health screening
8. Suicide screening
9. A comprehensive health history

On completion of the physical exam, a physician will classify the inmate according to medical need (Anno et al., 2004). These classifications are discussed in the following paragraphs.

Class 1 elderly offenders are basically healthy inmates who may be sent to any institution (Anno et al., 2004). Their housing and security classifications are essentially unimpaired by health effects of their elderly status. In fact, if these offenders are themselves assaultive, appropriate action (administrative segregation) should be taken for the safety of other inmates.

Class 2 elderly offenders are medically stable but require routine follow-up care and examinations, such as those with chronic illnesses (Anno et al., 2004). These individuals can also be housed in almost all institutions. As with class 1 offenders, class 2 housing and security classifications are essentially unimpaired by health effects of their elderly status. Likewise, if these offenders are themselves assaultive, appropriate action (administrative segregation) should be taken for the safety of other inmates; however, delivery of appropriate medical services will need to be brought to the inmates' cell or dormitory since they do have some health considerations that class 1 inmates do not share.

Class 3 elderly offenders require frequent intensive skilled medical care but can maintain their own activities of daily living. These would include patients on dialysis; those with severe lung disease, HIV, or AIDS; paraplegics; or those undergoing cancer treatment (Anno et al., 2004). These inmates should be housed only at special facilities designed to meet these extensive medical needs. They will seldom be a security risk to other inmates but are themselves at increased risk of being victimized.

Class 4 elderly offenders include inmates who require constant skilled medical care and assistance with activities of daily living. This includes those who require convalescent hospitalization. In this category would be unstable diabetics, advanced cases of HIV, quadriplegics, and inmates with terminal medical illnesses (Anno et al., 2004). These inmates should be housed only in some form of a correctional medical center. They will almost never be a security risk to other inmates but are themselves at increased risk of being victimized.

It is also important to note that any classification system for elderly inmates should include a protocol that distinguishes between inmates who entered the prison system before age 50 and those who reached that age while in prison. In essence, the data should note clearly and prominently if the offender falls within the category of an elderly first-time offender, a habitual elderly offender, or an offender turned elderly in prison. This is an important security consideration that most correctional administrators will find useful when running their institutions. Once the elderly offender has been appropriately classified and any necessary security precautions are resolved, prison staff will then be able to adequately ensure that the needs of these offenders are met. With continually changing legal requirements pertaining to disabilities, and the sobering reality that elderly offenders are increasing at a phenomenal rate, it will become increasingly important that facilities adequately meet the various special needs of the older disabled population. Two specific instances in which this has become a primary concern have to do with the Americans with Disabilities Act and concern for the terminally ill inmate. These two issues will be addressed in the following sections.

THE AMERICANS WITH DISABILITIES ACT

Uzoaba (1998) notes that in the United States, correctional administrators are compelled by law to comply with the provisions of the **Americans with Disabilities Act** (ADA). This act grants certain rights to citizens of the United States who are incarcerated. The act has been the catalyst to a legal landslide of cases claiming that negligent care had been delivered by various prison systems in the United States (Goetting, 1985; Uzoaba, 1998). The purpose of the ADA was clearly articulated by Congress. Among other things, two key purposes that apply to this chapter were the following:

1. To provide a clear and comprehensive national mandate for the elimination of discrimination against individuals with disabilities
2. To provide clear, strong, consistent, enforceable standards addressing discrimination against individuals with disabilities

Although the ADA has two separate titles, it is Title II of the act that is most applicable to inmates. This section involves physical plant conditions as well as access to programs and services. It is often the physical plant issues that most concern correctional administrators because they have the potential for exceeding the capacity of already tight budgets. Although the overall spending for corrections has increased along with the number of inmates throughout the nation, it has been found that even these larger budgets do not cover the specialized facilities and services required for facilities designed for the elderly and/or disabled. The main problems are with the cost to renovate already existing facilities since it is often the case that building a new facility with all the features required by the ADA is cheaper than modifying older buildings. Equipment to accommodate this population and the physical modifications needed for existing facilities can result in tight operating budgets being stretched beyond their imaginable limits.

To provide guidance to state and local governments concerning standards that should be met, the U.S. Architectural and Transportation Barriers Compliance Board has proven useful. This board generated what are referred to as the **Americans with Disabilities Accessibility Guidelines** (ADAAG). These guidelines apply to all facilities that were newly built or altered since 1992. However, it should be noted that the act does not require such changes if making programs and services accessible creates an undue administrative or financial burden to the correctional agency.

Appel (1999) makes note of several accommodations that are considered reasonable to allow for access to facilities and participation in programs and services for inmates. Appel points out the following requirements (among others) illustrated in the ADAAG as follows:

1. In general inmate housing areas, at least 3 percent of cells must be accessible to inmates with disabilities, and the cells should not all be in one special area.

2. In special housing areas, such as for protective custody, disciplinary detention, administrative segregation, detoxification, or medical isolation, there must be an additional accessible cell in each of these areas.
3. Noncontact visiting areas must have at least 5 percent of the cubicles accessible to both the inmate and staff, with at least 27 to 29 inches of clear knee space, and they must be at least 36 inches wide.
4. To be accessible to someone in a wheelchair, entrance doors must have at least 32-inch-wide clear travel space.
5. Water fountains must have spouts not higher than 36 inches, and the flow must be across the front of the fountain.

As can be seen, these are detailed guidelines, and correctional administrators will have to ensure compliance to evade liability. The challenge of providing activities and services that meet the needs of elderly inmates requires a new dimension of thinking (Anno et al., 2004). Anno et al. (2004) state that "as the inmate population ages, administrators need to consider special architecture, such as grab bars in cells, showers, and toilets; elevated toilet seats, stools, or benches in showers; and improved access to toilet facilities" (p. vii). In addition, consideration should be provided to ensuring that inmate programs are also accessible. This can often be accomplished by simply moving the location of a program to an accessible area, providing sign language and/or Braille assistance, running computers to open education programs to all inmates, and providing books on tape in the libraries.

Access to specific programs, such as education, addiction treatment, and vocational training, can result in increased satisfaction and health while in the prison. Further, participation in these functions can increase the offender's likelihood of receiving early discharge through good-time accumulation, and this participation can improve the prognosis of the offender's later integration into the community. Because of these factors, implementing the ADA requirements may be prudent for correctional administrators to follow beyond the simple legal liabilities involved. Indeed, incorporation of these accommodations beyond the bare minimal requirements may also serve to ultimately improve the plight of corrections in the future if these problems are addressed in a proactive manner. As Appel (1999) notes, the ADA is the law, and in much more than a monetary manner, compliance with the ADA is a classic case of "pay me now or pay me even more later." Thus, the long-term benefits for the wise correctional administrator will likely offset any of the short-term costs that are paid in the meantime.

THE CHRONICALLY AND TERMINALLY ILL INMATE

The growing number of elderly inmates with chronic and terminal illnesses affects correctional administrators in several ways. The annual cost of incarcerating this population has increased to nearly $70,000 for each elderly inmate compared to about

$27,000 for younger inmates kept in the general population. It is important to note that the elderly, the chronically ill, and the terminally ill overlap considerably. Thus, it is nearly impossible to discuss chronic or terminal illness without mentioning the elderly, and it is just as difficult to discuss the elderly inmate without noting chronic illnesses and terminal illnesses. For purposes of this chapter, **chronically ill inmates** are those inmates with an ongoing or recurring illness that requires that they be monitored closely to maintain their health status or to slow the progression of their disease or condition; examples include asthma, hepatitis C, heart disease, and diabetes. **Terminally ill inmates** are defined as those inmates who are known to have a fatal disease and have fewer than six months to live. To understand the magnitude of the health care problems pertaining to the chronic and terminally ill in prisons, consider the following:

1. In the prison system of New York, it has been found that the elderly inmates in their stay have an average of three chronic illnesses that must be treated during their incarceration (Greco, 2004).
2. In Texas, roughly 190 inmates over age 65 receive continual around-the-clock nursing care.
3. In Louisiana, inmates of Angola prison help care for the dying since they are often the only friends and family of the inmate. Scenes where coffins are carried by horse and buggy and are followed by praying inmates on their way to the prison cemetery are now a fairly frequent sight at this prison.

In 2000, approximately 18 percent of inmates in the Federal Bureau of Prisons were reported as being under care because of serious chronic illness. Common medical problems that were cited included diabetes, asthma, heart disease, HIV, and AIDS. Health care concerns regarding communicable diseases have been discussed extensively in Chapter 4, but the problems noted in that chapter are even more compounded and severe for the elderly population. Because it is clear that elderly inmates have considerably greater health care needs than younger inmates, prison administrators will have to contend with these costs.

Because elderly offenders have an increased risk of having one or more chronic diseases as well as the debilitating conditions that often go hand in hand with the aging process, elderly inmates should be placed in institutions that provide the full spectrum of health care services (Anno et al., 2004). This should include access to health care staff and emergency care 24 hours a day, seven days a week, including access to specialty medical services. Further, some of these offenders may be too frail or weak to attend to their own activities of daily living (e.g., eating, bathing, and waste management), and these individuals will need assistance. Anno et al. (2004) note that larger correctional agencies are developing nursing home environments to care for the frail elderly who require such extensive assistance. Finally, elderly inmates most often need different types of devices to aid them in maintaining functionality. Many agencies must provide walkers and/or canes, hearing aids, dentures, eyeglasses, supportive devices, warmer clothing, and extra blankets to elderly inmates (Anno et al., 2004).

All these services begin to sound as if the prison has become nothing short of a nursing home. It may well be that elderly offenders, particularly elderly first-time offenders, are not dangerous and that they are appropriate for early elderly compassionate release. **Early elderly compassionate release** refers to any program that is designed to place incarcerated elderly offenders in the community because of considerations regarding medical illness and the services involved with that illness. This has certain appeal when one considers the cost associated with keeping them incarcerated. If nonviolent elderly offenders over the age of 55 are released from state and federal prisons, the savings to correctional budgets have been estimated to be at least $900 million dollars during the first year of release alone. Such savings are phenomenal and would not jeopardize public safety if only used with those offenders who committed their first offense at an advanced age. For habitual offenders and those who grow old behind bars, the age of release could simply be raised to 60 or 65 to ensure that they are not capable of committing more crimes and to improve screening and assessment in the interest of public safety. From these groups, if the age was left at 65 and offenders at this point were released to community supervision, the cost savings is estimated to be another $175,000 per year.

It is important to keep in mind that these offenders selected for elderly early release would not simply be released on their own recognizance within the community. They would all be under community supervision, and those who were prior habitual offenders not only would be released later in the life span but also could (and should) be given more stringent parole supervision to include GPS tracking and/or electronic monitoring and citizen volunteers (see Chapter 15). These offenders can even provide community service at convalescent homes when they do not present a security risk, and some might even be able to obtain part-time employment to further offset costs. Thus, the threat to the public safety can be greatly minimized while providing humane alternatives to an elderly population that is better served outside the prison walls. The National Center on Institutions and Alternatives (2004) makes the following recommendations when formulating policy on possible elderly early release programs:

1. Release those who are 65 years of age or older
2. Release only those who were committed because of a nonviolent offense
3. Release those elderly offenders who have served a substantial part of their sentence (defined as one-third or more)
4. Release only those who are deemed to not present a significant risk to the community

Since some cases may warrant early release and since this may be prudent for many correctional administrators, programs should be developed that initially handle only a few released inmates, and these programs should be allowed to develop in a slow manner to ensure that public safety is not compromised. One program dedicated to the release of elderly inmates is known as the **Project for Older Prisoners** (POPS). This program was founded at the Tulane Law Center in Louisiana but is now directed from Washington, D.C. POPS uses volunteer law students to study cases of older inmates and determines whether they are safe to release. The program will not accommodate sex offenders or first-degree murderers.

It should be noted that POPS is very selective in the cases that it will accept. It is estimated that only about 10 percent of inmates interviewed are allowed elderly early release, and this is good, as it demonstrates that the screening and early release protocols need not result in the common fear that the "flood gates" will be opened for these offenders. Elderly candidates must be at least 55 years of age and must have already served the average amount of time typically served for their offense (again, a very stringent requirement). One other interesting point is that the victim or the victim's family is contacted, and their consent must be obtained if the inmate is to be released.

There is another point that is important to note regarding POPS. This program utilizes volunteers who provide the full range of services in determining release. In Chapter 15, it will become apparent that the use of volunteers is a strongly advocated approach within this book and within the therapeutic jurisprudence movement that is supported by this book. In fact, the POPS program is an excellent example of what therapeutic jurisprudence can offer to the correctional system, and it also demonstrates how this approach can be instrumental in solving problems associated with some categories of special needs offenders. The concept of therapeutic justice is discussed at length in Chapter 15, and it would be wise to refer back to the present chapter and other chapter readings (Chapter 3 on substance-abusing offenders and Chapter 5 on mentally disordered offenders) when reading Chapter 15. Finally, the fact that POPS contacts the victims and utilizes their input as primary in the decision-making process means that POPS also falls under the umbrella of restorative justice, which is another central approach to addressing special needs offenders and is also discussed in Chapter 15.

MAINTENANCE OF FAMILY CONTACT

It is important to understand that outside family contacts are a significant source of support for any inmate when they are in prison. Although they may have distance between themselves and their families, they will have the emotional security of knowing that someone does in fact care. They also know that there is something to return to when their prison sentence expires. This is can be important for inmates who value their families of origin. For offenders who come from disjointed or nonexistent families, this is not as likely to be true; thus, for the habitual elderly offender or the offender turned elderly in prison, this is not likely to be a significant factor since many of their family connections are likely to have been disrupted during their criminogenic past. Indeed, their families could be criminogenic and thus may simply perpetuate the problems for most of these offenders and their reform. Although these offenders may find the family support emotionally helpful, their odds of reforming are nonetheless impaired, and they are therefore likely to remain within the purview of the criminal justice systems. However, for elderly first-time offenders, the likelihood of having family bonds is much greater. Consequently, elderly first-time offenders are more likely to be negatively impacted by the distance imposed between them and their families.

For all offenders, their contact with family members is reduced to interactions via structured and supervised short visits, phone call privileges, and in some cases an occasional furlough. Even these forms of contact can be eliminated if the behavior of the inmate allows for disciplinary restriction of these privileges. Contact through the mail is an option, but even in this case the strain on marriages from such a limited form of communication can cause relationships to break. Further, the length of the sentence tends to be correlated with the likelihood of the relationship ending or being impaired. Thus, family unity and stability are greatly impaired, and this is precisely why those elderly offenders who have been in and out of prison throughout their lives are better adjusted; that is, they have already become acquainted with the lack of support.

Common reactions among elderly first-time offenders may include differing forms of withdrawal from the rest of the prison population (along with long-term depression and even possible suicide, depending on the type of loss and the personality of the inmate), or it may result in the inmate seeking out support from within the prison subculture. This support seeking can lead to institutional dependency since these inmates will have little else to turn to. Further, it is known (and even portrayed in some Hollywood films, such as *The Shawshank Redemption*) that older offenders with no support in the community who have been incarcerated for lengthy periods of time are likely to be apprehensive about their return and are at increased risk of suicide.

Thus, the ability of elderly offenders to maintain contact with persons outside the prison is very important (Uzoaba, 1998). Failure to ensure that relations of this sort are fostered affects their mental health within the prison and impairs their reintegration success once released. Uzoaba (1998) notes that if an elderly offender's crime involved a member of his family (especially with some form of sex offense), then it is not likely that he will receive visits or correspondence from the family. If an elderly offender also has problems with literacy, then there will be no ability to even maintain mail contact. Further, even if the offender is later released, his advanced age, coupled with his illiteracy, makes it all but impossible for that offender to truly reintegrate within the community. All this is important because it has been shown that offenders adjust better and reintegrate into the community more effectively if they maintain positive social contacts with family and friends in the community (Kratcoski & Pownall, 1989; Uzoaba, 1998). Thus, maintaining such contacts may alleviate a further decline in the health of these prisoners and the subsequent prison cost that is involved. Further, their likely reintegration into the community is enhanced, particularly among elderly first-time offenders. It is important that elderly first-time offenders be allowed to maintain such contacts if at all possible since this is the group that is most affected by separation and, ironically, the group that has the most incentive to reform on release.

GERIATRIC OFFENDERS IN THE COMMUNITY

Elderly offenders have the lowest rate of recidivism (Morton, 2001). One study reported that 45 percent of offenders ages 18 to 29 commit a new crime after release from prison, while only 3.2 percent of those over the age of 55 commit a new crime. In the state of New York's prison system, statistics that correlate age and recidivism show the following for each age-group:

Age	Likelihood of Recidivism
16–18	70.0%
45–49	26.6%
50–64	22.1%
65 and older	7.4%

According to Morton (2000), one option to consider with elderly offenders is an early release program that targets elderly prisoners who no longer pose a threat to society. Low-risk inmates may be suitable for special parole. Inmates having a moderate level of risk to the community might be able to be released but could be required to stay under electronic supervision. It is important that such electronic monitoring be carefully planned and implemented in the interest of both the community and the offender.

PREPRISON COMMUNITY SUPERVISION (PROBATION)

Because most elderly offenders do not commit serious crimes and because their rate of recidivism is low, they are perhaps good candidates for probation. However, this does not apply to habitually elderly offenders or offenders turned elderly in prison. Rather, it is expected that elderly first-time offenders will be the only elderly inmates who will be candidates for probation. This may even be true if they have committed a nonsexual violent crime that is in the "heat of passion" since these types of offenders are not likely to recidivate and these types of offenses do not usually reflect the true nature of the offender's psyche. This is important since it confirms that at least this subgroup of elderly offenders consists of good candidates for reintegration.

It is likewise true that the elderly first-time offender is likely to have immediate family support. This is particularly true if the offender did not commit a sex crime (particularly pedophilia, which has been noted as a problem among male geriatric offenders). It is the recommendation of this book that elderly offenders who have committed an act of pedophilia should be given incarceration because they have a poor treatment prognosis and are also the least likely to have family support.

For elderly offenders convicted of other types of crimes, the use of community supervision is an ideal way to process that group of offenders. This is true because of their lack of institutional dependency since they were ostensibly not in jail long enough to internalize the coping mechanisms associated with elderly offenders who are incarcerated for long periods of time. In addition, these offenders are more likely to have family support of one type or another. Thus, their less serious offending, their lack of being institutional dependent, and their likelihood of family support make the elderly first-time offender a better-than-average risk for release on probation.

POSTPRISON COMMUNITY SUPERVISION (PAROLE)

It is suggested that community supervision agencies work closely with the Social Security Administration to ensure that elderly offenders on community supervision are certified as eligible to draw benefits in a timely manner on release. Referrals to long-term care and assisted-living facilities and eligibility determinations for Medicaid should also be conducted. Finally, the task of finding a job is particularly difficult for the nonoffending elderly population, so this will naturally be problematic for offenders just released. Community supervision agencies should develop a community-based program that attempts to link these offenders with a job so that subsistence is at least moderately covered.

However, problems with motivation do often emerge with geriatric offenders. It is thought that older offenders are often hard to motivate because of their bleak perceptions of their future prospects. Some researchers have contended that educational and vocational programs have limited usefulness with these offenders (Wiegand & Burger, 1979). Further, many elderly offenders have few support systems (as discussed earlier), no permanent place to live, and serious health problems and tend to be harder to employ (Wiegand & Burger, 1979). Because of these drawbacks, they are often considered poor prospects for most comprehensive reintegration programs since it is viewed that these offenders are simply beyond assisting. Rather, these offenders are often inclined to simply wait for their ultimate demise, watching one day pass into the next with a depressive mood that undermines their ability to perform any of the necessary functions required by community supervision programs. As noted earlier in this chapter, elderly offenders who have spent long periods of time behind bars tend to have fewer living friends or family members who can lend assistance to their transition within the community. Many of these friends and/or family may have since died or moved on with their lives, having left the elderly offender on his own during years past. Thus, these offenders may be difficult to reintegrate.

In addition, parole from prison is usually contingent on good institutional adjustment, which is often demonstrated by participation in various programs within the prison institution. This type of participation is associated with improvements in risk management, improvement in behaviors and attitudes, and so on. Since most elderly offenders do not take active part in many prison programs, they may not be readily eligible for community release. Because of these and other reasons, elderly offenders have a less favorable prognosis and therefore do not obtain community release from prison any more than the average inmate; in actuality, they may receive it less. The result is that many elderly offenders do not even bother to apply for parole and instead consign themselves to ultimately dying within the institution.

Because of this, Uzoaba (1998) states that the parole system should recognize that elderly offenders are burdened with a double disadvantage: having a criminal record and an advanced age. Bias or ageism against elderly workers is itself a stigma difficult to overcome. Add to this a criminal conviction on record, and it makes it difficult for elderly offenders to gain economic stability while in the community.

Indeed, it may well be for some offenders with serious health care costs that prison becomes the preferred domicile. In fact, it may be speculated that just as the homeless have been known to commit petty crimes so that they can stay in jail during the winter months, elderly offenders may commit crimes later in life as a means of obtaining at least minimal medical care without enduring the financial burden. This may be particularly true if they have been unable to afford medical insurance, and this is likely to be the case for many of those offenders who have been recidivists. Although this may sound far-fetched, prison may be considered a feasible option for persons who are involved in a criminogenic subculture, particularly if they have been incarcerated in the past.

RECOMMENDATIONS FOR CORRECTIONAL AGENCIES WITH ELDERLY OFFENDERS

The appropriate programs should be available in locations that are physically accessible to the elderly offender (Uzoaba, 1998). These programs should be structured to facilitate the participation of older offenders rather than placing them in competition with younger offenders. Further, agency administrators should consider separating the basic education classes so that one group can be taught at a slower pace for older learners. This is important because elderly learners are at a disadvantage regarding short-term and quick-recall memory. Elderly learners experiencing retention problems because of their diminished short-term memory may be subjected to excessive ridicule by younger offenders. This can undermine any hope of getting these offenders to learn the skills that they will need to survive if they go on to live within the community. Thus, having separate classes will reduce the embarrassment and frustration that elderly offenders may feel when in the presence of younger offenders. In addition, many educators contend that learning for the elderly is improved and made more enjoyable if the teaching techniques are well designed to specifically meet their needs (Uzoaba, 1998).

Uzoaba (1998) states that correctional agencies should offer vocational programs incorporating arts and crafts geared to the needs of older offenders. These agencies should set aside specific areas for elderly offenders to read, play cards and checkers, and talk quietly to each other. Recreational programs should include activities that are geared toward maintenance of physiological health as well. Further,

Uzoaba (1998) points out that psychologists and counselors with special training in geriatrics should administer rehabilitation programs to ensure a greater awareness of the social, psychological, and emotional needs of these offenders (Goetting, 1983; Vito & Wilson, 1985). The need for specialized mental health professionals is great with elderly offenders. These professionals need to be well prepared to deal with offenders who present with dementia since dementia affects the elderly offender's ability to comply with supervision requirements.

Finally, Uzoaba (1998) provides several guidelines on training needs within many institutional and community-based supervision agencies. Specifically, he recommends that agencies offer specific training to custodial staff to more fully understand the social and emotional needs of older offenders, the dynamics of death and dying, the procedures for identifying depression, and a system for referring older offenders to experts in the community. Agencies should assess depressed offenders more frequently. Geriatric counselors should help older offenders make the transition to prison life. To facilitate the problems of handling older offenders, special in-service training geared to working with older offenders should be considered. Its objectives should be the following:

- To increase the staff awareness of their own biases and stereotyping regarding aging
- To provide basic gerontological information on the aging process and age-related problems
- To facilitate case management through improved communication and intergenerational skills
- To identify available community services and programs geared toward older offenders
- To provide the latest findings on age-related issues, such as sensory impairment, learning, memory, drug use and abuse, and health concerns (Hall, 1992)

CONCLUSION

From the statistics presented in numerous states, it would appear that elderly offenders will continue to be an increasingly serious concern for state and federal correctional agencies. This group of offenders is the fastest-growing group of offenders in the nation and is a virtual microcosm of the graying that is occurring throughout the rest of the nation. Correctional agencies will need to continue to provide services for this group of offenders because of legal requirements (such as the ADA) and fiscal considerations.

It should also be recognized that elder offenders are a diverse group both demographically and by the way that they are classified. This presents an even more difficult challenge in providing services to this group. This also makes it difficult to decide on housing considerations for these offenders within prison settings. Community supervision agencies are not as challenged if family networks are in place, but the ability of community supervision agencies to ensure adequate reintegration services is severely impaired with elderly offenders.

Typically, correctional programs are designed for younger offenders who have time in their life span to overcome some of the stigma associated with a criminal conviction. However, even beyond the concerns with stigma from having a conviction is the deviance from societal expectations of the elderly. Simply put, society does not expect the elderly to commit crimes, and thus society is often ill equipped to address issues surrounding such offenders. Both institutional and community corrections will need to increase and refine their services to the elderly or run the risk of creating either legal liability to the inmate or some form of public safety error with the community. Neither of these is a desirable option, making services for elderly offenders an even greater priority.

KEY TERMS

Elderly offender
Dementia of the Alzheimer's type
Habitual elderly offender
Offender turned elderly in prison
Elderly first-time offender
Institutional dependency
Age segregation
Age integration
Class 1–4 elderly offenders
Americans with Disabilities Act
Americans with Disabilities Accessibility Guidelines
Chronically ill inmates
Terminally ill inmates
Early elderly compassionate release
Project for Older Prisoners

REFERENCES

Aday, R. H. (1994). Aging in prison: A case study of new elderly offenders. *International Journal of Offender Therapy and Comparative Criminology, 38*(1), 121.

Aday, R. H., & Webster, E. L. (1979). Aging in prison: The development of a preliminary model. *Offender Rehabilitation, 3*(3), 271–282.

American Psychiatric Association. (2000). *Diagnostic and statistical manual of mental disorders* (4th ed., text revision). Arlington, VA: Author.

Anno, B. J., Graham, C., Lawrence, J. E., & Shansky, R. (2004). *Correctional health care: Addressing the needs of elderly, chronically ill, and terminally ill inmates*. Washington, DC: National Institute of Corrections.

Appel, A. (1999). Accommodating inmates with disabilities. In P. M. Carlson & J. S. Garrett (Eds.), *Prison and jail administration* (pp. 346–352). Gaithersburg, MD: Aspen.

BBC News. (1999). *Many elderly offenders "are mentally ill."* Retrieved from http://news.bbc.co.uk/1/hi/health/294252.stm

Fabelo, T. (1999). *Elderly offenders in Texas prisons*. Austin, TX: Department of Criminal Justice.

Goetting, A. (1985). Racism, sexism and ageism in the prison community. *Federal Probation, 54*(1), 10–22.

Greco, R. (2004). *Brief on older prisoner. New York: New York State Office for the Aging*. Retrieved from http://aging.state.ny.us/explore/project2015/briefs04.htm

Hall, J. (1992). *Managing the older offender*. Laurel, MD: American Correctional Association.

Johnson, E. H. (1988). Care for elderly inmates: Conflicting concerns and purposes in prisons. In R. McCarthy & D. Langworthy (Eds.), *Older Offenders* (pp. 268–283). New York: Praeger.

Jonsson, P. (2003). As prisoners age, should they go free? *Christian Science Monitor*. Retrieved from http://www.csmonitor.com/2003/0905/p01s01-usju.htm

Kratcoski, P. C., & Pownall, G. A. (1989, June). Federal Bureau of Prisons programming for older inmates. *Federal Probation, 53*(2), 28–35.

Morton, J. B. (1992). *An administrative overview of the older inmate*. Washington, DC: National Institute of Corrections.

Morton, J. B. (2001). Implication for corrections of an aging prison population. *Corrections Management Quarterly, 5*(1), 78–88.

National Center on Institutions and Alternatives. (2004). *Elderly study*. Retrieved from http://66.165.94.98/stories/eldst.pdf

Price, J. H. (2000). *Elderly and armed: Aging offenders*. Retrieved from http://www.findarticles.com/p/articles/mi_m1571/is_46_16/ai_72329012

State of Maryland Commission on Criminal Sentencing. (2001). Retrieved from http://www.msccsp.org/publications/aging.html

Teller, G., & Howell, R. (1981). The older prisoner: Criminal and psychological characteristics. *Criminology, 18*(4), 549–555.

Uzoaba, J. H. E. (1998). *Managing older offenders, where do we stand*? Montreal: Research Branch of Correctional Service of Canada.

Vito, G. F., & Wilson, D. G. (1985). Forgotten people: Elderly inmates. *Federal Probation, 49*, 18–24.

Wiegand, D., & Burger, J. C. (1979). The elderly offender and parole. *The Prison Journal, 59*(1), 48–57.

Wooden, W. S., & Parker, J. (1980). Aged men in a prison environment: Life satisfaction and coping strategies. *Gerontologist, 20*(1), 231–237.

LEARNING CHECK

1. These individuals are medically stable but require routine follow-up care and examinations, such as those with chronic illnesses.
   a. Class 1
   b. Class 2
   c. Class 3
   d. Class 4
   e. All of the above
2. The term "elderly offender" is used for inmates who are incarcerated at the turning-point age of ____________________ or later.
   a. 40
   b. 50
   c. 60
   d. 65
   e. 70

3. In 1990, it was found that among 179 "nonjustifiable" homicides committed by people age 60 and older, ______________________ had consumed alcohol before killing.
   a. 24%
   b. 34%
   c. 44%
   d. 54%
   e. None of the above

4. In the state of New York's prison system, statistics that correlate age and recidivism showed that ______________________ of inmates aged 50 to 64 were likely to commit another crime.
   a. 11.1%
   b. 29.1%
   c. 22.1%
   d. 34.1%

5. It is expected that elderly offenders, particularly first-time offenders, will continue to be a small minority of the criminal population.
   a. True
   b. False

6. The National Center on Institutions and Alternatives makes which of the following recommendations when formulating policy on possible elderly early release programs?
   a. Release those who are 65 years of age or older
   b. Release only those who were committed because of a nonviolent offense
   c. Release those elderly offenders who have served a substantial part of their sentence
   d. Release only those who are deemed to not present a significant risk to the community
   e. All of the above

7. It is the recommendation of this book that elderly offenders who have committed pedophilia be given incarceration because they have a poor treatment prognosis and are also the least likely to have family support.
   a. True
   b. False

8. This classification includes inmates who require constant skilled medical care and those who need assistance with activities of daily living.
   a. Class 1
   b. Class 2
   c. Class 3

d. Class 4
e. All of the above

9. ______________________ refers to any program that is designed to place incarcerated elderly offenders in the community because of considerations regarding medical illness and the services involved with that illness.
a. Early elderly compassionate release
b. Medical release for humanity
c. Medical reprieve for the terminally ill
d. Chronic illness release
e. None of the above

10. Assessment and classification to ensure that the right standard of care is given is designed to do which of the following?
a. Ensure that the inmate received adequate care
b. Ensure that precious resources are not wasted on inmates not needing more intensive care
c. Provide a guide when deciding housing and security levels for the offender to protect them and others from possible harm
d. All of the above
e. Both a and b but not c

ESSAY DISCUSSION QUESTIONS

1. Discuss the Project for Older Prisoners (POPS) program and explain whether you believe this is an effective method of early release for elderly offenders. Be sure to note which types of elderly offenders should be included in this program. Be sure to explain why by using elements of this chapter that support your answer.
2. Discuss the Americans with Disabilities Accessibility Guidelines (ADAAG) and how this impacts correctional administrators. In your opinion, do you think that correctional facilities should be required to provide the services recommended by these guidelines? Why or why not?
3. Identify and define the three types of elderly offenders. Compare and contrast each of these types of elderly offenders and explain how you would address each of these when providing correctional supervision.
4. Explain why assessment and classification of elderly offenders is so important. Provide a brief overview of the four classes of elderly offenders. Why are these considerations important for the elderly offender? Does society stand to benefit from correctly distinguishing between each class of elderly offender?

CHAPTER 15

RESTORATIVE JUSTICE AND SPECIAL NEEDS OFFENDERS

Chapter Objectives

1. Know and understand the basic tenets and concepts of restorative justice.
2. Demonstrate an understanding of how restorative justice can be ideally suited for processing many types of special needs offenders.
3. Understand how the community becomes involved in the supervision and the treatment process of special needs offenders. Discuss the various forms of community support for this type of case processing.
4. Understand the connections between therapeutic jurisprudence and restorative justice. Understand how intermediate sanctions provide a flexible range of sanctions that assist advocates of therapeutic jurisprudence and restorative justice in implementing effective supervision and treatment plans.
5. Identify, define, and discuss the various types of specialized courts that are evolving for many types of special needs offenders.

INTRODUCTION

For many people, the suitability of restorative justice applications to special needs offenders may not be immediately clear. Indeed, many people may not truly understand what is meant by the term "restorative justice." Likewise, many people may likewise be uninformed of the specific issues facing certain groups of offenders. Finally, the specific reasons for using this application with special needs offenders may not be readily apparent. Thus, this chapter will introduce the student to the notion of restorative justice and the reasons that this orientation should be considered. This chapter will also note some specific types of offenders (all discussed in the preceeding chapters) who might benefit from such an orientation. Finally, the interests of the victim and the community will be presented as being compatible with the interests and needs of specialized offenders.

The definition used for restorative justice is borrowed from researcher and advocate Thomas Quinn from his interview with the National Institute of Justice (1998). The definition provided by Quinn will be the working definition of **restorative justice** throughout this chapter. Specifically, restorative justice is a term for interventions that focus on restoring the health of the community, repairing the harm done, meeting victim's needs, and emphasizing that the offender can and must contribute to those repairs. Restorative justice considers the victims, communities, and offenders (in that order) as participants in the justice process. These participants are placed in active roles to work together to do the following:

- Empower victims in their search for closure
- Impress on offenders the real human impact of their behavior
- Promote restitution to victims and communities

Dialogue and negotiation are central to restorative justice, and problem solving for the future is seen as more important than simply establishing blame for past behavior. According to Van Ness (2002), this means that different approaches may be needed than those offered by typical criminal justice programs. These approaches might include mediation, conferencing, restitution, official apology, and other forms of amends. Van Ness (2002) contends that there are **nine components of restorative justice**:

1. Meeting of all the parties involved
2. Communication between the parties involved
3. Agreement or consensus between the parties involved
4. Apology provided by the offender to the victim and/or community
5. Restitution made from the offender to the victim
6. Change in the offender's behavior
7. Respect shown to all parties
8. Assistance provided to any party that needs it
9. Inclusion of all parties

When considering the nine components of restorative justice programs, some points should be added that are seldom emphasized. First, the offender will provide an apology, but this apology may likewise be given to the community if such is deemed therapeutic or beneficial to that community. Second, with respect to changes in behavior, it becomes clear that for such to occur, some form of therapeutic orientation would be observed. This is important because this demonstrates the "forward-looking" nature of restorative justice in that future change in the offender's behavior is designed to eliminate later recidivism. Third, respect should be given to both the victim and the offender. This is important for special needs offenders because many of these offenders (e.g., female prostitutes, mentally ill and nonviolent offenders, and drug addicts) may suffer from already lowered self-efficacy and thus will not respond well to programs that are overly punitive to nondangerous and repentant offenders. Fourth, assistance to any party implies that while the victim and the community will receive their just compensation, the offender also may need and even be entitled to some bit of assistance. This is important because many special needs offenders (again, consider the female offender who has a child, the mentally ill offender, the drug addict, or an offender with communicable diseases) may be in dire need of assistance, and this assistance may be the very thing that prevents any future recidivism. Finally, the sense of inclusion by all parties will foster communication and will be likely to increase the odds of success for the entire process.

COMMUNITY ATTITUDES TO TRADITIONAL SANCTIONS

Because of the expressed dissatisfaction that many citizens have with the standard criminal justice responses, restorative justice has substantial appeal. There is a significant body of research that demonstrates somewhat mixed attitudes when considering punitive versus liberal views on punishment (Doble, 2002). It is the premise of this chapter that restorative justice is a third option that addresses the vacillating concerns of the public regarding the punishment of offenders.

Indeed, when focusing on the extreme dichotomies in punishment (soft or liberal vs. hard or conservative outlooks), public opinion polls have found widely varying public attitudes regarding sentencing and punishment, depending on the sample area and time period that such polls are given. For instance, in Alabama it was found that when participants were asked to become familiar with 23 different criminal cases, they indicated that 18 out of 23 of the criminal offenders should be given some sort of incarceration (Doble, 2002). When this same group of participants were shown a public agenda video describing an array of alternative sanctions (intensive supervision, restitution, community service, house arrest, electronic monitoring, and so on) and then polled about their sentencing recommendation, incarceration was the majority in only four out of 23 cases (Doble, 2002).

The results have been fairly similar in North Carolina (Doble, 2002). Clear support emerged for the punitive sentencing scheme of making prison sentences longer and more restrictive. Almost two-thirds of the sample supported this view. At the same time, almost the entire sample (93 percent) supported the use of boot camps, community service, and restitution as a means for reducing prison overcrowding. Contrarily, states such as Delaware and Pennsylvania had large majorities that favored mandatory minimum sentencing laws.

On the other hand, a 1995 survey in Oregon found that 88 percent favored the use of mandatory treatment (a truly unusual concept) for offenders with drug and alcohol problems, even if it involved greater expense to the state. In Oklahoma, more than two-thirds of the participants favored the use of more mental health treatment, while 76 percent favored mandatory treatment for all drug addicts. Finally, in North Carolina, 79 percent favored psychiatric treatment for every mentally ill inmate, even if it costs the state more money (Doble, 2002).

From the research, it can be seen that there is support for both orientations and that there is some disagreement as to which is the best-suited general orientation. However, it is well established that the public is not antitreatment and that even some states that are punitive make some allowances for treatment-oriented programs, depending on the type of offender and the crime.

Further, there is at least moderate public support of intermediate sanctions. Intermediate sanctions reduce the need for prison and allow a progression of restrictions. This is important because many of the participants in the poll surveys just described expressed the concern that a prison sentence is unlikely to deter criminals from future crime and that it is unlikely to rehabilitate an offender. Thus, the public apparently does not have a high expectation of its prisons other than to be the great receptacle that houses inmates for a period of time.

Thus, the question arises as to whether there is a compromise between the punitive and liberal sentencing schemes and whether the use of intermediate sanctions can appropriately work as a compromise between the "opening of the criminal offender floodgates" (pertaining to standard probation) on the one hand and the further crowding of already overstuffed prisons on the other. The contention of this chapter is that restorative justice applications provide the compromise between punitive and liberal sentencing schemes and intermediate sanctions are the working tools that can be used to implement a restorative justice program.

Restorative justice might appear to be an awkward fit with special needs offenders since the impetus behind restorative justice deals largely with issues pertinent to the victim. But when the offender is a special needs offender, the manner in which the victim can realistically expect a gratifying social reaction against the offender is undermined by numerous special considerations. For instance, even if the victim desires a punitive approach when dealing with the offender, one's sense of "retribution" is probably less fulfilled when one learns that the offender is, say, a juvenile offender with mental retardation. Although one's initial instinct may be to "lock 'em up," it soon becomes obvious to even the victim that the effect on the offender is not the same as that on a normally well-adjusted member of society.

But it is clear from the popular literature that policy statements and practitioner guides have been directly connected with offender outcomes, including reduced recidivism and rehabilitation (Bazemore & O'Brien, 2002). This is a popular sell for many practitioners who are forced to deal with burgeoning prisoner populations in ways that are affordable but that also do not compromise public security or safety.

RESTORATIVE JUSTICE AND PUBLIC INVOLVEMENT

Bazemore and O'Brien (2002) have suggested that a restorative justice model needs three essential features to be successful. Incidentally, these features are also important to the specialized needs of special needs offenders:

1. A rehabilitation model does not always necessitate formal intervention. Instead, an informal support and social control system should be utilized that integrates the community into the supervision and treatment process.
2. Such a model cannot be fully focused on the offender alone; to do so will have the ironic effect of turning the community from the offender and will thus impair the offender's chance for long-term reintegration.
3. Such a model will require a fluid working relationship between those interventions concerned primarily with offender treatment, risk management, public safety, sanctioning, victim support, and prevention. The basis for such a network would be to repair the community as a core intervention support to the offender's long-term success.

While policymakers and other advocates may intend to move restorative justice toward a focus on victim needs (which are indeed important), the fact is that restorative interventions do hold substantial promise for most if not all special needs offenders. This is particularly true with child and adolescent offenders, geriatric offenders, learning-disabled and mentally retarded offenders, female offenders with children, offenders with health problems, and those offenders who are not predatory or violent (see Special Insert 15.1).

Special Insert 15.1. Restorative Justice Pros and Cons

Advantages	Disadvantages
Minor cases can be diverted from the formal process.	The term "restorative justice" tends to be vague and unclear.
Dispositions can be reached more quickly.	Due process issues can be unintentionally compromised.
The use of incarceration can be significantly reduced.	Possible resulting disparity in sentencing.
The image of the justice system can be improved.	
All parties can focus on similar goals and objectives unlike the standard adversarial process.	

Source: National Institute of Justice (1998).

Indeed, since treatment is recommended for so many offenders who have special needs and since treatment programs are often much more flexibly designed in the community, the notion of a restorative model can serve the offender well. At the same time, if such a process is utilized, the community will be involved, improving the level of "human supervision" of the offender while also providing a much larger support network. Further, victims who are willing to participate in such programs may find themselves gaining better compensation packages because the offender is held to a higher level of accountability than is the case with probation alone.

Restorative justice processes are often individually tailored to the victim. By the same token, they are likewise tailored to the offender. The offender has specific acts of redemption that are required to meet his or her sentencing requirements, and these acts are derived from the agreed-on contract established by the victim and the offender. This means that this "treatment plan" heals the victim, the offender, and the community and thus ensures that all parties work in congruence rather than conflict.

Bazemore and O'Brien (2002) note that there is now significant evidence that restorative practices can have a significant impact on recidivism (Umbreit, 1999). These researchers contend that most research shows that such programs either cause improvements in certain areas of offender reformation or, at worst, simply seem to work as well (and, by proxy, no worse) than other traditional programs. This is important because this approach helps inform and educate the community about the specific issues facing some of these specialized populations and likewise ensures that offenders with special needs do not have these needs ignored.

Since it is community support that is perhaps needed most in the reformation of special needs offenders, community education is critical. Many community members may have no idea how specific treatment needs can directly impact the likelihood of offender reintegration. Further, these same people may not truly understand that offender recidivism—and the future crime rate—is directly impacted by the successful rehabilitation and reintegration of the offender.

Offenders who are physically or mentally handicapped will naturally have difficulties finding jobs, particularly jobs that will at least pay the bills on a marginal level. Add to this the stigma of being a prior offender, and their chances in the job market are further diminished. However, employment is critical to successful offender rehabilitation and thus is critical to lowering their likelihood of recidivism.

Community members and employers may not realize this and thus may incidentally miss an opportunity to reduce crime in their locale through the rehabilitation of the special needs offender. Some local business owners may not realize that many states and federal agencies offer a variety of tax incentives to employers willing to hire such offenders. Naturally, if offenders are able to secure long-term employment, they are better able to pay restitution to their victims and to probation departments.

However, it is recommended under the auspices of restorative justice that the offender compensate the victim directly, not through some ambiguous state-administered program. This ensures that the victim has a say in the process of restitution and that one is given full compensation. Obviously, the whole process works better if the community is involved in the process as well. For example, in the case of a mentally retarded offender, having family involvement (if possible) with community involvement (certain churches, Big Brother or Big Sister organizations, the YMCA, and so on) to check on the offender and an employer who is able and willing to utilize such labor will ensure that the offender is properly supervised by informal networks of community members. These informal networks serve to ensure that offenders are conducting themselves in an appropriate manner and that their likelihood of making restitution to the victim is increased.

It should be noted that this does not even consider the role of a probation officer or other community supervision personnel. This discussion has also not considered the role of mental health specialists. However, previous chapters (see Chapter 5 on mentally disordered offenders and Chapter 12 on female offenders) have provided examples of numerous programs that have utilized collaborative efforts from public sector probation/parole agencies, community agencies, and private sector mental health contractors. Further, programs such as drug courts and mental health courts can employ restorative justice techniques that lend themselves well to such forms of therapeutic jurisprudence.

When considering the probation agency, the department can oversee and coordinate much of this but, more importantly, will play the role of liaison between the victim and offender to ensure that all court conditions agreed on by both the victim and the offender are met. The probation department will use an array of techniques known as intermediate sanctions to supervise the offender. Among these techniques are such mechanisms as electronic supervision (including global positioning surveillance), community service (which ideally should be linked to either the offense or the issues pertinent to that special needs offender), and house arrest (except during times of employment or other mandated appointments or activities).

Local police can enhance the supervision process without placing an extra burden on the police department staff simply by developing an effective Volunteers in Policing program and providing these volunteers with the task of visiting the domiciles and communities of those offenders who are returned to the community. These groups can also demonstrate concern to the victim by placing visits to the victim's domicile (if the victim is receptive to this) and ensuring that satisfaction with the process has been obtained. Human visits of this sort, as opposed to some obscure survey, convey genuine concern and provide the victim with another name and face to contact rather than a survey form to fill out.

The additional benefit is that volunteers are then given the opportunity to make a direct contribution to the justice system by working directly with the victims and offenders who are involved. This ensures that volunteers are utilized in a manner that is significant and should show them that their contributions are not taken lightly. Indeed, should they volunteer, the police department is taking them seriously in their desire to work in the justice system by involving them in a very important (yet fairly safe) and necessary task of "follow-up" in the justice system.

One other important point about the use of volunteers should be mentioned. The use of neighborhood watch programs should also be solicited. These members are often more than willing to observe and visit various locations to ensure that their localities are safe. Having these groups incorporated into the supervision process may be another way to supervise the offender. Further, the members of this watch, being members of the community where the offender resides, may likely know the offender and his or her family and thus may be in a position to provide supervision that is structured more as a genuine visit of concern (more as a relapse prevention than as a "you're busted" mentality) that may even be perceived as helpful by the offender and his or her family.

All these mechanisms demonstrate that volunteers, employers, families, and probation departments can provide supervision that is comprehensive yet receptive to the special needs of these offenders. This is important because the components of both care and supervision must be maintained. It is clear from the preceding examples that this requires participation from the community. This is the pivotal point to this entire chapter. Without support from the community, the likelihood of restoring the victim or reintegrating the offender is greatly impaired. Thus, a restorative justice model requires the participation of both the victim and the community.

Therapists, on the other hand, are responsible for the actual treatment and rehabilitation of the offender. Although this is the case, it should be noted that the efforts of the therapist can be enhanced by the active involvement of various community members. For instance, faith-based initiatives can be employed, and churches and religious treatment facilities may be willing to extend treatment plan objectives within their spheres of influence. Having the offender engage in cognitive yet spiritual forms of stress management, anger management, or addictions management may be beneficial for some offenders, presuming that the offender is receptive to this modality.

Other forms of community involvement may include "corollary" forms of therapy that are not necessarily central to the offender's crime or even their special need but are nonetheless adaptive activities that the offender can benefit from. For instance, the offender may smoke cigarettes or be overweight. In this case, the strong urging at the behest of the therapist to join a group for smoking cessation or weight control may not be directly relevant to the crime but nonetheless is more beneficial than harmful for overall social integration purposes. Further, more community members are supervising the offender, and the leaders of these programs can report progress to the therapist, who then increases the number of weekly human contacts that the offender has. Thus, on a social level, the offender is constantly under the watchful eye of community members who are addressing other needs of the offender.

Thus, therapists can provide another effective link with the community that enhances therapeutic objectives and supervision objectives simultaneously. This is important because this is the point to restorative justice. The victim, the community, and the offender are all critical to the success of this orientation. The victim must be acknowledged and given priority with this type of justice scheme, but for this to happen, the community must be involved in the process. The community becomes critical in providing the victim support (e.g., visits from volunteers of police agencies, emotional support, or spiritual support from area churches) and in providing supervision of the offender (neighborhood watch and so on). Finally, offenders must understand that restorative justice is intense and time consuming. While their needs are more likely to be met and addressed than in prison, they will be busy with numerous commitments and responsibilities. Indeed, this is not a justice scheme for all offenders, but it is perhaps the best modality for simultaneously meeting the specialized needs of this correctional population, providing justice and compensation for the victim, and ensuring public safety for the community, all the while keeping costs at a much lower level than straight imprisonment would entail. Finally, the offender will have to realize that this scheme of justice is not about freedom per se but about paying one's debt to society. This emphasis is likely to garner and maintain continued support from the community on a continual basis.

RESTORATIVE JUSTICE AND THERAPEUTIC JURISPRUDENCE

One subcategory of the restorative justice concept is the area of legal involvement known as **therapeutic jurisprudence.** According to Wexler and Winick (1996), therapeutic jurisprudence is the "study of the role of the law as a therapeutic agent." Essentially, therapeutic jurisprudence focuses on the law's impact on emotional life and on psychological well-being (Wexler & Winick, 1996). These are areas that have not received much attention in the law until recently. Therapeutic jurisprudence focuses on humanizing the law and concerning itself with the human, emotional, psychological side of law and the legal process. Specific examples would include mental health courts and/or drug courts that were discussed in previous chapters.

More specifically, therapeutic jurisprudence incorporates certain rehabilitative aspects, particularly those of the cognitive/behavioral variety. One type of these cognitive behavioral treatments encourages offenders to think through the chain of events that lead to criminality and then tries to get the offenders to stop and think in advance. This encourages an offender to introspectively figure out two things: (1) what are the high-risk situations, in my case, for criminality or juvenile delinquency, and (2) how can the high-risk situations be avoided or how can the situations be coped with when they do arise?

According to Neubauer (2002), modern courts have created numerous specialized courts that deal with specialized type of offenses and/or offenders. This approach is perhaps the most closely suited approach for handling many categories of special needs offenders. Common examples of specialized courts might include drug court, domestic violence court, drunk driving court, elder courts, and so on. These specialized courts are often tailored with a therapeutic justice orientation in mind. Neubauer (2002) contends that there are **five essential elements of specialized courts**, as follows:

1. Immediate intervention
2. Nonadversarial adjudication
3. Hands-on judicial involvement
4. Treatment programs with clear rules and structured goals
5. A team approach that brings together the judge, prosecutors, defense counsel, treatment provider, and correctional staff

Some court applications are better known than others. This chapter will provide brief discussions of drug courts, sex offender courts, and juvenile courts. Since drug treatment courts are one of the best-known applications of therapeutic justice, this type of court will be discussed first.

DRUG COURTS

Drug courts vary widely in structure, target populations, and treatment programs. The least distinctive way of creating a drug court is to establish one section of court that processes all minor drug cases; the primary goal is to speed up case dispositions of drug cases and at the same time free other judges to expedite their own dockets. Another type of drug court concentrates on drug defendants accused of serious crimes who also have major prior criminal records. These cases are carefully monitored by court administrators to ensure that all other charges are consolidated before a single judge and no unexpected developments interfere with the scheduled trial date.

Still other drug courts emphasize treatment. The assumption is that treatment will reduce the likelihood that convicted drug abusers will be rearrested. These courts will often mandate extensive treatment plans that are supervised by the probation officer. The sentencing judge, however, as opposed to the probation officer, monitors the offender's behavior. All in all, drug courts are thought to be a relatively successful method of combining both aspects of the punitive and rehabilitative components of the criminal justice system.

TEEN COURTS

Teen courts have also been referred to as peer courts. This is an appropriate term since the process literally includes a jury of the teen's very peers. The teens take the role of prosecuting and defense attorneys, jury members, and even judge in some jurisdictions. The young officers of the court are volunteers who are trained and supervised by professional volunteers. The structure of teen court varies by jurisdictions. The jury panel usually includes a combination of volunteers from the community along with former teen court defendants for whom jury duty is a punishment for their offense.

These programs, though restorative in nature and implemented by youth, by no means free offenders from their responsibilities to the victim and the community. One example is the Bronx Youth Court. The Bronx Youth Court is unusual because, operating with the permission of the city's Probation Department, it judges many serious crimes but attempts to ensure that restitution is provided. As stated previously, many of the judges, jurors, and lawyers are those whose own sentences included serving in youth court. Despite the "connection" that these youth may share, not many get any lenience. Of the roughly 70 youths who have appeared in the court during a two-year period, only two have been acquitted, and none has been arrested again (Sengupta, 2000).

Another program in Bend, Oregon, reported that 95 percent of its teen participants avoided being rearrested in the first 10 years of the court's existence (Neubauer, 2002). Research on this type of restorative justice model has generally been supportive, though there are critics who claim that the research has flaws in its design. Nonetheless, it appears that teen courts are popular with the media and society, and as a result they are most likely here to stay.

FAMILY GROUP CONFERENCES

Family group conferences, also sometimes referred to as restorative justice conferences, are a more recent development than victim-offender mediation and come from somewhat different roots, though there are many similarities. Barely a decade old, the family group conference is far less widespread than victim-offender mediation. In some jurisdictions, its use has been mandated by legislative action, while in others it is smaller in scope and optional.

Family group conferences are a process of bringing together an offender, the offender's immediate and extended family members and support persons, justice system representatives, and victims of the crime (possibly also including support persons) to make decisions about how best to respond. Typically, the details of the event will be shared, both the offender and the victim will have an opportunity to describe their experience and feelings, and the participants will develop and agree to a plan for handling the situation. Agreements usually entail some form of reparation to the victim, often including an apology, and may also involve community work and other restitution components.

One study on victim impact of victim-offender mediation in juvenile crime focused on serious or violent crimes (Flaten, 1996). Conducted in Anchorage, Alaska, the results of this qualitative study of seven juvenile cases concur with what is being learned from participants in cases of adult violent crime. Victims who choose to meet with violent offenders are largely interested in getting facts from the offender about the why and the how of the crime, telling the offender their own feelings and pain, and, in capital cases, teaching the offender about the person whose life was taken (Umbreit, Bradshaw, & Coates, 1999; Umbreit, Coates, & Vos, 2001). Restitution is often relegated to a secondary concern.

COMMUNITY CONFERENCES

The use of **community conferences** comes in a variety of forms: as court diversion for juvenile nonviolent offenders and juvenile first-time felony offenders, as an alternative to school suspension, to heal ongoing neighborhood conflicts, and as an aid in reentry into family and community after incarceration. The process used by community conferences consists of a three-part restorative conference structure: hearing what happened, letting everybody say how they have been affected by the situation, and then having the group come up with ways to repair the harm and prevent it from happening again (Mirsky, 2004). Community conferences are always voluntary. In a diversion case, the offender must admit to wrongdoing, and all parties must agree to go through the conferencing process instead of sending the case to court. If the case is resolved by community conferencing, the offender will not be given a court record (Mirsky, 2004).

MENTAL HEALTH COURTS

Mental health courts are designed to ensure that nonviolent mentally ill offenders are not warehoused in prisons, yet at the same time the goal of these courts is to ensure that these offenders are not being a nuisance for the community (see Chapter 5 for full details). Often, these offenders commit petty crimes and are homeless. Because of this and because most mentally ill offenders are not violent, informal interventions such as mental health courts are considered a much more effective method of intervention. These courts provide the offender with treatment and also provide the police and other community responders with a venue to utilize when processing these offenders. Mental health courts are adept at working with local agencies to both address the needs of the offender and protect the public's safety. Intervention and treatment specialists work with the judge to ensure that services are effectively delivered to the offender.

Research has confirmed the success of community conferencing. Abramson (2004) notes that "out of over 500 conferences, 99 percent have resulted in agreements, with over 90 percent in compliance with those agreements" (p. 2). Abramson also points out the importance of qualitative analyses of the "collateral impact" of conferences. According to Abramson, "so much of the research is about recidivism and participant satisfaction" (p. 3) that collateral impact is largely ignored. Collateral impact refers to the effect that conferences have on communities. The types of benefits that communities may receive are multidimensional, but ultimately community conferences are all about building relationships and building social capital. Specific things come out of conferences that people do work on collectively. In conclusion, Abramson contends that "social scientists talk about the importance of collective efficacy and social capital and that's what this is really about: it's using conflict to build communities" (p. 4).

Special Insert 15.2 outlines the varieties of restorative justice practices.

SEX OFFENDERS

One of the major problems with treating sex offenders (especially pedophiles) is their tendency to use defenses of denial, minimization, or blame to avoid responsibility for their acts. These techniques of evasion are often referred to as "cognitive distortions" and include attempts to explain away their behavior, such as "nothing happened," "something happened, but it wasn't my idea," or "something happened, and it was my idea but wasn't sexual." How justice officials respond to this can be critical at each stage of offender processing.

When discussing therapeutic jurisprudence, the key question revolves around whether laws, rules, court procedures, lawyers, and judges act in a manner that is either therapeutic or antitherapeutic. Do procedures utilized inadvertently promote cognitive distortion, or do they work to make such techniques less effective? The

Special Insert 15.2. Varieties of Restorative Justice Practices

Victim impact statements provide an opportunity for victims to express their concerns to the prosecutors and the court.

Victim impact panels give victims an opportunity to confront groups of offenders—not necessarily the one who committed crimes against them—and to talk about the anger and hurt caused by the crime.

Sentencing circles is a Native American approach that involves a wide array of interested parties, including those closest to the victim and offender and others likely to affect their future.

Citizen reparative boards are used in Vermont and elsewhere to determine the nature and details of the conditions of probation for convicted offenders. Trained volunteers provide offenders with a clear understanding of the impact that their crimes had on the community as well as an appropriate and relevant assignment to repair the damage.

Restorative justice sentencing plans use individualized strategies for the offender and the victim and are cost-effective sanctions that aid in repairing the harm. The individualized treatment plans are ideal for special needs offenders.

Source: Adapted from National Institute of Justice (1998).

hope is that court practices do not lend themselves to the sex offender's tendency to evade responsibility. However, as is well known to most court and criminal justice practitioners, most all criminal cases are pled out of court through the plea-bargaining process. In fact, over 90 percent of all criminal cases are pleaded out of court.

The prosecutor, because of the desire to obtain a conviction in an already over-burdened court, will often accept pleas of *nolo contendere* (meaning "no contest") that state that the offender is neither guilty or not guilty. This avoids the tendency of dragging cases out for extended periods of time in the pursuit of proving guilt when the offender will not admit to the guilt. Further, the offender is then free to bargain the sentence through either count or charge bargaining. This may lead offenders to reject offers of treatment directed at decreasing their deviant sexual arousal. This then means that the acceptance of *nolo contendere* pleas may undermine the possibility that treatment will be effective.

Thus, if courts refused to recognize *nolo* pleas or if judges refused or were less willing to accept these pleas in sex-offending cases (especially with pedophilia), the courts would essentially induce clients to engage in some level of cognitive restructuring where they are prevented from finding justification with their cognitive distortions. Further, judges can have an enormous impact on this process by rejecting *nolo* pleas and engaging in detailed questioning of the offender about the factual basis of the plea. Thus, a plea procedure that encourages a sex offender to make a detailed admission of guilt should work against denial and cognitive distortion, thus encouraging cognitive restructuring.

Thus, therapeutic jurisprudence perspectives on sex offenders and the plea process would suggest a revision of existing practices that, with the modified roles of lawyers and judges, can change the law's current reinforcement of denial and cognitive distortion. This would promote true internalization of their crime and their need for change and would thus improve chances at rehabilitation. Likewise, this is likely to bring more healing to the victims if they see remorse (something lacking in many sex offenders, especially child molesters) and genuine acceptance of responsibility. In such a case, victims are likely to have more satisfaction at the trial and sentencing stage and are also likely to have more satisfaction when restitution is made in earnest. Naturally, as has been noted before, victims should not be made to feel that they must forgive the offender; they simply need to know that an option that holds the offender personally accountable to them does indeed exist. Any further action should always then remain the choice of the victim.

MENTALLY DISABLED ADULTS AND CHILDREN

Probably the strongest argument in favor of community therapeutic jurisprudence for the mentally disabled is that it facilitates integration of the mentally disabled individual into the community. Cloistered in an institution far from the "real world," such an individual, even if his or her primary mental health problem is successfully treated, may find it difficult to acquire the psychosocial skills necessary for adequate assimilation in the community once released. Community justice is therefore thought to make it easier for the offender to acquire these skills and, at the same time, easier to find employment or other conditions in which the skills can be applied.

One often-touted argument is that mentally disabled offenders must become familiar with members of society (and vice versa) if they are going to have any chance at successful assimilation into the community. Otherwise, it is speculated that the mentally disabled will be discriminated against in subtle ways that can make it difficult for them to recover fully or function to the best of their ability.

FEMALE OFFENDERS

From the research and readings on female offenders (see Chapter 13), it should be clear that female offenders are, for the most part, ideally suited for an intervention program based on restorative principles. Indeed, these offenders tend to be "relational" in nature, both in terms of the majority of the crimes that they commit and in the manner in which they cope with incarceration. This means that most female offenders are intuitively ideal for a community-based response, which describes the restorative justice approach. Further, since most female offenders commit crimes related to drug use, the sex trade, or simple forms of theft and fraud, the types of offenses affiliated with this offender population are exactly those that are most amenable to restorative justice approaches.

Indeed, with respect to female offenders who are involved and convicted of prostitution and other sex trade offenses, they are often engaged in what are sometimes coined "victimless" offenses. While an individual "victim" may be lacking, the community is still adversely impacted by the activity, and this gives community members the opportunity to become active in eradicating this activity from within their local neighborhoods. Likewise, as was seen in Chapter 13, female offenders often are themselves trapped into such a lifestyle, and they are frequently as much the victim as the offender when looking at their prior socialization and development. Such unique characteristics mean that much of the female offender population simply testifies to the broader social ills in society that are clearly gender based. It will take community and citizen involvement to correct such problems, and this again demonstrates why restorative justice and/or therapeutic jurisprudence is ideal for this group of offenders.

Finally, it has been made clear that these offenders often have children and that prior to incarceration they were the primary caretakers for these children. The interpersonal and social dynamics related to this fact are both immediate and far reaching, as was noted in Chapter 13. The restorative justice approach is capable of ensuring that the mother–child bond is allowed to remain intact and is, incidentally, an effective approach for ensuring that offending mothers obtain the needed social services for their children while completing the requirements of their sentence. Thus, restorative practices that draw community members into the process provide a twofold benefit: they provide further informal supervision of the female offender (including oversight on parenting responsibilities), and they provide the female offender with a support network when performing parental responsibilities. These techniques are dependent, of course, on the type of sanction that is given to the offender. Because of this and because of the intuitive connection between this type of offender and restorative justice principles, it is recommended that the use of intermediate sanctions be maximized with this group of offenders.

THE USE OF INTERMEDIATE SANCTIONS

The interchangeable and flexible array of punishments associated with intermediate sanctions means that they are well suited for the variety of needs associated with specialized offenders. These types of sanctions also fit well within a restorative justice scheme given the informal and flexible nature of restorative justice approaches that consider the concerns of the individual victim and the individual offender. In fact, restorative justice should be seen as the broad overlay and intermediate sanctions as the detailed method of incorporating this orientation. Intermediate sanctions, as discussed in Chapter 1, come in many forms that are tailored for the type of offender. Some of the following examples are especially adaptable to a restorative justice approach:

Community service requires that the offender complete some task that helps the community or the victim. It is considered a form of restitution with labor rather than with money. Community service can be used as a sentence unto itself, or it can be an additional sanction that is added to a probation sentence. Community service lends itself well to restorative justice forms of case processing and provides a means by which the offender is held accountable but can provide a service that is pertinent to the reason for having offended, such as a domestic batterer who provides classes against family violence, a drug abuser who provides education to primary school children against drugs, and so on. This means that the service is helpful to the community and likewise is therapeutic to the client.

Another point with community service is that it can also be tailored to the specific victim if the victim desires. For example, the offender may be a youth who vandalized the home of the victim. If the victim's house needed exterior painting or some other form of general maintenance, the offender could be made to conduct such labor for the victim of the crime. This technique is likely to prove gratifying for victims who desire such forms of community service and will also assist the offender in reflecting on the person wronged and the crime committed.

Day fines are common punishments imposed on misdemeanor and lower-case felonies. These fines offset the cost of crime to the community and can be used to compensate the victim. It is important to note that fines are most often paid by offenders. It is also important to note that the fine amount is often set through the discretion of a judge. Given the rise of therapeutic jurisprudence and the use of other restorative processes, the victim can be given a say in this process, thus allowing for direct compensation to the victim and allowing the victim to set what he or she believes is adequate compensation.

Diversion is designed to limit the number and/or type of offenders entering prison. Obviously, this type of sanction is likely to be well suited for child and preteen offenders. Likewise usually deserving of this sanction are the learning disabled and mentally retarded. Note that all these cases presume that the offender is not necessarily violent.

Enhancement programs generally select already sentenced probationers and parolees and subject them to closer supervision in the community rather than regular probation or parole. Offenders placed on enhanced probation are typically those who have committed serious offenses deemed to be too serious for supervision on regular caseloads. This type of supervision might be especially appropriate for adolescent offenders who would not be sent to prison under the circumstances but whose behavior indicates that they may need more directive supervision. This also might be useful for domestic batterers who have been violent but only with one person. This offender may otherwise be safe in society but may need enhanced supervision for the protection of a specific victim.

Intensive supervision is most appropriate for many adult sex offenders. This type of sanction is used for offenders who would otherwise have been sent to prison. Often, jail or prison crowding influences the number of offenders placed on intensive supervision. This type of supervision emphasizes punishment and control of the offender in the community. In some cases, this may be therapeutic for the victim who simply wants to know that the offender is being supervised. This increased supervision is beneficial to the community welfare yet does leave the ability for the offender to maintain contact with relatives and support services that are in the community; thereby, it is hoped, their likelihood for treatment success will be improved.

Note that other aspects of intermediate sanctions, such as house arrest and electronic monitoring, fit nicely within the scheme of restorative justice and also enhance public safety concerns. But these aspects of intermediate sanctions are designed simply as controls on the supervision of the offender. Because they do not necessarily assist in "healing broken relationships," they are not included here. Again, this is not to say that such sanctions undermine restorative justice (they do not); however, the rationale for their use has little to do with compensating the victim, providing community involvement, or reforming the offender. Instead, custody issues (which are important) are the primary thrust of concern with these types of intervention.

VICTIM ATTITUDES TO RESTORATIVE JUSTICE

Restorative justice practices attempt to repair the harm resulting from crime in ways that benefit the victim, the offender, and the community, restoring healthy, positive connections wherever possible (Umbreit, Coates, & Vos, 2001). The use of conferencing by which crime victims are involved in some type of face-to-face meeting with the offender who committed the crime has had a substantial impact on the development of restorative justice.

Victim advocates are increasingly viewing victim-offender mediation (VOM) as an important option to have available for interested victims as long as it is clearly a voluntary choice (Umbreit et al., 2001). A survey of victim service providers conducted in Minnesota by the state's Center for Crime Victim Services (2002) found that the vast majority of respondents throughout the state believed that VOM is a valuable program and should be available in all courts. Beginning as an early skeptic of the process, the National Organization for Victim Assistance is now an active supporter of restorative justice and VOM. The victim advocacy movement has helped promote a balance between the needs and interests of victims and those of offenders within the VOM process.

Tension among these three groups can still be seen today in the VOM movement. Some contend that face-to-face mediation is unnecessary. Many in the victim advocacy groups find the word "reconciliation" to be an anathema. Others wonder whether mediation will be turned into a massive victim restitution program and lose its moorings as a program also designed to help offenders change.

In the 25 years since VOM began, interest in bringing victims and offenders into a variety of VOM formats has continued to grow. By 2000, more than 300 VOM programs were operating in the United States (Umbreit, 2000). Two-thirds of these were private community-based or church-based programs, while about a fourth operated under the auspices of corrections. Mediations reported were fairly equally distributed across the justice process occurring as a diversion from court, taking place between adjudication and disposition, or being included as a postdisposition option. The majority of cases involved juvenile offenders charged with vandalism,

Special Insert 15.3. Law Enforcement and Restorative Justice

According to the National Institute of Justice (1998), even law enforcement agencies have shown that restorative justice programs can be of added benefit. When the Harrisburg, Pennsylvania, police department randomly assigned citizen dispute cases to a mediation settlement program, they found that cases that were settled through restorative mediation processes were significantly less likely to need police assistance in the future when compared with those cases that involved a control group not receiving such intervention.

Indeed, for the cases referred to mediation, the number of calls for service to the same address dropped an astounding 83 percent (from 272 to 47 calls) compared to other cases that year that dropped only 17 percent (from 118 to 98). It is thought that the dispute settlement approach is better able to solve repeat problems and therefore provides long-term benefit in terms of future human resource hours used by police departments.

Source: Adapted from National Institute of Justice (1998) and Shepard (1995).

minor assault, or theft. Program staff reported pressures to mediate more serious cases. Many programs routinely work with burglary cases, and an increasing number are receiving referrals of far more violent crime. Perhaps one of the most dramatic examples of the growing acceptance of VOM within the United States is seen in the American Bar Association's 1994 endorsement of VOM and its recommendation that VOM should be available in courts throughout the country.

VOM is a process that provides interested victims of primarily property crimes and minor assaults the opportunity to meet the offender in a safe and structured setting with the goal of holding the offender directly accountable for his or her behavior while providing important assistance and compensation to the victim. With the support of a trained mediator (most often a community volunteer), victims are able to let the offender know how the crime affected them, receive answers to questions they may have, and be directly involved in developing a restitution plan for the offender to be accountable for the losses they have incurred.

PARTICIPANT ATTITUDES TO RESTORATIVE JUSTICE SANCTIONS

Most of the studies reviewed reported in some way on the satisfaction of victims and offenders with VOM and its outcomes. Across program sites, types of offenders, types of victims, and cultures, high levels of participant satisfaction were found (Umbreit, Coates, & Vos, 2002). Further, community participants, often volunteers, have also provided positive support and feedback on the use of restorative justice approaches (Boyes-Watson, 2004).

Both victims and offenders have expressed satisfaction with VOM across site locations and cultures and throughout different severities of criminal offense (Umbreit et al., 2002). High rates of satisfaction have been found in numerous studies that examine victims, offenders, and community participants. (Boyes-Watson, 2004; Umbreit et al., 2002). One recent study of VOM examined programs throughout six counties in Oregon and found aggregate offender satisfaction rates of 76 percent and aggregate victim satisfaction rates of 89 percent (Umbreit et al., 2001). Victims often reported being satisfied with the opportunity to share their stories and their pain resulting from the crime event (Umbreit et al., 2002). Even more telling is the fact that participants involved in face-to-face forms of mediation were more satisfied with the process than those participants who utilized a mediator between the parties (Umbreit et al., 2002).

Further, the active involvement of the community is just as important (Boyes-Watson, 2004). This is because communities are seen to be direct and indirect victims of crime and because communities are held to be responsible for maintaining social norms within the community (Boyes-Watson, 2004). Indeed, restorative justice elements should be seen as a form of community empowerment, and therefore the community volunteer is an integral component to the overall success of restorative programs. Because the police cannot possibly proactively stop all crime from happening and because it is simply impossible for the criminal justice court system to process every case with full due attention, it becomes clear that the community will have to absorb part of the responsibility in addressing problem behavior. Boyes-Watson (2004) discusses the use of community volunteers in the state of Vermont and notes that the number of volunteers within the Vermont system speaks volumes about the orientation of that state's correctional system and its view of the public as its primary client. Citizens in this system have a supportive relationship with paid probation staff in which they do meaningful work as unpaid but ideologically committed volunteers.

Indeed, the fact that these volunteers seek out this work and do so for free demonstrates their seriousness about the program rather than simply indicating the need for a paycheck, as is often (but not always) the case among many state- and county-level community correctional employees who find themselves suffering from burnout and stress related to excessive caseloads. These volunteers, therefore, are able to alleviate some of the stress for employees within probation and/or parole departments, particularly if these volunteers obtain a level of training where they can realistically provide specialized labor. This has the effect of reducing stress on the practitioners in the department while simultaneously involving the community. All the while, the services provided to the victim (and even the offender) are improved in the process since more careful (and possibly more caring) attention can be given to each case through the incorporation of volunteers. In closing on this issue, it should be noted that the extensive use of volunteers in community supervision has been found to be particularly effective in other countries, such as Japan (Reichel, 2002). Further, it should also be pointed out that the very father of probation, John Augustus, was himself a volunteer when he opted to have minor offenders diverted to his own home rather than having them processed through the jail system. This is important because it demonstrates that volunteerism can and should be incorporated extensively within the community supervision process if a truly restorative form of justice is to be met in this country. Such inclusion is the most likely avenue to successfully providing justice to the crime victim while meeting the specialized needs of the various special needs offenders who are becoming increasingly common within our criminal justice system.

CONCLUSION

Because restorative justice has a variety of applications, it is a paradigm that lends itself well to the tailored-to-fit needs common for successful reintegration of special needs offenders. The primacy given to victims—in fact, the very involvement of the victims—can improve the prognosis of many special needs offenders and thus holds promise of more effectively reducing recidivism among the special needs population of offenders. Community involvement will help educate the community on the specific problems unique to many of these offenders and should increase the level of supervision over the offender. Finally, community involvement will also assist the correctional practitioner in better meeting the competing roles of treatment and supervision, all the while empowering the community itself, which is ultimately the primary client of the criminal justice system.

KEY TERMS

Restorative justice
Nine components of restorative justice
Therapeutic jurisprudence
Five essential elements of specialized courts
Teen courts
Family group conferences
Community conferences
Mental health courts
Victim impact statements
Victim impact panels
Sentencing circles
Citizen reparative boards
Restorative justice sentencing plans
Community service
Day fines
Diversion
Enhancement programs
Intensive supervision

REFERENCES

Abramson, L. (2004). The community conferencing center: Restorative practices in Baltimore, Maryland. Retrieved from http://fp.enter.net/restorativepractices/cccbaltimore.pdf

Bazemore, G., & O'Brien, S. (2002). The quest for a restorative model of rehabilitation: Theory-for-practice and practice-for-theory. In L. Walgrave (Ed.), *Restorative justice and the law* (pp. 31–67). Portland, OR: Willan Publishing.

Boyes-Watson, C. (2004). The value of citizen participation in restorative/community justice: Lessons from Vermont. *Criminology and Public Policy, 3*(4), 687–692.

Doble, J. (2002). Attitudes to punishment in the U.S.: Punitive and liberal opinions. In J. Roberts & M. Hough (Eds.), *Changing attitudes to punishment: Public opinion, crime and justice* (pp. 148–162). Cullompton: Willan.

Flaten, C. (1996). Victim-offender mediation: Application with serious offences committed by juveniles. In B. Galaway & J. Hudson (Eds.), *Restorative justice: International perspectives* (pp. 387–402). Monsey, NY: Criminal Justice Press.

Minnesota Center for Crime Victim Services. (2002). *2003–2005 strategic plan for distribution of funds*. Minneapolis, MN: Minnesota Center for Crime Victim Services. Retrieved from http://www.ojp.state.mn.us/mccvs/02-05_Strategic%20Plan.pdf

Mirsky, L. (2004). *The community conferencing center: Restorative practices in Baltimore, Maryland.* Baltimore, MD: International Institute for Restorative Practices.

National Institute of Justice. (1998). *Restorative justice: An interview with visiting fellow Thomas Quinn*. Washington, DC: U.S. Department of Justice.

Neubauer, D. W. (2002). *American's courts and the criminal justice system* (7th ed.). Belmont, CA: Wadsworth.

Niemeyer, M., & Shichor, D. (1996). A preliminary study of a large victim/offender reconciliation program. *Federal Probation, 60*(3), 30–34.

Nugent, W. R., Umbreit, M. S., Wiinamaki, L., & Paddock, J. (2001). Participation in victim-offender mediation and re-offense: Successful replications? *Journal of Research on Social Work Practice, 11*(1), 5–23.

Reeves, H. (1989). The victim support perspective. In M. Wright & B. Galaway (Eds.), *Mediation and criminal justice: Victims, offenders and community* (pp. 44–55). Thousand Oaks, CA: Sage.

Reichel, P. L. (2002). *Comparative criminal justice systems: A topical approach* (3rd ed.). Upper Saddle River, NJ: Prentice Hall.

Roy, S. (1993). Two types of juvenile restitution programs in two midwestern counties: A comparative study. *Federal Probation, 57*(4), 48–53.

Schiff, M. (1999). The impact of restorative interventions on juvenile offenders. In G. Bazemore & L. Walgrave (Eds.), *Restorative juvenile justice: Repairing the harm of youth crime* (pp. 327–356). Monsey, NY: Criminal Justice Press.

Schneider, A. L. (1986). Restitution and recidivism rates of juvenile offenders: Results from four experimental studies. *Criminology, 24*, 533–552.

Sengupta, S. (2000). Youth court of true peers judges firmly. *New York Times*, pp. 1, 4.

Shepard, R. (1995). *Executive summary, neighborhood dispute settlement: An evaluation report*. Harrisburg, PA: Dauphine County Board of Directors.

Stone, S., Helms, W., & Edgeworth, P. (1998). *Cobb County Juvenile Court Mediation Program Evaluation*. Carrollton: State University of West Georgia.

Strang, H., & Sherman, L. (1997). *The victim's perspective*. RISE Working Papers No. 2. Canberra: Australian National University.

Strode, E. (1997). *Victims of property crime meeting their juvenile offenders: Victim participants' evaluation of the Dakota County (MN) Community Corrections Victim-Offender Meeting Program*. Unpublished master's thesis, Smith College School for Social Work, Northampton, MA.

Umbreit, M. S. (1999). Avoiding the marginalization and the McDonaldization of victim offender mediation: A case study in moving toward the mainstream. In G. Bazemore & L. Walgrave (Eds.), *Restorative juvenile justice: Repairing the harm of youth crime* (pp. 213–234). Monsey, NY: Criminal Justice Press.

Umbreit, M. S. (2000). *Handbook of victim-offender mediation: An essential guide to research and practice*. San Francisco: Jossey-Bass.

Umbreit, M. S., & Bradshaw, W. (1997). Victim experience of meeting adult vs. juvenile offenders: A cross-national comparison. *Federal Probation, 61*(4), 33–39.

Umbreit, M. S., Bradshaw, W., & Coates, R. (1999). Victims of severe violence meet the offender: Restorative justice through dialogue. *International Review of Victimology, 6*(4), 321–343.

Umbreit, M. S., & Coates, R. B. (2000). *Multicultural implications of restorative justice: Potential pitfalls and dangers*. Washington, DC: U.S. Department of Justice, Office for Victims of Crime.

Umbreit, M. S., Coates, R. B., & Vos, B. (2001). *Victim impact of restorative justice conferencing with juvenile offenders: What we have learned from two decades of victim-offender dialogue through mediation and conferencing*. St. Paul: University of Minnesota.

Umbreit, M. S., Coates, R. B., & Vos, B. (2002). *The impact of restorative justice conferencing: A review of 63 empirical studies in 5 countries*. St. Paul: University of Minnesota.

Van Ness, D. (2002). The shape of things to come: A new framework for thinking about restorative justice. In E. Weitekamp & H. Kerner (Eds.), *Restorative justice: Theoretical foundations* (pp. 1–20). Cullompton: Willan.

Wexler, D., & Winick, B. J. (1996). Therapeutic jurisprudence: An overview. Retrieved from http://www.law.arizona.edu/depts/upr-intj/

LEARNING CHECK

1. Interventions that focus on restoring the health of the community, repairing the harm done, meeting the victim's needs, and emphasizing that the offender can and must contribute to those repairs are examples of ____________________.
   a. Restitution programs
   b. Restorative justice
   c. Peacemaking criminology
   d. All of the above
   e. None of the above

2. In Oregon, it was found that ____________________ favored the use of mandatory treatment for offenders with drug and alcohol problems.
   a. 68%
   b. 78%
   c. 88%
   d. 98%
   e. None of the above

3. When considering public safety and community supervision, restorative justice should be seen as the broad overlay and intermediate sanctions as the detailed method of incorporating a form of supervision grounded in restorative principles.
   a. True
   b. False

4. In the state of Vermont, proof of community satisfaction of restorative justice programs is obvious because of the high number of ____________________.
   a. Volunteers who are involved in the process
   b. Cases that are processed
   c. Special needs offenders who are diverted
   d. All of the above

5. One positive outcome of restorative justice and community-based programs is that they help inform and educate the community about the specific issues facing some special needs offenders.
   a. True
   b. False

6. Which of the following types of programs are examples of restorative justice interventions?
   a. Citizen reparative boards
   b. Victim impact panels
   c. Sentencing circles
   d. All of the above
   e. Both a and b but not c

7. One disadvantage associated with restorative justice is that due process could be unintentionally compromised for the offender.
   a. True
   b. False
8. Which types of special needs offenders were specifically identified as being able to be better processed through restorative justice programs?
   a. Sex offenders
   b. Young childhood offenders
   c. Mentally disabled offenders
   d. Female offenders
   e. All of the above
9. One chief advantage of restorative justice is that all parties can focus on similar goals, unlike the standard adversarial process.
   a. True
   b. False
10. Which of the following is not one of the nine components of restorative justice?
    a. Apology
    b. Restitution
    c. Equality
    d. Inclusion
    e. Meeting

ESSAY DISCUSSION QUESTIONS

1. Discuss the advantages and disadvantages of restorative justice. Next, explain how restorative justice can ensure that the community is active in the offender's supervision within the community.
2. Discuss how restorative justice and/or therapeutic jurisprudence can be ideally suited for processing many types of special needs offenders.
3. Define and discuss two examples of specialized courts that are well suited for the special needs offender.

CHAPTER

PREDICTIONS AND SUGGESTIONS FOR THE FUTURE PROCESSING OF SPECIAL NEEDS OFFENDERS

16

Chapter Objectives

1. Define community justice. Understand why it is contended that community justice orientations are the best method for special needs offender supervision and treatment.
2. Be aware of likely trends with special needs offenders in the future.
3. Understand the challenges that are likely to face criminal justice practitioners in the future when supervising special needs offenders.

INTRODUCTION

This chapter signals the final word on special needs offenders in this book. Thus, it is important that this chapter not be a simple speculative excursion into vague possibilities. Rather, this chapter will bring to the surface some key points that have been noted throughout this book and will then provide some predictions based on these points and other trends noted in the United States and around the world.

This book notes throughout its pages that no matter what type of offender, the need for true collaboration among community agencies is critical. Numerous types of programs have been shown to be useful in aiding in the supervision process of these offenders. Likewise, innovative community-oriented programs (e.g., drug courts and mental health courts) have been shown to be effective in addressing the special needs of their targeted offender population. Because these programs have been shown to be effective, and because community supervision (particularly intensive supervised probation) can be effective with most offenders, it is the contention of this book that if offenders are to receive treatment, they should be treated within the community whenever feasible. This naturally harkens back to the contentions provided in Chapter 1, and it is for emphasis that this is again presented in this chapter. It is with this in mind that we proceed to the following points.

COMMUNITY INVOLVEMENT AND COMMUNITY JUSTICE

The community must be involved in the process. This means that the average citizen must know both of the offender and of any programs where they can be involved. This is important, and it requires that the agency provide aggressive advertisement and community awareness campaigns. Community supervision agents should visit not just the offender-client's home but also other homes in the neighborhood to increase the informal social controls and human supervision that are in place.

During the past decade, community supervision has seen partnerships emerge between police agencies, faith-based organizations, civic associations, social service agencies, and a wide range of other specialized organizations. In this emerging collaborative schema, community supervision agencies are looked at as the leader in addressing crime as a community-based social problem. Thus, community supervision agencies must often spearhead any conjoint community action when supervising special needs offenders. This is best achieved through the implementation of a community justice orientation. According to Clear and Cole (2002), **community justice** should be thought of as being simultaneously a philosophy of justice, a strategy of justice, and a combination of justice programs. When creating a community justice orientation within a given community, Clear and Cole (2002) note that there are three essential components: community policing, environmental crime prevention, and restorative justice.

Community policing employs methods of creating partnerships between the police and the community. This means that programs such as neighborhood watch, citizens patrol, and so on are utilized to create a working relationship between citizens and the police. Further, community policing is intended to make the police the friends of the community and will often be decentralized so that individual officers can mill about the community to build more personal and individualized relationships. This form of policing is likewise effective when dealing with diverse communities. Indeed, the community policing model has been found to be particularly effective in fighting problems of gang infestation within racial and/or ethnic-based communities. This is particularly true because often gang members will victimize weaker members of their own racial group (such as with Chinese gangs or Latino gangs and protection or extortion rackets), making it difficult for officers to detect such crime. Officers who are fluent in the primary language of such a community will have more informal exposure to community members and are often in a better position to detect such subversive victimization.

According to Shusta, Levine, Wong, and Harris (2004),

> Law enforcement agencies adopting the community policing strategy have not only become partners within a community but advocates for public well-being. As a result, the role of the peace officer, especially at the line level, changes dramatically. In addition, with increased contact between community members and police, there will be opportunities to educate the public as to the difficult practices and decisions that police have to make continually. (pp. 486–487)

Condon (2003) further notes not only how police will need to coordinate with the community citizen on a more effective level but also that it will be in the mutual best interests for police and community supervision officers to routinely collaborate. For community supervision officers, rising caseloads place an ever-growing burden on individual officers, and any supervisory assistance they can get makes their job (and the stress of that job) much easier to handle. Further, this makes the supervision process much more effective in detecting offender noncompliance. For police, the advantage is in the intensive background tracking that probation departments are able to provide as well as the ability to search the homes, persons, and lives of those who are most likely to be repeat problems while they patrol their neighborhood beats. This eliminates much of the headache associated with policing, particularly in communities that have a disproportionate offender population. Thus, community policing officers and community supervision officers work hand in hand quite naturally and with little extra effort needed to substantially improve the quality of oversight of the special needs offender.

This has been shown to have a strong effect on recidivism. As was mentioned in Chapter 9, programs such as Operation Nightlight were widely recognized for reducing violent juvenile crime in the Boston area (Condon, 2003). Programs such as these are useful in dealing with gang-related problems. These same programs are equally useful with other problematic offenders, such as pedophiles and domestic batterers.

In fact, it was noted in Chapter 1 that hard-core offenders benefit more from programs that are stricter than from programs that are less stringent. The long-term effects on recidivism are realized at a much better rate, and public safety is again much more improved.

The **environmental crime prevention** component of a community justice orientation will determine why certain areas of a jurisdiction are more crime prone than others (Clear & Cole, 2003). This is important in the prevention of crime and is specifically important when attempting to supervise special needs offenders. Areas rampant with drugs are important to locate to deter drug offenders from recidivism. In addition, areas of town where prostitution is known to occur should be monitored and supervised by community supervision and police officers to deter female offenders from engaging in the business of illicit sex services. Moreover, areas known to have gang problems should be saturated to diminish gang influence in that community and to improve the odds of former gang members on community supervision trying to get out of their previous lifestyle.

Restorative justice, as has been noted in Chapter 15, seeks to make the victim, the community, and the offender whole by restoring each to the state that existed prior to the crime. While restorative justice has been discussed extensively throughout this book, especially in Chapter 15, there still remains one other key point that must be stated in this chapter. Restorative justice is a global phenomenon that has been implemented to one extent or another in every continent in the world (Zveckic, 1994). Indeed, it is the prediction of this book that the United States will find itself being ever more synchronous with the rest of the global family and that this type of offender processing will become used with increasing regularity since this type of justice is ideally suited to tailoring sentences to both the needs of the victim and the unique issues challenging special needs offenders.

SPECIAL NEEDS OFFENDERS ARE HERE TO STAY

One thing is for certain: special needs offenders will continue to become a source of concern for an indefinite period in the future. Indeed, just as the population of the United States is becoming more diversified, so too is the correctional population. Female offenders continue to grow at a rate that outpaces that of male offenders, and the geriatric population is also growing at a rate that is faster than that of the younger population. Substance abuse continues to correlate with criminal activity, and high-risk populations continue to present with a variety of sexually transmitted diseases. Likewise, as clinicians become more adept at recognizing disorders, the diagnoses of disorders will continue at a higher-than-average rate in the offender population.

Further, this book has not addressed the issue of minority offenders (perhaps this will be dealt with in a forthcoming edition), but it is clear that the United States is becoming more racially diverse. This also translates to the continued fueling of gangs that are based on racial lines within the offender community. In addition, other offenders who are simply a specialized population (such as female and geriatric offenders) and/or those with specific mental health challenges are also frequently racial minorities. Thus, not only are special needs offenders likely to grow at a faster rate than other types of offenders, but they are likely to become more diverse. This means that caseloads for officers are likely to become much more complicated.

Maghan (1999) notes that inmates incarcerated today are more dangerous because of their unpredictability. The current prison environment is a breeding ground for violent offenders. According to Maghan (1999), the new generation of inmates is committing detected crimes at ever-younger ages of initial arrest, tends to be less and less educated (being illiterate, subliterate, and often learning disabled) and more unemployable, and is made up of an increasing number of racial minorities. This population also seems to be less affected by either punishment or rewards and is thus impervious to punitive sanctions and unmotivated by reinforcements or rewards for pro-social behavior. These offenders are also likely to be substance abuse offenders and drug addicts. They also tend to be less healthy both physically and emotionally. Maghan (1999) notes that current and future offenders will be characterized as follows:

- Be members of racial minority groups
- Not be healthy (average of 10 years older than physical age)
- Have sexually transmitted diseases, HIV, or tuberculosis
- Be overly emotional and lack impulse control
- Be children who are having children
- Be gang affiliated
- Be unmarried
- Be children of single-parent households

Thus, the offender population in general will tend to have many of the issues discussed in the preceding chapters of this book. This means that we are likely to see an even higher ratio of offenders who will qualify as special needs offenders. In addition, because of the continued high rates of incarceration, it is likely that there will be an increased amount of special needs offenders. Prison sentences are leaning toward lengthier periods, and this in turn will generate new forms of mental disorder, particularly with the rise of supermaximum facilities throughout the nation. Further, geriatric offenders and offenders with physical disabilities will become more frequent because of these lengthier sentences. This, along with the minority overrepresentation within the prison system, will ensure that the offender population will become ever more unique and specialized.

COMMUNITY SUPERVISION STAFF WILL HAVE INCREASING DEMANDS

Because special needs offenders are likely to continue to become an increasing concern within institutional and community-based corrections, there will be an increased demand for specialized knowledge and training among correctional employees. There is an increasing emphasis on working with special needs offenders. Training components for supervision officers working with special needs offenders should include familiarization and sensitization, educational and medical information about special needs offenders, techniques of dealing with many specialized populations, and in-depth and specialized training with specific groups for caseload management. This is the basis for the specialized needs caseload model discussed in Chapter 1, in which the officer assigned to specific special needs offenders is trained with special skills or training related to the needs of these offenders. Officers in this model of caseload management will need to be armed with strategies for managing special needs offenders.

Further, there will be an increased need for officers to be somewhat culturally competent. **Cultural competence** goes beyond mere sensitivity to multiculturalism and means that officers must thoroughly know and understand the formal and informal customs, traditions, language, and habits of a given cultural group. Asian and Latino gangs demonstrate this and the obvious need to be bilingual. Understanding the culture behind the actions can be pivotal among these groups. Further, when dealing with children and juvenile offenders, knowledge of family cultural dynamics can assist in the supervision and treatment process. If the parents are first-generation immigrants to the United States, they may be severely challenged in maintaining supervision over their children who may be more fluent in English than they are. In fact, they may even be dependent on their children for translation. Agency staff should be aware of these and other possibilities that may impede the effective supervision and/or treatment of the offender.

Regardless of whether the offender is mentally ill, mentally impaired/retarded, disabled, or simply not fluent in the English language, Anderson (1999) notes that staff should keep the following tips in mind when dealing with special needs inmates and offenders on community supervision:

- Talk directly to people if they are hearing impaired or have language difficulty. The ability to see facial expressions can assist in communicating to offenders who speak moderate English. In addition, those with hearing or speech disabilities may need to read lips to communicate.
- Use terms that the offender is able to understand. Keep in mind that learning disabilities and other impediments are common among this population and that wordiness or speaking in technical jargon can hinder effective understanding.
- Simplify instructions. Give one direction at a time to avoid confusion. If possible, put any directions in writing.

- When possible, establish and maintain a predictable routine for the offender who is mentally challenged. This can provide consistency in one's life and will improve stability. This is important for mentally challenged offenders, non–English-speaking offenders, and juvenile offenders.

As one can see, the process of simply communicating with some special needs offenders can be challenging. If a mentally challenged offender happens to also be non–English speaking, this generates even more objective specialized needs for that offender and also can increase the likelihood of recidivism and/or treatment relapse. In fact, even if the offender is fluent in English, a lack of training to detect specific clues of potential relapse can mean that community supervision officers will be less capable of providing public safety and protection. This can damage the reputation of the agency and thus undermine the ability of the agency to create effective networks with the community. Therefore, even the most basic training must be emphasized with officers dealing with special needs offenders, and, naturally, specialized and intensive training should be given to those who will be tasked with routinely working with a specialized type of offender.

THE MEDIA, COMMUNITY CORRECTIONS, AND THE SPECIAL NEEDS OFFENDER

This concern may seem to be an unusual addition to a concluding chapter on special needs offenders, but it is the contention of this author that the media can prove pivotal in the success or the failure of any program's ability to effectively deal with special needs offenders. One key, fundamental contention of this book is that community supervision agencies will need to establish community-based partnerships when establishing effective supervision over special needs offenders. The media can assist in facilitating the process and can also make the agency more visible so that community members will be apprised of programs that are being implemented. Indeed, the media can aid the agency in finding volunteers and agencies that are willing to lend a helping hand, thereby establishing a truly effective sense of community justice.

However, certain groups of special needs offenders, such as sex offenders, have drawn public attention and concern. This is understandable, but if such issues are not presented in the appropriate light, the public will tend to make erroneous deductions about special needs offenders, and this can completely destroy any agency's ability to implement an effective supervision scheme that is integrated with the community. **Media effects** are an important consideration in community supervision and refer to the effect that the media have on the public perception of offender supervision programs in the community. How the media report specific incidents can affect this. Further, when programs are successful and/or innovative, the media can provide effective coverage of these and ensure that the public is getting the most accurate information possible regarding both special needs offenders and community supervision.

Garrett (1999) notes certain points to consider when deciding on the involvement of the media in corrections. These questions have been adapted for community supervision agencies and demonstrate the potential concerns when the media are involved:

- To what extent will the media representatives disrupt the day-to-day operations of supervision personnel in the community? Will schedules and routine activities be hindered?
- How are offenders likely to react to the media coverage, and how is this likely to impact their ability to reintegrate within the community at large?
- How are people in the community likely to react to the coverage? Will this impair the ability of the offender to reintegrate within the community at large?
- To what extent can coverage impair public safety, particularly for prior victims?
- Will the coverage be likely to cause further trauma for previous victims and/or families of victims and/or the offender?

Thus, agency administrators who are attempting to build collaborative partnerships must foster good relations with the media and always be aware that the media can be a double-edged sword when presenting coverage on special needs offenders. This is particularly true with those who may be bizarre or unusual in appearance or mannerism.

SENTENCING MAY BECOME MORE INDETERMINATE

In January 2005, the U.S. Supreme Court held in *United States v. Booker* that federal judges no longer are required to follow the sentencing guidelines that had been in effect since 1987. The Court held that federal judges now must only consider these guidelines with certain other sentencing criteria when deciding a defendant's punishment. Because of this ruling and because of the trend toward community supervision, alternative sanctions, and restorative justice, it is speculated that sentencing will become more indeterminate.

Whether this is for the better or for the worse is not completely clear, but it has historically been the case that the criminal justice system operates on a spectrum with punitive philosophies at one end and reformative philosophies at the other. The previous 10 to 15 years have been reflective of a crime control model of criminal justice that has had an emphasis on mandatory minimums for sentencing as well as purely determinate sentencing schemes. Historically, the timing may begin to swing toward less restrictive prison sentencing that may lead to more use of community corrections.

While crime has decreased in the past few years, the populations within prisons and the resulting costs associated with this massive imprisonment continue to grow. Although increased imprisonment rates may be speculated to be the cause for lower crime rates, it may well be that other factors are at play. Since it is likely that multiple factors may account for the crime drop, there may be more need for the use of alternative sanctions, and this would not be a detrimental shift to public safety if programs like house arrest and global positioning satellite tracking are utilized effectively (see Chapter 1).

Therefore, in the long term, it is likely that we will see more and more special needs offenders within our community. Because these offenders are not necessarily more violent than other offenders and because of the continued use of community sanctions, it is the belief of this author that special needs offenders will become an increasing area of focus as community supervision continues to develop.

Further, Paparozzi (2003) notes that both international and national research has been effective at distinguishing those correctional programs that reduce offender recidivism from those that do not. In fact, the results from most of this research would provide a great degree of optimism for the effectiveness of community supervision. But the public perception of community supervision still remains negative because of misunderstanding and the failure of many agencies not only to provide clear evaluative data on their programs but also to publicize such data, especially in the media. Paparozzi (2003) states that "the absence of clear and convincing program evaluation data establishes the foundation for ideologically driven, as opposed to the more preferred evidence-based policies, programs, and practices" (p. 47).

This is a very good point because criminal justice policy is often driven by ideology and by media portrayals of the justice system. Paparozzi (2003) contends that when given a more research-based approach of analysis that is more or less objective, it will be found that a treatment-based approach is more likely to reduce crime the most on a long-term basis. This is the contention of this book as well (just as was indicated in Chapter 1). This support of rehabilitation (indeed, even forced treatment has some effect) will ultimately show that with rehabilitation-based offender supervision programs, there is a resultant decrease in recidivism rates within the same local area.

CONCLUSION

At the time of this writing, over 60 percent of all offenders who are in the custody of correctional systems around the nation are on probation or parole (Clear & Cole, 2002). Further, over 60 percent of these offenders receive some form of specialized treatment for some factor that led to their criminal offending. Thus, it is clear that there will be an increased need for programs relevant to special needs offenders. How community supervision agencies meet this need will affect public opinion toward these programs, in turn affecting the ability to gain community involvement and support. Thus it is that administrators within community supervision departments will become the lead advocates in demonstrating the usefulness and importance of community supervision with special needs offenders since it will be these personnel who will be tasked with supervising such offenders. Ensuring that the media correctly portray such offenders and that public perceptions of safety are kept intact will be the job and concern of these administrators. This reflects the fact that special needs offenders must be understood to have unique and specialized challenges that require attention from all of us since they are, in effect, part of the community in need. And it is the lack of attention to these needs that results in aberrant behavior—behavior that becomes criminal and disrupts our communities. Therefore, in closing, it is as if community supervision agency administrators must also play the role of community healer since they will have to ensure understanding from the numerous parties involved and it will increasingly be their role to foster collaboration from both the offender and all other members of the community at large.

KEY TERMS

Community justice
Community policing
Environmental crime prevention
Restorative justice
Cultural competence
Media effects

REFERENCES

Anderson, J. (1999). Special needs offenders. In P. M. Carlson & J. S. Garrett (Eds.), *Prison and jail administration: Practice and theory* (pp. 219–225). Gaithersburg, MD: Aspen.

Clear, T. R., & Cole, G. F. (2003). *American corrections* (6th ed.). Belmont, CA: Wadsworth.

Condon, C. D. (2003). Falling crime rates, rising caseload numbers: Using police-probation partnerships. *Corrections Today, 65*(1), 44–49.

Garrett, J. S. (1999). Working with the media. In P. M. Carlson & J. S. Garrett (Eds.), *Prison and jail administration: Practice and theory* (pp. 386–390). Gaithersburg, MD: Aspen.

Maghan, J. (1999). Corrections countdown: Prisoners at the cusp of the 21st century. In P. M. Carlson & J. S. Garrett (Eds.), *Prison and jail administration: Practice and theory* (pp. 199–206). Gaithersburg, MD: Aspen.

Paparozzi, M. (2003). Probation, parole and public safety: The need for principled practices versus faddism and circular policy development. *Corrections Today, 65*(5), 46–51.

Shusta, R. M., Levine, D. R., Wong, H. Z., & Harris, P. R. (2004). *Multicultural law enforcement: Strategies for peacekeeping in a diverse society* (3rd ed.). Upper Saddle River, NJ: Prentice Hall.

Zveckic, U. (1994). *Alternatives to imprisonment in comparative perspective*. Chicago: United Nations Interregional Crime and Justice Research Institute.

LEARNING CHECK

Note: The Learning Check for this concluding chapter simply consists of the following short essays for the student to consider on completion of this book.

ESSAY DISCUSSION QUESTIONS

1. Consider the various concepts that you have learned that are associated with community justice and restorative justice. Explain whether this is an improved method of public safety or whether this instead is likely to place the public at more risk. Explain and defend your answer.

2. What are the likely trends in the future regarding special needs offenders? How does multiculturalism relate to criminal justice processing of the special needs offender?
3. Consider the possible criminal justice trend toward indeterminate sentencing in the future. Do you believe that such a trend is likely? If so, how will this impact the special needs offender, and how will this impact society. If not, what is likely to be done when special needs offenders are processed through the criminal justice system? Explain your answer in either event.

GLOSSARY OF TERMS

Accepters accept the abuse as deserved and their fault. As a result, self-image is damaged, and the effects are long lasting and sometimes permanent.

Acquaintance rape is any rape in which the parties know each other but are not and have not been involved in any form of romantic activity with one another.

Adjusters usually have no negative effects because they put all blame and responsibility on the abuser.

Adlerian therapy examines a client's subjective perspective. This therapy emphasizes the importance of social interests and connections. The therapist often assists clients in changing their cognitive perspectives and often examines client birth order, inferiority complexes, and family constellations when delivering treatment.

Adolescent-limited offenders cease delinquency at some point in adulthood.

Age integration is the view that all inmates should be incarcerated in mixed environments with no concern over the age of the offenders who are incarcerated together.

Age segregation is the view that elderly offenders should be incarcerated separately from younger offenders.

AIDS is caused by the human immunodeficiency virus (HIV). A person infected with HIV may not present with observable symptoms for several years. Over time, the infection becomes increasingly difficult to control, and severe opportunistic infections, such as tuberculosis, hepatitis, and pneumonia, are much more likely to lead to death.

Alternative mental health pretrial supervision ensures that the community is alleviated of the additional expense from further jail space usage and that the offender is given quality supervision by someone trained and capable of ensuring that all criminal justice concerns are addressed.

Americans with Disabilities Accessibility Guidelines are various guidelines that facilities must comply with. Basically this means that in general inmate-housing areas, at least 3 percent of cells must be accessible to inmates with disabilities, and all the cells should not be in one special area; in special housing areas such as for protective custody, disciplinary detention, administrative segregation, detoxification, or medical isolation, there must be an additional accessible cell in each of these areas.

Americans with Disabilities Act ensures that access to complete programs and services is allowed to offenders who have physical or mental impairments (or record of such impairments) that substantially limit one or more life activities, as long as safety and security issues are not compromised.

Analysis stage has the objective to develop a thorough understanding of a problem.

Anger retaliation rapist strongly desires to harm women, and this offender actually has personal animosity toward women.

Antisocial personality disorder is a pervasive pattern of disregard for and violation of the rights of others that begins in childhood or early adolescence and continues into adulthood.

Assessment is the process that mental health practitioners use to gain information about an offender.

Assessment stage refers to both subjective methods of clinical interviews and observations as well as objective methods of test taking and mathematical models of offender profiling.

Attention deficit disorder is a disorder in which a person has difficulty paying attention and maintaining focus.

Attention-deficit/hyperactivity disorder shares many of the same symptoms as attention deficit disorder coupled with hyperactivity.

Authoritarian parenting reflects little knowledge of childhood development and often makes demands that are beyond the ability of the child at a given age range.

Aversion therapy is designed to achieve behavior change through classical conditioning techniques in which unpleasant (or aversive) stimuli are paired with responses from the offender that are undesired. This technique is often used with sex offenders and substance abusers to discourage their desire to engage in problematic behaviors.

Axes I, II, III, IV, and V are categories in the *Diagnostic and Statistical Manual of Mental Disorders* (4th ed., text revision) (*DSM-IV-TR*). **Axis I** consists of clinical disorders or conditions that may be the focus of clinical attention. **Axis II** includes both personality disorders and mental retardation. **Axis III** includes general medical conditions that are potentially relevant to the understanding or management of the individual's mental disorder. **Axis IV** includes psychosocial problems that can aggravate diagnosis, treatment, and prognosis of mental disorders possessed by an offender. **Axis V** deals with the overall functioning of the individual and is often referred to as the "GAF Scale."

Behavioral-oriented treatment incorporates learning modes of behavior that help the client meet personal needs through self-empowerment.

Behavioral therapy holds that long-term change is accomplished through action and that disorders are learned ways of behaving that are maladaptive.

Bipolar disorder consists of mood swings that go back and forth between manic and depressive states.

Bully indicators consist of the following observed behaviors: (1) intimidates and pokes fun, (2) incessant teasing that is hurtful, (3) embarrasses and ridicules, (4) loss of anger control, (5) pushes and shoves, (6) interrupts others, (7) center of attention with peers, (8) always blames others, (9) discourteous language and behavior, (10) lack of empathy toward others, (11) inability to apologize, and (12) makes excuses for their behavior.

Bully victim consequences are behaviors observed in victims of bullying and include the following: (1) missing school and/or poor grades, (2) decline in self-confidence, (3) depression, (4) anxiety, (5) suicidal thoughts, (6) sleep disorders, (7) nervous habits, (8) stress headaches, (9) loss of appetite, (10) inability to concentrate or stay on task, and (11) building of rage.

Category 1 batterers are the least dangerous and most treatable.

Category 2 batterers fall between the least violent and most violent groups and are the least predictable.

Category 3 batterers are very dangerous and not likely to complete treatment.

Certification implies a certain level of oversight in that a minimum standard of competency exists.

Chemical castration occurs when sex offenders are injected with drugs (most commonly Depo-Provera) to reduce the amount of testosterone in the offender's body.

Child exploiter is a juvenile sex offender that falls in one of two categories—undersocialized or psuedosocialized. For undersocialized child exploiters, abusive behavior is likely to be chronic and includes manipulation, rewards, or other enticement. The undersocialized child exploiter is motivated by a desire for greater self-importance and intimacy. For psuedosocialized child exploiters, abuse is motivated by a desire for sexual pleasure via exploitation. Psuedosocialized child exploiters tend to rationalize their behavior and feel little remorse or guilt.

Children of Incarcerated Parents Task Force seeks to alleviate much of the collateral damage done to society and individual trauma to children whose parent is sent to prison.

Chlamydia is a very dangerous sexually transmitted disease, as it usually has no symptoms; 75 percent of infected women and 25 percent of infected men have no symptoms at all. Infection can be cured with antibiotics. However, it cannot undo the damage done prior to treatment. Infected individuals are at greater risk of contracting HIV if exposed to the virus. Latex condoms can reduce but not eliminate the risk of contracting the disease during sex.

Chronically ill inmates are those inmates with an ongoing or recurring illness that requires that they be monitored closely to maintain their health status or to slow the progression of their disease or condition.

Citizen reparative boards are used in Vermont and elsewhere throughout the nation to determine the nature and details of the conditions of probation for convicted offenders.

Class 1–4 elderly offenders can be classified as follows: Class 1 elderly offenders are basically healthy inmates who may be sent to any institution. Class 2 elderly offenders are individuals who are medically stable but require routine follow-up care and examinations, such as those with chronic illnesses. Class 3 elderly offenders are inmates who require frequent intensive skilled medical care but who can maintain their own activities of daily living. Class 4 elderly offenders include inmates who require constant skilled medical care and those who need assistance with activities of daily living.

Classification stage includes housing, job, and educational assignments within institutions as well as treatment, vocational, and supervision schemes for offenders on community supervision.

Client-centered techniques emphasize that the therapist must be genuine, accepting, and empathetic to the offender-client.

Cognitive-behavioral therapy challenges the client to examine and question faulty beliefs when presented with contradictory evidence. Clients are encouraged to avoid a limited decision-making process (i.e., good or bad, black or white) and to become aware of their tendency to make quick judgments that may be in error. The therapist is often active and directive. This type of therapy is often highly structured and incorporates aspects from both behavioral and cognitive forms of counseling intervention.

Cognitive restructuring is when the offender constructs scenes that cast him or her or significant others in the role of the victim.

Cognitive therapy is based on the belief that faulty thinking patterns and belief systems cause psychological problems and that changing one's thoughts improves mental and emotional health and results in changes in behavior.

Collateral damage is the damage done to children due to the incarceration of one or both parents. This term is used most often when addressing female offenders who are separated from their children.

Common couple violence is an intermittent response to the occasional conflicts of everyday life, motivated by a need to control a specific situation.

Community conferences consist of a three-part restorative justice group that creates ways to repair and prevent further harm to the victim and the community.

Community justice should be thought of simultaneously as being a philosophy of justice, a strategy of justice, and a combination of justice programs.

Community policing employs methods of creating partnerships between the police and the community.

Community service requires that the offender complete some task that helps the community or the victim.

Comorbidity is when a person has multiple psychological disorders at the same time. Typically, two or more disorders are diagnosed by criteria in the *DSM-IV-TR*. This term is synonymous with the terms "dual-disorder" and "co-occurring disorder," which are all used to describe persons that have two or more psychological disorders.

Compulsive users are the true addicts who are seemingly unable to curb their addiction.

Conduct disorder is a complex group of behavioral and emotional problems that are experienced by some children. Behavior is typically aggressive and hard to control.

Confidentiality refers to information between a therapist and a client that ethically cannot be revealed by the therapist to other parties without the consent of the client.

Containment approach is based on the idea that multiple dimensions of offender supervision are necessary to optimize public safety, and this therefore requires numerous actors within the criminal justice and community setting.

Counselors are professionals who typically have training in particular areas, such as substance abuse counseling.

Cultural competence means that officers must thoroughly know and understand the formal and informal customs, traditions, language, and habits of a given cultural group.

Curiosity fire starters refers to a type of child fire setter who creates fires simply to observe the phenomenon out of curiosity.

Custodial sexual misconduct is any inappropriate sexual activity or harassment by correctional staff toward a person in custody.

Dangerous mentally ill offenders are reasonably believed to be dangerous to themselves or others and also have a mental disorder.

Date rape is a narrower term for rape that refers to nonconsensual sex between people who are dating or on a date.

Day fines are common punishments imposed on misdemeanor and lower-case felonies.

Day reporting centers are treatment facilities that offenders are forced to report to on a daily (or near daily) basis.

Dementia of the Alzheimer's type is a degenerative state of mental functioning among some aging persons.

Denyers tend to repress their sexual victimization. The true results of the trauma do not surface until later in life, usually because of some triggering event (e.g., marriage, loss of employment, sexual dysfunction, or death of a loved one).

Detoxification is designed for persons dependent on drugs and is typically found in inpatient settings with programs that last for 7 to 21 days.

Development of an individual education program is a process that is individualized to the objective and subjective needs of the offender according to his or her specific area of deficit.

Diagnostic stage refers to the process of diagnosing offenders on the basis of physical health or mental illness or on the types of challenges they may face.

***Diagnostic and Statistical Manual of Mental Disorders* (4th ed., text revision) (*DSM-IV-TR*)** allows mental health practitioners to label or diagnose individuals so that they can be better categorized for further treatment interventions.

Diathesis-stress model states that some people are more likely than others to develop various kinds of maladaptive behaviors or disorders when exposed to stress because of underlying physiological predispositions.

DID syndrome involves denying that a gang problem exists, ignoring the problem when it arrives, and delaying a response to the problem.

Disorder of written expression exists when writing skills, as measured by an individually administered standardized test, are substantially below those expected given the person's chronological age, measured intelligence, and age-appropriate education. This disturbance must significantly interfere with academic achievement or activities of daily living that require the composition of written texts.

Disruptive offender group describes a gang that possesses the following high-functioning group and organizational characteristics: (1) prison and street affiliation is based on race, ethnicity, geography, ideology, or any combination of these or other similar factors; (2) members seek protection from other gang members inside and outside the prison as well as insulation from law enforcement detection; (3) members will mutually take care of one another's family members, at least minimally, while the member is locked up since this is an expected overhead cost in the organization; and (4) the group's mission integrates an economic objective, and uses some form of illicit industry, such as drug trafficking, to fulfill the economic necessities to carry forward other stated objectives.

Disturbed impulsives are likely to have a history of previous delinquent behavior and/or to be psychologically disordered. They frequently come from dysfunctional families, have substance abuse issues, and possess learning deficits. Their offenses are impulsive.

Diversion is designed to limit the number and/or type of offenders entering prison.

Domestic violence refers to any violence between persons who are either involved in an intimate relationship or related by blood or marriage or between individuals who live within the same domicile.

Drug of choice is a drug that is consistently used with greater frequency than other types of drugs by a certain identifiable demographic group.

Drug courts include a nonadversarial approach to integrating substance abuse treatment with criminal justice case processing.

Dual diagnosis denotes the fact that the offender has two or more disorders.

Dynamic risk factors are those characteristics that can change and that are more or less influenced or controlled by the offender, such as employment, motivation, drug use, and family relations.

Dyssocial psychopaths exhibit aggressive antisocial behavior, but this behavior is simply the result of prior social learning from their subculture, their family, or other significant models of behavior.

Early elderly compassionate release refers to any program that is designed to place incarcerated elderly offenders in the community because of considerations regarding medical illness and the services involved with that illness.

Education and family history are records obtained when a person is being screened for a handicapped condition and may provide information such as history of dropout, truancy, or deficiencies in intellectual development.

Elderly first-time offenders are those who commit their first offense later in life.

Elderly offender is any offender who is convicted and is at least 50 years of age as determined by a comprehensive consideration of factors that include prior lifestyle, medical health, mental health, and the effects of prior incarceration on that individual's overall functioning.

Eligibility is the term for when an offender qualifies for an intervention program.

Enhancement programs generally select already sentenced probationers and parolees and subject them to closer supervision in the community rather than regular probation or parole.

Environmental crime prevention determines why certain areas of a jurisdiction are more crime prone than others.

Environmental manipulation helps get the domestic violence offender out of situations that are high risk for him and his potential victims.

Evaluation is the process by which the agency will determine suitability of an offender to a special education program.

Existential therapy is not a specific therapy but is designed more to help the client gain perspective on his or her life.

Experimenters initially use drugs simply because of influence from the peer group.

Exploitative pedophiles seek children primarily to satisfy sexual needs.

Extreme concern fire starters are children who set fires and who have an immediate need for some type of intervention beyond education.

Faith-based programs are treatment facilities that incorporate a strong religious focus into their treatment program.

Faith-based therapy is often a blend of cognitive and behavioral techniques that are grounded in scriptural instructions on the appropriate form of cognition or behavior.

False negatives occur when the offender is predicted to not reoffend, but the prediction turns out to be false.

False positives occur when the offender is predicted to reoffend, but the prediction turns out to be false.

Families and School Together (FAST) is a treatment program for adolescents that incorporates six research-based strategies that are used to build protective factors for youth.

Family group conferences are a process of bringing together an offender, the offender's immediate and extended family members and support persons, justice system representatives, and victims of the crime (possibly also including their support persons) to make decisions about how best to respond.

Family systems therapy includes other family members rather than simply focusing on one client. Family members can include anyone that is important to the client. The focus of this therapy is on communication between members and the problems that can emanate from familial relationships. Intergenerational aspects of behavior within families are also a source of attention. When used with substance abusing offenders, this therapy seeks to identify family routines, regulatory behaviors, rituals, or problem-solving strategies that have developed to deal with or encourage the substance abusing behavior.

Feminist therapy focuses on empowering women and helping women discover how to break free from some of the traditional molds that have kept them from succeeding.

Five essential elements of specialized courts consist of the following processes: immediate intervention, nonadversarial adjudication, hands-on judicial involvement, treatment programs with clear rules and structured goals, and a team approach that brings together the judge, prosecutors, defense counsel, treatment provider, and correctional staff.

Fixated pedophile presents with a long-standing, exclusive preference for children as both sexual and social companions.

Floaters are drug users who will usually focus more on using the drugs of other people, and they are more likely to maintain a moderate use of drugs.

Four standards of mental health care consist of the following tenets: correctional administrators must provide an adequate system to ensure mental health screening for inmates, correctional facilities must provide access to mental health treatment while inmates are in segregation or special housing units, correctional facilities must adequately monitor the appropriate use of psychotropic medication, and a suicide prevention program must be implemented.

Full-service gang units have responsibility for suppression, intervention, and prevention of gang activity within their jurisdiction.

Gang cross-pollination is when the gang has developed such power and influence as to be equally effective inside or outside the prison walls.

Gang exit strategy consists of a structured program that provides interventions for members of criminal gangs (most often street gangs) to desist from their membership. These programs consist of a variety of counseling interventions and life skills training that are often taught by facilitators who were once gang members.

Gang member assessment and intake is the phase that identifies interest and motivation of the gang member, the amount of gang involvement, and the member's family and social history.

Gang member case management involves individual support for the member but also requires ongoing group meetings for the ex–gang member.

Gang member intensive training and personal development provides training on interventions with gangs that implements separate curricula for male gang members and another for female gang members.

Gang sexual assault is committed by multiple offenders who simultaneously assault a single identified victim or set of victims. Often this type of sexual assault is associated with street gangs but can include prison gangs as well. This is distinguished from general group sexual assault simply by the gang affiliation that the offenders possess, and it sometimes serves as a rite of initiation and confirmation of loyalty and bonding to the gang.

Gestalt therapy does not emphasize the past or future but instead maintains that clients must focus on the "here and now" of their experience. Clients must resolve unfinished business in their life, exercise personal responsibility, and become associated with their feelings/emotions in a manner that is responsible while eschewing denial.

Global Assessment of Functioning Scale is useful in tracking the clinical progress of an individual in global terms, using a single measure.

Global positioning satellite systems use a series of satellites to monitor and locate offenders.

Gonorrhea is one of the most frequently reported sexually transmitted diseases. Infection can be cured with antibiotics. However, it cannot undo the damage done prior to treatment. Latex condoms can reduce but not eliminate the risk of contracting the disease during sex.

Group sexual assault is any situation in which two or more offenders sexually assault one victim.

Habitual elderly offenders have a long history of crime and also have a prior record of imprisonment throughout their lifetime.

Hearing, vision, and medical screening is a medical screening that includes vision and hearing tests.

Hepatitis A is a liver disease caused by the hepatitis A virus. It most frequently occurs through person-to-person transmission during community-wide outbreaks. Viral transmission can also occur through close personal contact (e.g., household contact, sexual contact, drug use, or children playing) and contaminated food or water (e.g., infected food handlers).

Hepatitis B is transmitted primarily through sexual activity among adults and adolescents, accounting for more than half of newly acquired infections. A vaccine exists, but there is no cure.

Hepatitis C is not a disease that causes many problematic symptoms. When symptoms do occur, they tend to be general and are usually not detected as symptoms of a more serious illness by the individual.

Herpes is painful and episodic; it can be treated, but there is no cure. Herpes is spread by direct sexual skin-to-skin contact with the infected site during vaginal, anal, or oral sex. Abstaining from vaginal, anal, and oral sex with an infected person is the only effective means of preventing the sexual transmission of genital herpes.

Histrionic personality disorder is a pervasive pattern of excessive emotionality and attention seeking, beginning by early adulthood and present in a variety of contexts.

HIV (human immunodeficiency virus) is a virus that attacks the immune system of a person. It is transmitted vaginally, orally, and especially through anal sex. HIV is also spread through infected blood or blood products and the sharing of drug needles with an infected person. When symptoms are experienced, they typically include flu-like symptoms, including fever, loss of appetite, weight loss, fatigue, and enlarged lymph nodes. Most who becomes infected with HIV will eventually develop AIDS and die of AIDS-related complications.

Home confinement with electronic monitoring is the most restrictive form of community supervision without actual incarceration and has also been used with offenders who have violated the terms of lesser forms of community supervision.

Human papalloma virus is the most common sexually transmitted disease; 33 percent of all women have this virus, which can cause cervical cancer (or penile cancer in men) and genital pain. Symptoms include cauliflower-like warts developing on and inside the genitals, anus, and throat. It should be noted that condoms provide almost no protection against contracting the disease during sex, and even more disturbing is the fact that there is no known cure.

Implementation of the individualized education program refers to the process by which educational services are specifically administered and include aspects such as predictability, supportiveness, and feedback.

Impulse charting is a method used to track points and times when certain thoughts and/or desires seem more intense.

Incapacitation is the process of simply removing offenders from society so that they cannot cause further harm to the public.

Incest experimentation is when young children close in age, size, and cognitive level engage in sexual acts that are more exploratory than gratifying.

Incest exploitation occurs when young children close in age, size, and cognitive level engage in sexual acts, but one child manipulates or forces the other child into sexual activity. This becomes more clearly a form of exploitation if reprimand does not decrease the activity by the overbearing child.

Incest sexual abuse is a sex act where there is considerable age or developmental difference between two children who are related by blood or marriage.

Institutional dependency is defined as the process whereby the elderly inmate exchanges his or her prior life identity with a prison-based identity with reference groups changing from outside friends and family to those persons within the institution.

Intensive supervised probation consists of the following: five face-to-face visits between the probation officer and the offender per week, a minimum of 132 hours of community service, a set curfew, mandatory employment, a weekly search for any new arrests, automated tracking of arrests using a state crime information system, and frequent yet random testing for drugs and/or alcohol.

Intensive supervision is used for offenders who would otherwise have been sent to prison.

Intermediate community supervision sanctions are those sentences that have differing levels of supervision, making the offender's sentence more structured than standard probation, but these sanctions are also considered less severe than a full prison sentence.

Interview files are a history of interviews with the offender, made to obtain a personal account of school attendance, educational level obtained, difficulties in school, and any special services received in school that may indicate previous placement in special education.

Intravenous drug users are people who inject drugs into their bodies with a needle.

Level of Supervision Inventory–Revised (LSI-R) is used to determine offender suitability for a given housing or custody status.

Licensure provides the legal right to see clients and receive reimbursement from outside insurance or government providers (payment from whom is referred to as third-party billing).

Life course–persistent offenders engage in delinquency that ultimately leads to criminal acts in adulthood.

Little Hoover Commission is tasked with providing recommendations to the state governor and legislature.

Low/definite/extreme risk arson offenders engage in fire-setting behavior that is typically a result of a lack of information about fire and its consequences. Definite risk arson offenders describes the fire-setting behavior as a reaction to some type of stress or crisis occurring in the life of the child and/or family. Extreme risk arson offenders include children who have an immediate need for some type of intervention beyond education.

Major depressive disorder is characterized by one or more major depressive episodes (i.e., at least two weeks of depressed mood or loss of interest accompanied by at least four additional symptoms of depression).

Malingering is when inmates falsely claim and consciously fake symptoms of an illness.

Marital rape is any sexual activity by a legal spouse that is performed or caused to be performed without the consent of the other spouse.

Masturbatory reconditioning involves having the client masturbate to an appropriate fantasy until he has an ejaculation.

Mathematics disorder consists of the following: mathematical ability, as measured by individually administered standardized tests, substantially below that expected given the person's chronological age, measured intelligence, and age-appropriate education; the disturbance in mathematical ability significantly interferes with academic achievement or activities of daily living that require mathematical ability; and if a sensory deficit is present, the difficulties in mathematical ability are in excess of those usually associated with it.

Media effects refer to the effect that the media have on the public perception of offender supervision programs in the community.

Megargee Offender Classification System is known to provide solid empirical support for classification and placement decisions.

Mental health courts emerged out of the recognition of inequities in the experiences of mentally ill offenders and two converging developments in the legal arena: therapeutic jurisprudence and the drug court movement.

Mental health diversion programs are a "no-refusal" policy so that the mentally ill are not jailed unless necessary for public safety.

Mental illness is any diagnosed disorder contained within the *DSM-IV-TR*.

Mental retardation refers to significantly subaverage general intellectual functioning existing concurrently with deficits in adaptive behavior and manifested during the developmental period.

Mentally Ill Offender Treatment and Crime Reduction Act was designed to improve access to mental health services for adult and juvenile nonviolent offenders.

Minnesota Multiphasic Personality Inventory (MMPI) is an objective personality adjustment inventory test that can be given to large numbers of offenders at the same time or individually as desired.

Minnesota Multiphasic Personality Inventory-2 (MMPI-2) is an objective personality adjustment inventory test that can be given to large numbers of offenders at the same time or individually as desired.

MMPI-2 Criminal Justice and Correctional Report (MMPI-2 CJCR) is perfectly suited to "match up" the offender's treatment plan with the level of security and serves as an additional double-check when making security decisions from the LSI-R.

Model of caseload delivery has to do with the process whereby offenders are initially assigned their community supervision officer.

Mood disorders are those disorders such as major depressive disorder, bipolar disorder, and dysthymic disorder.

Motor skills disorder consists of the following: performance in daily activities that require motor coordination substantially below that expected given the person's chronological age and measured intelligence (this may be manifested by marked delays in achieving motor milestones; the disturbance in the previous criterion significantly interferes with academic achievement or activities of daily living; the disturbance is not due to a general medical condition and does not meet the criteria for a pervasive developmental disorder; and if mental retardation is present, the motor difficulties are in excess of those usually associated with it.

Naive experimenters tend to be young (11 to 14 years of age), with little history of acting-out behavior. They are sexually naive and engage in one or just a few sexually exploratory acts with a younger child (typically two to six years old), using no force or threats.

Narcissistic personality disorder is a pervasive pattern of grandiosity (in fantasy or behavior), need for admiration, and lack of empathy, beginning by early adulthood and present in a variety of contexts.

Needs-principled assessment deals with the subjective and objective needs of the offender to maximize their potential for social reintegration and to reduce their likelihood of future recidivism.

Nine components of restorative justice are the main objectives of restorative justice interventions and include the following: (1) meeting of all the parties involved, (2) communication between the parties involved, (3) agreement or consensus between the parties involved, (4) apology provided by the offender to the victim and/or community, (5) restitution made from the offender to the victim, (6) change in the offender's behavior, (7) respect shown to all parties, (8) assistance provided to any party that needs it, and (9) the inclusion of all parties.

Not guilty by reason of insanity is a legal term used for those who are excused from their crime because of a mental illness, therefore making them innocent in a court of law.

Objective assessment is any test or assessment that is not influenced by the impressions and opinions of the interviewer, observer, or test administrator. These assessments tend to have closed response questions and lend themselves to quantitative analysis more than subjective assessments.

Objective needs are determined by society and the correctional agency and have to do with socially selected and acceptable levels of health and social functioning to ensure that legal conduct is maintained.

Offender turned elderly in prison is an inmate who has grown old in prison, has a long history in the system, and is the least likely to be a discipline problem.

Official halfway houses are residential settings for offenders who are court-ordered to stay at the facility as a supplement to their conditions of community supervision.

Opportunistic rapists demonstrate neither strong sexual nor aggressive features but engage in spontaneous rape when there appears an opportunity that makes the possibility look like an easy prospect.

Passive agents will tend to do as little as possible and do not have passion for their jobs.

Paternal officers protect both the offender and the community by providing the offender with assistance as well as praising and blaming.

Patriarchal terrorism consists of men who commit acts of spousal abuse because of a need to be in charge of the relationship and to control the woman by any means necessary.

Pedophilia involves sexual activity with a prepubescent child (generally age 13 and younger).

Penile plethysmograph uses a cup or band that is placed around the penis while the offender is in a private room. The offender is shown nonpornographic pictures of different categories of stimuli, and auditory stimuli are also provided.

Permissive parenting is characterized as nonresponsive to a child's needs. Parents of this style may be neglectful not only of the child's basic physical needs but also of his or her emotional needs.

Personality disorders are disorders that are characterized by an enduring pattern of inner experience and behavior that deviates markedly from the expectations of the individual's culture, is pervasive and inflexible, has an onset in adolescence or early adulthood, is stable over time, and leads to distress or impairment.

Physiological dependence is dependence that results because a drug produces pleasant physical effects. The dependent person must also exhibit signs of both tolerance and withdrawal to truly be physiologically dependent.

Pit bull batterers slowly burn in frustration and resentment before finally exploding.

Polygraph is the standard lie detector used to measure biological responses to deception.

Power assertive marital battering rapist desires a sense of dominance over one's spouse because of rigid sexist beliefs regarding the roles of men and women. This offender uses both physical assault and sexual assault as a tool of control and dominance in the relationship.

Power assertive rapist commits sexual assault simply to feel a sense of dominance and control over a female victim because of rigid sexist beliefs regarding the roles and rights of men and women.

Power reassurance rapists are typically not socially competent and may be quite introverted in thought and behavior. These individuals typically have a low sense of self-esteem and suffer from profound feelings of inadequacy, both socially and sexually.

Preintake identification is an observation made by law enforcement personnel during pretrial, detention, or sentencing that states that the offender has characteristics of retardation, learning disabilities, or other handicapping conditions.

Presentence investigation report is the file that includes a wide range of background information on the offender.

Primary psychopath is the "pure" psychopath in the sense of the word that is commonly meant in the general public.

Prison gangs are typically aligned along racial lines and are formed in prison environments to aid members in matters of criminal enterprise and basic survival.

Prison subculture is the surrounding lifestyle within a prison. Certain characteristics related to toughness, masculinity, and loyalty to fellow inmates are common within this subculture.

Probation with community service and restitution requires the offender to provide a certain number of designated hours of free labor to a given cause determined by the court. Restitution, on the other hand, is a stated amount of money that the offender must pay to the victim or to a state victim fund.

Prognosis refers to the likelihood of an offender to successfully reform and to simultaneously refrain from further criminal activity.

Project for Older Prisoners uses volunteer law students to study cases of older inmates and determine whether they are safe to release.

Projective assessments do not rely on the child's self-report. Rather, they try to get a "behind-the-scenes" reading of the child's mental state that is often safeguarded by a variety of defense mechanisms.

Protective factors can serve to reverse or hold in check many of the risk factors for delinquency and crime that the youth has been exposed to.

Psychiatrists are medical doctors who are typically involved with the criminal justice system only during times when inmates must be subdued with medicine or with seriously disturbed persons.

Psychodiagnostic method is a model of clinical assessment that is holistic and is intended to describe the client in a variety of ways.

Psychological dependence is dependence that results because a drug produces pleasant psychological effects. The dependent person must also exhibit signs of both tolerance and withdrawal to truly be psychologically dependent.

Psychologists have doctorates in psychology and typically have extensive education and/or experience in research, theories of human behavior, and therapeutic techniques.

Psychometric method of assessment emphasizes more objective use of tests and assessment instruments.

Psychopathy describes a condition among individuals who demonstrate behavioral patterns similar to persons with antisocial personality disorder. These individuals are known for their lack of sensitivity, empathy, compassion, and guilt.

Psychotropic drugs are those prescribed for mental health issues, and their effective use requires mental health practitioners to use the right dose of the right drug for the correct period of time.

Punitive officers see themselves as needing to use threats and punishment to get compliance from the offender.

Reactionary fire starters. Delinquent fire starters are supported by their peer group and engage in repeated intentional fire setting. Feelings of excitement and defiance are reported. Fire starting often is accompanied by other antisocial activities, such as drug or alcohol use, petty theft, or vandalism. No attempts are made to extinguish the fire. Feelings of guilt or remorse are rare. There is little fear of the consequences or punishment. Troubled reactionary fire starters have recent or chronic stressful events that trigger emotional reactions and result in fire starting. The fire represents the release of displaced emotions, such as frustration or anger. The fire also has the reinforcing properties of effect and attention. No attempt is made to extinguish the fire. There is no consideration of the negative consequences of the potential destruction.

Reading disorder consists of the following: reading achievement, as measured by individually administered standardized test of reading accuracy or comprehension, substantially below that expected given the person's chronological age, measured intelligence, and age-appropriate education; the disturbance in reading achievement significantly interferes with academic achievement or activities of daily living that require reading skills; and if a sensory deficit is present, the reading difficulties are in excess of those usually associated with it.

Reality therapy encourages clients to evaluate their present methods of day-to-day operation to determine if they are effective or debilitating. This therapy holds that people create their feelings by the choices they make.

Recidivism prediction stage takes assessment and diagnostic information into consideration to determine the basic level of risk that an offender holds for further offending, and this stage is usually the framework from which classification stage decisions are developed.

Referral is when an offender is recommended for participation in a special education program and usually occurs during the intake process or shortly after the intake process.

Regressed pedophile is a type of pedophile who probably had a fairly normal adolescence and good peer relations.

Relapse prevention programs train addicted populations to avoid high-risk situations that are likely to result in a lapse of further drinking or drug use.

Residential treatment homes are designed to house offenders in the community, but the offender is not ordered by the court to stay at the facility.

Response stage has three objectives: develop response options that are consistent with the information analyzed, select responses, and implement the responses.

Restorative justice is a term for interventions that focus on restoring the health of the community, repairing the harm done, meeting victim's needs, and emphasizing that the offender can and must contribute to those repairs.

Restorative justice principles are based on the notion that offenders need to learn about the impact they had on their victim(s) and in the process should develop a sense of accountability and remorsefulness.

Restorative justice sentencing plans use individualized strategies for the offender and the victim and are a cost-effective sanction that aids in repairing the harm.

Risk factors are a number of factors that have a high likelihood of leading to delinquent behavior.

Risk-principled assessment revolves around the protection of society and/or the safe management of correctional institutions.

Role identity confusion occurs when officers are unclear about the expectations placed on them as they attempt to juggle between the "policing"-oriented and the "reform"-oriented nature of their work.

Role playing is when offenders reenact their own crime scene(s) with another offender and take turns playing the role of their victim.

Rorschach Test explores for trauma in the individual and is very useful since many of the offenders who commit heinous crimes (such as murder) report some form of prior trauma.

Ruiz v. Estelle was an instrumental court case that established much of the groundwork for correctional responsibilities to provide adequate mental health care.

Sadistic pedophile is motivated by sex and aggression and selects children because of their sense of vulnerability.

Sadistic rapist is the most dangerous and the most likely to kill or permanently maim their victim. The primary desire of this offender is to simply cause pain to the victim.

Scanning stage involves looking for and identifying problems that a client may have.

Scheduled overmasturbation requires that the client routinely masturbate on a progressively more frequent schedule throughout the week.

Schizophrenic disorder symptoms are as follows: (1) delusions, (2) hallucinations, (3) disorganized speech, (4) grossly disorganized behavior, and (5) inappropriate affect.

Secondary psychopaths commit antisocial or violent acts, but this is due largely to severe emotional problems or mental disorders.

Security threat group is another name for jail and prison gangs.

Self-help groups are composed of individuals who meet regularly to stabilize and facilitate their recovery from substance abuse.

Sentencing circles are a Native American approach that involves a wide array of interested parties, including those closest to the victim and offender and others likely to affect their future.

Sexual abuse cycle is where older-generation family members sexually abuse children who in turn eventually become sex abusers themselves.

Sexual aggressive offenders are likely to have a long history of antisocial acts, poor impulse control, and substance abuse. Their sexual assaults involve force, and they are motivated by desires for power and control. Humiliation of the victim is common with this perpetrator.

Sexual assault is the act of forced penetration of any bodily orifice (vaginally, anally, or orally) or forced cunnilingus or fellatio involving violation of the survivor's body and psychological well-being.

Sexual compulsive offenders tend to commit repetitive acts and are seemingly unable to stop themselves. They are more likely to engage in acts such as voyeurism or self-exposure than the assault of a victim.

Sexual gratification rapist may simply desire sex and may be in a situation where he feels that force or coercion may successfully get the sexual intercourse that he desires.

Sexual sadism is a *DSM-IV-TR*–diagnosed sex-related disorder where the person gains sexual gratification from the infliction of pain or emotional harm to another person.

Sexually transmitted diseases are those that are transmitted from one person to another through sexual contact.

Social workers are individuals who might have a bachelor's degree, but most practicing social workers have a master's degree in social work.

Societal needs are concerned with those needs that most directly influence the likelihood of the offender's recidivism, and as a result, the agency must address these needs first.

Solution-focused therapy approaches of therapy emphasize the strengths and potential of the individual rather than the problems and dysfunctions.

Special needs offender refers to those offenders who (1) have some notable physical, mental, and/or emotional challenge; (2) these challenges prevent either a subjective or objective need from being fulfilled for that individual; (3) the lack of this subjective or objective need impairs their day-to-day ability to function within the confines of the criminal law; and (4) in addition, these offenders tend to be statistically unique from the remainder of the offender population and also tend to be prone to recidivism.

Specialized needs caseload model pertains to community supervision assignments to offenders who share common specialized needs such as substance abuse, sex offending, a given set of disabilities, and so on.

Spouse monitoring involves supervision on the part of the spouse (if and when available, though other family members may be able to assist) or significant other to complete a daily checklist on the offender's compliance with the treatment and to ensure that any therapeutic homework given to the client is being completed at the prescribed times in the week.

Static risk factors are characteristics that are inherent to the offender and are usually permanent.

Stranger sexual assault is defined as nonconsensual, or forced sex, on a person who does not know the attacker.

Subjective assessment process is an important yet less structured method of determining the security and treatment needs of the offender.

Subjective assessments are specific areas of subjective knowledge that can be helpful in assessing the childhood offender who kills.

Subjective needs are those felt by the offender and are those needs that the offender perceives to be important.

Subjective structured interview is simply a process whereby an interviewer will ask a respondent a set of prearranged and open-ended questions so that the interview seems informal (as if a conversation), yet because of the prearranged questions, a structure evolves throughout the conversation that ensures that certain bits of desired data are gathered from the respondent.

Substance abuse is when the recurrent use of a substance results in the failure to fulfill major life course roles (such as obligations at work, school, or home) or when such use results in physically hazardous situations, recurrent legal problems, or recurrent social or interpersonal problems caused or exacerbated by the effects of the substance.

Substance dependence is the repeated, nonmedical use of a substance even though such use harms the user or incites behavior in the user that harms others. Substance dependence can present as psychological and/or physical dependence.

Substance withdrawal is the development of a substance-specific maladaptive behavioral change, with physiological and cognitive impairments, that is due to the cessation of or reduction in heavy and prolonged substance use.

Syphilis can lead to serious damage of the brain and heart if left untreated. The most common way of contracting the disease is through vaginal, anal, or oral sex. However, it can be spread by nonsexual contact if the sores (chancres), rashes, or mucous patches caused by syphilis come in contact with the broken skin of a noninfected individual.

***Tarasoff* case** dealt with a perpetrator who stalked and ultimately murdered his victim. The legal rulings of this case and the resulting guidelines are applicable to virtually all cases where the client of a therapist is in jeopardy of physical harm.

Teen courts include a jury of the teen's peers. The teens take the role of prosecuting and defense attorneys, jury members, and even judge in some jurisdictions.

Terminally ill inmates are defined as those inmates who are known to have a fatal disease and have less than six months to live.

"The Big Four" includes the prison systems of Texas, New York, Florida, and California because they are the four largest and most prominent correctional systems in the United States.

Thematic Apperception Test explores for trauma in the child and is very useful since many of the children and teens who murder report some form of prior trauma.

Therapeutic jurisprudence is the study of the extent to which substantive rules, legal procedures, and the roles of lawyers and judges produce therapeutic or antitherapeutic consequences for individuals involved in the legal process.

Thought shifting requires that the offender shift his thoughts to aversive imagery. The sex offender may be allowed to view or think about some arousing image but then is trained to think about something aversive, like an approaching police officer.

Thought stopping is used to disrupt a deviant thinking pattern. The offender is given pictures of arousing images and is forced to stop his thoughts when the image is seen.

Token economy is a set of rewards that aim to link behavior with its consequences by the systematic issue of tokens or points contingent on behavior that is deemed appropriate and desirable by institutional staff.

Tolerance is indicated by a need for markedly increased amounts of a substance to achieve intoxication or the desired effect.

Treatment is the process whereby offenders are provided some form of intervention that will help them function within society without resorting to criminal behavior.

True negatives occur when the offender is predicted to not reoffend, and the prediction turns out to be true.

True positives occur when the offender is predicted to reoffend, and the prediction turns out to be true.

Tuberculosis is a disease caused by bacteria that affects primarily the lungs, though it can affect any organ in the body. Tuberculosis is spread through the air from one person to another.

12 steps to recovery is a self-help program that was created and is organized by Alcoholics Anonymous.

Vagal reactor batterers show reductions in measures of arousal during aggressive interactions with their partners—completely contrary to typical patterns during aggressive interactions that occur in other people.

Victim counselors primarily provide intervention services to victims of crime, particularly assaultive crime. These counselors may have been victims themselves at one time and thus are familiar with the trauma and anxiety associated with incidents of victimization.

Victim impact panels give victims an opportunity to confront groups of offenders (not necessarily the one who committed crimes against them) and to talk about the anger and hurt caused by the crime.

Victim impact statements provide an opportunity for victims to express their concerns to the prosecutors and the court.

Victim turned offender refers to the notion that many female offenders were themselves prior victims of either childhood abuse or some form of adult abuse, such as domestic violence.

Welfare workers view the offender more as a client than as a supervisee on their caseloads.

Wisconsin Risk Assessment System is an instrument that scores probationers on the predictors contained on a standardized list. From these data, the offender is classified as either high, medium, or low risk.

INDEX

A

B

D

E

G

H

M

R

S

U

V

W

Y